Los Angeles Times
Sunday
Crossword
Omnibus
Volume 5

by Sylvia Bursztyn & Barry Tunick

**Random House
Puzzles & Games**

New York Toronto London Sydney Auckland

Please address inquiries about electronic licensing of any products for use on a network,
in software or on CD-ROM to the Subsidiary Rights Department,
Random House Information Group, fax 212-572-6003.

This book is available for special discounts for bulk purchases for sales promotions or premiums.
Special editions, including personalized covers, excerpts of existing books, and corporate imprints,
can be created in large quantities for special needs. For more information, write to Random House,
Inc., Special Markets/Premium Sales, 1745 Broadway, MD 6-2, New York, NY 10019
or e-mail specialmarkets@randomhouse.com

Visit the Random House Web site: www.randomhouse.com

First Edition

Printed in the United States of America

10 9

ISBN: 978-0-8129-3683-4

ACROSS

1 Slippery tree
4 Gazpacho and cock-a-leekie
9 Acorn-bearing tree
15 Weasel word?
18 "Giant step" request
20 Name of eight Popes
21 *Pied-__* (part-time home)
22 "__ Little Teapot"
23 Copyright page abbr.
24 Filets in a fricassee
26 Wind up
27 Gleason's classic couple
29 Lukas of *Witness*
30 *McTeague* writer
32 Actor-diplomat John
33 Gilead soother
34 Cornerstone
35 Dish of 62A
37 Parliament peer
39 See men
41 Reiser and Rose
42 Polynesian image
43 Blue-green
45 Ecclesiastes words
47 Be impudent
48 Miller salesman
49 Break in the action
50 Estuary
51 An end to sex?
52 Forget the past
56 "__ now or never!"
57 Downtown horizons
59 Stands for Woods
60 Shrug's significance
62 Poultry products
63 Auctioneer's word
65 Soho streetcar
66 Actress Jacqueline
69 *The Good Earth* heroine
70 *Caffè* go-with
74 APB opener
75 Glen Campbell classic
79 *Star Wars'* Solo
80 Weeks *per annum*
81 Use the good china
82 Once more
83 Credit card consequence
84 Soup scoop
87 Zillions of years
88 Horne of music
89 Caucasian, to Polynesians
90 Pokerfaced
92 Accused's answer
93 WWII tank
94 Vibrate
95 Gets an eyeful
97 He played Sherlock
98 Hooray, to José
100 This may be a lot
101 "SNL" "French" family
105 Prizm producer

106 John and Ethel's actor brother
109 Violin's ancestor
110 Smash into
111 Make possible
112 *Mal* __
113 FedExed or faxed
114 Cleric's vestment
115 Lingered
116 Annoying people
117 Go to pieces

DOWN

1 Give forth
2 Wield the whip
3 "The rich get richer"
4 Surrender
5 Synthetic fabric
6 Above, in Berlin
7 Go by "Go"
8 Tin symbols
9 Bobby of Indy 500 fame
10 Of time, to Tertullian (anagram of 45A)
11 Cal. pages
12 Sitcom planet
13 Cobo and Cow Palace
14 Town near Racine
15 Explorer's attribute
16 Discontinued Dodge
17 Shoulder enhancers
19 Doesn't emulate Clinton
25 Niger neighbor
28 Designer St. Laurent
31 Melee
33 Come with
34 Bagel kin
35 Ending meaning likeness
36 "Let __ you a question"
37 An arm and a leg
38 Adequate
39 Tulips and jonquils
40 Anvil pounder
42 Lugs around
43 Truman Veep Barkley
44 Caine captain
46 Cushy
48 L x W's L
52 Feline crossbreed
53 Tour of duty
54 *Mrs. Miniver* star
55 Like "Friends'" Phoebe
58 Crane or Tremayne
61 The Latin I love?
63 Close or Ford
64 Caravan stopovers
65 Shinbone
66 Imperfect pitch?

67 Achilles' tale
68 Glenn Miller's instrument
69 Gibson garnish
70 Swahili title
71 Atmosphere tier
72 What Mensa means
73 Bury
76 Flawless
77 Uses a touchtone
78 Expression for an arch?
83 Actress Bebe or singer Billy
85 Rupee hundredth
86 Eats
89 Recycled leftovers
91 Lamentation
92 Grieg's Gynt
93 Indy pros
95 Do-do, e.g.
96 Made faux pas
97 Basque topper
98 Taj town
99 Not imaginary
100 "Dear" lady
101 Some special agents
102 Not at all hetero
103 First Bond film
104 Tartan pattern
107 "__ note to follow sol"
108 Many ft.

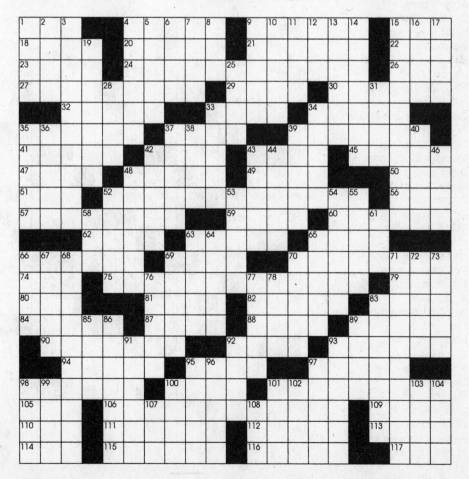

ACROSS

1 Adam of "Chicago Hope"
6 Prompted
10 *Like this*, for short
14 Brake part
18 Sporty Studebaker
19 "Dedicated to the __ Love"
20 __ Beach, Fla.
21 Involved with
22 Afternoon growth
25 Word of whoa
26 Sailing
27 *Mikado* role
28 Till bill
29 Club constituents
31 Divulged
32 Louis XVI coin
33 MTV "Real World"'s memorable Pedro
35 Billie who played Glinda
36 Snaky shape
37 Hipster's "Shake!"
39 Smoker and sleeper
40 *Speed* speeder
41 Bay Area coll.
42 Pigeon English?
44 Torn-off part
47 Postpone
50 *Seven* star
52 Go bad
54 Grey of tea fame
55 Actress Lena
56 Old Soviet scheme
59 Father's *hermano*
60 Courtesy
62 MRI precursor
63 I.e., i.e.
65 Historic plane __ Gay
66 "Clue" room
68 Crook, per Jackie Mason
70 Zorro's first name
72 Change direction
73 It's close to your hearth
76 Cider-song girl
77 Harry James hit
82 Pizzeria part
83 Egg container
85 *Mighty Aphrodite* director
86 Ireland, once
87 Bucephalus, e.g.
88 Marvin of soul
89 Memo abbr.
90 Birdie-bogie median
91 "Me __!"
92 Historian's forte
94 Some faculties
99 Prof's degree
102 Enliven
104 Hereditary ruler
105 It fits in a lock
106 *Silkwood* co-star
107 Rigby or Roosevelt
109 Fr. religious figure
110 Adjust a motor
111 He ate at Alice's
112 It can get iced
113 Top brass
117 "Suits me to __"
118 Say positively
119 The East
120 Gives a final performance
121 Profit counterpart
122 Salesclerk's call
123 Worn out
124 Fiery fragment

DOWN

1 Tijuana tips
2 Frays at the edges
3 Work dough
4 Skater Midori
5 Parking meter feed
6 Contrive
7 Strange, to Scots
8 Comic-book scream
9 Female
10 Chekhov play
11 Mogul Turner
12 Bouquet of roses?
13 Actor Rob
14 Spend
15 One way from L.A.
16 Baby bird?
17 Thicket of shrubs
18 __ worse than death
23 Chromosome sites
24 Greek pref. meaning half
30 Bus. degree
33 Full of zing
34 Use the Xerox again
37 Bottom of the *mapa*
38 Remote button
39 Soda pop option
40 Annette of *The American President*
43 Feat of Klee
45 *Battle Cry* author
46 Rorschach feature
47 Fudd, to Bugs
48 Inventor Whitney
49 '70 Nicholson flick
50 Mideast bread
51 Princeton plant
52 Jeweler's chalcedony
53 Use a missal
56 Iraqi coin
57 Rich commuter's home
58 Emergency CB channel
61 Rise ominously
64 Old Chrysler product
66 Golfer Ballesteros
67 Doogie Howser, e.g.
68 Donate
69 Is multiplied?
70 Finish spoiler
71 Mental flash
72 Ruin reputations
73 Oregon state tree
74 Balmoral river
75 Target for Testaverde
78 Float downriver
79 Ointment spoiler
80 Matzoh's lack
81 Bake in a kiln
84 Petits fours, perhaps
87 Help-wanted notice?
90 100-centimo units
91 Post-Plautus playwright
93 One of D.C.'s 100
95 Sunday *Times* extra
96 Vintner's vessels
97 Confectioner's staple
98 *Compos mentis*
99 Word group
100 *Catch-22* author
101 Molten metal impurities
102 Calyx leaf
103 Mickey's pet
104 Transmission position
106 Locust bean
108 The end __ era
110 King Cole's combo
114 Irritate
115 Wednesday preceder?
116 Shade tree

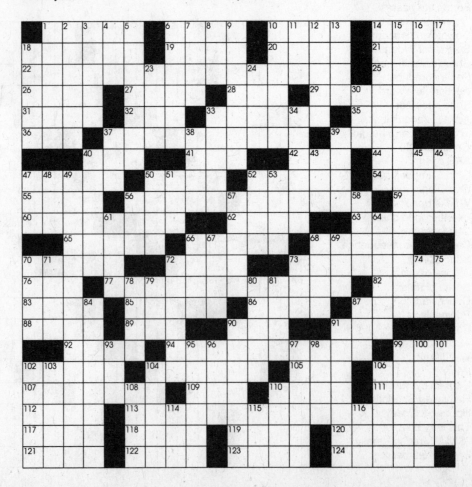

IN MOTHER WORDS: For the second Sunday in May

ACROSS

1 Woody plant
6 __-Pekka Salonen
9 Join the regatta
13 Flappers' flagons
19 What a player on the bench needs?
20 Make one
21 Skipping stone sound
22 Annual outdoor pageant
23 How we view ourselves, today?
26 Kind of energy or number
27 "Surf" platemate
28 Private ops
29 Polar to SSW
30 Alf and Mork
31 Canine shows?
34 Robin Goodfellow
35 Conrad's *The __ Sharer*
37 AWOLs' lacks
38 Cal or Georgia
39 Gift-wrap flourish
40 Aramis' *ami*
43 Raggedy fellow
44 And so on
45 Dine
46 "Seinfeld" character
47 Function
48 Golden rule opener, today?
53 A devil of a name
54 3, on a phone
55 Gas gauge reading
56 Off one's feed
57 Band booking
58 Aloof
60 Elm or Easy
61 One and only
62 Brooklyn institute
63 Time machine?
64 Eddy
66 SAT taker
67 It's left in the Louvre
69 Disharmony
71 "Mad About You" cousin
72 Paper product
73 Vestibule
74 Have the deed
77 Duke of Arles?
78 Like spiritual things, today?
80 Likewise
81 Depth charge
83 Be contrite
84 "Flying Down to __"
85 Carom or massé
86 Twist source
87 Sweet spud
88 Belfry denizens
89 Ornamented band
91 Fashion designer Todd
93 Actress Kay
94 Brief snowfall
95 Musician Metheny
97 Sturdiness symbol

98 Wagner marathon
99 Nose dose
100 *Luther* screenwriter Edward
102 Externally guided, today?
108 Nerd
109 Isle of leis
110 Overacting actor
111 Like Seattle
112 Leave high and dry
113 Humdinger
114 Popeye's goil
115 It has its tricks

DOWN

1 Losing ground?
2 Her match?
3 Lamb's kin
4 Card game
5 Bud container?
6 Still-life subjects
7 Doer of the lord's work
8 Spots on the tube
9 Oration
10 Smart __
11 Debtor's chits
12 CD ancestors
13 French quarter?
14 Sideways passes
15 Livy said it lovingly
16 Whatever, today?
17 Create cardigans

18 Biological bags
24 Tints
25 House coat?
29 Just in or out
31 Feel intuitively
32 A perfect match, today?
33 Collegiate climber
34 Small-minded
35 "Red Hot Momma" Tucker
36 Letter #VII
37 Praise
38 Extra inning
39 Jeeves, e.g.
41 *The Hairy Ape* playwright
42 Marsh plant
45 Evening do
46 Unit in a joule
48 Adroit
49 Leave unmentioned
50 Emotional peaks
51 Perry of "Friends"
52 Gateway abbr.
59 Fervid follower
60 Safe
61 Bradbury's __ *for Space*
62 Read over
63 LACMA's M
64 Meshach's "Dave's World" role
65 Like Asta's hair
66 Kind of wave or pool

67 Skedaddle!
68 Religious retreat
69 Songs sung singly
70 Dancer Charisse
72 Anthracite measure
73 On the __ (kaput)
75 In a daze
76 Chord component
78 Lute cousin
79 Apple mismatch
82 Wyo. neighbor
85 Dubbed one
87 Go yadda-yadda-yadda
88 Heston's Oscar role
89 *Doña __ and Her Two Husbands*
90 British poet Brooke
92 Loathed
93 Built supply
94 "Rose Marie" writer
95 Feline feet
96 Work without __ (take risks)
98 Chestnut kin
99 Operation Overlord's start
101 A California Santa
102 Speak with a Jersey accent?
103 Letter #XVII
104 One for the road
105 *Familia* member
106 Phase out
107 Turn an orange green

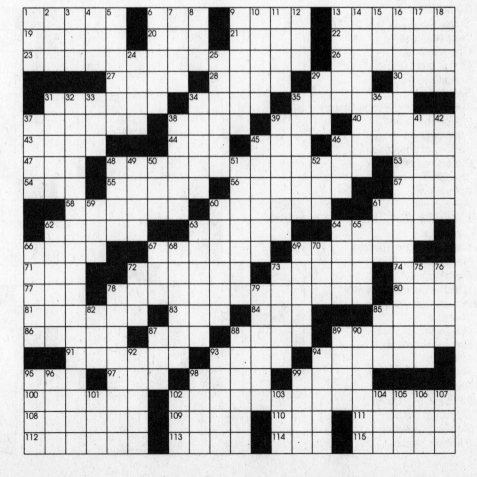

ACROSS

1 Kiltie's kin
5 ". . . we'll make a __ of a pair"
10 __ *pro nobis*
13 Beemer's rival
16 Armchair protector
17 Raincoat
18 Like some coffee
19 Soho optimism?
20 Hopi home
21 Where Simba signs?
24 Lunch list
25 Kol __
26 Slangy complaint
27 *Bus Stop* author
28 Ambassador's quarters
30 Avoid
32 Uses Elmer's
33 Parisian possessive
35 Ike's command
36 Christmas bell ringer
37 Menudo base
38 Capp and Capone
39 Novel by Simba Lewis?
42 __-ha!
43 Contemporary drag star
45 Orch. section
46 Before, to bards
47 Sharks-Jets set-to
51 Phylum subdivision
52 Thread rolls
54 Outperform
55 Good paper – or bad paper
56 Take habitually
57 Gravy spoon
58 Finger-paint
60 Band for a wedding
61 See 82A
63 Tune heralding Simba Claus?
65 Hodgepodge half
66 Pass over
67 Like __ of sunshine
68 Pisces neighbor
69 Thespians' union
70 Abby's twin
71 Help a waiter
72 Kerouac's *The __ Bums*
73 Luxurious
76 Boomer on the Thames
78 Nasser's org.
80 Dijon denial
81 Candy-counter giveaway
82 *Wind in the Willows* character
83 Cub-luring Simba?
86 Smothers brother
87 Pert
89 Home or bed add-on
90 Sales rep
91 Chiffons' "__ So Fine"
92 Brooks of Country
93 Begins to wake
94 Put in its place

97 Curtain color
98 Diagonal
99 Spendthrift's specialty
100 It runs through Florence
103 Betraying Simba?
107 Sing "Too Ra Loo Ra . . ."
108 London garden spot
109 Put on a border
110 Use a compass
111 Abigail, Alice or Ansel
112 Takes too much
113 Like Burns' mouse
114 Rice field
115 Novice

DOWN

1 Write computer programs
2 Simba the Peace Nobelist?
3 Photo folio
4 Bill __ the Science Guy
5 Jergens rival
6 Contest form
7 Migraine, e.g.
8 Ernesto, to Fidel
9 Bricklayer's burden
10 Eightsome
11 Navigator's nemesis
12 Do the math, sometimes
13 Enlist
14 Orbit's outer point
15 DNA constituents
16 It retains water
17 Word with pen or pill
18 Say again
22 __ dicta (incidental remarks)
23 Ferenc Molnár play
25 Of birth
29 Absorb
30 Patriotic org.
31 Oft-patched parts
32 Classify
33 Julius' avenger
34 Month in Tel Aviv
36 A walk in the park
37 Strong beats
40 Chabrier orchestral work
41 Like a stick-in-the-mud
44 Black-ink item
48 Trail behind Simba?
49 Polaroid inventor
50 Early birds?
52 Putdowns
53 Parasite
54 Oklahoma city
58 Superfluous
59 Reuners
60 Kingdom
61 Kingdom near Judah

62 Where Hawks dribble
63 Sprightly
64 Hit with a pitch
69 Peloponnesian War winner
71 Palm, Pebble or Pismo
72 Less fruity
74 Plum kin
75 Haws' partners
77 Caesar's betrayer
78 Steal a scene
79 Oil worker?
81 Musician's transition
84 Courtroom VIP's
85 Inventor's protection
87 Inviolable
88 Quiver contents
92 Tropical lizard
93 Burn a bit
94 Looked through keyholes
95 Sardonicism
96 Late for class
98 __ your time
99 Tried to dodge a tag
101 Dodger hurler Hideo
102 Many buttons
104 Make a mini
105 Jitterbug event
106 Notable time
107 Nap or nip opener

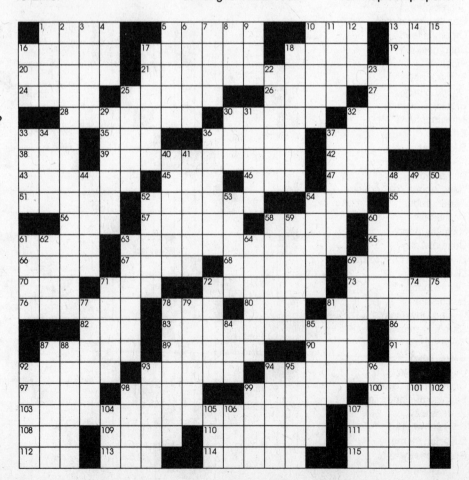

ACROSS

1 ¢ ¢
4 French actress Fanny
10 River of Burgundy
15 Washed out
19 Ark passenger
20 Horseshoes "almost"
21 Like tabloid tales
22 Tender ender
23 Where *on parle français*
24 Festive Eddie Cantor song?
26 Made angry
27 Philatelist or numismatist
29 Singular opera?
30 __ nous (confidentially)
31 Not at all sophisticated
32 Vulgarian
33 "Evil Ways" rockers
35 Calls on
37 Pleased-as-punch pop duo?
39 Secs., perhaps
40 Clever tactics
42 Babies' early syllables
43 Slicker place
44 Lorna of lit
45 Helps
47 Go back down
50 Red-lobster link
51 Onetime tickled stripper?
53 Trifling amount
54 '60s rocker Peter's kin
56 Clematis, etc.
57 Elevator man
58 Modernize
60 After daily or day-old
62 They're for drying or crying
64 "There's nothing __!"
65 Her and her
67 Buck and Bailey
69 Jolson and Jarreau
70 Well-pleased pop gender-bender?
74 Talk talk talk
77 Disdainful cry
78 Go to
79 States as fact
80 Trout tempter
81 Old dagger
82 Holds back
83 Morley of "60 Minutes"
84 Ecstatic Reaganomicist?
89 Milk option
90 L.A. help organization __ Niños
91 Solar heaters
92 Three, of a kind
94 Nervousness, in Napoli
95 Green gemstone
96 Leaving
99 Auto or pluto ender
100 Elated economist?
103 Join the competition
104 Gigantic
105 Musical show
106 Floral cluster
107 Columnist Le Shan
108 Elbe tributary
109 Ride without pedaling
110 Foster's river
111 The old college cry?

DOWN

1 Tony
2 Tex-Mex treat
3 Playful Pilgrim?
4 Gore and Camus
5 Does a take
6 Luke's father
7 Irk
8 Not e'en once
9 Give it a shot
10 Don a cardigan
11 Omen
12 ILO, OAS and NATO
13 It's nothing
14 Gelderland commune
15 Base blocks
16 Cardiologist's concerns
17 Gothic rib
18 Ingratiate
25 Apes
28 Nonclergy
30 Stash the Fender
32 He pays the price
33 Sluggishness standards
34 Confuse
35 Gaucho's cow
36 Horned goddess
37 Walkman creator
38 Saying
40 '95 visitor from Rome
41 One in the "L" column
44 Force unit
45 Where most people live
46 Market by machine
47 Fun-filled '50s candidate?
48 Hit 212 degrees
49 Smooch
51 Cha lead-in
52 Unhidden
55 Granola bit
57 Athena's symbol
58 Area code 801
59 Theda's colleague
60 Hit on the head
61 Cheese covering
62 Does It's job
63 Mined-over matter
65 Wrecks completely
66 "Laughing" scavenger
67 Guest work
68 Bobbles the ball
70 "Quantum Leap"'s Scott
71 In __ (before birth)
72 Billion-dollar Bill
73 Even once
75 District
76 Ernie's bud
80 Sri __
81 Break like glass
82 Less assertive
83 Well-groomed
84 Cochise or Geronimo
85 Handwoven carpet
86 MASH procedure
87 Neptune's neighbor
88 Gizmo
89 Anonymous
92 Puccini's prima donna
93 Mature
95 Joe, at Central Perk
96 Work like a beaver?
97 Verdi princess
98 Uh-huh
100 Circle section
101 MGM mascot
102 Its job is taxing

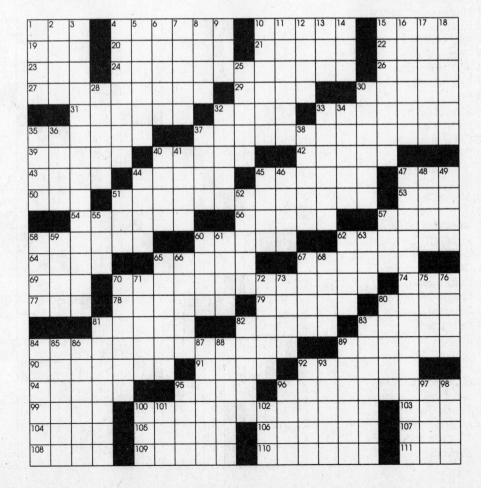

ACROSS

1 Keyboard key
4 Flat topper
9 Like the Six Million Dollar Man
15 Cold's kin
18 At the crest of
20 African lilies
21 Entirely
22 UNLV part
23 Ride on the runway
24 Memorable time
26 Leader of the pack?
27 Examples
29 Hoagie's cousin
30 Took a bough
32 Maids-a-milking, e.g.
33 Rigging holder
34 Gave as a reference
35 Base for salsa
37 Fight-card entry
39 Provincial potentate
41 Out of this world?
42 Wheel nuts
43 Marquis, e.g.
45 CIA agent, to some
47 Lesage's *Gil __*
48 Composer Boccherini
49 He married Kim
50 JFK predecessor
51 Pussycat pal
52 Loudspeaker system
56 Drumstick
57 Encircled by invaders
59 Corp. VIP
60 Judging groups
62 Stepped on
63 Prank
65 Joan of Art
66 Backslides
69 Girl with a hood
70 Big bugger?
74 "Who am __ say?"
75 *Song of the South* song
79 Ankh letter
80 __ *gratia artis*
81 Month before Nisan
82 Key ring?
83 Big Mama?
84 Catchers' catchers
87 Boss Tweed's bane
88 Lessen the mess
89 Celestial streaker
90 Dental alloy
92 Smooch
93 Conform to rules
94 Pistil part
95 Did the backstroke
97 Skiing hill
98 Author Gordimer
100 Hibernation spot
101 Australia and New Zealand
105 Mad. or Lex.
106 Maternity ward feature
109 Single-handedly
110 Craggy crest
111 Canine coating
112 Italy's last queen
113 Plenty of horn?
114 Have the deed to
115 Wanted-poster offer
116 Ritzy wrist watch
117 Faucet

DOWN

1 Hulot's creator
2 __ impasse (stymied)
3 Lunch-auction events
4 Writer Djuna
5 Vote in
6 Took the trolley
7 Skinny dippers?
8 Part of a chairman's name
9 Falls for it
10 Still as can be
11 Other, in Oaxaca
12 Subtle signal
13 Type type
14 Wolves' kin
15 Bosh
16 Irish export
17 Secondhand
19 Is part of a battery
25 Yon item
28 Like __ of bricks
31 Cop's quarry
33 It's on the record
34 *Odyssey* sorceress
35 Wealthy one
36 "For __ Know"
37 Construct
38 Today, in Torino
39 Changes direction
40 Matterhorn melody
42 Applied grease
43 San Diego pro
44 Senior one
46 Suds storers
48 He played Dracula
52 Rosie of *Fearless*
53 Mac maker
54 Montana pass?
55 Siddons of the stage
58 "__ in the bag!"
61 What CPA's crunch
63 Musical P.S.'s
64 Clear-witted
65 Frantically
66 Actor Neeson
67 Inner courtyards
68 20th-c. art movement
69 "__, I'm Adam"
70 Engine covers
71 Eradicated
72 Atelier item
73 Out of practice
76 Iloilo's island
77 Fact or figure
78 He gave us a lift
83 Fertilizer source
85 Rikki-Tikki-__
86 Bad-mouth
89 Condo cousin
91 Novelist or actor Graham
92 Roseanne, at first
93 Culmination
95 S&L client
96 Use effectively
97 Blarney or Rosetta
98 Brussels-based grp.
99 State openly
100 Andean capital
101 One of Woody's kids
102 Seasonal song
103 ". . . ere I saw __"
104 Daytime drama
107 Belli's and Bailey's forte
108 "__ out!"

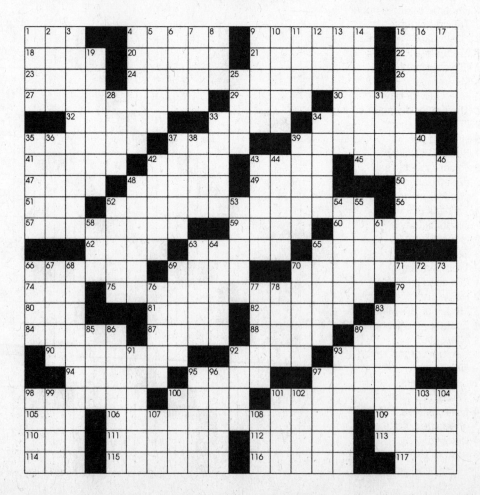

ACROSS

1 Tool with teeth
4 Social standing
9 Exemplars
15 Nocturnal predators
19 Butt end
20 Outlander
21 Apprehensiveness
22 Modish
23 Cross-country runner?
24 Tidbit from the *Rubáiyát*
26 Turner of tunes
27 Dead giveaways?
29 Singer Neville
30 Work a wedding
31 Deity of desire
32 Gloomy
34 Courage
36 Shrink away
38 Diameter divisions
39 Up and about
40 Safety org.
41 Ablush
45 WWII price org.
48 Show biz conglom.
49 Taking an ax to
50 Sra. Perón
51 Use an old phone
52 Relating to: Suff.
53 Plains natives
54 Scarborough events
55 Brake parts
56 Maker
58 Becomes insipid
59 Rome's Via __
60 Speak nonstop
64 Repulsive
67 "Theirs but to __ die"
68 Poe's Lee
72 Vizier's superior
73 Surgeons' garb
74 Actress Linda
76 Intensive suff.
77 Took the RTD
78 Speech feature
79 Doll, to Dali
80 Pen point
81 Bing's roadmate
82 Like an E-ticket ride
84 Not conned by
85 Sophia of the screen
87 Here's Howe
88 Weepy one
89 Mansard material
91 Herd orphans
93 Nemesis
94 In the air
95 Nap spots
96 Quest for the unknown?
99 UPC's C
100 Without warning

104 Yule fuel
105 At any point
106 Rootlessness
107 Foot marker
108 Put to work
109 Claret and burgundy
110 Says "Skoal"
111 Accumulate
112 Needle hole

DOWN

1 Freelancer's encl.
2 Pops the question
3 Pequod's quest
4 Pollux partner
5 Medicinal plants
6 "Dear" fellows
7 Palmer's pedestal
8 Extremity
9 Live in
10 Plow-making pioneer
11 Fielder's flub
12 Stratford stream
13 __ *Misérables*
14 L.A. – S.D. dir.
15 La-la interval
16 Static sound
17 Cruise ship
18 Fearsome
25 Bringing to heel
28 It may be gray
30 Tec's task
32 Maugham's Thompson
33 Of Frigg's mate
34 Cheeky children
35 Costa __
36 Stand-up guy
37 AMPAS award
38 Do a makeover
41 Narrated anew
42 Made well
43 Pandora released
  them
44 Who was on it
46 Treaty
47 As well
49 Pontificator's output
51 "Inka __ Doo"
54 Sort of satyrs
55 '40s star Durbin
57 ". . . a poem lovely
  as __"
58 Physicist Max
59 Santa Monica neighbor
61 Vote to accept
62 James of old Texas
63 Becomes frayed
64 Sort of wort

65 Melville opus
66 Lusty
69 Rhett and Scarlett's
  daughter
70 Typewriter option
71 Parts partner
73 On the way out
74 Desi's daughter
75 Singer Paul's kin
78 At that time
79 Stubborn
82 Mandamus, e.g.
83 Undoes
84 French river
86 Tenders
88 Lakers and Clippers
89 Indy entry
90 Light-__ (sweetheart)
91 Seals the fate of
92 "Come __!" (Get real!)
93 Union soldiers
95 Parthenon porch
96 *Trattoria* menu word
97 Optimistic
98 '50s film critic
100 Stable scrap
101 Juan's one
102 Roaring '20s, e.g.
103 London derrière?

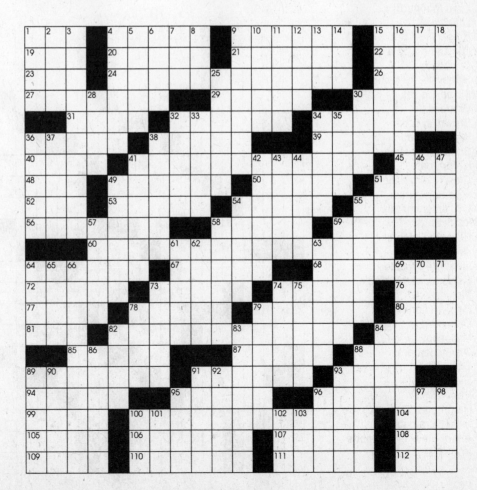

ACROSS

1 Guy's chum
4 Fred Allen's medium
9 Passbook bearers
15 Be profitable
18 Scent
20 Muscovy dukes
21 Catherine of __
22 First UN Secretary-General
23 Bathe
24 What a demagogue speaks with
26 Dentist's grp.
27 Silliness
29 Seine tributary
30 NaCl maker
32 More fashionable
33 Lively joy
34 Black tea
35 Fished
37 Infrequent
39 Napoleon victory site
41 Walks nervously
42 Cattle, once
43 Incite
45 Mason's Street
47 After happy or witching
48 Treat the turkey
49 Bristle: Pref.
50 __ in (pooped)
51 Little devil
52 Branching point
56 Consume a cola
57 Confusion
59 Splitsville, for some
60 Mixes the salad
62 Propensity
63 Brown, in Brest
65 Wyo. neighbor
66 Soak 34A leaves
69 Unfortunate
70 Close examinations
74 Red Book writer
75 L.A. amphitheater
79 Work at
80 Basketball center
81 Aachen article
82 Libreville's locale
83 Eagle or double eagle
84 Manufacturer
87 Barnyard grub
88 Driblet
89 Snapshot
90 Disencumbers
92 Goosefoot root
93 Did S&L work
94 Peevish
95 Hammett's The __ Curse
97 Main Norse gods
98 Anne, Emily or Charlotte
100 Applause
101 Nagging
105 Actress Ullmann
106 E.T.'s vehicle
109 Fiend's forte
110 Bartender's "rocks"
111 Truc or succ ender
112 Crinkled cloth
113 Lox emporium
114 Mpg part
115 Former follower
116 Raise spirits
117 Yank's opponent

DOWN

1 Ben Crenshaw's game
2 Tel Aviv calendar page
3 Prizes for amateurs
4 Pillaged
5 To have, in Le Havre
6 Pub missile
7 Black
8 Sugary suffix
9 "Gymnopédies" composer
10 Originated
11 Windmill part
12 Darner's aid
13 "Stars and Stripes Forever," e.g.
14 Stole
15 Mirror material
16 Helper
17 Ling or long lead-in
19 Merrymaker
25 Big name in Hawaii
28 Is indebted
31 Solitary
33 Unripe
34 Barbecue area
35 Plant louse
36 Wynonna's mom
37 Hazardous
38 Opposed
39 French underground
40 Kukla's pal
42 Jeweler's measure
43 Pallid
44 Designer Geoffrey
46 Pennines, e.g.
48 Malay isle
52 Sassy
53 Cornwall town
54 When duels were fought
55 Factotum, once
58 Egypt's __ Simbel
61 High or lark opener
63 Irish river
64 Propelled a bireme
65 Pry
66 Mosque VIP
67 Water nymph
68 Pay up
69 Ballerina's bends
70 Monastery master
71 Masters anthology
72 Cream
73 Church council
76 Southpaw
77 Poet Nash
78 Be brave enough
83 Wielded the gavel
85 Neck and neck
86 Soothing
89 Assume attitudes
91 Streetcar role
92 One heart and two hearts
93 Stowe villain
95 Lindy or lambada
96 Indignation
97 Expert
98 Oscilloscope sight
99 Playwright Elmer
100 Clue
101 Tree trunk knot
102 Zoological suffix
103 Khartoum waterway
104 Oversmooth
107 Thus far
108 One-spot

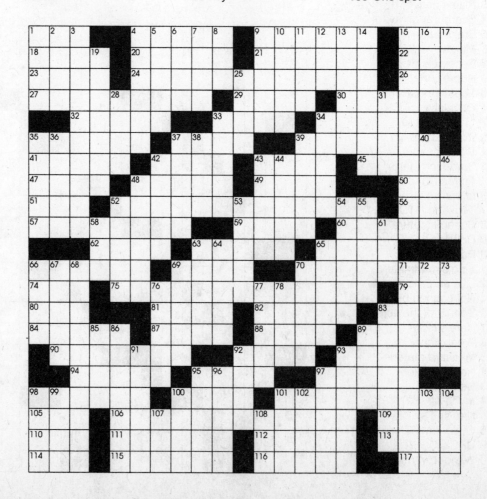

ACROSS
1 Pale
4 52A victims
9 Savage
14 Nave neighbor
18 Years on earth
19 *Calendario* opener
20 A week in Oaxaca
21 Score the same
22 Unprocessed
23 '40 Flynn flick
25 Pull up stakes
26 Raises in rank
28 Glasgow woman?
29 Afton or Avon
30 Gives stars to
31 Convention selection
32 Ruddy
34 Attorney Gloria
36 Impertinent
37 With all the extras
38 Farm equipment maker
39 Unpartnered
40 Hepster's exclamation
41 History-text chapter
44 Strong wagon
45 '80 Malle character study
48 Likewise not
49 Ending after lunch?
50 Try to persuade
51 Call forth
52 Swindle
53 Visa rival
55 Feel one's way
56 Vagrancy
58 Dry as dust
59 __ Haute
60 Hamlet or Horatio
61 Make waste?
64 Airport annoyance
65 Disregards
69 Unfortunately!
70 Poisonous
71 Jolson's "__ Boy"
72 Vengeance goddess
73 Buddhism branch
74 '93 Hanks-Washington hit
77 Math subj.
78 Nay canceller
79 Slow times
80 Eye colorer
81 Le Louvre, e.g.
82 Just about
84 Attacks
86 High trumps
87 Evel doings?
88 Museum in Brentwood
89 Interrupt the dance
90 Seaside
91 Camry competitor
92 Mallow family member
95 Ready the razor
96 '36 Gable-Tracy classic
99 "__ Got Sixpence"

100 Composer Satie
101 "The love __ young day!": Motherwell
102 Highway of '42
103 Pouring party
104 Agora arcade
105 Pepe the toon
106 Fingerprint features
107 Verb for Popeye

DOWN
1 Get out of shape
2 Gelling agent
3 '47 Holiday-Armstrong jazzfest
4 Ardent enthusiast
5 Combined
6 Shimon of Israel
7 CGS units
8 "__ gather"
9 Feudal fidelity
10 Roast host
11 Prince's was purple
12 Symbol of industry
13 Minstrel's song
14 Esteem
15 '77 Bogarde-Gielgud fantasy-drama
16 Spared from harm
17 Washstand item
20 The Ancient Marner?

24 Harriet or Horatio
27 Wed
29 Actor McDowall
31 Leaves for lunch?
32 __ *à deux* (dual delusion)
33 Milk, to Moreau
34 Put 2 and 2 together
35 Amiri Baraka, né __ Jones
36 Before power or plexus
37 Philosopher John
39 Hero's horse
40 Sub's viewer
42 Mega-meow
43 Arnie's entourage
45 Musical chipmunk
46 Hillside ridge
47 Piano key, to some
50 Dermal opening
52 Noted *Graf*
54 Lynx and leopard
55 Icy
56 __ *cum laude*
57 Exclusively
59 There's an *x* in the middle of it
60 Leary the comic
61 Indefinite
62 Out of wind?

63 '45 Flynn-Smith Western
64 "Hello" girl
65 Perfect-game adjective
66 '52 Scott-Massey railroad saga
67 One who essays
68 Those in the know
70 Caches for cash
71 Atomizer mist
74 The Wright idea?
75 Make smart?
76 Hark!
77 North African capital
81 Chair's concerns
83 California's motto
84 6D's language
85 Earth bearer
86 Wheel cover
87 It's between second and third
88 Blunder
89 Pancho's pal
90 Some babies
91 Short, quick cut
92 Hawaiian port
93 Eye area
94 Line of clothing?
96 Terra's star
97 Nut-brown beverage
98 Pres. before Herb

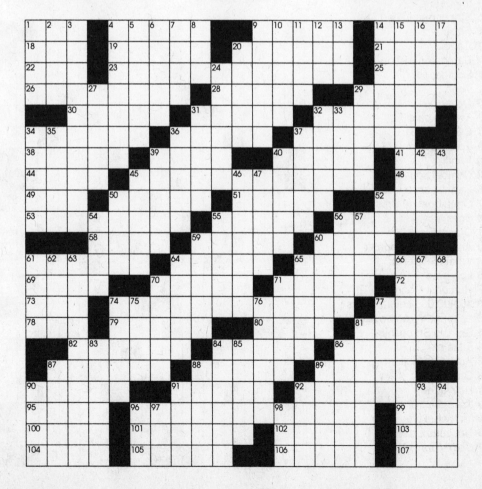

ACROSS

1 What some may work for
6 Chocolate substitute
11 Cubic decimetre
16 Emulated the Afton
17 The Lord, to Livy
19 Writ of __ corpus
20 Loch of song
21 Ferris-wheel whereabouts
23 Out in the open
24 Happy-face arc
25 Defensive tactic
26 Sea inlet
27 Funny Foxx
28 Twist or stomp
29 Doctrines
30 Piano-key material
32 ". . . have you __ wool?"
33 Islamabad's locale
35 Stock mkt. division
37 Energy units
38 Luxuriant
40 Hebrew letter
42 Triumphant expression
44 In front of the bow
45 Discipline an adolescent
47 Silents' comic Ben
51 Of no avail
53 Unlawfully obtained, to poets
55 Stat or meter lead-in
56 Frolic
57 Canter
59 San Antonio shrine
61 Engrossed
62 Tune
63 Ooze
65 Orange coat
67 Caesar's 151
68 Forehead
70 Pundit
73 Combat souvenir
75 Renaissance sword
77 Open boat, to Brits
79 Boss
81 Dracula, e.g.
83 Ancient sect member
84 What plotters do
86 Low card
87 Humorist George
88 16,900,000 square miles
89 Letterman's home state
91 Shirt, in Shropshire
94 Bible bk.
96 Adhesive friction
98 Guided
101 Hold tight
103 Take the trolley
105 Tiresome types
106 Not quite closed
107 Coin's front: Abbr.
108 Commandment verb
110 Cocoon occupants
111 Struck mighty blows
112 Victoria's grumpy remark
115 Space cadets
116 Goods thrown into the sea
117 The end __ (milestone)
118 Garbo and Salinger
119 Dictator's aide
120 The start of four words?
121 Lachrymose

DOWN

1 Untidy one
2 Shakespeare farce
3 __ to the wise . . .
4 Fast time?
5 "77 Sunset Strip" 's Byrnes
6 "B.C.," e.g.
7 Charm
8 Court order
9 Snake-eye?
10 Phrenologist's reading matter
11 Slip
12 Philippine tree
13 What Ivan inspired
14 Collecting leaves
15 Emerson specialty
16 Botanist's study
17 Praising faintly, perhaps
18 Sunday speech
19 Alts.
22 Home tweet home
24 Tokyo tipple
28 Valleys
29 Down-Under fish
31 Safari servant
33 Thick soups
34 Blue, in Baja
36 Historian Bruce
39 Axis extremity
41 Pedestal percher
43 "How's that again?"
44 Is ambitious
46 Bullring bravo
48 Whoopee-cushion planter
49 Beseech
50 Announcement
51 In working condition
52 Whole bunch
54 Rhett set?
58 Ocean fish
60 A SALT concern
64 High regard
66 Reduce a reputation
69 Inflicts
71 Terrarium growth
72 Rouse
73 Haggard woman
74 G&S specialty
76 Made yarn
78 Extremity
80 Scorch
82 Andean adieu
85 Way into la casa
88 Erstwhile S.F. mayor
90 Conks out
91 Looks daggers
92 Even though
93 Devastate
95 Italian river
97 Overdoing drinker
99 Hash house
100 Go formal
102 Of benzene: Comb. form
104 Rough sketch
106 Whirlpool rival
109 Switch positions
110 Fourth-down option
111 Wild plum
113 Managed
114 West of Hollywood
115 USN division

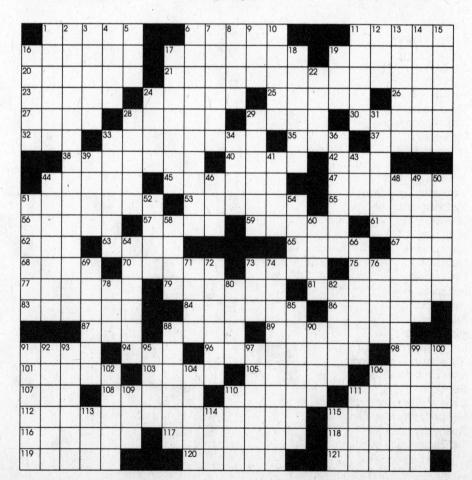

ACROSS

1 Hack
4 They give skiers a lift
9 Leave high and dry
15 Not many
18 Stomach
20 She came out in '97
21 Customize
22 Island in the *fleuve*
23 Colombian city
24 Shooting range orders
26 Heavy D's genre
27 Diagnostician's concerns
29 Merriment
30 Don't exeunt
32 Makes eyes at
33 Track transactions
34 Female demon
35 Floater
37 Woody Herman band
39 What some scouts seek
41 Michael Caine's Cockney
42 Tissue layer
43 Black, to bards
45 Sculled
47 "Oops!" evoker
48 Tamperers' hamperers
49 End-table neighbor
50 Wrath
51 Not wide, for short
52 Query to a speeder
56 Bigger than med.
57 Beside __ (irrelevant)
59 Light
60 Izaak Walton emulator
62 Broadway statuette
63 Bos'ns' bosses
65 Magic spell opener
66 Printing process
69 Unchanged
70 "Beg, steal __": Newley lyric
74 Onassis, familiarly
75 "__ you see the whites . . ."
79 It means environment
80 Crag
81 Greek war god
82 Say "hi"
83 Where every rose has its thorns
84 Chasten, in dialect
87 Annie Oakley
88 Sponsorship
89 Young pigeon
90 Like pupils in the dark
92 Drug addict
93 Brooks
94 Locations
95 N.A. or S.A.
97 Pickle flavoring
98 Survivals from the past
100 Tiny bit
101 Devout

105 Initials not at the '80 Olympics
106 Don't shoot!
109 Ireland, for 12 years
110 Get the bronze?
111 Smoothly courteous
112 Water weasel
113 Football play
114 Cabinet dept.
115 Marshals' men
116 Sugar source
117 Antique form of antiquity

DOWN

1 D minus CIC
2 Russian inland sea
3 Hotshot
4 More succinct
5 Sanctify
6 Winglike structures
7 '17 revolutionaries
8 Ship plank's upward curve
9 Wading bird
10 Makes docile
11 Abounding
12 *Arabian Nights* name
13 98.6 deg., e.g.
14 Foster's "Beautiful __"
15 Order threatening to Rogers or Shakespeare?
16 Verve
17 Grieved
19 Shoe style
25 Matured
28 CSA's Robert __
31 Young *hombre*
33 Gall
34 Hawaiian isle
35 Didn't exist
36 Mohammed was his prophet
37 McCullers' lonely hunter
38 She, in Chartres
39 Chewy candy
40 Maestro Koussevitsky
42 Kind of weeny
43 Tub: dial.
44 Certain Africans
46 Forest fauna
48 Japanese religion
52 Paid court
53 Diminish
54 Br'er or Peter
55 Sign up
58 WWII torpedo boats
61 Union vets' assn.
63 Bistros
64 Improper
65 Comic Johnson's namesakes

66 Feedbag filler
67 Palm leaf
68 Resort near New York
69 Zuckerman instr.
70 It means dream
71 Shoot back
72 Indian, e.g.
73 Prenatal places
76 Neck backs
77 Excrete
78 Entreat
83 Escorted
85 Et __ (and others)
86 Make mends, or amends
89 More *than* one or two
91 Inca *oro*, to Pizarro
92 Two-toed sloth
93 Consumers, usually
95 Irish chieftain's tax
96 Sioux or Siouans
97 Insertion mark
98 Blues singer Brown
99 Jacob's brother
100 Lupino namesakes
101 Pianoforte, for short
102 Baptism, e.g.
103 Europe-Asia mountains
104 Lascivious
107 Lots of oz.
108 Plunder

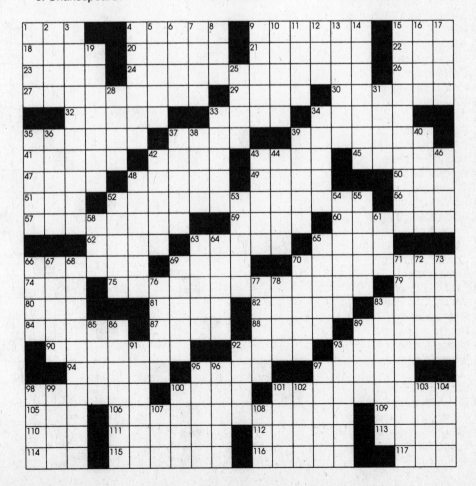

ACROSS

1 Disdainful cry
4 Rapunzel's pride
8 Coffee, to some
12 NATO and SEATO
17 *Jacta __ est*
19 Teen woe
20 "__ your debt!"
21 Come to terms
22 Daytime-Emmy winner Walton
23 Mindless routine
24 Dred Scott, e.g.
25 Stop
26 Porter's passionate paean?
30 Abounded
31 Band aids
32 Towards the wake
33 Dale's trailmate
34 Beaujolais cousin
36 The birdy bunch?
38 '89 play about Capote
41 Give it a whirl
43 Take potshots
44 The man from UNCLE
45 Former cygnet
46 Comment about a Renaissance woman?
50 34A's color, often
51 Endure
52 Emerald Isle
53 Sweater size
54 Plus
55 Soft core
56 Makes videos
58 Escrow participant
59 One of the wealthy
60 Dixie drink
61 Reach 212 degrees
62 Public regard
65 Kind of heating
66 Sound the tocsin
67 Shropshire chap
70 On the qui vive
71 Folksinger Phil
72 Fine sediment
73 Canapé covering
74 *The Full Monty* climax?
79 Caesar's bad day
80 Table scraps
81 Poet Dickinson
82 Wyatt of the West
83 German article
84 Help to do wrong
85 Neapolitan nervousness
86 Athena's symbol
87 Luau loop
88 Glitch or hitch
89 *Schindler's List* locale
92 Starting to set things right?
99 After 57D, menu option
100 School for Raoul

101 Actor Mischa
102 __ tight ship
103 City on the Missouri
104 Destroy a paper trail
105 Project Mercury grp.
106 Solvang neighbor Santa __
107 DNA constituents
108 Bivouac shelter
109 First-aid cases
110 Ship's rope

DOWN

1 Muslim's pilgrimage
2 Alaskan islander
3 Writer Hermann
4 Angel's ride
5 "Feed __, starve . . ."
6 Division word
7 Shorten sail
8 Clunker
9 Gather
10 __ *le roi!*
11 Work without __ (take risks)
12 Calm down
13 Intermediary
14 Steep cliff
15 Miss Durbeyfield
16 Behold
18 *

20 Lone Pequod survivor
27 Surrounded by
28 The Bucs stop here
29 Devastation
34 Grind together
35 "__ She Sweet?"
36 Yeltsin
37 Verve
38 Square-dance maneuver
39 Kitchen appliance
40 Below
41 Place for a plaster
42 Pat. __
43 Union unit
44 Throat culture finding
45 See 53A
46 Restorative resort
47 Martini munch
48 Molokai patient
49 Fashion's Calvin
55 LuPone or LaBelle
56 Oklahoma city
57 See 99A
58 Kind of, colloquially
59 Actors John and William
60 Artist Jasper
61 Mild
62 REM opener
63 Give the slip

64 Falk or Fonda
65 *Ivanhoe* writer
66 Writer Cather
67 Lion of Oz
68 Surmounting
69 Lawn waterer
71 Jack's giant, e.g.
72 Make incisions
73 Ancient zither
75 "It's __ deal"
76 Nullified
77 Pablo's pal
78 More recent
84 Virgil hero
85 Short sock
86 Scarlett's kin
87 Willowy
88 Indignant derision
89 One of the inn crowd?
90 Jeer
91 Warren of "Which Way, L.A.?"
92 Doubleheader half
93 North African port
94 Outperform
95 Pain from strain
96 Went under
97 River structure
98 Do nothing
99 Mechanical tooth

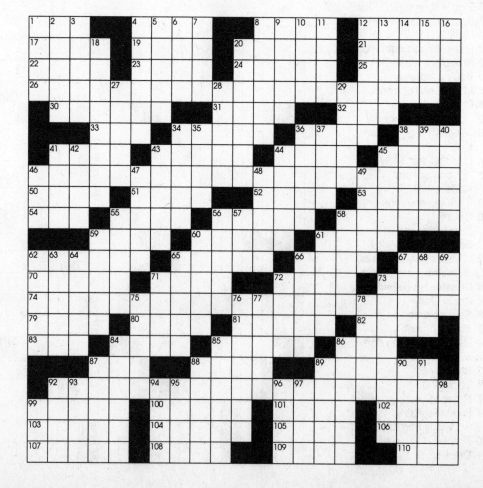

ACROSS

1 Where Radar worked
5 Earth
9 I-beam cousin
13 Left over
16 Customer's cost component
18 Bandleader Bill
19 Hawaiian port
20 Negative connective
21 Top Hun
22 Careless quickness
23 Tempo slowing: Abbr.
24 Fifteenth Tarzan Ron
25 Multiple personality anthem?
28 Portuguese plaudit
29 Parched
30 Change
31 Way out there
32 Put in stitches
35 Shirr thing?
36 Peronista's idol
38 Crowd sound
39 Gloria Bunker Stivic?
44 Till compartment
45 Berry Gordy's birthplace
46 Ploys
47 Prado or Louvre
49 And so on
50 Barrister's wear
51 The Captain's Tennille
52 Semi-semicolon
54 Not barefoot
57 Goes out with
59 Mythical Goldfinger
60 "Like that's not totally obvious!"
61 Go for the gold?
62 Customer with expensive taste?
65 __-Pekka Salonen
66 "You __ here"
67 Splits
68 Mountain air?
69 Once again
70 The start of something new?
71 Ever so long
72 __ it out (persevere)
73 Mil. unit
75 Grumble
77 Map book
80 Star in Carina
84 Wedding cake layer
85 Laborer?
87 Make concessions
88 Self-esteem
89 Scepter companion
90 Ottoman official
91 Skillful
92 Malt-drying kiln
93 Takes minutes
97 Not on duty

98 "Wow, how mediocre!"?
104 Try to win over
105 Ganges garb
106 Self-help shelf sign
107 Where Arthur went
108 Miss the mark
109 North Carolina college
110 Astrologer Sydney
111 Slew
112 Tennis term
113 It vies with Vogue
114 Tri-Star's owner
115 Give a hand to

DOWN

1 Study of #s
2 Aesthetically pretentious
3 ". . . one way to __ cat"
4 Mr. __'s Holiday
5 Overcharges
6 Commencement
7 "Tell __ the judge"
8 Mortgage, e.g.
9 Husky-voiced
10 '67-'70 African state
11 Beatles' "__ Loving"
12 Hero or villain
13 Precipitous person?
14 Eight bits
15 It blows hot and cold
16 Carnivore's craw
17 Really pitiful
18 Put on plastic
26 Stingy
27 Satan's specialties
31 Best, to Lloyd's
32 Lay down the lawn
33 L.A.-N.Y. flight path
34 Freshly painted
36 MGM has two
37 Compete
38 Withstand
40 In high dudgeon
41 Wayne's word
42 Ruffles rackmate
43 Boring tool
44 Bluefins
47 Demonstrate for Dior
48 "Eek" evoker
50 Conveys lightly
51 Lamasery locale
53 Sign of spring
54 Extend across
55 Oda inhabitants
56 Halfhearted try?
57 Postpone
58 Pig's digs
59 She always had a bad hair day
62 Took the stump
63 African country

64 Hulk or Paul
69 Say bluntly
73 Sunup
74 What CLU's sell
76 Color lightly
77 Ekberg or Baker
78 Colorizer Turner
79 Polygraph detection
80 Locust bean
81 Where to find peas on earth?
82 British actress Mary
83 Aerobat's arena
85 Rain __ (come what may)
86 Quinn or Kildare
87 B.C. part
88 BSA troop part
91 Parakeet's perch
92 "__ the nerve!"
93 Mountain ash
94 No __ (keep out)
95 Bowie or Brinkley
96 Old hat
98 What video means
99 TAE or TSE pt.
100 Major-__
101 Pot for a podrida
102 Coward who was knighted
103 Phase out

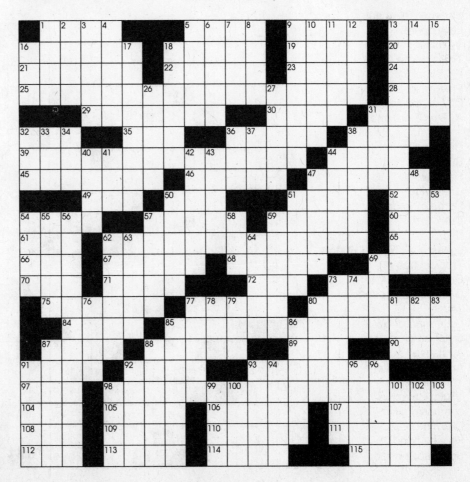

ACROSS

1 Stage backdrop
6 The girl from uncle?
11 Prolonged quarrels
16 Moe or Curly
17 Signify
19 Official seal
20 Largo and lento
21 Guest book
23 Bugs' foil
24 Smoked
25 Deep moan
26 Screen's Gardner
27 Trudge
28 Mockery
29 First or reverse
30 Helped with the dishes
32 Juan or Pedro
33 Astronomer's interval
35 Toe total
37 Contrary current
38 High-ranged sax
40 Nancy Lopez's grp.
42 Little dickens
44 Sired
45 African fly
47 Crusaders' concerns
51 Burgundy
53 Shirt for a she
55 Tempt
56 Balance sheet entry
57 Lully opera
59 Viral disease
61 That *femme*
62 Floral necklace
63 Freelancer's encl.
65 City on the Moselle
67 A, B or E, for short
68 "__ homo"
70 Dear, in Dijon
73 Surveyor's nail
75 Hebrew A
77 Unmoving
79 Horde member
81 Dunk
83 "No cord . . . can . . . hold so fast __": Robert Burton
84 Tropical tree
86 Corpulent
87 Gamma ray product
88 Jaunty
89 Letterman or Swift
91 Galahad garb
94 A relative?
96 Antacid ingredient
98 Turmoil
101 "Rule, Britannia" composer's kin
103 Learning branches
105 Fill with pride
106 Schusser's need
107 Phon and son enders
108 Interest arouser
110 "Et tu, __?"
111 Heartbreak, for one
112 Lincoln's appeal
115 Land ownership
116 Summer TV fare
117 Exposes shams
118 Worships
119 Cosmetician Lauder
120 Warbucks, for one
121 Patches up

DOWN

1 Kowalski cry
2 Showing practicality
3 Used a lasso
4 Borodin's prince
5 My, to Marie
6 Malapropping comedian
7 Truly
8 Phillips U. site
9 Swindle
10 Floor, to Fleur
11 Demon
12 Self-esteem
13 Volunteer
14 Dug deep
15 Regular date
16 Dance components
17 Au __ (up-to-date)
18 Corrigenda
19 Mineral spring
22 Time past
24 FDR's dog
28 Strong point
29 Plasterboard
31 Status
33 Shows off
34 38A neighbor
36 Most agreeable
39 S-shaped molding
41 Jesus, to Giuseppe
43 Stag party attendee
44 Cuts in two
46 Tracks up?
48 Currency unit basis
49 Surpass
50 Be *really* mad
51 Poland's Lech
52 Morse symbol
54 Austen opus
58 Come down in buckets
60 It means foot
64 Stress
66 N. Rhodesia, now
69 French star
71 Gown for Ginsburg
72 Danny Kaye's *Up* __
73 Holden's final film
74 Just fortunate
76 Residue
78 Pianist Pogorelich
80 TV's "I've __ Secret"
82 Many, in Midlothian
85 Respirations
88 Era
90 It means bone
91 __ d'
92 Sole supports?
93 Pay phone word
95 Injury
97 Verbal noun
99 Motherless calves
100 '36 Olympics hero
102 Tea cake
104 Firmed the muscles
106 He says
109 Ers
110 Malt weevil
111 Got carried away?
113 Stage signal
114 To be announced, for short
115 Check the water

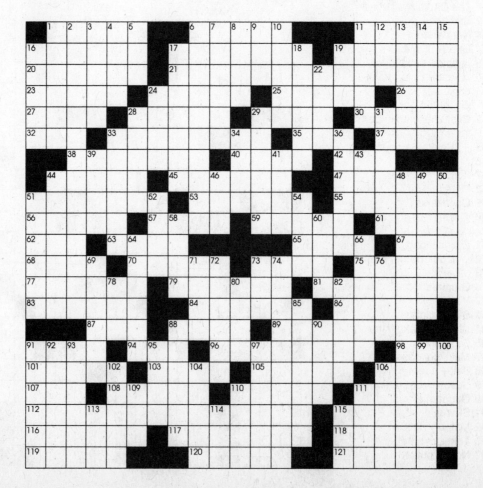

ACROSS

1 Sailor's saint
5 First deadly sin
10 Sauna site
13 Say whodunit
19 Britt __, the Green Hornet
20 Ritzy drive
21 The way
22 Prim partner
23 Baker's doozie
26 Ado
27 Snookums and Sweetums
28 *Battle Cry* writer
29 South Americans
30 Have a go at
31 Before or after head
32 Libreville's land
34 Destiny-determining
35 Honorable
37 *Certainement*
38 Abner's radio chum
41 Jolson standard
44 Dimwit
45 *The Forty Days of __ Dagh*
46 __-Magnon
47 Come again?
48 A few
49 Barber a bush
51 Comic-book bang
52 Part of a list
53 Society swells
55 Queen, in Québec
56 Sand, to some
57 Sow sound
58 San Pedro point
59 Two lines in rhyme
63 Tetons or Sierra Madre
65 Edith, to Archie
66 Weaver's *Alien* character
67 Copped to the cops
68 Choir attire
69 Actor Delon
70 Sidesplitting
73 Shapeless shape
77 Eat in style
78 Make spotless
79 Cherubic figure
80 Early Anka title
81 Was winning
82 Pressed a suit
83 Where Anna taught
84 Lillehammer's land
85 Gay '90s, e.g.
86 Vie for votes
87 "I say!"
90 Star-trashing do
92 Bridge support
93 Sodom or social closer
94 Traveler's aid
97 Sum
99 Glynis' johns?

100 *Born Free*'s Joy and kin
102 What NSF checks do
103 Room to rise
106 Light cavalryman
107 It's nothing
108 "Life is just __ of cherries"
109 Actor Bogosian
110 Suffixes
111 Road sign
112 Billiards shot
113 100-meter run

DOWN

1 Blow up
2 Father Damien's concern
3 *Play __ for Me*
4 Valhalla Allah?
5 Logician's assumption
6 Mouse or squirrel
7 Wedding words
8 Morning moisture
9 Cosmic cycle
10 *Sliver*'s Stone
11 Giving the finger?
12 Bedazzles
13 A hand, clapping
14 Zagreb's land
15 Terra __

16 Sisyphus agenda item
17 Gotten an eyeful
18 Goes amiss
24 Spiffy
25 Ark blueprint unit
32 Folklore figure
33 Freud pupil
34 Source
35 Word on a coin
36 Take as one's own
39 Astronomer's Muse
40 Instant
41 Madras mister
42 Hose down
43 Poker "bullet"
45 Sexy scent
48 Kabob rod
49 Goody-goody
50 Long-ago letter
51 Composer Alban
53 Physicist Harold
54 Desi's drum
55 Actor Auberjonois
56 Secluded vale
58 Mini-whoppers
59 Rock-a-bye rocker
60 More unctuous
61 On your feet again
62 Ballet maneuver
63 __ avis

64 Unknown auth.
65 Unsmiling
67 Burned up the road
68 Capacious
70 Succ or truc finish
71 *Casablanca*'s Claude
72 Mosque leaders
73 Pewit or pipit
74 Court concern
75 Out __ limb
76 Hudson or Half Moon
78 Candy box standards
80 Scale starters
82 Dancer's partner
83 March monarch
84 Worth mentioning
87 More land?
88 Moves furtively
89 Typesetters' no-nos
91 Pound part
94 Ballet's Shearer
95 Ones against
96 Pref. meaning mind
97 Baker preceder
98 Sob sister?
99 It holds your breath
100 "Burke's Law"'s Burke
101 Snow-going slider
104 Lamb's father
105 Mgt. school prof.

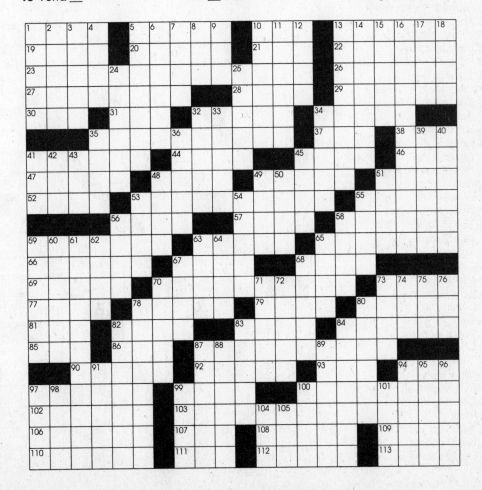

ACROSS

1 Before Christ and British Columbia
4 A magus
10 *Chanteuse* Edith
14 Twist nemesis
19 Rarer than rare
20 Former S.F. mayor
21 Early Andean
22 French painter
23 Shipshape
26 Prolonged pain
27 Hamlet et al.
28 Stevenson monogram
29 Has permission
30 Unseat, in rodeos
32 Became
33 TGIF pt.
34 Japanese cabbage
35 Close
36 Switch position
39 Photoelectric cell
40 Cheap seat site
43 Genealogist's word
44 Turf segment
45 Leguminous vine
46 Kiln
47 Act as usher
48 It means community
51 Winter blanket
53 Move erratically
54 Experience
55 Santa or Vera follower
56 Forest god
57 __ and bear it
58 Leander's love
59 UC Irvine mascot
62 Small pellets
63 Love affair
66 The Spanish?
67 Actor's cosmetic
70 John of Wales
71 Entice
73 Dig for 99A
74 "Gentle on My Mind" musician
76 Listen!
77 Wrongful act
78 Son of Jacob
79 Last Stuart monarch
80 Thorax
82 Two-wheeled vehicle
83 Numerous
84 __ up (got smart)
85 Sugar unit
86 Diva's ditty
87 Turk's topper
88 Chum
89 Theater's Grosbard
90 Minor matter
94 Svc. woman
97 Coll. degrees
98 Photos
99 Adit exiter
100 Small leftover
101 Comic Carvey

102 Show gratitude
104 Pep
105 Lanka lead-in
106 Computer menace
107 Step series
109 Announcer's asset
113 Viscounts' superiors
114 Hodgepodge
115 Lord, in Lod
116 Guido's note
117 Confound
118 Pale coloration
119 Life sacrificer
120 Patriotic org.

DOWN

1 London or Triborough
2 Stoolie
3 "Old Folks at Home" river
4 Hiatuses
5 ". . . and one for __"
6 California county
7 Plain-woven fabric
8 Sweetsop
9 Richard the Anonymous
10 Caribe
11 __ 500
12 Old radio's Goodman
13 To the greatest degree
14 Bumptious one
15 Othello's bane

16 Have expertise
17 Dusk, to Donne
18 Pen full of oink?
24 Notre Dame bench
25 An alphabet's end
31 Damage
33 G-man
34 Fret
35 Killed at a tilt?
37 Exploit
38 Lavish party
40 Nanki-__
41 "Once __ a midnight dreary . . ."
42 Nabokov nymphet
44 Magnitude
47 "Roseanne"'s Gilbert
48 Milan's La __
49 "Believe It __"
50 Is up to snuff
51 Exhausted
52 Crack agent?
53 Wharton's Ethan
54 Entice
57 E. Flanders capital
58 Time of day
60 Separately
61 Sharpness criterion
62 Mini or poodle
63 Inclined
64 Chili con __
65 Finished

68 Unprincipled
69 Genghis or Kublai
72 Coarse file
75 Go bankrupt
77 Coin flipper's call
78 Mideast strip
80 Med, for one
81 Hippy dance?
82 Eccentric
83 Allot
84 Existed
86 '70s African despot
87 1040 and W-2
88 Darling
90 Meager
91 Christie's Belgian
92 Sluggishness
93 Get one's bearings
94 Admonished
95 She played Jessica
96 Julius or Augustus
101 Couple
103 Pork Chop or Hamburger
104 Over-proud
105 Actress Thompson
106 Bustle
107 Red or Black
108 Wee bit
110 Samuel's teacher
111 Scenery chewer
112 Planner page

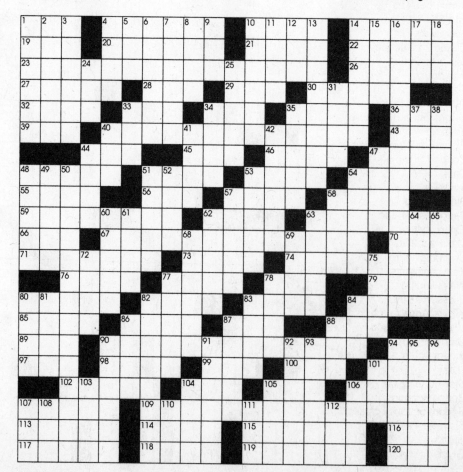

ACROSS

1 Like Liverpool's Four
4 Capacitance unit
9 Irascibility
15 Stalag GI
18 Magnificent mausoleum site
20 Idaho's Coeur d'__
21 *Si, si,* asea
22 Lyricist Gershwin
23 Dig site
24 They're out of your mind
26 *Bellum* opposite
27 Star quality?
29 Nixon nix
30 Attractive
32 Ruler of Palestine
33 Schooner feature
34 Grew weary
35 Bird dog
37 Granola ingredient
39 Time for a test
41 Out doors
42 Look amused
43 Tend tables
45 Give a talk
47 Uncivil
48 Tea party crasher
49 ". . . and to __ good night"
50 Ripen
51 Watney's, for one
52 It's out of your mind
56 Pop favorite?
57 Pirandello's people
59 *Show Boat* composer
60 *Allons!* in Allentown
62 VMI or RPI pt.
63 Look and look and look
65 Bean town?
66 Kris Kringle
69 Book jacket part
70 HOMES' biggest
74 He wed Jackie
75 It's out of your mind
79 Lakers' assn.
80 Beseech
81 Bard baddy
82 Correct the wheels
83 State as fact
84 Theater seater
87 Lip service?
88 Rani's wrap
89 Gaggle members
90 *Konditorei* specialty
92 Flea-flicker finale
93 Intersection
94 Laid booby traps
95 First-class stuff?
97 Jeweler's unit
98 Brawl
100 Sentry's station
101 Leisure

105 Specs supporter
106 It's out of your mind
109 Gas or pit ender
110 3-3, e.g.
111 Stir up
112 Beatrice's beloved
113 State of pique
114 Sponsor's spots
115 *The Right Stuff* role
116 Red as __
117 Mazatlán Mrs.

DOWN

1 Cultivate crops
2 Juárez water
3 It's out of your mind
4 Makeup man Max
5 Audibly
6 Tear apart
7 Stake on the table
8 German article
9 Bears' lairs
10 Hilton rival
11 Wine: Pref.
12 Body of *eau*
13 It's closed in a wink
14 Vacation options
15 They're out of your mind
16 By mouth
17 Like paraffin

19 Beatty's Bening
25 A Karamazov
28 Wraths
31 89D, for short
33 Certain Louvre oil
34 Uranus' child
35 Near East inn
36 Jubilate
37 Certain gens.
38 Well-off
39 Home of La Scala
40 Rev. 20 threat
42 Eye light
43 Crisp cracker
44 *Crooklyn'*s Woodard
46 __ *Sabe* (Tonto term)
48 Penultimate state
52 Linnet's kin
53 Giraffe's kin
54 Tie type
55 Aden neighbor
58 Twice XXVI
61 Camel component
63 Counterfeit coins
64 Cantina snacks
65 Louis, in Lugano
66 '37 *Elephant Boy* star
67 Headlock?
68 They're out of your mind

69 Thresher's tool
70 Uses muddlers
71 They're out of your mind
72 Portly, plus
73 Seen less
76 Had a taste for
77 Like some twangs
78 How sad!
83 Fills with fizz
85 Writer Ambler
86 Fugitive
89 INdTV's Al
91 Famed streetcar
92 Soft core
93 It's often underfoot
95 "Northern Exposure" stroller
96 Michaelmas daisy
97 Social standing
98 Greek salad cheese
99 Takeover try
100 Tub stopper
101 Do the deck
102 Fragrant tree
103 California trailblazer
104 Valencian verb
107 Hawaii's Mauna __
108 Columnist Le Shan

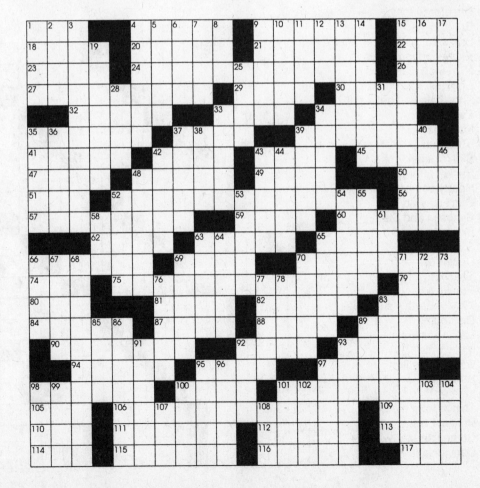

ACROSS

1 A month in Masada
5 Hurried home?
9 Ambassador's asset
13 Conspirator with Brutus
18 __ avis
19 Country's Tucker
21 Fever
22 Gobbled down
23 Music based on a Hoffmann tale
26 Oil source
27 Like Hardy's Jude
28 Succinct
29 Hospitality enjoyers
30 Single-pipped dominoes
31 Watery fluid
32 Like hard rock: Pref.
33 Removes mist
36 Coats with frost
37 He wrote "Diana"
40 Approver's expression
41 Dickens villain
42 TV's "Lonesome George"
43 Square-dance group
44 Theater's McAnuff
45 Certain hall decor
48 Eight pts.
49 Syn. opposite
50 Director Sidney
51 Breathing sound
52 Sra.'s daughter
53 Expanded, as pupils
55 Nine-inch measures
57 Emphasis
59 They help you get a grip
60 Psi follower
61 Madame Curie
62 Young'un
64 Skiers' aids
65 Basket rummy
67 Hearty companion
68 Can't stay up
69 Simpson and Starr
70 Brit. isle
72 S.A. city
73 December wish
77 Teachers' org.
78 Prankish fairy
79 70% of Earth's surface
80 Distributes
81 LAPD officers
82 Mat words
84 Bodily appetites
85 Strip site
87 Irritated
88 Things from the blue
89 Bristle: Pref.
90 Comedian Marty
92 Canvas holder

93 Introduce
97 Muslim prophet
98 Bing's December dream
101 Dvořák or Bruckner
102 Director David
103 Bound bundle
104 Ostrich cousins
105 Billiards move
106 Stir on the water?
107 Alcott and Irving
108 Actor's assumption

DOWN

1 Florence's river
2 Smear on
3 M.A. part
4 Nocturnal mammal
5 Gazes intently
6 Spikes punch
7 Affix your John Hancock
8 Tint
9 Camry competitor
10 Kind of prejudice
11 Wholesomely pretty
12 Ball booster
13 Nonchalantly
14 Wisdom goddess

15 December wish
16 Worship system
17 Tarzan's family
20 Apollo's twin
24 Ladder step
25 Alhambra neighbor El __
29 Thin porridge
31 Vision
32 Butler, on the screen
33 Tzara's movement
34 Improve writing
35 Eight-day holiday
36 Was uncontrolled
37 Car co-ops
38 "Adonais" subject
39 Book of charts
41 Shows annoyance
42 Former Gold Coast
45 Jaded
46 Exterior
47 Incomplete sents.
52 Sahibs' kin
54 Not taped or filmed
55 Kind of a hit
56 Mph center
57 Xmas temp
58 Refuse
60 Med. specialty

61 Takes notice of
62 Petruchio's Kate
63 Selassie
64 Spanish snacks
65 Encrusts
66 Narrow ridge
68 Rapidity
69 Hits with horns
71 Orient
73 __ and sinker
74 Zeniths
75 Talisman
76 Gets cozy
81 Brandy goblet
83 Confessions of faith
84 Behind
85 Lines in letters
86 SW Indians
88 Modern religion
89 Use an atomizer
90 Mosque leader
91 Zola heroine
92 Pitcher
94 Shot and shell, for short
95 Fetal membrane
96 Existence
98 Edmonton's prov.
99 Got or hot closer
100 Line of clothing?

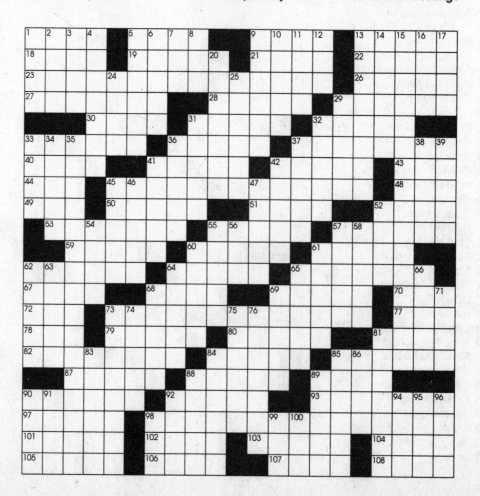

ACROSS

1 Take the primrose path
6 Discard
11 Balkan capital
16 Trailing
17 Herald, Pershing and Times
19 Vegas naturals
20 Raises
21 Los Alamos sights
23 *Psycho* name
24 Narcotic shrubs
25 Nero's nothing
26 GPA spoiler
27 "Outland" comic penguin
28 It means "of ankles"
29 Capital by a fjord
30 Freezing rain
32 For each
33 Chayefsky play *The __*
35 Sixth sense
37 Puts 2 and 2 together
38 What a self-reformer turns over
40 Do a garden chore
42 Eng. subject
44 With 91D, a Caribbean leader
45 Oblique
47 Evoke
51 Most lethargic
53 RSVP request
55 Kind of oil or republic
56 Fed the kitty
57 Doggone!
59 *Swan Lake* role
61 Election losers
62 Stuttgart st.
63 The pen
65 Alleviate
67 Share
68 High, in Haiti
70 White-haired horses
73 Singer Tennille
75 Basel's river
77 Shout at the soloist
79 Arthur's nephew
81 Wine holders
83 Sioux
84 Flag's fiftieth
86 "__ without end . . ."
87 Koppel or Kennedy
88 __ San Lucas
89 Hudson Bay borderer
91 Rob Reiner's dad
94 Ancestry-oriented org.
96 Kitchen conveniences
98 Peruke
101 Face-cream additives
103 Boglike
105 Burning

106 Biblical graffito opener
107 Norm, for short
108 Verdi's Miller
110 Indo-Iranian
111 Sweet wines
112 '45 Bette Davis hit
115 Waterloo
116 Break a promise
117 Lumbar anaesthetics
118 Mar
119 Popish Plotter
120 Bergen's Mortimer
121 Good-time Charlie

DOWN

1 Bright blanket
2 What one who wasn't born yesterday didn't just fall off
3 Granulates, as potatoes
4 Pangolin's menu
5 QB's gains
6 Crush completely
7 Social convention
8 Words of cheer
9 Itinerary abbr.
10 Laborers
11 Bear's orders
12 It means egg
13 Had a vendetta

14 Certainly
15 Plus factors
16 '45 jazz innovation
17 __ a whip
18 Smirched
19 Academic subj.
22 Conductance units
24 Welles' citizen
28 Archer Wilhelm and son
29 Combination punch
31 One from south of the border
33 Rough wool fabrics
34 Barley fibers
36 West Point frosh
39 Actress Adams
41 Observed
43 Stevedores' union
44 Town near Colton
46 Articles
48 Boxer's hazard
49 Began a canticle
50 Flavors
51 Rushed
52 The Andrews Sisters, e.g.
54 Nothing in Nîmes
58 "__, a bone . . ."
60 Secular

64 Walks across
66 Flubs
69 Flute on and on
71 Okinawa town
72 Slang for a sailor
73 Argentine aunt
74 Wambaugh's *The __*
76 Mata
78 Hwy.
80 Away, sans OK
82 Informed
85 Athabascans, e.g.
88 Turning point
90 Gull friend?
91 See 44A
92 Tennis star Gibson
93 Rat, e.g.
95 Ex-dictator Idi
97 Cockney's "Right on!"?
99 Unimpaired
100 Film classic *Beau __*
102 Plods
104 Grates
106 Soprano Anna
109 Script ending?
110 English composer
111 Chick's chirp
113 So-so grade
114 Cardplayer's cry
115 Dental deg.

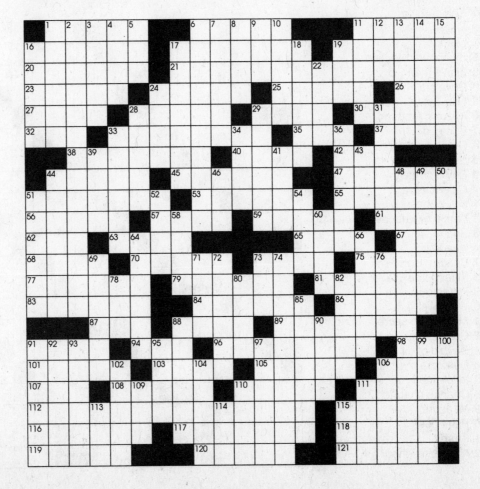

ACROSS

1 TV alien
4 Shooter's game
9 Actors' assumptions
14 Arcing shots
18 Store-hrs. word
19 Spartan slave
20 Ere
21 Of Fr., Ger., G.B., etc.
22 Bravo's cousin
23 Total try
25 Flurry of activity
26 Hung-jury result
28 Nom de plume
29 Bias
30 Starsky's partner
31 Yet
32 Like an egghead
34 Act parts
36 Hyatt or Hilton
37 Saluted
38 Waterproof boot
39 Wrestler Brazil
40 Noodles, in Naples
41 Rugged mountain
44 "Are you __ out?"
45 Wind up in the black
48 Begone beginner
49 Batter after Babe
50 Hoopster
51 Potpourri part
52 Magus
53 Languor
55 Symphonic section
56 Finn's friend
58 Revelers' romp
59 Like Esau
60 Arizona Amerind
61 Sun god
64 Grasping devices
65 Backs with bucks
69 Royal or navy
70 Calendar page
71 Hay cubes
72 Toque or tarboosh
73 Sodom fleer
74 Heads up!
77 Beach resort
78 Maestro de Waart
79 Paramour
80 Wear well
81 Membrane secretion part
82 Cold as ice
84 Devoid of dinero
86 Democrats' symbol
87 Influenced
88 Change channels?
89 Measure
90 Plant pest
91 Sturdy
92 Naples neighbor

95 Pastoral places
96 "You're kidding me!"
99 Sturdiness symbol
100 Spiked club
101 Disinclined
102 '40s riveter
103 Scap or spat ender
104 Scroll holders
105 *Philadelphia* director
106 Lay out money
107 Mystery's Josephine

DOWN

1 Element element
2 '53 title role for 14D
3 Filled in the gaps
4 Constitution
5 Martyr's mementos
6 Abdul's Almighty
7 Car co-op
8 Queue after R
9 Coffee-cup warmup
10 Rubbish
11 Writer Anita
12 Cross i's?
13 Make waves?
14 Actress Caron
15 By far
16 Salty

17 Classify
20 Contradict
24 Dermal design
27 Stereo component
29 Caesar or Cobb
31 Off the sauce
32 Swiss port
33 Comic Rudner
34 Swine's slop
35 It's paddled in the rear
36 Informal, in a way
37 Snicker syllables
39 Like marshland
40 Country's Cline
42 Opera box
43 Parliament member
45 What laders load
46 Goalpost part
47 Dolorous drops
50 Yastrzemski
52 Pavlova portrayal
54 Golfer's goal
55 African tribe
56 Muscle-bone link
57 Latin lesson word
59 Medal or award
60 Series opener
61 Equal to the task
62 Trudge

63 On the fritz
64 Fare exchange
65 Traitorous
66 Lose your nerve
67 Best-selling Betty J.
68 Poker-faced
70 Changed abodes
71 Horny bills
74 Actor Bridges
75 Move like the Blob
76 Not at all 31D
77 Sudden rush
81 Expressed grief
83 Poker bumps
84 Skirt's topper
85 Carrier's course
86 He sailed on the Beagle
87 Asparagus unit
88 Rage
89 One who takes a gander?
90 Opera's Gluck
91 Wineglass part
92 Call it quits
93 Story
94 Informal assent
96 Son of Jacob
97 'Tis the night before Christmas
98 Francs, for short

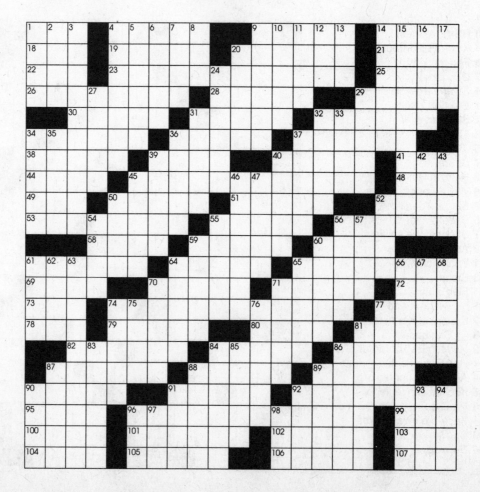

ACROSS

1 Nun's followers, in Israel
7 Area south of Atlas Mts.
13 Not at all *grand*
18 Heavenly
19 Beseech
21 Tetragrammaton expansion
22 Chews out
24 Swashbuckler Flynn
25 Lace again
26 Land west of Nod
27 Burmese measure
28 Night noise
29 Region
30 Hoover was one
31 Pose anew
33 Big drink
34 School before jr. high
35 Great Laker Jerry
36 Small drink
39 Before legs or level
40 Gamal Abdel
43 Discontinue
44 Via, con and aque enders
46 Ancient Italian
47 More brazen
48 Amtrak upper
49 Square things?
50 Verbose
51 Depleters
54 Bob and Carol and Ted and Alice
55 Alpine abode
56 Kinte family saga
57 Computer datum
58 Ham preserver?
59 Made a reservation
61 Single
62 Pop-top feature
63 Divided, as a road
64 Loire city
65 Garment for Gracchus
66 Cagey ones
68 Menlo Park name
69 Jested
70 Caddoan Indians
71 One who whimpers
72 Prayer series
73 Cretan summit
74 Bread spreads
75 Gold and Barbary
76 Comm. coll. degs.
77 Pop group
79 A few bucks?
80 Tibia site
81 Ref. book
83 Seize illegally
85 Pueblo foes
86 Chaucer piece

90 Wahine's welcome
92 Sesame
93 Seed covering
94 Peggy Lee signature tune
95 Bestower
96 Monopoly holding
100 Sluggish
101 Mutual agreement
102 Catherine, for one
103 Folkloric fiends
104 Rome's epic
105 Sets firmly

DOWN

1 Express derision
2 The small type?
3 Means of communication
4 Otherwise
5 Caboodle companion
6 Plotter
7 Classic rock singer?
8 Ugandan name
9 Hwy. Post Off.
10 Ft. above sea level
11 Open car
12 It means chief
13 Wild Asian dogs
14 Deserves
15 Socks it to, judicially
16 What pianists tickle
17 Russian wagon
18 Irish exclamation
20 __-Unis
23 Red-coated cheese
30 Merriment
31 Gloater's pronouncement
32 Raleigh's rival
34 Crosswordy worker
35 Gushed
37 Thinks
38 Meticulous one
40 A, but not A-flat
41 What you can't tell?
42 Covets, e.g.
43 __ it (calmed down)
45 Cardboard box, briefly
46 Anwar, et al.
47 Comes to a stop
48 Shattered
50 Gives a ring
51 "ER" role
52 Dead ones are doubles
53 Regular date
55 Kind of cable

56 Salon solutions
59 Flaxen
60 Customize
65 Make salad
67 Faith, to Feydeau
68 Certain fisher
69 Soprano Sutherland
71 Adjust
72 *Reines'* mates
73 Posting
75 Clawed, as a crustacean
76 Barber's __ *for Strings*
78 Bizarre
80 Activity
82 Thither
84 Italian art center
85 Entreated
86 Pied-à-__
87 Shun
88 Slants
89 Wagnerian role
91 All singing, all dancing
93 One against
94 Richard Simmons' bane
97 Bear lair
98 Like: Suff.
99 Doctrine

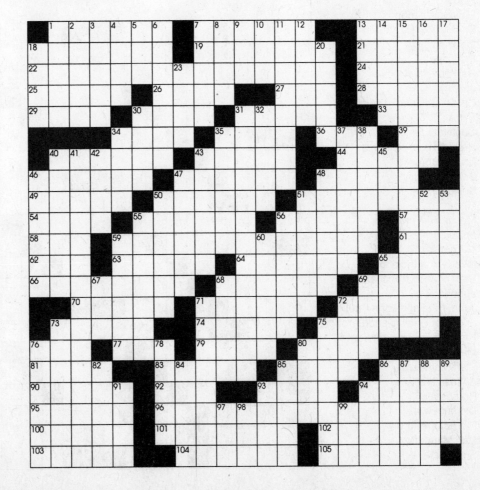

ACROSS

1 The slammer
5 Glitch
9 "You're it!"
12 Bisect
17 Solothurn's river
18 Gold
20 Hawkeye's home
21 Advantage
22 The Bambino
25 Kind of wave
26 TV control
27 Subtle sarcasm
28 Confederates
29 Gossip
30 Up for __
31 Religious sculpture
32 "__ the Walrus"
33 Play
34 Horticulturist
37 Caper
40 Bagel alternative
42 *Life with Father*'s Clarence
43 Tumult
44 Miffed
45 Writes IOU's
46 "__ girl!"
47 Formicary dweller
48 Kookaburra
52 Pallid
53 Hawkeye's friends
56 Sadat
57 Modifies
58 Incensed
59 *As You Like It* locale
60 Jet
61 Cause longlasting anger
63 Extra
64 Captivated
67 Heraldic borders
68 Be dictatorial to
70 Bonzo's cousin
71 Surrounded by
72 Memento __
73 Mechanical practice, once
74 Merganser
75 Invaders of India, once
76 Start of a Poor Richard aphorism
80 John, Paul and John Paul
81 Friend of Shelley and Byron
84 Haven from the humdrum
85 Malleable metal
86 Staff members
87 Actress Mai
88 Prances
92 Did sum work
93 "V" actor Andrew
94 Like Manderley
95 Small nails
96 Words of support
98 Sun circler
99 Siberian city
100 Drench
101 Second-hand
102 Uppsala citizen
103 Dashboard stat
104 Caribou, e.g.
105 Sun. talks

DOWN

1 Nickname for Louis
2 Border lake
3 Chekhov "sister"
4 Confine
5 Bow of obeisance
6 Off-the-wall
7 "I smell __!"
8 Rev the motor
9 Dots on maps
10 Out, in baseball
11 Heater
12 Extreme ill will
13 Ply the sky
14 Disney doggy duo
15 Italian ways
16 90-deg. tube extension
19 Ballet's Shearer et al.
20 Weather map line
23 Bears, to Brutus
24 Window case
28 Little women
30 "Anitra's Dance" writer
31 More 52A
33 Mild curses
34 Dancers Marge and __ Champion
35 Corroder
36 Old soap "__ Hope"
37 1/16 oz.
38 Japanese language
39 What *South Pacific* sings there is
40 Greek literary language
41 French feudal family
44 Runnered shoe
46 Texas ballplayer
49 Capacitance unit
50 Largest lemur
51 Kind of tooth or talk
52 Grad
54 Annoyed
55 UCI, UCLA and UCSD
57 To pieces
59 Shower time
60 Links legend Sam
61 Use the oven
62 Pauldron, cuisse and greave
63 Miserable
64 Bacchanal cries
65 Heavy foil
66 Lawn waterers
68 IOU subjects
69 Once around the sun
72 Made cat calls
74 High-sounding
77 Hamlet's jester
78 Actress Elg
79 North Sea port
80 Central point
82 Having movable covers
83 "__ Fidelis"
85 Leather processor
87 Drummer's implement
88 Bring about
89 Washer cycle
90 Less fierce
91 Rosebud, etc.
92 ". . . maids all in __"
93 Vainglory
94 Grimace
95 A.D.'s precursors
96 __ Kippur
97 How some parcels come

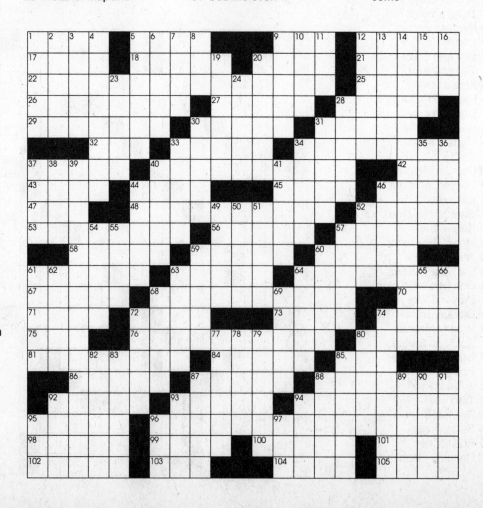

ACROSS

1 ". . . a __ unto my feet"
5 Hard-bed bear
9 Comeback of a kind
13 Job for the bunco squad
17 Away from the wind
18 Sooner city
19 Place after place
20 "It is easier for __ to go . . ."
22 Pre-landing formation
25 Humbert's obsession
26 Drawstring bag
27 Actor Jeremy
28 Tossed the dice
29 *Pretty Woman* man
30 Stoles and shawls
31 Outdo
32 Jerez product
35 Causes distress
36 What some may talk
37 Puts the kibosh on
38 Living thing
39 Saharan
40 Cinder or citron ender
44 Not quite never
45 Arsenio Hall catchphrase
47 Ride an updraft
48 Keats specialty
49 *Carmen* composer
50 See 60D
51 Tedious task
52 Kind of sweater
54 The old __-ho
56 Actress Fleming
57 Hurler Hershiser
58 Feydeau specialty
59 Abrupt
60 Black eye
63 "Shush!"
64 Kitchen container
68 McCartney's band
69 Dip donuts
70 City of Lights
71 Tell's canton
72 Enthusiastic
73 Play mind games with
76 Table-talk collections
77 Bigfoot of Asia
78 Breezy
79 Stand for a sitting?
80 Executive's enclave
81 Mettle
83 Smacking of the sea
84 Kevin of "Kojak"
85 Being overfond
87 '51 Reagan co-star
88 Humdinger
89 Wise one
90 Coated cheese
91 Town south of Tampa
95 Reveal
96 Like bankrupt businesses
98 Shrank back
99 Maturing agent
100 Mayberry tippler
101 3-in-1, etc.
102 Forest forager
103 Silent assents
104 Gets the point
105 Treasury offering

DOWN

1 Haley-Bolger co-star
2 Cosmetic addictive
3 Go all gooey
4 Bloodline
5 Severe poverty
6 Emulate Izaak
7 Meerschaum
8 Toothpaste-approving grp.
9 Alienate
10 Giza pyramid builder
11 Dilemma duo
12 Is proprietor of
13 Skedaddles
14 Be in charge
15 ". . . inch, and they'll take __"
16 Taxi ticker
20 "Enough __!"
21 Youngster
23 Champagne buckets
24 Losing oomph
30 Belt belt
31 Invigorating
32 Busybody
33 Believer in karma
34 Do very, very well
35 He gorged on gourds
36 Cooling-off period
38 Gem setting part
39 Upstairs
41 Craziness criterion
42 Rendered hogfat
43 Bailiwick
45 Onions go-with
46 Pamphlet
49 Ear benders
51 Actor Sarandon
53 Type of runner
54 17-syllable poem
55 Before, before "before"
56 Take to the station
58 Humorous
59 December song
60 Bend with the breeze
61 Bee flats
62 "I really put my foot __!"
63 "Star Trek" alien
64 Hugh or Mariah
65 North African city
66 Poets' inspiration
67 Gone upwards
69 "Nothing __!" (no way!)
70 It's based on basil
73 Discouraged
74 Rambles
75 Père Goriot's creator
76 French tapestry town
80 Of our star
82 Military attack feature
83 Became bitter
84 Forcible restraint
85 Michelangelo masterpiece
86 Sheepish?
87 Hand drum
88 Piaf's "__ en Rose"
89 Suture
90 __ Carlo Menotti
91 Venue
92 The O in B&O
93 Compete at Camelot
94 Choir recess
97 Dawn deity

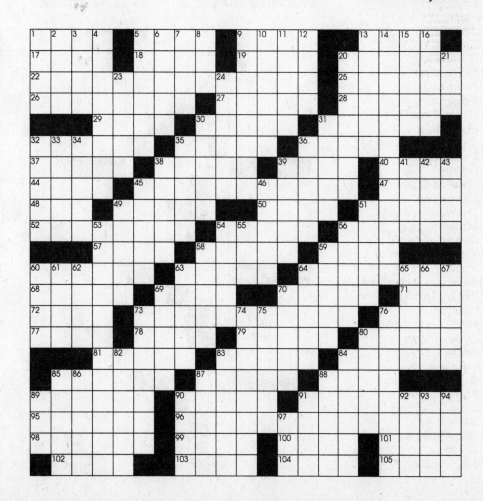

ACROSS

1 Bowe blow
4 Blow your own horn
8 Preceding periods
12 Long-dist. run
16 Expert
17 Old Greek colony
19 Skirt style
20 Goshawk's grabber
21 Song about a swagman
24 Nautical order
25 Draw out
26 Comforts
27 Augie March's creator
28 Corrects
30 Hindu goddess
31 Joker
32 Moselle tributary
33 Cackleberry
36 '54 Horse of the Year
43 Be hoity-toity
45 *Herr*, here
46 Once-stylish jacket
47 Cease, asea
51 Rocky hill
52 Suppose
54 Drench
55 As long as
56 Bar orders
58 Playwright John Millington's kin
59 Frame, in a way
60 Single units
61 Unk's bro
62 Shake a leg
70 Emir's asset
71 Pedro's pigeon
72 Indigent
73 G- and T-men
77 Mandarin, e.g.
79 Sandburg and Sagan
80 Pentateuch
81 Courted
82 Snow, to Scots
84 Irish patriot
85 Down-easter's state
86 Matterhorn, e.g.
87 Mystery writer's Oscar
89 First words from the moon
94 Baseball's Red or White
95 Pickle flavoring
99 Function
100 March's was the 15th
102 Aquarium flora
104 Edible root
108 Links bearers
111 Sunday rejoinders
112 Suspect's out
113 W.H. Auden poem
116 '29 emotion
117 British notables
118 Tire layer
119 Four-in-hand

120 Very, in Vichy
121 Where Greeks left their gift
122 Is mistaken
123 Yore

DOWN

1 Fat chewers
2 Cajuns' first home
3 Caspian caviar
4 *Carmen* creator
5 *Reine*'s mate
6 Arbor preceder
7 Jazz players' jobs
8 Draw forth
9 Evil anagram
10 Means' destination
11 Place for swells?
12 Asian weight
13 Airline to Ben-Gurion
14 De __ (over again)
15 Had the facts
18 Enraged
19 Chateaubriand novel
20 The railroad section-gang worker
22 Roll-bk. bearer
23 Actor Arkin
27 Misbehaving
29 Rep's counterpart
31 Are in the past

34 Caught on
35 10 to the hundredth power
37 "Lord, __ I?": Matt. 26
38 Dodger announcer Scully's namesakes
39 Gas for a light
40 Locomotive's sound
41 One of the Gaels
42 Regrets
43 March or mambo
44 Singer Lopez
47 D.A.'s helper
48 Competitor
49 One against
50 Porgy
52 Experienced one
53 Mortar's mate
57 Chatterer
58 Was in session
60 Actor Ferrer
61 RNA minus oxygen
63 Casual greetings
64 *All That Jazz*'s Bob
65 Restitution
66 Garment worker's union?
67 Expression
68 Ex-Python Eric
69 Saclike structure

73 Sphere opener
74 Certain Indian
75 Certain Indian
76 Indian breads
77 Type of dict.
78 Beer flavorings
81 Corduroy component
83 Gone by
88 Bunyan's implement
90 Former flame?
91 Kind of winks
92 Norse anthologies
93 Hammer part, to some
95 Noodle
96 Conceive
97 Edible seed
98 Flogged
101 Result of a schism
103 Alan and Cheryl
104 Absorbed
105 Winged
106 Have a repast
107 Sacred Egyptian bird
108 Coventry cleaner
109 Of aircraft
110 Withered
113 Asian new year
114 High'r than
115 By __ (very much)

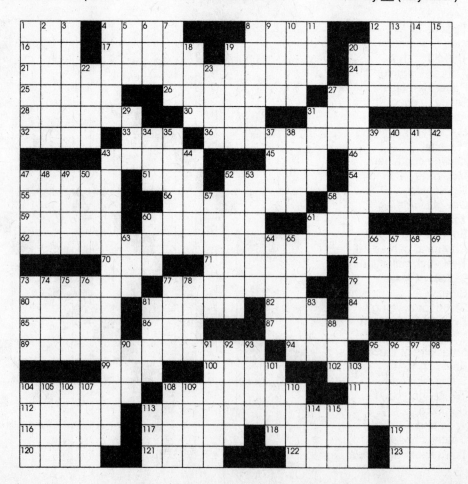

ACROSS

1 UCLA part
4 S.C. motto *Dum spiro,* __
9 Legal kickback
15 Rip, hack, whip or chain
18 Outback birds
20 *Acteur* Delon
21 Neptune neighbor
22 Hagen of the stage
23 It's a long story
24 Dinosaur confection?
26 Mars or Mercury
27 Seeing the world
29 Nile vipers
30 Developed into
32 Poe crow
33 Lute marking
34 Organ offerer
35 Syrup sources
37 Dieter's dread
39 Chop-shop props
41 Greek strongman
42 Herb for salmon
43 Scissors case
45 Experience 57A
47 '60s sprinter Wyomia
48 Wild fight
49 Rhett's last word
50 Ebenezer's expletive
51 Joad or Jones
52 What confectioners did?
56 Zsa Zsa's sis
57 Really great feeling
59 Takes a chair
60 Kind of horn or hound
62 Detail
63 Sorta saunter
65 Pylon shape
66 100 céntimos
69 Intl. relief org.
70 Lazybones
74 Inuit's knife
75 Gutsy girl's makeup?
79 Vintage auto
80 Panhandle
81 Army outfit
82 Three minutes for Marciano
83 Be a kvetch
84 Hose woes
87 Point at the table?
88 Sty cry
89 Alamo defender
90 Cops' collars
92 Egg yellow
93 Billy the Kid
94 Comfort quaff
95 Tizzy
97 Sings like Merman
98 Under-counter compartment
100 Wedding cake feature
101 Certain siren sounder
105 H⁺, for one
106 Pure sweetness explained?

109 Boy-watch
110 Moving vehicle
111 Feeling like a million
112 Twist of fate
113 Leo's lodge
114 Whatsoever
115 Church assemblies
116 "Eight Miles High" group
117 Balderdash!

DOWN

1 "__ we forget"
2 Poetic tentmaker
3 Stuffed with bonbons?
4 Mercury models
5 Unadorned
6 Make bread – or bring home the bacon
7 Call up
8 Word on a dime
9 After Ballet or Charlotte
10 Go volcanic
11 Paper-or-plastic totes
12 Santa __ winds
13 Food fish
14 In __ (basically)
15 Sweet squares?
16 A bit smashed?
17 Walk in water
19 Telly on the telly

25 Sailor's tale
28 Dec. 24 and 31
31 Wheedle
33 Form 1040 returner
34 Taking action
35 Photo finish
36 "Here's looking __, kid!"
37 "SNL" 's Radner
38 Not windward
39 78D's organic part
40 Uncle Tom, e.g.
42 Strauss' material
43 Paul in *The Hustler*
44 Flavorful
46 One of those
48 *Jules and Jim*'s Jeanne
52 Annie of "Designing Women"
53 To munch, in München
54 Teem
55 Dogie's domain
58 Make haste
61 Humpback's home
63 San Quentin's county
64 Declaim
65 Pokey or pen
66 Queen's Head and King's Arms
67 Turgenev heroine

68 Hip to sweets?
69 Dog, to Darius
70 What Lou Grant hated in Mary
71 Sweet strength?
72 Like the twilight zone
73 Friend of Ms. White
76 __-percha
77 Sag
78 Firm earth
83 Smart employer (would you believe)?
85 Get large
86 Leaves the union
89 Something from the blue
91 Painfully
92 Play area
93 Wallace and Noah
95 Imposed penalties
96 Yorkshire city
97 X or Lazy J
98 Met star
99 Leather color
100 Jackson 5 member
101 '50s TV horse
102 Frankenstein aide
103 Ad award
104 B'way's original Tony, Larry
107 Rooter
108 Sis, to Sonny

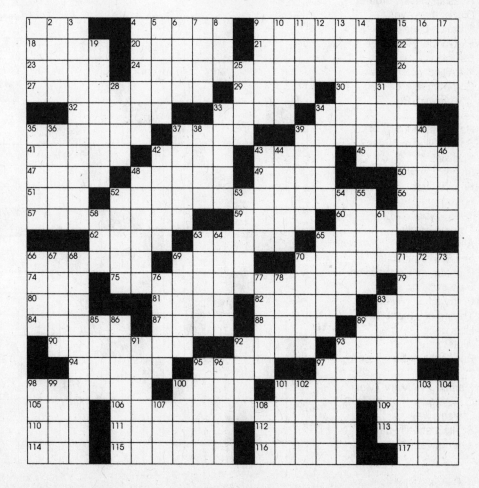

ACROSS

1 "Go, team!"
4 Trite
9 Noted bareback rider
15 Major leaguer
18 "How sad!"
20 Do stand-up?
21 Gets on the soapbox
22 Journalist's question
23 Left at sea?
24 Comedy brother
26 Réunion, *par exemple*
27 Puts up a fight
29 Fan's fave
30 Made airtight
32 WWI battle site
33 Highland valley
34 "Who steals my __ . . ."
35 Autobiography
37 Dry ink
39 Fidgety
41 Beatles' "Free as __"
42 Ring out
43 One with will power?
45 Marks in a margin
47 Gen.'s underlings
48 African antelope
49 Mansard feature
50 Weasel's prey
51 Angled annex
52 Russian classic brother
56 Bigger than avg.
57 Breakup cause
59 Ex-Dodger Hershiser
60 Bar man
62 '44 Allied victory site
63 Common taters
65 __-Cynwyd, Pa.
66 Forswear
69 Raised platform
70 Spring-filled mattress?
74 Kiwi kin
75 Inventor brother
79 Freeze over
80 Lob's path
81 "I'm __ you"
82 Turning point
83 Alliance
84 Indian monotheists
87 Problem-solving session
88 Be a good boy
89 Chihuahua chicken
90 Traded at a meet
92 He's deep
93 Water channels
94 Put on the radio
95 "__ on first?"
97 Marianne or Mary Tyler
98 O.K., e.g.
100 Chase away
101 Scylla's equally-bad
   alternative
105 Coffee dispenser
106 Tale-telling brother
109 Spanish jar
110 Patient's payment
111 Apollo 13 astronaut
112 Stendhal's charterhouse
   site
113 Reichstag refusal
114 Positive about
115 Short-tempered
116 Workout workup
117 Chew the fat

DOWN

1 They may be beaten
2 Very much
3 "Paper Doll" brother
4 Wisconsin athlete
5 Seed enclosures
6 Genteel
7 Pops the question
8 __ *Miz*
9 "Johnny B. __"
10 *Loot* playwright
11 Actress Arlene
12 Graph extension?
13 Against
14 Puts forth
15 "Bye, Bye Love" brother
16 Function
17 Was short
19 Semi-comas
25 Memorable comic
   Kamen
28 Crossword diagram
31 __ were (so to speak)
33 Ingrid's last role
34 Actress Rosie
35 Attacked with a spray
36 Salerno neighbor
37 Cecil's buddy
38 Rawboned
39 Go up against
40 Floor in a *maison*
42 Dialogue writer
43 Learned on the
   grapevine
44 Chair man
46 Dump closure?
48 More malefic
52 Opening bars
53 Excite
54 Kansas City neighbor
55 Gentleman's gentleman
58 As a rule, as an abbr.
61 Mercenary's
   opportunity
63 Sea dogs
64 Sitcom sample
65 Unpressed
66 Latin I word
67 Tennis' Becker
68 Studio mogul brother
69 Had a three-star meal
70 Cellar dwellers
71 Righteous brother
72 *Maitre*'s milieu
73 Of a '20s art movement
76 Exercised suffrage
77 Halting words?
78 Off-the-rack items?
83 New Orleans street
85 Top crop
86 Takes up the whole sofa
89 Game gambit
91 Greek mountain
92 Prosperous period
93 Prepare a disk
95 Puppy, e.g.
96 Ms. Golightly
97 Poppa's partner
98 Pants part
99 Hydrox rival
100 Bandleader Fields
101 Sticking place
102 Put on staff
103 Pelvis bones
104 Went into depth?
107 C - XLIV
108 Dr. Welby, et al.

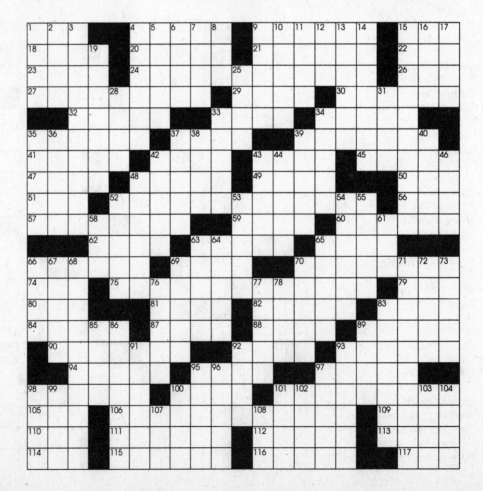

ACROSS

1 Blubber
5 Wee pranksters
9 One of the wealthy
13 Telemarketing danger
17 Twice *cuatro*
18 Limp-watch painter
19 Dyed-in-the-wool
20 Dug the dirt
22 *Sister Act* sister
25 Trip to the store
26 *Eroica* or *New World*
27 Long-limbed
28 Self-rewarding quality?
29 Hittite city
30 Fab Four's oldest
31 Gainsays
32 Like this word
35 Robert E. Lee sighting site
36 Spree
37 Oil source
38 She works under pressure
39 Lacquer layer
40 Viking's landing site
44 Trig function
45 "Sister, Sister" sister
47 City near Buffalo
48 Six-footer, of a sort
49 Hazard
50 Comrade in arms
51 '60s greeting
52 *Manon* composer
54 Mythical maze commissioner
56 Pitcher's slab
57 Pesky plant
58 Harley rider
59 Made the rent?
60 Uprising
63 April payment
64 Golden-brown stone
68 Tampico ta-ta
69 __ *Joy of Man's Desiring*
70 Like the designated driver
71 Pop favorite
72 River in Cumbria
73 Singing sister
76 Trend
77 *The King* __
78 Baal, for one
79 United rival
80 Gullible one
81 Computer key
83 Tend the boiler
84 Solitary
85 Khrushchev
87 Mouseketeer O'Brien
88 Sisters
89 Dissolved substance
90 Nurse Barton
91 Live uneventfully

95 One who dotes
96 Swinging sister
98 Kitchen adjunct
99 Type of rug or code
100 Caesarean delivery?
101 Discordia's Greek counterpart
102 Like a certain Susan
103 Extra benefit
104 See 36A
105 Corporate ID

DOWN

1 Hood's weapons
2 Needing liniment
3 "To __ it may concern"
4 Escape hatch?
5 ESL student's bugbears
6 Word of honor?
7 Stratagem
8 RSVP's second
9 *Carmen* highlight
10 Play Nemesis
11 Leo's neighbor
12 Suffering the fantods
13 Waterbed's lack
14 Dreiser sister
15 "It's __" ("See you then")
16 Café cartes
20 The year *Future Shock* came out
21 AES' opponent
23 __ out (end gradually)
24 '89 Morgan Freeman role
30 Have a ball
31 Often handwritten book
32 Northeast India state
33 Dishes
34 Delivers diatribes
35 Breaking point
36 Is a kegler
38 Went for it
39 Use crayons
41 Bedouin
42 Paella part
43 Oracle
45 Ism item
46 Lions' prides
49 Opens oranges
51 Less tainted
53 "Sisters" sister
54 Snafu
55 See 21D
56 "Understood"
58 Swiss port
59 Rome's river
60 Pro __

61 Paradise paradigm
62 Became contestants
63 King of the high C's
64 Memorable funnywoman Fields
65 Play to the balcony
66 Long-distance call?
67 Polishing mineral
69 Pontius Pilate's prefecture
70 Serpentine
73 See 12D
74 Flare-up
75 Weather-map line
76 Nanki-Poo's disguise
80 Filleted
82 After-dark club
83 More urbane
84 Car-wheel attacher
85 Of a swelling
86 '40s actress Massey
87 *Tess* character Angel __
88 Peachy-keen
89 Enervate
90 Give a hand
91 Kill a bill
92 Piloting pref.
93 Baby branch
94 Exxon's ex-name
97 Finish with

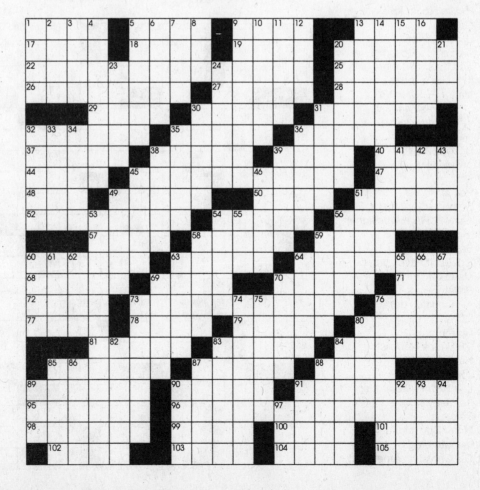

ACROSS

1 Unruffled
5 Fergie's first name
10 Dull Jack's lack
14 Festal
18 Postal map division
19 Town near Minneapolis
20 Mirren who plays Tennison
22 *Lucky Jim* writer
23 Frisbee, e.g.
24 "Father Knows Best" father
26 Typesetter's concern
27 Iron and Bronze
29 "Lou Grant" reporter
30 Florence gallery
32 Get back with
35 Kiri Te Kanawa, e.g.
37 Isle of Man point
38 It means outside
39 "Major Dad" dad
43 Pool parlor?
46 Exclamation oft-used in *Stalag 17*
48 Beethoven wrote *für* her
49 Cat-__ tails
50 Cob's mate
51 Camper's cover
52 Burn balm
53 RN's ASAP
54 Let off steam
55 __, Bravo, Charlie
56 "Make Room for Daddy" daddy
60 Division word
61 Kind of inspection or service
63 "O! The blood more stirs to rouse a lion than to start __": *Henry IV*
64 "__ live as cheaply . . ."
66 Video game locale
67 Hard hikes
68 Decorticated
69 Twaddle!
70 Kol __
71 Postal worker
72 He played Adam on "Ellen"
73 *Father of the Bride* father
76 Highest powers
79 Sandbox set
80 It doesn't have a leg to stand on
81 British composer
82 All hands on deck
83 "Wha?"
84 Run-through
86 '78 Peace Nobelist
88 Norman Vincent __
89 Journal ending
90 *Life With Father* father
93 Kennedy's cape
94 Pointers
95 Motor City gridders
96 Immature egg
98 Old Chrysler nameplate
101 Takes five
103 Clue-sniffing canine
104 Athirst
105 *Daddy Long Legs* "daddy"
109 Journey
113 Without bounce
114 Vitamin B type, __ acid
115 Of a satellite
116 Make bacon
117 WAC center
118 Bunch of bits
119 They make the grade
120 Tin lizzie

DOWN

1 He's no gentleman
2 Uris hero
3 __ *Misérables*
4 Portuguese overseas province
5 Placid
6 Hubbubs
7 Josh
8 "Wheel of Fortune" buy
9 London department store
10 Purgative
11 Delibes and Durocher
12 His, in Le Havre
13 Kyoto cash
14 Social blunder
15 Mine, to Mlle. Piggy?
16 Torte town
17 Spot of wine?
21 Vietnam's __ Van Thieu
25 Mellow-toned Mel
28 "You get what you give," to PC users
31 Actress Soleil Moon __
32 Lariat
33 Do your best
34 "Bachelor Father" "father"
35 Moses or Molly
36 Outlander
37 Moreno's Oscar role
40 Tie in
41 Turning parts
42 "What's in __?"
43 *Father's Little Dividend* father
44 Fivesome
45 Bruckner or Dvořák
47 Checks the flow
52 Reebok rival
53 __ leg (hurry up)
54 Cause for an NC-17
57 Herded to a corral
58 Heat unit
59 Shandy man
62 Was up?
65 Douse
66 Containing gold
67 Copenhagen park
68 Ballet position
69 Use the tub
70 Himalayan country
71 Things to draw
74 Monkeys have 'em; apes don't
75 Krypton kin
77 Spartan slave
78 Stockholmer
84 Make fun of
85 Scam
86 Jimmy of "NYPD Blue"
87 Peter or Paul
88 Story action
91 __-Lorraine
92 Also-rans
94 Après-ski quaff
97 Trap
98 Surrealism precursor
99 In perpetuity
100 Anna's adopted land
101 Have confidence
102 Emulate Perry White
103 A Saroyan
106 Burgle
107 Provence preposition
108 Balin or Claire
110 Acerb herb
111 Nest-egg acronym
112 Boy's name?

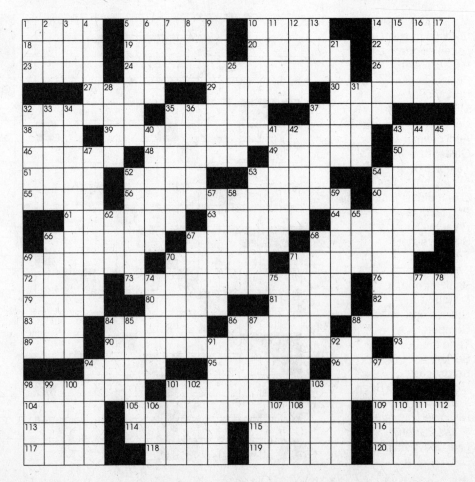

ACROSS

1 L.A. layer
5 Friday was one
8 Like omega
12 Gossip, slangily
16 Pola's rival
17 Mary Todd's mate
18 Dodger pitcher Nomo
19 "Sesame Street" regular
20 He led the Comets
21 Decalogue
24 Copyread
25 Your, of yore
26 '97 Chris O'Donnell role
27 Clean-air org.
28 Sue Grafton genre
30 Military storage site
31 Sweet madeira wine
35 Indira Gandhi's attire
36 *Hud* star Patricia
37 Pertaining to planes
38 Actress Thurman
39 Where gull meets buoy?
41 In fleeting fashion
45 Parishioner's seat
46 Jordanian capital
48 Actor Ossie's wife
49 Richland, Ill., county seat
50 Fronded houseplant
51 Filly or colt
52 Place for a slicker
53 Category
54 Well ventilated
55 View from Catania
56 Down front?
57 Impetuous ardor
58 Chili con carne's con
59 Tape-deck button
60 Rigged voting districts
64 UCLA's crosstown rival
67 Cow hand?
69 UK awards
70 Spike or Sara
71 General under Dwight
72 Be nurse to
73 Lime sources
75 Cutlet?
76 In the buff
77 Socks
78 Marsh plant
79 Wind rush
80 Drunken revel
81 Bldg. unit
82 Like severe judges
85 Sushi bar selection
86 It hangs by the neck
87 *Zwei* from *drei*
88 Parks or Ponselle
89 Norway's patron saint
91 Underfed-looking
93 Full of froth
95 Office crew member
98 Memorable comic Paulsen
99 Dolphin habitat

100 Cote matriarch
101 Sat in the sidecar
102 Go all goo-goo-eyed
107 Mournful melody
108 Boiling over
109 "The Eve of St. __"
110 Live and breathe
111 Was a thespian
112 Give them a hand?
113 Defendant of '49
114 Suede feature
115 Low man at the opera

DOWN

1 Not quite legit
2 "Don't Cry Out Loud" singer
3 Single-named folksinger
4 Adjective for Paree
5 Guisewite's comic
6 Comply with
7 Ballpoint or felt-tip
8 Dance where you really get down
9 Pass word
10 Young Lennon
11 Cargo unit
12 Night vision?
13 Roadhouse
14 Command to Fido
15 Males
16 Some of those things
18 Ballyhoo
19 Use
22 Peanut butter style
23 Beloved adverb?
25 Tonsorial touchup
29 Brian Boru's land
30 Kentucky contest
31 Deals out
32 Herculean exertions
33 Polishing material
34 Show sleepiness
36 What it is?
37 Sothern and Jillian
39 More secure
40 Melodramatize
42 Rap-sheet listing
43 Actor Lloyd's family
44 Serengeti sprinter
47 CSA state
50 In shape
52 Pan handler?
53 Sculptor Oldenburg
54 Give a leg up
57 Identifying device
58 Time span
60 Pantheon member
61 '70 film *Count __, Vampire*
62 Hebrew prophet
63 Linear lead-in

65 Beetle's boss
66 Catch cache
68 Top binary digit
71 Sapporo sash
72 Something to talk about
73 School bully, e.g.
74 Finds totals
75 Wacko
77 Porkpies and panamas
78 Japanese religion
79 Aphoristic
80 Dracula portrayer Lugosi
82 Wanted-poster word
83 One of a Dumas trio
84 Score unit
90 Where Timbuktu is
92 Aries-Taurus time
93 Huck and Mickey
94 Writer Joyce Carol __
95 Use a besom
96 Advantages
97 Marsh plant
99 Bible travelers
100 II Chronicles follower
102 Timeworn
103 Be rivals
104 Zsa Zsa's sis
105 __-jongg
106 *Richard III*'s McKellen
107 Pat with cotton

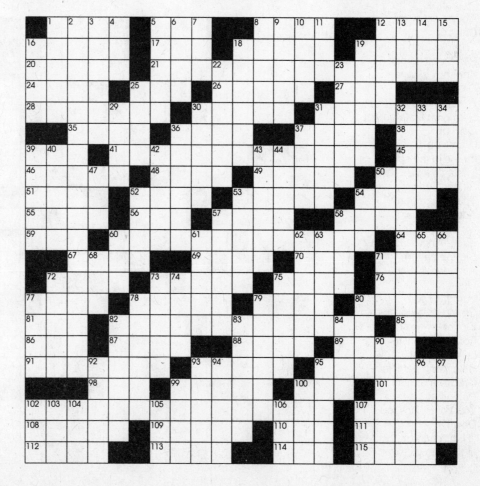

ACROSS

1 Piglet's parent
4 Journalist's question
7 Little bighorn
11 Is borne on the breeze
16 Bird-bill area
17 Short trip
18 Early English royal house
19 Married *mujer*
20 Stamp on a box
23 Fuel for lorries
24 Ferdinand II's home
25 Negative vote
26 L.A. Times section
28 Lower the lights
29 Two foursomes
30 Jam or pickle
31 Is down with
32 Endorses
34 "I'm Alive" musicians
35 Pronoun for Priscilla
36 Old hand
37 Oxford tutor
38 __ *culpa* (I'm guilty)
39 Wordplayer's ploy
40 Stamp on a bill
45 Lorelei Lee's creator
47 Hide away
49 Hamelin vermin
50 Mansard makers
52 Like a perfect game
53 __ glance
55 Coffee-set part
56 Drink up
59 "Thanks, don't mind __"
60 Place-setting part
63 Kennedy's cape
65 Dealer's choice
66 A diam. crosses it
67 Stamp on a statement
71 OAS pt.
72 Wraps up
74 It runs in the spring
75 Tristan's love
76 Skater Sonja
78 Trial separation?
80 Addams cousin
82 It's always in poetry
83 Everything, in Essen
84 Pie-top pattern
86 Avoirdupois unit
88 Lingers
89 Father or son
90 Stamp on a dossier
94 Singer's warmup notes
95 Former ring king
97 Lenin loyalist
98 Solar wind particle
99 Crackers or nuts
102 Podium pauses
103 West of Hollywood
104 Down
105 "Hut!" chanter
106 In the know
108 Skip town
109 Diadem
111 "Wudja say?"
112 Funnywoman Boosler
113 Facilitate
116 Stamp on an envelope
119 Made emends
120 Stable sound
121 Altos or Alamitos article
122 Effortlessness
123 "Cheers!" in Chartres
124 Carve on crystal
125 Person addressed
126 Orderly grp.

DOWN

1 Warranted inquiry?
2 Elaborate
3 Sand blaster?
4 See 4A
5 See 4A
6 Way of thinking
7 Jean-__ Godard
8 Unyielding
9 Fundamental folkways
10 Mr. Maverick
11 Bitty
12 Fire bug?
13 Stamp on a check
14 Cressida's love
15 Tim of the Angels
16 Anarchic state
18 Your, among Friends
19 Wheel radius
21 Parking place
22 Strain
27 Best-known Montague
30 To opposite
31 Night sound
33 *The Crucible* setting
36 Coastal hwy.
37 Forensic aid letters
40 Articulated
41 Bar legally
42 Two of these and it's curtains
43 Not perf.
44 Yield
46 Scepters' companions
47 Chiffons' "He's __"
48 Stamp on a parcel
51 Pet name
52 More agreeable
53 Writer Seton
54 Large Mexican seaport
55 Nullify
57 Conceals from sight
58 Borderlines
61 Make cable stitches
62 "Tag" seekers
64 Nonpareil
68 D.A.'s helper
69 TV's Dr. Art
70 "__ fool I've been!"
73 Official stamp
77 Airline to Ben-Gurion
79 Sauna mister
81 Score half
85 More frigid
86 At deuce
87 Like 1 or 3
88 Disobey the Decalogue
89 His rights are often read
91 Panicky
92 Like the ten o'clock news
93 Preschooler
94 Donnybrooks
96 Intertwined
99 Call for help
100 Marshal Dillon portrayer
101 Farm equipment maker
104 Kind of tooth or talk
105 Oldest settler in the West
106 Falstaff's quaff
107 Fades
110 Department in NW France
111 Royal initials
112 *Mi casa __ casa*
114 Air-conditioner spec
115 Net-hitting serve
117 "That's gross!"
118 Tic-tac-toe trio

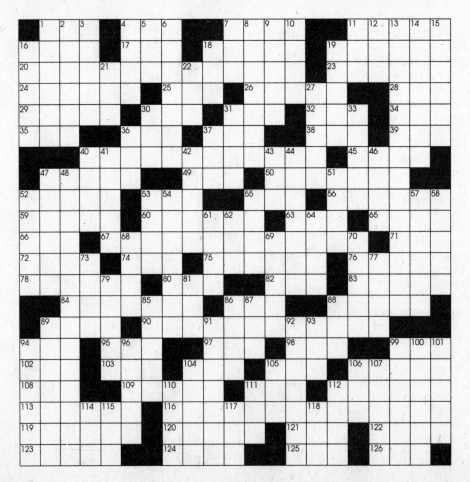

ACROSS

1 Stay in style
5 Gods' blood
10 Make tracks
15 Light carriage
19 Sax type
20 Carp kin
21 General assemblies
22 Domesticate
23 Dash or happy opener
24 Job visitor
25 Architectural order
26 Cupid, to Romans
27 Country singer with comedian
31 Chor and chlor enders
32 NEA abbr.
33 Prepare for struggle
34 Before bay or bed
36 Cadabra opener
38 Inter __
40 WHO's last
43 Singer with gangster
49 Land amid a *mer*
50 Treats squeaks
51 Heel
52 Opera's Gluck
53 Male cat
54 Egglike decorations
55 Fashions
56 Old English coin
57 Sweet potato
60 Bill of fare
61 Joker
62 An 007 with poet
69 Cal. column
70 Lop or dog ender
71 Chasmlike
72 Washbowl
75 Mystery writer Michael
76 Baby's bed
78 Caesar's 2050
79 Billy Baldwin's brother
80 Join forces
81 Ireland, for a dozen years
82 Danish coin
83 Columnist with contralto
89 Syn. opposite
90 Rivers, to Rivera
91 Explosive abbrs.
92 Conked out
93 *Foucault's Pendulum* author
94 Designer Chanel
96 Underwear
98 Actor with ape
107 Hamlet's thing
108 Incensed
109 Hidden supply
110 Tried companion
111 Dromedary feature
112 African nation
113 Displayed humanity, perhaps
114 Dye for 7D
115 Liability to pay
116 Lazarus and Goldman
117 Prepare
118 Attic height?

DOWN

1 Tie to the mast
2 "It's __ big mistake!"
3 Ollie's partner
4 First sergeant
5 Peace goddess
6 Before shoulder and feet
7 It grows on you
8 Eight, in Ecuador
9 Squabble
10 Car rides
11 Be a buffoon
12 Actor Santoni
13 Indigo
14 *Guarding Tess* star
15 Clermont's power
16 Injury
17 Bible book
18 Aye, ashore
28 "My Way" writer
29 "__ a Little Prayer"
30 *Dies* __
34 Element 14: Pref.
35 Swelling reducer
36 Talented
37 Big drum
38 Shrewdness
39 Minus
40 City by the Skagerrak
41 City on the Tevere
42 Bitty biter
43 Strictness
44 Tommy of *Gentlemen Prefer Blondes*
45 Sofa
46 Ornate
47 One from the heart
48 Stately movements
55 The going rates?
56 Slightly tainted
58 Actress Lee
59 What Fe means
60 Professional's path
61 Like ducks' digits
63 Uniform materials
64 Devilfish
65 Scottish county
66 Diffuse through membranes
67 Severe supervisor
68 TV's DeGeneres
72 TJ's location
73 Country singer Jackson
74 Denomination
75 __-European
76 Minimal money
77 Long inlets
80 Form an AFL local
84 Old chest
85 Scratch inducer
86 One more
87 MacDonald partner
88 Rice dish
93 Site of two Napoleon victories
94 Ultra antonym
95 Curved pointed arches
96 Induced ennui
97 Toffee-nose's adjective
98 Adhesive
99 Metrical foot
100 Small amount
101 Disable
102 Days of knights
103 Palm variety
104 *Mila 18* author
105 Wimple wearers
106 "__ life!"
107 Prof's degree

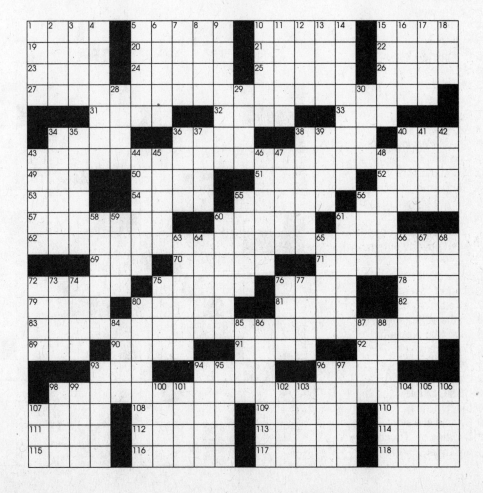

ACROSS

1 A little juice
4 Mary's little follower
8 Sec
12 Newts
16 Poet-harpist
18 Fable finale
19 Alternative to nuclear
20 Zhivago's love
21 Tell it to the world, loudly
25 Feigns
26 Puts on guard
27 Employs torsion
28 Irene Cara hit
29 Sheep shelters
30 Do a bar exercise
31 More than one opus
33 City east of Pasadena
34 Climb a pole
35 Depot, for short
38 The __ (Jericho phenomenon)
42 Timetable abbr.
43 Distaff GI
44 Trouser size
45 Hodgepodge
46 Vegas venture
47 __ Hoa (Viet city)
49 Neth. Antilles isle
51 Stirs up
52 To the ocean
54 Pluck
55 Interfere
56 Completely kaput
60 Squishes squash
63 Machinate
64 Cravings
67 Opening
68 Asparagus sprig
70 Childe Harold author
71 Choose
73 Makeup artist?
74 Gendarme, to some
75 They're tagged at tag
76 Mind: Comb. form
77 Proverbial consequence, when poverty enters the door
85 Benz closer
86 Hinged covers
87 Introductory comment
88 __ the other (either)
89 Deal with problems
90 Cuts grain
91 Pen residents
92 Cartoon cry
95 USMC biggies
96 Fleet felines
99 Capote classic
103 Downey of "Touched by an Angel"
104 "Pomp and Circumstance" composer
105 Climbing plants
106 Feels remorse
107 Aerie
108 Rough file
109 Need
110 Driver's peg

DOWN

1 Pecs' neighbors
2 Raja or rishi lead-in
3 CSUN teacher
4 Lenya
5 Sandy's syllables
6 Impair
7 Wingding
8 Artist Jasper
9 Islands in the Seine
10 __ and Away
11 Foamy
12 Spritelike
13 Pianist Waller
14 Horse's gait
15 Blackjacks
17 Sailor's bag
18 Newfoundland native
19 Steady flow
22 Puts asunder
23 Quemoy neighbor
24 In debt
29 Pilsen citizen
30 Porcelain
31 Popish Plot inventor
32 Coat with gold
33 Actress Plummer
34 Gross-out artist
35 Sound
36 Ribbed fabric
37 __ for news
38 Complex network
39 Oscar or Tony
40 Popeye's nemesis
41 Idle scribble
47 Chirp
48 Young actor Lukas
49 Zeal
50 Tumult
51 Hold sway
53 Stay attached
54 Dali's wife
55 Hand, to José
57 Cheaters
58 Gershwin's "I Got __"
59 Bring to heal?
60 Ten cents
61 Cation antonym
62 Drudge
65 Sonata movement
66 Animal track
68 Trombone part
69 Speckled birds
70 Falls for it
72 Tote by boat
74 Go wild about
78 Knock to the ground
79 First bettor
80 East Russian range
81 Land layer
82 Suitors
83 Before city or circle
84 Wise old man
89 Defraud
90 Summarize
91 Cockiness
92 Brought into being
93 Siouan
94 Resistance units
95 Captains' boats
96 Elegance
97 A month in the contrée
98 Capt. Hook colleague
100 Pay or shin ender
101 '33 govt. agency
102 Yacht's course

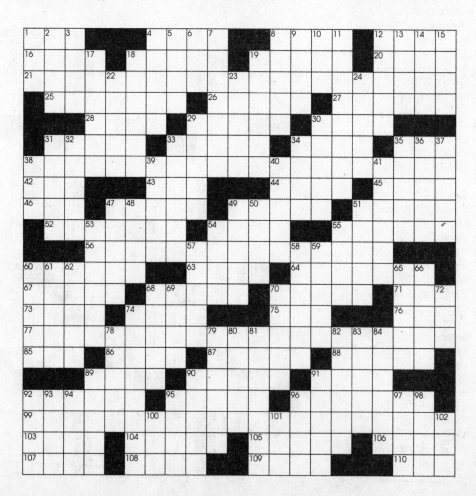

ACROSS

1 TV E.T.
4 Tributary
10 Honshu port
15 It may be hard to swallow
19 Taradiddle
20 Assert sans proof
21 Laker or Clipper
22 Understanding words
23 Hill builder
24 Garner's big cheese role?
26 Halves of turns
27 Shore dwellers
29 Map out
30 Ladies of Spain
31 Carotid, e.g.
32 "To __ not to . . ."
33 Like feathery clouds
35 Certain surplices
37 *What's Cheese Got to Do With It* subject?
39 Spanish highs?
40 Show place?
42 Calliope's sister
43 Dubbed ones
44 Dove's goal
45 Heal the Bay concern
47 Overacting actor
50 Words before T
51 A big cheese in hotels?
53 Journal ending
54 Pure or simple
56 Bill and Bennett
57 Wee drop
58 Move about a 64A
60 Mardi Gras group
62 Time, to Tomás
64 Pivot point
65 Dagger
67 Scotland's __ Green
69 Paleo's opp.
70 Flick where Kevin was the big cheese?
74 21A's org.
77 Rural lodging
78 Lawrence's land
79 *Golden Boy* writer
80 Secret Svc. guy
81 Shadow on the Lido
82 Make amends
83 Bailiff's bailiwick
84 Big cheese in talk shows?
89 Reproductive cell
90 Shallowness
91 Like Poe's bug
92 Like some idols or arches
94 City near St. Louis
95 Slog through surf
96 Nouveau riche, perhaps
99 Animated critter
100 Chuck Berry's big cheese?
103 Skosh

104 It means height
105 Playwright's ploy
106 Before neck or check
107 Unit in a joule
108 Revue part
109 Settle a debt
110 Regular date
111 Sunbeam

DOWN

1 "Oh me, oh my"
2 Queue
3 '87 cheesy thriller?
4 Tex-Mex treat
5 Slides over
6 Composer Bernstein
7 Irish district
8 Self-opinions
9 Ask for an ans.
10 Striped wildcat
11 Jungle jaunt
12 Stravinsky ballet
13 Flooey starter
14 Jazz great Tatum
15 Conquistador Francisco
16 "What a piece of work __!"
17 Official emissary
18 Like one evil?
25 Make topsy-turvy

28 Some 30A, for short
30 Dramatist John Van __
32 Induced ennui
33 Jeweler's units
34 Give __ (try)
35 Playbill listing
36 Miscellaneous mix
37 Pay stub abbr.
38 Recently
40 Pitched quarters?
41 Aesop's also-ran
44 Model's assumption
45 Pack away
46 Aachen article
47 Old sitcom's really big cheese?
48 Pronto
49 Inter-off. note
51 Socks or Sylvester
52 Shorthand pro
55 Is down with
57 Cub Scout unit
58 Indian princess
59 Bunyan's Babe, etc.
60 Poilu's cap
61 __ avis
62 Score halves
63 It means resident
65 Smugly earnest

66 Serving on a skewer
67 Narrow valley
68 Unthinking repetition
70 "L.A. Law's" Harry
71 Space lap
72 Went to the polls
73 Redolence
75 Young Simpson
76 Stud fee?
80 *My Cousin Vinnie*'s Marisa
81 "__ you again!"
82 Wrong, to Rob Roy
83 Jerusalem hill
84 Vaqueros' ropes
85 Use a key
86 Zen goal
87 Kampala's land
88 Comic Dangerfield
89 Skated smoothly
92 Bond baddy Gert
93 Oranjestad's isle
95 Powerful party post
96 "I nearly busted __ laughing"
97 O'Hara's home
98 Nervous
100 Honey holder
101 Last of the sugar?
102 Apt. ad abbr.

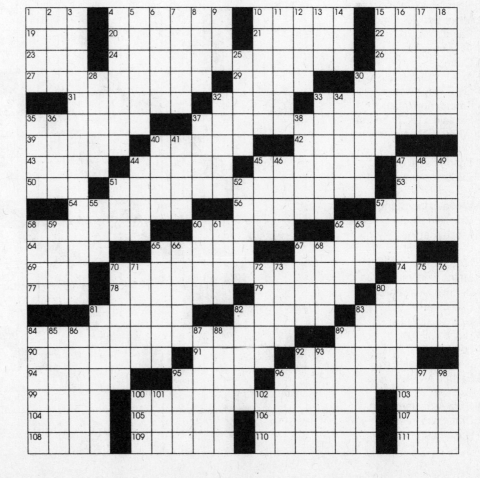

ACROSS

1 Pendulum path
4 Turner and Cantrell
9 Bring charges against
15 Table scrap
18 Surreal Salvador
20 Ecclesiastes words
21 Hemlock, e.g.
22 Former Mideast grp.
23 Like __ of bricks
24 "__ news"
26 *Muchacho*'s uncle
27 The Lone Ranger, for one
29 Stetson and stovepipe
30 VIP? Not he!
32 Psychologist Havelock
33 Fifth-c. marauders
34 Calligrapher's stroke
35 Spruces
37 Claim on property
39 Most succinct
41 ". . . __ backtalk!"
42 Mrs. Copperfield
43 Roe parent
45 Lake, port and canal
47 Excited
48 Be partial to
49 It sent up Apollo
50 Student's stat
51 John, to Ringo?
52 Nonmanaging part-owner
56 Major Babylonian god
57 Sauntered
59 APO opener
60 Grumble
62 Antiprohibitionists
63 Off-B'way awards
65 Tractor and trailer
66 He paid a fee to be free
69 Where Shiraz is
70 Not confident
74 Scap or spat ender
75 Exclusive event
79 __ vomica
80 Wood of the Stones
81 One little piggie's menu
82 Prexies' aides
83 Dentist's deg.
84 High rooms
87 Metric work measures
88 Beerish beverages
89 Silly ones
90 Grandiloquent
92 Half a half-pint
93 Lorry fuel
94 Get rid of waste
95 Earth
97 Tendon
98 Grapevine items
100 Christmas trees
101 Hush-hush
105 Hebrew lion
106 Tacit menace
109 Edible tuber
110 Marsh
111 Infuriate
112 Raised capital?
113 Box at the gym
114 "You're it!"
115 Further down
116 It means moon
117 Concorde, e.g.

DOWN

1 First mate?
2 Pro __ (proportionately)
3 Like executive sessions
4 Longtime baseball czar
5 Iotas
6 Pinta follower
7 So be it
8 Work on quilts
9 Of certain buzzers
10 Is priced at
11 "Coffin nails"
12 GIs' hospitality org.
13 Oklahoman
14 Throw support to
15 Hippie's "great!"
16 Incursion
17 Helen's homeland
19 Vague notion
25 Steer clear of
28 It means oil
31 Coffin
33 Vena cava site
34 Family car
35 Lake, volcano and language
36 Metal bar
37 Adored
38 Monopoly token
39 Flavorful
40 House of hide
42 Hills' companions
43 Trap
44 Damages
46 German river
48 Oil-change discard
52 Hamlet's sleeve-knitter
53 American revolutionary
54 Ejection
55 Writer Godden
58 Nocturnal one
61 Two before toe
63 Simian
64 *Psycho* name
65 Goes bonkers
66 Folksinger Ives
67 Standoffish
68 JFK's favorite novelist
69 Creamy white
70 Maria's song "__ Pretty"
71 In secrecy
72 "Blossom" family name
73 Outdo
76 Powerless to move
77 Advantage
78 Kind of swoop
83 Emulates Miss Marple
85 Fast-food phrase
86 Turned suddenly
89 Chromosome part
91 Old sect member
92 Main point
93 Composer Walter
95 Military encirclement
96 Doric or Ionic
97 Outpouring
98 Huck's transport
99 Nitrogenous compound
100 Commotion
101 Unfeigned
102 One of *les yeux*
103 Ages
104 Legal wrong
107 Choler
108 Orgs.' centers

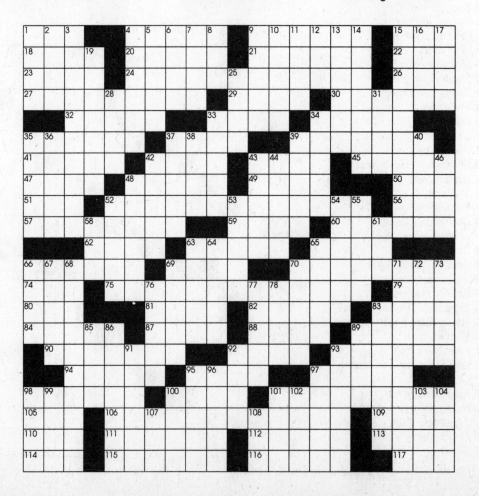

ACROSS

1 Eiger, e.g.
4 Map collection
9 Schnoz
15 Sunday bench
18 It's in a jamb
20 Exultant
21 Unpigmented
22 Eng. neighbor
23 Irish Rose fancier
24 Dotty painters?
26 Zero
27 Mindreader
29 Hook worm
30 Harvested
32 Scrabble pieces
33 Percipient
34 It means disease
35 Hooded reptiles
37 Red planet
39 Kidd or Kirk
41 Provence town
42 Ankles
43 Iodine source
45 Capp's li'l one
47 Flamingo or Rodeo
48 Large car
49 Away from the wind
50 Uno, due, __
51 Abby's twin
52 Eagle Scout type?
56 Actress Arden
57 Insincere compliance effort
59 Sty cry
60 Inflated
62 Pledge of combat
63 Committed to memory?
65 Café carte
66 Improve
69 Drink hard
70 Song under a balcony
74 Angled annex
75 Resort east of Los Angeles
79 Equip
80 La Gardner
81 Concerning
82 Grazer's grub
83 Camp clothes?
84 CD's and 45's
87 Coin flip
88 Be fond of
89 Lying face down
90 Maria Schwarzenegger, née __
92 Celebration
93 Raked with nails
94 It means feet
95 Bus. degrees
97 Cat calls
98 April event
100 Agra attire
101 April in Paris?
105 Luau sight
106 Polyphony
109 Upset
110 Ceramic ware
111 Handled
112 Carroll's rabbit chaser
113 Irish or Mulligan
114 Welcome item?
115 Scraped
116 Hot light beam
117 Possesses

DOWN

1 Furniture style
2 Earring site
3 Very close range
4 Winesap and Gravenstein
5 Ménage amount
6 Lane of The Planet
7 Jane, to Bridget Fonda
8 Shell-destroying tracer
9 George of the Bears
10 Fran's friend
11 Final notice?
12 It's the old way?
13 Ensnare
14 Linguist's stone
15 Located precisely
16 Penna. port
17 Unite closely
19 Out of service?
25 Wading bird
28 "__, poor Yorick"
31 Pequod skipper
33 Squeeze dry
34 Before work or weight
35 Small weight unit
36 U. of Maine site
37 Adam's addressee?
38 Jai __
39 Uriah Heep, for one
40 Chutzpah
42 Succinct
43 Couric of "Today"
44 African antelope
46 Organ pipe part
48 Stain
52 Snafu
53 Impend
54 Manon and Tosca
55 Ebbed
58 Kind of trip
61 Press for payment
63 Takes wing
64 __-ski
65 Reagan aide
66 Comprehend writing
67 Lisa Marie's dad
68 Lowest burning temperature
69 Domingo, for one
70 Milk or hand ender
71 Lewis' Martin
72 Mme. de Poitiers
73 Pelted, in a way
76 Windy day fliers
77 Eyes amorously
78 Court order
83 They're in your chest
85 Shell propeller
86 Brandy cocktail
89 Conspiracy
91 Capulets' town
92 Truman's __ Deal
93 Middle position
95 Photo finish
96 Engender
97 Chop finely
98 Urban blight site
99 Olympus VIP
100 Ginger cookie
101 Screen's Negri
102 Journalist Jacob
103 Entreaty
104 Attaches patches
107 Seagoing initials
108 Chum

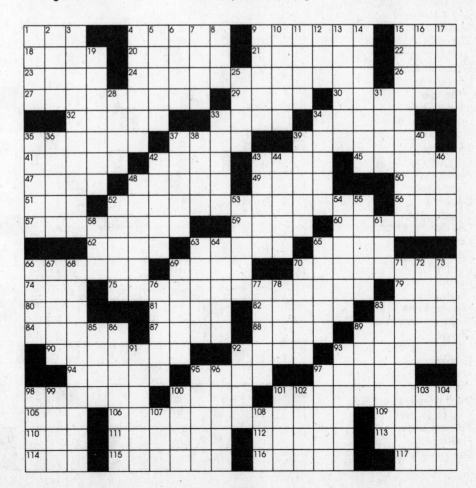

ACROSS

1 Christie's Miss
7 "Better not!"
11 Gratis
15 Trot or canter
19 Place to park an ark
20 Water vessel
21 Spinks or Panetta
22 Impolite
23 Makes your house a coffeehouse?
26 Vivacity
27 Out of whack
28 Sotheby's signal
29 Lady's man
30 "Cheers' " Carla
32 Hops dryer
33 Hat or head follower
34 Pre-Nadia sensation
35 Significance
38 Christiania, today
40 Blackthorn fruit
41 Knight's backup
42 Besides
43 Grads-to-be
46 Caffeine delivery system?
49 Food fish
50 __ gallery
52 Sheltered, at sea
53 Now, later
54 Not nearly near
55 Irish export
56 CAT's do it
57 Thin Man pooch
58 Blueprints
59 "My Way" writer
60 Word from Snerd
61 Life sentences?
62 __ de soie
63 It's in the bag
64 Go to coffee heaven?
69 Fall behind
72 S&L closer
74 Give a leg up
75 Piscator's purchase
76 Misery cause
77 Gleaming
79 Satan's realm
81 Like Dorothy's slippers
83 Condescend
84 Place for a pig?
85 Bumper bruise
86 Kachina maker
87 Colonize
88 Feels guilty about
89 "Enjoy the kaffeeklatsch?"
92 Coterie
93 "A mind __ terrible . . ."
94 Exceedingly
95 Advice to Nanette
96 Without feeling
98 Perls' therapy theory
100 Stop on the way home?
101 Al Bundy's wife
102 Finless fish
106 Like some tales

107 Spelling of "90210"
108 Sleep like a cat?
109 Bo-Peep's loss
110 Mil. misbehavior
112 Coffee-inspired courage?
116 Rawboned
117 Hill or camp preceder
118 Spellbound
119 Foresight
120 Predator's quest
121 Out of kilter
122 Dominance
123 Come to

DOWN

1 '52 Mitchum film
2 Café bouquet
3 Ghostbuster Harold
4 Conjurer's word
5 Laddie's love
6 Biblical suffix
7 Rum, to some
8 Was in the hole
9 Finish with
10 Victorian novelist
11 Botanist's concern
12 Try for a part
13 Aurora, to some
14 Transshipment center
15 Kermit's color
16 Most sanctified coffee?
17 Crete's highest peak
18 Olympic maximum
24 Gibson garnish
25 10-4 predecessor
31 Isn't out of
33 Story action
34 Novelist Tillie
35 __ Solemnis
36 "The man without a country"
37 Moving men?
39 Made thread
40 Ward of "Sisters"
41 Coll. Board warmup
43 Thud cousin
44 Queen of la France
45 Heavy decaf?
47 Marina moorer
48 Derby site
49 Casa component
51 PBS benefactor
56 Take to court
57 Come on TV
58 Part of a pod
60 Family room
61 Flower forerunner
62 Third degree, to some
64 Has permission
65 Big Three meeting place
66 1859 Titusville find
67 Go around the world
68 Slyly shy

70 A matter of degrees?
71 The Balcony writer
73 Till bills
76 Try the trifecta
77 Parsley portion
78 Monopoly's buy
79 Tin Man's lack
80 A deadly sin
81 TV exec Arledge
82 Hairstyle of old
83 Consider
85 Casablancan's coverall
86 Indianans
87 Self-satisfied
90 Tree bump
91 Unhandy
94 Kilmer of The Saint
97 Command
99 Voluble
100 Plunder
101 "Peanuts" girl
103 Uncanny
104 The Band member Helm
105 Pay out
107 Weather deity
108 Sonoma neighbor
109 Fit of anger
110 Heidi's home
111 Kids' card game
113 That's awesome!
114 Congressional output
115 Actress Tanguay

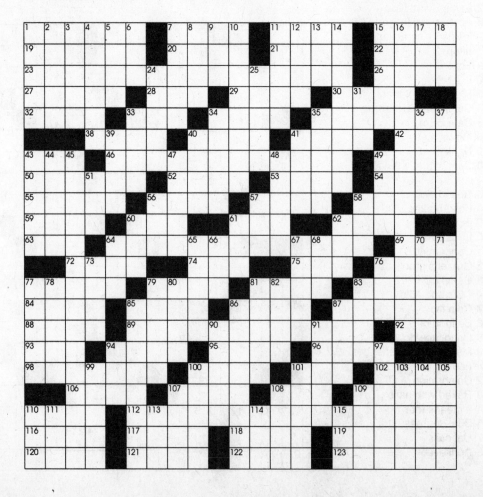

ACROSS

1 Fad
6 Pasture portion
10 Salary limit
13 Clothing
17 *Casino* star Stone
18 Ran in panic
19 Docs' bloc
20 Sonora "so long"
22 Kind of pigeon or device
23 Lose freshness
24 Savalas steed
26 *Tiny Alice* playwright
27 Boldness
29 Nab
30 Journalist Lindstrom
31 Wooded valley
32 Desiccated
33 Join
35 Circus structure
36 Get a lode of this
37 Peck part
38 Recorder, e.g.
39 Sad song
40 *Annie* role
42 Tennis exchange
43 Ruby or Sandra
44 Charles or Louise
45 Monopoly buy
46 Peace pipe
50 Pert
52 Boxing match
53 '53 Eddie Fisher hit
54 Evade duties
55 Musical transition
56 Nile nicknames
57 Actor Silver
58 Rotters
59 Chesterton sleuth
61 Stover of Yale
62 Japanese apricot
63 Sand hills
64 Tars' toddies
65 Weighs heavily
66 Duchamps disciples
68 Timid
69 Kingdom
70 What a single gets you
71 Blessings
72 Profound
73 British isle
74 Pie shell
75 Pinocchio's papa
79 Unruly kids
82 Singer Frankie
83 Small bays
84 Tombstone initials
85 Is on the ticket
86 Toulouse topper
87 Pick nits
88 Church liturgy
89 Mr. Baba

90 Sharp
91 Long-handled tool
93 Settee kin
94 Literature's "Papa"
97 State for sure
98 Give meaning
99 Clear tape
100 Gone by
101 *Giant* star
102 Old Chevy model
103 Burger side
104 Longing
105 Earth's quadrillion
106 Writer St. Johns

DOWN

1 *Love in the Time of __*
2 Old Nash model
3 Prospero's servant
4 Basketball defense
5 Chang's twin
6 Business
7 Red Bordeaux
8 Made over
9 First place?
10 Hepster's "dude"
11 Convenience
12 Sense of taste
13 *Corregidora* author Jones
14 Classifieds, e.g.
15 Humdinger
16 Panning out loud
17 Cranston's alter ego
21 Flood
25 Be situated
27 Duck's dad
28 Esophagus
32 Peachy!
34 Void companion
35 Monopolize, as phones
37 Maladroit medico
38 '64 Grant role
39 Fleur __
41 Gets fuzzy
42 Scoundrel
43 Pythias' pal
45 Euphoric states
46 Works on taffy
47 94A was her dad's dad
48 Name source
49 Sherman and Patton
50 Medicine man
51 __-camp
52 Entertains
53 It means study
54 Old Italian coin
55 French toast
56 Out of sorts

59 Picky
60 Heaviest part
61 Curtain
63 Clock faces
65 Chick chirps
67 Sanctions
68 Goes up
69 Ward off
71 Soft cheese
72 Printer's apprentice
74 Massacre
75 Is sovereign
76 Commonplace
77 Oberon's queen
78 Kitchen gadget
79 Astronomer Tycho
80 Sovereigns
81 Skunk or skink
82 Margin
83 Warning
86 Plead
87 Witches' gathering
88 Long arm?
90 Was cognizant
92 "Mary __ little . . ."
93 Property owner's paper
95 "A rose __ . . ."
96 Over there, once
98 Bus. notice abbr.

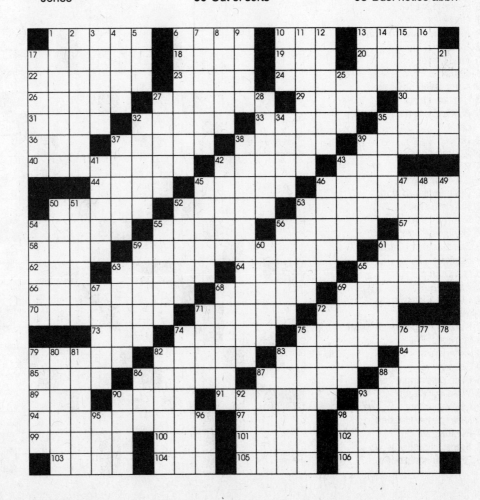

ACROSS

1 *The Grass Harp* writer
7 Emporium
11 Reagan role
15 Arthralgic
19 Leguminous tree
20 Sound from Socks
21 Substance from seaweed
22 Yippee!
23 Tina Turner's paean to cows?
26 Ambiance
27 Questionnaire last line
28 Washington bill
29 Alter course
30 Bergman role
32 Try out
33 Sectarian's suff.
34 Let use
35 It was reunited in '76
38 Order to fly?
40 What snobs put on?
41 Aretha's realm
42 Blubber
43 RR's Star Wars
46 Vikki Carr's milk manifesto?
49 Steer clear of
50 Chino neighbor
52 No-win situations
53 Small spasms
54 Big brass
55 Feed the computer
56 Makeup artist?
57 Uncivil
58 Anti-gun activist Brady
59 Geezer
60 Feel unwell
61 Cousy or Crosby
62 Actor Sean or Chris
63 Hesitater's sounds
64 Bowie-Queen cud-chewer carol?
69 Hi-tech LP's
72 Aggregates
74 Prohibition, e.g.
75 L.A.-Yuma dir.
76 Put canines to work
77 Sends by rail
79 Herman of toons
81 Canine of films
83 Béchamel or béarnaise
84 Hacks
85 "La Douce"
86 Pass over
87 Severe supervisor
88 Merely
89 Kern-Mercer cow melody?
92 Humorist Bill
93 Antagonist
94 Lascivious
95 Pref. meaning wine
96 Yves' colleague
98 Library section
100 Newscaster Hughes
101 Ply the sky
102 Sign of sensitivity
106 Projectionist's need
107 *Mon Oncle* star
108 Not keep up
109 Puccini opera
110 It follows Hosea
112 Blondie's lactic lyric?
116 Grad's exam
117 Baby in pink
118 Penultimate piggy's portion
119 Objective
120 Sordid
121 Edible tubers
122 Drawers of ships
123 Increases

DOWN

1 Boston family name
2 Obtuse opposite
3 Lanes
4 Eightsomes
5 Layer cake layer
6 Cochlea site
7 Disbursed
8 Colossal
9 Gold for Goya
10 It follows Psalms
11 Having a portal
12 Borodin's prince
13 She played Mindy
14 Insured's payments
15 Be expectant
16 Byrds' bovine ballad?
17 His match?
18 Pro vote
24 Romance-novel heaver?
25 Obtuse
31 Elver's elder
33 Greek I
34 Quart kin
35 Before mail or box
36 Isle near Venezuela
37 Parrotlike bird
39 Drop clues
40 One side of the Urals
41 Pallet
43 Zest giver
44 Plasma provider
45 *Man of La Mancha* moo-d music?
47 Of some purpose
48 Torn-off parts
49 Freberg or Laurel
51 Passé
56 Pot top
57 Sturgeons-to-be
58 Didn't I tell you?
60 It costs to take them out
61 Madonna outerwear
62 Post opp.
64 See 63A
65 Retrofitter's reinforcer
66 Snoop
67 Brief fight
68 Cable network
70 Fake drake
71 Stockholmer
73 __-daisy
76 Kind of corder
77 Mock
78 35A capital
79 Physical strength
80 During
81 Change the Constitution
82 Storage for forage
83 Radio's Vic and __
85 Body of concepts
86 Docile
87 Count (on)
90 Early days
91 Russian river
94 Recline
97 Cave
99 London tube?
100 Soul singer Lou
101 Cabby's customers
103 Grate stuff
104 Potpourri product
105 Red deer
107 Contract condition
108 Trouser size
109 __ avail
110 Run like Clinton
111 . . . man __ mouse?
113 Entertainer Peeples
114 "__ dirty rat!"
115 Pen-point part

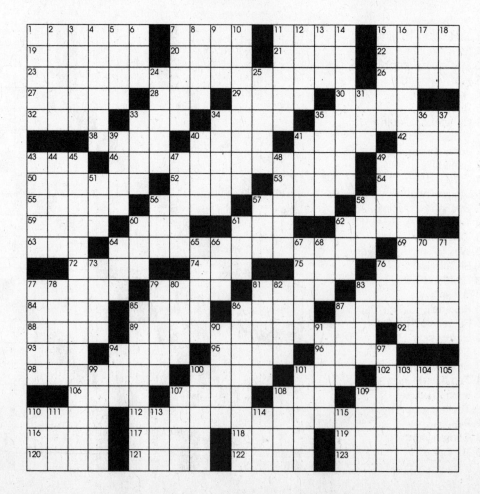

ACROSS

1 Tee preceder
4 One who's up, to bleacher bums
9 Refluxes
13 Ty Cobb, the Georgia __
18 Stupid
20 Menotti opera hero
21 The pen, in Penzance
22 Sesame Street denizen
23 Cake decorator
24 Kin by marriage
25 Quantity discounts
27 News-gathering service
30 Tallow source
31 Synagogue pointers
32 Vassals or lords
36 One who mistreats
39 Is obligated
41 Essayist's nom
43 Congo Bantu
44 "For unto us a __ given"
45 Bike accessory
48 Silk, in Sedan
49 Social standing
50 Eve's opposite
51 Christmastide
52 Composer Kaspar and kin
53 Knacks
54 Animals
56 Country music's "Cowboy"
57 Bears or Musketeers intro
59 Eight-pt. units
60 Litter's littlest
61 But, to Brutus
62 Alley alliance
66 Chance
69 Nine inches, in Nottingham
71 Raised platform
72 Musical "Matthew"
74 Rose perfume
76 Shrimp cousin
78 Curse
79 It means mountain
80 Shipshape
81 Christopher's bear
82 Divide
83 Diplomacy
84 Nude
88 It means seven
89 Digit
90 Petrarch's porch
91 Dark shades
92 Deep valley
93 Having a handle
95 Once more
96 Two words after take or make
97 Eastern utility
105 Long johns
108 Uncultivated areas
109 Too
110 Painter Rousseau
111 H.S. junior's hurdle
112 Ornamental stud
113 Rhythmical cadence
114 Purgative ingredient
115 "Que __ . . ."
116 Diaries' spans
117 He wrote "To Helen"

DOWN

1 Emulate Ben Bradlee
2 As __ (per se)
3 Peter Pan pirate
4 Kiss, in Cassis
5 "I __ a crook"
6 Baby powder
7 Bangkok resident
8 "There'll __ an England"
9 Incited further
10 Jongleurs
11 Betty the toon
12 Calumny
13 Show cat
14 Expunge
15 Organized insect
16 Fr. company
17 Stag attendees
19 Most obstreperous
26 Centaurs' home
28 Brings actions
29 Hulot portrayer
33 Collective treatment
34 W. Australian town
35 Behalfs
36 Resources
37 Actor Powers
38 NAFTA signatory
39 Lodging place
40 Sums, for short
41 Scholar's collar
42 *Padrone*'s dough
45 Hall of Famer Rod
46 Entertain
47 City on the Rhône and Saône
49 Screen's Leslie
54 Artful Dodger's mentor
55 Totalities
56 Hints
58 Construction girder
59 Nibble steadily
60 Less civilized
63 "Gem of the Mountains"
64 Amaryllis plants
65 Hopeless one
67 A Fury
68 ". . . attempting to find a __ it will be shot": Twain
70 Way to go
73 Latent
74 Ekberg of '50s films
75 Mortise partner
76 "Horseback hockey"
77 Papal tribunal
78 Writer Aphra
81 Eucharist plates
82 Freighter freeloader
85 Tallinn's country
86 Canary broom
87 Son of Jonathan: Ezra 8
88 Aforementioned
92 Treasure and hope
94 Oak nut
95 Sacrifice site
96 Hognose snake
98 Has an evening meal
99 Seine feeder
100 Buster Brown's dog
101 Raines of the screen
102 Kind of case or cover
103 Frogner Park site
104 Memorandum
105 Hesitation sounds
106 Wedding story word
107 See 39D

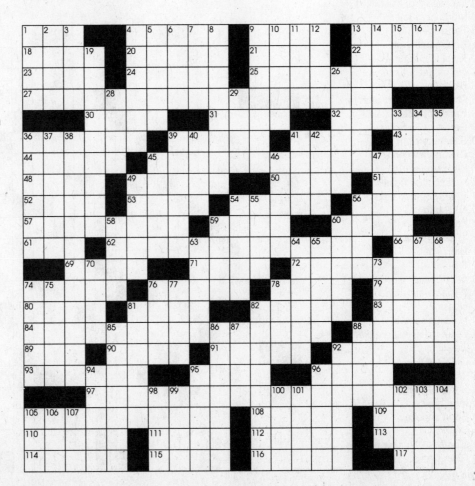

ACROSS

1 Caterpillar, e.g.
6 Check mate
10 Listen in on
13 Big rollers?
17 Off-the-cuff comment
18 Now, to *niños*
19 Three make one
20 Sentry's command
21 Wrong-way holiday hopper?
23 Got carried away?
24 Scandinavian city
25 Beautifies
26 Japanese dog breed
28 Rose water ingredient
29 Nerve
32 Kind of feeling
33 __-dieu (prayer bench)
34 At present
36 Masonic symbol
37 Roses-red link
38 Tea holder
39 Rather formal
41 Be garbed in
43 Misdirected movie genre?
47 Pesky insect
50 The Spanish?
51 Req. for payment
52 Apportion
53 He played Paladin
54 Queue before Q
56 Unbleached, as textiles
58 Ingrid or Ingmar
60 Fate
61 Enlarged thyroid
62 River of Burgundy
64 It's *chaud* time
65 Blunder
66 Misdirected *Misty* director?
68 Parking place
69 Barracks bed
70 Salisbury sight
71 Diamond weights
72 Works on skirts
73 Having repercussions
75 Sharp-toothed eels
76 NYC part
77 Freeze, as windows
78 "Take __ Train"
81 Ump's call
82 Doleful
83 Bare peaks
84 Wrong-way Hitchcock classic?
90 Nautilus captain
92 Of an Italian winemaker
93 Day light
94 Olds' oldie
95 White lie
97 Senate "yes"
99 Inert gas
100 Short snooze
101 Distort
102 Modify
104 Riding whip

106 Seasoned stew
108 Gorge
109 Food fish
110 Disoriented Irangate figure?
115 Give the eye
116 Make unusable
117 Iris layers
118 Genoese admiral Andrea
119 Slimness standard
120 Founded, for short
121 Cultivate
122 Xenophobe's concern

DOWN

1 It comes with your order
2 Fabulist George
3 *Kidnapped* auth.
4 Absolutely necessary
5 Not up yet
6 Divert
7 They can be gross
8 Coffee dispenser
9 Golden Gate locale
10 Slow down from a run
11 Actor Quinn
12 "Raven" maven
13 BB's, e.g.
14 Wrong-way breakfast option?
15 Make less severe
16 Put into memory
18 Unexpected
19 Italian port
22 Scamps
27 Spillane's __ *Deadly*
28 Humbling feeling
29 Accelerator
30 Klee contemporary
31 Grassy mead
33 Sneak peek
35 Possess
38 Crack from the cold
39 Kitchen set
40 Thus far
42 Popeyed
44 Steal
45 Becoming weary
46 Loads programs again
48 Gray matter?
49 Ism items
53 Born companion
54 Casablanca's country
55 Disoriented regional charmer?
56 "__ a Go-Go"
57 José, Buddy or El
59 Seth's son
60 Misleading practice
61 Secluded valley
62 "The Waltz King"
63 "I need to get __ the country for a while"

66 Part of the pot
67 *My Name Is Aram* writer
72 Cache
74 Yorkshire river
75 Composer Gustav
76 Composer Sammy
79 Bub or cap lead-in
80 Harrovian's rival
82 Semi-coma
84 Chinese sauce
85 Repress a memory
86 Customary practices
87 Noah place like home?
88 Match the bet
89 Pull along
91 Crackers or nuts
95 Prefer
96 PR concern
98 Horse play?
100 USNA part
101 Milker's seat
103 Have an opening for
105 Part of a set
106 Cambodian coin
107 Beef-rating grp.
109 *Uno, due,* __
111 Cornelius Tacitus' birth year
112 Mentalist Geller
113 Make a connection
114 *Star Wars'* Solo

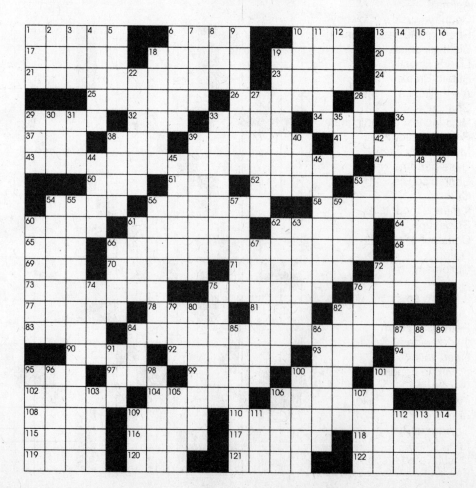

ACROSS

1 Fridge foray
5 Take it in stride
9 "Ripeness __," said Lear
14 __ mater
18 160 sq. rods
19 Less assertive
20 Hot seasoning
21 *Serpico* author
22 Street academy
26 Shuns
27 Yes-person
28 Ready to listen, to CBers
29 Disencumbers
30 Epsom event
31 Bee flats
32 Rain-plain terrain
35 Dry plaster painting
36 "The wind blows out of the __ the day": Yeats
39 Last place?
40 Expanded eye part
43 Racecourse circuit
45 African succulent
46 Bus. school subj.
47 Suffers ill health
48 Locate
49 Big-ticket item
50 School wall climbers
51 Small change
53 Low couch
54 Kal-El's home planet
56 WWII medalist Murphy
57 *Star Wars* heroes
58 Funny farm
62 Offend
65 More peculiar
66 Minister's aide
70 Absurd
71 Chair back part
72 Yule candies
74 Biblical verb
75 It means mountain
76 *Graf __*
77 Curve components
78 What Pahlevi was
79 W.C.
80 Some grill work?
84 Little, to Luis
85 Derring-do
87 Is entitled
88 Pan handlers
89 Exclusively
90 Use an atomizer
91 *Rubáiyát* name
93 "Horny-handed sons __": Kearney
96 Stand
97 Safekeeping
100 Majority owners
104 Taken, to McTavish
105 Boldness
106 Emulated Marceau
107 Rainbow
108 Don't go
109 Avarice
110 Asian ruler
111 See 51A

DOWN

1 Informer
2 Molar malady
3 Angers
4 Delineate
5 Manifests
6 Uncles, in Uruguay
7 Conger-line member?
8 Safeguard
9 Sleepy Hollow's Crane
10 Not on the up-and-up
11 Ethereal
12 Lawyer's deg.
13 "Tell it __"
14 Loves, in 50D
15 Lakes, in Lausanne
16 Bonito shark
17 Grp.
19 Molt
23 Facial feature
24 Ally of 57A
25 Lint trap?
30 College officials
31 By chance
32 Pancake portion
33 Exactly opposite
34 Writer Cleveland
35 Blackthorn fruit
36 Kind of pig or hen
37 Kind of drab
38 Deadly
40 Sincere
41 Hockey maneuver
42 Kind of button or attack
44 Writes
48 Ancient oracle
50 Liguria's land
51 Washington sound
52 Biblical region
53 Showroom models
55 Underworld VIP
56 A lick __ promise
57 Grade-schooler's break
59 Wishful ones
60 Was inactive
61 Prom, e.g.
62 False god
63 Author Lofts
64 Martin or McQueen
67 Rowdy one
68 Trail
69 Guiding beliefs
71 Piquant
72 Sideshow barker
73 War god
76 Coventry coin
78 Intermittent
80 Invigorating
81 Bore witness
82 Kal-El's new planet
83 *Wind in the Willows* writer
86 Mickey or Andy
88 Memorable stargazer Sagan
90 Find solutions
91 Different
92 Humor
93 Makes choices
94 Campus grp.
95 Singer Turner
96 Like Hubbard's cupboard
97 Classical or conductor lead-in
98 Man in *Pretty Woman*
99 Emerald Isle
101 Mph center
102 Brink
103 Concorde, e.g.

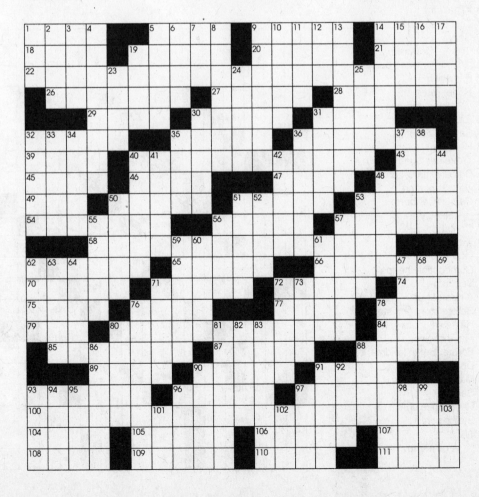

ACROSS

1 Hipster's man
4 Hitchcock
10 Applaud
14 Church projections
19 Barbecue residue
20 "Michael Hayes" star David
21 Auld lang syne
22 Dutch treat
23 Debtor's ploy
26 Rockies resort
27 Swarm
28 Symbol of 29A
29 Rather's network
30 Lissomely agile
32 Marx's instrument
33 Hubbub
34 With 98A, stylish
35 "You bet!"
36 Kind of session
39 Station or revolution ender
40 Constitutional safeguards
43 1/1000 of an inch
44 Dot on a die
45 Rat-race course
46 Uttered
47 Artistic movement
48 Done in, as dragons
51 Coarse tobacco
53 Hurtled into second
54 Virginia caverns
55 Measure for 101D
56 "That ain't __!"
57 Test by touching
58 Chore
59 The __ for Burning
62 "I __ fir yew and balsam"
63 Exemplar
66 Under restraint
67 '52 Nixon address
70 Randy's rink partner
71 Savile Row pros
73 Recent
74 Traveler's agenda item
76 Celestial flare-up
77 New York nine
78 Can, in Canberra
79 __-majesty
80 Contend
82 Awarded
83 Inter
84 Combustible heaps
85 Vacuum
86 A number of
87 Before story or sister
88 Half a sawbuck
89 Make choices
90 Former Berlin landmark
94 Do something
97 Mariner's catcher
98 See 34A
99 Resistance unit
100 Stable scrap
101 Wings
102 "__ in a name?"

104 Sling contents
105 Droop
106 Helen, in Jalisco
107 __ box (the tube)
109 What paperhangers do
113 Monetary gain
114 Mallomar shelfmate
115 Tapeworm
116 Score the same
117 Laments loudly
118 Aromatic drinks
119 ". . . war to __ wars"
120 PST pt.

DOWN

1 "__ falling star . . ."
2 Squared stone
3 Supposition
4 Formic or nitric
5 80's slogan "__ the place!"
6 The von Richthofen married to D.H. Lawrence
7 Guys and Dolls chronicler
8 Ferrara's nobility
9 Homer Simpson's interjection
10 Orchestral clasher
11 Mauna and Sina closers
12 Biblical lion
13 Very clear
14 Certain marbles
15 Elegant

16 Retail Clerks Union member
17 Dutch commune
18 Mateo or Miguel
24 Annual exam
25 Dazzling effect
31 Aroused anger
33 Nile biter
34 "Snug as __ . . ."
35 Nautilus cousin
37 She loved Radames
38 Perform on the piano
40 Sign the register
41 Sideless wagon
42 Numb
44 Compassion
47 Housekeeper's concern
48 Kind of decision
49 Tropical climber
50 "He's making a list __"
51 Sneakers and loafers
52 Receipt for a fedora
53 Touch, for one
54 Woodcutter's machine
57 Militant symbols
58 Savoir-faire component
60 Franklin invention
61 Hot rodders' grp.
62 Chatter
63 Crowfoot plant
64 Poker-player's move
65 Golf course sections

68 Gridiron group
69 VIP of the desert
72 Clamorous
75 Welsh lake
77 Mrs. Ike
78 Bass brass
80 English river
81 Lasso
82 "This is a __ for a picnic!"
83 German composer Theobald
84 Pizza or peach pastry
86 Kind of check
87 Fool, on Fairfax
88 Suitable
90 Chess goals
91 Human trunks
92 Shouted
93 Pond
94 Danger signals
95 "You __ out for yourself!"
96 Tantalized
101 Publican's offering
103 Cornucopia
104 "Take arms against __ . . ."
105 Laurel or Freberg
106 Jacob's well site: John 4:20
107 Kind
108 Payable
110 Exist
111 Indian language
112 Marionetter Baird

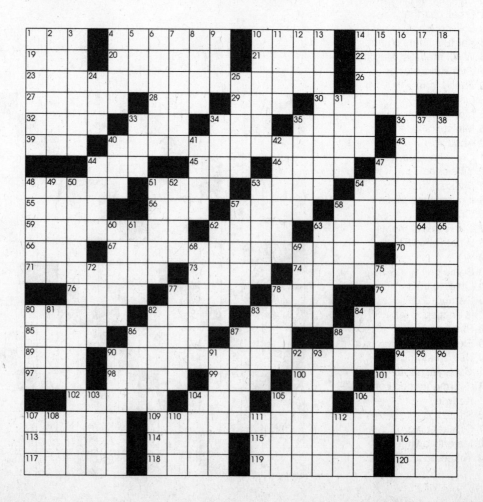

ACROSS

1 Magic Johnson, briefly
6 Frost
10 "Nightline" name
13 Practice punching
17 It means male
18 Fellini's world
19 Bygone bird
20 Costume for Markova
21 MAYOUD
23 Guitarist Clapton
24 At the apex
25 Whirlpool
26 Beau tie?
28 Salt water
29 Allude to
32 Ocean off Eur.
33 Donald or Daffy
34 Shade
36 After 31D, perfectly
37 Reset readout
38 Thérèse, e.g.
39 Jai alai ball
41 Turner on the radio?
43 THREE QUARTER
47 Iron-pumper's pride
50 Hoodwinked
51 WWII boat
52 Semester
53 Taj __
54 Strong-arm man
56 Adorable ones
58 Almond confection
60 Guest work
61 Coming or going, e.g.
62 Weird Al parody
64 Polar to SSW
65 Carte start
66 PWITHAL
68 TWA datum
69 What slanderers sling
70 Dickens title opener
71 "Bonanza" theme player Al
72 Dozen in a box?
73 Populated
75 Gate guard
76 Like bees or beavers
77 Smithy sight
78 Estimator's words
81 Ali stats
82 PC system
83 Slow flow
84 THE OTHER ONE
90 Hold your horses
92 Chores
93 BPOE member
94 The mind's I
95 Ex-ember
97 PC storage abbr.
99 Young adult
100 Place for a peke
101 Satyrs' revel
102 Use stealth
104 007 or 86
106 Duke's town
108 Knotmaker
109 Treat meat
110 JOANB
115 Run without moving
116 Keen
117 Dismissal
118 Light on one's feet
119 It's a loch
120 Zing
121 Patella place
122 Another Gabor

DOWN

1 Rotating piece
2 __ shoestring
3 Put into the mix
4 Desire desperately
5 Knight of the road
6 Ramada or Radisson
7 Cameo stone
8 Turmoil
9 French clown painter
10 *Vaca*'s mate
11 Mrs. Bunker
12 Disney dwarf
13 Part of Old Glory
14 US PUT IT
15 Observe Yom Kippur
16 100 paise
18 Grumble
19 "__ halls with . . ."
22 Spoke formally
27 George C. and Martha
28 Poor Richard, really
29 __ au vin
30 Letters of credit?
31 See 36A
33 *La Forza del* __
35 Maui music maker
38 Dateless
39 Grazing ground
40 See 68A
42 Gern for a Libra
44 Baba au __
45 Dollars for dollar, e.g.
46 In a hollow way
48 Steinbeck's row
49 See 12D
53 Study of numbers
54 TNT part
55 HEAD
‾‾‾‾
HEELS
56 Greenish glaze
57 Draw forth
59 Singer Coolidge
60 Gaucho grounds
61 Scandalous suffix
62 Copy cats?
63 "Give me __-case scenario"
66 Become boring
67 Cotton cloth
72 Merely
74 Meerschaum
75 Tone down
76 After 79D, Mao's tome
79 See 76D
80 Pan-fried
82 Oracle site
84 Lennon in-law
85 Cravat clasp
86 Cortege component
87 Not him
88 Darner's aid
89 Rocker Orbison
91 Tick off
95 A TV Addams
96 Slyly malicious
98 A color purple
100 Leap forward
101 Series ender
103 Eris' brother
105 Satchel
106 Painter Jim
107 Hoss' big brother
109 Beanie or gimme
111 Renoir's refusal
112 What's up when you're caught
113 GOP center
114 Arthur or Lillie

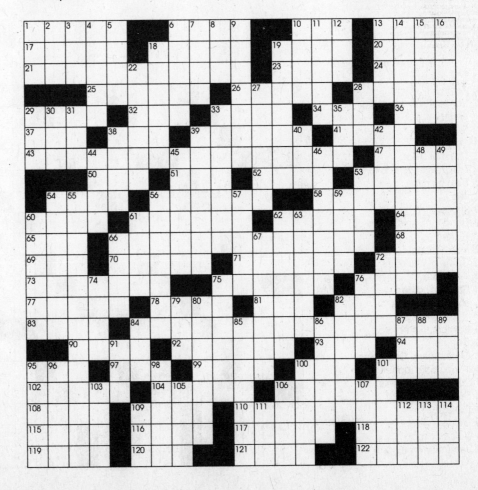

ACROSS

1 Make free of
4 Hotel Bible
10 Mom's mom
14 Atoll material
19 Serve a winner
20 __ you (your turn)
21 Indian VIP
22 Entertain
23 Some reunion photos
26 Goes into depth?
27 Palm leaf
28 __ Fail (Irish coronation stone)
29 Veteran actor Philip
30 LaBelle
32 Nitwit
33 Elmer, to Bugs
34 DDS's org.
35 Art Deco master
36 Hook, as a crook
39 Sibilant sound
40 Windsors and Stuarts
43 Brace
44 Harbor boat
45 Telecast
46 Dig for diamonds
47 Come in third
48 Make ready again
51 Saucy lass
53 Tea unit?
54 Be in bees?
55 Vivacity
56 Shoshone
57 "Eh?"
58 *Chanteuse* Edith
59 Cataleptic
62 Leave with the tide
63 Full of life
66 AP rival
67 Longest-running radio serial
70 Damage
71 Told
73 Marshal Dillon
74 *Guys and Dolls* doll
76 Belgian river
77 Jab
78 Hasten
79 Bend for Baryshnikov
80 Risked
82 Non-fictional
83 Game of chukkers
84 Tikal tribe
85 Square footage
86 One of the ages
87 __ out (renege)
88 Cambodia's Angkor __
89 Grippe
90 Clintons and Coolidges
94 Toothpaste topper
97 20 hundredweights
98 Strays
99 Fuse abbr.
100 Globe
101 Volcanic rock
102 Japanese immigrant

104 Pay dirt
105 Lao-tse's way
106 Become separated
107 Hurry off
109 The UN, ideally
113 Ford or Pyle
114 Lendl
115 Lake near Syracuse
116 ". . . and sold for endless __": Housman
117 Less foolish
118 Actress Irene
119 Singer Johnny or Mabel
120 Boston great Williams

DOWN

1 Chance-taker's event
2 Daedalus' son
3 Dynamos
4 Midas touch result
5 Compton-Burnett
6 Position troops
7 Beethoven's Third
8 __ *vez* (again)
9 In no manner
10 Modern dance's Martha
11 Hat or check opener
12 Soldier insect
13 Tit for tat, for one
14 Social classes
15 Leave out

16 Be hereditary
17 Seek answers
18 __ *Sylphides*
24 Printer's purchase
25 Cpl. O'Reilly
31 Suit to __
33 Face or fight lead-in
34 In __ (in hot water)
35 Poet who inspired *Cats*
37 Truant trooper
38 Orange or Tangerine
40 Dull routine
41 Penny or Lois
42 Classic Chevy model
44 Singer Turner
47 Sail support
48 Happen again
49 Run away secretly
50 Kin conclaves
51 Meditated
52 List entry
53 Go from first to second
54 Female prophet
57 Squander
58 Long nap?
60 Hauled
61 Nonpareil
62 Asp or adder
63 TV
64 Piano teacher Boulanger
65 Kilmer opus

68 Quantity
69 Knight wear
72 Lost
75 __ on the back
77 Media part
78 Arizona Amerind
80 Loony
81 Woody's kid
82 Great!
83 Partner of circumstance
84 More, in Moratalla
86 Make weary
87 "Horse designed by a committee"
88 Network
90 Addams uncle
91 *Our Gang* member
92 Slugabed
93 Connoting the contrary
94 Frolic
95 Madison or Vermont
96 Analyzed sentences
101 Welcome symbol
103 Silk, to Sylvie
104 WWII Gen. Bradley
105 __ down (soften)
106 Marquee name
107 Put in stitches
108 __ *de coeur*
110 Gardner of film
111 __ Kippur
112 Humorist George

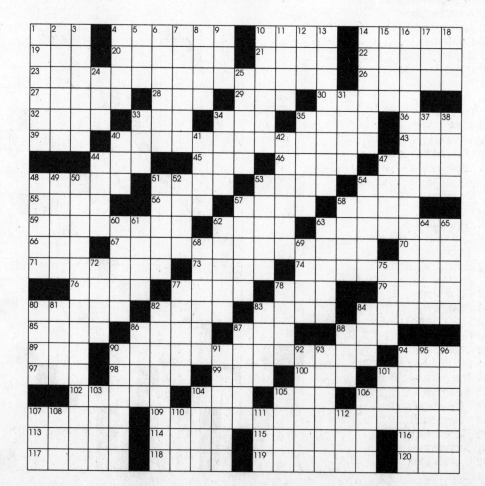

ACROSS

1 PC alternative
4 '40s hit "Maria __"
9 Where Francis was from
15 Bounder
18 Nigeria, Algeria, etc.
20 Miser Marner
21 Photocopy predecessors
22 Aeolian poem
23 Harald III's capital
24 Saturday night fever complication?
26 Big boy
27 Changes places
29 Active one
30 Cold and wet
32 Approves
33 Prospectors' props
34 Latin lovers' words
35 Army careerists
37 Horned hopper
39 Signify
41 Unmoving
42 Fronded plant
43 CNN's Bernard
45 Do better
47 Roman historian
48 Actress Marisa
49 Block of stamps
50 "__ Clear Day . . ."
51 Wine consideration
52 String player's problem?
56 Dance floor move
57 Chevy speedster
59 Snorri story
60 Eye lights
62 "Must've been something __"
63 He led the Comets
65 Irritated state
66 Steak go-with
69 Staff member
70 Punchless pills
74 Do the same as
75 Wind section infection?
79 Onassis nickname
80 Transgression
81 Unique item
82 Del Monte competitor
83 Surgery souvenir
84 Bluefins
87 After 16D, Eliot hero
88 First name in fashion
89 "Bell Song" opera
90 Composer Legrand et al.
92 Sets down
93 Justice Abe
94 Arthurian sword holder
95 Racetrack fence
97 Loud, as a crowd
98 Suite site
100 Domesticate

101 Without visible means of support?
105 Massage
106 Scat singer's surgery?
109 Abba of Israel
110 Freudian concern
111 Ancestry
112 Leslie who played Lili
113 *Lohengrin* lass
114 Sma
115 Kane's castle
116 Other side
117 Sixth sense, to some

DOWN

1 Give berth?
2 Transept projection
3 String section sickness?
4 Pieces of Bacon
5 Swingy trills
6 Composer Siegmeister
7 Couch quickies
8 Nile reptile
9 Extra room, often
10 Triangle trio
11 Move deeply
12 TGIF part
13 World Cup sport
14 Put in solitary
15 Composer's complaint?

16 See 87A
17 Refuse to admit
19 Chef's study
25 Yikes!
28 Caddie alternative
31 NYSE rival
33 Terror *haute* ?
34 Campanile or belfry
35 Lavender flower
36 Architect Jones
37 Arizona college town
38 Hydrox rival
39 Ling-Ling, for one
40 Jeans material
42 Strong point
43 Big name in china
44 W.C. of the blues
46 Track trips
48 Sketch on skin
52 Wasteland
53 Trojan beauty
54 Krazy Kat's mouse
55 Mrs. Kramden
58 By way of
61 Time for *les vacances*
63 Backpacked
64 Put on a pedestal
65 Thrown
66 Bygone days
67 St. Laurent scent

68 Athletic musician's ailment?
69 Cecil B.'s niece
70 Ballerina's bends
71 Soprano's distress?
72 Pan or di ender
73 Fathers foals
76 Aristocratic
77 Spooky-movie extra
78 Pool-table top
83 Mrs. Smith's rival
85 They'll make a play for you
86 Place for pumps or platforms
89 Lariat end
91 Digestive tracts
92 Marina sight
93 Salinger heroine
95 REM opener
96 "Waiter, may I see __?"
97 __ *With a View*
98 Shell occupants
99 Bobsled cousin
100 Forum finery
101 Getz or Kenton
102 It's in the trunk for a change
103 Get smart
104 Get the picture
107 Coal holder
108 Strongest club?

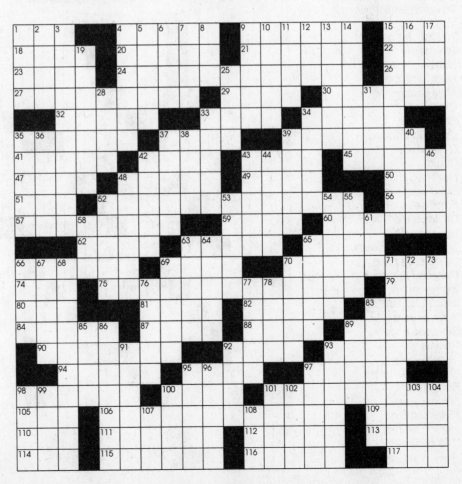

ACROSS

1 Letters from Greece
5 Johnny's successor
8 Before soda or sandwich
12 Sterilize
16 Cabaret, in Calais
17 "__ got it!"
18 Excelled
19 Startle
20 Of Athens
21 Hunt for jobs
24 Timber wolf
25 Downcast
26 Bowler's button
27 Big boy?
28 Tended wounds
30 Trot and canter
31 Aromatic alcohol
35 Mets, Nets or Jets
36 Trouble quantity?
37 Philatelist's unit
38 A Gershwin
39 Statute
41 Get into full swing
45 KO count
46 Paragon
48 Litmus reddener
49 Parka parts
50 Tobacco or Abbey
51 __ up (enlarged)
52 Toss in the microwave
53 Fixes fences
54 Walden, for one
55 Descartes
56 Half and half
57 Rajah's helpmeet
58 *Maja* painter
59 Creative field
60 Strike it rich
64 Cwt. hundredths
67 Day division
69 Cupid
70 Never alternative
71 Subdivider's map
72 Small salamander
73 Driving force?
75 Bundestag city
76 She loved Narcissus
77 "Mine eyes have __ . . ."
78 Respond to stimuli
79 Blockhead
80 Indo-European, once
81 Your, of yore
82 Blow one's top
85 Recline
86 Anger
87 Holiday precursors
88 Barn birds
89 "What __ say?"
91 "Tsar of all the __"
93 Heavy hammers
95 PTA people
98 Head or nog opener
99 Director Frank
100 Red or Irish
101 First father
102 Give the gist
107 With 40D, "The Woman," to Holmes
108 In re
109 Warbucks ward
110 Space-age assent
111 Twilled fabric
112 Chicago area
113 Honey wine
114 Hale or Hari
115 Estimator's words

DOWN

1 Dynamo part
2 Knock for a loop
3 Indolent
4 Min. part
5 Holy war
6 Eager
7 To this time
8 Where the toys are
9 Finishes last
10 Component
11 Plant plot
12 Meager
13 Sidekick
14 Genesis vessel
15 Aye or yea
16 Like Capt. Picard
18 Arab chiefs
19 Foster's river
22 Followed trails
23 Edits, in a way
25 Round of four
29 Satirist Mort
30 Lamp inhabitant
31 "Eight __ a-milking"
32 Work perfectly
33 Mountain nymph
34 Come to earth
36 Change place?
37 Poke
39 Sign of fall
40 See 107A
42 Jeer at
43 Actor Paul
44 Gin go-with
47 Wonderment
50 Actor Scheider
52 *Nuit* color
53 Student's specialty
54 What antes start
57 Kind of control
58 Grad's garment
60 Crude cabin
61 Emerge from the egg
62 Hillocks
63 Producer Carlo
65 Baha'u'llah follower
66 14 pounds, in Perth
68 Personal
71 For each
72 Jawaharlal
73 Apportions
74 Roan's repast
75 Seethes
77 Recipe direction
78 Light yellow-green
79 Loose skin fold
80 Seaweed product
82 Altitude
83 Meal part
84 Coll. athletic grp.
90 Less distant
92 Establish
93 __ cum laude
94 Plant pest
95 Annoying
96 Valentino dance
97 Pintail duck
99 *Teatro* cousin
100 Word of whoa?
102 *2001* computer
103 Eastern Nigerian
104 Overly
105 Overacting actor
106 Hemispheric org.
107 Metric or morphic lead-in

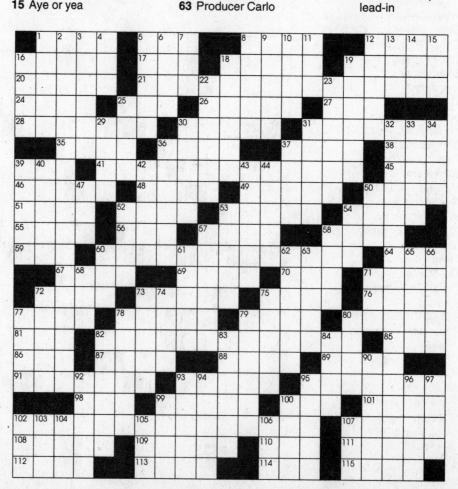

ACROSS

1 Extemporize
6 Bliss
9 L.A.'s Union
12 Suppose
18 Main squeeze
19 Strike dumb
20 Haole's wear
21 Actress Dahl
22 Certain synagogue
23 Bike race bypass?
26 Electron collector
27 Gave a bite?
28 Took on
29 Put up stakes
30 Oz visitor
31 Instant lawn
32 Walk the floor
33 Fire-alarm part
35 "__ Kick Out of You"
37 Huron's neighbor
38 Clan war
39 Check the water?
42 From __ Z
44 Deli-catered sausage?
47 Pres. Fujimori's land
48 Bicycle built for two
50 Beryllium symbols
51 Shipper Onassis
52 Forgoes
54 Firebug's felony
55 Jones who played Morticia
57 Fretful
58 Lane of Metropolis
59 Om, e.g.
60 Wash. airport
61 Catchall abbr.
62 Sitcom cancellation cause?
65 New newt
68 She gave us *Scruples*
70 Mertz and Merman
71 Nimble
72 Chiffons' "One __"
74 Lighting designer's doodads
76 Burnable piles
77 Odd
78 John, to Jock
79 Afore
80 Holy city?
81 After 86A, Sharks' home
82 Controversial *Psycho* setting?
86 See 81A
87 *Double Indemnity* bus.
88 Microorganism
89 Pied Piper's prey
90 Cover story
92 Vamp of silents
93 WACs' sacks
94 Pool tool
95 Shaping tool
98 Astrologer Sydney
101 Urbane
103 Diamond club
104 Furtive one

105 Attorney's reckless binge?
108 Oscar winner Woodward
109 Snail __
110 Army address?
111 Scull's sculler
112 Prevention units?
113 Bratlike
114 Barbecue buttinsky
115 Go for it
116 Salvers

DOWN

1 ". . . __ 'clock scholar"
2 Disease of the downgraded?
3 Servile follower
4 Aimless
5 Tournament "free pass"
6 Blasé
7 Had chits out
8 Still and all
9 Water channel
10 __ Haute, Ind.
11 Assistant
12 UK air arm
13 Gofer's task
14 Trolley sound
15 Clark of Metropolis
16 Never again?
17 Be short of

18 ASAP in the OR
24 Atheist Madalyn
25 Barely beats
27 Stable youngster
31 Plant part
32 Arrange bulk mail
34 Lasts longer than
36 Paradise paradigm
37 Turns inside out
38 End of the work wk.
39 Gimmicky government office?
40 Olympian aggressor
41 Go to the dogs?
42 __ *of Two Cities*
43 Diviner's deck
45 Writer Vicente Blasco __
46 Coffee set part
47 Gyro holder
49 Spanish pair
53 Abbr. on an env.
55 Slyly spiteful
56 Collar continuation
57 Loses a sunburn
59 Attic comedy writer
60 Sound setup
62 Coral Gables' county
63 Bears witness
64 Heat units
66 Singer Payne

67 Cicely who played Pittman
69 Dream, to Dumas
71 Word pt.
72 Japanese mountain
73 Privy to
74 LAX watchdog
75 Shy person
76 __ sci
78 "Big Blue"
80 40% of TV
83 Clear the board
84 Broken bread
85 Lacking slack
88 Red rock
91 Split ingredient
92 Butler who plays Grace
93 Log lodge
94 Have in stock
96 Writer Grey's namesakes
97 __ out a living
98 Saratoga stats
99 Denote
100 '60s do
102 103D, to Caesar
103 Smokey or Yogi
104 Kind of cream or grapes
106 Bonelike?
107 After polka or peri
108 Make a note

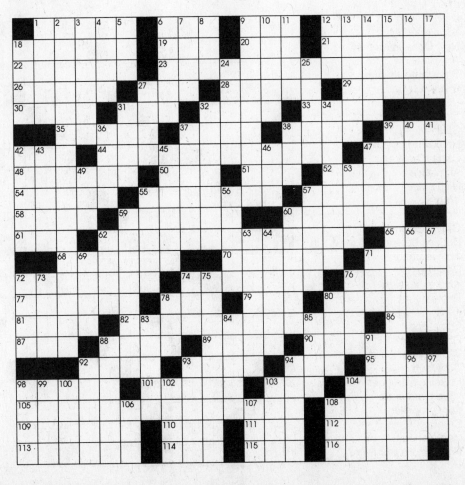

ACROSS

1 D-day beach
6 Give it a go
9 Eavesdrops electronically
13 Slovenly
19 Ear lender to Antony
20 Cry companion
21 *Exodus* author
22 Latin epic hero
23 Nursery rhyme opener
26 Demented
27 Extravagant
28 Rock's Young
29 Actress Taina
30 Horseshoe score: Abbr.
31 Electrical unit
34 Overwhelm
35 USPS penultimate
37 Mescal
38 "__ lively!"
39 Coop occupant
40 It means tissue
43 Encircles, to poets
44 Golf hole marker
45 Opposing vote
46 Dues payer
47 "Bei __ Bist Du Schoen"
48 Columbia, in song
53 Chang's companion
54 I.M. the architect
55 At a distance
56 Jedi's foe
57 Drug-testing org.
58 Bible reading
60 New Orleans French
61 Any day now
62 Snowmass feature
63 River at Lyon
64 Utter disdain
66 Floral neckwear
67 Soul
69 He played Lestat
71 Certain nest egg
72 Add spice
73 Nice noise
74 Wary
77 Hr. part
78 Gravel Gertie's daughter
80 Begone beginning
81 Act the traitor
83 Dead heat
84 Kind of session
85 Prima donna
86 Fussy Felix's roomie
87 Cozy room
88 Fourth base?
89 Black eye
91 Confused
93 Folksinger Seeger
94 More clamorous
95 Punt propeller
97 Cruet contents
98 Mad as heck
99 *Witness* director Peter

100 Shows vanity
102 Erin
108 Bloomer or Earhart
109 Garment borders
110 Existed
111 Shaq pack member
112 Ira wrote them
113 Lenient
114 Potato bud
115 Discharges

DOWN

1 Leftover scrap
2 Blade the blades
3 Pal in Paris
4 Chinese dynasty
5 Short sock
6 This and this
7 Mystery writer Rendell
8 Bow wood
9 Engine adjustment
10 Actor Alan
11 It may be hard to take
12 Yacht heading
13 Spanker and jib
14 Extend
15 Switch positions
16 Dorothy Parker's retort to "Age before beauty"
17 Anguish attack
18 Flanders river

24 Artificial bait
25 Purpose
29 Long, long time
31 High home
32 '79 Judy Davis film
33 Not neg.
34 Unbending
35 Cosmetic stick
36 See 25D
37 Splendor
38 Masters' river
39 Curved-billed bird
41 Sinew
42 It's played at Dodger Stadium
45 Bond
46 Silents' Murray
48 Show shock
49 In addition
50 Bovine comment
51 Wonder Woman, for one
52 Before
59 Aurora, in Athens
60 Screen's Lombard
61 Mayday!
62 Bowler's set
63 Green-feathered finch
64 Clubs, e.g.
65 Urbanite's milieu
66 What you're in when you're on hold

67 Aral, e.g.
68 Divided
69 Upscale pancake
70 Join the 10K
72 Secret seeker
73 Censure
75 Stay suspended
76 1984 or 2001
78 Bitterly sneering
79 For the time being
82 Half a diam.
85 Solved, as puzzles
87 Marina __ Rey
88 Anti-orthodox belief
89 Defile
90 Leap over
92 Young Simpson's sis, et al.
93 Cinquains, e.g.
94 Flat paper?
95 Iridescent stone
96 West Point 11
98 NYC stadium
99 Kong's handful
101 Actor Wallach
102 Common article
103 Lamb's dam
104 Descartes' conclusion
105 Wood runner
106 Service call?
107 Hesitating sounds

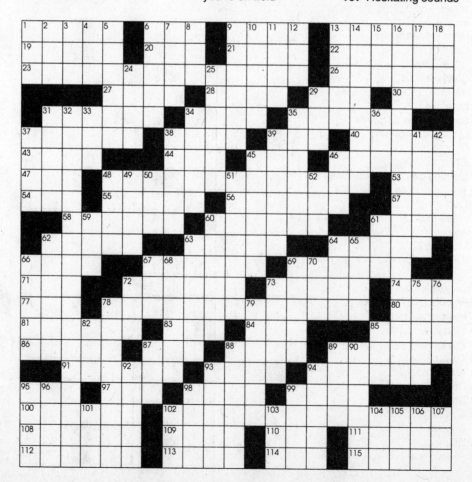

ACROSS
1 P.M. wear
4 Smart as __
9 Muscle-bone connectors
15 The price is right on it
18 Carl Sagan's sci.
20 '53 Ladd role
21 Long hooded jacket
22 Menu words
23 Dissolute one
24 Beat back middle age?
26 Hi-tech scanner
27 Santa Fe Trail town
29 Nonpareil
30 Chicago suburb
32 Stones' "Get Yer __ Out!"
33 Beatles' "Back in the __"
34 Lacy mat
35 Mollify
37 Lasso dogies
39 Main meals
41 Chews the fat
42 Caddies' cargo
43 Miss Toga?
45 Full of gunk
47 __ avis
48 Sham rocks
49 Design
50 Mined-over matter?
51 Escort's offering
52 Postquake retrofit law?
56 Alley
57 Manon composer
59 Rickenbacker and Richthofen
60 Silver and Scout
62 Wee bits
63 Hoops player
65 Lose strength
66 Guarantee
69 Boot bottom
70 CFO's concern
74 The buck stops her
75 Machiavellian option?
79 Caesar salad ingredients?
80 Beaver's oeuvre
81 Dilute
82 Cools one's heels
83 Midge
84 Get around
87 Hoskins in Hook
88 79A, to us
89 Where rice is raised
90 Zodiac arachnid
92 Rapierlike
93 Professional's path
94 Greek theater
95 Incursion
97 Make parallel
98 Except possibly
100 Nut house?
101 It follows
105 Zodiac cat
106 Small songwriters' site?
109 This, señorita
110 No, to Nanette
111 Pioneer
112 Golfer Calvin
113 Prepare prunes
114 "__ luck?"
115 High regard
116 Asked, as questions
117 Designer label inits.

DOWN
1 Cowpoke's pal
2 He played on "B. Miller"
3 Reading-breeding areas?
4 School of New York Realism
5 "__ Silvia, what . . .?"
6 "Not another step!"
7 Filmdom's Jones, to pals
8 Fido or Fluffy
9 Composer Saint-__
10 Get the impression
11 Jordan's queen
12 Misadd
13 Bell's assistant
14 '50s TV flying hero
15 Seedy stable adjuncts?
16 Kirghiz range
17 Airport area
19 Rowing race
25 Footwear
28 They're behind most spectacles
31 Stick in the fridge?
33 Underdog's dream
34 "Avenger" Rigg
35 Vamoose
36 Tara belle
37 Put the counter to 000
38 Steed feed
39 Sturdy wagons
40 Spendthrift's specialty
42 Makes the wild mild
43 "Star Trek" arena
44 Birchlike tree
46 Certain evergreens
48 The __ 52D (Eudora Welty work)
52 See 48D
53 Enthusiastic
54 Does as Gregorians
55 Matt Lauer's gig
58 113A homophone
61 Stimpy's co-star
63 TV reporter Roberts
64 By oneself
65 Decrees
66 Finds totals
67 Drenches
68 Partial settlement?
69 Sap
70 Pretend
71 Unpleasant publisher?
72 See 84A
73 Nymph chaser
76 "__ the bag!"
77 Coat fabric
78 Fashion or passion
83 Uses mouthwash
85 Took mass transit
86 Railroad support
89 Jill's burden
91 Nosegays
92 Oast or lehr
93 Was too much of a good thing
95 100 paise
96 Waker-upper
97 Mountain ridge
98 Bone near the biceps
99 The light stuff
100 Park in London
101 Liz played her
102 Cheers, to Che
103 1, 101 and 10
104 Ketch kin
107 Natalie's dad
108 Bk. addendum

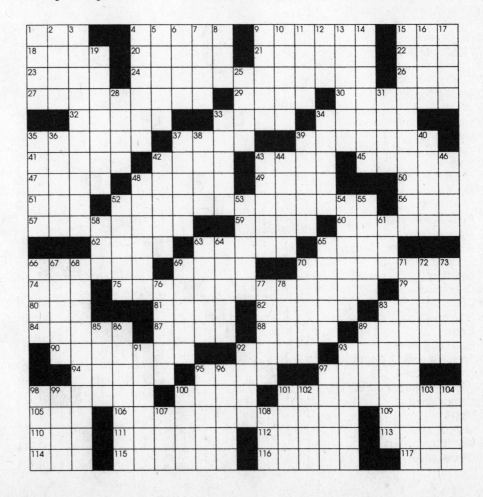

ACROSS

1 Datum
5 O with a bar through it
10 Kiddie's piggie
13 Graduated
19 A singing Guthrie
20 *The Kiss* sculptor
21 Lyricist Gershwin
22 Twain's town
23 "Jumpin' Jack Fish" group?
26 Like sharp pencils
27 Clear brandy
28 Approve
29 Value for taxes
30 Chaplin brother
31 Join the competition
32 Stared steadily
34 Just picked
35 Chief catchers of the day?
37 Weasel's prey
38 __-Pekka Salonen
41 RLS's doctor
44 Palindromic names
45 Makes i's
46 When DST starts
47 Gallic and prussic
48 Stir on the water?
49 Nobel or booby
51 __-a-brac
52 Trendy's concern
53 Remedy for fishy breath?
55 Kama __
56 Timber trees
57 Conductor Klemperer
58 Train of thought
59 Making 10 with two
63 Make it happen
65 Waste away
66 Contract stipulation
67 Little lions
68 "Lois & Clark's" Dean
69 Severe
70 "Fishin' Impossible" star?
73 Marina mooring
77 "__ Rhythm"
78 Passenger's peeve
79 Many millennia
80 A singing Guthrie
81 Back burner?
82 Life story
83 O for goodness' sake?
84 Complain
85 Sign on a door
86 Rep.
87 Fish story writer?
90 "Whither shall __ from thy presence?": Ps. 139
92 What grumps are out of?
93 Campaigned
94 Mph kin
97 Mollycoddles
99 Kett of the comics
100 Official approval

102 Victoria's consort
103 *Mary Pompanos* tune?
106 Lassie's breed
107 Party member?
108 Man of Le Mans
109 Oscar winner Thompson
110 Paid attention to
111 Fort near Monterey
112 Recording star?
113 *Phantom* prop

DOWN

1 Destinies
2 Set in order
3 Make murky
4 Tattled
5 Unimportant
6 Mellifluous
7 Periphery
8 "__ the season . . ."
9 Queen's subject
10 Meandering mender
11 Mountain nymphs
12 Cushy
13 Apart
14 Clothes quarters
15 Not quite right
16 Bravely devoted to fishing?
17 M.A.'s A

18 Bradbury and Charles
24 Video-game features
25 Seeps
32 "The Love Boat"'s MacLeod
33 Saying
34 Got severe stage fright
35 RLS's mister
36 "__ hell": Sherman
39 Montana pass?
40 Video-game arena
41 Play for fun
42 Environmental pref.
43 What Rick called Ilsa
45 Pebbles' pet
48 Composer Alban
49 See 97A
50 Baptism, e.g.
51 Red tan?
53 Trig function
54 Immoderate imbiber
55 Barking place?
56 Flounder, for one
58 Certain sib
59 Ecclesiastic split
60 Bedevil
61 "Trawl It Like It Is" sole singer?
62 Oxidize

63 Castro's country
64 "Dear" lady
65 Stand for speakers
67 RC or Pepsi
68 Pachelbel opus
70 Actress Midler
71 Change chemically
72 Gaucho's gizmos
73 Not even fair
74 Debtor's letters
75 Mag wheels?
76 Potent potable
78 Summarized
80 Do the twist?
82 "Rhoda"'s Harper
83 King of Tyre
84 Takes a peek
87 Purim queen
88 Chubby
89 Music award
91 Ebbets or Soldier
94 Terra __
95 Frost lines?
96 Kind of preview
97 A musical B
98 Lotion ingredient
99 The bouncing bawl?
100 Drainage pit
101 Rain cats and dogs
104 Fwy. police
105 Weeder's tool

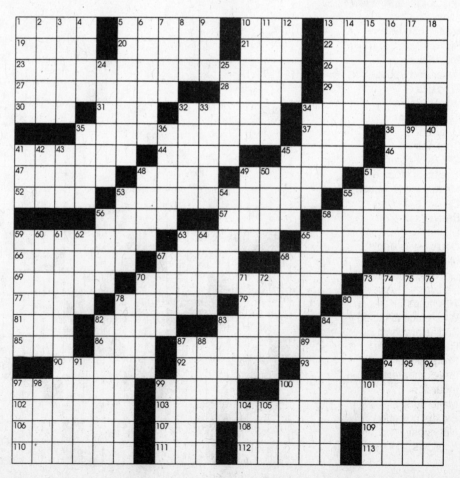

ACROSS

1 Overindulge
6 Snooty sort
10 Action figures?
14 Indifferent
18 Pierre's chair
19 Dear, to Domenico
20 Links alert
21 Not fooled by
22 Through __
25 Seneca's student
26 It vies with Vogue
27 Another name for Abby
28 Col.'s command
29 Horse-opera hat
31 Perpetually
32 Watching machines?
33 DJ's transitions
35 Chump
36 Asta or Fala
37 Go through __
39 A pop
40 Kind of blade
41 Bon follower
42 __ Aviv
44 Ex-New Yorker editor Brown
47 Costume
50 In the mode
52 '54-'77 alliance
54 Mideast missile
55 Mine, in Monaco
56 Through __
59 Grade schooler
60 Charm with flattery
62 Carry on
63 Bridge defenders, often
65 Moose's mates, e.g.
66 Hang gracefully
68 East of Eden name
70 100,000 BTU's
72 The Grateful Dead's Bob
73 They clean your clothes
76 Make like a masseuse
77 "Through __"
82 "Would __ to you?"
83 Dismounted
85 Like "The X-Files"
86 Knight wear
87 Eyeballed
88 It has roots and many
   branches
89 Certain microchip
90 Whence Cossacks came
91 George I's veep
92 Prune
94 Put through __
99 Wimbledon unit
102 '94 Reeves hit
104 Bush II's veep
105 Stable particle
106 Showed up
107 Sully or stain
109 He danced onscreen with
   Deborah

110 Finished
111 They can take a yoke
112 Nabisco nibble
113 Come through __
117 Give, for a time
118 Away from windward
119 Housing project?
120 Stab in the conscience
121 Countercurrent
122 Term for Tim
123 Your Erroneous
   Zones writer
124 Half an Austen title

DOWN

1 Put on the back burner
2 Warehouse platform
3 Ship of fuels?
4 "A mind __ terrible . . ."
5 Time-consuming
6 Disharmony
7 Hit squarely
8 Gp.
9 Arab sultanate, to some
10 "Son __!"
11 E, in Morse
12 Mother Hubbard, e.g.
13 Spanish muralist
14 Gets in touch with
15 Get it through __
16 Others, to Orozco

17 Crazy as a bedbug
18 Cry from a coop
23 Jay's rival
24 "Here __ again!"
30 Clean-air gp.
33 Have in inventory
34 It's left behind
37 Gregory Hines specialty
38 Auditory
39 Time Machine people
40 Fender or Stratocaster
43 Forti finale
45 Nice night
46 Does sum work
47 Chew the fat
48 Bird on an Aussie coin
49 See through __
50 Pal
51 Shorts support
52 Shoot the Canon
53 U2 member The __
56 Uno, due, __
57 Give a grant
58 Minimal high tide
61 Humor writer Bombeck
64 Dole out duties
66 He loved Lucy
67 Leave the lounger
68 It's owed on the road
69 Soulful Charles
70 Coal carrier

71 Western U.S. dance
72 Glowing effect
73 Do Sun Valley
74 Never say this
75 But, to Brutus
78 Bacterium
79 Low land?
80 Cleveland of letters
81 Punjab princess
84 Song of lamentation
87 Crew member
90 Resided
91 Does Spade work?
93 General Amin
95 "__ we're the Monkees"
96 ". . . when the rainbow is
   __"
97 Midday tryst
98 Band of baddies
99 Angles' counterparts
100 Come forth
101 On edge
102 It's a wrap
103 Whittled
104 Get Shorty's Palmer
106 Noncandidate Powell
108 Hit like Ruth
110 Sleazy saloon
114 Finger complement
115 Word of cheer
116 Be in arrears

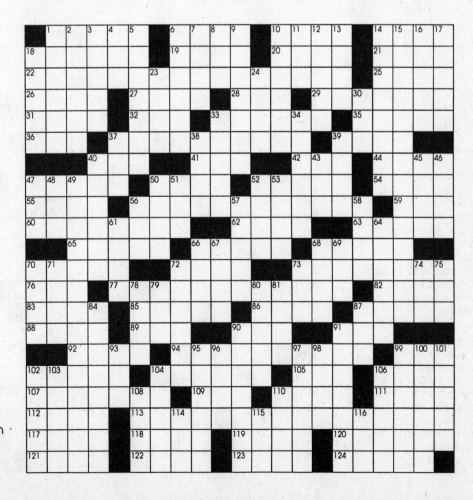

ACROSS

1 Ascend
6 Computer units
10 Pat gently
13 Makes memos
17 Pickled-pepper picker
18 Basic belief
19 Seven hills city
20 Prowl car, to cops
21 Worthless opportunity?
23 Eagerly craving
24 *Quo Vadis?* baddie
25 Mythical high-flier
26 *Fried Green Tomatoes* director Jon
28 Watts up?
29 Grandiose
32 *Bellum* opposite
33 Very, to Verlaine
34 89D homophone
36 Seek answers
37 Fled on foot
38 Signal to the USCG
39 He may take liberties with women
41 Optimistic
43 Inadequate idea on the way?
47 Big seller in bear markets?
50 Olde King's Head order
51 Iowa college
52 "... let __ as happy as we can": S. Johnson
53 Tie the knot
54 Empathize
56 "Poor man's silver"
58 Feathers of a bird
60 Cowl guy?
61 Benz or Jag alternative
62 *Psycho* setting
64 Palindromic nickname
65 An end to Man?
66 Vocalize in vain?
68 What Hester wore
69 Write a P.S.
70 Johnny or Ole
71 Rock singers?
72 Book value?
73 African language
75 Razz the comic
76 Wipe out in battle
77 Impressionist Edouard
78 Andy Taylor's son
81 Fabric for a *bailarina*
82 Pool hall?
83 *Manon* melody
84 Useless stimulant?
90 Stop up
92 Stonecrop family plants
93 Mare's morsel
94 Round starter
95 Before, of yore
97 CSA's R.E.
99 Lah-di-dah ways
100 Misjudge
101 Place for a dip?

102 Onetime Chevy model
104 Lithuanian capital
106 Brave
108 Grace period?
109 Pall partner
110 Skeptic's inconsequential request?
115 __ *la vie*
116 Without concentration
117 Arch types
118 Hobbes, for one
119 Get rid of
120 Music's Paul or Brown
121 Sorrel horse
122 *Élève's* milieu

DOWN

1 IRS employee
2 Actor Cariou
3 Give __ whirl
4 *M*A*S*H* extra
5 Bric-a-__
6 Sweethearts
7 Caravansaries
8 Gumshoe
9 Acid from tallow
10 Peace proponent
11 Friendship
12 Oyster area
13 Jupiter's mate
14 Empty options?
15 Cavaliers ride on them

16 Baby bird?
18 Beat soundly
19 King's __ (huge sums)
22 *The Grass Harp* writer
27 Velvety felt
28 The even prime
29 Gay '90s, e.g.
30 Mythical piper
31 Claire of *Ninotchka*
33 Rest for a while
35 Bit of a joule
38 Realtor's aim
39 Frosty, for one
40 Umbrella radius
42 Mess meat
44 Turkey option
45 Long cold spell?
46 Eighth rock from the sun?
48 Crisp cotton cloth
49 Laughing scavengers
53 Pack animal
54 Post-'45 conflict
55 Trivial trouble?
56 Retiree's support
57 Make the word go away
59 Traffic light part
60 Bad atmosphere
61 *Show Boat* tune
62 Wholesale-retail margins

63 Verdi hero
66 "And __ goes"
67 Judicial comments
72 Scandinavian saint
74 Make sound
75 Park front first
76 Measles mark
79 Ballet step
80 In a perfect world
82 Like hen's teeth
84 Ripen
85 Museum manager
86 Symposia
87 Back from to
88 Big time
89 *Sheep*
91 Antiquated
95 Play charades
96 Capulet in-law
98 Duck
100 Pioneering sitcom
101 Anti-altruist
103 The under-the-hill gang
105 Maladies
106 Charge answer
107 Actress Nelligan
109 USMA pt.
111 Id kin
112 Time past
113 N.J. neighbor
114 Modern art?

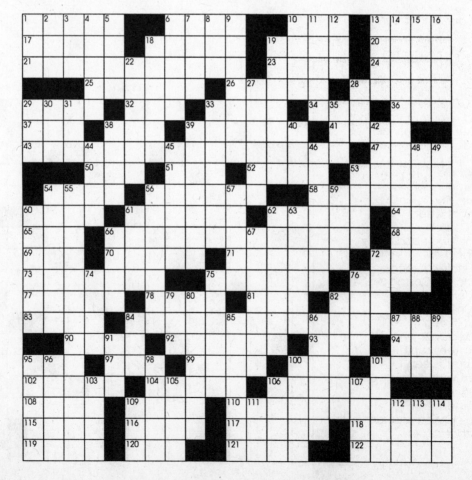

ACROSS

1 Ring inset
4 *Tio*'s brother
9 Get less green
14 Missing at reveille
18 Roaring Twenties, e.g.
19 Steel, to Camille
20 Romeo's hometown
21 Repulsive
22 ''My country, __ of thee''
23 Pitt-Freeman suspenser and Rock Hudson satire
25 ''I've Got the Music __''
26 ''A bed by night, __ drawers by day''; Goldsmith
28 It's in
29 Ebbs
30 Characteristic
31 Overdetailed
32 Kind of license or justice
34 J.S. Bach's J
36 They get high twice a day
37 Solidify
38 Have __ for living
39 Amahl's night visitors
40 Soviet labor camp
41 What the U.S.A. makes
44 Joe from France?
45 Kurosawa epic and Macaulay Culkin hit
48 Squeezing snake
49 Poem's pussycat pal
50 Explode
51 Water colors?
52 Makeup artist?
53 Candle wax source
55 Slips a Mickey to
56 Rust, mildew or smut
58 Forever and __
59 Spunk
60 Interrogate
61 Crude container
64 Crime-spotter's group
65 Guilty
69 Go first
70 Paying passengers
71 Fees to get free
72 Of Providence's st.
73 Mentalist Geller
74 Cruise drama and Caron weeper
77 Get a D
78 Time beyond measure
79 Metal bolt
80 Wrinkle remover
81 Domino's game?
82 Chauffeur
84 Act fraction
86 Rationality
87 Composer Gustav
88 Doctor of literature
89 December air
90 Dromedary, for one
91 Tin Man's lack
92 Georgia seaport
95 ''Unfortunately''

96 Elizabeth Taylor epic and Woody Allen farce
99 Put into service
100 Newman's Own rival
101 Diverts
102 British architect Jones
103 Ball booster
104 Goes blond
105 Went white
106 Port on the Rhine
107 On the down side

DOWN

1 ''__ grip on yourself!''
2 Rock's Burdon or Clapton
3 Sutherland-Gould comedy and Goldblum-Davis shocker
4 En __ (chess term)
5 Explosive ingredient
6 Fairway scar
7 Coral growth
8 Coastal bird
9 Rest period
10 Alexander Pope's device
11 Little lake
12 Write finis to
13 Sodium symbols
14 Have upward mobility?
15 Newman racing story and Hanks fantasy
16 Ancient Mexican

17 Marvin and Meriwether
20 Chapter and __
24 MGM or RKO
27 Get the lead out
29 A piece of the pie
31 54-40 alternative
32 __ Verdes Peninsula
33 North African port
34 Esau's twin
35 Boston maestro
36 Poisonous weed
37 Hawaii hipshakers
39 Wed
40 It may go from E to F
42 Biblical boatwright
43 Hair splitter?
45 RFD's R
46 What Karl's manifesto manifested
47 Provide gear for
50 George Eliot's Adam
52 Judy's daughter
54 Lay man
55 Overfond one
56 Teddy Roosevelt's word
57 Kissing couple?
59 Deserve
60 TV's ''medicine woman''
61 See 107A
62 Prefix with space

63 Joan Crawford moral tale and Jeremy Irons drama
64 Silicon chip
65 It's paddled in the rear
66 Terry Gilliam tour de force and Streisand drama
67 ''Hungarian Rhapsody'' writer
68 Piece of Bacon
70 High-temp state
71 Stable sites
74 Run on a flute
75 Cell block?
76 Southwest celebration
77 Edible pine seed
81 Sunshade
83 Indian monkey
84 Acted as usher
85 Reins in
86 Untamed
87 Indonesia's language
88 Feel vibes
89 Constellation __ Major
90 Jack or joker
91 Heist amount
92 Yemen capital
93 On the Black or on the Red
94 Give ear to
96 Banana Republic rival
97 ''__ Yankee Doodle Dandy''
98 Pen part

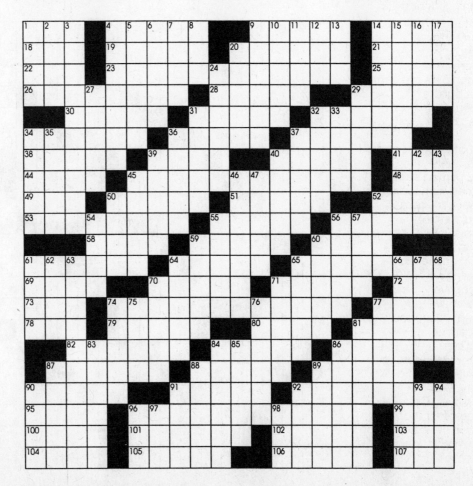

FOR ADULTS ONLY 54

ACROSS

1 Sat. or Sun., to most
4 Gushes
9 Make up your mind
15 Coming-out party girl
18 Minimountain
20 Varnishkes ingredient
21 She played Sabrina
22 Wrath
23 Quito quaff
24 X-rated dental problem?
26 Estuary
27 Who knows and who cares
29 Docs for ducks
30 Pleased no end
32 Casablanca's Claude
33 Plays the perfecta
34 Kind of council
35 And the Band Played On writer Randy
37 Detroit gridder
39 Venice canal cruiser
41 Poet Neruda
42 Nikon need
43 SOS!
45 Short shot
47 Country bumpkin
48 Wow!-evoking
49 Isaac's eldest
50 Pizarro's gold
51 Midori on ice
52 X-rated abyss?
56 Comics' Krazy __
57 Liberal
59 Harem units
60 French perfume center
62 Brits' bars
63 Impertinent
65 Biting bug
66 '95 De Niro film
69 It's hot when it's coaled
70 Floatability
74 Nod or mod ender
75 X-rated ilium feature?
79 Schooner's cargo
80 Predicament
81 Verdi villain
82 Dishonor
83 Read on the run
84 Bringing ruin
87 Receptive
88 Pocket fluff
89 Cinema Superman
90 Serpentine
92 Dog biter
93 Become bloodshot
94 Mrs. Ricardo et al.
95 Thank God
97 He played Chips
98 Hang glider shapes
100 Joined the competition
101 Like muscle-toning exercise

105 Mideast weapon
106 X-rated with no frills?
109 Kind of coin or trash
110 To's correlative
111 Wobble
112 U.S. Grant's rival
113 Deer sir?
114 Trekker or X-phile
115 Jockey Eddie
116 Dolefully
117 Administrative ctrs.

DOWN

1 Laker O'Neal
2 French accent
3 X-rated award?
4 Yarn coils
5 Corfu neighbor
6 Sports junkies' network
7 Grinch's victims
8 Airline to Oslo
9 Officer-to-be
10 Looks for
11 Poetic paeans
12 Hockey great Bobby
13 English or Canadian river
14 They're used in a wink
15 X-rated expressions?
16 Clinton's canal
17 Rosary part
19 17th-c. French explorer

25 Post-revenge status
28 Onetime Yugo driver?
31 Bard's river
33 Intimate
34 Infield out
35 Parsley portion
36 Like some cuisine
37 Certain punches
38 Poop
39 Minimalist composer Philip
40 Bayeux Tapestry, e.g.
42 Yoga position
43 Takes notice
44 Opinion piece
46 Be a caddy
48 Yogi's sidekick
52 Main force
53 Finishes out of the money
54 Pay no mind
55 Breakfast-in-bed props
58 Demic or dermic lead-in
61 One-time bridge
63 Military blockade
64 Matching crime?
65 Hotel patron
66 Sleeve end
67 Crook's cover

68 X-rated big number?
69 Tent parts
70 Swahili sahib
71 X-rated facts?
72 Horrormeister Barker
73 Mocha's country
76 Religious
77 Keep score
78 Off-Broadway Tony
83 Tranquilizes
85 ''Sometimes you feel like __ . . .''
86 Eartha Kitt film Anna __
89 It's put before Descartes
91 Pearl harborer
92 Lose color
93 English portraitist George
95 Hamelin visitor
96 Printer's proof
97 Carpenter's pin
98 Memorable actor Howard
99 Pound of poems
100 Career summary
101 Think-tank product
102 Auctioneer's ''amen''
103 Where Basra is
104 Wheel teeth
107 Kind of rm.
108 Salk and Pepper

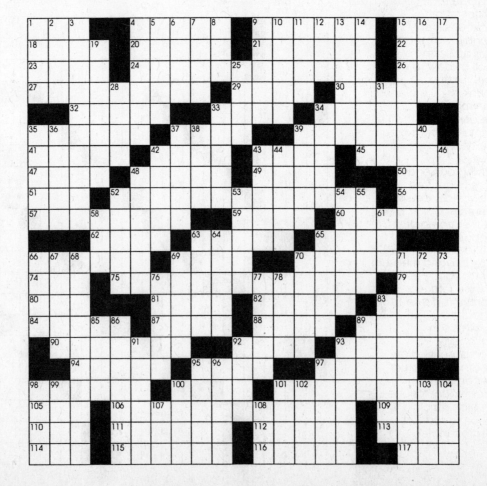

ACROSS

1 Davenport or divan
5 *The Metamorphosis* writer
10 Rink roller
15 Sidewinder sound
18 Baby whale
19 Blockhead
20 Oedipus' riddler
21 Toque or tarboosh
22 Hap Arnold's org.
23 Upgraded classic novel?
25 Clark's *Mogambo* co-star
26 Five-and-ten
28 Atremble
29 Hatch the Senator
31 What some are sworn to
32 Central Asian language
33 Camera stand
34 Lizzie's makeup?
35 Does the butterfly
36 Future flapjacks
37 Baseball clubs
40 Hair care lair
42 Madder family members
43 Tough elastic wood
44 Superlative Sound?
48 Kitchen shortening?
51 Was explicit
53 Word-building game
54 Trident-shaped letters
55 Eyre head?
56 Beef grade
58 Israel Philharmonic maestro
59 Italian air base for U.S. troops
61 Tomcats, in Toledo
62 End up profitable
63 Memorable netman Bobby
64 One of the Fates
66 Spooky sort
68 Relay-race parts
69 Car option
70 Caustic
73 See red?
74 Upgraded Watergate figure?
77 Clairvoyant's claim
78 Deviate
80 Shares an apartment
81 La Bombeck
82 Like some buns
83 *La __ de ma tante*
85 Focus group member?
87 Chintzy
88 Gaggle member
89 Ability
93 A, as in Athens
94 Supremely bad
95 Move for Margot Fonteyn
97 NL or AL award

98 Improved dessert?
101 English river
102 Ten decibels
103 Disco's Donna
104 Canteen contents
105 Racetrack fence
106 Sugary suffix
107 Live coal
108 That is
109 Baa maids?

DOWN

1 Gulf War missile
2 Camel stop
3 Sweetheart
4 Makes change?
5 Cat kin
6 For this purpose only
7 Super-hot, like some chili
8 Laker Bryant
9 Worked on a submarine?
10 Gives the oration
11 Uniform color
12 Not at all stuffy
13 Stick with a kick
14 Appealed urgently
15 Superlative gunslinger?
16 Rescuer
17 Lose a lap

20 __ und Drang
24 Strabismus
27 Kin of "sahib"
30 *Hud* director Martin
32 Terrible time for tots?
33 Jeer at
35 Tireless transport
36 Explosion
37 Coll. degrees
38 Nile reptile
39 Improved metropolis?
40 State of pique
41 Author-critic James
42 United voters
44 Pride members
45 Point __ return
46 Dome-cile
47 Cows and sows
49 In __ (at the original place)
50 H.S. junior's exam
52 Rugged rocks
54 Remains unsettled
56 Gratifies fully
57 Anglo-Saxon letter
58 Corday's victim
59 Woody's heir
60 Penthouse asset
61 Auctioneer's finale
62 Elite alternative

64 "Drove my __ to the levee . . ."
65 Easy canter
66 Getting close
67 Deity of desire
69 Briskly self-assured
70 Tootsy wrapper?
71 You can believe it
72 Books reviewer
74 Downscale
75 Has faith in
76 Heavy reading
79 Genie's gift
81 Landscape spoiler
82 Individualities
83 *Kiss Me Kate* composer
84 Beatles' "I'm a __"
85 Beatles' feel-good doctor
86 Leave open-mouthed
87 Rumba relative
88 Singer Eydie
89 Babble
90 Croupiers' implements
91 Skiers' valley
92 "Wake Up Little __"
94 Protective place
95 USNA pt.
96 Finless fish
99 Stereo annoyance
100 Night or light lead-in

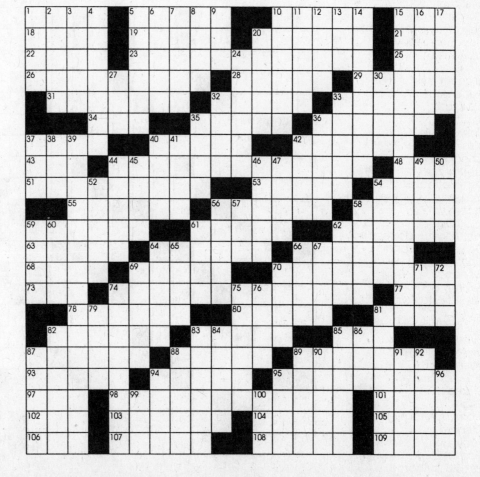

ACROSS

1 Hebrew hero
7 Vigor, in Venice
11 Ballerina Plisetskaya
15 Stiff-necked
19 Refugee's refuge
20 Take chances
21 Satan's specialty
22 It means wine
23 Rock oldie about a swimming sweetie?
26 '95 Branagh *Othello* role
27 Cuts the mustard?
28 Snake charmee
29 Like the Mojave
30 Pack of pennies
32 View from Toledo
33 Have another birthday
34 Track-meet projectile
35 Irrational tendency
38 Merchandise mover
40 Craziness criterion
41 Sand, to some
42 "Tastes great!"
43 Nursery chant start
46 Poolside camcorder output?
49 For whom the bell tolls
50 Dogie leash
52 Paquin of *The Piano*
53 Kiln kin
54 Tanning target
55 The 23rd, for one
56 Zane or Jane
57 TV screen word
58 Cowboy flick
59 He's looking for a fight
60 Bleachers bellower
61 Peruvian money unit
62 Measuring standard
63 Winner's take
64 Dangerous swimming practice?
69 Is suffering from
72 Holly
74 Bulls do it
75 Cheer starter
76 Georgia or Cal
77 Banks of baseball
79 Mousetrap cheese, e.g.
81 Strong suit?
83 __ Brava
84 Write on the dotted line
85 De Lesseps' canal
86 Domestic chicken
87 Concoct
88 Granny or Gordian
89 Pool-life storywriter?
92 Goon
93 Chutzpa source
94 BLT dressing
95 Professor 'iggins
96 Jazz motif
98 10D composer
100 Stamp sheet
101 Share
102 Tra or ooh follower
106 Ensnare
107 Lucy's kid
108 Post- opp.
109 English author John Cowper __

110 Katmandu's continent
112 Prolific poolside-reading writer?
116 Masher's target
117 Neck of the woods
118 Have the facts
119 *Peter Pan* penner
120 Let loose
121 Trolley car quarters
122 Gape
123 Bug or bee

DOWN

1 Le __ du printemps
2 Son of Jacob
3 '68 headline hamlet
4 They're hit in Vail
5 Thine and mine
6 Abbr. not describing HST or DDE
7 Hiawatha, for one
8 Post-wedding fling
9 "Sort of" suffix
10 "Oh, What a Beautiful Mornin' " musical
11 Rate
12 Dyed-in-the-wool
13 Feminine force
14 "The sky is falling!" crier
15 French doughboy
16 Enjoy the heck out of a hot tub?
17 "Minuet __"
18 Barn bellow
24 Most of Israel
25 Maine college town
31 End the indecision
33 Came to rest
34 Boy or Bono
35 "__ my case"
36 Blue shoe material
37 Bahrain bigwig
39 Navelless man
40 DMV feature
41 John, in Genoa
43 Greek's A
44 Fundamental
45 Patient swimmer's stroke?
47 Has coming
48 "Behold, *mon ami!*"
49 Burmese's neighbor
51 Type
56 Generation problem
57 Overmuch
58 Three __ match
60 E-mail alternative
61 Poland China's place
62 There's one at home
64 Majors or a general
65 Island southwest of Majorca
66 Fanatic
67 __ out (relax)
68 Sort of slick

70 Become troublesome
71 Form
73 Washday residue
76 Thee, in Paree
77 Glacier ridge
78 Beatle in the back
79 Harbor markers
80 Piloting prefix
81 Post-Connery Bond
82 On the road
83 Puck or Bocuse
85 Painful poke
86 Overmeticulous
87 Stand in line
90 Back-comb
91 Oliver wanted more of it
94 __ *culpa*
97 Knocks for a loop
99 One of the bunch
100 Pie nut
101 It's above a king
103 Cognizant
104 Cata or hydro ender
105 Brains or brawn, e.g.
107 She changes color
108 Punt front
109 Blueprint
110 He lost to Franklin
111 Bottom of the *mapa*
113 Man-mouse link
114 Santa __ winds
115 Louis Freeh's org., once

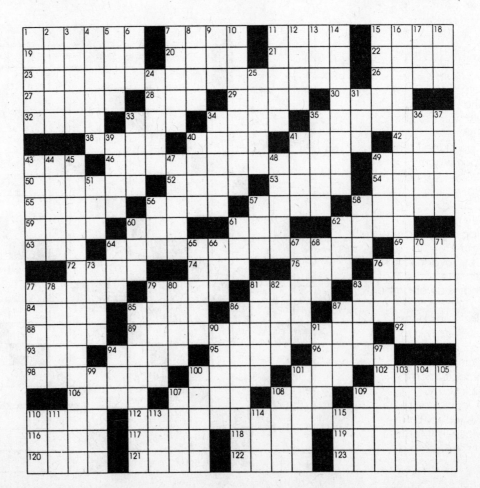

ACROSS
1 Invites
5 Underground lava
10 "J'accuse" writer
14 Old Lincoln?
18 Eat caramels
19 Trojan War epic
20 Diving ducks
22 Break or bird opener
23 Newcastle's river
24 RIGHT
26 Perry's penner
27 Quod follower
29 *Raiders of the Lost Ark* villains
30 Crackbrained
32 Used an ATM card
35 Early late-night host's kin
37 Branch headquarters?
38 George Hamilton's pride
39 RIGHT
43 Giant Giant
46 *Three Sisters* sister namesakes
48 Strike from the record
49 One-armed bandit's arm
50 Yokohama drama
51 The nose knows it
52 River to the Moselle
53 '90s party
54 "Platypus Man" star Richard
55 Fate
56 RIGHT
60 Vase-shaped jug
61 Be munificent
63 Wagnerian *Ring* leader
64 Christian soldier's direction
66 Ryukyu religion
67 Golfer Julius
68 Hugh and Mariah
69 Binaural box
70 "Wheel of Fortune" buy
71 Igneous rock
72 "Of wrath," in a hymn
73 RIGHT
76 Soccer coach Mihalovic
79 Snakes in lakes
80 Jazz drummer Cole
81 Van Gogh subject
82 R&B's Johnny
83 Contract
84 Pier __ Pasolini
86 Philo Vance creator __ Dine
88 Shout "Yes!"
89 Biblical ending
90 RIGHT
93 *Citizen Kane* studio
94 Mower's milieu
95 Worker's ret. act
96 Pianist Erroll
98 Beefsteak, for one
101 Stroke the strings
103 Mustachioed surrealist
104 Help a hood
105 RIGHT
109 Like old bubbly
113 Chevalier classic
114 Moshe of Israel
115 Like legal pads
116 Mantilla material
117 Field worker
118 Out of shape
119 It means within
120 Gazed at

DOWN
1 Do Shakespeare
2 Diffident
3 Merry Prankster Kesey
4 Win the Series in four
5 Emperor of Japan
6 Ended a flight
7 Whitney's invention
8 Fuming
9 Shelley wept for him
10 Eva's sis
11 Atlanta arena
12 '84 ZZ Top hit
13 Shoemaker's holemaker
14 Disgorge videos
15 Escapade
16 Actor O'Shea
17 Spread served in bars
21 Quit the Union
25 Feydeau specialty
28 Barbell sequence
31 Kind of friendly?
32 Welcomed the judge
33 "Where's __?"
34 RIGHT
35 Software bootlegger
36 Nintendo forerunner
37 *Separate Tables* Oscar winner
40 Slope-roofed shed
41 Camel cousins
42 World Series maximum
43 RIGHT
44 Darkroom needs
45 Bronze place
47 Freestanding closets
52 Fly by the __ one's pants
53 Related anew
54 CD container
57 Like a dialogue
58 *Grumpier Old Men* co-star
59 Words of honor?
62 Compass point
65 FDR's Blue Eagle
66 Beale or Baker
67 Russian wolfhound
68 Where you play keno in Reno
69 Military encirclement
70 String section member
71 Orff's *Carmina* __
74 Chipmunk munch
75 Teases, in a way
77 *Duino Elegies* poet
78 He dealt in pelts
84 College Board warmup
85 *Cat's Eye* author Margaret
86 Woody plant
87 They move you
88 Common concluder
91 Ruler
92 Entebbe's country
94 Tacitus' tongue
97 Long arm
98 Pack a pipe
99 Off-Broadway award
100 "From the desk of" note
101 Eye sore
102 Comparison word
103 An end to evil?
106 Apprehend a perp
107 Solderer's metal
108 Bamboom sticks?
110 Produce eggs
111 Trick taker
112 Jane's husband

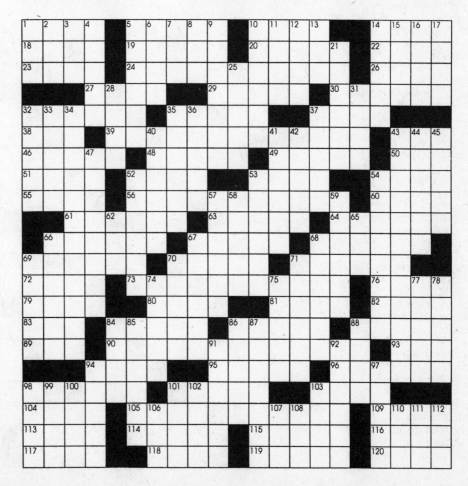

ACROSS

1 Hang loose?
7 Faux
11 Fiddler on the reef
15 Petty clash
19 Isis was his sis
20 Novelist Morrison
21 Atmosphere
22 Carpet quality
23 Soviet leader who cooked on a liner?
26 Make a list?
27 *Waiting for Lefty* writer
28 Dinghy dipper
29 Haley-Bolger co-star
30 Be afraid
32 Breather
33 Young scamp
34 Celebrate
35 Venus __
38 Cosmonaut Gagarin
40 So long, in Salerno
41 "I cannot tell __"
42 Present, in Soho
43 Actress Dawber
46 American leader veto in'?
49 Aerobics prop
50 About-faces
52 They're picked out
53 Fight site
54 Use a prie-dieu
55 Cafeteria totes
56 Word on a fuse
57 Third of three
58 Magnetic flux density unit
59 It's served in prison
60 That lass
61 Atty.'s honorific
62 Parking ticket payment
63 Edible tuber
64 French leader who liked everybody?
69 Hungry Horse or Hoover
72 Not home
74 Speak Pekingese?
75 It's a new start
76 A number of
77 Lost on purpose
79 Swab on a stick
81 Asian language
83 Be skeptical
84 Thousand or Dumbarton
85 Evita's husband
86 Brag loudly
87 Make a hit
88 Motel room, e.g.
89 Rational Jordanian leader?
92 60A, objectively
93 Saturn or Mercury
94 Yves and Calvin's colleague
95 Sword handle
96 Autumn pear
98 Lair
100 Bears do it
101 Bailey's bailiwick
102 Funny Foxx
106 Like a bump on __
107 What the Beaufort scale measures
108 Plea at sea

109 Indian lute
110 Sound system
112 British leader who's so certain?
116 Many buttons
117 Novelist Paton
118 Door to daylight
119 Shows the way
120 Motown's Marvin
121 Playful pinches
122 Rex's tec
123 Use Calvin Klein's cologne?

DOWN

1 Organ offerer
2 "All joking __ . . ."
3 Reeboks alternative
4 Plucky
5 Wagons-__ (sleeping cars)
6 L.A. Philharmonic first-name part
7 Sandal part
8 Witching or happy
9 Groove-billed cuckoo
10 Plants red herrings
11 Hidden hoard
12 German industrial region
13 Contemporary art?
14 Mysterious
15 Chairback feature
16 Canadian leader who shunned counterfeiters?
17 Chicken-king stuffing?

18 Olympic maximum
24 Standup guy
25 Shirley of *Goldfinger* fame
31 Hook partner
33 Rainbow
34 Hose and house lead-ins
35 '66 James Coburn role
36 Perimeter enclosures
37 Noted diarist
39 Where remains may remain
40 Find fault
41 Center of rotation
43 Glazier's gunk
44 Awesome hotel lobbies
45 Libyan leader who's a wacky boxer?
47 Bart's dad
48 Baghdad native
49 Come across?
51 Something to eat or drink
56 "Gotcha!"
57 '60s mind-bender
58 Jackie and Duke's teammate
60 Skittish
61 Second sight, for short
62 Mrs. Andy Capp
64 Fowl bawl?
65 Committing perjury
66 "Raven" writer's monogram

67 Eats away
68 Three before O-U
70 Gentle pace
71 Taxi ticker
73 Toward sunset
76 Ham, to Noah
77 Rough partner
78 City on the Red River
79 "Shush!"
80 Sharp taste
81 Fad doll
82 Bash thrower
83 Shaping devices
85 He played O. Madison
86 Barney fans
87 Winter blanket
90 "__ Man Loves a Woman"
91 Disconcert
94 Reset readout
97 Turning point
99 Beethoven dedicatee
100 Communicates silently
101 The numbers game
103 Practice piece
104 Has the gumption
105 Get garbed
107 Prepare presents
108 Use a muddler
109 Check mate
110 Nonsharer
111 ". . . __ woodchuck could chuck wood"
113 Baba or Pasha
114 Somerset stream
115 In the past

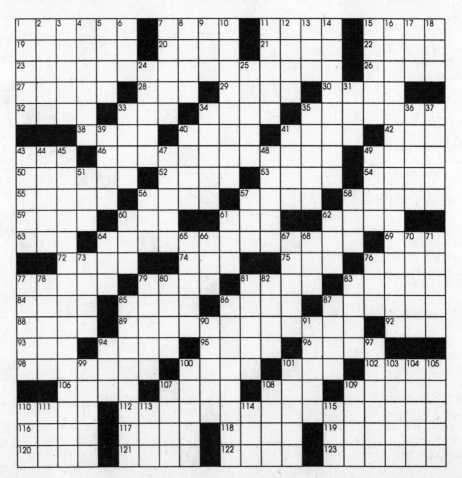

ACROSS

1 __ favor
4 Nobleman
10 Public perception
15 Comic Carvey
19 Horation?
20 Lawrence's stamping ground
21 Floor specialist
22 Top or trop ender
23 Wild bunch
24 Bali misdial?
26 Chuck-wagon fare
27 Stretched out
29 Flying bowman
30 Get extra mileage from
31 Wild and crazy guys
32 Talks talks talks
33 20A, to 7D, e.g.
35 Lofty groups?
37 Indian apology?
39 Longtime Angels owner
40 Some designer clothes
42 Alternate identity
43 Words of cheer?
44 John __ Jingleheimer Schmidt
45 Report card inspector
47 Copy tapes
50 Poker ''bullet''
51 Clooney hit, on Honshu?
53 ''Right you __!''
54 Lily-livered
56 Jackson and King
57 Greek peak
58 Well-mannered
60 Has progeny
62 Clinton preceder
64 Perched on
65 Take it easy
67 Maestro Menuhin
69 Compete at Henley
70 Ted Lewis' Arabic hit?
74 British garden spot
77 Mattel male
78 Queen of whodunits
79 Audition awards
80 Tilting-tower town
81 Carnival booth
82 Longtime bridge whiz
83 Reaction to a pun
84 Turkish superhero?
89 The Red Cross isn't for it
90 Foreshadows
91 Polio pioneer
92 Danube tributary
94 Burdon and Bogosian
95 LSD or HCl
96 Whirlybird nests
99 Bray of pigs?
100 Kitschy Samoan light?
103 Minerva's domain
104 Turning leaf?
105 Split to become one
106 Costa Rican volcano
107 Flyer to a flower
108 Husky's haul
109 Shortened slats
110 Tall thin tower
111 Bow wood

DOWN

1 Ostentation
2 Aerosol target
3 Cuernavacan comic?
4 Stonework
5 Persian cats?
6 Sweater size
7 English horns' kin
8 Orange coat
9 Trygve's successor
10 Pianist José
11 Drink with o.j.
12 Vestry vestments
13 Awed remark
14 Drop a popup
15 Abridges
16 ''I've Got __ on You''
17 Mid-Atlantic state?
18 Victoria's consort
25 Comes closer
28 Hideouts
30 Take turns
32 Lone star?
33 Mint family plant
34 Athens attractions
35 Dear, to Dante
36 McCarthy's comm.
37 Not quite yet
38 Von Richthofen, for one
40 Lord's lady
41 Windows picture
44 Jazz jargon
45 Denver of Hollywood
46 Cries of triumph
47 Mideast VIP?
48 Major in astronomy?
49 Verb for Scotty
51 Early comic Krazy __
52 Paddy Chayefsky hero
55 Irving's sleeper
57 Matchless?
58 Urban oasis
59 Plains tribe
60 Iran statesman Bani-__
61 ''This __ Country''
62 Letters from Greece
63 Royal pronoun
65 Diva Maria
66 A Nightmare __ Street
67 Bulldog's school
68 Paradise paradigm
70 Mercury, etc.
71 Veldt mammal
72 Comic Legion leader
73 Sixty minutos
75 Actor Morales
76 Have a yen for
80 Utah town
81 Left in tiers
82 Role for Rita
83 Wrestle
84 Famed pyramid builder
85 Antenna
86 Periphery
87 Break loose
88 Scolded
89 Kind of urge or scream
92 Fracas
93 Chan portrayer Warner
95 Swear it's so
96 Aesop's also-ran
97 Newspaper source
98 Pot-au-feu
100 Article written by Rimbaud
101 Carte start
102 It may move you

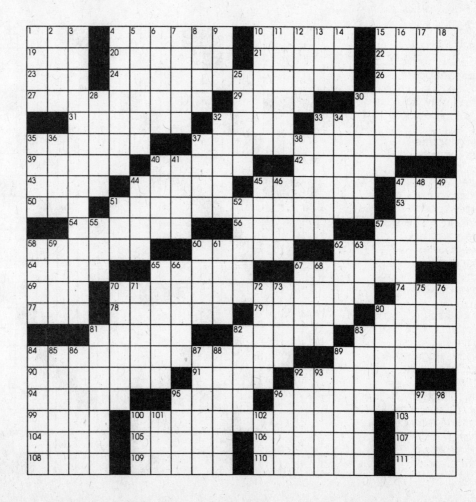

ACROSS

1 Muffler
6 Nigeria, Algeria, etc.
10 Fall guy
13 Tihs, e.g.
17 New Guinea part
18 Engagement ring?
19 Valley NW of Los Angeles
20 Cut the crop
21 An exclamation of doubt would be __
23 Pizazz
24 Archipelago unit
25 Whinnies
26 Interoffice items
28 Charles, Clete or Ken
29 Like some lingerie
32 Aussie animal
33 Sitarist Shankar
34 Tyrrhenian, e.g.
36 Christian, e.g.
37 Fleecy female
38 Needle holder?
39 "He's a __ mission"
41 Eyes, poetically
43 Donne's line would be __
47 Meet Me __ Louis
50 Cgs unit
51 Photocopier button
52 True, to Trudeau
53 Hang gracefully
54 What wild oats are
56 G.I. Blues co-star Juliet
58 Mogambo star
60 Galoots
61 Inhumane
62 Deadpan comic Jack
64 It may get boxed
65 Extreme abbr.
66 Sartre's play would be __
68 Ref's ring decision
69 Bolo, e.g.
70 Martini partner
71 Cold showers
72 Last of a gang?
73 Under
75 Untrustworthy
76 Pretzels' partner
77 Poetic justice, e.g.
78 In years gone by
81 Have a rivalry
82 Walton or Wanamaker
83 Frank's Rat Pack pal
84 Words of woo would be __
90 Cow for beans, e.g.
92 It's over a buck
93 Big time
94 Versailles agreement
95 Ostrich lookalike
97 Salon service
99 Musical sign
100 Cervine creature
101 Charon's ferry crosses it
102 What a beatnik beat
104 Union soldiers
106 Lead ore
108 Saddle or step start
109 Tea time
110 Dickinson's line would be __
115 Q.E.D. center
116 Kitty feed
117 More disgusting
118 '02 headliner
119 Antis' answers
120 Potent potable
121 Takes tiffin
122 First copy

DOWN

1 Body shop?
2 He sang of Minnie
3 "Simpsons" mart clerk
4 Like underdone omelets
5 Go back for a pass
6 Pref. with pedic
7 Seating for the masses
8 Spain's last queen
9 Islands NW of Jamaica
10 Minuteman's home
11 Stockpile
12 Mat win
13 King Cole's combo
14 "Tea for Two's" show would be __
15 Further from florid
16 Beethoven wrote just one
18 Rabbit-hair yarn
19 Grad student's class
22 Putting on the hits
27 Develop
28 Lush setting?
29 Meadowland
30 Leatherworker's tool
31 Cartoon collectible
33 Trolley's big brother
35 Goddess of the dawn
38 Seedless plant
39 Composer Gian Carlo
40 Collector's suffix
42 Jazz's Charlie Parker
44 Cat calls
45 Shows "I Love Lucy"
46 Seriousness
48 Gingrich, once
49 Intense fear
53 Prohibitionists
54 Amadeus antagonist
55 Mercouri's movie would be __
56 Actor's type of jitters
57 Slog through snow
59 They take to the hills
60 Top the offer
61 Escutcheon smutch
62 More substantial
63 Eastern prep school
66 Use a missal
67 A merry Oldsmobile, perhaps
72 Detachable trailer
74 Once it was enough
75 Come to terms
76 Hamburg highway
79 Sch. lobby
80 Official reprimand
82 Dracula's creator
84 Work for "the company"
85 Hard to pin down
86 One who cheers
87 ". . . Just kidding!"
88 Gal's pal
89 Boxcars component
91 Pother
95 He played Clampett
96 Ballerina Shearer
98 Key material
100 Roof edges
101 Fencing weapon
103 Procures
105 Guitar cousin
106 Moola
107 Bochco's "__ Blue"
109 Wide companion
111 Unaccounted-for GI
112 Palm leaf
113 Crosswd. clue
114 Besides

MOVIE MUNCHIES

ACROSS

1 Big cheese in Holland
5 Purchase-order order
9 Broad bean
13 Shipper's box
18 Story
19 Oahu veranda
21 Tree of life site
22 Morgan of myth
23 '76 road-race comedy
26 Pica alternative
27 Roosevelt or Rigby
28 "Better to have __ and lost . . ."
29 Upped the ante
30 Crime writer Buchanan
31 Rolls in Reno
32 Raise the steaks?
33 Juiced-up jalopy
36 Apollo 13 actor
37 Pacific Palisades canyon
40 Labor Dept. arm
41 Uniform jacket
42 __ With Love
43 A long time follower?
44 Pueblo enemy
45 After 60A, '91 Bates-Tandy hit
48 R&D room
49 "__ U.S. Pat. Off."
50 Over easy, like omelets
51 Did a takeoff on
52 Low-voiced lady
53 Magic town
55 Like leisure suits
57 Corresponds
59 Aries and Taurus
60 See 45A
61 Did business
62 Hit list?
64 Meals for money
65 When it's darkest, proverbially
67 "So that's it"
68 Williams Sr. or Jr.
69 Healthy
70 Old energy org.
72 Krypton, e.g.
73 '61 Tushingham film
77 Nada
78 A piece of Freud's mind
79 Scottish loch
80 "Time in a Bottle" singer
81 Add a fringe
82 Kneejerk responses
84 Ty Cobb, the Georgia __
85 Largest Indian tribe
87 Beatles' "She's a __"
88 Harmless trick
89 Deprecating word

90 He played Stanley
92 Hit Gregorian record
93 Accumulates, as interest
97 "What __ in the neck!"
98 '61 Poitier-McNeil drama
101 Starbucks specialty
102 Give commands
103 Reddish brown
104 Antitoxins
105 "__ been my pleasure"
106 WWI German admiral
107 Münster mister
108 Too, in Toulouse

DOWN

1 Ess kin
2 Arlene or Roald
3 Sheltered, at sea
4 One of the Furies
5 Marzipan base
6 Native Israeli
7 Table-talk collection
8 Sidekick
9 Give a lift?
10 Runs out of gear?
11 Pinochle score
12 One, no matter which
13 Where to change your spots?
14 Vatican treasures
15 '88 Cleese-Curtis-Kline comedy
16 London art museum
17 Gimlet or goggle ender
20 Forbidden
24 Reverse
25 Overly intricate
29 Linenlike fabric
31 Film-scorer Elfman
32 Fix the fairway
33 Many minutes
34 Pref. meaning bone
35 '40 John Ford Oscar winner
36 Alicante approval
37 Lugged around
38 Intaglio material
39 East L.A. rockers Los __
41 Watches over
42 Made videos
45 Prepare Parmesan
46 Talk and talk and talk
47 Won at chess
52 Side-by-side figure?
54 Mandolin kin
55 Male mallard
56 Basketball center?
57 Idaho's Coeur d'__
58 All agog
60 Typesetter's options

61 Do bonsai
62 Detroit pro
63 Siouan language
64 Groundwork
65 Mutt
66 Cayuse's cry
68 Refuge
69 After future or culture
71 Liz played her
73 Windflowers
74 Sam Houston, e.g.
75 Continent separators
76 Emotionally amok
81 It was conquered in '53
83 Nabokov's nymphet
84 Eulogize
85 Gods' gulp
86 Roguish
88 Process part
89 Lord's lodging
90 Timbuktu's country
91 Get __ on the back
92 Cut short
94 Mouse manipulator
95 Pref. meaning France, Italy, etc.
96 Lose it
98 Tummy muscles
99 Japanese drama
100 Summer tea additive

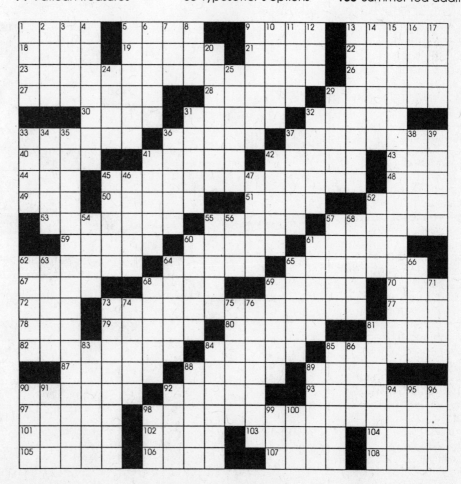

ACROSS

1 Be out of
5 Say "cheese"
10 Fresh fish?
13 Tooth type
19 Novel set in Tahiti
20 Chair designer Charles
21 Oscar nominee Stephen
22 Draw breath
23 Card-carrying Reaganite?
26 Whisks off whiskers
27 Concerns
28 Chemical endings
29 "Baby Blues" baby boy
30 Coquettish
31 "When I Was a __"
32 Wine sediment
34 Declined
35 Actor whose roles are a gamble?
37 Me, to Mimi
38 "Serves you right!"
41 Legal eagle
44 City near Buffalo
45 Four gills
46 *Avis* output
47 In two places at once
48 Memorable San Francisco columnist
49 Lots and lots of ergs
51 Non-Arabic 1102
52 2.5% of a snooze?
53 Comic who made it look like child's play?
55 Guatemalan Maya site
56 Finely appointed
57 Be dependent
58 Computer key
59 It was wild and woolly
63 Fearsome
65 Stuck on the runway
66 Local groups?
67 *Tu* plus *tu*
68 *The Valley of Horses* author
69 Like loose diamonds
70 Movie baddie who was right on target?
73 Sax-playing Simpson
77 Pinta pole
78 Speeders make it
79 Gold and silver holders
80 How some love
81 Danube port
82 Rotunda's crown
83 Opera's Gluck
84 Delilah undid him
85 Shout heard at the Olympics
86 Wine, in combinations
87 Cabaret singer who played the numbers?
90 Betray
92 __ *Is Born*
93 Quill pen point
94 San Francisco's __ Valley
97 Film critic Neal

99 "What __ mind reader?"
100 Collection-plate collection
102 Caught in the Net?
103 Actress-writer who hits the deck?
106 Christmas carol opener
107 Half hexa-
108 Common sense
109 Fast, to Françoise
110 Has a spoonful
111 AARP members
112 __ la Paix
113 Storyline

DOWN

1 Spock's forte
2 Essential acid
3 Memorable game-show host Bert
4 *The Mikado* hero
5 Butler or maid
6 Get by
7 Devilkins
8 She played TV's Caroline
9 Exaggerator's suffix
10 Kind of group or benefit
11 Take a break
12 Goes yadda-yadda
13 Thanksgiving Day snapper
14 Live in
15 "Have you no __?"
16 Puckish painter?
17 Flamenco shouts
18 Interlace
24 Least healthy
25 Canadian official
32 *10*'s 10
33 Bridle attachments
34 Post or Dickinson
35 Actor Michael's dad
36 Ring advantage
39 Ply the sky
40 Rained hard?
41 Chew the fat
42 News letters
43 Administered
45 Weak
48 Quarters or halves
49 Heckle
50 Nothing but
51 Uris' __ *18*
53 Makes memos
54 Army bigwigs
55 William of Uri
56 Bridge, in Avignon
58 A fast buck
59 Long colorful dress
60 Chronicles
61 Of Aggie Christie's sleuth?
62 Chandon's champagne partner
63 Arrange by ZIP code

64 Baby-faced
65 The cost of belonging
67 Ming thing
68 "Let's Make __"
70 Pythias' pal
71 West African river
72 Put in the mail?
73 Priest of the East
74 Bar proof?
75 One mo?
76 Writer Rand
78 They're toasted
80 '64 Leslie Gore tune "__ Know"
82 Tension suspension
83 Perfume from petals
84 Cold symptom
87 She was in *Ecstasy*
88 His son was Set
89 Embrace
91 Most glamorous guests
94 It was nothing to Nero
95 ". . . and __ grow on"
96 Everglades bird
97 Hero's opposite
98 Time-half bridge
99 They'll make a play for you
100 Expression for an arch?
101 Say if you're coming
104 Neighbor of Syr.
105 Bird on an Aussie coin

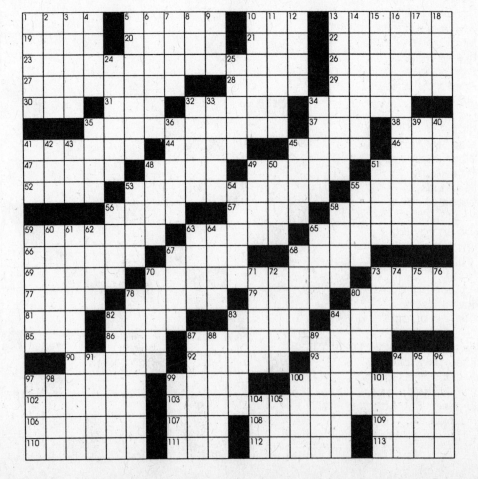

ACROSS

1 N.Y. play producer Joseph
5 Virus named for an African river
10 NATO or SEATO
14 Henry VIII's house
19 First-Amendment lobby
20 Philippine Muslims
21 Jai __
22 Lyre-holding Muse
23 Hollywood goings-on?
26 Lit up
27 Overfills
28 Make into law
29 Puts on a happy face
30 Be precarious
31 After 50D, "The Big Valley" actor
32 __ bifida
33 Zee, as in Penzance
34 To be, to Bernadette
35 Playground purchase
38 One in the 500
41 Overdue Redford-Newman caper film?
44 Scandinavian rug
45 Gelling agent
46 Tasmanian pine
47 Of "The Raven's" auth.
48 Sow and sow
49 Fill in
50 What bugs you about your bed?
54 Watchful
55 Blissful
57 Gets an earful
58 Pascal
59 Chanukah treat
60 Styx transport
61 Actress Ina
62 Eponym of 64A
64 Celestial streaker
65 Was part of
68 *Affaire de coeur*
69 Holy toast?
71 Corrida kudos
72 Put the squeeze on
73 Powder-room powder
74 Bad, in Baja
75 Swiss modernist painter
76 "Put __ Happy Face"
77 Prop for a long experiment?
81 Exodus commemoration
82 "Emperor," for one
84 Mars' counterpart
85 What 5 might mean
86 Arrives at LAX
87 Make quake
88 Breeding ground
91 Strongly built
93 Muslim mendicant
94 Arm-bound
96 It may be filthy
97 Actual L.A. suburb?
99 Before a live mike
100 *The Good Earth* character
101 Poem part
102 Praise from a critic
103 Stops on the way home?
104 How it all started?
105 Deler's choice
106 Conked out

DOWN

1 Donner, Brenner or Khyber
2 Have __ (converse)
3 Dialogue writer
4 Journalist's prize
5 Chewed the scenery
6 Arbor
7 Celestial spheres
8 Comic Costello
9 Contends confidently
10 "Magic bullet"
11 Smart finale
12 Pick players
13 'Twas now
14 __ up (allying)
15 Pressing for
16 Opera by Tex Wagner?
17 Dakota's cousin
18 Big to-dos
24 By and by
25 Like neon and argon
29 Gives it a whirl?
31 Fashion's Geoffrey
32 Steal
35 Croats and Serbs
36 Once-over givers
37 Test for flavor
38 Devil-may-care
39 Flulike disease
40 One-horse Mexican resort?
41 Tutu material
42 Like Toledo?
43 Suspicious
46 Panky preceder
48 Done in
50 See 31A
51 Leitmotif
52 Shimon of Israel
53 Where we live
54 Stand for
56 What it's worth
58 *Jungle Book* bear
60 Brute strength
61 Ball star
62 It's often wreaked
63 Containing NH_2
64 Yo-Yo Ma's instrument
65 Tattle
66 Appomattox signature part
67 Fawn's family
69 Marching orders?
70 Show a good time
73 Late for class
75 Rock instrument
77 Offers
78 Getting the quarterback
79 Wedding dress feature
80 Hillside house row
81 "Gymnopédies" composer
83 Dreiser's *Sister __*
85 Earl the Pearl
87 It's a wrap
88 Saber handles
89 After Chou
90 Dig deep
91 Mess maker
92 Salade niçoise ingredient
93 FDR's Scottie
94 Elizabeth of *Lone Star*
95 Like batik fabrics
97 Criminal clique
98 __ es Salaam

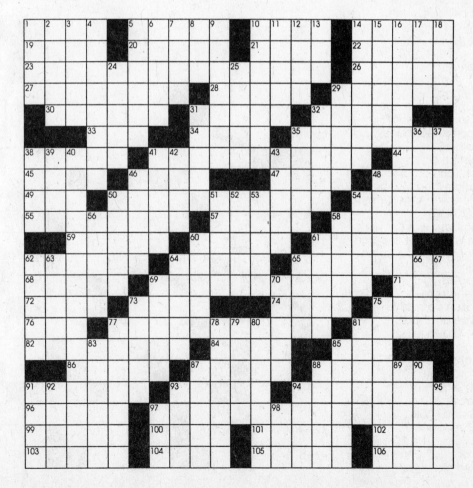

ACROSS

1 Flung or fetched lead-in
4 It runs in the woods
7 Pre-*vu*?
11 *The Trial* writer
16 Heavy mud
17 "When __ door not . . ."
18 Snake's secretion
19 Bahama islands
20 Sinclair Lewis' valorous evangelist?
23 Joins forces
24 Not nearly neat
25 Not in the closet
26 Ice house
28 __ Aviv
29 Televised
30 Steady trot
31 Pepsi cooler
32 They're after your VW
34 Opry adjective
35 Work undercover
36 Chew the fat
37 Prefix prefix
38 Chin attachment?
39 Teachers' degs.
40 Singing in the pain?
45 Word with off or up
47 Disseminate
49 The longest time?
50 Strut and fret upon the stage?
52 Gallivants
53 Paperless pooch
55 Big old bird
56 Regulars' orders
59 __ ease (edgy)
60 Farthest point
63 ". . . kerchief and __ my cap . . ."
65 Dispatched dragons
66 Bando or Mineo
67 Laundered-money holder?
71 Not at all sm.
72 Environmental sci.
74 Article in Le Monde
75 More like Andersen's duckling
76 Kinshasa was its capital
78 Send another telegram
80 Doctor's office sounds
82 Ike
83 Red as __
84 Trendy green
86 Italian possessive
88 Give and take
89 Give and take
90 Role for a lackadaisical danseuse?
94 Lipton liquid
95 Time frame
97 Jackie's O
98 Grand finale?
99 Ticket agent?
102 Wrigley Field flora
103 Conger line member?
104 Two-piece top

105 Wood thickness
106 Bathysphere inventor
108 Dispensable candy?
109 Genesis 5:9 topic
111 Paris accord?
112 Cheerleader follower
113 Dancer Juliet
116 Wine Country tour advice?
119 19th-c. poet Sidney
120 Still as can be
121 One of three articles
122 Lacking slack
123 Actress Verdugo
124 Ustinov *Quo Vadis?* role
125 LBJ beagle
126 Hospital areas

DOWN

1 Embellishment
2 Weapons warehouse
3 Chaucer pilgrim
4 Give autographs
5 Hard-rock bridge
6 Ham Fisher's fighter Joe
7 Cub house
8 Was seductive
9 Brazilian novelist Amado
10 Starch prefix
11 Relations
12 Somme chum
13 Ready for accounting?

14 Prepared to be knighted
15 Walkways
16 Tablelands
18 Vintner's vessel
19 Harbor markers
21 Ablush
22 Carry with effort
27 Common daisy
30 Set up the punch?
31 Qum home
33 Zeno's Z's
36 Swerve, at sea
37 '93 treaty signatory
40 Role for Marie Wilson
41 Ravens' havens
42 Elvis, in Paris?
43 Swain's pitch
44 Was of use
46 Louis XVI coins
47 Consolation
48 No place to leave candles?
51 Mystical marking
52 Stage platform
53 Spit in the ocean?
54 Swedish university town
55 Whimper
57 Uncle Tom's owner
58 Like Georgia Brown
61 Wildebeests
62 Darner's aid

64 Elvis, in Italy?
68 First name in fashion
69 Actor Quinn
70 Dada's daddy Tristan
73 100 centesimi
77 Place __ on (prohibit)
79 100 paise
81 Computer foiled by Dave
85 Arizona political name
86 Dame __ Hess
87 Three, in Thrace
88 Tango quorum
89 A few
91 Writer Ring
92 He was slain by a sling
93 I am in Managua
94 Drink too much
96 __ to (mention)
99 Last place
100 Old editor's mark
101 '92 also-ran
104 He played Paladin
105 Young boxer
106 Panhandle
107 Happify
110 Frigga's mate
111 Baseballer Mel or Ed
112 Flanders' river
114 Finish in front
115 Swell place?
117 Acapulco gold
118 Seashell seller

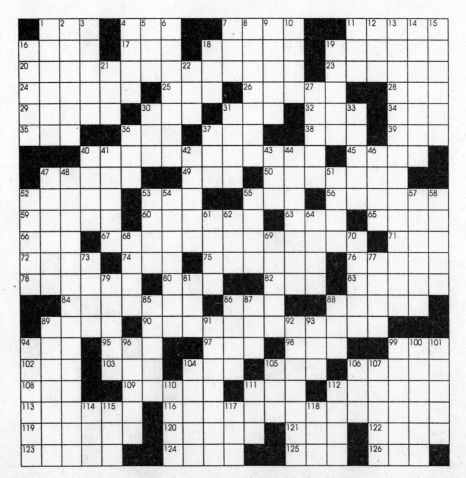

ACROSS

1 __ up (wolf down)
7 No time at all
11 Give 'em a hand?
15 Popeyed
19 Scarlett and Maureen
20 Sweet sandwich
21 Trattoria menu word
22 Peace advocate
23 Raymond Chandler classic
26 Sandy, silty soil
27 They may be coded
28 Pay extra?
29 Twice CCLVII
30 Gung-ho
32 Musical pause
33 Vaudeville family head
34 Five-time presidential candidate
35 Did the deck
38 Beatles' second film
40 Memorable actress Merande
41 Nancy who played Suzie Wong
42 Nay canceler
43 Flow's backwash
46 '77 Fleetwood Mac hit
49 Waited on the line
50 "Star Trek" trek
52 Ardor
53 Otologist's specialty
54 Eagled on a par 3
55 Pitchers
56 On Liberty writer
57 Crawl, perhaps
58 Old __ (the flag)
59 Spare bones?
60 Put on the dog?
61 "El Dorado" writer
62 Caterwaul
63 Mystery writer Josephine
64 '66 Left Banke hit
69 Pkg. carrier
72 Resonate
74 Animation frame
75 '50s Dem. candidate
76 Hajji's leader
77 Trap in a sea inlet
79 Long pass
81 Like a breezeway
83 Shul teacher
84 Like some tales
85 Rain-gutter site
86 Helen or Lamar
87 Commotion
88 Fraud
89 '64 Zombies hit
92 "__ yer old man!"
93 Path of a pass
94 Surgery souvenir
95 Melville opus
96 Surge
98 Dead Souls author Gogol
100 Sis' sibs
101 Reuben bread
102 Trigger treat
106 Vulgarian
107 Praiseful song
108 Doozie
109 Herod's domain
110 After 58D, gosh!
112 '62 Steve Lawrence hit
116 Hasenpfeffer base
117 Alley Oop's gal
118 City on the Moselle
119 Landward
120 Chances
121 He and she
122 Move to the music
123 Mugs

DOWN

1 Make great progress
2 Midwest air hub
3 Exposes
4 You've got to take it
5 Court concerns
6 L.A.-Yuma dir.
7 Pirates' __ Roger
8 La Douce
9 Otherworldly
10 Balderdash!
11 Sammy or Ossie
12 Alt.
13 Cheer rival
14 Some payment plans
15 Stray from the script
16 Philip Roth award-winner
17 39D, in old Rome
18 Thing on a ring
24 Like Phoebe on "Friends"
25 Yoke support
31 Commuter's transport
33 Ice in the water
34 Miami golf venue
35 Bunch of buzzers
36 He makes forays for morays
37 Warbucks or Longlegs
39 Poultry products
40 Swashbuckler's delight
41 War movie river
43 Turn inside out
44 "Rebel Rebel" rocker
45 '26 Eddie Cantor classic
47 Novelist Cynthia
48 More recent
49 Onetime Leno rival
51 MGM motto opener
56 .001"
57 Wok sauce
58 See 110A
60 __ Paulo
61 Spanky, to Alfalfa
62 Referendum choice
64 A question of motive
65 Pinnacles
66 Network, to Variety
67 Mother feted Apr. 22
68 Napoleon's marshal
70 Picasso
71 He played Sifuentes and Simone
73 Combustion residue
76 __ a Camera
77 Fictional Frome
78 Certain New Zealander
79 Brotherhood-based religion
80 Walkie-talkie word
81 Parker and Hazard are old ones
82 Having as a hobby
83 Has misgivings about
85 Snail, chez Bocuse
86 Four and fore, for for
87 T on a test
90 Marilyn, at first
91 Karnak's country
94 __-pitch
97 __ it out (endures)
99 Slips through the cracks
100 Off-the-beaten-track path
101 Fit for swells
103 So long of the south?
104 Land at Orly?
105 Mall events
107 Patriot Nathan
108 Falafel holder
109 "__ Joy of Man's Desiring"
110 A personal question?
111 Hoodwinked
113 Ah's partner
114 Hollywood honcho Wasserman
115 What a sitter makes

ACROSS

1 Half the SAT
5 Chorister's goal
9 MVP opener
13 Work at the copy desk
17 Cairo's river
18 Month after Av
19 It's in Mexico
20 Yahoos
22 Sentimental outlaws?
25 Etcher M.C.
26 Going lickety-split
27 Lots of lots
28 Team in the most NBA finals
29 Use UPS
30 Use the hibachi
31 Uses the tub
32 First *Wochentag*
35 M.O.'s M
36 Seder staple
37 Planetary paths
38 Lucre lover
39 Like some losers
40 Laddie's luv
44 Man-shaped mug
45 Wooden gangster?
47 "To Sir With Love" singer
48 "Hold on Tight" group
49 Like a bad apple
50 Small spasms
51 Illuminated
52 Friend of bill?
54 Gear part
56 Baedeker cousins
57 Gomorrah gala
58 Becomes boring
59 Outrigger
60 Shostakovich
63 Locked passageway?
64 God of wine
68 Honey-mustard alternative
69 Lung division
70 Kind of sack?
71 DDE's command
72 St. Louis landmark
73 Fishy gunslinger?
76 Baby's bed
77 Bric-a-__
78 Disassemble
79 Spicy cooking style
80 Oodles of ergs
81 "__ moi le déluge"
83 Pencil-chewing, e.g.
84 Bad trip, man
85 Pattern
87 From now on
88 Faux pas
89 Gretel's brother
90 Toy car maker
91 Blue-plate items

95 Beethoven's Third
96 Slow-moving mobster?
98 Body shop worker
99 Jackie K's second?
100 Like Poe's bug
101 Italian smoker
102 Calendar boxes
103 Queue after Q
104 Sagacity symbols
105 "Mystery!" hostess Diana

DOWN

1 Crowds
2 "Just __, skip and . . ."
3 Fork feature
4 How Abe did it?
5 Meeting a raise
6 He played Chan
7 Item in a chest
8 Before hat or hand
9 Actress Melina
10 Father of Horus
11 Superman's makeup
12 Smidgens
13 Phony
14 Evasive Old West reprobate?
15 "With this ring, __ wed"
16 Priva and profi closers

20 Type of birthday card
21 Grads-to-be
23 Mental flashes
24 Asked for ID
30 Cow's cognomen
31 Stock holders
32 *Psycho* setting
33 Rounded molding
34 Agnew's nattering negativist
35 Right may make it
36 Cadge
38 Like some terrariums
39 He went from "L.A. Law" to "NYPD Blue"
41 "Self" starter
42 Musical sign
43 Dines at eight
45 Boccherini or Cherubini
46 Key ring?
49 Magus gift
51 Daffy
53 Bungling outlaw?
54 Great Chief Justice
55 Gran finale
56 Palm part
58 Cellist Casals
59 Edible pine seed
60 Lackluster

61 Lenny Bruce's mother Sally __
62 Native of old Peru
63 Common ailments
64 Old gold coin
65 It's in the blood
66 Coming in handy
67 On the wagon
69 Irish export
70 Aladdin's ally
73 Felon who fences
74 Please's partner
75 Car parts department purchase
76 Anthologizer
80 Influence, slangily
82 Jigsaw puzzle parts
83 Mint family member
84 Mingles well
85 Was brave enough
86 Front of a plane?
87 Rimes
88 Witch's work
89 Shape a log
90 Snowmass transit
91 Refuse transport?
92 Piedmont province
93 Like the i in like
94 Start a run
97 In time gone by

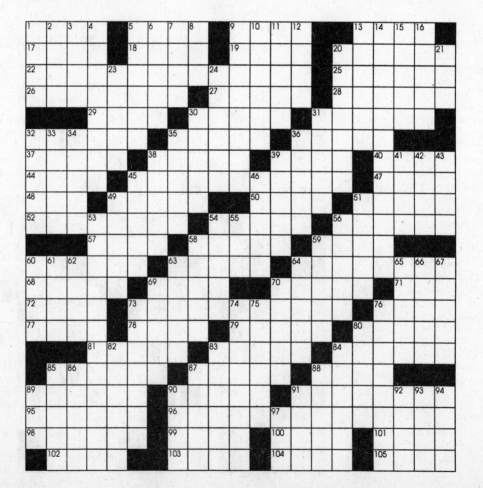

ACROSS

1 ''B.C.'' buck
5 Polio fighter Salk
10 Fuse, to glassmakers
14 Some Luce magazines
19 French *accent*
20 Suspect's need
21 It's better than never
22 Love, Italian style
23 The whole revue?
26 Diagonal spar
27 Rastafarian's idol
28 Sign up for class
29 Dense hair mass
30 Love seat
31 Environmentalist
32 Moonshine
33 Particle in a cyclotron
34 Graceful cadence
35 Superlatively small
38 Emmy winner Cicely
41 What the boiler room crew has?
44 RR stopover
45 Goldie who played Benjamin
46 Porch for Pericles
47 Golden Rule word
48 Retail store
49 What ''will be'' will be
50 Masses of incoming bees?
54 Hipsters made it
55 Future cynic?
57 Patronizes Avis
58 More musty
59 *The Bell Jar* writer
60 Slalom markers
61 ''. . . amount to __ of beans . . .''
62 Medieval merchant groups
64 ''Star Trek: DS9's'' Shimerman
65 The whole gang
68 Late Ford
69 Bunco squad equipment?
71 A long way
72 Truck-stop stoppers
73 Procrastinator's promise
74 Pearl Mosque site
75 Kitty or Piggy
76 Ozark matriarch
77 Make no-nonsense Thanksgiving plans?
81 Singer Lenya
82 Boat's birthplace
84 Syngman of Korea
85 Ghostly greeting
86 Trouser sizes
87 Horned deities
88 Crêpe kin
91 Stuffed grape leaves
93 Literary category
94 Senior's souvenir
96 Thrown for __
97 Wisest 18th-c. philosopher?
99 Breaks like the day
100 Dietrich's Marlene
101 Vedder or Van Halen
102 Tractor-trailer
103 Handlelike parts
104 Playbill listing
105 ''Mairzy __''
106 South's bridge opponent

DOWN

1 Big Mama
2 Feels fondness for
3 Like aerobicists
4 Genetic change
5 Olympic speedskater Dan
6 Blast from the past
7 Inoffensive
8 Attorneys' assn.
9 The Ob runs through it
10 Cauliflower clusters
11 Dangerous element
12 ''__ be 64D day in hell . . .''
13 Golfer's gizmo
14 Attack wildly
15 Effect
16 Why to beachcomb?
17 Orwell's real first name
18 Clockmaker Thomas
24 007 auto __ Martin DB-5
25 *A Nightmare __ Street*
29 Mann's __ *Kröger*
31 Eye light
32 Trumpeter Al's kin
35 Coins coins
36 Old Age
37 Downtown L.A.'s Forum
38 Burmese neighbor
39 NIMBY's Y
40 Panoramic trees?
41 Stoner's supply
42 Cause for a suit
43 Kicks on fourth
46 Actress Loretta's kin
48 Like ling
50 *Tribute* playwright Bernard
51 Psychoanalyst Erich
52 Piece of the past
53 __-trump (bridge bid)
54 Uses a swizzle stick
56 ''__ forgiven!''
58 ''Barnaby Jones'' co-star Mark
60 Halloween dido
61 NYC's __ Fisher Hall
62 Wheat centers
63 'Umble Heep
64 See 12D
65 Periphery
66 He ripped Tweed
67 One of the Gaels
69 Reaches new heights
70 Hogarth's *The __ Progress*
73 Big bucks
75 Sci-fi flick site
77 Nerve impulse gap
78 RTD center
79 ''Star Trek'' officer
80 Went back on a promise
81 French châteaux river
83 Roman garden goddess
85 Sounds like a boombox
87 Senses
88 Seem seemly
89 ''. . . Pussycat went __''
90 Barrels along
91 Pop art?
92 *The Good Earth* character
93 Karmann's car-design partner
94 He taught Luke
95 Make mittens
97 RN's touch
98 Tokyo, once

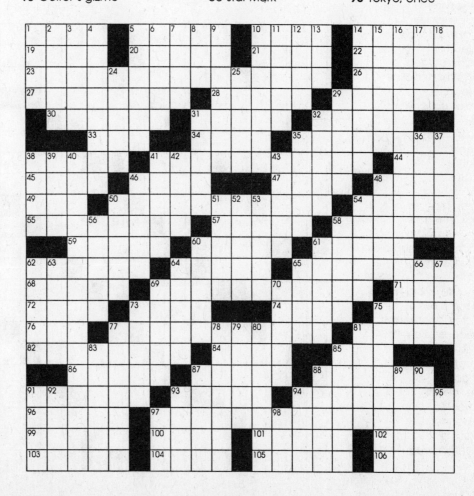

ACROSS

1 Symbol of sovereignty
4 Hits the bottle
9 Tantalize
14 Flows back
18 Grassland
19 Vase handles
20 Val or Joyce
21 Pound pest
22 Vegas opener
23 Detonators
25 Animal enclosures?
26 Having a pH over 7
28 Actress Garr namesakes
29 Dealers in meters and feet
30 Correct text
31 Not yet expired
32 Turn to toast
34 Not at all *grande*
36 A one and a two
37 Frasier's ex-wife
38 Uses aglets
39 Small-scale
40 __ Verdes Estates
41 It runs when broken
44 Periods of note
45 Pram, in Peoria
48 Long, long time
49 Certain older IBMs
50 Cross-examine
51 Principal pipes
52 Out of the harbor
53 Conjecture
55 Portage burden
56 Most after deadline
58 Fair feature
59 Sideburns shortener
60 Bindle stiff
61 War of words
64 Mideast martyr
65 Look like
69 Brooklet
70 Polio pioneer
71 Prepared pears
72 Play with robots
73 Gerry Adams' org.
74 Pregame warmup aids
77 "Circle Game" singer Mitchell
78 Big house or pig house
79 Like some seals
80 Square decameters
81 Mite-caused malady
82 Tackle-turned-actor Alex
84 Plantation building
86 Pert girls
87 Long speech
88 Aviator Markham
89 Gin partner
90 Like some shutouts
91 Sunbathing site

92 Condemned to exile
95 Piccadilly potables
96 Zaire, once
99 Cassowary cousin
100 Dueler's stride
101 Old sayings
102 Writer Chekhov
103 Some dashes
104 Sacred chests
105 Woodland deity
106 Projection room pile
107 Squealer, or squeaker

DOWN

1 Spanish stew
2 Royal, to Raul
3 Nervous wreck
4 Armful for Moses
5 Cruising cyberspace
6 Mind your __ Q's
7 Unstress
8 Coterie
9 Nineveh's river
10 Spanish hero
11 *Amo, __, amat*
12 Cal. page
13 Crisis centers
14 Elbow grease
15 Roquefort relative
16 Bed onboard

17 Mouth off at
20 Ring a bell
24 Roman alternative
27 Designer Hardy
29 Composure
31 PVC center
32 Miser Marner
33 Jam
34 Skirt fold
35 Planet of the apes
36 All-time bestseller
37 "That Lucky Old Sun" singer
39 Indian corn
40 Previous conviction
42 Says, in teen talk
43 Sandfly
45 Bouquet thrower
46 "__ Grace"
47 Continued
50 Fortitude
52 Element element
54 Word-of-mouth
55 Room on a liner
56 Gets upset, perhaps
57 Not up yet
59 Fanatical
60 Toast starter
61 Plumbing problem
62 Ireland, in Irish

63 Monetary carte blanche
64 Gives R's and G's
65 "Message received"
66 Raspberry
67 Fencer's move
68 Iroquoian folks
70 Virtuoso's violin
71 Do "Deck the Halls"
74 Beatnik's headwear
75 Its banks are Swiss
76 Malibu or Mandeville
77 "Down on Me" singer Joplin
81 Underlings
83 Gets to one's feet
84 Profession
85 *Norma* numbers
86 Genghis Khan, for one
87 Green power?
88 Like some kids' clothes
89 *Mère's soeur*
90 Viny valley
91 Land map
92 Radius, e.g.
93 Samms or Peel
94 Prepare to lift prints
96 Kind of relief
97 Writer LeShan
98 Jam ingredient

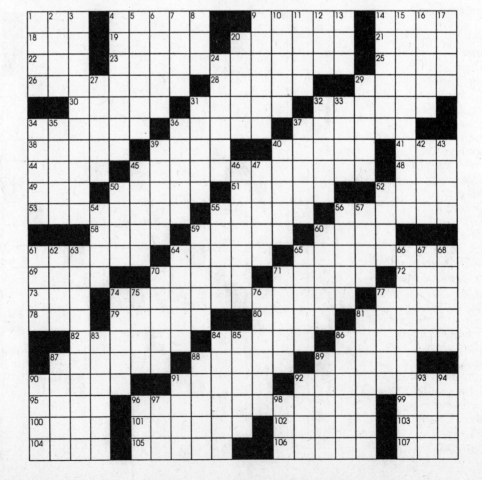

ACROSS

1 Came together
4 Adjective for the Four
7 Ollie's biggest friend
11 Plumed hat
16 Gossipy Barrett
17 It's put before the carte
18 String quartet fourth
19 Unemotional
20 TV policewoman
23 Streisand standard
24 Outer edge
25 Kipling stripling
26 Lamb Chop's handler
28 Before band or box
29 Kemo Sabe's companion
30 Master's subject?
31 Hush-hush org.
32 Word often mispunctuated
34 Not safe
35 Consult
36 Balloon shaper
37 Worm holder
38 Come down with
39 Hillary Clinton, __ Rodham
40 *Carousel* choreographer
45 Myth-laden mountain
47 Kite's claw
49 Rugged mountain
50 Ben Jonson comedy
52 Early computer language
53 Gray horse
55 This clue's number, less I
56 Gave the slip
59 Put on edge?
60 They're the best
63 Alway
65 Blight
66 Broke bread
67 Framed French captain
71 "__, Oprah, Oprah . . ."
72 Computer interface jack
74 "__ Were a Rich Man"
75 "__ what your country . . ."
76 Famed ombudsman
78 Na is its symbol
80 Anatomical vessel
82 Provence prepositions
83 "This place is __!"
84 United Nations Day month
86 Follower of Ivan?
88 Chef's stock
89 Necessity
90 Dickens dip
94 Coke cousin
95 English cathedral city
97 Rancor
98 Spreadsheet info
99 Army bed
102 Abbr. on a map
103 Sugarloaf locale
104 Early p.m.
105 Deep black
106 Took things the wrong way?
108 Flexible blackjack card
109 *Mea culpa*'s admission
111 A month in Marseilles
112 Latter preceder
113 Red and white among the greens
116 Monte Cristo's creator
119 Place to park an ark
120 The apple of __
121 Ahab's affirmative
122 Glazed fabric finish
123 Final authority
124 Mercedes' brand-mate
125 Shampoo partner
126 F or G, but not H

DOWN

1 Bandleader Vaughn
2 *The Little __ That Could*
3 "'Tis!" response
4 Lose strength
5 Jenny in *Love Story*
6 Broadway angels
7 Old Cadillac feature
8 *William Tell* composer
9 Maui howdy
10 Barrie babysitter
11 Sault-Marie link
12 After yoo?
13 French naturalistic novelist
14 Crater on Mauna Loa
15 *Swan Lake* role
16 Flat floaters
18 Energy
19 Vent malice on
21 Swellhead's problem
22 Hobbyist's buy
27 Bright star in Orion
30 Deep-dish dish
31 Army outpost
33 Milker's aid
36 Bay State cape
37 *Fantasia* frame
40 Spiny-leaved plant
41 Israel's Meir
42 Beatrice inspired him
43 II more than 55A
44 "P.S. I __"
46 Cold-shoulder
47 "It's just __ divine!"
48 Cooperstown local legend
51 Where the Amazon starts
52 Wrangler's wear
53 Take your hat off
54 Toward a stream's source
55 Sky or mind ender
57 Tangle up in
58 Cherished ones
61 Tarbell and Lupino
62 Some HMO employees
64 Young salamanders
68 Wheel's wheels
69 Put a stop to
70 Catch in a trap
73 Twitches
77 Cupid, to some
79 Absolute
81 Museum pieces
85 Louisiana marsh
86 Actor John or William
87 "__ Buttermilk Sky"
88 Maj. gen.'s subordinates
89 Makeup applied with a wand
91 Age for a *quinceañera*'s debut
92 New York natives
93 Semi-semicolon
94 Pageant prizes
96 Low-calorie
99 HUAC target
100 Chicago cow owner
101 Short-winded?
104 "O come, __ faithful"
105 Middle Brady daughter
106 Instant lawn
107 Pickup, e.g.
110 Da-*dah*, e.g.
111 Co-star for W.C.
112 "Dogs"
114 Return receivers
115 Saint, in Santos
117 The __ Affair (1797-98 scandal)
118 Pumpernickel ingredient

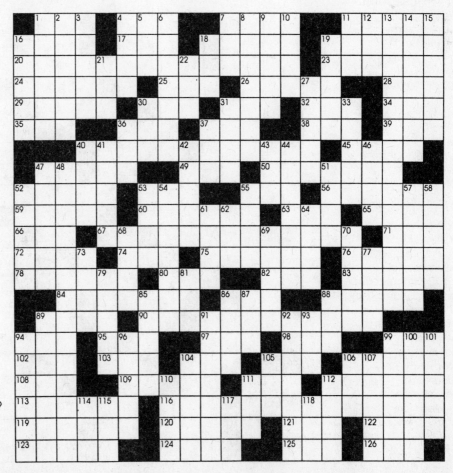

ACROSS

1 Deli sandwich
4 Floats downriver
9 Lake near Studio City
15 *Cabaret* co-writer
18 Orpheus' instrument
20 Relieve
21 *Norma* and *Martha*
22 *He Got Game* director
23 Part of a set
24 Local actor who could express well?
26 Friday, for one
27 Politic
29 Letter opener
30 Deflect
32 In fact
33 Colon kin
34 ''Understood''
35 Full of jargon
37 As of
39 Comedian Carol
41 Stones' ''Get Yer __ Out''
42 Like 2000
43 Him and her
45 Atomizer mist
47 Break in the action
48 Yeats heroine Maud __
49 Despise
50 Water cooler
51 Debate side
52 Lucy's mischievous mate?
56 Lower in the meadow?
57 Nuts and bolts
59 Places of refuge
60 Get at
62 Get carried away
63 Bag and box openers
65 Large knife
66 Slow to catch on
69 Have a falling out?
70 '70s dove Eugene
74 Capek classic
75 Catty columnist?
79 Go quickly
80 Rhea's cousin
81 Indian princess
82 Rite site
83 Tennis' Mandlikova
84 Made choices
87 North Carolina college
88 Like the Mariana Trench
89 Hair fringes
90 Turn into a prune
92 Lascivious partner
93 Eisenhower or Nehru
94 Uncompromising
95 Be scared of
97 Screwdriver part
98 Gorgeous guy
100 Hindu funeral custom, to some
101 Named above

105 It's often in hock
106 Sharp satirist?
109 Pitti Palace river
110 Two-time link
111 Like the hills
112 Blood line
113 Eroded
114 There's one on DDT
115 Uncle Tom's oppressor
116 Follow the reaper
117 What some may surf

DOWN

1 Like Gainsborough's boy
2 Bobcat
3 On-the-road comic?
4 In a risqué way
5 Tin Pan or Shubert
6 Custard cousin
7 Under stress
8 Charlie Chaplin's brother
9 Bears the bags
10 Ricki's rival
11 Goneril's father
12 Tell legend locale
13 Guilelessness
14 Gives out tasks
15 Instant playwright?
16 Hold up under
17 Stooped
19 Everlasting
25 Cheese choice
28 Udders
31 Prexy's subordinate
33 Grumpy coworker
34 Author Godden
35 Slender, graceful girl
36 Nyro or San Giacomo
37 Thrust and parry
38 What privates can't pull
39 Outmoded VCRs
40 Lunch with a crunch
42 French châteaux river
43 Show place?
44 Cabs
46 Hedge shrubs
48 Like some eggs
52 Checker move?
53 Director Haines
54 Vixen's mate
55 Liner support
58 Joanne of *Red River*
61 It means wax
63 Turn down
64 Musical chipmunk
65 Dogfight
66 Sandwich cookie
67 Speed deterrents
68 Sincere actress?

69 Hoops, for some
70 Toned down
71 Grateful homer hitter?
72 Depend
73 You'll get a rise out of it
76 Foster
77 '96 Presidential candidate
78 Played piccolo
83 Metal cutter
85 Colleen's cognomen
86 Analog alternative
89 Invited
91 Countenance
92 Not of the cloth
93 Air in basketball
95 Aesop specialty
96 Chopin's ''Butterfly,'' e.g.
97 West African river
98 Great white hunter?
99 Spreadsheet fodder
100 Ikea competitor
101 He never calls; he never writes
102 The going price?
103 As to
104 Word above WALK
107 Rule, for short
108 Harridan

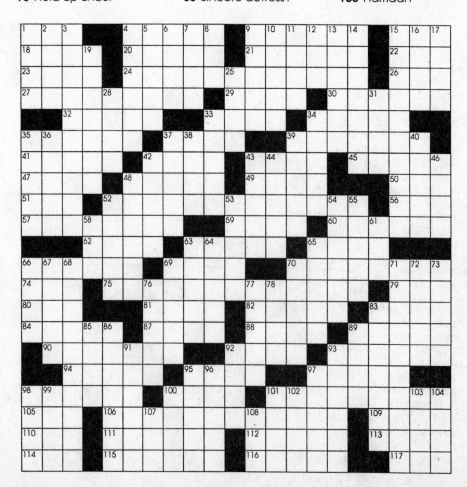

SUNDAE SUPPLEMENT

ACROSS

1 Hamelin vermin
4 Beatles' "Sexy __"
9 Play things
14 Memento __
18 Before this time
19 Trim a limb
20 Breadth of fresh hair?
21 Military group
22 Zing
23 Man's summer outfit
25 WWII battle site
26 Sever
28 Thickening things
29 Feels pangs
30 Of an Islamic republic
31 The unreal McCoy
32 Reggae immortal Bob
34 Laundry ironing machine
36 Loy of Hollywood
37 Landing sites
38 Ancient Greek city
39 Heavenly headwear
40 Spoof
41 Morris Dees' org.
44 Heaven, to some
45 Co-starring comedian
48 Detroit org.
49 3, on a phone
50 Province on the Yangtze
51 Kingly or queenly
52 Lasting impression
53 Outdoor
55 Seen less
56 Rockers __ Dan
58 "It's a Sin to Tell __"
59 Salome's septet
60 Sierra Club founder
61 Make a chess move
64 Capt. Nemo's creator
65 Hull-scraper's bane
69 Pluckable
70 Musician's transition
71 Early wonder drug
72 Overacting actor
73 Fuss
74 Essential aspects
77 Manila moola
78 Metro maker
79 Meets end to end
80 One of Chekhov's three sisters
81 Less furnished
82 Prolonged prayer period
84 Do a hitch
86 Short snowfall
87 Thorny twigs
88 Mount a play
89 Bagel traymate
90 It grips a bit
91 Memorable Lamb Chop handler
92 Tanzania component
95 Superlative review

96 '60s psychedelic rockers
99 Silver container
100 Say seriously
101 Too
102 Ire
103 Farrow of film
104 Bare peaks
105 They last for days and days
106 Layer cake layers
107 Misbehaving

DOWN

1 Uses a gavel
2 *African Queen* writer
3 Finishing with a flourish
4 Pretty passes?
5 Obscure
6 Tunes for two
7 Hollywood pioneer Thomas
8 Ballad or buccan ending
9 L.A. County Fairgrounds site
10 A Staub in the park
11 *Mr. Holland's* __
12 Canadian prov.
13 Matching pieces
14 Brawn
15 Hitting the bottle
16 "When the Frost is on the Punkin" poet
17 Leno's Dancing __
20 Goshawk's grabber
24 Writer Nora
27 Volcanic gas element
29 Where to book matches
31 Traffic cone
32 Tin or zinc
33 Mary Kay competitor
34 Miata maker
35 Historian Durant
36 Portuguese province
37 LEM opener
39 Hereafter
40 Beeps
42 Jezebel's deity
43 Out of whack
45 "Wake Up Little __"
46 Ran out of the tub
47 Uncle Miltie
50 Satan's realm
52 Injection fluids
54 Insurance quote
55 Play it again
56 __ the net (browses via mouse)
57 She played Ginger
59 Slots spot
60 Hospitalers' island

61 Rugged cliff
62 Helper
63 Edgar Lee Masters creation
64 Roman hearth goddess
65 WWII battle area
66 Red firecracker
67 Surgical beam
68 Atlanta university
70 Stupefies
71 Crack the case
74 Maritime
75 Above, in Abensberg
76 Lucrezia of Ferrara
77 Neutrino postulator Wolfgang
81 School jackets
83 Edmonton team
84 Procrastinates
85 With time to spare
86 Identify
87 "Well done!"
88 Malinger
89 Scout's honor
90 Mild expletive
91 Old weapon
92 New Mexico people
93 "Summertime," for one
94 Try for a part
96 Word of honor
97 Hail at the Forum
98 Sprat's anathema

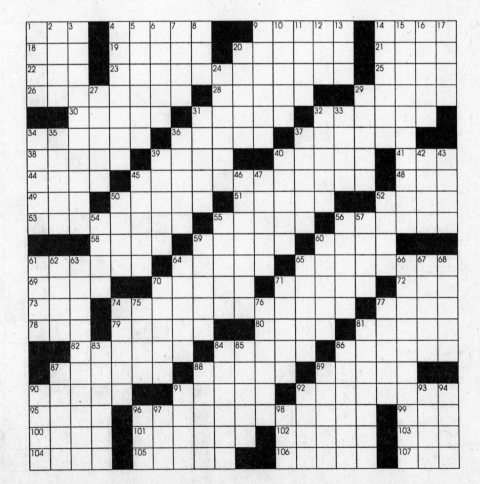

ACROSS

1 Attacks with hen grenades
5 Of cities
10 C&O and B&O
13 Changes chemically
19 Cozy corner
20 Poke fun at
21 Three before O-U
22 Like some physicals or flowers
23 Imaginative writer?
26 Diva Kathleen
27 American tree
28 Goes out with
29 Waxed histrionic
30 Podium pauses
31 *Muchacho's* uncle
32 Michelangelo masterpiece
34 '83 Nicholas Gage bestseller
35 Writer's rounds?
37 Guy's chum
38 It's not gross
41 Silky hound
44 Am and bamb enders
45 They're fit to be tied
46 Mop 'n __
47 Naive
48 Staff insignia
49 Iron and lock openers
51 Extinguished candles
52 Watched
53 Fido's vote for best writer?
55 __ *qui peut!* (Run for your life!)
56 What sweeps sweep
57 "__ cow!"
58 Prizm competitor
59 Settle, as quarrels
63 Rub the wrong way
65 Twist creator
66 Disengage
67 Hill or camp preceder
68 Godmother, often
69 Put into memory
70 Raises a writer?
73 Facial feature
77 Prop for Harpo
78 Appearance
79 Without concentration
80 All set to go
81 More E than N
82 Top execs
83 Matic or syncratic start
84 When, in Rome
85 Scandinavian rug
86 Possessed
87 Novel-writing?
90 Join
92 Ostentatious
93 Scott Joplin opus
94 Early comic Krazy __
97 Happen to
99 Old stringed instrument
100 First-stage interviewer
102 Deity's mouthpiece
103 Late-night writer?
106 Attic room
107 Medico
108 Loosen a brogue
109 "How sweet __!"
110 Spirited mounts
111 *Paradise Lost* character
112 More ignoble
113 Young guinea fowl

DOWN

1 Between *nous*?
2 Champion of dance
3 Driving impulses
4 Nonfat
5 Impossibly ideal
6 Ebb
7 Subside
8 Hair color
9 The start of something new
10 O'Hara's *A __ Live*
11 Mend anew
12 Gains a lap
13 Gargantua's creator
14 Glossy cosmetics
15 Bruckner or Dvořák
16 Snubbing a writer?
17 Chaucer's miller had one
18 *Call of the Wild* vehicle
24 Robin's *Birdcage* co-star
25 Rehab candidates
32 Triptych third
33 "Knock __!"
34 Major staff acronym
35 Discard
36 United worker
39 Craps natural
40 The more they dry, the wetter they get
41 Minor drinking problem?
42 Fish outing
43 It's right on the farm
45 Slick
48 Condo cousin
49 __ around (be playful)
50 Capacity
51 Trunk cover
53 *Marjorie Morningstar* writer
54 "__ in a name?"
55 Breakaway body
56 Do smithy work
58 Wee
59 Narc's target
60 __ *and Cleopatra*
61 Writer's output?
62 "Hee Haw" humor
63 Make dinner
64 "__ it going?"
65 Active military service
67 JFK and RFK, e.g.
68 Permit
70 Miss Two-Shoes
71 Printer's incomplete line
72 Enlighten
73 Veteran actress Richards
74 Bled in the wash
75 Anomalistic
76 Colo. neighbor
78 Picket-line handouts
80 Robust
82 Cooled the Chardonnay
83 "__ you so!"
84 Lunar period part
87 Isaac of sci-fi
88 (A), (B) or (C)
89 Jughead's pal
91 Mother-of-pearl
94 Notre Dame's Rockne
95 Home on high
96 Romeo's rendezvous
97 Quagmires
98 Part of *esse*
99 __ mecum (reference manual)
100 Mil. titles
101 Ponch on "CHiPs"
104 Worn-down end
105 Pig-poke connection

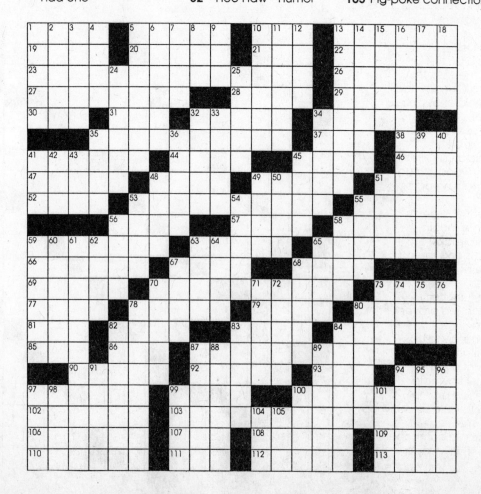

ACROSS

1 Bric-a-__
5 Hipster's music
10 Celebrated
15 Queue after Q
18 Give a makeover
19 Similar
20 Make bubbly
21 Garden evictee
22 Oils, to pharmacists
23 Bargain stopover?
25 It's big in London
26 Without reservation
28 Macho men
29 "__ you so!"
31 Chrysoberyl kin
32 What the conductor knows
33 Cubs and Explorers
34 Actress Irving
35 Three-speed threesome
36 Woodward or Worley
37 Engine hum
40 Tack-y?
42 Like B but not P
43 A verb for you
44 Can't forget?
48 Back again
51 Either-or process
53 Holdup man?
54 Laundry unit
55 Congo tributary
56 West Pointers
58 What holds hold
59 Heineken rival
61 Home of La Scala
62 Ford or forest follower
63 Damages
64 Freebooter
66 Helix
68 Midianite invader of Israel
69 He wrote of Roo
70 They'll get your vote
73 DOD branch
74 Darning?
77 Vintage vehicle
78 Says "nyah-nyah"
80 Pink potables
81 Like batik fabrics
82 Statistician's middle number
83 Soup scoop
85 River to the Irish Sea
87 Old folkie Richie
88 Ran out of gas
89 Ignore the alarm
93 Overturn
94 Enjoy
95 Cogitate about
97 "Smoking or __?"
98 Superego?

101 Reliever's credit
102 Palindromic pharaoh
103 Cal Ripken Jr., e.g.
104 Rita Hayworth role
105 Chor and chlor concluders
106 Ave. crossers
107 Peanuts' Peppermint
108 Abattoir waste
109 Dessert-tray item

DOWN

1 Eye or high ender
2 Piece of the past
3 Journalist Rogers St. Johns
4 Dye and drug ingredient
5 Google or Rubble
6 Mournful poem
7 Gideons' giveaway
8 Not hurt
9 Stroke a cat
10 Thighbones
11 Break the bank?
12 Works a shuttle
13 When France is bakin'?
14 Daintiness
15 Championship basketball move?
16 Stylishly slim
17 Is inclined
20 He dealt in pelts
24 Houdini feat
27 An end to sex?
30 Inflection
32 Dweller by the Morava
33 Dirties
35 Sordid
36 Dr. Salk
37 Gridiron protection
38 Tell's canton
39 Déjà vu episodes?
40 Air apparent?
41 50% prefix
42 Bit of a shock
44 Chestnuts' kin
45 Volcano in Vietnam?
46 Traffic tracker
47 Tommy's gun
49 Go unchecked
50 Olfactory worker?
52 Nuclear weapon
54 Wahine's porch
56 Delicious drink?
57 Brown brew
58 Tea wagons
59 __ En-lai
60 Two in a row?
61 Thigh-high skirt

62 *Casablanca* hero
64 Mature
65 Sad to say
66 Wild plum
67 Iron-pumper's pride
69 High plateaus
70 To be, to Brutus
71 Miss-named
72 Pregrown grass
74 Pluvial unit
75 Commands
76 Collapse in the clutch
79 First place?
81 Take into account?
82 Plan
83 "Step __!"
84 Did standup?
85 Of molars and cuspids
86 "Yikes!"
87 Looks for prey
88 Prognosticator's pack
89 Volume setting?
90 Evans or Evangelista
91 The Donald's ex
92 Worse than late
94 Roasting rod
95 Workers' relief initials
96 Observe the Sabbath
99 Time-line time
100 Have __ at

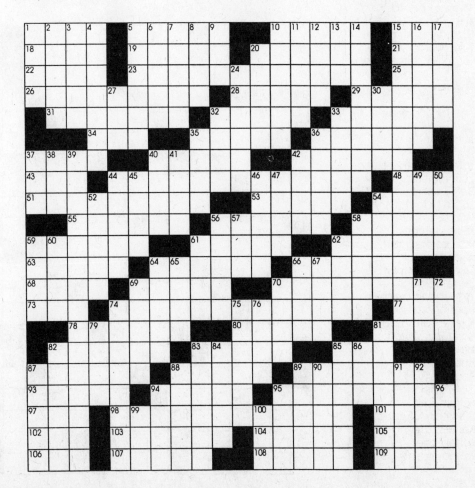

ACROSS

1 Stray strands
6 Tango feature
9 Freelancer's encl.
13 Dress for Lamour
19 Leaving word
20 Avail oneself of
21 What comes to those who wait?
22 Writer Glyn
23 Drink way too much
26 Black gum tree
27 Alternate clock sound
28 Washstand item
29 Pop favorite?
30 Use a crosscut
31 Olympic diver's no-no
34 TV palomino
35 Seattle b-ballers
37 Zebra or donkey
38 Predicament
39 Key letter
40 Like Murphy's professor
43 Masher's target
44 Exalting poem
45 KGB counterpart
46 Arrow poison
47 Pirate-flick prop
48 Insured's payment
53 Conway or Curry
54 Geisha girder
55 Donne and Bradstreet
56 Ethnic
57 "Now __ heard everything"
58 Tympanum stimuli
60 Rule over
61 *Fargo* filmmaker Joel or Ethan
62 Anguish
63 Aura
64 Daredevil's deed
66 Fan
67 Brezhnev
69 Elk
71 Baton Rouge inst.
72 Cast aspersions
73 Gen. Powell
74 No, to Nanette
77 N.C.'s seashore
78 Baltic port city
80 Not professional
81 Depended
83 Capt. of industry
84 Coffee, slangily
85 Respond to an alarm
86 Front of a plane?
87 Former Ford model
88 Agricultural worker
89 It may be gross
91 Smithies
93 Flour bag
94 Galway's and Rampal's instruments
95 Girl of an '05 song
97 Aerialist's fallback
98 Rudely brief
99 Roundup eats

100 Word with card or check
102 Lobbyists' employers
108 Delon and Resnais
109 Overhaul
110 Crossword creek
111 TV screen-in-a-screen
112 Barrio store
113 *Henry IV*'s Glendower
114 Squid squirt
115 Throws out a line

DOWN

1 Bark accompaniment
2 Ox tail?
3 Pose for a portrait
4 Black-eyed veggie
5 Brunei bigwig
6 Reagan nickname
7 Writer Dinesen
8 Bill-signing souvenir
9 Prepared prunes
10 Lent a hand
11 Song's jingle-jangler
12 Uncommon sense
13 Catholic educator Mother __
14 Earth crust's most abundant metal
15 It's often carved in stone
16 Class or caste
17 Vincent Lopez theme song
18 Gain girth
24 Make an on-the-trail tail fail
25 Ear piece
29 Miss Piggy, to Miss Piggy
31 Young pigeon
32 Shooting down, oater-style
33 It's often glossed over
34 Man with gilt feelings?
35 Israel's Yitzhak
36 Dastard
37 Sailor's saint
38 Fight-night highlights
39 Musical selections
41 Hot-dish stand
42 San'a is its capital
45 Hungered after
46 __-de-sac (dead end)
48 Neat as __
49 Given to eavesdropping
50 Born as
51 Investigating
52 John, to Jock
59 "Batman" sound
60 Chinese ornamental tree
61 Share of the loot
62 *Emma* writer
63 Expressed
64 Some doctors do it
65 Itty-bitty

66 Trumpet call
67 Retriever, for short
68 Votes in
69 Grown girls
70 Confederate st.
72 What slanderers sling
73 Hook alternative
75 Caravan campsite
76 *Da* opposite
78 Getting wind of
79 Pops out of the VCR
82 UN labor org.
85 Poppycock!
87 Imperfect serve
88 Weems was one
89 Publicize
90 Rule in red
92 __ charge out of (enjoys)
93 Shoe leather
94 One-in-a-million
95 Picket's foe
96 He ate at Alice's
98 All hands on deck
99 Show delight
101 Vegas cube
102 Country club employee
103 Mentalist Geller
104 *Cat __ Hot Tin Roof*
105 Enterprise initials
106 Socks, to Chelsea
107 D.C. has lettered ones

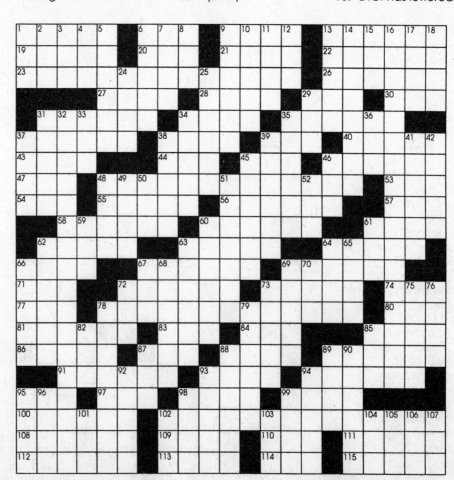

ACROSS

1 Sole support
5 Move crabwise
10 Dutch treat
14 Union member
19 Joan of Art
20 Weirdo
21 Barely cooked
22 Leaves home?
23 Challenged by conscience
26 Fix the fairway
27 Spend the summer
28 Small cities
29 Tommy Lee's ex
30 Houdini specialty
31 Onetime Saturday night activities
32 Strip for breakfast?
33 Eng. neighbor
34 As far as
35 Filer's hazard
38 Like some canes
41 Hindu Kush country
44 Posting at LAX
45 Burn balm
46 Transport to Tel Aviv
47 Robbers' rods
48 Mai or juin
49 Londonderry tune
50 Everywhere
54 Garand or Winchester
55 John Jr., to John
57 English racecourse
58 Masked merrymaker
59 Very sharp
60 Joe of "Hill Street Blues"
61 Craze
62 Aplenty
64 Kind of colloquial?
65 Athenian leader
68 More than adequately
69 Offering ambiance
71 Laders' org.
72 Grow weary
73 Quahog
74 Cartesian connection
75 MRI exam
76 Denver-Chicago dir.
77 Use in-lines
81 Composer Saint-__
82 Inferior verse
84 Water bearer
85 Chick's Laker sidekick
86 Silly goose
87 Paid out
88 Pokes fun at
91 Mine features
93 Love of Paris
94 Fills to repletion
96 Nantes aunt
97 Magyar capital
99 Sign of stress
100 Lyricist __ Jay Lerner
101 Languish
102 Sponsorship
103 Hopalong William and activist Malcolm
104 Wax bananas?
105 "Holy moley!"
106 FedExed or faxed

DOWN

1 Friendly fille
2 Car-wash cycle
3 Bureau and Euro enders
4 It's just murder
5 Decarbonize burnt toast
6 More than sore
7 Rhyme for really
8 Were ahead
9 Grave words?
10 Samuel Butler's Utopia
11 Praises faintly?
12 Arsenal's supply
13 __ culpa (confessor's phrase)
14 Nomadic Arab
15 Aftershock
16 '81 Newman-Field film
17 Hammer or tongs
18 Germanic earth goddess
24 Reproductive gland
25 "Whole __ Shakin' Goin' On"
29 Two "Monday, Monday" singers
31 Military brass
32 Bonkers
35 Sacred song
36 Of some purpose
37 High-tech dart gun
38 Cinderella Liberty star
39 Inter __ (among other things)
40 Expectant parents' ideal
41 Share and share __
42 Most popular, slangily
43 Snow place like home?
46 Growing outward
48 Parrot or ape
50 Taking too much interest in one's work?
51 Printer's proof
52 Old-time footwear
53 "It's __!" ("Piece of cake!")
54 Of Anglo-Saxon writing
56 School for Raoul
58 Cuomo or Andretti
60 River in Picardy
61 Word processing command
62 Like some communities
63 Essential acid
64 Stable section
65 Saucy
66 Vivacity
67 Lacking
69 Oop from Moo
70 Celery center
73 Foot faults?
75 Wieners and bratwursts
77 They trade dollars for quarters
78 Seed anew
79 Win, place and show
80 John Jr., or John
81 Besmirch
83 Having talent
85 Entrapments
87 Family car
88 Border lake
89 Floor of a bâtiment
90 Canary cousin
91 Torn-off part
92 Circle overhead?
93 Dance to chants
94 "Cut it out!"
95 SSS pt.
97 Keep out
98 Hindustani mister

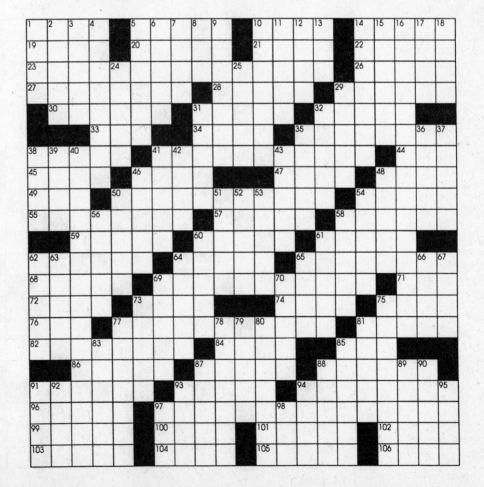

ACROSS

1 Long loose garment
7 It's a long story
11 Guinness from London
15 Their calling is calling
19 NBA's Grant
20 '90s Attorney General
21 Storage for forage
22 Run-on sentence?
23 *Sunset Boulevard* co-star
26 Beginning of eight words?
27 Cabinet department
28 Caboodle companion
29 SSW U-turns
30 Not worth arguing about
32 Taj attire
33 Arctic explorer
34 Mental faculties
35 Wolfe's *The __ of the Vanities*
38 Hen's pen
40 A head
41 Frank Herbert book series
42 Like Carnaby St. fashions
43 Terminus
46 Go mad with frustration
49 Hit like Ruth
50 Lorraine's pie
52 Dufy contemporary
53 Bacchanalia
54 Seeger or Sampras
55 Strong drives
56 Santa Fe Trail stop
57 Gratis
58 Baby in the bulrushes
59 Sunday closing
60 Casual greetings
61 Mutt, to Jeff
62 Chow
63 Lille lily
64 Small-time
69 Colgate closer
72 Equestrian gait
74 Rambo rescuee
75 Campers
76 "Jewel Song," e.g.
77 Fashion's Hardy
79 Top-of-the-line
81 Popeye kid __ Pea
83 Buckets
84 Pew area
85 Heavyweight wrestling
86 That's a laugh
87 They're from the hearth
88 Tough trip
89 Paradigm
92 Iris locale
93 Spread the frosting
94 Reached for the floor
95 Out of
96 Do Time?
98 Carry the current
100 Green acres?
101 Automatic transmission
102 Not quite closed
106 Piquancy
107 Act as accomplice
108 The "It" Girl
109 Let off the hook
110 Comedian Martha
112 Mint plants of song
116 Versatile fiber
117 Operator
118 Bacterium
119 Slipped into
120 Boxcar cargos
121 Ham, lamb or Spam
122 Sea swirl
123 Scottish exports

DOWN

1 Mating game?
2 Heart line
3 Tuck's title
4 Strategy subsection
5 Pain from strain
6 Sagebrush st.
7 Bert's tormenter
8 Noodge
9 What CDs earn
10 Cliff road
11 Phoenix birthplace
12 Trumped-up tales
13 Yale alum
14 Ordinarily
15 Detached
16 Pot-smoking, to some
17 Less than e'er
18 Avant-gardist
24 Giraffe cousin
25 __ job (working)
31 It's for the money
33 Ingenue, e.g.
34 Towers community
35 Convexity
36 Postal beat
37 Barely beats
39 Newspaper pioneer
40 Iberia's named for it
41 Schoolyard challenge
43 Peer
44 "The Flying Finn" Paavo __
45 Lipase, for one
47 "Let __ you a question"
48 Pulitzer's paper
49 Primer pooch
51 1200 mos.
56 XXX's first X
57 Fervid follower
58 Dogpatch Daisy
60 SRO show
61 Fido's offering
62 Letters from Miami
64 What CPAs crunch
65 Downs of England
66 Studio area
67 Night vision?
68 I have shrunk?
70 Alvin of dance
71 Out of vogue
73 Be olfactorily offensive
76 Excellent rating
77 Playful act
78 Kublai's visitor
79 Like some offerings
80 Give vent to
81 WASP penultimate
82 Ka-boom!
83 Guilty or not guilty
85 Prism's revelation
86 Birthright
87 Show muscle
90 Zimbalist, Jr.
91 Jumbo shrimp
94 Kramden's conveyance
97 Jane's "Frasier" role
99 Ocean trenches
100 Round reviewer
101 Like beer heads
103 Meadows or Mansfield
104 Pistol-packing
105 Fen flora
107 Bound for Tahiti
108 Arctic explorer
109 Pack away
110 Letter from Greece
111 Irish airline __ Lingus
113 Last of the sugar?
114 Obviously embarrassed
115 It was banned in '72

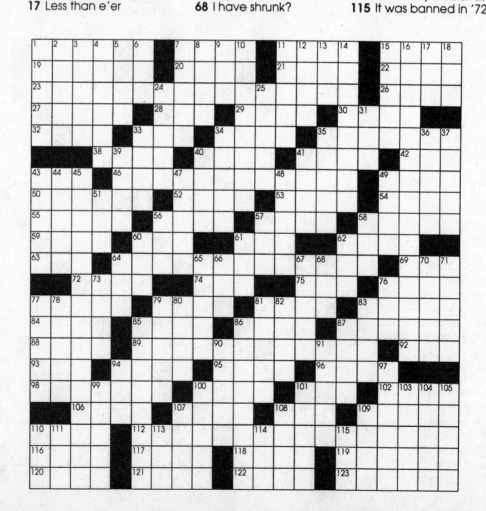

ACROSS

1 Scored the same
5 Pinch pennies
10 Has a bawl?
15 Nick and Nora's dog
19 Coty or Clair
20 Of the spirit
21 Overtheatrical
22 Helicopter feat.
23 When to tread carefully in the forest?
26 Count's counterpart
27 Thai dish __ krob
28 Earth's quadrillion
29 Daft
30 *Palme d'Or* award site
32 Gets there
34 Gait rates
35 Vocally
36 Plop or plunk opener
37 Knight spot?
38 Cardinal's title
41 Pontifical Mass vestment
44 Elation lack?
46 Current slower
47 Couples club?
48 Unkeyed flute
49 Düsseldorf duck
50 Con game
51 Drill insert
52 Poor sound system south of San Francisco?
56 Baseball's Boyer
57 World's third-largest city
59 Pitcher Blue
60 Want water
61 Fencer's move
62 S&L customer
63 Crepe de __
64 *Jane Eyre* writer
66 Allowance for waste
67 "Take my wife" comic
70 Garrets
71 Get shut out in Scrabble?
74 Plastic __ Band
75 ABA member
76 Former shahdom
77 Bread and drink
78 Pesky insect
79 Japanese play
80 Not disparage lumber?
84 *Mildred Pierce*'s Ann
85 Glacier fissure
87 *Golden Boy* writer
88 Cote quote
89 Like Wilde or Levant
90 Dealt mighty blows
91 Plasterboard
95 Memorable actor Vito
97 Eddy
98 Prehistory writer Jean
99 *24 horas*
100 New Age subject
101 Crisis for a tailor?
105 Dudley Do-Right's love
106 Rub the wrong way
107 Kweisi Mfume's org.
108 ". . . can't believe __ the whole . . ."
109 Saratoga stats
110 Eggy cake
111 Force units
112 Couturier Christian

DOWN

1 Play fare
2 Direct elsewhere
3 Type in
4 Little, to lassies
5 Perdition risker
6 Does macramé
7 Wayfarer's stops
8 Asian aborigine
9 Some college athletes' goal
10 French feudal fortress
11 Kon-Tiki, etc.
12 "If __ be so bold. . ."
13 Aussie avian
14 Stratified rock trough
15 Pennsylvania, in Washington
16 Be ritual-intolerant?
17 Ripped or zipped
18 "__ fair in love . . ."
24 Midnight dreary visitor
25 Ipso follower
31 Welk's intro intro
33 Greek Orthodox adornment
34 "*Dona Nobis* __"
35 Friendship
37 Anna of the Met
38 Sicilian city
39 Chews the fat
40 One of the Earth's quadrillion
41 White lies
42 Puccini piece
43 Arctic absence?
44 Willy-__
45 Preclude
48 Debussy contemporary
50 Missile launcher
52 Hinds' hes
53 Pistil part
54 He played Phileas Fogg
55 "__ Billy Joe"
56 Double features?
58 Kind of raid or hose
60 Dull sounds
62 Smelled awful
63 Prepared apples
64 Mel or Mont
65 Axle attachment
67 Toys that "walk the dog"
68 Pre-med course
69 Christopher of "Law & Order"
71 Not very poetic
72 Football feature
73 Put down words
76 Innate inclination
78 Incandescence
80 *Carrie* co-star William
81 Party's standard-bearer
82 Nostril nudgers
83 Ecologist's concern
84 Peter of "Everybody Loves Raymond"
86 Important organs
88 Heebie-jeebies
90 Rapid
91 Conehead in the corner
92 He lost to Ike
93 "Would I __ you?"
94 Ink-jet alternative
95 ". . . *in corpore* __"
96 Gave lines
97 Box at the gym
98 Muslim prayer call
102 Taunting cry
103 Unapproving vote
104 Past do?

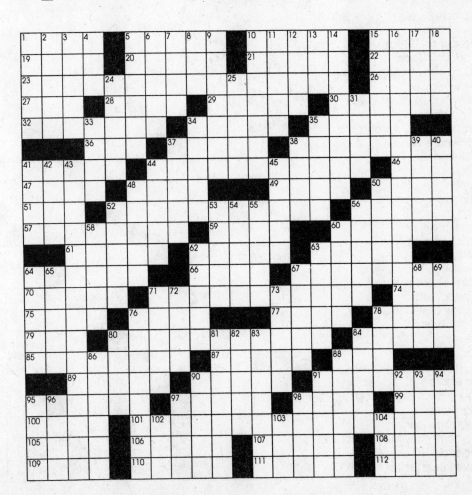

ACROSS

1 Drape borders
5 Mother Hubbard's quest
9 Layered hairdo
13 Dundee dude
17 Composer Satie
18 Composer Siegmeister
19 Molokai neighbor
20 In __ (prosperous)
22 Actor for the ages?
25 Ark rider's descendant
26 Arctic walkwear
27 Backless couch
28 Equalized
29 Old French coins
30 Quoted from
31 Former fiancées
32 Crossword legend Margaret
35 Water lily
36 Rather expensive
37 Significant person?
38 Used augers
39 In this way
40 Ransom the carmaker
44 Made a right
45 Ten-year molar?
47 Territory of most rulers
48 Corn or form lead-in
49 Sculptor or actor George
50 Actress Skye
51 Cut it out
52 Hairdo on ''Happy Days''
54 Boop the Toon
56 10 p.m. in Los Angeles, e.g.
57 Be worthy of
58 Haydn and Hemingway
59 ''The Vamp''
60 Broadway's Josh and Ella
63 Mideast's Moshe
64 Painting prowess
68 Clio or Obie
69 Jupiter's mate
70 Sun Valley locale
71 Half a laugh?
72 Bank (on)
73 Soldier's long-term assignment?
76 Blueberry or Bunker
77 Joint where you met Santa?
78 Is beholden
79 Bobby and Cordell
80 Night watch
81 Feels sore
83 Eccentric orbiter
84 A Thousand and One __
85 He worked at the Factory
87 The __ Not for Burning
88 High in fat
89 Budapest person
90 ''__ say'' (doubter's phrase)
91 Wooed
95 Take into custody
96 Timely sitcom?
98 Cooks with gas?
99 Swenson of ''Benson''
100 Fiend's forte
101 Nondairy spread
102 Sun. speeches
103 Noncommercial comm'ls.
104 Noted Graf
105 Caledonian loch

DOWN

1 Music's Dame Myra
2 Leprechaun land
3 Picasso contemporary
4 Prepared kebabs
5 William Wyler classic
6 Actor Edward James __
7 Riviera resort
8 It's a scream
9 You can get it by yourself
10 Sports sections
11 In the future
12 '50s TV sleuth Peter
13 Croatian or Serbian
14 With The, Shakespeare's timely play?
15 Sheepish
16 Chapeaux supports
20 Hold dear
21 Chianti color
23 Meatman Mayer
24 Prepped for the press
30 Reef component
31 Caesar's last word
32 Require the defroster
33 ''__ 'clock scholar''
34 Switzerland's Stein-am-__
35 Union unit
36 Fake
38 Start
39 Tugboat greetings
41 Shirk work
42 Two pills, perhaps
43 Mulligan or slumgullion
45 Darlings
46 Cronus or Oceanus
49 Get straight?
51 Conversation piece
53 Beatles' annual refrain?
54 Jambalaya-fest locale
55 Anti-smog gp.
56 Guisewite's comic
58 Trousers
59 Little terrors
60 Shakespeare's ''herald of the morn''
61 Wister of Westerns
62 Powerful blow?
63 Seashore sites
64 NC-17 film attendee
65 Dark-meat option
66 What the trick candle did
67 ''Gimme an A!'' etc.
69 Gem
70 Has an off day?
73 Companions
74 Pink azaleas
75 Nanki-Poo's love
76 ''Do Not Forsake Me'' movie
80 Ecclesiastical agent
82 Abysses
83 Lake near Cornell
84 Rhyme's adjective for Jack
85 Toad features
86 Go along
87 Diving birds
88 Former talk show host O'Donnell
89 More, to Morales
90 One liner?
91 Letters to answer
92 Drummer Cozy
93 Musical Duke's monograms
94 R.A.F. decorations
97 Abbrs. for ''that is''

ACROSS

1 Eton elevators
6 Rule-book pro
9 Lop the crop
13 Rascals
19 Immobile
20 Sense of self
21 Pretensions
22 Compost component
23 EARHART
26 Loch denizen, to some
27 Freezes over
28 Deadly pale
29 *Semana* segment
30 Horny little devil?
31 Sundial necessity
34 It turns on the cooker
35 Icy
37 DreamWorks' Spielberg
38 Collins or Crawford
39 Letters from Mom?
40 Hopping mad
43 Rob the actor
44 Word with ears or
   thumbs
45 Brazil's __ Paulo
46 Had a colt
47 Chicken-king link
48 NEWHART
53 Shake a tail
54 *Si*, here
55 Cozy corners
56 Refrigerator ancestor
57 Letters on stamps
58 Gotham area
   footballers
60 *New World Symphony*
   writer
61 'Riting, perhaps
62 Cops' collars
63 Friend of Cecil the Seasick
   Sea Serpent
64 Classroom show?
66 Landlocked land
67 Give notice of
69 Gel alternative
71 Loan letters
72 Paris station Gare __
73 Annie and Arsenio
74 R as in Greek
77 Help the checker
78 SMART
80 Josh
81 Hole in your shoe?
83 First person in Prussia?
84 Dakota resident
85 Tend
86 Garage charge
87 ''Yecch!''
88 Contented cat's
   comment
89 Playground staples
91 Fall
93 Supersmall
94 Rose Bowl prologue
95 RWR's Star Wars
97 Monkees' ''__ Believer''
98 Dance partner

99 Falana or Montez
100 Capital of the state of
   México
102 BOGART
108 Cobo and Omni, e.g.
109 Artist Bonheur
110 Show conclusion
111 Help after school
112 Charles, Andrew et al.
113 GI absentee
114 Christina's dad
115 Intoxicating

DOWN

1 Say the wrong thing?
2 Rural lodging
3 Passed the puck to
4 '90 one-man
   Broadway hit
5 Waller's piano style
6 Buy more Time
7 The best ones are AA
8 Antagonist
9 Oatmeal additive
10 Two by four?
11 The Cadets
12 Erstwhile airline
13 SST center
14 Genesis subject
15 Radio spots
16 MOZART
17 Strait-laced
18 Transude
24 Religious relic
25 Chemical in '60s
   headlines
29 GP's and OB's
31 Shoulder warmer
32 STEWART
33 Park in NYC
34 Goes it alone
35 It doubles in division
36 Nest-egg acronym
37 Emulate St. George
38 Men in red or
   black suits
39 Café or diner
41 Back-combs
42 Mystery writer's prize
45 Handler
46 Modern message
48 Quick pic
49 What cyclotrons
   generate
50 Trike rider
51 *Four Seasons* writer
52 Korean GI
59 Returns home?
60 Paucity
61 Cricket wicket sides
62 Tropical fruit
63 Bring up for discussion
64 Hawaii hip-shaker
65 NAACP, e.g.

66 DKNY or YSL
67 Heston role
68 Naval officer
69 Army officer
70 Geraldo's hurrah
72 NYPD rank
73 Fonda or Ford
75 Swinging thing
76 Tote-board info
78 Upstanding
79 Airport waiting area
82 __ Diamond Phillips
85 Satchel's mom
87 Actress Thurman
88 Of an endocrine organ
89 Pretzel topping
90 Phantom
92 New England univ.
93 Trunk
94 Swindle's eponym
95 Banner spangler
96 Golden, in Genoa
98 Clumsy craft
99 Hibernation spot
101 One for *los libros*
102 Mazatlán Mrs.
103 Org. to which Jordan
   belonged
104 Paint property
105 Greek vowel
106 Bacillus shape
107 Dixieland's Kid

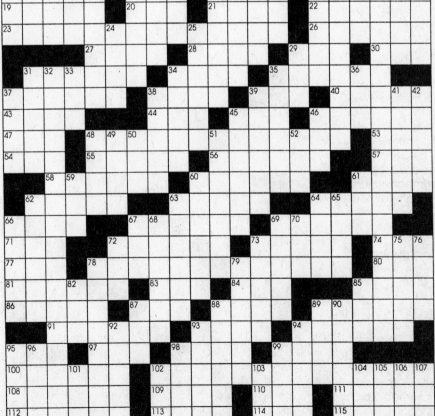

ACROSS

1 Crack agent?
5 Cherished ones
10 Sundance's sidekick
15 Diamond headwear
18 Mouse manipulator
19 Sponsorship
20 Dada photographer
21 Friend of the *famille*
22 Not at all *bueno*
23 Tied L.A. area?
25 Mother Teresa, for one
26 Ani, e.g.
28 Comfortable
29 Reach on the radio
31 Sighs, e.g.
32 Leafy course
33 Swindled
34 Masonic symbol
35 Site of La Scala
36 Used Ameslan
37 Adroit
40 Paris divider
42 Abdominal organ
43 Dinghy thingy
44 Tied steak?
48 What bartenders check
51 You owe them
53 Vaquero's rope
54 Take your best shot?
55 HIO₃ salt
56 Seesaw neighbors
58 Talk show host Gibbons
59 Cervantes
61 Trauma cause
62 Colorized
63 ''_ been a pleasure . . .''
64 Rival of Estée
66 Two after tic
68 Place for a slicker
69 Fable feature
70 Pests
73 Enzyme ending
74 Tied cakelet?
77 Go one better
78 Eaves dripper?
80 Prefix meaning lung
81 Curds complement
82 DEA, e.g.
83 Old photo tint
85 Spelloff
87 Wisdom goddess
88 Beckett's no-show
89 Artist Marc
93 ''_ luck!''
94 Comeback court star
95 Utopia Hilton?
97 Chopin's Concerto _ Minor
98 Tied wagon?
101 Paramecium shape
102 Programmable product
103 No-goodnicks

104 Showed ''M*A*S*H''
105 Earthquake aid org.
106 Pretty wide shoes?
107 Enclose
108 Battle field?
109 Nanny Drescher

DOWN

1 Insensate
2 Make _ (move merchandise)
3 ''Chill!''
4 Make doilies
5 Be a dilettante
6 Causing goose bumps
7 Maturing agents
8 It provides zest
9 Fast way to the UK
10 Role for Keaton, Kilmer or Clooney
11 Single
12 Hector's home
13 Chinese playwright _ Yu
14 Lightest element
15 Tied biters?
16 Tickled pink
17 Felt nostalgic
20 Clams and fins
24 Worked on the Pequod

27 Mary _ of cosmetics
30 Writer Rice or Tyler
32 _ Fein
33 Eyelashes
35 Architect _ van der Rohe
36 Dalmatian's distinction
37 Friend of Ms. White
38 Equilibrium center
39 Tied cargo haulers?
40 Nasty brat
41 To be, in Toulouse
42 Smeltery refuse
44 Current events?
45 It may be last on the list
46 Last name in the U.S.A.?
47 Brian Boitano's bailiwick
49 Dumbfound
50 Fokker foe
52 Vulgate version
54 Man of La Mancha
56 Volume setting?
57 Gained the day
58 Quart's cousin
59 Isinglass
60 It's expanded
61 Miniblind part
62 ''Ac-cent-_-ate the Positive''

64 With anger
65 Canal to Buffalo
66 Vegan's protein
67 Power particle
69 Hajj destination
70 La _ Tar Pits
71 Pre-school group?
72 Hale, Hari or Harriet
74 Topmost place
75 Go against
76 Foot or fathom
79 Copyright symbols
81 Go gradually
82 Immediately
83 Flew like Lindy
84 Perfect places
85 Split component
86 It's a chick thing
87 Still breathing
88 V-fliers
89 Tedious task
90 Comic Viking
91 Source of the bile
92 The beast, not the priest
94 High-hat
95 One of AA's 12
96 Shepard in space
99 Transvaal leader _ Paul Kruger
100 Sold-out notice

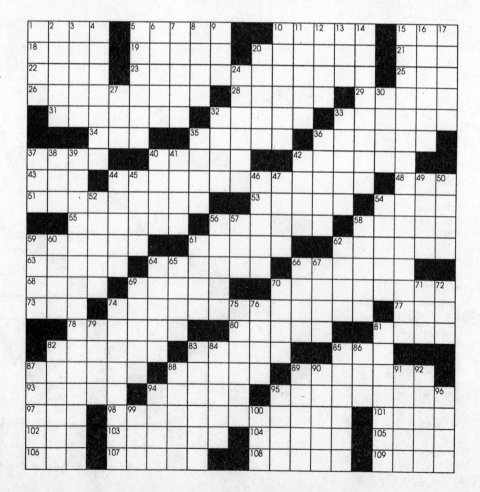

ACROSS

1 Ticket parts
6 Ex-ember
9 Light-years away
12 King of the Fairies
18 Surfer slang adjective
19 Female kudu
20 Where speedometer needles rest
21 Attraction
22 Tampered with
23 They bring pizzas
26 *Gorillas in the Mist* director
27 Ramses' predecessor
28 '50s TV's "__ of the Jungle"
29 Center
30 "I've __ to London . . ."
31 Banana Republic rival
32 Picnic cry
33 Wee pranksters
35 Lagoon surrounder
37 Hostile to
38 __ ex machina
39 Method
42 Head for the hills
44 They work with editors
47 Large glen
48 The Confessor King
50 "Give __ try"
51 "Caught you!"
52 Irish actor Moore
54 Pro __ (perfunctory)
55 Streaked gray animal
57 Announcements
58 Deuce beater
59 Strut
60 Professional man?
61 Sportscaster's shout
62 Erector set member?
65 U.S. 66, e.g.
68 Writer Gay
70 Buy a term policy
71 Husky coat?
72 Artist Jackson
74 Sizzling social engagement
76 Host's hostee
77 Actress Mimieux
78 Limbo need
79 Cereal grass, once
80 Old Faithful, e.g.
81 __ avis
82 They do a lot of skimming
86 Be overpersonal
87 Manhattan transit till '55
88 Sicilian volcano
89 Sudden silence
90 "Same here"
92 Cordage fiber
93 Lapidary display
94 Beyond dampish
95 As soon as
98 Love, in Lyon
101 Win by __ (edge out)
103 Pounds and pounds
104 Mythical moneybags
105 Soft-drink biggie

108 Scout's find
109 *Children of a Lesser God* director
110 Paperless pooch
111 It's lent or bent
112 To-do list
113 Samantha's "Bewitched" mother
114 WKRP or KCRW
115 Subject to strain
116 Unsporting

DOWN

1 Take potshots
2 They work on canvas
3 "Handle at once!"
4 Wasn't colorfast
5 Charlie Chaplin's bro
6 Make sense
7 Coal dust
8 It may be taken up in sewing class
9 Super gung-ho
10 Molecule mites
11 Parks of Montgomery
12 It fits in a lock
13 Goodyear and Fuji fliers
14 9/9/56 Ed Sullivan guest
15 Felt bad about
16 12D homophones
17 Cardinal's residence

18 Take rudely
24 Ticked off
25 Less moist
27 Baby powder
31 All smiles
32 Make more attractive
34 Haggard's "Okie" town
36 Ethno-pop singer Haza
37 Interim
38 Narcs' agency
39 Ernie Pyle or Ed Murrow
40 Lotion ingredient
41 Longings
42 Baseball's Grove or Gomez
43 Flip over
45 Vituperative speech
46 Vietnam base __ Sanh
47 Face mask?
49 Golfer Alcott
53 "Believe __ not!"
55 Invigorating
56 Item in red
57 Kol __
59 Moral maxims
60 Wheat flour component
62 Rorschach feature
63 Disrobe
64 "Swords into plowshares" prophet

66 Stun gun
67 Admission
69 Utah ski spot
71 Bull's order
72 Bonfire heap
73 Somewhat circular
74 *2001* computer
75 Philharmonic or Pops
76 Adventurous tale
78 Herpetological hugger
80 Gumption
83 Near, as beer
84 *12 Angry Men* director
85 Place west of Nod
88 Breadmaker?
91 Peon or esne
92 Good, to Gonzalez
93 Leave the building
94 Concern
96 Some comes from Mars
97 Valencian verb
98 *Days of Grace* author Arthur
99 Sort of average
100 *Metamorphoses* poet
102 Of the peacock network
103 Eye drop
104 Melchior and mates
106 AR, TX, DE, CO, etc.
107 Net-tickling serve
108 Wee bit

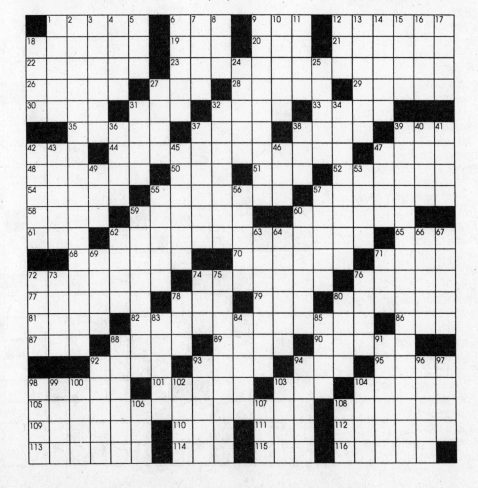

ACROSS

1 USAF arm
4 Use an atomizer
9 __ up (botch)
14 Attack like Brutus
18 Biblical ending
19 Investigation
20 Plot
21 Cut down
22 "Who __ kidding?"
23 Certain writ
25 Hero of a '22 play
26 Fiddled, in a way
28 Video game character
29 Don duds
30 Came on TV
31 Dilemma duo
32 D's preceder?
34 Legendary
36 Strikes the Stooge?
37 '80s pitcher Boyd
38 Tape holders
39 The hi sign
40 Blow taps
41 Ax-handle wood
44 Abbrs. on "as is" bins
45 Like old tigers
48 Cote call
49 Baronet's title
50 Racing shell
51 Snow-white bird
52 Kind of soda or sandwich
53 Bogie-Bacall film
55 Birchlike tree
56 Ravel work
58 Jazz home
59 Twenty make a team
60 Defense mechanism?
61 Peace in the Middle East
64 Element 86
65 Lassie's castle
69 Faneuil or Tammany
70 Calligraphy stroke
71 An Olympia and a Venus
72 French-born diarist
73 Nile nipper
74 Genesis edifice
77 FDR's on it
78 LBJ's VP
79 Enlighten
80 Table-talk collections
81 Witch craft
82 He was Dillon
84 Grasse gracias
86 Failed square knot
87 Can't stand
88 Collecting, to many
89 Pool stroke
90 Out-and-out
91 Asia's Ulan __
92 Textbook addendum
95 Small simian
96 Florida resort
99 Startling syllable
100 Memorable actor Tamiroff
101 Carotid, e.g.
102 Tempest sprite
103 Antlered animal
104 Tape deck abbrs.
105 Pesky plants
106 Saxophonist Mulligan
107 Bruce or Spike

DOWN

1 Garment worker's union?
2 Aer- cousin
3 Mahogany family tree
4 Globes
5 Used a missal
6 Like most choirs
7 Retired
8 Pro vote
9 Sneers at
10 Evonne's court rival
11 Auto take-back
12 Outback bird
13 Director Craven
14 Menelaus' kingdom
15 Place of worship
16 Leave your seat
17 Husking contests
20 Give a fright
24 Workplace pariah, nowadays
27 Cancels publication of
29 Rolled at Reno
31 Disheveled shack
32 Proverbial right-maker
33 Everyone, in Essen
34 Pat down
35 Condor condo
36 Poet Neruda
37 Peripheral
39 Novelist Evelyn or Alec
40 Barrel diameters
42 Kind of mash or cream
43 Emmett Kelly persona
45 Leave town fast
46 Read the Riot Act to
47 Utah rail center
50 Postwar Japanese leader
52 Role for Liz
54 Break in the action
55 Sound
56 Doughy delight
57 Folksinger Phil
59 Tie the knot
60 Fashions
61 Bygone ruler
62 Yesterday's dinner, today
63 Like ABC
64 Mariner's hazards
65 A United Arab Emirate
66 Clothing tag
67 You do what he says
68 York, to Lancaster, once
70 Reuben cheese
71 Kassebaum of Kansas
74 High-sounding fellow?
75 Frankfurt's river
76 Streisand
77 Pulls a gun
81 Bumptiously
83 French cathedral city
84 GM's M
85 Jet magazine rival
86 Staple seller
87 "Take __!" ("Beat it!")
88 Detested
89 Director René
90 Dressing-room symbol
91 Bit's big brother
92 Crawford's ex
93 Lecter, to Hopkins
94 Ox-cessory?
96 Margery of rhyme
97 About 120 square yards
98 Caddy sack

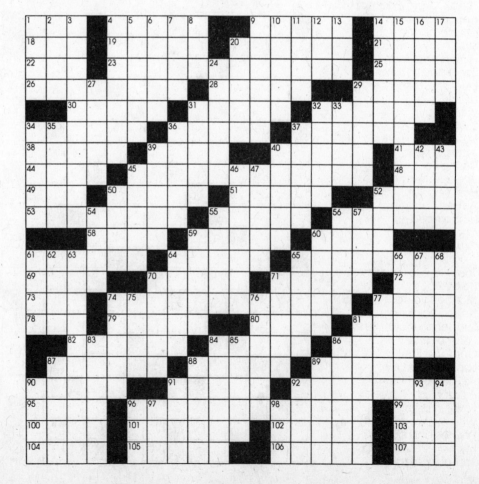

ACROSS

1 You have to work at it
4 Church-group gathering
10 Skiing turn
14 Try a tidbit
19 Poetic pugilist
20 Wise one
21 Reactor part
22 Squeegee, e.g.
23 Deprecate Custer's defeat?
26 Draw forth
27 *The Jungle Book* bear
28 They're rated in BTU's
29 "Fine, Houston"
30 Grass blade
32 Name for a colleen
33 Mamma follower
34 "Who am _ say?"
35 Hit a fly—or a fourbagger
36 Surfer's milieu
39 Do batik
40 Contemptuous Chase-Aykroyd comedy?
43 Buddy, in brief
44 Caddle's burden
45 Went underground
46 Beat's Cassady
47 Furtive follower
48 PC-phone linkup
51 Andy's pal
53 County festival
54 Normand of silents
55 Fail to mention
56 90210, e.g.
57 Chance to participate
58 Like double-entendres
59 Flops
62 Revamp
63 Deer meat
66 Cockney's cows?
67 Pompous VIP?
70 Canada's Grand _
71 Severe
73 Towards the harbor
74 Publicity-hound's goal
76 "What's _ for me?"
77 Midas' complex?
78 Dig this
79 Dry as dust
80 Craze
82 Budget opener
83 Square on campus
84 Energizer animal
85 Foster a felon
86 Kirghiz range
87 Astronaut Grissom
88 Northern seabird
89 Woodstock stuff
90 Mock fried cakes?
94 PST part
97 Early bird?
98 Clunk kin
99 Just miss a putt
100 Pop questions
101 Uris' _ *18*
102 Sophia of the screen
104 Bren or Sten
105 Formicide victim

106 "We've Only Just _"
107 Craft or coach opener
109 School for snubbery?
113 It separates in-laws
114 Wodehouse word
115 Mekong, etc.
116 Palindromic songstress
117 Beginning
118 Burgles
119 Lollipops and lemon drops
120 Diva Merriman

DOWN

1 Set up a haymaker
2 Chicago cow owner
3 Burke of . . . *Oz*
4 "And _ bed"
5 Parsley, perhaps
6 Rodin's "The Burghers of _"
7 Huge glacier
8 Clothes for the masses?
9 Aloha boa
10 Porpoise pack
11 Captured
12 Act human
13 Jockeys, boxers, etc.
14 Aviary syllables
15 Opera set in Egypt
16 Rioting scoffers' slogan?
17 Gumshoe
18 Until
24 Apollo's son
25 Like some subdivisions
31 "The cute Beatle"
33 *Courage Under Fire*'s Ryan
34 Horned goddess
35 Yarn coil
37 Where Perry won
38 Turnpike tariff
40 Beaver's œuvre
41 Denny's rival
42 "Got all your ducks _?"
44 Letter after aleph
47 Curbside cry
48 Leveled the lawn
49 Astrologer Sydney
50 Hissed at church windows?
51 Montezuma subject
52 _-en-scène
53 "Oh, darn!"
54 Edison's Park
57 Basic point
58 Slow flow
60 Old village by the Tiber
61 Course division
62 Small mill spills
63 Irritated
64 Utah's Hatch
65 Penurious

68 Fresno fruit
69 Rhea's anagrammatic daughter
72 Fit of anger
75 Sinclair Lewis birthplace _ Centre
77 Backcourt player
78 Be a bouncer
80 Lucille's final feature film
81 "Snug as _ in . . ."
82 Thrash about
83 Crack wise
84 Help a waiter
86 Pain in the neck
87 Coffee maker's concern
88 Couples-only craft
90 Way across town?
91 Liquids and gases
92 Twisted mass
93 What you will
94 Con artist's target
95 Onetime student
96 A river runs through it
101 Size after sm.
103 Rouó's glance
104 Catch hold of
105 A second time
106 31D's instrument
107 Portuguese holy man
108 Pewter component
110 Hotdog's problem
111 They show your age
112 Fat or fraidy follower

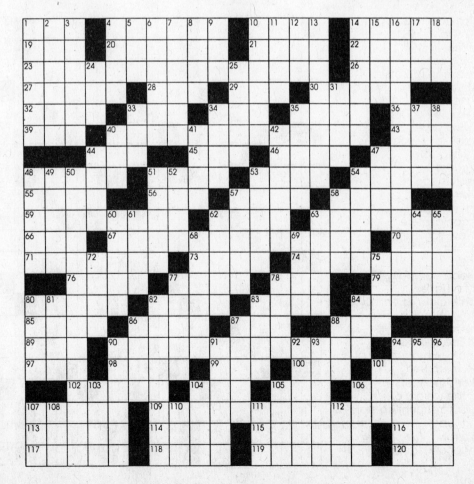

ACROSS

1 Hack
6 Day-care attender
9 Record replacers
12 Pasadena parade
18 Eight on the ice?
19 Detroit org.
20 PC perch, perhaps
21 JFK Jr.'s aunt
22 Hardens
23 Beer to cry into?
26 Expert
27 Baseball's Brock or Boudreau
28 Hollywood Park, e.g.
29 Dossiers
30 Pound the keyboard
31 Inflation cause?
32 Polynesian carving
33 NCO's addresses
35 Do a take
37 He gave us a shot in the arm
38 Peak point
39 QB coups
42 __-owned (used)
44 Con artist's motto?
47 Ayatollah predecessor
48 Pellucid
50 Pitcher projection
51 Wintry chill
52 Lily of the valley stem type (anagram of A CREME)
54 Plato's plaza
55 Quick comebacks
57 Holy Grail finder
58 Actor Musante
59 Sewing or family follower
60 Mozartean factotum
61 Pref. with ceps or ceratops
62 Young Transylvanian brute?
65 Big Apple—or burger
68 London's river
70 Squash and such
71 F.Y.I. circulator
72 Narcotics
74 Pigskin snappers
76 Cow hands?
77 Singer Richie
78 London derrière
79 __ New York minute
80 Gabfest
81 Let use
82 Sly soap company?
86 Put to the test
87 Infomercials, essentially
88 Idée __
89 Best, to Lloyd's
90 Like Ede citizens
92 Accomplishment
93 PGA members
94 Baker's shortcut
95 Test the weight of
98 Olivia's frequent co-star
101 Brings up
103 On a roll
104 Winger or Paget
105 Gymnast's seagoing fans?
108 Cooper's product
109 Evaluator
110 Hirt and Haig
111 Is doubled?
112 The '48 state
113 What -vores means
114 ###
115 Be worth the effort
116 More diffident

DOWN

1 She played Shirley
2 Cold symptoms?
3 He went to seed
4 Author Harte
5 Sycophant's reply
6 Remedial teacher
7 Pearl Harbor site
8 Night or light lead-in
9 Superhero's alter ego
10 __ Lama
11 Job particular
12 __ Comedy Jam
13 Be smarter than
14 "__ the loneliest number"
15 Old channel changer
16 Back forty unit
17 Pianist Myra
18 Italian carmaker
24 Photo from a film
25 Giraffe kin
27 Lo-cal
31 Metal eater
32 Future frog
34 Dukedoms and baronies
36 Inter __
37 Informant, informally
38 Mont Blanc, e.g.
39 Scotland?
40 Lady of Spain
41 Hoe house?
42 Edward of "Get Smart"
43 Strictness
45 Tips off
46 Las' followers
47 Capone feature
49 Jimmy
53 Like Pegasus
55 Takes the RTD
56 Time on the throne
57 __ the lily (overdecorates)
59 Greenhouse shrub
60 Jaclyn and Kate's co-star
62 Behindhand
63 They need to be seconded
64 Bandleader Tito
66 Anti-AIDS org.
67 He played Huxtable
69 It's out on a limb
71 It follows the Sun.
72 Large-mouthed pot
73 Like Hamelin's piper
74 Cowardly one
75 Discomfit
76 Give a party
78 Hum bug
80 Heart of the matter
83 Mob-scene member
84 Perch
85 Pass sentences?
88 Guy, to Ado Annie
91 Singer Neneh
92 Screenwriter Horton
93 An apóstol
94 Cabbage or kale
96 Less governed
97 Not vertically challenged
98 Major suffix
99 103D's mother
100 Remainder
102 Abba of Israel
103 Juno's counterpart
104 Hyphen's big brother
106 Abbrs. for gram and Greek
107 East is right here
108 Twice, on prescriptions

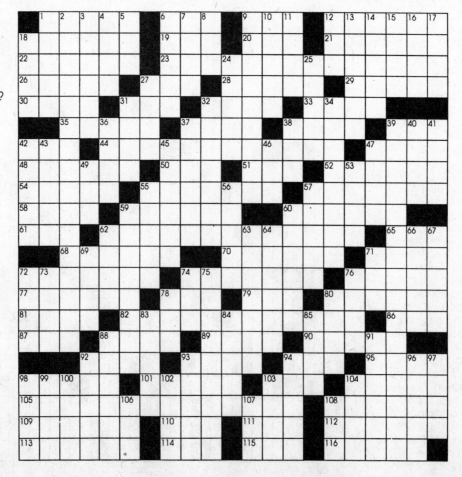

ACROSS

1 Baryshnikov's birthplace
5 Flowing locks
9 High court actions?
13 Nanny's baby
16 Playing it closer to the vest
18 Libreville is its capital
19 One of Woody's kids
20 Nev. neighbor
21 Menacing phrase
22 Indian, e.g.
23 Skim along
24 Bolivian resource
25 Spooky shipboard situation?
28 Stir-fry pan
29 Plum kin
30 It grows on you
31 Torch-bearing coin
32 She's born to be shorn
35 I, in Ulm
36 Medieval association
38 They play at Shea
39 Female aerial-ist?
44 Obi, e.g.
45 Referee
46 World record?
47 Aaron's sister
49 El, pluralized
50 Who's Who entry
51 Cong or Minh lead-in
52 Begone beginning
54 Rotary-phone feature
57 Lose it
59 Tot's toe
60 Ecstatic cling?
61 Business letters?
62 Thoroughbred novelist?
65 Stein's rose-rose link
66 Highest degree
67 Find a way around
68 Implied
69 Burned up the road
70 Tetra less one
71 Workshop fixture
72 Cable choice
73 Cattle call
75 Erie Canal terminus
77 Western Hispaniola
80 Iron men?
84 Like Ranger John Reid
85 Always on one's toes?
87 Gymnastics coach Karolyi
88 Pitchers' errors
89 Where Tell did dwell
90 At the moment
91 Surge
92 Folksinger Ives
93 Orchestra section
97 Psychochemical letters
98 How to miss actress Arthur?
104 Taunter's cry
105 Florence sits on it
106 France's longest river
107 Hebrew prophet
108 Personal
109 Steed speed
110 "Get Happy" composer
111 Lavender holder
112 Advanced degs.
113 Serve with sauce?
114 "Our Gang" dog
115 Caught in the act

DOWN

1 __ avis
2 "__ a Kick Out of You"
3 Role for Rita
4 Fabulous fellow?
5 Like Rambo
6 Red as __
7 Biblical life saver
8 Sicilian city
9 Where to see Manon in Milan
10 Corsage component
11 More melancholy
12 Puts in turf
13 Movie gear for Indy Jones?
14 Eat crow and talk turkey
15 Merci, in Merzig
16 Inner ear?
17 Script doctor's output
18 "A-ha!"
26 Not so mean
27 Waters down
31 Lucie's dad
32 Big Band, e.g.
33 Lord or lock lead-in
34 A drop in the ocean
36 Certain square dancer
37 One for los libros
38 Supreme sacrificer
40 Buffalo pro
41 Judge in '95 headlines
42 Poured down
43 Impassive
44 Military encirclement
47 Main companion
48 Computer accessory
50 Count with lots of numbers?
51 Pay a call on
53 "Holy cow!"
54 Force
55 Pref. meaning within
56 Vulnerable mafiosi?
57 Commonplace
58 Garfield or Felix
59 Alfresco meal
62 Castro's capital
63 Sheepish?
64 Starbucks option
69 AA member's club?
73 Shows in the daytime
74 Not even!
76 Something from the blue
77 Word to Dolly
78 7D's craft
79 Qualifiers
80 Lesser Antilles language
81 Publican's place
82 Environmental pref.
83 Attach a button
85 They have nothing original to say
86 Soup serving bowl
87 Balderdash!
88 __ Aires
91 Melancholy
92 Quotable catcher
93 Walking stick?
94 Low dice roll
95 Big bashes
96 Add zest to
98 Tinting tubs
99 Snafu outcome
100 Play preceder?
101 '68 Open champ
102 In those days
103 Boater or sailor

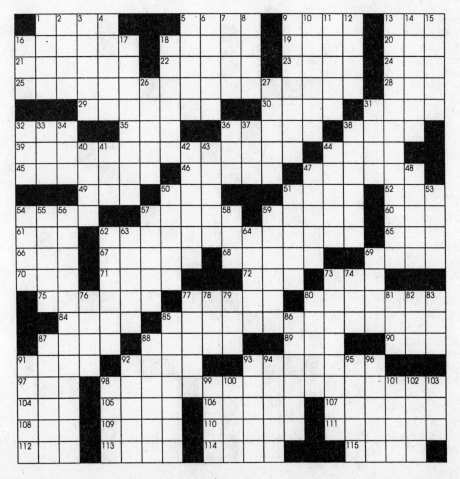

ACROSS

1 Tree-covered valley
5 On edge
10 Make a coin vanish
14 One in a long line of sausages
18 Hydrox lookalike
19 Come to terms
20 Postal map divisions
22 Iroquois enemy
23 Overcast
24 Town where you can eat up the scenery?
26 Rioja or rouge
27 Pvt. addresses?
29 Tra and ooh followers
30 Simultaneity
32 Nudnik's kin
35 Perform __ (sing alone)
37 Rickenbacker and Richthofen
38 El Dorado's riches
39 Bedroom community?
43 Times and Times Mirror, for short
46 Sugar units
48 Kael's __ It at the Movies
49 Rides updrafts
50 Pref. meaning self-acting
51 Birth of a notion
52 Liquid lump
53 __ were
54 Dial __ Murder
55 They come out at parties
56 Well-regulated city?
60 Beehive cousin
61 Value system
63 Dizzy and Daffy
64 Match socks
66 Hurries over?
67 Poker bump
68 Former
69 Papeete's place
70 Berlin products
71 Gambling game, __ de fer
72 Mayberry moppet
73 Icebox burg?
76 Some U.S.A. personnel
79 Treats squeaks
80 Away from the storm
81 It has Swiss banks
82 The Counterfeiters writer
83 __ Aviv
84 Nancy of Sunset Boulevard
86 Wild boar, e.g.
88 '39 role for Flynn
89 Slugger's stat
90 Wide-open town?
93 Runner Sebastian
94 Oversupply
95 Alvin of dance
96 Great white birds
98 Mirage
101 Eyes, in architecture
103 Kiss, in Castile
104 Camelot character
105 People-watcher's place?

109 End of the shoot
113 Tattled
114 Without a __ (smoothly)
115 Moses' mountain
116 Symbol of peace
117 Unique
118 Lorelei Lee's creator
119 __ fro
120 1984 or 2001

DOWN

1 Nipper or Checkers
2 Do a human thing
3 Meadow
4 Scout's second adjective
5 Derek who played Claudius
6 "I hate it!" sounds
7 Mil. rations unit
8 Notre Dame bench
9 Decays, as paper
10 Conditioned-response pioneer
11 Aida air
12 Discounted by
13 Gym pad
14 Jerry or Jerry Lee
15 Pupil's locale
16 Future hombre
17 Mourn aloud
21 It's just under a cup

25 Flanders city (ATLAS anagram)
28 Little pointers?
31 Untouchable Eliot
32 Hepster's exclamation
33 Tanker cargo
34 Domestic quilters' community?
35 Lets
36 Chimney accumulations
37 '48 film __ With Judy
40 Whitman's bloomers
41 Holy scroller?
42 Perturbs
43 City of orange?
44 Crucial meeting number
45 Hone
47 Petits fours and bear claws
52 Mayo, e.g.
53 Andre of tennis
54 Catalogs in batches
57 "Ten Cents __"
58 Stallion sound
59 The shape the world is in?
62 Word before a hike
65 Second in command?
66 Double-edged sword
67 Ivanhoe's bride

68 "From __ stand" ("In my view")
69 Comb component
70 "How could you stoop __?"
71 Tom of techno-thrillerdom
74 Is out of
75 "Rawhide" theme singer
77 "__ a Grecian Urn"
78 Genders
84 Kon-Tiki's resting place
85 Cape Kennedy event
86 Artfulness
87 Most crafty
88 Peacock tail features
91 Just for __
92 Chaplin's first feature film
94 Euphoric
97 Obstreperous
98 White House rejection
99 A party to
100 Window ledge
101 Not falling for
102 Mlle. Chanel
103 Granola ingredient
106 Sneeze and wheeze
107 Early Angeleno Pico
108 Japanese airline
110 She's such a deer
111 Palindromic name
112 Pricing word

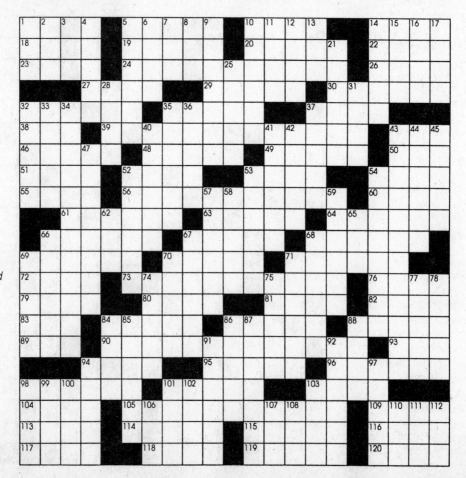

ACROSS

1 Pres. or amb.
4 Pasture youngster
10 Boxcar rider
14 Military storage place
19 Bruin of fame
20 Come to conquer
21 Foretoken
22 Shake the Etch A Sketch
23 Tryster's choice
26 Backslide
27 __ mirabilis (notable year)
28 Anaïs
29 Bit in a horse's mouth
30 Recipe verb
32 One going in the right direction?
33 Helios, to Romans
34 Snoop's aid
35 Booby, gooney or dodo
36 Roy or Reiner
39 Mag wheels?
40 New Hampshire's challenge
43 Iberian eye
44 Nothing doing!
45 Holm or Richardson
46 Told taradiddles
47 Sticking place?
48 Ort, often
51 Summoned Jeeves
53 Famed freebooter
54 Iris center
55 Aphrodite's love
56 It often follows you
57 Succumbed to strain
58 Buffalo or Pecos
59 Immense
62 Mislead
63 Walter Mitty's forte
66 Flightless ratite
67 Diner's dichotomy
70 Place for hydrotherapy
71 Put up the SRO sign
73 Drive insert
74 Tickled beyond pink
76 Tom's Polly
77 Role for Reeve or Reeves
78 Cross-shaped letter
79 Chili con carne's con
80 Louvre locale
82 Political patronage
83 Red planet
84 Polished plane
85 They're big in Hollywood
86 Soccer score
87 __ vobiscum
88 Elfin
89 South, south of the border
90 Passenger's pick
94 Look pooped
97 "Nightline" name
98 Fullerton neighbor
99 Likewise not
100 Listener's loan
101 Verdi princess
102 Christ Stopped at __
104 You get it with your order
105 Bear foot

106 Roles are his bread
107 Led the way
109 Risk taker's tossup
113 Absurd
114 Writer Sarah __ Jewett
115 Einstein or Schweitzer
116 Zip
117 Presents
118 Spick-and-span
119 Friday, often
120 S.F.-L.A. direction

DOWN

1 Go by boat
2 Had a pressing engagement?
3 Snips off superfluity
4 Shorts supports
5 Photog's abbr.
6 Chekhov opus
7 Simplistic
8 Elysium
9 Ransom Eli Olds' car
10 Tribute
11 Leave off a list
12 Crenshaw or Hogan
13 Like a Möbius strip
14 Deceive
15 Q.E.D. center
16 Shopper's option
17 CIA precursor
18 Golf accessory
24 Capek classic

25 Flaubert's hometown
31 Droughty
33 News hour, often
34 Boast
35 Bouquet thrower
37 So. Cal. music festival locale
38 Be a kegler
40 Place for gloss
41 Capital punishment?
42 Musical that won Best Picture
44 Rocket launcher
47 Unorthodox religion
48 Wise ones
49 Whodunit deed
50 Coffee-drinker's determination
51 Bonnie or John
52 Ogee, e.g.
53 Sleeping-bag filler
54 Grape variety
57 One of the inn crowd
58 Bellhop's burden
60 Garish lights
61 Giving no slack
62 Imbibe
63 Cry to the projectionist
64 Kind of fence
65 Marina moorer
68 Channel swimmer Gertrude
69 Rip or zip

72 The Bridge of San __ Rey
75 Farthest from the pin
77 Qantas mascot
78 Prepare for takeoff
80 Nuisance
81 Malarial woe
82 Trident-bearing god
83 Bryn __
84 Chosen number?
86 Baby in pink
87 Go stealthily
88 Advocating
90 Humble homes?
91 "Not __!" ("No way!")
92 At hand
93 Broke like the day
94 Peaceful protests
95 Venus' love
96 Treat a sore throat
101 Essen expletive
103 Stooped
104 Moth variety
105 Theda's rival
106 D.A., e.g.
107 He'll make a hog of himself
108 Macaw kin
110 It's all in vein
111 Raven maven's monogram
112 60 minuti

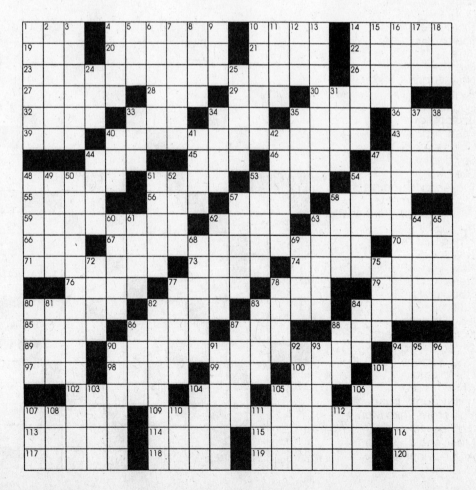

ACROSS

1 Toon tycoon
6 Ball or strike
10 Shortwave operator
13 Assembly phase
17 Screened messages?
18 Big star's small role
19 Mystique
20 Mah-jongg oblong
21 Now, Judy Collins?
23 Hand or foot
24 Firearm fodder
25 Where Césars are given
26 Recaps, often
28 Inexperienced
29 Subterfuge
32 Served the purpose
33 Quarter fraction
34 A real looker
36 Ironically funny
37 ID datum
38 Brief moment?
39 Zero on stage
41 Opera villain, often
43 Now, Foreigner?
47 Corporate abbrs.
50 Solo in space?
51 Dye pot
52 It's a loch
53 Draft status?
54 Too content
56 Car hood, to Sir Harwood
58 Fort Apache force
60 ROM's R
61 More osseous
62 Short vowel mark
64 Yore
65 Even one
66 Now, Grass Roots?
68 As well
69 Finger grip
70 Logical flaws
71 Faisal's family
72 Hajji's leader
73 Say again
75 Like liters
76 Tucked in for the night
77 Made a memo
78 ''. . . kerchief, __ in my cap''
81 Magnon intro
82 100 square meters
83 Tar's toddy
84 Now, Eagles?
90 Stereo ancestor
92 Stood up to
93 FM slot
94 It's all the rage
95 Dad or hickey lead-in
97 Omega, electrically
99 Riga resident
100 Oh, to Otto
101 Charon's river
102 Unpleasantly pungent
104 Valli of The Third Man
106 It divides to multiply
108 MacDonald's spread
109 Arduous journey

110 Now, Association?
115 Broadway bomb
116 Nora, to Nick
117 That is
118 They'll give you the news
119 Rocket deviations
120 Stable scrap
121 DeSoto and LaSalle
122 Bedouin bigwig

DOWN

1 Babies in blue
2 What Caesar said to Cleo?
3 '60s war area, to GIs
4 One who says uncle?
5 Sweet Liberty star
6 Sized up, as joints
7 Oldest prophetic book
8 Sign on a summer house?
9 '62 film The __ Day
10 Search
11 Come up
12 Prepare for framing
13 Walk of Fame symbol
14 Now, Outsiders?
15 Bugs bugs him
16 Showy-flowering plant
18 Distrustful ones
19 Without frills

22 Of Patagonia's peaks
27 Determined
28 Mousse alternative
29 Pack animal?
30 ''Get that away from me!''
31 Galilee, e.g.
33 Tin Cup star
35 Word of cheer?
38 Booty
39 They were blue in Yellow Submarine
40 Mormon letters
42 She didn't like Ike
44 It's often dull
45 DeCarlo who played Lily Munster
46 Self-denier
48 Freight measure
49 James Bond's bailiwick
53 In charge of
54 Kerry or Kerrey
55 Now, Jackson Five?
56 Symbolic logic system
57 Ragged-edged
59 Monopoly bd. words
60 PG, e.g.
61 Trunk, in Tottenham
62 Out of focus
63 Makes waves?
66 Roe housing?

67 Car jack mechanism
72 ''__ to differ''
74 Park in New York City
75 Ticked off
76 Diva's big moment
79 Homer Simpson's neighbor
80 Large and innocent, as eyes
82 ''O Canada,'' e.g.
84 La-la lead-in
85 Colossal
86 Ford's Corolla rival
87 Top Ten tune
88 Sit in judgment
89 Talk-show topic
91 Auction action
95 Pitcher Dizzy's brother
96 City near Gainesville
98 Montessori or Muldaur
100 ''This place is __!''
101 Hawthorne's home
103 Scamps
105 Where hooks go
106 State for the record
107 '86 Rob Reiner film Stand __
109 Number for the show?
111 Writer LeShan
112 Work on something?
113 Compete
114 Musical sense

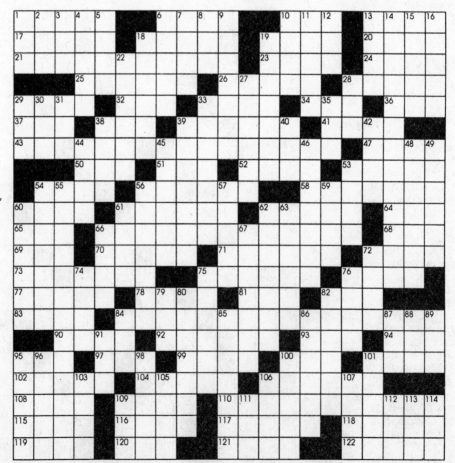

ACROSS

1 Drink with sashimi
5 Leonardo's Lisa
9 Guadalajara girlfriend
14 Peacock's pride
18 "Come __" ("Enter")
19 Check books
20 Trite
21 Meter lead-in
22 HOO
26 Beasts of Burdon?
27 Silverdome team
28 Make a difference
29 Backchat
30 Companies
31 Venetian resort
32 Urn odist
35 Brushed leather
36 Transmit by 67D
39 British Princess
40 WATT
43 Chem. room
45 Walden or Golden
46 Doctorate hurdle
47 Fedora feature
48 It's hot when it's coaled
49 Retic or ridic ender
50 Oops! evokers
51 It may be frozen or liquid
53 From now on
54 Hack for hire
56 Cosmetics-counter name
57 Hang out
58 WEN
62 Trailing
65 Subsequently
66 Jacks, often
70 Dumbfound
71 Beyond blasé
72 Subject to change
74 What a swabbie swings
75 Entertainer Minnelli
76 Wrap-around dress
77 Separate
78 Wood, in Oaxaca
79 L'eau land?
80 WARE
84 Southernmost U.S. county seat
85 Mournful poems
87 Attains justly
88 Tippecanoe's running mate
89 Of the Diamond St.
90 Sitcom sample
91 Narrow inlets
93 Light
96 Begin fighting
97 Fifteen percent might pay for it
100 HOWE
104 Cache for cash
105 Treasure collection
106 Cat Nation people
107 "__ girl!"
108 Streep's and Stover's alma mater
109 Horse opera
110 Checks the water
111 Jack Sprat's diet

DOWN

1 Sea plea
2 Dragonwyck writer Seton
3 Potter's oven
4 Joined up
5 Heats and spices cider
6 Aeolian poems
7 Zilch
8 Studio
9 Six-pack site?
10 They often cross Firsts
11 Trek stops
12 One-liner
13 It may be foiled
14 Pre-taps call
15 "__ you know!"
16 Spillane's __ Jury
17 False witness
19 Vive's opposite
23 Latin lesson word
24 L'__ Temps (Ricci perfume)
25 Rice growing ground
30 Burning needs
31 On the up-and-up
32 On the fritz
33 WWII plane __ Gay
34 Attach
35 Trade at a meet
36 Basin or Baker
37 Michigan metropolis
38 Feydeau forte
40 Lodz locale
41 African antelope
42 Ghosts writer
44 Snoopy's is root
48 Fake
50 You can catch it in the act
51 "Since you __ . . ."
52 Touch the heart
53 Readied the razor
55 Island east of Spain
56 Villa-building family
57 Cell components
59 Fierce gazes
60 Pianist Boulanger
61 Baskerville beast
62 Java neighbor
63 South Pacific character
64 Watership Down rabbit
67 Modemed messages
68 Actress Esther
69 Animal track
71 Frank or Jesse
72 Facade
73 Carrillo and Gorcey
76 Heel type
78 Annual exam
80 "__ Kick Out of You"
81 Not this, not that
82 Smacking of the sea
83 Brushed beagles
86 Fit to be tried, at tiffin
88 Kipling's Rikki-Tikki-__
90 Miff
91 Kings, in Castile
92 Bargain bin abbrs.
93 __-bitty
94 '50s VW Karmann-__
95 Carter of Broadway
96 Turnstile feature
97 Pickens or pickings
98 Mention for merit
99 This señorita
101 Musical syllable
102 The anti-Brady bunch
103 Sun shade

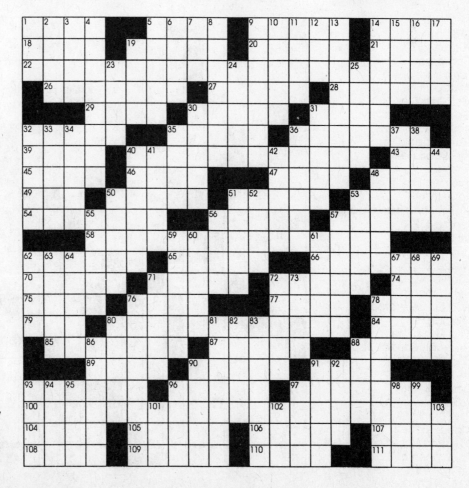

ACROSS
1 Jabber?
5 Sweeping
10 Pi follower
13 Londoner's local
16 Sonora flora
17 Nerd
18 Dolorous drop
19 Written with four sharps
20 Greek theater
21 Guaranteed luxurious garment?
24 Asian desert
25 "Johnny B. __"
26 Brian Boru's land
27 Test tube
28 "It's the __, stupid!"
30 It's a natural
32 Flying wedge
33 In place of
35 Tot's timeout
36 Henry the Brave
37 Koufax the Dodger
38 Acute or obtuse fig.
39 Guaranteed seafood dish?
42 Drawer of ships
43 Plantation pest
45 Egoist's words
46 Hagiographer's abbr.
47 Potemkin setting
51 More agreeable
52 Revolt
54 Towel off
55 AT&T pt.
56 Put to work
57 Consecrated
58 Farm fraction
60 At capacity
61 Mr. Dillon
63 Guaranteed bakery staple?
65 Questionable
66 The Charleses' dog
67 Sunbeams
68 Live and breathe, e.g.
69 Polar toiler
70 It might end with a bang
71 Tend a tot
72 Trojan hero
73 Have-nots have them
76 Graceful girls
78 "Sort of" suffix
80 Half a toon twosome
81 And God Created Woman star
82 King Guz subject
83 Guaranteed diet staple?
86 Linguist's suffix
87 Devoutness
89 Designer Perry
90 768 tsps.
91 Ring highlight
92 Makes money
93 S&L strongroom
94 Town north of Torrance
97 Not pro
98 It freezes your flippers
99 Greenbacks or gelt
100 Singing Swedes
103 Guaranteed numismatists' prides?
107 Slander in the press
108 Obtained
109 Airport near Paris
110 Laker Rodman
111 Help
112 Sean Lennon's mom
113 Chow mein chaser
114 Just know
115 Hasidim or Mennonites

DOWN
1 Portuguese folksong
2 Guaranteed salad base?
3 Like Spock
4 Like some Western stars?
5 Twig broom
6 One before 8D
7 In the old days
8 One before fire
9 One of the Tweedles
10 Violinist's need
11 She played Benjamin
12 Copenhagen coin
13 Felt for
14 Apprehensive
15 Milton of comedy
16 Sprocket
17 Goldberg of Ghost
18 Playwright Rattigan
22 Rebellion
23 Get even for
25 Contort
29 Ablaze
30 PGA's Snead
31 Get the lead out
32 Overly showy
33 Babe in the woods
34 "Dedicated to the __ Love"
36 St. Francis' town
37 Put in the pantry
40 Utilize
41 Bo and John
44 Hearth goddess
48 Guaranteed cafeteria staple?
49 Ego
50 Friend in battle
52 Lusitania sinker
53 Screen's McQueen
54 Impurity
58 Saw eye to eye
59 Havana mujer
60 Records handler
61 Matter for Einstein
62 Pasty-faced
63 Fried chicken option
64 Hudson and Ford
69 Make possible
71 Scotch servings
72 "... to __ of beans"
74 Medicine measure
75 Winder kind
77 Justice or license lead-in
78 In a perfect world
79 Greet the general
81 Sitcom bunch
84 Ignited
85 Exit
87 Steering section
88 Entirely
92 Chutney ingredient
93 Zapata crony
94 Hired hoods
95 Warbucks' ward
96 Too trusting
98 Barreled along
99 Twin Cities' st.
101 "__ ever so humble..."
102 Everyone, or every one
104 Tent bed
105 IRA options
106 Peg for Peete
107 UNLV penultimate

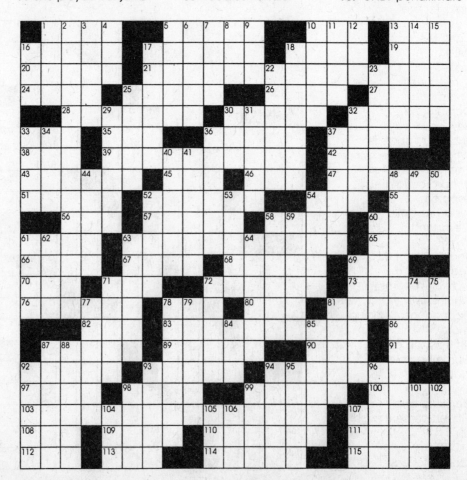

ACROSS

1 Frisbee, e.g.
5 Nature photog Adams
10 Roller on the river
13 Surg. sites
16 Mills or Fargo
17 County Kerry capital
18 Northern French river
19 Young yipper
20 Union meeting place?
21 Skywalker saga installment
24 Submissive
25 Episcopal clergy member
26 Braving the waves
27 It's poison in crosswords
28 Evangelical meeting
30 Put on hold
32 Racing shell
33 Yon ship
35 French roll-call response
36 ''__ your debt''
37 Swimming in suds
38 Aurora, to some
39 ''Eeyeww!''
42 Comic Conway
43 Off the straight and narrow
45 Mortar mixer
46 Café alternative
47 Fills with joy
51 Pad size
52 Delicate
54 Apt. ad abbrs.
55 Actress __ Dawn Chong
56 Campsite vehicles
57 Not at all Saharan
58 ''__ sow, so shall . . .''
60 Lee or Paretsky
61 __ gin fizz
63 South-of-the-border silver center
65 Pub purchase
66 Praise
67 Hotfoots it
68 Actor Andrew or singer John
69 Spigoted server
70 Little dickens
71 Tawny
72 Word group
73 Obeys a parental instinct
76 Philosopher Blaise
78 Gardner of Mogambo
80 Dakota's kin
81 Mother Courage creator
82 It's a cinch, in Osaka
83 Like some queues
86 __ polloi
87 Underwater apparatus
89 They were made by jerks
90 PBS benefactor
91 Call a spade a club
92 Exhausted
93 The ancient Marner?
94 Was a noodge

97 They can fold right in front of you
98 Bus Stop author
99 Whitman namesakes
100 He wrote a Book
103 Syntactically subordinate section
107 Cartoonist Feiffer
108 From KA to ME
109 Chihuahua cheers
110 It's a circus in there
111 Skillful
112 It means stop
113 ''Die,'' like a man?
114 Exorbitant
115 Superlatively good

DOWN

1 Former majority leader
2 Common-concern coteries
3 Weave in and out
4 Jaguar or Cougar
5 Betel palm
6 Durban's province
7 Insult
8 More often than oft
9 Deighton of spy-fi
10 Quart's kin
11 Safety org.
12 ''That's amazing!''
13 Share feelings
14 Without civility
15 Sales talk
16 Water container
17 ''Jeopardy!'' info
18 ''That makes a lot __''
22 Like a lout
23 Crunchy veggie
25 Evian competitor
29 Heart, liver, lungs, etc.
30 Start of Tanzania's capital
31 Gush feeling
32 Dirties
33 Diploma adornment
34 Haberdashery section
36 ''__ kick from champagne''
37 '70s sound setup
40 Give __ to (fire)
41 Blazers' rivals
44 Praised extravagantly
48 Commuters' concerns
49 Deserve
50 Pants part
52 Cereal seed
53 Antibody carrier
54 School for Hercule
58 Like a center of rotation
59 ''The __ the fathers . . .''
60 Shopping binge
61 Careless mistake
62 The priest, not the beast
63 Muse of comedy
64 Flynn namesakes
69 ''Mind-blowing!''
71 Domestic cat
72 Raccoon kin
74 Asgard god
75 The pokey
77 Meal part
78 Gives out tasks
79 Blue hue
81 Sanctify
84 Freon or neon
85 Oxford arch
87 Completely calm
88 Settled down
92 Waterproof boot
93 Display disdain
94 Kind of cuisine
95 Memorable ''Matter of Fact'' columnist
96 Escape from
98 Twiddle your thumbs
99 Carry on
101 Retained
102 No. 1 suffix?
104 Start to snooze
105 Letterman's network
106 Eng. subject
107 Pugilist's poke

ACROSS

1 Agcy. discontinued in '73
4 Fill fully
8 Stick broom
13 Bust stop?
16 Beatles' call to Jude
17 Make cole slaw
18 __ day's work
19 Stole or shawl
20 Unburden
21 Boyfriends and girlfriends
23 "Manhattan" lyricist
24 Spare
26 Customary practice
27 Military blockade
29 Many VW's
30 L.A. museum benefactor
31 Cockcrow
32 Brynner namesakes
33 Active one
34 Powdered starch
35 Interstice
38 Caltech's forte
39 Pull the plug
43 United competitor
44 Picnic places
46 Not imaginary
47 *Peer Gynt* penner
48 Tolstoy topic
49 Israel's Moshe
50 Volvo rival
51 Healers' gp.
52 Multinational crime-fighters
54 Tabard and Wayside
55 '96 Gibson-Russo suspenser
59 Small Dodge
60 Tarantino opus
64 Man in *Pretty Woman*
65 House on the Hill
67 Take the trolley
68 DuPont product
70 Debussy's sea
71 Trend
72 Say "nyah-nyah"
73 On the job, for short
74 Sealed packages
77 Synthesizer inventor
78 Like some sandpaper
79 Pier group
80 He married Mary II
83 The other side
84 "Muskrat Ramble" writer
85 Start the season
86 Beat 4-3, e.g.
87 Make cotton candy
89 Coats on coatis
90 Pamphlet parts
92 Freaked-out
95 It means "as if"
97 Singer Carpenter
98 Fidelity
99 Sound from Socks
100 Gets engrossed
103 Juliette Gordon Low's gp.
104 Staff member
105 Point to the east
106 Between, to Racine
107 '70s series "__ Ramsey"
108 Name for a chowderhead?
109 The T in THC
110 "Sexual Healing" singer
111 Tut's cousin

DOWN

1 Woody plant
2 River past Notre Dame
3 *Tale of Two Cities* hero
4 Sun specs
5 Heavenly butter
6 Work the bar
7 The Begleys
8 It's heard in a herd
9 Gray matter
10 Number out of a hat?
11 Low note?
12 It makes you feel kneaded
13 Toot your own horn
14 Few and far between
15 Well put
17 Nasal appraisal
18 __-Hungarian Empire
19 "Stop pouring!"
22 Shea Stadium borough
25 Scissors case
28 Famous flag-raising site
30 Bridge expert Charles
31 Screen's Arlene
33 Screen's Shelley or Robert
34 Random guess
35 Joes who got the Bill
36 Serve well done?
37 Hog haven
38 Al Jolson classic
39 Beatles' "From Me __"
40 Corsica's owner
41 Eat like a king
42 Zaire border river
43 Castor and Pollux
44 E. Germany
45 Dr. Dre or Heavy D
50 Slyly malicious
51 "Gunsmoke" star
53 Protector of the crown?
54 "I don't know __ so far as to . . ."
56 Cpl. Klinger's goal
57 Deity's channeler
58 Raspberry sauce
61 Numismatist's prize
62 Pleistocene epoch
63 Alternative to Midway
66 Boring
69 Thai specialty __ krob
71 Io, e.g.
72 Salad server
74 The even prime
75 Intake intake
76 Twist together
77 Titles on French envelopes
78 Rhythmic
81 Moderate orange color
82 UC VIP
83 A boxer makes it
87 Harsh
88 Novelist's bailiwick
89 Paying passenger
90 Indianapolis pro
91 Theater in the round
92 Mrs. Rubble
93 Hippy flowers?
94 Natural talent
95 Throw in the towel
96 Pakistani language
97 Create cardigans
98 Delany of "China Beach"
99 Faux follower
101 Lode stone
102 Col.'s command

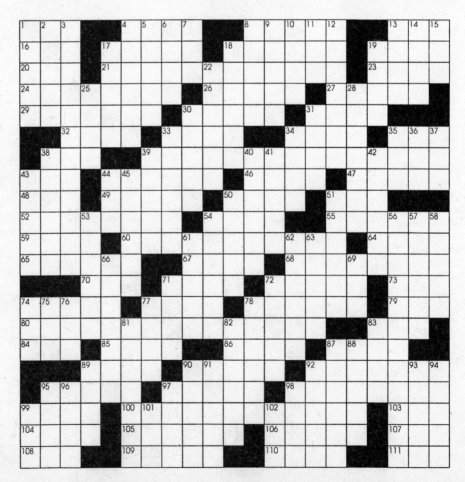

ACROSS

1 Shopaholic's hangout
5 Santa Fe neighbor
9 Cheese that's made backwards?
13 Potter's purchase
17 Yours, in Tours
18 Thrice minus twice
19 "__ Smile Be Your . . ."
20 Hoodwinked
22 Excess poundage
25 Front line?
26 Places in harm's way
27 Smidgens
28 NYC's __ Island
29 Like Texas' star
30 Vamoose
31 Disclaims
32 Making a sitcom episode
35 Underground filmmaker Jonas
36 Coat cloth
37 Robert wrote them
38 Like some CD sets
39 ". . . in corpore __"
40 Festival
44 Edible seaweed
45 The real thing
47 Slammer
48 Where *Cav* and *Pag* play
49 Undignified
50 One for the road?
51 Observe Yom Kippur
52 Foretell
54 Treasury offerings
56 Votes to accept
57 Pleas and meas enders
58 Black or flower follower
59 Aspersion
60 '96 Tom Arnold role
63 Damsel's retort to the villain
64 Clergy aides
68 Rain checks?
69 Swinging stride
70 Perspective
71 19th-century Scottish explorer
72 Countercurrent
73 '64 Supremes hit
76 Hamster's home
77 Rhymin' Simon
78 Grand-slam HR quartet
79 WWII wolf-pack member
80 Like footballs and baseballs
81 Dakotas' kin
83 Greek strongman
84 Kathy Bates' Oscar-winner
85 Lacking principle
87 Ore extract
88 Smothers and Snyder
89 Stopped in traffic
90 Capacitance unit
91 They're watching
95 Rabbit ears, e.g.
96 Mash notes
98 Delicate
99 Bonnie of PBS's "To the Contrary"
100 *Nez* neighbor
101 Plumber's U
102 Gives in to gravity
103 Bombs doing stand-up
104 Workout units
105 Anxious

DOWN

1 French Sudan, today
2 The least little thing
3 What insiders are in
4 More probable
5 Becoming buff
6 It's a matter of degrees
7 Folksinger Phil
8 Place for swells
9 Poe poem
10 Nile and Mississippi areas
11 Starting lineup
12 Large-scale
13 Right triangle ratio
14 O'Neal-MacGraw film
15 *Tiny Alice* playwright
16 We get on in them
20 Andiron
21 No and J
23 Branding tools
24 Meter feed
30 Male and female
31 "No man is an island" poet
32 Chaplin role
33 Gimlet kin
34 Dialogue writer
35 Timid
36 Hideaways
38 Top honchos
39 Picabo Street, e.g.
41 At the apex
42 Fabric fuzz
43 Olympian aggressor
45 Brought to bay
46 Water-loving weasel
49 Comic Elliott
51 Butterfly or frog, e.g.
53 Youthful passion
54 Original
55 Have to pay
56 Parallel to
58 Old recording star?
59 Slight
60 Take it in stride
61 Mock fanfare
62 Asian tongue
63 *Ora pro* __
64 Billy the Kid, e.g.
65 Track down
66 Gung-ho
67 Run-down
69 Decca or Deutsche Grammophon
70 Scandinavian *santé*
73 In a sweeping fashion
74 Blooper-reel fodder
75 Half a Beatles title
76 Tape dispenser?
80 The sky, sometimes
82 Halloween haul
83 Oxygen eater
84 T and A, e.g.
85 Zones
86 *West Side Story* heroine
87 Kiri Te Kanawa, e.g.
88 Blooming bulb
89 Like Peck's boy
90 Took it on the lam
91 '40s film critic James
92 Certainly not Mr. Cool
93 Rugged cliff
94 Cable TV sports award
97 Easter opener?

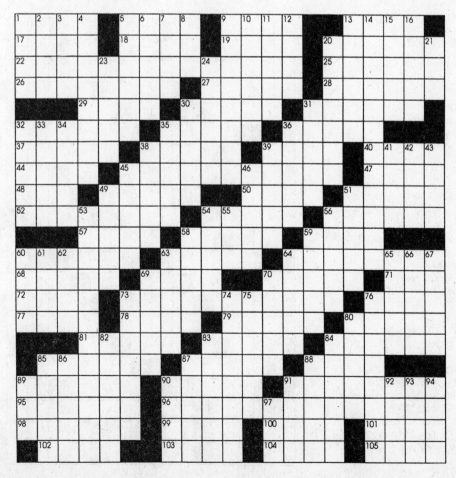

ACROSS

1 Old store counter
7 Ditty
11 Kobe's teammate
15 Nose out
19 Visalia's county
20 Mideast queen
21 Lima and llama land
22 Fridge foray
23 Wagner lovers
26 __ facto
27 Saudis and Iraqis
28 Son-gun link
29 Borscht or bisque
30 Print indelibly
32 "El Paso" cantina owner
33 Eland cousin
34 Pool-table topping
35 Pilgrims' Indian friend
38 Arthur Marx's instrument
40 __ sci.
41 Fairbanks, to friends
42 Ruffle feathers
43 He played it again
46 Mellencamp lovers
49 Indians' home
50 Quonset hut, e.g.
52 Radames' love
53 Flash Gordon villain
54 Risqué
55 Walking __ (elated)
56 II Chronicles follower
57 "No sweat!"
58 Snooze fortieths?
59 Band for a wedding
60 Twelve *meses*
61 Pt. of NATO
62 *Shane* star
63 Danson who married Mary
64 Purcell lovers
69 Base bigwigs
72 Telecommunications unit
74 Crackers, bananas or nuts
75 Give the gun?
76 Closed
77 Teaser ad
79 Rough water
81 Half a Melville title
83 Hospitalers' island
84 Nashville's McEntire
85 Singer Jones or Jackson
86 Something for one to do
87 Talk about you when you're gone?
88 Clerics' vestments
89 Gershwin lovers
92 Dawn deity
93 United __ of America
94 Common tater
95 *Rarae* __ (unusual ones)
96 Bonzo's cousins
98 Nabokov's Lolita
100 Shoot the breeze
101 Playwright Christopher
102 Wisecrack
106 Lewis of "Ellen"
107 Jerusalem Temple site
108 Mystery writer Grafton

109 Bee, Em and Ena
110 Norse narrative
112 Saint-Saëns lovers
116 *The Virginian* writer Wister
117 V.P., e.g.
118 "As 108D as __ in a rug"
119 Barrio store
120 Mangel-wurzel, e.g.
121 Make over
122 Stuffing stuff
123 Confer as a gift

DOWN

1 Flower essence
2 Pack animal
3 The Sundance Kid, e.g.
4 *Algiers* setting
5 Cockney's pains?
6 Salt source
7 Glitch result
8 Lady Chaplin
9 Affirmative action?
10 Chaucer's and Boccaccio's patient one
11 Rain drain
12 Fab Four flick
13 Ender for dull or drunk
14 Ahab's harpooner
15 Susan's daytime character
16 Ravel lovers
17 USO audience
18 Maestro de Waart
24 Like "Married . . . With Children"
25 "That this too too __ flesh . . ."
31 Harbor boat
33 Take rudely
34 *Easy Rider* star
35 Saxophonist Rollins
36 Bridge game part
37 Gives thumbs up to
39 Not quite 76A
40 Put twos and twos together?
41 Toastmaster's place
43 Hurling, curling or birling
44 Palmer, to his army
45 Joplin lovers
47 Buzzing instrument
48 PR concern
49 Saharan
51 Banyan fruit
56 Go no further
57 The Renaissance, e.g.
58 Used to be
60 SOSer's need
61 Unmatched
62 Fugitive's flight
64 Minimum team
65 Surrounded by
66 Carpet fuzz
67 Mover and shaker

68 Stitch or arch ender
70 Expenditures
71 Doesn't go
73 *Amo*, __ . . .
76 Mule of song
77 Big shrimp
78 Pass on
79 Influence
80 Like #4 pencils
81 "Water Lilies" painter
82 Father of the Reo
83 Ponder
85 Chamberlain, infamously
86 Florida plains
87 Catch sight of
90 Boor
91 Like some seals
94 Its sequel was *Ayesha*
97 Calamaries
99 Factory
100 Pancho's pal
101 Fiddle with the facts
103 Not rented
104 Give __ (try)
105 "Applesauce!"
107 Adrian of "T.J. Hooker"
108 Comfy
109 Palliative plant
110 Cry convulsively
111 Knock the socks off
113 Loggers' lopper
114 Atty. assn.
115 Go back down

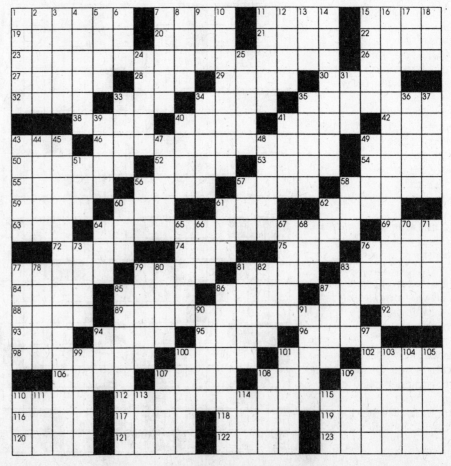

ACROSS

1 Suntan lotion abbr.
4 VCR button
9 Slender hunting dog
15 Thespian Thurman
18 Henbane or horehound
20 Andrea the admiral
21 Harmonious agreement
22 "... _ a lender be"
23 Like Pegasus
24 Vexation examination?
26 Dauphin's dad
27 Wisconsin river
29 What you used to be
30 Estée's competitor
32 Aviary sound
33 The price of freedom
34 Rome's Demeter
35 Gives gloss
37 Exploit
39 Sparta's sometime foe
41 Unspoken
42 Thumb nail?
43 Rob's dad
45 Fable follow-up
47 Massage target
48 Mother-of-pearl
49 Miscellaneous collection
50 José's hurray
51 Brewed beverage
52 Annoying agitation?
56 Old eggs?
57 Takes a plane to Cuba?
59 Father of Phobos
60 Bygone flag symbol
62 Sacred chests
63 Irritable
65 *Vaca*'s mate
66 Trinket
69 Rare-coin rating
70 AWOL's lack
74 Mouth piece
75 Troubled troops?
79 Kung _ chicken
80 What bartenders may
   ask for
81 Strike one as
82 Onionlike veggies
83 Flabbergast
84 What ticks you off
87 DeMille's Delilah
88 What we have
89 Pool-table topper
90 Walk waveringly
92 Not out
93 Marsh plants
94 Reverent
95 Door to ore
97 /
98 Gorgeous guy
100 British quarters
101 Gym or lab gear
105 Bloomers worn 'round
   the neck?

106 Pressured pinniped?
109 Breton or Briton
110 Answer to the Sphinx's
   riddle
111 Follower of Lao-tzu
112 Spain's patron saint
113 Oft-patched part
114 Aesthetic expression
115 Sleek
116 Senator Thurmond
117 August hrs.

DOWN

1 Pillow cover
2 Soccer's "Perla Negra"
3 Hysterical Huxley tome?
4 Cochran and Fisher
5 Café Américain, to Rick
6 A Nova Scotian
   language
7 Give as a source
8 It covers a lot of ground
9 Rice-wrapped fish
10 Adams the
   photographer
11 Lo-cal
12 Take advantage of
13 Like some pickles or delis
14 Meanwhile
15 Chaotic cubicle?
16 Armstrong's landfall

17 "*Vissi d'arte*," e.g.
19 GSUSA member
25 *La Californie* or *La
   Virginie*
28 Convene
31 He follows the news
33 Code B
34 Panamanian port
35 CPI and GNP
36 Czech diacritical
   mark
37 Friday request
38 Neutral color
39 Blubbers
40 Go 50-50
42 To-do items
43 Bailiff's bailiwick
44 Tin Pan or Shubert
46 Bunker's creator
48 Meter feed
52 Cute Little Rascal
53 Headquartered
54 Farmers' 42D
55 Viscounts' superiors
58 Boxer's blow
61 It's heard from the
   herd
63 Used a stopwatch
64 Sharks, to Jets
65 Takes care of loose
   ends?

66 Radar dot
67 Deputies
68 Troubled tennis term?
69 Less bound
70 Jacques, in a round
71 Jittery gridder?
72 Filmy fabric
73 Whetstones
76 Phoenix material
77 Rose Parade feature
78 *Poulet* product
83 WWII comic GI
85 Self-important
86 85D ones
89 'Bama's Bryant
91 Nouveau artist Klimt
92 Locale
93 Curvy course
95 Heeling
96 He went through hell
97 One of Puck's places
98 Mrs. Colin Powell
99 Expensive
100 Go bankrupt
101 _ were
102 House of Lords
   member
103 Glob and gran enders
104 Leave in, after all
107 Incipient seafood
108 Filling sta. operator?

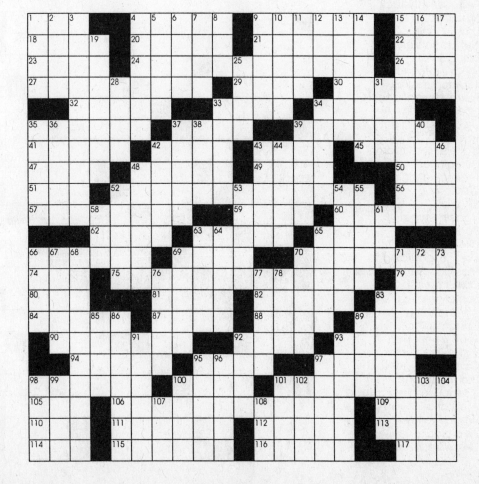

ACROSS

1 Part of a stable family
5 Enemy
8 Sudden pain
12 Story line
16 "The Great George M."
17 Try-square shape
18 "__ far, far better . . ."
19 Words to live by
20 Egglike
21 When French artists kick back?
24 Big or Larry
25 Do the hole thing?
26 Mustang's brakes?
27 Sodium symbols
28 European economic union
30 Killarney's county
31 At a loss for an answer
35 Wax-coated cheese
36 Indian VIP
37 Litmus reddener
38 Bulldog backer
39 Stop procrastinating
41 Winning, in a French pub?
45 Young Cratchit
46 Vespiary denizens
48 Toe the line
49 Chicago stopover
50 8A or 38D
51 Siamese employee, onstage
52 Sign off on
53 Petrol-driven truck
54 Mac input
55 Line-__ veto
56 Net judge's cry
57 Bikini atoll isle
58 What ranters raise
59 16D namesakes
60 French tent pitcher?
64 __ out (withdraw)
67 Do a column right
69 To coach a thief
70 Caltech workroom
71 Humdinger
72 Telemarketing danger
73 Water lily
75 KP, e.g.
76 Vaccine type
77 Bock or Beck's
78 Like poles do it
79 De __ (according to law)
80 Massachusetts university
81 Drink from a bowl
82 Sampling of a French parodist?
85 Pastoral place
86 Tony winner Hagen
87 Without purpose
88 One way to get to the Promised Land
89 It's spoken in Islamabad
91 Antarctic Ocean arm
93 Within the law
95 As a group
98 Like Willie Winkie

99 Arrange
100 Title for Angelico
101 Close
102 French Dolly Levi?
107 Where the toys are
108 Off the ground
109 Little laugh
110 "How was __ know?"
111 A la King?
112 Liability
113 Laver's pitcher
114 Nicotine go-with
115 Of the Gaels

DOWN

1 Double-feature half
2 Lots of French trouble, no?
3 Was a marauder
4 Wind up
5 Cartoon cat
6 Yves' colleague
7 Santa's helper
8 Landing place?
9 Thin in tone
10 Pops the question
11 Ebenezer's expletive
12 Light refractor
13 Was in charge
14 Turkish chamber
15 Diminutive dog
16 Baseball's "Georgia Peach"
18 Spain and Portugal
19 Monet or Debussy
22 In, for now
23 Punctual
25 Like a Carrey character
29 Ho Chi Minh Trail locale
30 Sagal of "Married . . ."
31 Frightening
32 Little French pretenders?
33 She could have danced all night
34 Mint product
36 Sales incentive
37 Solidifying agent
39 Be in store for
40 Twain's pauper Tom
42 Kidded around
43 '59 film __ the Top
44 Drum with fingers
47 Tennis' Shriver
50 Start of Brazilian place names
52 Ken of "L.A. Doctors"
53 Closes an oxford
54 Make i's
57 Horsehead or Crab
58 Like Dorothy's slippers
60 Escort's offering
61 Out of style
62 Mice or men
63 Mix flick
65 Part of a service

66 Oklahoma city
68 Nasser's org.
71 Mary's TV boss
72 Defunct treaty org.
73 Kenzle of "Mad About You"
74 Nashville songfest
75 Of the highest peer
77 Out-of-focus object
78 Atone for
79 Veracruz capital
80 Time in office
82 Most Solomonlike
83 Peanut, e.g.
84 Big fish in a small can
90 100-meter runner
92 Gulliver's creator
93 Con __ (like café olé?)
94 Old number?
95 One way to get to first base
96 "Wake Up Little __"
97 Leather addition
99 One-pot meal
100 Greek salad cheese
102 Inflate the expense account
103 Heady brew
104 Laura Petrie's hubby
105 Got fed up?
106 Medic's bag
107 2.0 GPA

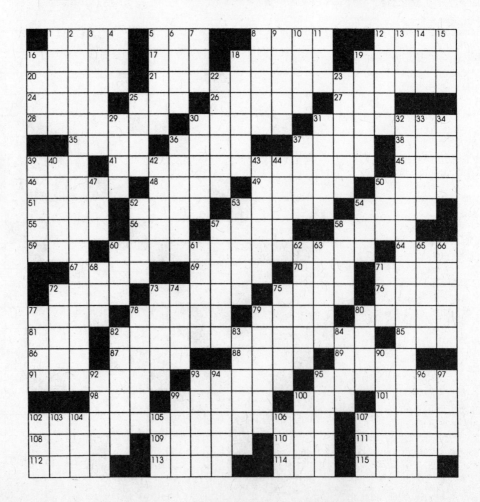

ACROSS

1 Very French?
5 "__ talk?"
10 Entrain or enplane
15 Took the gold
18 Make smart?
19 Egglike
20 Before best or punch
21 Clean-air gp.
22 Colleague of Hap and Ike
23 Oregon
25 Vegas put-down?
26 "Dick Van Dyke Show" co-star
28 Of cities
29 Wilson or McKinley
31 Verbal comebacks
32 Bend a bit
33 Kind of values
34 Gloucester catch
35 Diaphanous
36 Apt
37 J.S. or P.D.Q.
40 Palate part
42 Certain scout's find
43 Pvt. pension plan
44 Famed American orator
48 Small amount
51 California red wine
53 "Mairzy __"
54 __ En-lai
55 Underwear material
56 ". . . but __ chosen"
58 Queeg captained it
59 Word of warning
61 Deserve
62 New Math term
63 Foe
64 Major German port
66 Scandinavian sea
68 An option for Hamlet
69 Melancholy
70 Creating clergy
73 Strike dumb
74 Clive Bell says it "is not necessarily true"
77 Loserless game
78 Ornamented band
80 Anaheim athlete
81 Force unit
82 Hawthorne's Hester
83 Ingrid's last role
85 Monarch, to Monique
87 Flexible
88 Kind of soprano
89 Contract provisos
93 Serengeti scavenger
94 Tokyo main drag
95 They're in clover
97 ". . . kerchief, and __ my cap"
98 Fabian Society leader
101 Fight-night highlight
102 It makes connections
103 Uncle Tom's nemesis
104 Lint trap?
105 Pronoun for 56D
106 Longs, for short
107 "That's someone __ problem"
108 Fashion-consciousness
109 Hound sound

DOWN

1 Thunder god
2 It's quickly spread
3 Make a clean slate
4 Make a limo longer
5 Yellowbelly
6 Turn away
7 *Ora pro* __
8 Nora, to Nick
9 Conductor de Waart
10 Table clearer
11 Ready to pour
12 First *jardinero*?
13 Turn state's evidence
14 Indigo manufacturer
15 '85 Starship hit
16 For all to see
17 Cooper's Bumppo
20 Senator Thurmond
24 Horse opera heavy
27 Kine word?
30 Dark clouds, perhaps
32 Window base
33 TV's X, e.g.
35 Petrol, for lorries
36 Coffeehouse standard
37 Show, for one
38 Shipper Onassis
39 '29 Warburg-Smith tune
40 Negate
41 Asian communist
42 Ukase issuer
44 Milk-producing plant
45 Assist or attend ender
46 Dickens' Drood
47 Dinghy or dory
49 Top-notch
50 Something one can't do
52 Bowling unit
54 Log lodge
56 French female
57 Prior, to poets
58 Adorable one
59 __ carotene
60 Once it was enough
61 Persian word?
62 Tito, for one
64 Mark a trail
65 One way to learn
66 *Quel fromage!*
67 Des Moines neighbor
69 Flemish town
70 One of Chekhov's three sisters
71 Diarist Anaïs
72 Directive to Dobbin
74 Still up for grabs
75 *The Human Comedy* writer
76 Conductor Akiro
79 Meg or Nolan
81 Emulate Adam and Eve
82 Working at a trade
83 Categories
84 Harriet's hubby
85 Speak nonlinearly
86 Lord's Prayer start
87 Lab vessel
88 Anglican headdress
89 "American Pie" car
90 Retailer's brand
91 *Élève's* locale
92 Jolly Roger part
94 Jokes or chokes
95 Go after flies, or hit them
96 Dance component
99 Foray for morays
100 Nus to you

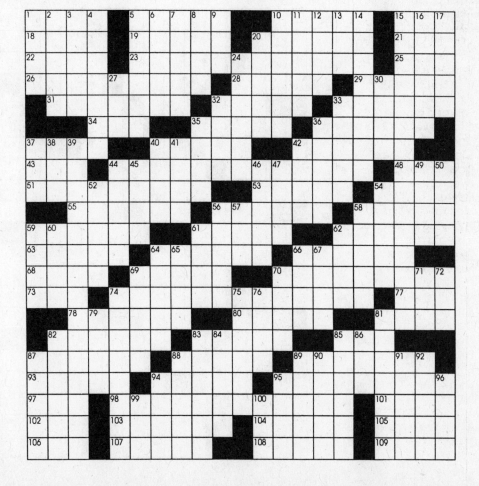

ACROSS

1 Key letter
4 "Olde" emporium
10 Land at sea?
15 Spielberg smash
19 Silver of the screen
20 Sci-fi writer Ellison
21 Love affair
22 Jamb closer
23 "Batman" sound
24 Deluxe diapers?
26 Bric-a-__
27 Hard-line
29 Nashville attraction
30 Warm, in a way
31 Nicaraguan natives
32 Control
33 Like the Cyclops
35 "I'm __ and singin' in the rain"
37 Chaplin *Gold Rush* meal?
39 Restore free speech to
40 "__ live in a yellow . . ."
42 Thickening things
43 They often have it
44 Great Dame?
45 Flash light
47 SSNs, sometimes
50 Trail the pack
51 Contemplative TV dad?
53 Entertainer Peeples
54 Trial separation?
56 Turner's machine
57 ". . . for __ good men"
58 Jagger's group
60 Slender wineglass
62 Like Amos?
64 F in music?
65 Fall for a crooner?
67 Of the eye
69 Dada pioneer
70 Gladiator tourney?
74 Blade the blades
77 Aye, ashore
78 Expressionist Mark
79 Morrison's group
80 Four Tops leader Stubbs
81 It means milk
82 Walk destination
83 More ominous
84 Last bill you'll ever pay?
89 Bats' bailiwick
90 She has lots to show you
91 It can take a shuttle
92 Costa Rican volcano
94 Fragrant iris root
95 Earth sci.
96 Stuff in the Smithsonian
99 Nice night?
100 *Star Wars* aggressor?
103 Carnivore's craw
104 Mind find
105 Manila hemp
106 "You'd Be So __ Love"
107 Century 21 rival
108 Lewis' Timberlane
109 Erik of ballet
110 Size up
111 Firmament

DOWN

1 Money players
2 Owl's yowl
3 Organized trespassers?
4 Wing-ding
5 "__ there" ("Don't give up")
6 Gluck opera __ *ed Euridice*
7 Maps out
8 Huff and puff
9 SASE, e.g.
10 Cloudy rounded patch
11 Istanbul inn
12 Broadway trophy
13 Drop from the team
14 Many mins.
15 Out of work
16 Watercourse
17 Equivocate
18 Leave the Union
25 "__ be the first to know"
28 Conquerees of 1533
30 His job is a snap
32 Ruffled feathers
33 "I'm just a prisoner __"
34 Theban queen
35 Like some carburetors
36 Author Seton
37 Jamie of "M*A*S*H"
38 Harpo Productions honcho
40 Stuns
41 Guesses at LAX
44 Compass pts.
45 Bed board
46 Pierre's pate
47 Kiss-and-tell exes?
48 Gaul's god
49 Tools with teeth
51 Cool with cubes
52 French abbey town
55 Wind up
57 Org. for Doogie Howser
58 Do in
59 Ripped or zipped
60 People
61 Oaxaca wolf
62 Controversial coverings
63 One of Rita's exes
65 Kids' caretaker
66 "Yippee!"
67 Spanish eyes
68 Actor Jurgens
70 Hallmarks
71 Fighter Marciano's real first name
72 Way of saying things
73 Cheers regular
75 Exceeding
76 Sinewy
80 Sachet scent
81 Nymphets, per Nabokov
82 "What a __ am!"
83 Actor Robert's family
84 Tongue-in-cheek
85 Poet Pablo
86 Is different
87 Chevy Chase character
88 James of "Star Trek"
89 Flat-topped toppers
92 Accumulate
93 Go back to blonde
95 Writer Shirley Ann __
96 Gardner namesakes
97 Stool pigeon
98 Putting position
100 Smidgeon
101 Like college dicts.
102 PBS benefactor

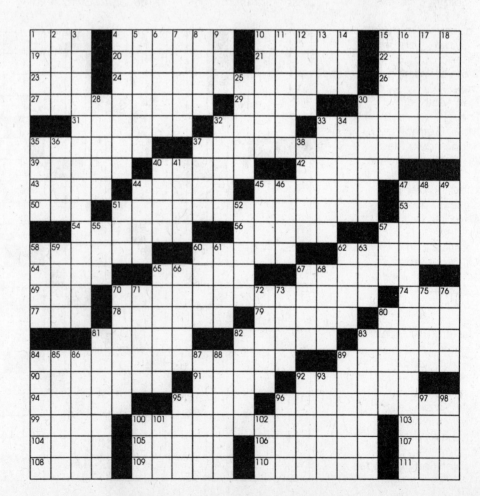

ACROSS

1 Prosecutor's problem
6 Lewd look
10 Go into depth?
14 Sun-worshipper's deity
18 Most of North Africa
19 Disturb
20 Type of rug or code
21 Rosalind of *The Joy Luck Club*
22 BRIEFS
25 Bovine bunch
26 Other than this
27 Hard labor
28 Juniper juice
29 Car or truck
31 We, *oui?*
32 Barley bristle
33 Edna St. Vincent __
35 Everything, in Essen
36 Med school teachers
37 SHORTS
39 Dietrich's Marlene
40 "My Gal __"
41 Chopin's Concerto __ Minor
42 Thumbs-up vote
44 Make-meet middle
47 Counterfeit
50 TV's T
52 Skillful lawmaker
54 Call it quits
55 *The Good Earth* character
56 DRESSES
59 Eggs pluribus?
60 CD holder's record
62 Lifeline locale
63 Before city or circle
65 Como or Mason
66 Barcelona beach
68 Praise
70 __ la vista
72 Settled
73 Turned off the sound
76 Strip bark?
77 HOSE
82 Broad bean
83 Matterhorn matter
85 Corday's victim
86 Verve
87 In the cards
88 Sabra dance
89 "__ my brother's keeper?"
90 Quilters' party
91 Use a tuffet
92 Air-cond. spec
94 JACKET
99 Fuse-box unit
102 Female zebras
104 Massages
105 Gridiron's Grange
106 Danube tributary
107 Thoreau's essayist friend
109 In the thick of
110 Enterprise android
111 Dry Spanish sherry
112 Use an old phone
113 BELT
117 A big fan of
118 Chester __ Arthur
119 Alaskan port
120 Commendation oration
121 Great Lakes salmon
122 Law degs.
123 Worth a B
124 Dig down deep

DOWN

1 Reception room
2 Short-tailed monkey
3 Saharan stopovers
4 It's of miner concern
5 Ship's overhang
6 Important Roman family name
7 Successful slap shot
8 Lille lily
9 Hard to pin down
10 What DJs may do
11 Lyricist Gershwin
12 Brash
13 Danny, Sammy or Stubby
14 Hector's feller
15 SOCKS
16 "College Bowl" host Robert
17 Stem joints
18 Pay out
23 Revelers paint it red
24 Bamako is its capital
30 Onetime English Leather rival __ Karate
33 Impressionist Claude
34 Refuge
37 Some are grand
38 Leon Uris' __ 18
39 Debark
40 L.A. Strip
43 Many millennia
45 Peace proponent
46 Sail support
47 Charlie Parker's genre
48 Schnozz extension
49 PANTS
50 Where 14D died
51 Shrieker's sound
52 What rulers hold
53 Alley Oop's girl
56 Craggy crest
57 Baby oysters
58 Point of view
61 Toot your own horn
64 Skim
66 Accused's answer
67 Washday residue
68 Potter's purchase
69 Minuscule suffix?
70 Ort meal
71 It flows through Florence
72 Rocky's wife
73 Mineral spring
74 Twelve hours from morn
75 Unc's bro
78 Latin lesson word
79 Smash into
80 Swarms
81 Waugh or Wilder
84 Downfall
87 Oregon state tree
90 Just developing
91 Made staid
93 Naval initials
95 French race course
96 Split, slangily
97 Was valedictorian
98 Kill a bill
99 Isaac of sci-fi
100 Get by
101 Stand-in
102 Front-line physician
103 Containing NH_2
104 Small round hill
106 Beatles' "If __"
108 Squished circle
110 CD for a DJ
114 Bounder
115 Griffith Park attraction
116 Tint

ACROSS

1 Sunday service
5 Volume setting?
10 Room at the top?
14 Mom's mom
18 Side by side?
19 Speaker's prop
20 Emanations
22 Subterfuge
23 Hose holder
24 Playful deer's cry?
26 Freshly
27 Ms. Gardner's namesakes
29 Fly apart
30 Contest the ruling
32 Solomon's forte
35 Cremona craftsman
37 Deseret, today
38 Modern musician Brian
39 Deer UC site?
43 A Sprat preference
46 Draw forth
48 Conger catcher
49 Memorable actress Sharon's kin
50 Enzyme ending
51 Joan of Art
52 Dermal defect
53 Normandy battle town
54 Use a natatorium
55 Iran's Bani-__
56 Hooves?
60 Take __ (snooze)
61 Computer-connected
63 Dance's Ruth Saint __
64 At an angle
66 Ledger items
67 Annie of "Designing Women"
68 Desi Arnaz and 71D
69 Fiesta *noche*, often
70 Twist or stomp
71 The Lusitania's line
72 Bodybuilder's exercise
73 Sincerely woodsy?
76 "__ the Sun in the Morning"
79 Second generation member
80 Nabisco nibble
81 Sufferer's suffix
82 Chalet feature
83 Grazing ground
84 Beany's buddy
86 Dasher's master
88 Let on or let in
89 Check the check
90 Main deer drag?
93 L.A.-N.Y. flight path
94 Melville title part
95 Song's lead-in
96 Excites
98 Tenor Enrico
101 Asian mountain system
103 Cools with cubes
104 The least little thing
105 Composer Peter Schickele's antler ego?
109 It grows on you
113 Go hither and thither
114 Oozy muck
115 An archangel
116 Curtain color
117 Nimble
118 In a bit
119 With time to spare
120 Stationery quantity

DOWN

1 Besmirch
2 Is multiplied?
3 "*Comprende?*"
4 Bar food
5 Big Bird's street
6 Panama and pillbox
7 Philharmonic name part
8 Drumstick
9 Insect-repelling plant
10 Coconut oil acid
11 Thine and mine
12 Be a worrywart
13 Chi preceder
14 Where axes cross
15 Letter from long ago
16 Out of the harbor
17 Whimper
21 It's carved in stone
25 Peripheral
28 Viva __ (orally)
31 Go by Go
32 Bandleader Ted
33 Home to one in six humans
34 Deer's staff of life?
35 Pennsylvania, in Washington
36 Jim Ryun, e.g.
37 Writer Sinclair
40 Search missions
41 __ time (now)
42 Timbuktu residents
43 Deer diversions?
44 Omsk and Tomsk natives
45 Lure
47 Hokey
52 In __ pique
53 South Carolina river
54 On the payroll
57 It means tooth
58 Command to Fido
59 Intimidates
62 Pot top
65 Suffragist's initials
66 Applied plaster
67 Samuel Richardson novel
68 Amicus __ (friend of the court)
69 Milan's La __
70 Simple column style
71 Batista foe
74 Bullwinkle's pal
75 Pay tribute to
77 Like ewe?
78 Lyons heads
84 Captains of industry
85 They're bent in bars
86 Moses' mountain
87 Tiffany lamp, e.g.
88 Amaryllis relative
91 Fingerless glove
92 In roguish fashion
94 It's wrapped in Egypt
97 Music Center employee
98 Geos and Reos
99 At the apex
100 Sound of the '20s?
101 "You could hear __ drop"
102 Wheels of fortune?
103 Scand. country
106 Carte start
107 Bosom companion?
108 Vacuum's lack
110 Jim's Ventura
111 A CPA might recommend one
112 Planter's punch punch

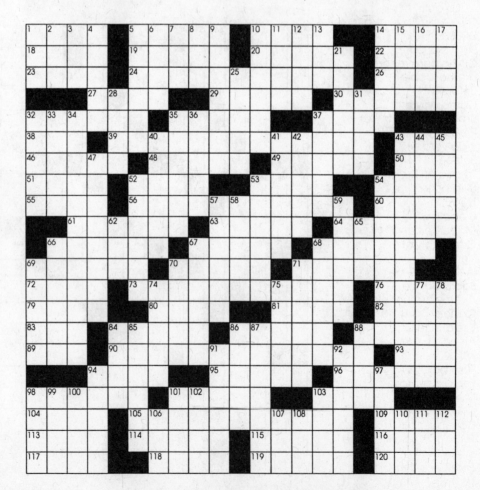

ACROSS

1 From front to back
5 Sit in the sidecar
9 Uppercase letters
13 D.C. subway
18 Pot for a *podrida*
19 Wax histrionic
21 Unctuous
22 Playwright Fugard
23 Miller's tale about Willy Oweman?
26 Literary motif
27 Too large
28 Spa near Lake Geneva
29 Rural crossings
30 Actress Skye
31 Bloodhound's cue
32 Gracias, in Grasse
33 Actress Kidman
36 Homeowner's holding
37 Handwoven hanging
40 Q.E.D. center
41 Conscience-stricken
42 *Salome* songs
43 Place-kicker's prop
44 Unburden
45 Runyonesque masked musical?
48 Thompson of "Caroline in the City"
49 "Give Peace a Chance" figure
50 Of one of Chekhov's three sisters
51 Wind and will preceders
52 Nuisance
53 Sex Pistols' "__ in the U.K."
55 "Peanuts" part
57 Places to schuss
59 Pinnacles
60 Cutlass kin
61 Smidgen
62 Composer Gustav
64 Used Elmer's
65 Way to LAX
67 Hunt's "__ ben Adhem"
68 Actress Nettleton
69 Biblical verb
70 Cray or pay suffix
72 Fat or fraidy follower
73 Simon's overwhelming comedy?
77 Marked a spot
78 New newt
79 "__ la!" (Gallic "wow")
80 Get on the soapbox
81 __ cava
82 Pavlov's bell, e.g.
84 Complaint
85 Augustus or Julius
87 *Sunset Blvd.* name
88 Devoutness
89 Ort meal
90 Legendary nitery
92 Wynonna's mom
93 "Time" piece
97 Early Sooners
98 With *The*, Wasserstein's Caribbean account?
101 Promote
102 "If This __ Love"
103 :), on-line
104 Stolen stuff
105 Winnows
106 El __, Texas
107 Comply with
108 *Show Boat* author Ferber

DOWN

1 Numbskull
2 Alt.
3 Czech river
4 Hancock or Hale
5 Prune and polish
6 Figure of speech
7 Spanish pair
8 Character in *The Iliad*?
9 Right triangle ratio
10 Target
11 Blueprint
12 Antonym ant.
13 Sleep on it
14 Codes of conduct
15 Hellman's flowery drama?
16 Carthage's nemesis
17 Music to toreadors' ears
20 Oedipus' complex counterpart?
24 Old Greek coin
25 Reading expert Wood
29 Calyx leaf
31 Fathers foals
32 Pushes the envelope?
33 Tiber tyrant
34 *Three Sisters* sister
35 Williams' rotter drama?
36 "That is __" ("I mean")
37 Danish dwarf
38 Campanella teammate
39 1923 literary Nobelist
41 Sounds of relief
42 Theater's Stella or Luther
45 Singer Eydie
46 Duodenal problem
47 Ate at eight
52 Fence support
54 First Amendment lobby
55 VCR button
56 Face on a fin
57 Jolly Roger part
58 Singer Lenya
60 Guardian Angels founder Curtis
61 Form
62 Attacks with spray
63 Sternward
64 Soccer scores
65 *On the Beach* author
66 Actress Verdugo
68 Hawaiian hardwood tree
69 Requiring rinsing
71 Purim's month
73 Grayline passengers
74 Celeste and Ian
75 Scale starters
76 Siskel and Ebert
81 Matter for the DMV
83 Unpretentious
84 Florentine painter
85 Gleason co-star
86 Spumante source
88 Perfectionists take them
89 Caucasian, to Polynesians
90 Has a bawl?
91 Yours, in Tours
92 Viking launcher
94 Doofus
95 Trotsky or Uris
96 Valencian verb
98 Street-smart
99 Care-limiting gp.
100 Spare part?

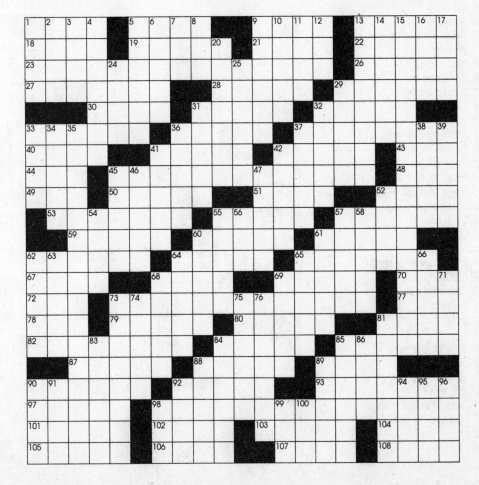

ACROSS

1 Romans preceder
5 Oafs
10 KGB counterpart
13 Baby food
16 Kegler's consolation
17 Sugarcoated nut
18 Get out of office
19 Before this time
20 Cold mold
21 Y
24 Lo or chow follower
25 Make noise in bed
26 Mayberry moppet
27 Isn't ungrammatical?
28 Baja border town
30 Maestro Kostelanetz
32 Walks wearily
33 Whiffenpoof word
35 Escort's offering
36 Mame's onus
37 Ultralight wood
38 The whole shebang
39 Y
42 Vanity fare
43 Like haunted houses
45 Big bang causer
46 Job-hunter's edges
47 Bar man?
51 RFK foe
52 Orff's *Carmina __*
54 Darlin'
55 Acapulco gold
56 Deborah's *King and I* co-star
57 Muscateer?
58 Paradise paradigm
60 Jupiter's mate
61 Deep-dish dishes
63 Y
65 Element element
66 Seven Hills city
67 Type of prof
68 Prop for Groucho
69 Hwy. through Malibu
70 Fleecy female
71 Coal hole
72 Cure
73 High rooms
76 Birth-control pioneer
78 ASCAP rival
80 Potential pike
81 Noh kin
82 Bolshevik
83 Y
86 Sodom survivor
87 "Well done!"
89 Mythical nymph
90 3-3, e.g.
91 Baton Rouge inst.
92 Use the egress
93 On __ and a prayer
94 Liberate
97 Amount to be raised?

98 Golfo de México contents
99 "Look away" song
100 Chops meat?
103 Y
107 Copland ballet score
108 Back burner?
109 Skin growths
110 Peruvian mammal
111 Domingo's domain
112 Bit of a joule
113 Nonprofessional
114 Propose as explanation
115 Had been

DOWN

1 Vaulted choir cover
2 Y
3 Lopez or Alvarado
4 Champagne choice
5 Sing like Bing
6 1944 Gene Tierney title role
7 Forest grump?
8 Telephone trio
9 Salerno six
10 Adorable one
11 Dot on a map
12 Had haddock
13 BBQ milieux
14 Docket

15 PC interface jacks
16 Ted, on "Cheers"
17 Power generator
18 Fish-eating hawks
22 Colorful cager
23 Wicked material?
25 Suddenly churlish
29 1973 film *The Day of the __*
30 TV E.T.
31 Music teacher Boulanger
32 Hedonist
33 Wild party
34 Kal Kan competitor
36 Field of flowers
37 Fit in
40 Loggers' leavings
41 Mesmerized
44 Coming in handy
48 Y
49 Cubist Rubik
50 Motel module
52 Puffery part
53 Caroline, to Ted
54 Hudson or Ford
58 Longtime soap "The __ Night"
59 Royal headband
60 Esau's brother
61 Veep's boss

62 Hawkeye's home
63 Head set?
64 Genesis hunter
69 Participant
71 Miff
72 "He is __"
74 Ring refs' calls
75 In __ (in the original place)
77 Road covering
78 Bigger pictures
79 Pop singer Carey
81 Darin hit "Mack the __"
84 Mattress appendage
85 #1 Hun
87 1959 film that won eleven Oscars
88 PG, e.g.
92 Backslide
93 Ecstasy opposite
94 Mideast peninsula
95 Precise
96 Run for your wife?
98 Out of the harbor
99 Pickpockets
101 Like a bagatelle?
102 Serpentine squeezer
104 Echolocation user
105 Speak Pekingese?
106 Mrs. Andy Capp
107 Corny line?

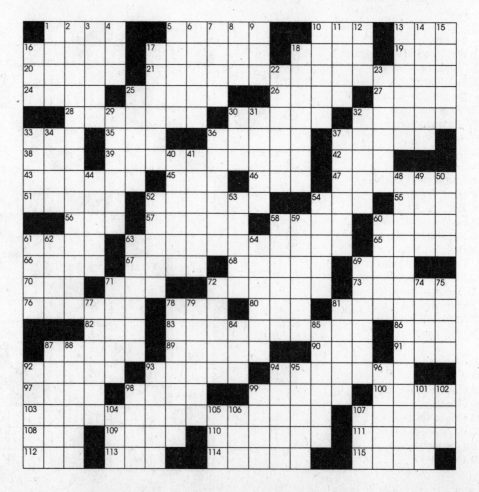

ACROSS

1 Durango dinero
6 Morse T
10 Vonnegut or Weill
14 Air apparent?
18 Go from medium to small
19 Contrarian
20 *Night* author Wiesel
21 "__ My Heart"
22 From break-table snacks
25 Labor Dept. arm
26 Live on the edge?
27 Use a missal
28 Fifth-century invader
29 Professionally moral
31 Needle pts.
32 Lizzie's makeup?
33 Low dice rolls
35 Bridge bonanzas
36 Rested the feet
37 From a honeymoon haven
39 Now, on "ER"
40 Mistletoe mo.
41 SRO show
42 Pooch, parrot or Persian
44 Crawford's ex
47 *Fiddler* fellow
50 Swing a sickle
52 Pilfer
54 Tighten copy
55 Saudi or Iraqi
56 From a battle cry
59 Rutherford or Harding
60 San Mateo County city
62 Take notice
63 Raccoon family member
65 Lead the way
66 Get an out-of-state license?
68 Muslim paradise feature
70 Kinky character
72 "Art of Love" poet
73 Vinegar variety
76 Nev. neighbor
77 From an H.G. Wells tome
82 Bear with a soft bed
83 Iodine source
85 Like loads
86 *Rocky III* boxer Clubber __
87 Hemingway heroine
88 Noodle topping?
89 Rocky pinnacle
90 Note dropped from 49 Down
91 1040 people
92 Get hot under the collar
94 From an Eastwood flick
99 Behold
102 Make a point
104 Plain toast?
105 Cat tail?
106 Fender dent
107 Coleridge's was ancient
109 "__ Blue?"
110 Eurasian river
111 Pop of rock
112 Spots for teens?
113 From a love match
117 Barking place?
118 Like bucks and boars
119 Stickums
120 MOCA tour leader
121 Qualifying race
122 In the thick of
123 Window frame
124 Break the bank?

DOWN

1 Fear
2 City WSW of Leipzig
3 Strains
4 Long-distance call start
5 Doubting Thomas
6 Vietnam battle site
7 Gump or Griffith
8 Queue before V
9 Snobbish
10 Barking lot?
11 Inuit's knife
12 Priest's duties
13 Cricket event
14 Produce manager's concern
15 From a cow or a cat
16 Old Irish alphabet
17 Successful slap shots
18 Heaps or lots
23 Horne solo
24 Throw
30 FDR follower
33 Menudo base
34 Caught sight of
37 Maiden name preceder
38 Queequeg's captain
39 Pipe part
40 Folkloric demon
43 Anti-smog gp.
45 It provides zest
46 Ante up?
47 Prof's aides
48 Christian, e.g.
49 From a Golden State tourist town
50 It's put before Descartes
51 Comic Philips
52 Aerobics prop
53 "Yippee!"
56 Woodstock stuff
57 TV's Ms. Morgenstern
58 Singular opera?
61 Brannigan
64 Brut rival
66 On any occasion
67 Lifesaver flavor
68 Put up paintings
69 *La fiesta brava* cry
70 Monotheistic Indian
71 Birth of a notion
72 Ender for ect, end, mes or pseud
73 Coal holder
74 "__ Yankee Doodle Dandy"
75 Packard, but not Hewlett
78 Detest
79 Tokyo, once
80 Becomes too much of a good thing
81 Fifty-fifty share
84 Having satyriasis
87 __-owned (second-hand)
90 Orchestra section
91 Collapse to the center
93 Boyz II —
95 Had a little lamb?
96 Rig on the road
97 Attack
98 Teheran tender
99 Exhaled audibly
100 V-8, for one
101 Boutros-Ghali's homeland
102 Tennis put-away
103 Hidden hoard
104 Best of the best
106 Strobe-lit club
108 Austen opus
110 "X-Files" topic
114 Former ring king
115 Malabar Coast port
116 Additionally not

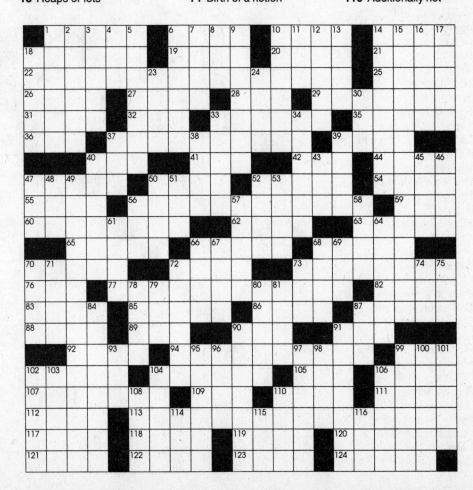

ACROSS

1 Unaltered
5 __ la vista
10 Flung or fetched opener
13 Union members
19 Film fragment
20 Blood of the gods
21 Sign on a summer house?
22 Jughead's pal
23 Avocados
26 Happening lately
27 Guinevere's lover
28 Aparicio or Tiant
29 Analyzes sentences
30 It makes a shade of difference
31 Done, to Donne
32 It's good for knotting
34 Process leather again
35 1960s "Bella Linda" band
37 Gelderland commune
38 Foot docs' org.
41 Prancer pulls one
44 Sharp-tongued
45 Trudge
46 Kith kith
47 Birdie beater
48 Shed tears
49 Prep for the game
51 It goes with the floe
52 GI absentee
53 Hollywood Golden Age actress
55 Of Benedict
56 Blue books
57 Flower forerunners
58 Unlike eternity
59 Train trailer
63 Foppish fellow
65 Tout
66 Long-legged shorebird
67 TV's T
68 Clematis, e.g.
69 Beatles' "A Hard Day's __"
70 He bunched the Bradys
73 Ring out
77 Most cubmasters
78 Specialty
79 Alley Oop's girl
80 Class conehead?
81 Give __ whirl
82 Babe in the woods
83 Odets contemporary
84 Don't keep in memory
85 Leo's lair
86 Monkees' "__ Believer"
87 Muscle car, often
90 "That's __ me!"
92 See 84 Across
93 Dawn deity
94 Name for a cook?
97 London Bridge site Lake __ City
99 Thompson of TV's "Family"

100 Broker's business
102 Solvang neighbor Los __
103 Insincere sobs
106 Remember
107 Pronoun for you and me
108 "__ thy father and thy mother"
109 Of the Gaels
110 Designer Laura
111 Papers the house
112 Converges
113 Mob scene

DOWN

1 Get really steamed
2 Ease
3 Christopher Robin's father
4 Heroic saga
5 Miami racetrack
6 Walken and Danson
7 Carom or masse
8 Bare peak
9 Dadaist Jean
10 Show off
11 Homes on high
12 "Friends" role
13 Trojan War Lycian leader
14 Grabbed the tab
15 West African capital
16 1948 de Havilland drama
17 Aachen article

18 Square-dance units
24 With 25 Down, Silas Marner writer
25 See 24 Down
32 Golf hazards
33 Value
34 What the trick candle did
35 Country singer Vince
36 Ferry tail?
39 CD bootlegger
40 Catfish hunter
41 The Tyrrhenian, e.g.
42 Jurisprudence
43 Chutzpah source
45 Long shots?
48 It could be hard, soft or flat
49 Impact sound
50 Giuliani, to pals
51 Places off-limits
53 The majority
54 Dogpatch dude
55 Meerschaum
56 Angelou, e.g.
58 Render a verdict
59 Like Funt's camera
60 Ply the sky
61 Paper Moon director
62 Folksinger Phil
63 Credit card result
64 Aweather's opposite

65 "__ Yellow Ribbon 'Round . . ."
67 Unable to decide
68 1930s screen legend Lupe
70 Martin's TV partner
71 Salad servers
72 Dangerously out of control
73 Sound from an Angora
74 UK part
75 Perfect service
76 Imperfect service
78 In a superlative way
80 "It just __ get any better"
82 Tuscan town
83 Stern with a bow
84 FTD delivery
87 Get ready
88 Passions
89 Fanatic
91 Maritime
94 Lamb Chop's handler
95 Human trunk
96 Underdog's dream
97 Part of a dia
98 Malt brews
99 Loch Lomond local
100 Turpentine source
101 Crystal gazer
104 Bit of resistance
105 Deer dear

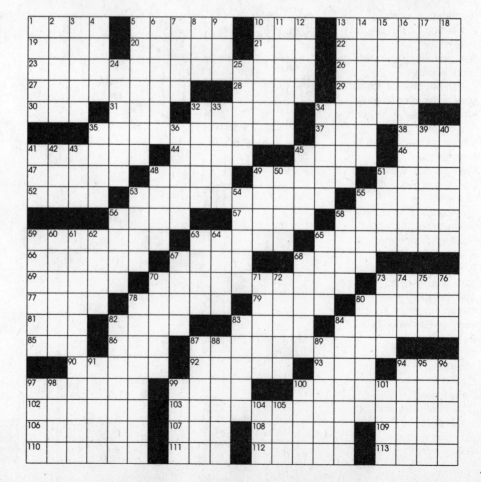

ACROSS

1 Word below 120 Across
5 Elbowroom
10 Table mountain
14 Put out candles
18 Jon Arbuckle's pooch
19 Its towers were topless
20 Beth's preceder
22 Walesa
23 Band of baddies
24 Spoiled deejay?
26 In times past
27 Napoleon and Josephine, briefly
29 *Feliz año* __
30 "Nerts!"
32 Comics captain
35 Plumed hat
37 Pillow cover
38 Director Grosbard
39 Authority's artifice?
43 Educational inst.
46 Time being
48 "Get Happy" composer
49 "This is between __ them"
50 Money for an AARP member
51 Get in here
52 Seed enclosure
53 Pluto or demo ender
54 Fancy fastener
55 Lowdown
56 Realizes rapture?
60 Be an also-ran
61 Washington airport
63 Piece maker
64 Heavy herbivores
66 Profession
67 *The Crucible* setting
68 __ grâce
69 Couch potato's control
70 Wise ones
71 Kick out
72 Ragnarok ruler
73 Try to hate?
76 Away yonder
79 Spanky and Alfalfa
80 It's controlled in Washington
81 Dodge trucks
82 Evening in Eboli
83 Right-angle shape
84 Prove innocent
86 Hindu mystic
88 *The Maids* writer
89 L.A.-S.D. direction
90 Stylishly corrupt?
93 __-Cat (winter vehicle)
94 __ San Lucas
95 Having flaps
96 Like Hyundais
98 Composure
101 Mutton cut
103 Manger visitors
104 Bluesy trumpet effect

105 Fight to pay costs?
109 Overcast
113 To boot
114 It takes a bit
115 Carrier's beat
116 Upsize
117 Calendar capacity
118 Mule team?
119 The going rate
120 What hang in hanging ten

DOWN

1 Pointer or pinscher
2 Turkish chamber
3 Finish in front
4 Arid Israeli area
5 A piece of cake
6 A positive sign
7 Inflation cause
8 Paperless pooch
9 Come from the source
10 "That's what little boys are __"
11 Ht.
12 Dry, in Durango
13 Shrinks' gp.
14 Jack Benny theme "Love in __"
15 Big star at night
16 "__ homo"

17 Curds complement
21 Half a dash
25 Whitehorse is its capital
28 Early Persian
31 Case or core lead-in
32 *Sic transit gloria* __
33 Crazy as __
34 Standard epic movie?
35 "ER," e.g.
36 Hamburger and Pork Chop
37 Scythe's sweep
40 Lifelong job
41 Insistence on perfection
42 Tribe from Missouri
43 Be ambivalent about military spending?
44 First to cry "TGIF"?
45 Lethe locale
47 Salad bar sprinkle
52 In Morpheus' arms
53 *Fierce Creatures*' John
54 Book protector
57 Mythical menace
58 Forayed for morays
59 Certain cutthroats
62 Ignited
65 Illyria invader
66 Bronze Star and Purple Heart
67 Juvenal's genre

68 Universal
69 They're stranded
70 Mar. 17 honoree
71 Left the Enterprise
74 "No __ talk to me": Housman
75 GATT concern
77 Theater-in-the-round
78 Betray
84 Pull an all-nighter
85 Hit over the head?
86 Get straight
87 Most ants
88 Tar's toddy
91 Almost
92 Green-lighted
94 Some roses' is red
97 Untilt
98 Putting position
99 Far from florid
100 Sax-playing Simpson
101 Work the wok
102 Navigation station
103 Aussie's buddy
106 Powerful PAC
107 Popinjay
108 Have misgivings about
110 Start of three John Wayne titles
111 What "will be" will be
112 Sportscaster's shout

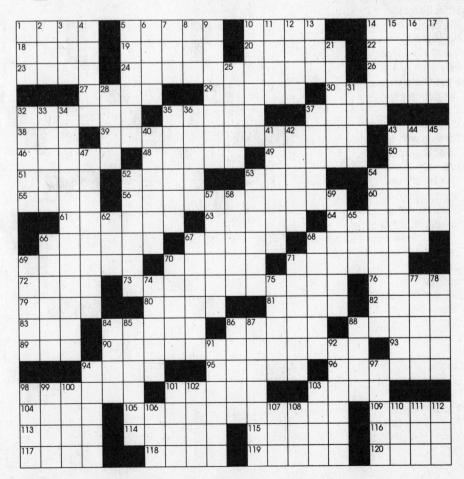

ACROSS

1 Wasn't colorfast
5 You put them into your food
10 Dip chip
15 Monks' titles
19 County south of Colusa
20 Reynolds competitor
21 __ wintergreen
22 Seat at bridge, or anagrams
23 Big deal in the Coral Sea
26 Isinglass
27 Ointment, per MD's
28 Burundi Bantu-speaker
29 Uses a stopwatch
30 All squished
32 Spring ring thing
34 1995 Horse of the Year
35 Midwest air hub
36 History-text chapter
37 "Man at the Crossroads" artist Ben
38 Place of seclusion
41 Cronus or Oceanus
44 Big deal on the slopes
46 "Scots wha __ . . .": Burns
47 They're big in Hollywood
48 Billboard
49 Leave unmentioned
50 __-majesté (detraction to dignity)
51 Litter bearer
52 Big deal in cartoons
56 Fills fully
57 Vocal vibrations
59 Filly filler
60 Eyes like pies, e.g.
61 Transfer a plant
62 Tim of *Annie*
63 It's heard in a herd
64 Puts up with
66 Eclectic mixture
67 Aromatic
70 Like legal pads
71 Big deal in romantic songs
74 Likewise not
75 Spirogyra, for one
76 __-dieu (kneeling bench)
77 Totes that barge
78 Court order
79 Bat stat
80 Big deal in Arizona
84 Secret supply
85 Cobra foe
87 Correct texts
88 Swindle
89 Strong point
90 Electoral list
91 More or less
95 Toodle-oo
97 She played Cagney
98 Band for a wedding
99 One foot wide?

100 James Jones, at heart?
101 Big deal in statuary
105 English anthemist
106 Aviary syllable
107 Qantas ad cutie
108 Beanstalk protector
109 Granny or Gordian
110 Smarts
111 "Our revels now are __"
112 Nuremberg defendant

DOWN

1 "I declare!"
2 Blackmore's Doone
3 Mournful poem
4 Edmond O'Brien film noir
5 __ rasa (blank slate)
6 Please no end
7 Linen shade
8 Craggy crest
9 Aristide subject
10 1066 invaders
11 Broadcaster
12 Keys to *la cité*
13 Follower of Ivan?
14 Outgrowth
15 Thighbones
16 Big deal in salvage stories
17 Writer Sholem

18 Stick around
24 Rose guard
25 Two by four?
31 "Look __ dancing!"
33 Minestrone morsels
34 Monk's monody
35 Early TV dragon
37 Sounds of relief
38 Auto engine parts
39 Support for Seurat
40 Pee Wee of Brooklyn
41 It's held for questioning
42 "M*A*S*H" cook
43 Big deal in disaster movies
44 1962 Jackie Gleason film
45 No-good
48 Barn buildings
50 Truman's birthplace
52 Wimped about
53 "__ Never Know"
54 Madame Curie
55 *Los* __ (the others)
56 Military encirclement
58 Circe's niece
60 Croats and Ukrainians
62 Like spy dispatches
63 California's Jerry or Willie

64 Bedside buzzer
65 Baggins of *The Hobbit*
67 Genesis 7 topic
68 Nibble tidbits
69 Arboretum item
71 Degauss a tape
72 Five after four
73 Jule of Broadway
76 Shelters
78 Summoned Jeeves
80 Gruesome
81 Holm of the movies
82 Stockpile
83 Japanese carved collectible
84 What the doctor ordered
86 Stemmed glass
88 *Heart of Darkness* writer
90 Wild plums
91 Biathlon equipment
92 Before hop or hog
93 Looks from Groucho
94 Sycophant's syllables
95 Whippoorwill's bill
96 Tar's tale
97 Narrow valley
98 Tobacco or Thunder
102 Be in arrears
103 Male delivery
104 La-la lead-in

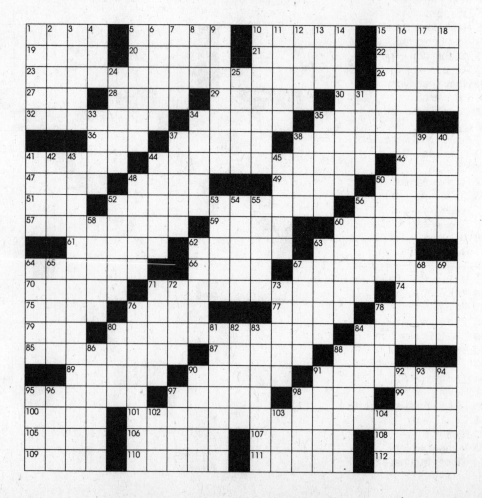

ACROSS

1 Highland dance
6 Norway's patron saint
10 Mystical Muslim
14 Part of the plot?
18 Evening do
19 Vegas game
20 Map out
21 Fabrication
22 Wordless Johnny Mercer song?
25 Field shield
26 Actress Lena
27 HOMES penultimate
28 Ballerina's pivot
29 Small crown
31 Rodin's thinker?
32 Ump's NFL counterpart
33 Like Corvettes
35 Riled up
36 Mag wheels?
37 Charades player?
39 Aunt Bee raised him
40 Spur a cur
41 Antiquity, in antiquity
42 Matchless?
44 New Year's Eve word
47 Mercutio's friend
50 Filly feature
52 Tolkien hero
54 Boyz's place
55 Goddess of discord
56 Silent broom pushers?
59 Janeane's . . . Cats & Dogs co-star
60 Gymnastics phenom Nadia
62 Tag and bag leaders
63 Odalisque's abode
65 Chew the scenery
66 Liquid lumps
68 Abyss
70 Out-and-out
72 Botch completely
73 Like Hals' cavalier
76 She starred for Ingmar
77 Mystifying to Marceau?
82 Melville novel
83 Mars' counterpart
85 Carl or Francoise
86 Bring down the house?
87 Graph detection
88 Ernie's straightman
89 Para. neighbor
90 Posed for pix
91 Contemporary art?
92 It'll last for months
94 Silent relative?
99 Daft
102 Board members?
104 "Children should __ . . ."
105 E-mail address ender
106 "Galloping dominoes"
107 More spacious
109 Initials on exports
110 Choir member

111 Privy to
112 Cope Book author
113 Ball-Fonda silent movie?
117 Christmas tree topper
118 National flower
119 Essayist's pseudonym
120 Antiseptic tincture
121 Went into depth?
122 Fulda feeder
123 Actress Laura
124 Helps nefariously

DOWN

1 Frustrated
2 Breaking points
3 Castle with lots of steps
4 School lobby
5 Like lower-cost drugs
6 The staff __
7 Work on the docks
8 Circumference segment
9 Highway robber
10 Globe
11 Vist or fist closer
12 Word with dress or Dan
13 Prefix with European or Chinese
14 Knock the socks off of
15 Trade Shields for Yarnell?
16 Pinker in the middle
17 Dash E
18 Dealt mighty blows
23 Provo suburb
24 Birnam or Belleau
30 Coolio's music
33 Comeback court star
34 Army
37 Mine, in Milan
38 Lalique or Lacoste
39 The nose knows it
40 Opening word?
43 Pres. who started NASA
45 City on Seward's Bay
46 Big cheese in Holland
47 Kind of rm.
48 El Dorado's treasure
49 Wordless Chaka Khan number?
50 "Eek" evokers
51 Poirot's pal
52 Potential Guinness Book entry
53 Rules, for short
56 N.Y.C. opera
57 What Johnny done Frankie
58 Jitterbug's dance
61 Average guy?
64 Like sailors on leave
66 Tom's Jerry Maguire co-star
67 Disney King
68 Do wickerwork
69 Cling to

70 Thick slice
71 Put on the payroll
72 Music from Jamaica
73 Designer Claiborne
74 Vichy veto
75 Mars or Mercury
78 Bavarian river
79 When spr. starts
80 ". . . amber waves of __"
81 Overdue
84 Champion skier Ingemar
87 Past-due amount?
90 Irate, to Ralph Kramden
91 Smelling salts component
93 "__ live and breathe!"
95 He has interest in interest
96 1930s lawman Eliot
97 "American Pie" man Don
98 It's a bit like a whit
99 He took Manhattan
100 Squirrel's stash
101 Compact
102 The Times goes to it
103 Heart line
104 Coop group
106 LED closer
108 Brontë's governess
110 Abu Dhabi VIP
114 Take habitually
115 L'eau land
116 ID info

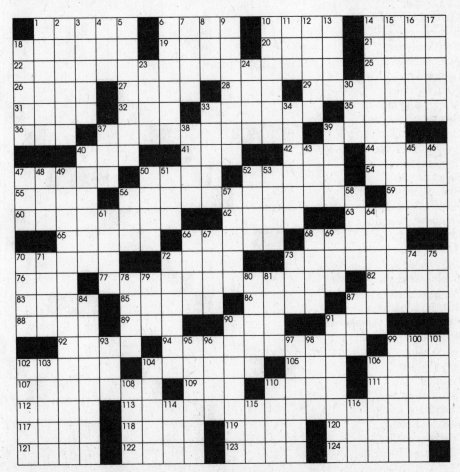

ACROSS

1 It falls in fall
5 Line for Lassie
10 Standup guy?
15 Romanov ruler
19 Pasture portion
20 Dragon puppet
21 Role for Tierney
22 Here, to Geraldo
23 Lack of icy storms?
26 Felt guilty about
27 Process leather
28 Ova easy?
29 High-temperature state
30 Border order
32 Livingstone's greeter
34 Trojan beauty
35 __ Abdel Nasser
36 Haig, Hirt and Hirschfeld
37 Stimulating nut
38 Contract stipulations
41 Bonkers
44 Misty forest creature?
46 Conquistador's quest
47 *Dos* cubed
48 Am, in Amiens
49 Falstaff's quaffs
50 Way out there
51 Jenny or nanny
52 Whirlwind writer?
56 Use in-lines
57 Voluptuary
59 End in __ (draw)
60 It did Romeo in
61 Actor Neeson's namesakes
62 Finishing nails
63 African language group
64 Gives third degrees
66 One for *die Bücher*
67 Kipling character
70 Seeps slowly
71 Sultry people?
74 Prohibition promoter
75 Rocker Osbourne
76 Theda's colleague
77 Attys., usually
78 Hit with a pitch
79 J. Davis led it
80 Overcast kid show?
84 Pram propeller
85 Building site sights
87 Where Artemis' temple was
88 Phone or ring lead-in
89 Ranking members
90 Items in red
91 Trounce
95 Detroit suburb __ Pointe
97 Child in the kitchen
98 Verb for Scotty
99 Feathery nonflier
100 Flat floater
101 Storm over a defendant?
105 Strong smell
106 Prevention unit
107 Tittles
108 Inhuman brute
109 Vague
110 Liberated
111 Bizarre
112 Ottoman officials

DOWN

1 Stays the course
2 Verve
3 Where to book matches
4 Copayment, e.g.
5 Wigwams
6 Gray matter
7 Chamonix's environs
8 *Herr,* here
9 Violinist Jascha
10 *Shōgun* writer James
11 Like some health bread
12 Sierra Club founder
13 Refugee relief org.
14 Vocal compositions
15 Apron material?
16 Precipitate precipitation?
17 Cave Bear clan creator
18 Carousel, e.g.
24 London tube?
25 Stormy screen star Lupe
31 Ottoman official
33 Org. founded in 1949
34 Armed robbery
35 Feminist Germaine
37 Pickling liquid
38 Up to the task
39 Homer's inspiration
40 Philosopher Kierkegaard
41 Head cheese?
42 Needing acetaminophen
43 Storm over Dorothy?
44 Pieces for Steve and Eydie
45 *Bullitt* director Peter
48 Butterflies, perhaps
50 Japanese dog breed
52 Doctorate hurdle
53 World __ (1939-45 event)
54 "Read __ weep"
55 Where the hit tune isn't
56 Berlin products
58 Alvin of dance
60 They're from hunger
62 "Aw, don't __ at me"
63 JFK adviser McGregor
64 Organic groceries name
65 Oscar-winning composer Miklos
67 Role for Rita
68 Qum home
69 Before 10001 on an SASE
71 Owls' yowls
72 Greenlanders' knives
73 *Time Machine* people
76 __ *the Apes*
78 Fishhook feature
80 Chuck alternative
81 Gave in
82 Maynard G. Krebs' pal
83 New York neighbor
84 The retired Judd
86 James Stewart Western role
88 Go by
90 Kind of conical cap
91 UFW's Chávez
92 Neutral color
93 Atlanta college
94 They're carved in stone
95 "Rhoda" co-star David
96 Famed London acting sch.
97 What 6 may mean
98 Joke target
102 Heston role
103 Former franc fraction
104 Inner ear?

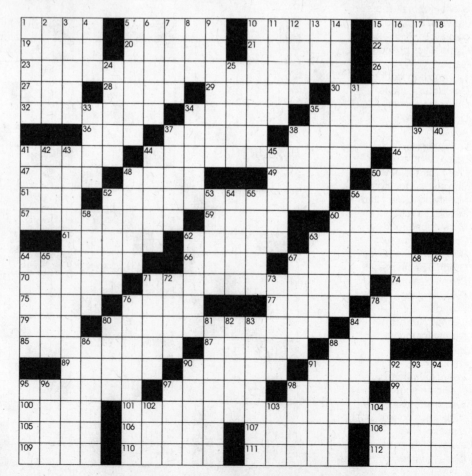

ACROSS

1 Up to it
5 Plays on the links
10 Paulo preceder
13 Best bud
16 It's dropped onstage
17 Arizona New Age center
18 Villainous Venetian
19 "__ Little Teapot"
20 Places for plasters
21 Oft-filmed H.G. Wells story
24 Watch over
25 Erstwhile Strip club
26 Bambi's dad
27 Demolish
28 Movie musicals' Grayson
30 Selling point
32 He takes the bait
33 Sinking signal
35 *Wasser,* across the Rhine
36 Peaceful protest
37 Prince's "When __ Cry"
38 Caesar salad ingredients?
39 Second-year students
42 Spud bud
43 Unprecedented events
45 Hail, to Caesar
46 Canonized *mlle.*
47 Leave the dumps?
51 Confuse
52 Offal smell?
54 High hill crest
55 What 'arry gave 'em?
56 La Brea pit filler
57 Its first is for fools
58 Yale Bowl hosts
60 Magnani or Moffo
61 Taxi's drop-off point
63 Empire State campus
65 Operation Overlord start
66 Outland penguin
67 Lotto variant
68 Downtown's __ Forum
69 One-tenth of MDX
70 Anybody, to Bugs
71 Egotist's pronouns
72 "__ we here?"
73 Takes a breather
76 Short sock
78 "Faugh!"
80 Put into service
81 Duke's town
82 Slo-pitch pitch
83 Cicero's plaint
86 Tribulation
87 Western spread
89 Asian primate
90 LP center?
91 Enzyme end
92 Andy's adjective
93 Cartridge content
94 Bonsai raisers
97 Barker of filmdom

98 One for the book
99 *Twelfth Night* role
100 Cairo's river
103 Romantic music classic
107 Change a bill
108 __ kwon do
109 Opera set in Egypt
110 Quantity
111 Highway maneuver
112 Stately tree
113 Get nosy
114 Opened wide
115 Sit for Seurat

DOWN

1 Feel pangs
2 Standard security vehicle
3 McCartney of Wings
4 Mommy's triplets?
5 Architect Frank
6 Early Greek theater
7 Partner for Clark
8 Op cit. and ibid.
9 Bando or Mineo
10 Nasser successor
11 Popeyed
12 TV "Batman" sound
13 Teach or Kidd
14 Dumbfounds

15 Morning TV's Matt
16 Mach 2 flier
17 Agitate
18 Deeply felt
22 Stat for Shaq
23 Actress Minnie
25 State of confusion
29 Cologne counter courtesy
30 Not be up to snuff
31 Hidden loot
32 Bergman's *Gaslight*er
33 Davenport or divan
34 *Metamorphoses* poet
36 Picturesque
37 Knock off a king
40 Millinery accessory
41 Carry too far
44 Hefty chunks
48 Certain kitchen appliances
49 Bone by the biceps
50 Dull Jack's lack
52 Kyoto quaffs
53 Loin cover
54 Fierce *chat*
58 Sun Bowl site
59 Lecherous looker
60 Conductor Kurt
61 Composer's closer

62 Informed about
63 Revue unit
64 Easy deuces in the NBA
69 Defoe's shipwreck
71 Clement quality
72 At what locale?
74 Santa Fe Trail stop
75 Barrie baddie
77 *Ed Wood* Oscar winner Martin
78 Taylor's only husband
79 Observes Yom Kippur
81 Karan or Summer
84 Peace, to Piotr
85 Charm
87 Alfalfa or Buckwheat
88 Country song?
92 Careless quickness
93 Radio Shack owner
94 Fit condition?
95 Ammo unit
96 He looked up to his lady
98 Ace topper
99 Cognac honorific
101 *Picnic* playwright
102 Words of honor?
104 Triple-A giveaway
105 Harridan
106 Actress Thurman
107 Rock blaster

ACROSS

1 Seafarer
4 Sachet release
9 Calaboose
15 Tun of a kind
18 Rude anagram
20 Does some roadwork
21 Compassionate
22 The I's have it
23 Periodic tbl. datum
24 Alexis A. Benet moves to __
26 Hardly Mr. Right
27 A ring says you have one
29 Have coming
30 Lamented
32 Original
33 Count tree rings
34 Frost starter
35 Adroit
37 Maestro Masur
39 Counting everything
41 Burton who plays Geordi
42 Potion portion
43 Hot new star?
45 Antarctic birds
47 He was terrible
48 Got along
49 *The Wizard* __
50 A crowd, in Cremona
51 Size after sm.
52 Vera Rae Woddle moves
to __
56 Gardner of *Mogambo*
57 Capital on the Paraná
59 Vikings' destination
60 Scamp
62 Bothersome one
63 False appearance
65 *Garçon*'s girl
66 Trinidad's island partner
69 Bed board
70 NBC symbols
74 A verb for you?
75 Sarah O. Beakman moved
to __
79 Chicken-king stuffing
80 Actor Cariou
81 It's out on a limb
82 Imamu Amiri Baraka, né __
Jones
83 Close-fitting
84 Like Morse messages
87 Maui music makers
88 Take __ (swim)
89 Potsdamer's please
90 SPCA opener
92 PGA members
93 Medal candidates
94 Romeo and Juliet
95 Club's emotion?
97 Legendary fleece finder
98 Dodger dog
100 *Norma* number
101 Eighty, to Abe

105 Unit in a joule
106 Midori Amalfi moves to __
109 Vittles
110 Word to a Latin lover
111 Belittling word
112 Fades away
113 Seine tributary
114 Fled on foot
115 Leaves the couch
116 Haas of *Everyone Says
I Love You*
117 A thole holds it

DOWN

1 Sand or speed follower
2 Political cartoonist Tony
3 Dean Verona moves to __
4 Interval setter
5 Secret schemers
6 Wickedness
7 Carter of "Gimme a Break"
8 Eliot's monogram
9 Peek performer?
10 Bizarre
11 Harbinger
12 Bradley International
letters
13 Protector of the crown?
14 Vacation destinations
15 Hal Vuarnet moves to __
16 Author-critic James

17 Lincoln in-law
19 "Mellow Yellow" singer
25 Pinlike?
28 Even once
31 How berserkers run
33 1995 Stallone role
34 Eloise's hotel
35 Ascent
36 Bandit's arm?
37 Chosen, today
38 Kind of friendly?
39 Say it's so
40 1950s actress Bella
42 Ships' crane
43 Countryless man Philip
44 Los Angeles County
Museum __
46 John and Yoko's son
48 City near Sacramento
52 Zorro's first name
53 Play to the balcony
54 Liver-and-bacon
appetizer
55 Jong or Kane
58 Fitness center
61 Bill Gates, e.g.
63 Bell-bottom bottom
64 Commissar and
commodore
65 Man of morals
66 Baby powder

67 Oft-split snacks
68 Ben E. Gordon moves
to __
69 Unsteady
70 Louvre locale
71 Antonio Cho moves to __
72 Fonda film
73 Pundits
76 Verges on
77 What boomboxes do
78 Change the decor
83 Desert wind
85 MBA subj.
86 A problem with horns?
89 Porgy's woman
91 More macabre
92 Resound
93 Pick on
95 Éminence __ (privately
powerful person)
96 Eton elevators
97 Pilate's protectorate
98 Depreciation factor
99 Role for Marie Wilson
100 Des Moines neighbor
101 *Herr*'s helpmeet
102 Sty cry
103 Parks or Ponselle
104 Washbasin partner
107 He wed Jackie
108 Pussycat boatmate

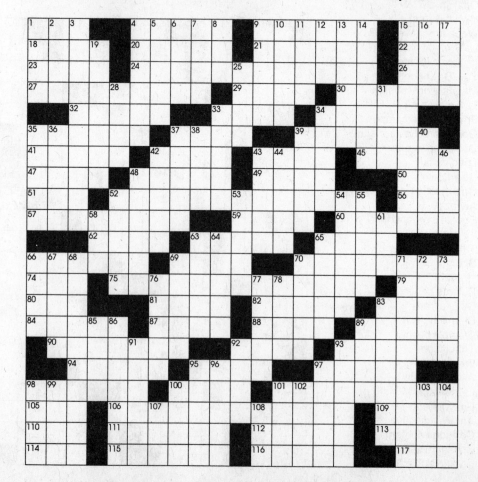

ACROSS

1 LAPD dispatch
4 Implant
9 Exemplars
15 Sarge's sack
18 Ta-ta, in Taranto
20 A color purple
21 Unsophisticated
22 Pizarro's plunder
23 Muenster mister
24 Unassuming broadcaster?
26 Speak Persian?
27 *Sound of Music* song
29 Ages and ages
30 *Grumpy Old Men* star
32 Hindjends
33 Caddie alternative
34 "I'll have the same"
35 Many Miamians
37 Fake
39 Boulevard dividers
41 Lacking backing
42 Put to flight
43 St. Laurent's mentor
45 Fictional Frome
47 Bill-signing souvenirs
48 Word-processing command
49 Yours, to Yves
50 Two minute eggs?
51 Final analysis
52 Unvarnished exercise equipment?
56 Swabbie's swabber
57 Tarts and trifles
59 Cotton block
60 Saunters
62 Osiris' sis
63 Lip shiner
65 Common tater
66 Gat or rod
69 Become better
70 Certain snobs
74 Down a brownie
75 Basic yet risky?
79 __ *jacet* (here lies)
80 Give __ shot
81 It's got you covered
82 Genghis' gang
83 Chute opener?
84 Geeky guys
87 Matches the bet
88 On the safe side?
89 Actor Theodore
90 Gilligan's Island inhabitant
92 Wineglass part
93 Lech of Poland
94 "__ Caesar's ghost!"
95 Calamities
97 Malden and Marx
98 Lunar feature
100 Red-tag event
101 Cartographer's concern
105 She played Cleo
106 Simple country girl singer
109 Marvin of Motown
110 Top tortes
111 Julia, on "Seinfeld"
112 Onetime "Mr. Television"
113 La Bombeck
114 According to
115 Come back after a close-down
116 Talk a blue streak?
117 Two of nine?

DOWN

1 Massage target
2 Parti-colored
3 More modest investments?
4 Fire-gone conclusion?
5 He hit 61
6 Bulls' orders
7 Tanguay and Perón
8 Animal sanctuary?
9 Greek gods' blood
10 Intimidate
11 O'Neill title trees
12 Linen vestment
13 Dangled
14 Honeybunch
15 Folksy Fonda flick?
16 Sweet sandwich
17 Municipality
19 Joan of Arc, Maid of __
25 Lions or Tigers or Bears
28 Ebb
31 Palace protector
33 Provide for parties
34 Deserve
35 Like Batman or Robin
36 TV doc Art
37 Arranges by ZIP
38 Elephantine
39 TR's Bull __ Party
40 Former Alpine duchy
42 Musical pauses
43 Sign on a *puerta*
44 Type that leans to the rt.?
46 Cat tails?
48 Poet Rukeyser or novelist Spark
52 Fabulous fellow
53 *Christ Stopped at __*
54 *Star Wars* baddies
55 Postal beat
58 Put on the dog?
61 RR's Star Wars
63 Aladdin's ally
64 Watering places?
65 Get home in a hurry
66 Trigger puller?
67 Popish Plot perpetrator
68 Unadorned astronomer?
69 Walker in the woods
70 Stephanie Zimbalist's dad
71 Minimalist playwright?
72 Cavaliers ride on them
73 Actress Gia
76 Personal plus
77 "__ my boy!"
78 It gets bored
83 Loot
85 Lowdown
86 He may be approaching 70
89 Roseanne, once
91 Pass out of the pen
92 Ooze
93 *Ring* writer
95 He played McQ
96 Johnson's vaudeville partner
97 Eucalyptivore
98 NFL no-no
99 Post-wedding fling
100 Boat's berth
101 Gained girth
102 To be, to Bizet
103 Praiseful song
104 Thumbs-up votes
107 Man of Luang Prabang
108 What situps strengthen

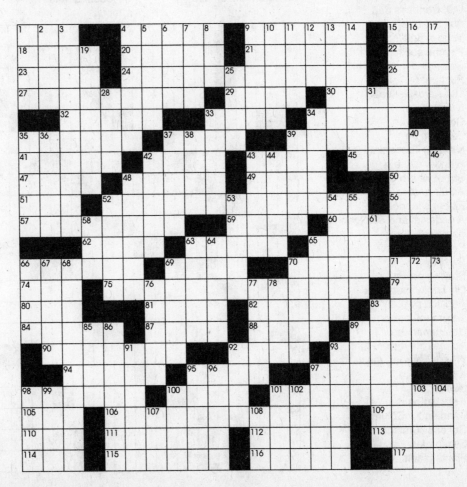

ACROSS

1 Missing the mark
4 Skin layer
10 Filtered
15 Thomas Wolfe hero Eugene __
19 Colonial descendants' gp.
20 Tyke who stayed at the Plaza
21 Treasure stash
22 Flower of one's eye?
23 It runs in veins
24 Counterfeit copiers?
26 Kelly or Krupa
27 Big wheels in Vegas?
29 Wales emblem
30 Unaccompanied sacred song
31 Recipients
32 Née
33 They may take liberties with women
35 Aunt Jemima and Uncle Ben
37 Devilishly cavalier?
39 Items in a chest
40 Chef Julia
42 Crosses foils
43 Book value?
44 Part of a service
45 Horse house
47 D.J. Conner's dad
50 Ask for alms
51 Time to fight?
53 Psyche section
54 Smoothed things over?
56 Pushover
57 104 Across's foreign minister
58 Cockpit cover
60 Looks to be
62 Maestro Toscanini
64 Wanderlust, e.g.
65 Street where usted live
67 An 82 Across
69 Fibber's fabrication
70 A pedestal and no pigeons, perhaps?
74 Stadium souvenir
77 Swabby
78 Staying power?
79 Lily family members
80 Audition award
81 Before roll or bar
82 Countenances
83 Actress Hayes or Hunt
84 Where Thoreau rescued a pet?
89 Had a colt
90 It should be due
91 Bandleader Columbo
92 Golfer's concern
94 Escapades
95 Plants plants

96 Tennessee's trolley
99 Frequent Ye follower
100 Weeping's worth, in this world?
103 No-win situation
104 Eshkol's successor
105 Strawberry, in Seville
106 Draw out
107 Scheherazade's place
108 Kingsley and Bradlee
109 Marshal Earp
110 Tailless game animal
111 Def Jam genre

DOWN

1 Aerosol target
2 Vegas game
3 Dream dance duo?
4 Stands up for
5 Gladdens
6 Make an itinerary
7 "Just add water" products
8 You can believe them
9 Humpback's home
10 Those who get done unto
11 Use a compass
12 Whomp
13 Preceding period
14 Parisian prepositions
15 Professional men?
16 Retort to "Am not!"
17 Frisco gridders
18 Fly from Africa
25 Mare's-tail, e.g.
28 Trouser sizes
30 Cereal grass
32 Bundled cotton
33 Like some .38s
34 Journalist St. Johns
35 Unattractive mass
36 Not at all genteel
37 Starts partner
38 Madison predecessor
40 Hint for Holmes
41 Like #4 pencils
44 Steinbeck's was red
45 Con man's plan
46 Wee ones
47 First-nighter fan?
48 Substance from seaweed
49 It's strictly taboo
51 Bound like a bunny
52 35-inch blades
55 Sturgeons-to-be
57 Misc. ending
58 Unorthodox religion
59 "Summertime," for one
60 Insult
61 Robert of Bull Run
62 Bldg. units
63 Second notes
65 Birchbark boats
66 Take __ for the better
67 Balanchine ballet
68 Cows and sows
70 Shoulder warmers
71 Works the bar
72 Pours down
73 "Where is the life that late __?"
75 Not windward
76 Be in the offing
80 Don't just stand there
81 Computer aces
82 Hollywood landmark __ & Frank
83 Abe's attribute
84 Composure
85 County Kerry's capital
86 Get a __ edgewise
87 Marcel who remembered
88 Get more fed up?
89 Like Spenser's queene
92 Hofbrau handful
93 Hollywood Park, e.g.
95 Accused's answer
96 E.T.O. battle town
97 Verdi princess
98 Bring in the sheaves
100 Vets' org.
101 Second or secret closer
102 Passed the puck

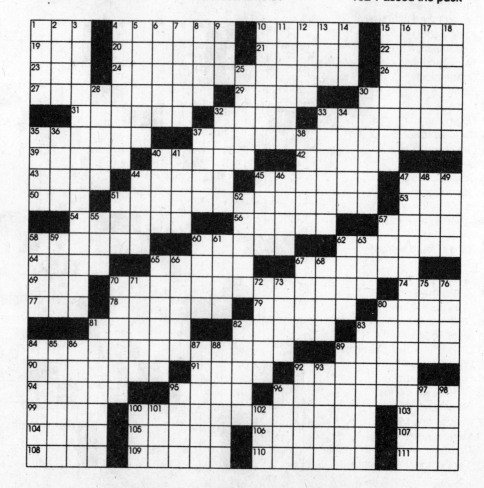

ACROSS

1 Old video format
5 "... owed by so many to __": Churchill
10 Tell all
14 Make like lava
18 Ill-tempered tsar
19 It's down in the mouth
20 Stairway section
22 With 98 Across, *Ecstasy* star
23 Twelve-tone composer
24 Touchy child star?
26 Well-developed country?
27 Tuxedo junction?
29 Transactions of interest
30 Buchwald output
32 Muumuu cousin
35 In two places at once
37 Post-season game
38 Sighting subject
39 Cantankerous comedy legend?
43 Bear, in Baja
46 Truck with tyres
48 It checks Rex
49 Deeds' needs
50 Become blighted
51 Popular wisdom
52 Given a darn
53 Doozies
54 Measuring standard
55 Ship's prow
56 Testy Western sidekick?
60 *Quo Vadis* character
61 Hoity-toity
63 Drop and fall openers
64 San Diego pros
66 Leads off
67 Blubbers
68 Thimble Theatre star
69 It may be V.S.O.P.
70 Singer Lopez
71 Where a congregation congregates
72 Lyricist Lorenz
73 Dyspeptic presidential candidate?
76 Hamites' land
79 Singular opera?
80 Bank holdup?
81 Long. crossers
82 Actress Best
83 Abner's radio chum
84 Walking stick?
86 Old West Indian language
88 1950s Ford fiasco
89 Syn., to ant.
90 Irascible writer?
93 Leaving after dinner?
94 Stand for speakers
95 Sign of stress
96 Cotton-rayon, etc.
98 See 22 Across

101 A Montague
103 All smiles
104 Resort near Ventura
105 Short statesman?
109 Certain Celt
113 Simon does it
114 Katey of "Married ..."
115 Salt and pepper, e.g.
116 Like raw linen
117 Hecuba's home
118 Quebec's Levesque
119 Checker move?
120 Fawn's father

DOWN

1 Drop cloth?
2 Primitive fruit picker
3 Camel component
4 Gloomy depression
5 *Valley of the Dolls* writer
6 *Avis* output
7 It's a wrap
8 Corner shape
9 Ambushes
10 It's inspired
11 Depict
12 Cairo cobras
13 Ten decibels
14 Plant in a crowd
15 Pres. Fujimori's land
16 Colorful cheese
17 Actor Ed or Keenan
21 Shrink back
25 Lady Liberty's handful
28 "Calm down, now"
31 Is proprietor of
32 Selects
33 Underway
34 Fractious fictional fellow?
35 "These shoes __ too small for me"
36 Alternative agenda
37 Unimpressed
40 Tips off
41 Miss Saigon et al.
42 Noted diarist
43 Irritable explorer?
44 Evening event
45 Four H.R.E. emperors
47 Fabric-store bargains
52 Put the kibosh on
53 Fergie's former father-in-law
54 Stripped of finery
57 Cook meat
58 Openings caused by boring
59 Rain drains
62 Sixty *minute*
65 Time-change mo.
66 Get in a lather
67 Jane Eyre's creator

68 Snap decision maker?
69 He lives *la vida loca*
70 Run on a flute
71 Neck stretcher
74 Ad awards
75 Beethoven dedicatee
77 Charlie McCarthy's trunkmate
78 Obeys the sentry
84 Capone feature
85 Show places?
86 Floor specialist
87 Narrative
88 Salmon tail?
91 Thunder roll
92 Most proficient
94 Dagwood's dog
97 Adds a border
98 Forlorn
99 Not quite closed
100 It's often held in diners
101 Fashion or passion
102 __ even keel
103 Bren and Sten
106 Ring or phone opener
107 Emulate Johnny Appleseed
108 Who, to Hulot
110 Do Shakespeare
111 Hershiser's was 2.26 in 1988
112 Schlep

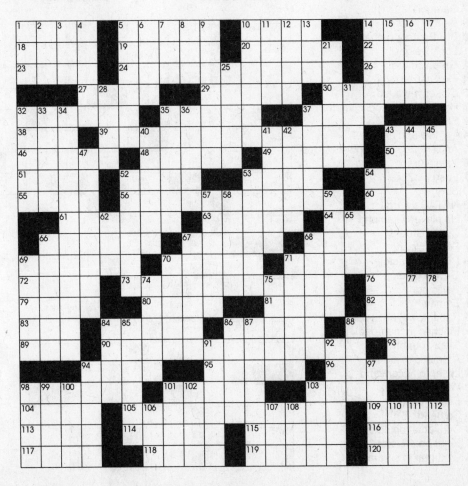

ACROSS

1 Pack groceries
4 Scorch
10 Outdoors
15 Bonkers
19 Grassland
20 Buckeye
21 Printer's proof
22 Hold sway
23 Vein glory?
24 Robin's Spanish sweetheart?
26 It means land of the Aryans
27 Harvey Mudd and Mills
29 PC screen symbols
30 Hide a bug
31 Harem chambers
32 Best, to Lloyd's
34 Water hazard
36 O.K., e.g.
39 Agnes' "Bewitched" role
41 Where Chichén Itzá is
45 100% of the workers?
48 Finish work, finally
49 Bay Area's __ City
50 Daisy, Ginnie and Fannie
51 L.A.-S.L.C. direction
53 Back-to-the-past style
54 Long intro?
55 Trojan's foe
57 Category
59 Beauty spot?
60 Pre-Easter purchase
61 Long weight?
62 Green shade
64 Pkg. carrier
66 Closes a wound
67 Hot dish for a cool climate?
71 Shad or shark
74 "__ live and breathe!"
75 Ancient Egypt neighbor
76 Yale alum
77 Easy trio?
80 Bury
82 NATAS awards
84 He played Clampett
86 Comic Brooks
87 Forest clearing
88 PBS benefactor
89 Goya's golds
90 Baltic port
91 Enmity
93 Paper towel analyses?
98 Pinched in the nose
100 Slept soundly?
101 Aromatic mint
102 Loser to Netanyahu
104 Whack skeeters
105 Poilu's cap
106 Sautéed
109 Conversation piece
111 Eight on the side?
115 Clothmaker's frame
116 Buyers soaked in remorse?
119 Bambi's Faline, e.g.
120 This señorita
121 Proverb
122 Warehouse platform
123 Parsley, often
124 Senior member
125 Stage setting
126 Steelies' bagmates
127 "Fantasy Island" prop

DOWN

1 Coalition
2 Flying start?
3 Isle of Man man
4 At a future time
5 Artist Marc
6 Staff members
7 Hillcrests
8 Osaka assent
9 Last stop
10 Oaxaca worker
11 Eliel Saarinen's son
12 Gives it a whirl
13 Like some TV news shows
14 Ishmael, to Abraham
15 Calmly explore for oil?
16 New Age emanation
17 Custard cousin
18 Abode in a bag
25 A or Asia follower
28 Petrol-driven truck
30 Expectant dads, perhaps
32 Radio wave receiver
33 Two to one, e.g.
35 Sharer's possessive
36 Signed over
37 Egg producer
38 U.S. Grant's rival
39 Actor Morales
40 Held on the stage?
42 It's found on the spine
43 Traffic director
44 Sporty little Dodges
46 Big name at the South Pole
47 Come after
52 Coffeehouse cuppa
55 A/C spec
56 Novelist Jaffe
57 Big name at the North Pole
58 Discounted by
63 Yecch!-evoking
65 Sandal, mainly
67 Tarzan turned interior decorator?
68 Covered with frost
69 Cold dessert
70 Vietnam Memorial designer Maya
71 Bout
72 Wedding acquisition
73 Washington, for one
77 Out of whack
78 "I __ differ"
79 Necklace fastener
81 Emitted odors
83 Bradbury *Chronicles* site
85 Brazen
89 Gumbo goody
90 Violinist's need
92 Alemannic article
94 One with the lowdown
95 "It's __ never"
96 ". . . land of __ and . . ."
97 Keyboard artists?
99 Make sense of semaphore
103 It could be poison
105 Used a prie-dieu
106 Took it on the lam
107 Pink potable
108 Greek I
110 __ Park, NY
111 *To Live and Die __*
112 Fan's fave
113 Barreled along
114 Bigfoot of Asia
116 Gave birth to
117 WWII price org.
118 Bark accompaniment

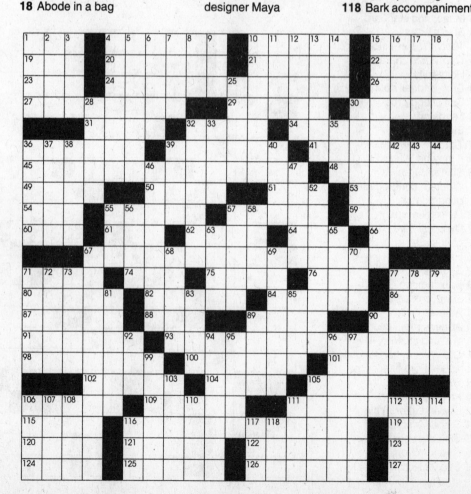

ACROSS

1 Funny and hip
6 The Badger St.
10 Cave critters
14 Bachelor's study
18 Fire insurance?
19 "Are you __ out?"
20 Mixed bag
21 Purely academic
22 BEAR
25 UAW center
26 *Moi*, to a *roi*
27 U2 singer
28 For closer?
29 Lasting forever
31 Join forces
32 Judge in 1995 headlines
33 Across the sea
35 Edge along
36 GPA deflator
37 GET
39 Stonehenge builder
40 Past do?
41 Señor Guevara
42 "Your room __ mess!"
44 Sky or mud ender
47 *Camille* creator
50 Lightheadedness source?
52 Joined the jam
54 It gives the orchestra an A
55 Finian's land
56 TRESSES
59 She played Mrs. Charles
60 Impoverished
62 Periodontist's concern
63 Gossip tidbits
65 James, Jimmy and John
66 Ref, colloquially
68 Put a cap on
70 They're taken for a walk
72 Tear in despair
73 Slash in number
76 Opry adjective
77 TUNE
82 Play piccolo
83 *Aves* have them
85 Friday request
86 Versifying astronomer
87 Gunpowder alternative
88 Give autographs
89 Zimbalist's TV org.
90 Healthful hangout
91 Impair
92 Ill at ease
94 BIDDING
99 It's S. of S. Dak.
102 Louisiana creek
104 Twenty minutes of hockey
105 Isn't any more
106 "The Things __ for Love"
107 It can be a drag
109 Nanty __, Pa.
110 Etta of old comics
111 __ facto

112 *Familia* members
113 GAVE
117 To be, to Satie
118 "Would __ to you?"
119 Wampum item
120 In a genteel manner
121 Lip or cheek
122 No longer holds up
123 Hankerings
124 Works like a beaver

DOWN

1 Tumblebug
2 Shopaholic's favorite phrase
3 Like Snickers
4 Misreckon
5 Marine layer?
6 Sift
7 Death Valley's county
8 U.S.-Canada canals
9 Disintegrate
10 "The Hub"
11 Andy Capp's quaff
12 Like some bathroom walls
13 Tenderhearted
14 Panhandle town
15 UM
16 Wreck completely
17 It's a wrap
18 Sole pattern

23 Smidgen
24 Uncommon, to Cato
30 Ethnic suffix
33 Detest
34 Spitzlike dogs
37 Insult a rapper
38 UCLA anagram
39 Chaplin prop
40 Defoe or Day-Lewis
43 Word usually in brackets
45 Elbow's need
46 E and G, e.g.
47 "Agnus __"
48 Where remains may remain
49 TIES
50 Layers and layers
51 Stop procrastinating
52 Railroad branch
53 Mrs. Colin Powell
56 D.C. VIP
57 Guitar tuner's mnemonic
58 Valley north of L.A.
61 "Surprise!" response
64 Logger's cry
66 Lemon peel
67 Eve's grandson
68 Smirk
69 Frigid

70 Tight wrappers?
71 "__ said was . . ."
72 Cookbook content
73 Some trial evidence
74 As well
75 It sounds like you
78 Maybe, maybe not
79 Research room
80 Motorized bike
81 Arab league member
84 Backs for office
87 Faux follower
90 Waited for news
91 Sporty Ford
93 Visceral
95 Gomorrah galas
96 Ruffle feathers
97 Scottish exports
98 Gosh darn, or worse
99 Patrick, to Auntie Mame
100 1950s Fords
101 It's shaken or taken
102 Falls for it
103 Moreno's Oscar role
104 Comedian Poundstone
106 Supernatural sisterhood
108 Old Egyptian sacred bird
110 Tatar sovereign
114 Set, as sail
115 Stand for Woods
116 Like Oz's woodsman

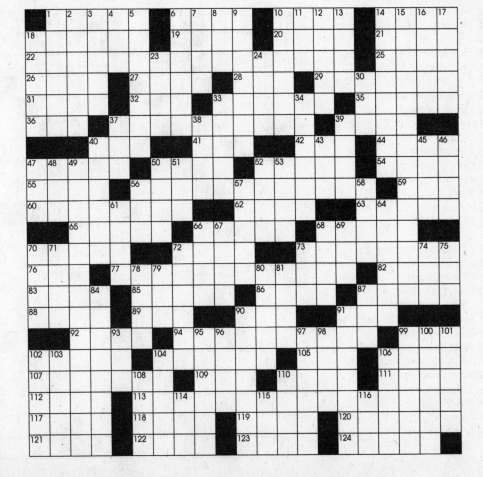

ACROSS

1 Take it on the lam
5 Chosen number?
8 Lunch is on him
12 Piner for Narcissus
16 Humdingers
17 "__ note to follow sol . . ."
18 He commits grave crimes
19 Merman or Mertz
20 Melodramatize
21 Summer garb?
24 34 Down is a mild one
25 Helpful hint
26 Jalopy
27 It's not returnable
28 One for the books?
30 Like salmon skin
31 Famished
35 Red-headed rover
36 X-marked item
37 "The Jeffersons" theme "Movin' __"
38 *Uncle Tom's Cabin* girl
39 Tennis deuce followers
41 Empty trunk problem?
45 Disobey the Decalogue
46 Hellene
48 Before hearted or headed
49 Show the ropes
50 Unpartnered
51 1996 Tony winner
52 His words are gospel
53 Made-up
54 "Abide with Me," e.g.
55 A shot
56 Curator's concern
57 They can't pass the bar
58 "__ today, gone . . ."
59 Conductor de Waart
60 Haven for aloha shirts?
64 Catch a monarch?
67 Ballpark figures
69 Puccini piece
70 Old musical note
71 Movie-ticket seller
72 Tizzy
73 He has long hair and models
75 Ersatz
76 One to grow on
77 First name in espionage
78 Official purchase?
79 Fine sediment
80 Blarney or Rosetta
81 'Tis the night before
82 Fashion addict's anthem?
85 Enterprise initials
86 What corporals call captains
87 Columnist Archerd
88 Airport near Paris
89 Exuberance
91 Antagonistic
93 "Since you __ . . ."
95 Turndown
98 Clay, today
99 Out of line
100 OK, at the corral
101 Actor Richard
102 Writer of *The Big Sleepover*?
107 Truffaut's __ *et 107 Down*
108 Previously-__ (used)
109 Leaves off the list
110 OIN SHRDLU opener
111 Wrinkle removers
112 Be nurse to
113 Cartoon skunk Le Pew
114 Teammate of Newk and Duke
115 Vidal's Breckenridge

DOWN

1 "The Voice of the Xtabay"
2 Ensemble meetings?
3 Porter or Stout
4 It's on the tip of his Tung
5 Panache
6 Clanton gang foe
7 Field of Mars
8 Sandbank or sandbar
9 High-flown
10 Yorkshire river
11 "Nel __ Dipinto . . ."
12 It'll knock you out
13 Where they read the Trib
14 She's apt to brood
15 Cheer, to Che
16 Thirteen Popes
18 Revolve round an axis
19 Warden's worry
22 Camry competitor
23 The Mother of us all
25 It has an edible shell
29 It's on the cuff
30 Pitch woo
31 Maliciously sly
32 Wardrobe consultant?
33 French spa
34 "Shoot!"
36 Menelaus' kingdom
37 Porter's "Miss __ Regrets"
39 Feel the same
40 Feel very afraid
42 Abrupt
43 Hercule's creator
44 Oklahoma oil center
47 Biblical ending
50 UAR member, once
52 AAA giveaways
53 Large tome
54 Every other hurricane
57 "Seinfeld" or "Cybill"
58 Fraud
60 Well-chosen
61 Talmudic teacher
62 In fact
63 "Popeye" heavy
65 Is worthy of
66 Baobab and deodar
68 Farrow of film
71 Used a tuffet
72 Mario of Berkeley fame
73 Bowling unit
74 Gossamer
75 Expertise area
77 Interlace
78 "White Christmas" writer
79 Cunning
80 Individuality
82 Blew a mean sax
83 Keepsakes
84 Prexy's running mate
90 Omen
92 Made the wild mild
93 "The way of __ in . . . the sea": Prov. 30:19
94 Emulate Baiul
95 RFD's R
96 Gladiatorial ground
97 Smaller portion
99 Wile E. Coyote's supplier
100 Hairy Himalayan
102 Poppycock
103 Blow away, in a way
104 Hostel
105 Halter or bandeau
106 Stocking stuffer
107 See 107 Across

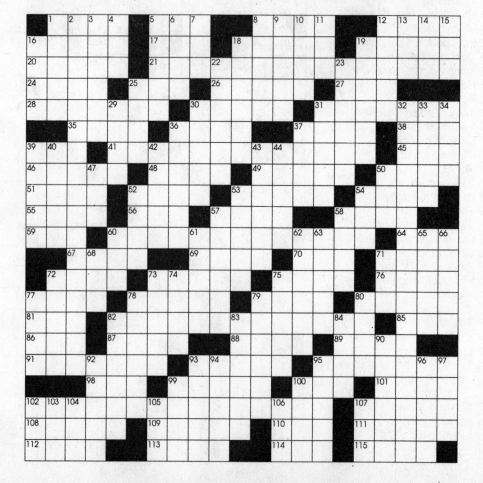

ACROSS

1 Richard of *Primal Fear*
5 Cry from the crib
9 Spill the beans
13 Vamoose!
16 Scuttlebutt
18 Strips for breakfast
19 Napoleon victory site
20 Environmental pref.
21 Journalist Fallaci
22 Enraged
23 Eye area
24 Your, of yore
25 Expressing ecstasy
28 Require overtime
29 Stash away
30 Rose's Broadway beau
31 Tend
32 Cat's-__
35 Emulate Savion Glover
36 It keeps a cook tied up
38 Hound's tooth
39 Nip-and-tuck procedure
44 "Yesterday" or "Tomorrow"
45 Trail to California
46 Fake
47 A long way away
49 Youngest "little woman"
50 Star Wars in D.C.
51 Hit like a Fielder
52 "Ay, there's the __"
54 Garret
57 Dew or view ender
59 #, to a proofreader
60 The mind's I
61 Drop a popup
62 Days Inn deadlines
65 Early-morning riser?
66 Frequent further follower
67 Potato pancake
68 Lacking lucre
69 Muffet diet staple
70 Turkish topper
71 They'll make a play for you
72 Have a mortgage
73 X, to Xenophon
75 Sailor's morning warning
77 Nautical order
80 It's the wurst
84 Loch or Eliot
85 Sitcom sweetener
87 Wild and crazy guy
88 Small flock
89 Museum pieces
90 Posting at LAX
91 Show a little cheek
92 Elisabeth of *The Saint*
93 Gibraltar and Dover
97 High times
98 Took a long look around
104 Do a Little bit
105 Dinghy's thingies
106 Whiskers
107 Nat Cole hit "__ Boy"
108 Ex-GI
109 Do more than ask
110 *Jungle Book* bear
111 Like a bikini
112 Mister and Asner
113 Piscator's purchase
114 It's a great deal
115 Ares' sister

DOWN

1 Maharishi, e.g.
2 Saudi sachem
3 Sorrel horses
4 Els with tees?
5 Corday's victim
6 Without __ in the world
7 Early feminist Lucretia
8 Once again
9 Gainsborough masterpiece
10 1960s gathering
11 Fred's first partner
12 It's not fair
13 Stepping out of line
14 *The Book of Changes*
15 Trifled
16 Molder
17 Consecrate
18 Bodybuilder's pride
26 Prayer ere fare
27 Bess' man
31 Hernando's hand
32 Signs of softness
33 It's put before the carte
34 Pallid
36 In the past
37 Waterman invention
38 Smithies
40 RN's ASAP
41 Campbell's lid
42 *Rabbit, Run* writer
43 It means nose
44 Piquancy provider
47 Sweetheart
48 Bach composition
50 Pennsylvania Ave. pet
51 Satchel Lee's father
53 Thinner than thin
54 Fall faller
55 It's just one thing after another
56 Problem for Imelda Marcos
57 Subordinate
58 Margarine container
59 Filled the hold
62 Swank
63 Potboiler producers
64 Valuable collection
69 Genie's offering
73 Warns
74 Ecstatic cling
76 Cub pack parts
77 Yale's is New
78 Denver-Chicago dir.
79 No matter which
80 Conductor Caldwell
81 Had the fare
82 See the point
83 Time-line time
85 Court title
86 "Cowboy's Lament" town
87 Used a ray gun
88 Put on plastic
91 Urbane
92 Make quake
93 Old hat
94 Lose on purpose
95 Harness part
96 Indian lute
98 Kind of cream or grapes
99 Recedes
100 Arrangement
101 New Mexico people
102 Casserole candidates
103 Napoleon's marshal

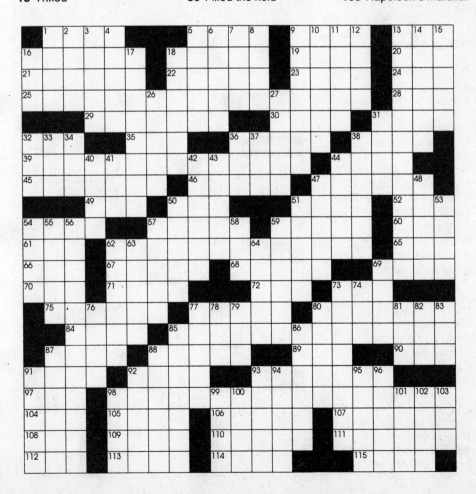

ACROSS

1 Telemarketing danger
5 Book-jacket praise
10 Internet messages
15 Tom or billy
19 Chez O'Hara
20 LEM opener
21 Thomas with three Emmys
22 Geographical datum
23 Rocker Benatar?
26 Throws on the floor?
27 Guadalajara gold
28 Justice Black
29 Writer Eudora
30 Smooth, to surfers
32 Occupy, as demons do
34 Lugosi and Karolyi
35 Beth's preceder
36 Say the wrong thing?
37 1996 also-ran
38 They're for the birds
41 Exotic dance diva Lili
44 Impressionist Little?
46 Unknown ordinal
47 Scrabble oblong
48 Homer's son
49 Writer Wiesel
50 Mohammed Khan's title
51 -kin kin
52 Baseball legend Aaron?
56 "Spirit of '76" figure
57 In-your-face quality
59 Yesterday, in Ypres
60 "We __ by nine a.m. than . . ."
61 German poet Rainer Maria
62 Add up
63 Colonial news source
64 "Why __ hard to . . .?"
66 City on the Oka
67 Miami-Miami Beach connector
70 Navigators Islands, now
71 Mystery writer Grafton?
74 What Caesar said to Cleo?
75 Certain MOCA oils
76 Utopia writer Thomas
77 Nothing but
78 Empty crossword
79 It has Swiss banks
80 Rock musician Morrison?
84 Louella rival
85 Du Pont product
87 Not at all eager
88 Stood for office
89 Film dubber's concern
90 Cattail environment
91 Merrymaking
95 European hot spot
97 Erik, on "CHiPs"
98 Sport for heavyweights
99 Non? Non
100 Polo grounds?
101 Actress Barrymore?

105 "Here comes trouble"
106 "Oh, how __ to get up . . ."
107 Silly Soupy
108 Gem for a Libra
109 Rather and Rowan
110 Peter and a Wolfe
111 Moppets
112 Canasta play

DOWN

1 Barbershop prop
2 Lorre's Maltese Falcon role
3 Io's hundred-eyed guardian
4 __-jongg
5 Middy, e.g.
6 Items in chests
7 Golden Rule word
8 "Go, team!"
9 It'll make you stout
10 Strive to equal
11 Dillons of "Gunsmoke" and Rumble Fish
12 Bohemian
13 UN labor org.
14 Palm reader's prediction
15 Jan.-Feb. followers
16 Actress Struthers?
17 ZZ Top hit
18 Sleuth Rawlins

24 His and his
25 Not topside
31 Table extender
33 Roy Rogers, né Leonard __
34 Built-in bunk
35 To have, in Le Havre
37 Faith of music
38 "__ Want for Christmas . . ."
39 Old number?
40 Go fifty-fifty
41 Pencil remainder
42 Cash cache
43 Writer Twain?
44 She played with a Ball
45 LSD advocate Timothy
48 See 1 Across
50 Evangelist McPherson
52 Ultralight wood
53 Midwest air hub
54 Boneless cut
55 Word to Dolly
56 First in Flatbush?
58 Music's Puente and Jackson
60 TV's "Virginian" James
62 Esteem unit?
63 Make leakproof
64 Abraham's son
65 Abraham's wife

67 Cameo shell
68 Encompassed by
69 Jedi instructor
71 Actress Feldshuh
72 Seed protection
73 Refinement
76 The old soft shoe
78 Pool occupier?
80 Small-scale
81 "Strangers in the Night" exchange
82 Liberty's handful
83 Most foolhardy
84 It's often wreaked
86 Ones with nothing original to say?
88 Derelict
90 "Eureka!" is California's
91 Indian coin
92 Jeweler's eyepiece
93 Arcadian
94 Intersection sign
95 Telecommunication unit
96 Federal safety org.
97 Tree for a partridge
98 He gave us a shot in the arm
102 1960s military base __ Sanh
103 "Que Sera, Sera" singer
104 Big gobbler

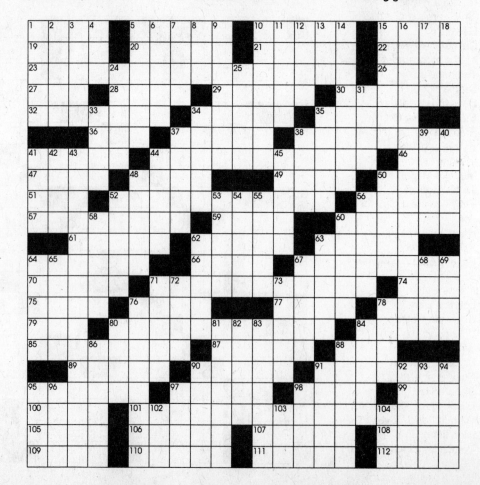

ACROSS

1 California trailblazer
5 Loses it
10 Toothy tool
13 Cried like a jenny
19 Catania landmark
20 Reddish brown
21 Flamenco cry
22 Shoemaker's order
23 Agar, etc.
26 More than right
27 Adjective with arts or accounting
28 Vexation to Lady Macbeth
29 Made cents
30 Farm animal?
31 A geisha may tie one on
32 Discoveries
34 News personality Connie
35 Give detailed instructions
37 Attila follower
38 Phi follower
41 French underground
44 *Vier und vier*
45 Cowpoke's pal
46 One layer?
47 Curaçao neighbor
48 Labor Dept. arm
49 Donny's sis
51 Midi terminus
52 God, to González
53 He may be over 80
55 Singer Lawrence's partner
56 See 10 Down
57 Norway's patron saint
58 Soviet emblem part
59 #, * and @
63 Makes moues
65 Meals
66 Suit __ (fit perfectly)
67 How it all started?
68 Sidewalk seat site
69 Humorist Hamilton
70 1957 Sinatra song
73 Mineralogist's scale
77 Director Buñuel
78 Use the tub
79 Rising setting
80 French artist Dufy
81 Simplicity epitome
82 Doesn't keep up
83 Peter Gunn's girl
84 Famous law man
85 Chew the fat
86 A sea of Japan
87 Early TV husband-and-wife team
90 Of cities
92 Like Esau
93 Marilyn's monogram
94 Which of you
97 Shown with a nimbus
99 Anchors' backdrops
100 He rakes it in

102 Attraction
103 "Bully for you!"
106 Coca's co-star
107 Cupid or Quayle
108 Wine quality
109 He follows the news
110 Mother's whistler?
111 Charlie Chaplin's brother
112 17th-century recording star?
113 Perfect place

DOWN

1 Hajj destination
2 Interstate 180?
3 Cove
4 Pro __
5 Manuscript copiers
6 What monkey see?
7 Zenith
8 The Edgar honors him
9 In the doldrums
10 With 56 Across, a daily special
11 Not quite
12 Setting setting
13 Pamphlet
14 Shaq might get it
15 John who played Gomez
16 Those in Thomas Moore's song were endearing

17 Besides that
18 Monopoly card
24 See 113 Across
25 "Billie Jean __ my lover . . ."
32 Microfilm sheet
33 "__ to Be You"
34 Kind of mail or letter
35 Benchwarmers
36 Hologram producer
39 Motorcyclist's must
40 Surmises
41 Crackers or nuts
42 Actress Meyers
43 Like some statuses
45 Econ or psych teacher
48 Berke Breathed's penguin
49 Go all gooey
50 Latin I verb
51 Senseless state
53 One and only
54 Moola
55 Be slack-jawed
56 Ordinary guys
58 Test the weight of
59 Colonel Klink's clink
60 Western Nigerian
61 Perfect cure
62 Heater stat
63 Trodden track

64 In years gone by
65 Toast to the chef?
67 Byte parts
68 Sized up, pre-heist
70 Conestoga
71 Hope chest wood
72 Like Spain's plain, mainly
73 "You Bet Your Life" host
74 Comic caveman
75 "Wudja say?"
76 Underhanded
78 Striped fabric (anagram of BE A DEARY)
80 Builds, as a bar tab
82 Left-leaning
83 Be
84 Brunch cocktails
87 Hit __ (sack out)
88 "I hate to __ run . . ."
89 Chad's singing partner
91 Drive out of bed
94 Overcaffeinated
95 *Buch der Lieder* writer
96 *Loot* playwright
97 NBA no-no
98 Wings for Amor
99 NBS norms
100 Pork portion
101 Pier foundation
104 Chump
105 *Uno e due*

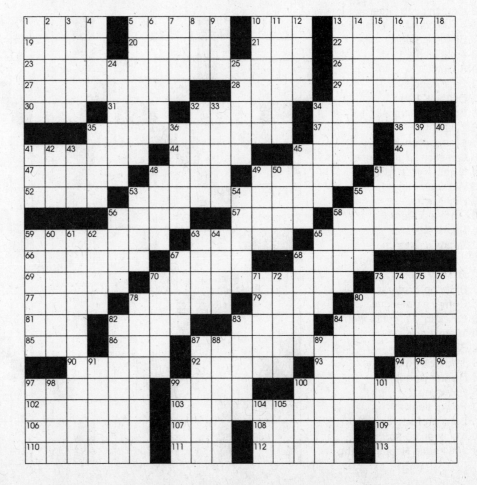

ACROSS

1 Before canto
4 BLT layer
9 French racing track
15 Bleacher creature
18 Trade-in's status
20 1836 battle site
21 Aviator Earhart
22 Airport abbr.
23 Shankar of the sitar
24 Money to go?
26 Before Sydow or Stroheim
27 Hamelin stiffed him
29 TV Times span
30 Movie theater
32 Arrive at
33 Docket entry
34 Class AAA, in baseball
35 Detangler's targets
37 *Under Siege*'s Busey
39 Inhibitions
41 West African capital
42 Gin flavoring
43 Potter's purchase
45 Barbershop sounds
47 Give Life support?
48 Push the right buttons?
49 All-night dance party
50 It means model
51 A, as in Austria
52 It means Joe Green
56 __ de coeur
57 Beauty contests
59 Aesir leader
60 Scamp
62 Halloween, etc.
63 Daphnis' lover
65 Snowmass transit
66 Lulu
69 Islamic branch
70 Geneticist's groupings
74 It's all in your mine
75 Woolgathering
79 Highly rated
80 State a preference
81 Sorcerer's stick
82 Sends cables
83 Clowns for the camera
84 Destiny
87 Birthright barterer
88 Currier's colleague
89 Glockenspiel components
90 Miami track
92 Biting bug
93 Two-seated carriage
94 Painter Degas
95 Brown out?
97 Power peak
98 Bank protectors
100 Not even so-so
101 1961 song Hepburn sang

105 "__ we having fun yet?"
106 Rodeo city?
109 Sci-fi submariner
110 Army address?
111 Made unusable
112 In existence
113 Satchel
114 Admin. centers
115 Bee flats?
116 Renoir's classmate
117 The hot *saison*

DOWN

1 Pat baby on the back
2 Actor Morales
3 Speculator's technique
4 ABC's
5 A, as in Israel
6 Spelunker's spot
7 One-tenth of an ephah
8 Negative connective
9 Freeway features
10 Game-show host
11 Submissive
12 Heidi's height
13 Pellagra preventive
14 Sage soundbites
15 Great excitement
16 Cyclotron smashee
17 Barrie babysitter
19 Enlightenment leader
25 On the road
28 Sidekicks
31 You name it
33 Lowlife
34 Movie magnate Louis B.
35 Log *Z*'s
36 Boulanger of music
37 Lip enhancer
38 Top of the line
39 Refuge
40 Heidi's creator
42 Closes
43 Words to live by
44 Piaf's __ en Rose
46 Make thread
48 Mrs. Tanqueray's creator
52 Auctioneer's aid
53 Opposite
54 W.E.B. or Blanche
55 More than sore
58 "Yikes!"
61 Johnnie Ray hit
63 Porcelain ware
64 Dharma follower
65 Tricycle trio
66 Pan handler
67 Naomi's daughter-in-law

68 Fetching dogs?
69 Stoner's supply
70 Chartres chapeau
71 Historical horseman
72 Colonel's bird
73 Talking back
76 Take an oath
77 Patrick of the Knicks
78 Brando film __ *Zapata!*
83 Freeway challenge
85 Fabricated
86 Quest for the unknown?
89 Aberdeen accent
91 Relent
92 Gruesome
93 Norma Desmond's boulevard
95 More miffed
96 Antiquated
97 Complete the puzzle
98 Pirate's punishment
99 LaSalle of "ER"
100 1990s Cabinet member
101 A Venus' place
102 Screen's Ken or Lena
103 Give forth
104 It's pulled on a pulley
107 XIV half
108 Easter entrée

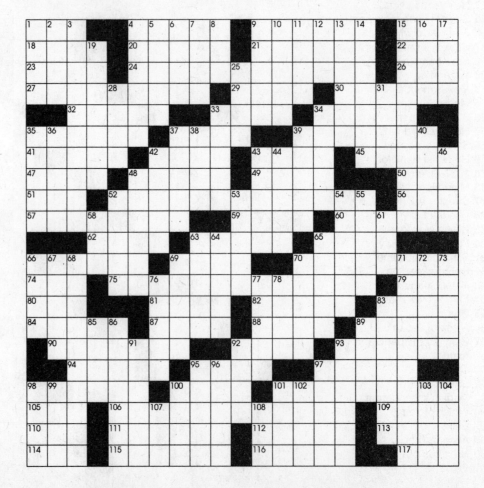

ACROSS

1 "Get lost!"
5 Hidden hoard
10 Former shahdom
14 Russian industrial center
18 Holy circle
19 Thrown for __
20 Old empire near Egypt
22 Authentic
23 Sweet-milk cheese
24 De Niro's teasing role?
26 Use the good china
27 Felicitous feature
29 Salinger's *Franny and* __
30 Come forth
32 Kids
35 Asian capital
37 Ice-cream thickener
38 Quick to learn
39 Like a healthy cat?
43 The price is right on it
46 Transudes
48 Orange coats
49 It means bone
50 Fifth-century invader
51 Cleveland's Hershiser
52 Detail
53 German crowd?
54 "__ My Heart"
55 Mondavi's valley
56 Ethical liar?
60 Staller's syllables
61 Committee rules
63 __-dovey
64 *Get Shorty* writer Leonard
66 Old London gallows
   ground
67 Long-eared leapers
68 Teaser ads
69 Street or seed
70 Bangs a gong
71 Scratched
72 ITT pt.
73 Owl's perch?
76 D-Day GI carriers
79 Biographer Leon
80 Easily-bruised items
81 Old man, in Oldenburg
82 Lateral or librium opener
83 Bio word
84 AAA or EEE
86 Eyed flirtatiously
88 NC-17 film attendée
89 Avant-garde painter
90 Pollyanna motto?
93 Cookbook phrase
94 As soon as
95 Irritate
96 Ski slope surface
98 Lake below Cornell
101 White sale offering
103 Plucky
104 Act as accomplice
105 Fighter plane?
109 Bygone bird
113 Before hand and bag
114 Uncanny
115 Arles' river
116 Aura
117 First name in
   architecture
118 Untouchable Eliot
119 Treated squeaks
120 Barely beat

DOWN

1 Pronoun for Pru
2 Bore
3 Pay extra?
4 Zing
5 Tenor Enrico
6 Woeful word
7 Mechanical tooth
8 Non-sharer
9 Of an external parasite
10 Worth its weight __
11 Country bumpkin
12 "What __!" (some
   bargain!)
13 It's nothing
14 Franciscans, for one
15 Israel's Golda
16 Warbled
17 Kandinsky colleague
21 Merry, in Mérida
25 Lock, stock and barrel,
   e.g.
28 More opposite
31 BLT dressing
32 Medea's husband
33 One of the Met set?
34 How pots of tea are
   made?
35 Displays disdain
36 Plant swelling
37 Bandleader Shaw
40 Harlem, to Manhattan
41 Moneyman Malcolm
42 Dairy carton imprint
43 Spelling's sullen series?
44 Foreshadows
45 Folkloric figure
47 Cooperate
52 Istanbul inn
53 Dispossess
54 Pounded
57 Peruvian plains
58 Do without
59 Change G's to PG's,
   e.g.
62 Abner's radio crony
65 First gear
66 Make an offer
67 Syllables from Santa
68 __ jour (today's special)
69 Chianti region
70 "I __ differ"
71 Stick in the salad?
74 Property divider
75 Leap, in La Paz
77 Veil material
78 Shankar's instrument
84 Hockey attacker
85 Should it happen that
86 Person with a title
87 Napoli's patron saint
88 It has its quarks
91 Twist and stomp
92 Let off the hook
94 Better – or best
97 Pie portion
98 *Con Air*'s Nicolas
99 Code for A
100 Period of revolution?
101 Orpheus' instrument
102 Horned goddess
103 DNA constituent
106 Doll since 1961
107 Key letter
108 PAC-man?
110 Of ancient vintage
111 Shar-pei or shih tzu
112 Be short

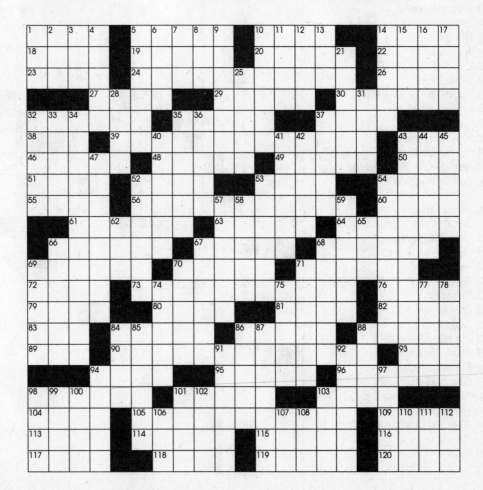

ACROSS

1 Use a cotton ball
4 Thick piece
9 Fuss and squirm
15 Run up __
19 Dander
20 Push destination?
21 Channel swimmer Gertrude
22 Pepper source
23 Salt source
24 Oz hopeful
26 Lothario's look
27 Mickey Mouse movie
29 Poe preceder
30 Like tyros
31 Zorro souvenir
32 In a delicate manner
34 Caught a line drive
36 Rugmaking, e.g.
38 Grieve
39 Countesses' consorts
40 Make smart?
41 Motor City 11
45 Drape border
48 Type or sort
49 Browning work?
50 Edit film anew
51 Tikal dweller
52 She was born that way
53 Ray and Moro
54 Of Innocent or Urban
55 Rueful
56 A is one
58 Extra on "The X-Files"
59 Wheel things
60 Hepburn Oscar-winner
64 Mollycoddles
67 Goalies' milieus
68 Agamemmon's son
72 "__ my case"
73 World Wide Web locales
74 Family living on chicken feed?
76 Wee prankster
77 Sat. TV sports org.
78 Unicycle, mostly
79 Beyond begrimed
80 Sticky stuff
81 Golden, to de Gaulle
82 Resents
84 Day saver
85 Dial rival
87 Punjabi princess
88 Aviator Markham
89 Pointed teeth
91 Cherry Garcia, e.g.
93 All hands on deck
94 *Homo sapiens* member
95 George Hamilton and Rod Stewart's ex
96 Murky
99 Lord of Thor and Loki
100 Chennault's WWII group
104 "Well, looky here!"
105 Tear apart
106 Play Nemesis
107 Mediterranean port
108 Archaeologist's hunting ground
109 Make-meet middle
110 House plant sprayer
111 On edge
112 Vacation venue

DOWN

1 Frisbee, e.g.
2 Neck of the woods
3 Wall Street selling scene
4 Aircraft carrier protector
5 Trembled
6 Scattered, as seeds
7 Clark's *Mogambo* co-star
8 Beatles' "__ Blues"
9 *8 1/2* director
10 Romantic interlude
11 House leader Tom
12 Ear-to-ear expression
13 "Hold on Tight" group
14 Perfect number?
15 Lacking principles
16 Warm-water predator
17 Tree-lined walkway
18 Amalgamate
25 Modern fabric
28 Wilson predecessor
30 Fr. neighbors
32 Keno kin
33 Ambiences
34 Korean capital
35 Breathe hard
36 Twentieth-anniversary gift
37 Elizabeth II, for one
38 Gene genius
41 Washington airport
42 Gets into shape
43 Cartoon skunk Pepe
44 ". . . think __ think . . .": *The Little Engine That Could*
46 Gothic Jane
47 Baseball immortal Willie
49 Potpourri packet
51 Othello's fellows
54 Ballet bends
55 Old Alka-Seltzer spokesymbol
57 "__ far, far better . . ."
58 She played Tina
59 Actor Woody
61 More standoffish
62 Writer Joyce Carol
63 Pesterer
64 Predicament
65 Shell rival
66 Consider
69 1997 Masters winner
70 Atlanta university
71 Thread holder
73 One-horse vehicles
74 Maestro Walter
75 Less couth
78 "As you __"
79 Necktie
82 Beethoven's birthplace
83 Actor Stewart or Farley
84 Give ear to
86 Tasty dishes
88 Shamelessly bold
89 Tedious task
90 Anglo-American poet
91 Michigan metropolis
92 Ted of "The Love Boat"
93 Rock the comic
95 They often have it
96 FedExed or faxed
97 Lion-tamer's prop
98 Eastern discipline
100 Bro, sis et al.
101 Non-Arabic 56
102 "Let's call __ draw"
103 Lock, stock and barrel?

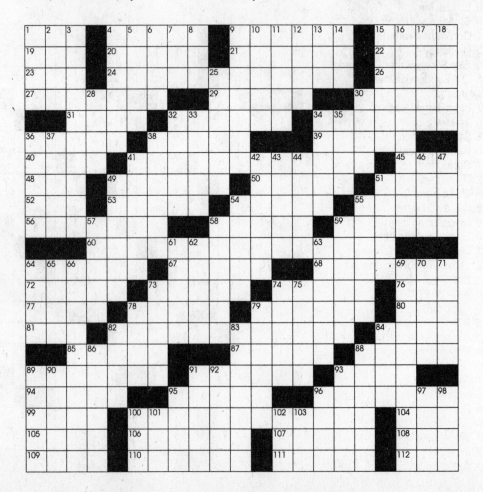

ACROSS

1 Pen name
4 "Just Another Day" singer Jon
10 Influence
15 Mouth off at
19 Marriage agreement
20 Inn, in Istanbul
21 Caterpillar, e.g.
22 Like __ out of hell
23 Cheer alternative
24 George Washington's close friend
26 Oaxaca wolf
27 They're knockouts
29 Complaint, colloquially
30 Be of use
31 Passes pleasantly away, as time
32 Learned justice?
33 Art Deco
35 Purity spoilers
37 1940s home front effort
39 Library listing
40 Writer Muriel
42 Immigrants' island
43 Russian city
44 Eva-Saint center
45 New people
47 "Da __ Ron Ron"
50 Pref. with fume or form
51 Bud and Kelly's parents
53 Go yadda-yadda
54 Crusoe's discovery
56 Common code
57 Passport stamp
58 Well-mannered
60 Part of Ethiopia's capital
62 Sharp, as a tack
64 Melville mariner
65 Water Lilies painter
67 "Hogan's Heroes" locale
69 Put an end to something?
70 Ben's cast-iron design
74 Switch positions
77 Brand near the Brillo
78 Close opened envelopes
79 Cat-__-tails
80 TV reception trouble
81 Edible pine seed
82 Like old chestnuts
83 The T in THC
84 Dumbarton dance
89 Raleigh neighbor
90 Signs up
91 Pastoral path
92 Stevie Wonder's "My __ Amour"
94 Nickname for someone skinny
95 Modem speed unit
96 Stayed the night
99 Dorothy's dog
100 Gold for Greg Louganis
103 Keogh kin
104 Like left-hand pages
105 Tantalus' tearful daughter
106 National, for one
107 Flask sampling
108 1990s Series champs
109 Rome's river
110 Extends one's Life
111 I.e.'s e

DOWN

1 Partiality
2 Wait at the light
3 Unheated housing
4 Site for Michelangelo
5 Messages by modem
6 Have a cow?
7 Where Van Gogh painted
8 Ottoman officials
9 Treas. Dept. unit
10 Lawyer's employer
11 Town in "The Cowboy's Lament"
12 Carmina Burana composer
13 Sunscreen label letters
14 April payment
15 Tea trays
16 On the bus
17 Texas border river
18 Like some glances or kisses
25 How some are taken
28 Reagan's "shining city on __"
30 Fresh as __
32 Chartered
33 Old TV's "What's __?"
34 Made goo-goo eyes
35 Way station
36 Rubber roller
37 Having an I problem
38 Picture puzzle
40 It's a long story
41 Use a prie-dieu
44 Media rep?
45 Amorphous mass
46 Hocus- kin
47 Fading away early
48 Conical kiln
49 Not hurt
51 Prepare prunes
52 Violin of value
55 Off-the-rack item?
57 Routing preposition
58 Grade-school grade
59 Lima's locale
60 "My Way" composer
61 First phone caller
62 Fix potholes
63 Bullring "bully!"
65 Hod workers?
66 Upright
67 Mild disturbance
68 Broadway bestowal
70 Extras
71 Of kidneys
72 In Casablanca, who said "Play it again, Sam"
73 Glitch or hitch
75 Nick's Thin Man wife
76 Crawled, perhaps
80 Comic opener
81 Illumination units
82 Indian tongue
83 Carapace carriers
84 Mother of Pearl
85 Smitten
86 Prepared Parmesan
87 Like cherries jubilee
88 Singer Cyndi
89 Indiana university
92 Drug-free
93 Thicket fence?
95 Party invitation inits.
96 Capt. Hook's first mate
97 Discordia's Greek counterpart
98 Enthralled
100 Prov. seen from Detroit
101 Full deck, to Romans
102 Bright, briefly

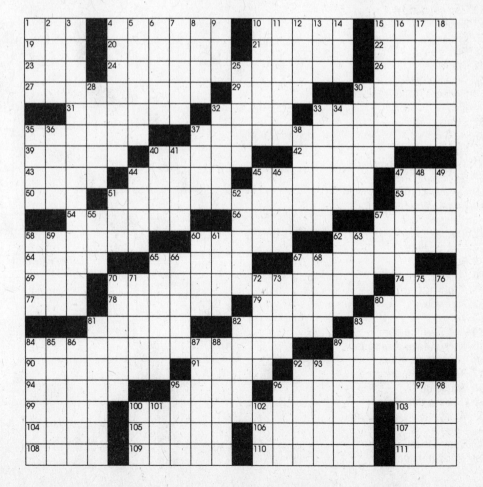

ACROSS

1 Young salamanders
5 Fashion's Geoffrey
10 Part of www
13 Socks can be found here
19 Ice in the water
20 "__ so sure about that"
21 Where the CSA was organized
22 Entertain
23 Persian's protective presence?
26 Reformer Bloomer
27 Moments
28 TAE middle
29 Reward poster word
30 Inflation problem?
31 Thai cuisine's __ krob
32 Bark barque
34 Have __ to eat
35 Feline's remote feature?
37 Commuter's transport
38 *Kidnapped* auth.
41 Bombay bigwigs
44 *Village Voice* bestowal
45 Chest muscles, to some
46 Young fox
47 Zee, to Zorba
48 Asian salt lake
49 Pool or loan follower
51 Ms. Moreno
52 Use carbon 14
53 Rogue River Ragdoll?
55 Eliciting a "mee-oo-ww!"
56 She's a flirt
57 Trace
58 Diva Kathleen
59 Rockers Rage Against the __
63 Open
65 Held up
66 Layabouts
67 Tropical hardwood
68 Browse on the Net
69 Ladd's "come back" role
70 Frightening feline flick?
73 Flying jib, e.g.
77 Shapes logs
78 Call a halt to
79 Fowl bawl
80 Virile
81 About 120 sq. yds
82 Toe woe
83 Very dry
84 Like Ben the bear
85 Walker, in sign language
86 Continuous sound
87 Persian's nature preserve?
90 Brings up
92 Dickens title opener
93 What makes MADD mad
94 Lincoln's st.
97 Commits to memory
99 Word in an octagon
100 See
102 Display
103 Gray and black Birman's masterpiece?
106 Yarn measure
107 Need an elixir
108 Leave one's seat
109 Pinochle low card
110 Size up
111 Bisected fly?
112 Paul of *Melvin and Howard*
113 Utah ski spot

DOWN

1 Sam Spade's secretary
2 Thrown
3 L.A. Olympics statue
4 Modern muralist
5 Something "Extra!"
6 Waxes dramatic
7 Puts a stop to
8 Lamb's was Elia
9 DDE's command
10 Swedish mystery writer Per
11 One by one?
12 Theda the Vamp
13 Disadvantage
14 Doesn't go
15 007 or 86
16 Fantasizing fictional feline?
17 Composer Siegmeister
18 Did Time?
24 Kawasaki competitor
25 Nantes aunt
32 What Che wasn't
33 Like Pisa's tower
34 States plainly
35 Leaflet leaf
36 Water softening agent
39 Bo Peepish?
40 Lingered
41 Stewart, Serling or Steiger
42 Powerful D.C. lobby
43 Jacuzzi spout
45 Historian's forte
48 British composer
49 Be in a whirl
50 "Baywatch" type
51 Pro __ (proportionately)
53 Before rickey and rummy
54 Plumed hat
55 Jersey kid?
56 Bog
58 Icy detachment?
59 Accident
60 Stick
61 Star of *The Invisible Manx*?
62 Some turkeys
63 Service charges
64 Funnywoman Martha
65 Easy two-pointer
67 Compared to
68 Muscle-bone link
70 Surrender stipulations
71 VIP
72 Cairo, in *The Maltese Falcon*
73 Lacking
74 Hill dweller
75 "__ be back"
76 Corrosive liquid
78 Spirited steeds
80 Physician
82 Opportunities
83 Trades at meets
84 Epicure
87 "Misty" singer
88 French star
89 *Potemkin* setting
91 Comic Kovacs
94 Zero, to Nero
95 Program part
96 Kentucky college
97 Mother of the Gemini
98 Two December days
99 Double or triple, often
100 Strait-laced
101 Volcano in Vietnam?
104 Alpo rival __ Kan
105 Palindromic preposition

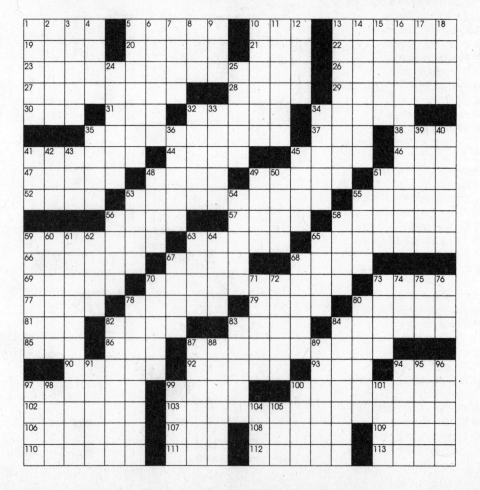

ACROSS

1 Punch variety?
5 Mel or Mont
10 Inclined from the perpendicular
15 Goatee locale
19 Water color?
20 Watts Towers builder
21 Most of Israel
22 German article
23 City slavery?
26 Numbered rds.
27 Oinker
28 Beame and Burrows
29 ". . . partridge in __ tree"
30 Sib's kids
32 Spruced (up)
34 Pesky insects
35 Popular 1970s talk show
36 Guitarist Paul
37 Liter's little brother
38 Klutzlike
41 Goes up against
44 Liner's loser level?
46 "Bill __, the Science Guy"
47 Pueblo pot
48 Boyfriend
49 U-Haul rentals
50 Give the eye
51 In the manner of
52 Womanizer's kit?
56 Deep sleep
57 Loki's forte
59 Bag and rags preceder
60 Motown recalls
61 "No one is __ that he cannot live yet another year": de Rojas
62 Rotgut or redeye
63 LAPD collars
64 Tanker accidents
66 Not falling for
67 Somewhat
70 Michael Caine breakthrough role
71 Baseball team's problem?
74 Ahab's affirmative
75 What pluviometers measure
76 Brogue bottom
77 Courtroom vow
78 City on the Jumna
79 Casual Friday no-no
80 Control to the max?
84 Eccentric
85 Anomalies
87 Tickle pink
88 Schoolmarm's hairdo
89 Helps a hood
90 Eye a guy
91 Give satisfaction
95 Fresno County neighbor
97 Signified
98 Lie in the tub
99 A month in Montréal
100 Comet competitor
101 Screw up insurance?
105 U.S. mint?
106 Form's first space
107 Stir from sleep
108 Cashew cover
109 Very French?
110 Wax nostalgic
111 Finito
112 The Beaufort scale measures it

DOWN

1 Genies' homes
2 Rig out
3 Molds, mildews and mushrooms
4 Randy's skating partner
5 Unethical gifts
6 Cantered easily
7 Orgs. for liberals and dentists
8 Zip
9 Beach houses
10 Filmdom's Funicello
11 __ a beet
12 Gelling agent
13 Stag party staple
14 Post-sunset periods
15 Snack for Seinfeld
16 Stamp on a wedding invitation?
17 Arrow poison
18 Caledonian loch
24 Java joints
25 MOCA display
31 *Bus Stop* author
33 Pooch's passenger
34 __ the works
35 Rock guitarist Eddy
37 Drink
38 Crow
39 It may run while you walk
40 Topanga's Theatricum Botanicum family
41 Head of the glass?
42 "__ want is a room somewhere"
43 Secret proverb?
44 "Don't let yourself __ astray"
45 Weasel out of
48 Biblical plague
50 Pep
52 Unabridged
53 Pent and hex add-ons
54 Loin cover
55 Buzz-tone producer
56 Suitable material?
58 General Powell
60 O'Hara portrayer
62 Ridiculous blunder
63 Blue or book closer
64 Painter Andrea del __
65 Scotland yards?
67 It has wings and flies
68 Marching band music holder
69 Vintage designation
71 Boxing boundaries
72 Caps and spans enders
73 Ridicule roundly
76 Apropos
78 Ena, to Bambi
80 Mun or mon ending
81 Borneo language
82 Essential acid
83 Alternative to nature
84 Shake from shock
86 Agile goats
88 Defied
90 Less numerous
91 Gaggle component
92 Japanese porcelain
93 *Oliver Twist* villain
94 Triangular street sign
95 It may be rigged
96 What a door may be
97 Leonardo's Lisa
98 Skim along
102 Trumped-up tale
103 His veep was George
104 Like some recruits

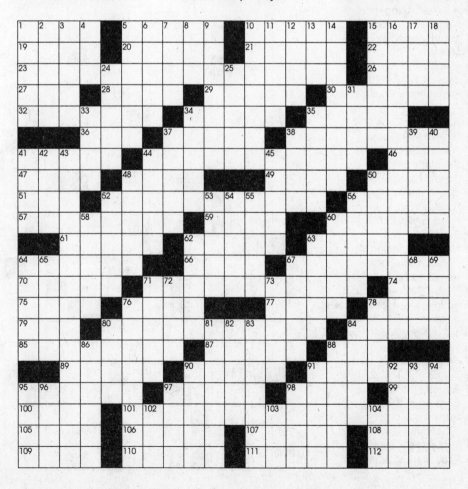

ACROSS

1 Work for "the company"
4 Insult
10 Transmission position
15 Arduous journey
19 Pain for a princess
20 Bellhop
21 Strictness
22 71 Down's instrument
23 Hockey Hall of Famer
24 Low-population metropolis?
26 Plasm preceder
27 Filament element
29 Sham rocks
30 Out of line
31 Sans editing
32 It's a ball
34 *Tapestry* or *The Wall*
36 Quarterback's option
39 Big name in San Francisco
41 Certain Mozart works
45 Start of a letter
   to a hiker?
48 Vanish without __
49 Circumspect
50 SASE, e.g.
51 Hebrew letter
53 "__ the bag!"
54 Reunion, *par exemple*
55 Search for springs
57 Davis of *Thelma and Louise*
59 Adlai's running mate
60 Nancy Drew's boyfriend
61 Tummy muscles
62 Noggin
64 Neighbor of Syr.
66 Jane of Thornfield
67 Entertaining Pacific cruise?
71 Guitar legend Hendrix
74 A really big shoe?
75 Sink or swim, e.g.
76 "Coincidence? I think __"
77 Scholar's goal
80 John or John Q.
82 Reckoned wrongly
84 A deadly sin
86 It has Swiss banks
87 Earn
88 New Zealand parrot
89 Person from Perth
90 Apropos of
91 "Hotel California" band
93 Teddy Roosevelt's made-up
   troops?
98 1973 Woody Allen comedy
100 Watery mixture
101 Political group __ List
102 Terrif!
104 Robert __ of Virginia
105 Exchange discount
106 Sunset has one
109 "That cuts __ with me"
111 Disperses
115 Silas Marner's machine

116 Bloodsucking jurist?
119 Our omega
120 "Alice's Restaurant" singer
121 Indian lute
122 Turkish hospice
123 Administered
124 Jughead or Butt-head
125 Play ground?
126 March event?
127 Sculptures and such

DOWN

1 Name for a Dalmatian
2 Land on Lake Titicaca
3 Kitten's plaything
4 America's marsupial
5 Semisoft cheese
6 Lets loose
7 It means people
8 The start of something
   new?
9 *Red River* star
10 ". . . __ went to Manderley
   again": *Rebecca*
11 Musical abbrs.
12 Jim Croce's "__ Name"
13 I and E, e.g.
14 It follows directions?
15 Brainy briny?
16 Roll partner
17 Dufy contemporary

18 Be cognizant of
25 Scare
28 *Pretty Woman* director
   Marshall
30 Em, to Dorothy
32 Powerless pill
33 Brooklet
35 Fluffy scarf
36 Dickens' Drood
37 Writer Zora __ Hurston
38 Ventured
39 Barley bristles
40 "This round's __"
42 Flavorful
43 Steel, in St. Lô
44 Have a hunch
46 It goes against Time
47 Photo finish?
52 Romantic missive
55 Dit go-with
56 Orchestra tuner
57 Like secluded
   communities
58 __'acte
63 Roof edge
65 Wild fracas
67 Easy-as-pie nursery
   rhymester?
68 Flat-topped topper
69 Little-known
70 Indefinite ordinal

71 After 78 Down, big-band
   leader
72 Like Utopia
73 Homer's helpmeet
77 Triptych third
78 See 71 Down
79 Go formal
81 Advancement
83 Words of cheer
85 Listless
89 Hot under the collar
90 Dostoyevsky's Myshkin, e.g.
92 Ninth mo.
94 Orestes' sister
95 Took precedence
96 Entertained
97 Parrot or ape
99 Impressive Impressionist
103 Way to go
105 Legend builder
106 Mattress support
107 Made a dash
108 Indy Jones, to Ford
110 Turkey neighbor
111 Surgery souvenir
112 Pound of poetry
113 Caboose site
114 Faced the fax?
116 Civil War org.
117 It's often carved in stone
118 Docs' bloc

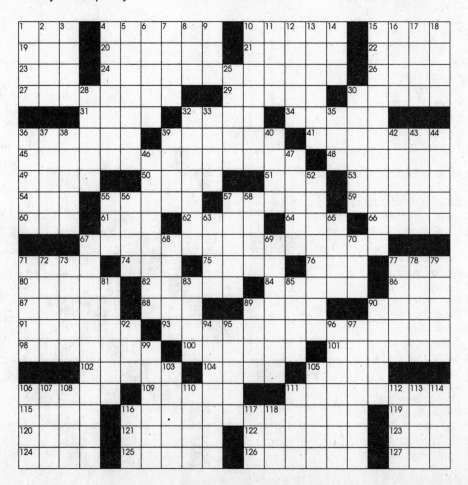

ACROSS

1 Fair game site
7 Take it in stride
11 Fifth gear
15 It has a Minor part
19 Get there
20 *Vaca*'s mate
21 Follow the leader
22 Chutzpah
23 Viking's favorite takeout?
26 Eye of the wolf?
27 Pro and con
28 Mongrel
29 Serve with sauce?
30 108 Down's mistress
32 Goes no further
33 Memorable candidate Paulsen
34 Succumb to strain
35 King or queen
38 Chance to play
40 Poster mailer
41 Smack on the mouth?
42 "That's it!"
43 Daily grind
46 Viking's favorite curse?
49 Polar explorer Richard
50 Supported
52 Env. enclosure
53 Pedicure pentad
54 Clinton's canal
55 Nevada peak
56 Playlet
57 Stovetop stuff
58 Impurities
59 Gift wrap flourishes
60 Alejandro's aunt
61 Awesome, in teen slang
62 Door upright
63 Crossword bird
64 Viking's favorite actor?
69 TGIF part
72 It brings people closer
74 Snoop's aid
75 Mother of Memnon
76 Make a cable stitch
77 Bias
79 Ruin a candid shot
81 Sunup
83 French Franck
84 Catapult
85 French river
86 Roy's co-star
87 Kanga's crony
88 500 locale, for short
89 Viking's favorite height?
92 Fiber fuzz
93 Freudian concern
94 Cozy rooms
95 Clarinet cousin
96 "How about we . . ."
98 *Tale of Two Cities* knitter
100 Dandling place
101 Scratch the surface
102 A Karamazov
106 Pelion sat on it
107 Pitcher of hoppiness?

108 Ready follower
109 Lithe-limbed
110 Show shock
112 Viking's favorite sleuthing duo?
116 Nothing doing?
117 Well-ventilated
118 One for the road
119 Goal
120 When hands meet
121 Grandma, to some
122 Approach
123 Sheriff's bands

DOWN

1 Pool shot
2 Disaster movie master Allen
3 1995 Stallone role
4 Most inclusive
5 Hails at the Forum
6 100-sen unit
7 Glass of Guinness
8 Get the show on the road
9 Miss the mark
10 ". . . best of all __ worlds"
11 Silver or Cigar
12 Crane's cousin
13 Ring highlight
14 Mesmer's forte
15 Where Aesop shopped
16 Viking's favorite boxer?
17 Out of the pink?

18 Cold porter
24 Mere
25 Privileged people
31 Many buttons
33 Cow poke
34 Host's hostee
35 Sound-stage props
36 George : Batman :: __ : Robin
37 Land down under
39 Like Andersen's duckling
40 Bangkok resident
41 Do macrame
43 Dance from Cuba
44 Muckraker Sinclair
45 Viking's favorite classic film?
47 Herr Schindler
48 "Knock __!"
49 Nature's speed bump?
51 Windy City transports
56 Title for Gilbert or Sullivan
57 Big house or pig house
58 Ward, to Beaver
60 Cover for a Mac?
61 Corgi or collie
62 Last yr.'s sophs
64 Spicy
65 *Ghosts* writer
66 Good name for a lawyer?
67 See 13 Down
68 Drag or lag ender

70 Miss America headwear
71 Throat culture finding
73 No more than
76 Sardine can opener
77 Recoiled
78 Fencer's move
79 Back up?
80 Burden
81 *Speed 2* villain Willem
82 Tonic-yielding plant
83 This is in French
85 1971 Heston role
86 Shorthaired dog
87 Perpetually
90 Firmed up
91 Where Bowie fell
94 HMO's pros
97 Has in the crosshairs
99 Town near Snowmass
100 Nairobi's land
101 Subspecialty
103 Workshop clamps
104 Coeur d'__
105 __-foot oil
107 Quarters for trolleys
108 Cinema canine
109 "__ extra cost"
110 Pink lady's need
111 Foofaraw
113 Crossword creek
114 Feel remorse
115 Catskills snoozer

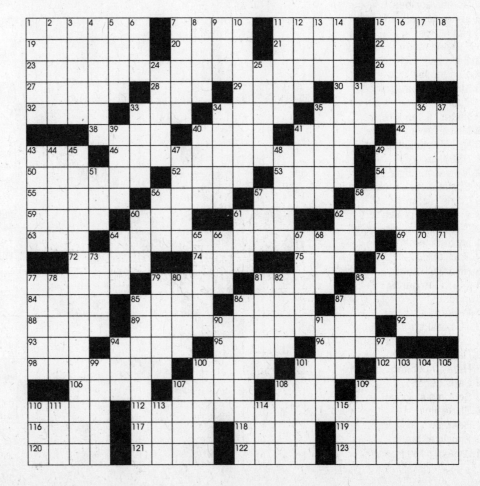

ACROSS

1 Daddy-O
5 George, née Mary Ann
10 St. Louis landmark
14 Roe and doe
18 Move for Midori Ito
19 TV Hercules Kevin
20 Permanent setting?
22 Go cold turkey
23 A, B or AB
24 Student astronaut's resolution?
26 Elbow-wrist connection
27 Vivacity
29 Like fresh lettuce
30 New England hockey player
32 A Brit's may be sticky
35 Whence the Phoenix rose
37 Do finger painting
38 Time gone by
39 Aspiring actor's resolution?
43 She looks at books
46 Ossie of *Get on the Bus*
48 Lyricist's contribution
49 Rawboned
50 Cause friction
51 At all times
52 Trig ratio
53 Husky food?
54 Verb of the past
55 Some vaccines
56 Letter carrier's resolution?
60 Hops dryer
61 Sudden storm
63 Sells via machine
64 Gushes feelings
66 Moonshine machines
67 Toon duck
68 Plates of salmon?
69 Island NW of Tahiti
70 __ killing (cleaned up)
71 *Streetcar* cry
72 Ring around the moon
73 Scuba diver's resolution?
76 Osiris' sister
79 Amused expression
80 Circumcision ceremony
81 Icy detachment
82 Back talk?
83 Hillary Clinton, __ Rodham
84 "__ in the hand . . ."
86 Indent
88 Weirdo
89 TV breaks
90 Dress designer's resolution?
93 Raised fiber
94 Hera's husband
95 Sans sense
96 Sonoma stopover
98 Show films
101 Beau tie?
103 Play like Pan
104 Breaks new ground?

105 Caterer's resolution?
109 Baba au __
113 Came to rest
114 Sole mates?
115 MOCA display
116 Don Corleone
117 A lot
118 Petty clash
119 Roe and Doe
120 Three-sided sword

DOWN

1 Butter bit
2 Eagle Rock college, for short
3 Zing
4 Glossy
5 What the heir bags
6 Shylock's offering
7 Exasperate
8 UK honor
9 Moved to tears, perhaps
10 St. Francis' town
11 Uses a gavel
12 Thunder sound
13 Ad __ committee
14 Young pigeon
15 Nut house?
16 __ *kleine Nachtmusik*
17 Head the cast
21 Alternative to JFK

25 Gets the patient ready
28 Triangle sides
31 One of Donald's nephews
32 Walks wetly
33 "__ at the office"
34 Reporter's resolution?
35 Without a key
36 Make confetti
37 Writer John Gregory
40 Majorette's moves
41 Weather word
42 Dessert tray items
43 Playwright's resolution?
44 Prizefighters' prizes
45 Helps in heists
47 1980's Mideast __ wars
52 "Hogan's Heroes" house
53 Chinfest
54 Less focused
57 Circumvents
58 Suggest a specialist
59 Leave the federation
62 Suffix for mod or nod
65 __ de mer
66 Went bad
67 Iron Butterfly's "In-A-Gadda-__"
68 Powerful
69 __ cum laude

70 Cambria neighbor __ Bay
71 Like the sea
74 Last writes?
75 Frequently
77 Whitman's "__ America Singing"
78 Mawkish
84 *Night of the Hunter* screenwriter
85 Borderland
86 Church assembly
87 Joy
88 You can go for a dip with one
91 Most pleasant
92 Surprise endings
94 Piquant
97 Chutzpah
98 Faux
99 Popular pop
100 Cayuse control
101 Surmounting
102 Stadium since 1964
103 The elder Dumas
106 Zeros
107 Dieter's last resort?
108 Westphalian product
110 Cheer leader
111 Shoshonean
112 A Pep Boy

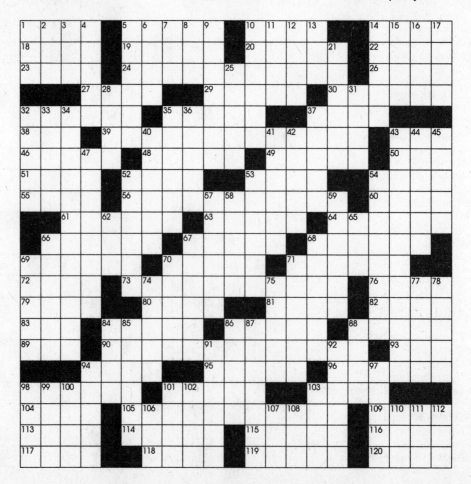

ACROSS

1 Guinness from London
5 They make you smart
10 Do nothing
14 Brew base
18 Ancestor of six Israel tribes
19 Singer Cherry
20 Achilles' tale
22 The O in B&O
23 Shaman's wisdom
24 Clean campuses?
26 Foot five
27 Turn green?
29 Children's doctor?
30 London insurer
32 Bright-colored shell
35 It means healing
37 On __ with (equal to)
38 Orange Cty. campus
39 Polished soap?
43 Know, in Knightsbridge
46 Iraqi port
48 Wispy white clouds
49 1994 Geena Davis film
50 Follower of Paul or Benedict
51 Sultry Sommer
52 You put your foot in it
53 Conn the actress
54 Nabokov prof
55 Articulates
56 A break from grime?
60 Hubbubs
61 Smart remarks?
63 Lover
64 Tuttle of radio's "Sam Spade"
66 Streetcar's Blanche
67 Predicted
68 L.A. soccer team
69 Pan the choreographer
70 Early Belafonte song
71 "I take my __ to you"
72 Erstwhile Atlanta arena
73 Detergent development method?
76 Jabber?
79 Sexton or Sassoon
80 Two in a row?
81 ". . . __ it Memorex?"
82 Divisive word?
83 Blah blah blah: abbr.
84 Welcome the judge
86 Stamp sheets
88 Bullion piece
89 It means ten
90 Cleanliness advocate?
93 Zsa Zsa's sis
94 Domino dots
95 Unkempt
96 Hardy partner
98 Kobe robe
101 Dylan's "The Mighty __"
103 Nod neighbor
104 Caesar's fateful date
105 Washable?
109 Septennial affliction
113 Salty seven
114 Irish playwright Brian
115 Green power
116 Isthmus of Kra dweller
117 Merchandise mover
118 Domed church part
119 Skiing turns
120 Longings

DOWN

1 Surf shelfmate
2 A sign from above
3 Audio receiver
4 Biz rival
5 Speak whiningly
6 Impose, as taxes
7 *Enero* to *diciembre*
8 For each
9 Crooked mouthpiece?
10 In __ (replacing)
11 "Oh me! Oh my!"
12 Half-turns
13 Evian, in Evian
14 Detroit, the __ City
15 "Yo! Yeoman!"
16 Distributed disinformation
17 Put in the round file
21 Oracle locale
25 Monarchist's cry "Vive __!"
28 Thatch source
31 Behindhand
32 Cuts up stew meat
33 Florida town
34 Prevent ring-around-the-collar?
35 Eat crow and talk turkey
36 Correspond
37 Longhorn rival
40 Off-the-wall answers
41 Hit squarely
42 California date center
43 What triggers a cleaning session?
44 Like some bagels
45 Present in English class?
47 Make another offer
52 Crystalline rock
53 Reduce in reputation
54 Candle base
57 Fad dolls
58 Watts Towers builder Simon
59 __ a pancake
62 Runner Sebastian
65 It means gums
66 Strip of a stripe
67 Chin warmers
68 Gaudy
69 Had aspirations
70 Woody's Annie
71 Antidogma doctrine
74 Strawberry colts
75 Dunk food
77 Range in the home
78 Wreck a car
84 Give it a whirl
85 Advance warning
86 Fallback strategy
87 Suitability
88 Word in a Latin hymn title
91 Cal Ripken, Jr., e.g.
92 They got here first
94 Band after bandits
97 One of Kwanzaa's principles
98 Lip service?
99 Think of it
100 Fast finish?
101 Don't stick it in your ear
102 Adaptable trucks, for short
103 Dutch port
106 Lyricist Gershwin
107 Preschooler
108 Seine sight
110 Charades' "little word"
111 Campbell's container
112 Casual greetings

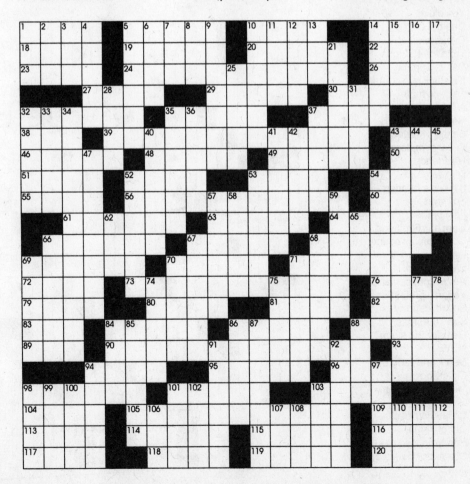

ACROSS

1 Slow boat
4 As Solomon would've done it
10 On the rocks
14 Police protection?
19 __ pro nobis
20 Hemoglobin shortage
21 Funnywoman Martha
22 Did standup?
23 MGM
26 Golfer Nancy
27 Viewpoint
28 Guy in Jamaica
29 Coal holder
30 Break in the action
32 Heading for overtime
33 Fish for a fish stick
34 Cartoon Chihuahua
35 Mute emoter
36 Enough for checkers
39 Punt pusher
40 MD
43 Oct. preceder
44 Dracula, at times
45 La-la lead-in
46 Do the first show
47 Isolated rock
48 One who obeys orders
51 Measles mark
53 Wildebeests
54 Serpentine
55 Workbook section
56 Yon bloke
57 Driblet
58 Devastate
59 Take the tour bus
62 Self-important
63 It's stuck in a corner
66 Tabby's mate
67 ATM
70 Rocker 88 Across __ Jovi
71 Beetle's sergeant
73 Fever symptom
74 Residence
76 Desideratum
77 It takes a beating
78 Fell for it
79 First name
80 Liner surroundings
82 Coral Gables county
83 Lethal weapons
84 Weeny head
85 Activist priest Malcolm
86 Vegan's protein
87 Scand. country
88 See 70 Across
89 Gear for the slope?
90 NOW
94 Derek and Diddley
97 Cigar end
98 Mrs. Shakespeare
99 Divining tool
100 Collar, copwise
101 Out of shape
102 Poet who inspired Cats
104 Conductor Calloway

105 __-jongg
106 Penne and such
107 Flawless
109 UFO
113 Duino Elegies poet
114 Join the cheerleader
115 Flew without copilots
116 Old soap
117 Moved smoothly
118 Starts to snooze
119 Romantic rendezvous
120 Age of distinction

DOWN

1 Beefsteak, for one
2 Astronomy Muse
3 Wisconsin collegian
4 Carry on
5 Concert ending?
6 Sunday speech
7 Personify
8 MGM mascot
9 Sweet tuber
10 Writer Washington
11 He slew 25% of the world's population
12 It looks out for you
13 Hates with a passion
14 Assesses
15 Deity of desire
16 SPCA
17 Mao-Tung link

18 "Oh yeah? __ who?"
24 Antiquity, in antiquity
25 Witch doctor's practice
31 Sunday closing
33 1940s jazz buff
34 Haymarket Square event
35 Do a swab job
37 Powerless
38 Nashville attraction
40 Place setting setting
41 Predetermine
42 "Absolutely not!"
44 Choices A and B
47 Fit of anger
48 Does a slow burn?
49 Gibson garnish
50 BMW
51 Nut case
52 Artist Mondrian
53 Smutty stuff
54 California roll, e.g.
57 Small quantity of dope?
58 Gallivant
60 What a cinema seat may be
61 Citizen Kane prop
62 Nebulous
63 Story lines
64 Mideast heights
65 A Hatfield, to a McCoy
68 Short of funds

69 Valhalla Allah?
72 Audition for a part
75 Memorable San Franciscan Herb
77 Actor Willem
78 Go up in flames
80 "__-da, life goes on . . ."
81 Dove notes?
82 Decline in activity
83 Worth a B
84 Simple ending?
86 The __'clock news
87 Mythical weeper
88 It needs work
90 Caught dead to rights
91 Hallmarks
92 Knotted
93 Exuberant expressions
94 In comparison with
95 Playing around?
96 Spenserian section
101 Musical measure
103 Aral or Caspian Sea, really
104 Doofus
105 Dial __ Murder
106 Where to find peas on earth?
107 Pique experience
108 24 horas
110 It comes in gobs
111 JFK arrival, once
112 Came together

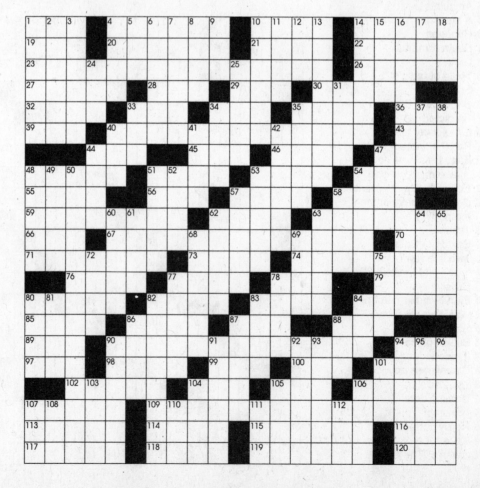

ACROSS

1 Con job
5 Some drummers do it
9 Poet exiled in 8 A.D.
13 Open-handed hit
17 One of Chekhov's three sisters
18 Target of the silly rabbit
19 Bargain holders
20 Raised
22 Fasten-ating bit of foliage?
25 Survive
26 Good enough
27 Solemn ceremonies
28 Hid out
29 Pull strings?
30 Intense
31 International A-list
32 Sheepish?
35 Strauss' material
36 Having more marbles?
37 Fido's fetter
38 McDormand's Oscar movie
39 Have a yen for
40 Eye colorer
44 Makes a choice
45 Existential swamp shrub?
47 Glazier's insert
48 Oscar nominee Stephen
49 One who takes a gander?
50 Off-the-rack items?
51 Pinnacle
52 Dexterously
54 Kudos for Callas
56 Shucked
57 Feats of Klee?
58 The hard stuff
59 Deal with it
60 Strong
63 Like older Brie
64 "Jeopardy!" e.g.
68 Sweater size
69 Job, John or Jonah
70 Where matzos are broken
71 Bedazzlement
72 Role for Ronny Howard
73 Herb that's a wash?
76 Moon, over Milano
77 Starr's predecessor
78 Takes advantage of
79 Admiral's adverb
80 Less coarse
81 Paperless pups
83 Old chum
84 Skimpy
85 Right now
87 Butler portrayer
88 Junk in the box?
89 Critical time
90 Of hearing
91 Adjective for Hagar

95 DNA expert's concern
96 Blue bloomer?
98 Be a noodge
99 Historian's Muse
100 Ceramist's need
101 Radius companion
102 Get smart
103 Witnesses
104 Moola
105 Outcomes lacking losers

DOWN

1 Parlor piece
2 Clump of clay
3 Chills and fever
4 Earl's superior
5 Stabilize
6 Poet's Muse
7 Run-on sentence?
8 IV times XVI plus I
9 Zone of the unknown
10 Trickster's target
11 1984 Wilder comedy *The Woman __*
12 UK decorations
13 Legislative body
14 Orchid that makes waves?
15 As __ (usually)

16 1990s White House wannabe
20 Gives some slack
21 Blade wetter
23 It's done in Hollywood
24 __ *bragh*
30 It may be free or blank
31 He looks both ways
32 Botanist's concern
33 Father Damien's concern
34 "__ Joe's"
35 Gatsby's love
36 Latin dance
38 Proverbial rushers-in
39 Relinquish
41 Banister
42 Memo start
43 Rank tennis players
45 Cracker snacker
46 Wild companion
49 Lead the way
51 Apartment mgr.
53 Flowers that hate waterlilies?
54 Hits on the head
55 It follows Da Doo
56 Watercolorist Winslow
58 Keeps afloat
59 Officer-to-be

60 Mess maker
61 Stock ticker output
62 *Trinity* writer
63 Bathroom hangups
64 Disney Hall designer
65 Favorite hangout
66 O'Hara, to Tara
67 Exhausted
69 Tend to the turkey
70 Arthurian sword holder
73 Meat market maven
74 Bridgetown is its capital
75 Harlem theater
76 Where Gulliver was very big
80 County festivals
82 Remus, Sam and Vanya
83 Eddie and Debbie's girl
84 Report-card inspector
85 Where Van Gogh painted
86 Oklahoma city
87 Duplicity
88 Runway walker
89 Crest closer
90 Fundamentals
91 Be down with
92 Java neighbor
93 Queue
94 Gay Nineties, etc.
97 Near mist

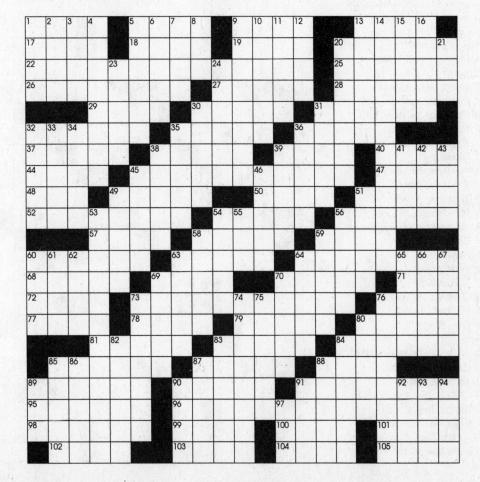

ACROSS

1 Chicken chomper's choice
5 Gold standard?
10 Ploy
14 Quahog
18 Fiend's forte
19 "__ of star-crossed lovers"
20 UHF's U
22 O for goodness' sake?
23 Use the Underwood
24 Person who forgot the words?
26 Bible preposition
27 Part of speech
29 Easy mark, perhaps
30 *Call of the Wild* writer
32 Quantum theory physicist
35 Lullaby's cradle supporter
37 King of the apes?
38 Swiss stream
39 Wordless American anthem?
43 Highest honor
46 Renders insensate
48 Dot on a map
49 Unit costs
50 Your, among Friends
51 Of wrath, in a Latin hymn
52 Playwright Wilson
53 Actress Skye
54 It means wing
55 Wash. body
56 Lunch too good for words?
60 To laugh, to Lafayette
61 Old, gold money
63 Bardot's baths
64 Post and Dickinson
66 Steal
67 Sierra Nevada lake
68 Porpoise, possum or person
69 *Planet of the Apes* author
70 *Subpoena duces* __ (CUT ME anagram)
71 Distract
72 Whitewash ingredient
73 Wordless state?
76 Impedance measures
79 Mendicant's request
80 Memorable screen sexpot Diana
81 Deserve
82 Flow slowly
83 Go out with
84 O with a bar through it
86 Macbeth, in Act I
88 Operettist Franz
89 Be off
90 What you hear instead of discouraging words?
93 Tell's canton
94 Dotty
95 Atmospheres
96 Signoret Oscar film __ *the Top*
98 *Little Men* writer

101 Besmirches
103 Bad-luck charm
104 Sheep's clothing?
105 Wordless ode to abodes?
109 Tar in Tarragona
113 Pianist Gilels
114 WWII plane __ Gay
115 No-goodnik
116 "Sorry!"
117 Say it isn't so
118 Classical conflict
119 Dix and Knox
120 Faint

DOWN

1 More than moist
2 Collegiate climber
3 Puppy bite
4 Project Mercury hero
5 Point on Oahu
6 "__ is the lowest form of wit"
7 Smash into
8 Second in command?
9 Homage
10 __ wrong way (irk)
11 1997 Peter Fonda beekeeper role
12 Use a swizzle stick
13 Fork-tailed seabird
14 Newscaster Connie
15 Come to earth
16 Bird's sax
17 Satellite
21 Fit like __
25 Cap or gown lead-in
28 Early N.Y. publisher
31 Wallet greenery
32 Go into a tizzy
33 Hijacked ship Achille __
34 Industrialist who forgot the words?
35 Where the hearts are
36 Port __ Angeles
37 Steven S.'s actress wife
40 Very small
41 Singer Jackson
42 Indian princesses
43 Barbarian who forgot the words?
44 Kate's co-Angel
45 Brontë's Jane et al.
47 Gulls or rooks
52 Closely trimmed
53 Nonliteral phrases
54 The wrong path?
57 You can count on it
58 Short Bible book
59 Blissful state
62 *Hercules* frame
65 *Mlle.*'s mom
66 Tillie, in old comics
67 Mideast capital
68 Helen of "Prime Suspect"
69 Like one who's "been there, done that"
70 "It Takes __ Tango"
71 Rigg and Ross
74 Puffy swelling
75 "Do I __ Waltz?"
77 Stiller's spouse
78 Mast pole
84 Just one of those things
85 __ rail (have the inside track)
86 Top of the world, to ancients
87 Emphatically and reflexively she
88 Clinton aide Panetta
91 Chiang's realm
92 Actress Tammy
94 "Gee whiz!"
97 Yoke support
98 Dazzled
99 Togo's capital
100 Eagle or double eagle
101 Noxious mist
102 Capital on a fjord
103 Fair
106 One for *los libros*
107 Overly
108 Biblical epic *Ben-*__
110 Incipient seafood
111 Clean-air gp.
112 Say "what?"

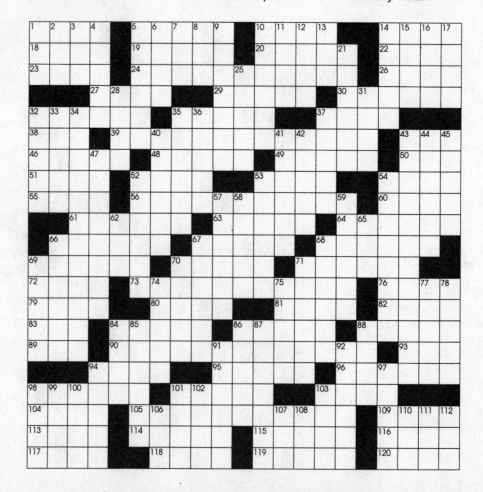

ACROSS

1 Persona non __
6 Clobber
10 London subway
14 Meaningless syllables
18 Of Crees or Crows
19 Saturn trailer?
20 Where port is left?
21 Grow weary
22 B in Botany
25 A Walton girl
26 *Dos* cubed
27 Up __ good
28 Procure
29 Mars
31 Not e'en once
32 Low note?
33 Painful struggle
35 Tickle the fancy of
36 Ex minus five
37 C in Cinema
39 Somber
40 Baby bloomer
41 "Muskrat Ramble" composer
42 Stage signal
44 Lay eyes on
47 __ broke (risk all)
50 *Typee* continuation
52 The Doors' "Riders on the __"
54 Numbered hwys.
55 __ contendere
56 A in Art
59 Dian Fossey subject
60 In full force
62 Arch type
63 Emmy-winning Ed
65 On the wagon
66 Give the brush?
68 Polished plane
70 Deepest lake in the lower forty-eight
72 Actor Penn or Bean
73 "What's My Line?" expert
76 Channel 14 and up
77 D in Design
82 Virginia of Virginia
83 Held up under
85 Butler's belle
86 Tarzan's truelove
87 Hepster's exclamation
88 Peak point
89 Pop-top opener
90 Sound at the circus
91 Texas' Houston
92 DeMille's genre
94 B in Business
99 Lower, as lights
102 Disconcerted
104 Add via keyboard
105 Letter from Greece
106 . . . *in corpore* __
107 Hall of *South Pacific*
109 Follower of Christ?
110 Brummel or Bridges
111 Toward the center
112 Sovereignty symbols
113 A in Anthropology
117 Wheezy chest sound
118 Nigeria, Algeria, etc.
119 "Read 'em and __"
120 U. of Oregon site
121 Daddy's triplets?
122 Clockmaker Thomas
123 With a twist?
124 Plow-making pioneer

DOWN

1 Thalia and her sisters
2 Wealth
3 Detest
4 __ kwon do
5 Counting everything
6 Old racer Oldfield
7 Likewise
8 Bro, to Sis
9 Highfalutin'
10 It gets under your skin
11 GI's R&R spot
12 Diver's danger
13 Unstress
14 More muggy
15 C in Criminology
16 That old Dodge?
17 High-strung
18 Chuck's relative
23 The fourth Mrs. Chaplin
24 Garr of *Dumb & Dumber*
30 Light years away
33 Prognosticator's pack
34 Construct cryptograms
37 Dastard
38 Tide controller
39 Onyx and opal
40 Ouchie or owwie
43 Where Tell did dwell
45 Le Pew or Le Moko
46 It flows through Flanders
47 New homonym
48 Wall or ball ender
49 F in Food Science
50 No longer stuck on
51 Like the Hatter
52 Looks pooped
53 Hard hike
56 Had a little lamb?
57 Auctioneer's warning
58 Fragrant spice
61 Not up yet
64 Only now and then
66 *Fearless* director Peter
67 Tennis' Mandlikova
68 Dough to go
69 As well as
70 Euphonium cousin
71 Just __, skip and . . .
72 Sea dog
73 Go for the gold
74 Hindustani mister
75 Mary's "Ink" co-star
78 Coll. cadets
79 Solver's shout
80 Borg of tennis
81 Island near Kauai
84 They're overhead
87 Two cents worth
90 Largest of the Ryukyus
91 Reconnoitered
93 Uganda's Amin
95 Made __ for (promoted)
96 Within arm's reach
97 1980s fashion look
98 Kra dweller
99 Fonteyn or Farrell
100 Harmonizing
101 Toon squirrel's sidekick
102 Norway coastal feature
103 Nimbi
104 Mole-colored
106 Military encirclement
108 Southwest art colony
110 Transvaal trekker
114 Wimbledon unit
115 Kareem, before 1971
116 Color

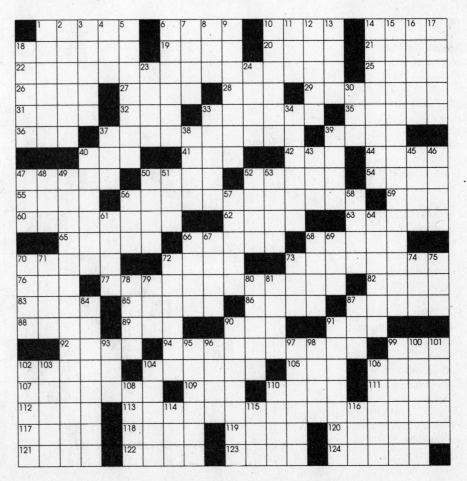

ACROSS

1 Blazing
6 Sign of bigfoot?
9 It was once yours
12 Early malls
18 Bunsen's invention
19 Half MCCX
20 Down front?
21 London's __ Garden
22 Prayer
23 "Shropshire Lad" line
26 __ a wet hen
27 Marcello's mine
28 Juan's January
29 End table?
30 Before bag or ball
31 Perfect number?
32 Hot mos.
33 USPS districts
35 Aspire
37 Silk shade
38 Far in front?
39 Lao-tse's way
42 Intersected
44 Suggestive sitcom
47 Leatherworker's tools
48 Urge strongly
50 Bastille Day season
51 Hardly old-fashioned
52 Where the Mud Hens play
54 Shorthand pro
55 Come-hither look
57 Jurassic Park's Richards, et al.
58 Muses' domain
59 Comes in feet first
60 Mustachioed movie critic Gene
61 Rip, hack, whip or chain
62 Hitchcock mystery
65 Kisser
68 Beethoven overture
70 Cowboys, at times
71 Simons-Marks 1931 hit "All __"
72 Chaucer's "The __ Tale"
74 Dredged for frying
76 Fly catcher?
77 Pre-toddler
78 "Yuck!" of yore
79 French thread
80 Snake-haired Gorgon
81 AARP pt.
82 Revolver
86 Fam. reunion attendee
87 Type of gray or tray
88 Actor Ossie's wife
89 Family chart
90 Con men?
92 Buttonlike
93 Garb for Ginsberg
94 What Dorian Gray didn't
95 Take a little off the top
98 Links rarity

101 In excess of
103 Leaves at 4 p.m.?
104 Divide at the deli
105 Eventually
108 Front-runner
109 Gets ready to drive
110 It's inspired
111 Positive point
112 Pay no heed
113 Fords that failed
114 Egoist's pronouns
115 Go one better
116 Flightless birds

DOWN

1 Luminous radiations
2 Time for superstition
3 More than eccentric
4 Early Ford rivals
5 Seaside soarer
6 Thespian Booth
7 Recording studio effect
8 Twelve hours from morn
9 Whatchamacallit
10 Julia Ward and Gordie
11 Three trimesters
12 Do one's part
13 Miss the field goal
14 Biscuit bakers
15 Tear
16 Initial offering?

17 Charon's river
18 Fail utterly
24 It means nerve
25 MTV's Tabitha
27 What's cooking
31 Fox or turkey trailer
32 Consent giver
34 Insectivorous plants
36 Hair do
37 Sinaloa o Sonora
38 Smidgen
39 Flapper era expression
40 Everyone Says I Love You actor
41 Chicano bears
42 High plateaus
43 "Cast of thousands" member
45 Hoist anew
46 Raven maven
47 Kirghiz range
49 Switch positions
53 Treats squeaks
55 Narrow valleys
56 Gen lead-in
57 ". . . like __ of elephants"
59 Traveler's timesaver
60 Rockers __ Dan
62 Govt. guys
63 "The truth shall make __"

64 7Up rival
66 Entertain
67 Bee quest?
69 Bags or rags preceder
71 Kind of no.
72 Oscar-winner Sorvino
73 De la Fresange of fashion
74 In shape
75 Remains after dinner
76 Just the type?
78 Birds do it; bees do it
80 Go for the gold?
83 Witch doctor's practice
84 Having eyes, poetically
85 Norse narrative
88 Feeling remorse
91 Corsica or Capri
92 No-cigar earner
93 Charlie Allnut's love
94 Storytelling slave
96 Champagne buckets
97 Scant
98 Novel ending
99 Overwhelmed
100 Says, in teenspeak
102 Smile joyfully
103 Beginner
104 Utah flower
106 Townships, briefly
107 Likely
108 Jack-in-the-box top

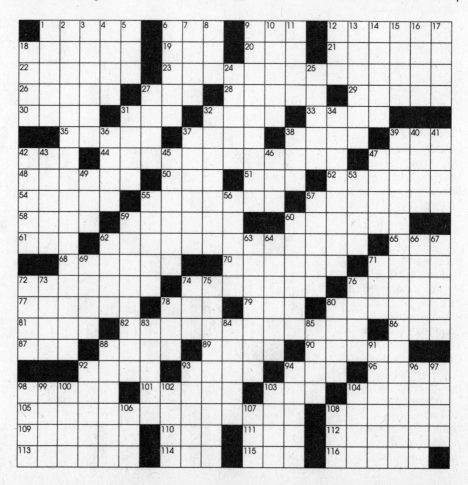

ACROSS

1 Baking quantity
6 Boston orchestra
10 Site for sites
13 It's ova now
17 Greetings from the fiftieth
18 Fergie's first name
19 Dossier
20 Realtor's aim
21 Baseball stand-in?
23 Check writing
24 Ensnare
25 Sorcerer's specialties
26 Goodwill, for one
28 African mammal
29 Shoot the breeze
32 Org. in Tom Clancy books
33 Homer-hitter's gait
34 Psychology I
36 Cartoon collectible
37 Royal pronoun
38 Pregrown grass
39 Get __ welcome (enter triumphantly)
41 Sign of The Times?
43 Decade in a Japanese penthouse?
47 Beetlejuice's Baldwin
50 Aurora, to some
51 Queen Mercutio described
52 California county
53 Ravine
54 Rough in the diamond?
56 Get on video again
58 Luau music-maker
60 Adjective for 2000
61 North-of-Sunset area
62 Enlarge the house
64 Word from a bird
65 Bobble the ball
66 Undercover choices?
68 It's often broken
69 Former fort
70 Army outfits
71 Brahms' birthplace
72 Lady's man
73 Humbert Humbert's creator
75 Hungarian coin
76 "Dear" fellows
77 Dovish deity
78 The African Queen writer
81 Iron or Bronze
82 FedEx rival
83 Gossip or grime
84 Governor's repeat pardon?
90 Terse turndown?
92 Stately dance
93 Like zinfandel
94 Golden Girl Arthur
95 Coll. degrees
97 Harry-Jack link
99 Hardly Mr. Cool
100 Head cheese?
101 Help in dirty deeds
102 Become troublesome
104 They bought up the Broadway

106 Land rovers
108 Big name in Champagne
109 Palindrome start
110 Dove's cry?
115 Quel fromage!
116 Memorable character actor Fritz
117 Mideast money
118 1956 97 Across rival
119 They're accommodating
120 Put to the test
121 Shoots the breeze
122 Roof supports

DOWN

1 Ewe might say that
2 Soul singer __ Sure!
3 Anthracite measure
4 Where the toys are
5 Irish national symbol
6 Entertainer Abdul
7 Celestial spheres
8 Good buddy
9 Satirist Harry
10 Far-ranging
11 Haute monde members
12 It makes the pool larger
13 Durango direction
14 Clotheshorse?
15 Windshield woe
16 Calyx component

18 Non-patterned fabrics
19 Bedeck
22 Fake drakes
27 Raid
28 Griffith Park attraction
29 Barracks bed
30 Say what?
31 Shipper Onassis
33 Take __ (bite)
35 Mop 'n __
38 Pack on board
39 Hindu god's incarnations
40 Sun spot?
42 France, under Caesar
44 Cut the crop
45 Popular Western?
46 "Oh no, __!"
48 Creamy pastries
49 Ate caramels
53 Sten and stun
54 Automaker Enzo
55 Nonkosher conductor?
56 Return to fashion
57 Utah university town
59 Hawaiian coffee name
60 Brezhnev
61 U2 pilot?
62 After 63 Down, classic Cukor comedy
63 See 62 Down
66 Salad veggie

67 Copied cassettes covertly
72 Italian actress Virna
74 Not conned by
75 Laverne De Fazio's friend Shirley
76 Nimble
79 Sparkler
80 Showed
82 Hullabaloo
84 Mouse-o-phobe's cry
85 Daisy- or day-care center
86 Plant diseases
87 Not neap
88 Churchill sign
89 Put away groceries?
91 Sockdolager
95 Stag movie?
96 Squirrel snack
98 Fiery fragment
100 Monks' hoods
101 Playwright's ploy
103 Pueblos' enemy
105 Confederate
106 Grand Forks' st.
107 Dull brown
109 Near the rear
111 Peeples of "Fame"
112 Palm leaf
113 Namath, in 1977
114 Acapulco affirmatives

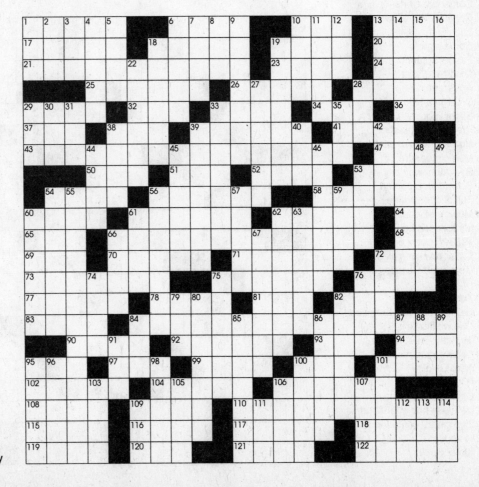

ACROSS

1 __ to (should)
6 Cow hand?
10 Ardor
14 USGS publications
18 Make the scene
19 Poetic tentmaker
20 As well
21 "I nearly busted __ laughing"
22 Sport for the exuberant?
25 It's at the end of the line
26 Restaurateur Victor
27 Be on the lookout for
28 Mazatlán Mrs.
29 The one that got away
31 To be, to Bernadette
32 Cruciform character
33 __ dictum (incidental opinion)
35 Place of berth?
36 Psalm 23 comforter
37 Scandinavian gambling spot?
39 Peppy
40 On PBS, he can cook
41 Water tester
42 Magnon intro
44 Change for a five
47 Ore chore
50 Aretha's realm
52 Parody
54 Put down blacktop
55 Comedian Chris
56 Conflict over "Chantilly Lace"?
59 Some bipeds
60 Faucet adjunct
62 Oxidize
63 Apparent
65 Change a bill
66 Slight light
68 Prepared to be shot
70 North African capital
72 Metric measure
73 Saskatchewan city
76 Scepter companion
77 Full of cheap wine?
82 Music's Mitchell
83 My fodder's house?
85 1923 Nobelist poet
86 Cellar dweller's place
87 Composer Camille Saint-__
88 Ht.
89 Turndowns
90 Barney, on "The Simpsons"
91 Like wallflowers
92 Typical "TRL" viewer
94 Slushy condiment?
99 Aero Oslo?
102 Pinnacle
104 Clipped or hacked
105 Versatile truck, for short
106 Egg cream component
107 In vogue
109 Kin of Spain
110 Wise __ owl
111 Future prune
112 Sacred slitherers
113 Noble spice?
117 Archipelago unit
118 "Hawaii Five-O" locale
119 Appomattox signature part
120 Changes chemically
121 Have to have
122 Revue part
123 Aubade time
124 Joins the team?

DOWN

1 City on the Douro
2 Toward the top
3 Bottled spirit?
4 Sarcastic exclamation
5 Isolde's beloved
6 Hide out
7 City on the Om
8 Acorn, in 2020
9 Flipped disk
10 Emiliano or Carmen
11 Elm City collegian
12 Lou Grant, offscreen
13 Fireplace fodder
14 Mrs. who misspoke
15 Fishy film?
16 Blender button
17 Cowman?
18 Venomous viper
23 Grand jeté, for one
24 Prudish person
30 Stanley or Davis
33 Convex molding
34 Accompany
37 Have an egg?
38 Check mate
39 Spot for a snooze
40 City near Union Gap
43 Use your scull
45 Eternally
46 Transmitted
47 Jean of Dada
48 Trifling amount
49 Game player's drink?
50 Hoe house?
51 'Neath's opp.
52 Made webs
53 Nuisance
56 Bronzemaker's buy
57 Groom carefully
58 Joey and Chandler's friend
61 Greek salad choice
64 MTV VIP
66 Fortitude
67 Swimming units
68 Look sullen
69 Alley __
70 Pink drink
71 Seed enclosure
72 Connecticut's Ella
73 Docs' degrees
74 Gloucester's cape
75 Minn. neighbor
78 Vanessa's sis
79 Delibes or Durocher
80 Silent screen comic Harold
81 Vittles
84 Trite
87 That lass
90 Grabbed a line drive
91 What hams may chew
93 Slim swimmer
95 Amount produced
96 Ballerina's bend
97 *Pride and Prejudice* penner
98 Jazz players play here
99 Soothe
100 Butterflies, frogs, etc.
101 Emma of "Dynasty"
102 Plain rain terrain
103 Earp's men
104 One in a million
106 Address an audience
108 GI mail centers
110 Several
114 __ Beta Kappa
115 Schnozz extension
116 Antique auto

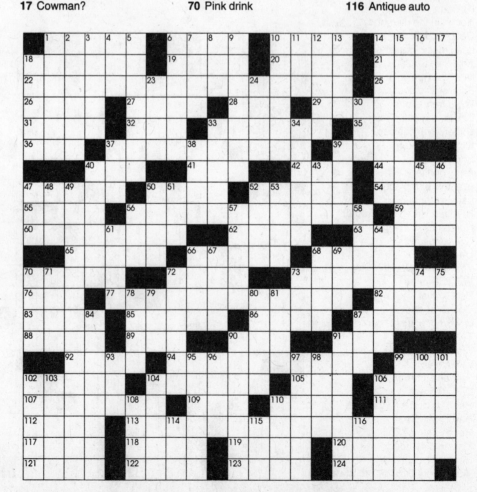

ACROSS

1 Swedish pop group
5 "Mr Natural" cartoonist R.
10 Mild oath
14 Lots of lots
19 Nostradamus, e.g.
20 Condor-minium?
21 Car bar
22 Heavy metal poser Pat
23 After ALL
26 One of Donald's exes
27 Land lost to the ocean?
28 Out of practice
29 Engineless aircraft
30 Worked in the woodshop
31 Some MOMA holdings
32 Dieters' dreads
33 To be, to Bernardo
34 "Yeah . . . right!"
35 Airway to Rome
38 You can go by it
41 After ALL
44 Extremity
45 Icelander's catch
46 State of pique
47 Actor Curtis or Danza
48 Modem rating unit
49 Speak with a Jersey accent?
50 After ALL
54 Man with a mission?
55 Play's closer, often
57 Wouk's The Winds __
58 O. Henry's real name
59 Sub spotter
60 Bar fare
61 Nile delta city
62 Roomer
64 Ecclesiastical agent
65 "Valley Girl" hangout
68 Rich tapestry
69 After ALL
71 Personal
72 Fargo director
73 High in fat
74 Lobby's cousins
75 Secret Svc. guy
76 Bambi's aunt
77 After ALL
81 Game with men
82 In a melancholy manner
84 Blood line
85 Iowa college
86 Popish Plotter Titus
87 Gaggle members
88 Long green
91 1963 Chiffons hit "He's __"
93 What Hammerstein hammered out
94 Play to the balcony?
96 According to __
97 After ALL

99 Palliative plants
100 Asian tongue
101 Track events
102 Peerless person
103 Yeats' Gonne and Whittier's Muller
104 Rowan Atkinson character Mr. __
105 Poet Lazarus' namesakes
106 ID datum

DOWN

1 Thin Man pooch
2 Heart throbs
3 Ms. Abzug
4 Hope's state
5 Lope
6 Made over
7 Caches for ashes
8 Mine, in Milano
9 Like a seller's market
10 Del Shannon's "__ to Larry"
11 Out doors
12 Cause satiation
13 Doll since 1961
14 Can-do quality
15 City east of Los Angeles
16 After ALL
17 Juli or equestri ender
18 Brown meat
24 Patagonia's peaks
25 She coined "radioactivity"
29 Merrily
31 Photo finish
32 Sparkle
35 Love affair
36 Harden
37 Hognose snake
38 Crowning part
39 Handwriting feature
40 After ALL
41 Become liable for
42 Reebok rival
43 "I had rather be __ . . .": Othello
46 Sweetheart
48 Ballet studio prop
50 Steps on the scale?
51 Carp kin
52 It's two steps before F
53 Happy or Grumpy
54 French doughboy
56 Boston airport
58 __ Verdes Estates
60 Exhales loudly
61 "Sleeping Prophet" Edgar
62 Shoestrings

63 U. of Maine site
64 Queen Victoria, to no one
65 Seles rival
66 "__ Made to Love Her"
67 Dancers Miller and Reinking
69 Small mill spills
70 Think out loud
73 Street show
75 "Look for __ label"
77 Humidity
78 Pentagon procurement problem
79 Gives grub
80 Not at all stiff
81 Deceive
83 Split, slangily
85 Tender touch
87 Coated cheese
88 Bombay-born conductor
89 __ cum laude
90 Hunt's "Abou Ben __"
91 Pillow cover
92 Alley's gal
93 Eroded
94 Hold back
95 To be, to Bernadette
97 Airline focal point
98 Like many Sp. nouns

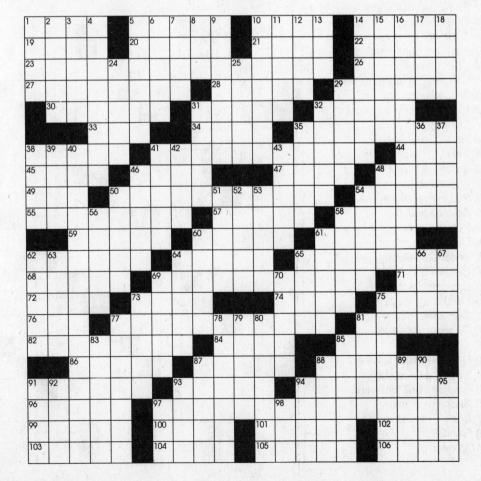

ACROSS

1 Hair fringe
5 Punch, to Judy
9 Scrooge McDuck, e.g.
14 Moist
18 Guessing game phrase
19 Homerer of the Braves
20 *Swan Lake* tempter
21 Inter __ (among other things)
22 TABLE
26 Stop yourself
27 One of the inn crowd
28 Jong and Kane
29 Zhivago's love
30 Get the lead out
31 Viennese artist Schiele
32 Overindulge
35 Debonair
36 Juicy fruits
39 The water's swell
40 CABINET
43 Red-carpet rater
45 Cuckoos
46 Guitar bar
47 Shoppe sign word
48 Clown's cognomen
49 Three before V
50 Construction site sight
51 ABC News' Roberts
53 The Great Pretender, e.g.
54 Of epic proportions
56 "I dunno" gesture
57 Tubb of country music
58 SINK
62 Champagne-o.j. mix
65 Grace periods?
66 Michael Jackson or David Letterman
70 Hale Jr. and Sr.
71 Take __ (venture)
72 Oktoberfest prop
74 A month in Montréal
75 Place for a slicker
76 Colorful duck
77 Potpie pieces
78 Old chestnuts?
79 Wyler epic *Ben-__*
80 COUNTER
84 Eye of the wolf?
85 Lost
87 Takes the Pledge?
88 Germaine or Jane
89 Either Holbein
90 One thing after another?
91 Soothing ointment
93 Gale and hail followers
96 Short vowel mark
97 Chex, Trix and Kix
100 RANGE
104 All over
105 Gladden
106 Mah-jongg oblongs
107 Macgregor, to Rob Roy
108 Make, as a way
109 Gets carried away
110 Like Brie or Camembert
111 NIMBY's Y

DOWN

1 Cry to Cratchit
2 Roman Eros
3 The longest river
4 Persistent critics
5 Word not in *The Godfather*
6 Kincaid of 1960s beach party flicks
7 Pounds and pounds
8 Puzzles
9 Kit hobbyist
10 I.e., i.e.
11 Winnow
12 Samuel's predecessor
13 Loose cannon
14 Seeing socially
15 Billy Baldwin's bro
16 Uris' __ *18*
17 Foots the bill
19 At some remove
23 Like Sabin's vaccine
24 Mexico's __ Laredo
25 Sardonic humor
30 Executive enclave
31 Eat off the land?
32 Hide away
33 Colorful horse
34 Detestation
35 Cinematographer Nykvist
36 Put in one's debt
37 Bring to mind
38 Portly and petite
40 The Congo's continent
41 Northern constellation
42 Abner or Pansy
44 Left at sea
48 They were big in the 1940s
50 Salad green
51 Tuna style
52 Eyeballs
53 Aerosol propellant
55 Hard black wood
56 Compass points
57 Swellhead
59 Pillage for plunder
60 Ezio's *South Pacific* role
61 Ostrich lookalikes
62 SST speed word
63 Troy, to Romans
64 It means mother
67 Face in the mirror
68 Birdie beater
69 Stage platform
71 Protection
72 Kind of fence
73 Gymnasts' goals
76 MTA convenience
78 The usual state
80 Memorable mission
81 Sticks to it
82 Tropical fruit
83 Says OK
86 Wily, in a way
88 Jocundity
90 El Greco's birthplace
91 *John Brown's Body* writer
92 "Lively" septet
93 Bandleader Artie
94 R&B's Tony! Toni! __!
95 Meaningful sign
96 Rosary part
97 A little lower?
98 Gwen, in *Damn Yankees*
99 Boom, or box
101 Non-Arabic 551
102 Domenico's deity
103 Write finis to

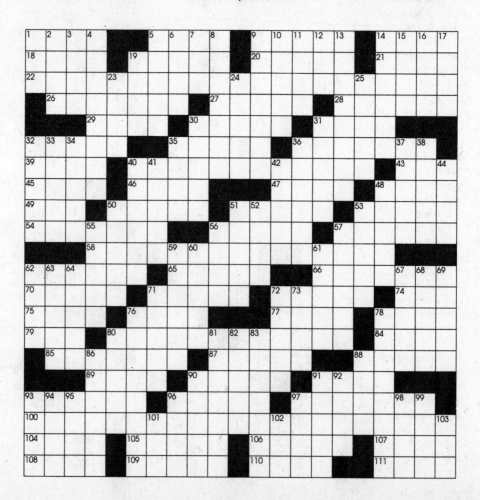

ACROSS

1 *Love Story* composer's kin
5 Groucho persona
__ T. Firefly
10 Felon's flight
13 Congregate
19 "Not to mention . . ."
20 Front of a plane?
21 Name before Jah or Sha?
22 He played Lawrence
23 Saintly mini-meal?
26 Penultimate state
27 It blew its top in 1883
28 Caesar's bad day
29 Sounded grate-ful?
30 It may be last on the list
31 Mutt, to Jeff
32 The stuff that reams are
made of
34 Rica or Brava
35 Saintly finger food?
37 Paint property
38 Keyboard key
41 Temporary locks?
44 Oliver of *Oliver!*
45 Gets the bronze
46 "Simpsons" mart manager
47 Venus de Milo, once
48 Mental faculties
49 Hormone regulator
51 Custard kin
52 Wheedle
53 Saintly plutocrat?
55 Oil film
56 Trout tempter
57 Appearance
58 Leading *Sturm und Drang*ster
59 Woodstock attendees
63 Ringling ding-a-ling
65 Kept waiting
66 Tony and Oscar
67 "__! and it was gone"
68 Be inclined
69 Cats, in Catalonia
70 Saintly triangle side?
73 Stayed fresh
77 Be an eager beaver?
78 Threw down the gauntlet
79 Hero's home?
80 He works under pressure
81 What CD's earn
82 Watson, to Bell or Holmes
83 Himalayas' Nanda __
84 Stephen King shocker
85 Start of Brazil's biggest day
86 Palindromic nickname
87 Kermit's saintly crew?
90 Underground chamber
92 Parks and Ponselle
93 Doggie bag item
94 Prefix prefix
97 Plot
99 Immunity fluids
100 From Hungary, e.g.

102 He gives you fits
103 Saintly South Pacific
spot?
106 Field marshal?
107 Shakespeare title's
second word
108 Princess Caroline's
mother
109 Inner drive
110 Built an aerie
111 ID on a 1040
112 Assuaged
113 Tireless transport

DOWN

1 Potato pancake
2 On guard
3 Abraham's son
4 Marinate
5 City Hall holdup?
6 7Up, in ads
7 __ song (cheaply)
8 Inuit's knife
9 He played it again
10 Pioneer
11 Gives fits?
12 Be lonesome for
13 Circulate
14 Books with legends
15 Lift one's spirits?
16 Saintly cordiality?

17 Sommer of *The Oscar*
18 Try for a part
24 Did more than nod
25 Spoke shrilly
32 Michelangelo
masterpiece
33 Have __ for life
34 Monks' melody
35 High point
36 Menudo ingredient
39 Cochise or Geronimo
40 Stayed the night
41 Tic-toe tie
42 El Dorado's riches
43 Thurman of *Gattaca*
45 It's a chore
48 Lord and lock lead-ins
49 Flush, or blush
50 He has his pride
51 Pluto's pest
53 Pool tools
54 High, as a kite
55 Auctioneer's "amen"
56 Toppers
58 Heredity element
59 Traditional Scottish dish
60 "__ Be Your Man"
61 Saintly snack?
62 Nautical nose
63 Manage
64 Put in film

65 He loved Lucy
67 Combustible heap
68 Blooming bulb
70 "I __ Anyone Till You"
71 Plant swelling
72 Certain birthmark
73 Chocolate shape
74 First mate?
75 Pricing word
76 Give it a shot
78 Changed the baby
80 Photocopies'
predecessors
82 *Alice Doesn't Live
Here* __
83 Cul-__ (dead end)
84 Wed
87 Staircase parts
88 He heard a Who
89 Swoop and seize
91 Kindled anew
94 Buck or Bailey
95 Stove
96 Over
97 Strike dumb
98 Showed up
99 Sauna sites
100 Historians' specialties
101 Grade enhancer
104 Sweet 16, e.g.
105 Nest-egg acronym

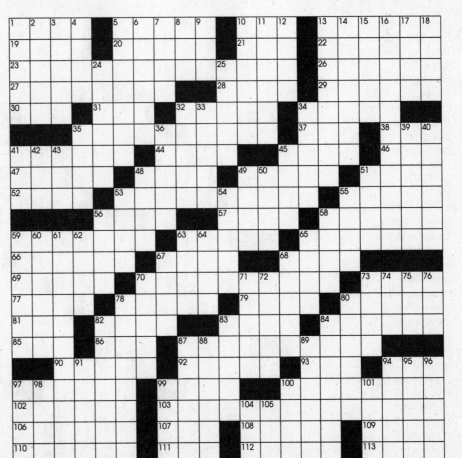

ACROSS

1 Freon or neon
4 RFM opener
9 After 8 Down, *U.S.A.* writer
15 "Here comes trouble!"
19 Plate scrap
20 Snow place like home?
21 Turn on
22 Mexican dance __ doble
23 Tell it like it isn't
24 Marcel's dream state?
26 Three make one
27 Went bonkers
29 Coming in handy
30 Jotted down
31 River through Sudan
32 Polliwogs and piglets
34 Spits in the food?
36 Equanimity
38 Melodious Mel
39 DC-10 or 747
40 Karenina or Karina
41 Straight Sidney?
45 Rugged mountain
48 Sonny's sib
49 Reduce in reputation
50 Declaim
51 __-dieu (kneeling bench)
52 There's a big one on your foot
53 Not right
54 Contemptible one
55 "See what I mean?"
56 Like Brady Bill supporters
58 Passé
59 Juggle OUR HAT?
60 Majestic Horatio?
64 Kools' competitors
67 Time machine?
68 Charge in court
72 Last Italian queen
73 Cellar dwellers
74 Comic Viking
76 Like Willie Winkie
77 Rob the actor
78 Skirler's skirts
79 Big name in the Renaissance
80 Short reply?
81 Luau loop
82 Topple Jane?
84 Pique condition?
85 Spendathon
87 At bay
88 Bears the bags
89 Dignified older woman
91 Five who sang "In the Still of the Night"
93 Bygone
94 Napoleon's fate
95 Donnybrook
96 Not taboo

99 40% of TV
100 Massages Maurice?
104 It may have a big head
105 They're kept under lids
106 Factory-direct store
107 "Amazing __"
108 Dick was his veep
109 Observe the Sabbath
110 Looks like a villain
111 Played at Atlantic City
112 Signal at Sotheby's

DOWN

1 Play the links
2 Cashew cover
3 Gertrude in the bigger picture?
4 Undulate
5 Be in accord
6 Tramp
7 Debtor's letters
8 See 9 Across
9 More pallid
10 Bandleader Shaw
11 Mate and music openers
12 Apt. manager, to some
13 Bear in a *bosque*
14 To-be-cont. story
15 Toward Harlem
16 Bret's home ground?

17 Wickerwork willow
18 Brits' bonnets
25 Underground Railroad leader
28 Tilting tower town
30 Far from far
32 McCoy, to Kirk
33 Zones
34 Vent malice on
35 "Twittering Machine" painter
36 Elbows on the table?
37 Pungent root
38 Comic's necessity
41 Madagascar mammals
42 Cigarette claim
43 *The Tempest* role
44 Himalayas' __ Devi
46 Wheel's wheels
47 Marquis, e.g.
49 Explorer Vasco
51 Jordanian tourist mecca
54 Pundits
55 War, in Oaxaca
57 Graff of "Mr. Belvedere"
58 Loathe
59 With __ of salt
61 *South Pacific* character
62 Oscar de la __
63 Brought up the rear

64 Vend
65 Emollient source
66 Sinclair's subterfuges?
69 Markophile's demand?
70 Aladdin's ally
71 Condor-miniums?
73 More like the Magi
74 Leder is its lead-in
75 *Bellas* __ (fine arts, in Aragon)
78 Banjo setting?
79 Prints on p. 24, e.g.
82 Strong drive
83 Bears witness
84 Fair-to-middling
86 Most wan
88 Spilled the beans
89 Discourage
90 Certain daisy
91 1960s revolutionary Bobby
92 Birchlike tree
93 Take the silver
95 Deal out
96 Leading man?
97 Nevada town
98 It can be good or dirty
100 Bout routs
101 She has a habit
102 Oriole's origin
103 FDR's Blue Eagle

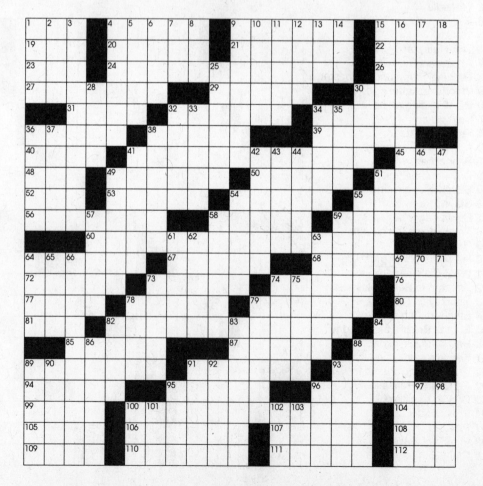

ACROSS

1 Special performance
5 *Shul* teacher
10 Clooney's "__ Italiano"
15 Take an ax to
18 "Enough to make __ laugh"
19 Cook's cover
20 Get back
21 Actress Bartok
22 Hemmed in
23 *Lives of a Bengal Lancer* star
25 Be laid up
26 Air infomercials
28 Wickerworker's purchase
29 Norse fate goddesses
31 Goldwyn and Beckett
32 Helped with the dishes
33 Bricklayer's hammer
34 Cent or se preceder
35 More elegant
36 Pyramus loved her
37 "Is that a __?"
40 Oscar-winning Keaton
42 Lunar feature
43 Bk. before Jeremiah
44 Mental health discipline
48 Flow's backwash
51 Emulated Phileas Fogg
53 Carroll character
54 She said, "Kiss me, my fool!"
55 Wielded the whip
56 Copyist
58 Hindu rope-climber
59 *The Count of Monte __*
61 Color tone
62 Hit hard
63 Delivers diatribes
64 Severe poverty
66 MGM or Miramax
68 Early birds?
69 UC campus
70 The right way
73 Beyond dampish
74 Camera adjunct
77 It fits in a socket
78 Cargo carrier
80 Robert wrote them
81 A lot
82 Florida beach
83 *Peter Pan* song "__ Grow Up"
85 It runs in the woods
87 Lose
88 Strike dumb
89 Decant
93 Frome of fiction
94 Meat jelly
95 Really easy jobs
97 Two before tau
98 Divided into two classes
101 Successful stud
102 Come down with
103 Abalones
104 Harriet's hubby
105 Effortlessness
106 Settings for medical dramas
107 A Lott of Washington
108 Noggins
109 Shack out back

DOWN

1 Mad about the guy
2 DNA and RNA
3 Caterpillar, e.g.
4 Have a go at
5 Huck or Jim
6 Four before a slash
7 Chutzpah
8 Pebbles Flintstone barrette
9 Ltd. relative
10 Profession
11 Took steps
12 Secure a sloop
13 Whopper topper
14 1945 Rossellini classic
15 1956 Elvis classic
16 Demonstrate
17 John of "America's Most Wanted"
20 O'Donnell or O'Grady
24 Old Hudson model
27 Bitter herb
30 English river
32 Rat Pack pal
33 Octagon or oval
35 Saudi king
36 Draw outlines
37 Not quite the truth
38 Fit-fiddle middle
39 In the driver's seat
40 Force unit
41 Like some tea
42 Corn holder
44 Diplomatic assignments
45 Lower Broadway area
46 Tough
47 Peace-prize winner Wiesel
49 Camembert cousin
50 Medieval minstrel
52 Places in the cellar?
54 Fundamental
56 "Put a sock in it!"
57 One for the road
58 Goes back for a pass
59 Men of oar?
60 Go unchecked
61 Pins back?
62 Go up in flames
64 Writer Grace
65 At any point
66 Boot bottom
67 "__ chic!"
69 Commuter's problem
70 Peacemaker maker
71 Caustic soda
72 Hemlock kin
74 Puccini opera
75 Mexican muralist José
76 Tony-winning Tommy
79 Trattoria menu term
81 Husband and wife
82 Vacillate
83 Jag or Jetta, but not Jeep
84 Web user's woes
85 Shoe leathers
86 Chip-shot path
87 Get into the flow
88 Pasty-faced
89 Domino's game?
90 __ a million
91 Bathsheba's husband
92 Laconic
94 High point
95 Fitting question
96 It's for the birds
99 Like some vbs.
100 Criminal clique

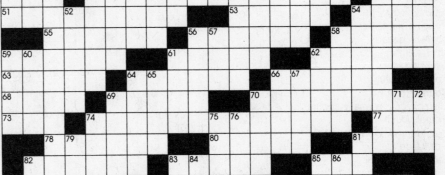

ACROSS

1 Woodstock wallow
4 Foolish fellow
10 It's sometimes shocking
14 Soak in the tub
19 Bio bit
20 Pique
21 Biologist Metchnikoff
22 Second of two
23 What Santa was when he fell on his face?
26 Numbers below the score?
27 Winter whiteners
28 Son-gun link
29 Signs off on
30 Flavorless
32 Peter Gunn's girlfriend
33 "Alice" spinoff
34 Appropriate
35 Money for a car, maybe
36 Director Grosbard
39 "Dear old" fellow
40 Blue with fatigue?
43 Picnic dispenser
44 Work undercover
45 It may be living or dead
46 Do the job
47 Ring out
48 Beach east of Orlando
51 Ross national product?
53 Type
54 Surfer's wagon
55 He's way off base
56 Delighted exclamation
57 Isolated hill
58 Cow hand?
59 Like live appearances
62 Dog's breath
63 Ding-a-ling
66 Don's king
67 Paradoxical vessel?
70 Name made of musical notes
71 Apples' mismatch
73 Cinder ender
74 Like the Avila Adobe and the Bradbury Building
76 Exigency
77 Amuse to the max
78 Pigeon English?
79 Low-voiced lady
80 "L'chaim," e.g.
82 Marquee name
83 Keystone cutups
84 Young chicken
85 Olympic gold-winner Katarina
86 Primer pooch
87 Waterston or Wanamaker
88 Road sign
89 Barbecue buttinsky
90 Gem of a Hamlet phrase?
94 Orienteering need
97 Avail yourself of Vail
98 Bridal shower?
99 Invader from Asia
100 Tilde bearers
101 Sleeplike state
102 Try to get a rise out of

104 Rabid
105 End the indecision
106 Bill of "Real Time"
107 Taps on a table
109 Prepare to scold?
113 It's one for the books
114 Compulsion
115 Like the Oscars
116 What Seuss's Horton heard
117 Pesky plants
118 Hagar, to Sarah
119 Strong
120 Collectible doll

DOWN

1 Aggregated
2 Where Amin was mean
3 Lacking, with "of"
4 Gallivants
5 Exchange market trader
6 Jesuits' founder
7 Looking __ number one
8 Workers protection org.
9 Ball-bearing item?
10 Stole a glance
11 Troubles
12 Zilch
13 Computer or combo component
14 A life science
15 "Got two fives for __?"
16 Precocious R&B noble?
17 Female lobster
18 Vocalized pauses
24 She's born to be shorn
25 Confined
31 Shakespeare's "herald of the morn"
33 Whimsically strange
34 "Consarn it!"
35 Hotelier Helmsley
37 Principal part
38 Like Andersen's duckling
40 New Deal org.
41 Uh-huh
42 Alternatives for olives
44 Dover delicacy
47 Big seller in bear markets?
48 Lorre's *Maltese Falcon* role
49 Possessive person?
50 Put on someone else's act?
51 Comestibles
52 Actress Anderson
53 Nairobi's land
54 Superlatively bad
57 Virile
58 Hotfoots in
60 Syn.-ful fellow?
61 Husky's haul
62 Opposite
63 Bye word
64 "Take __ out of crime"

65 Ornamental scheme
68 Interact
69 Denny's rival
72 Where chicks hang out?
75 Lifeboat inventory item
77 Act squirrely?
78 Answer the summons
80 "Jabberwocky" opening
81 Cry from the sty
82 Philadelphia arena
83 "Cosby" co-star Madeline
84 Actress Wray or Bainter
86 Tibia locale
87 "Clue" room
88 Shavian monogram
90 Has faith in
91 Safe from the sun
92 Don sackcloth
93 Faithless
94 1980s punk do
95 *Cocoon* actor Don
96 Country's Dolly
101 Felix or Socks
103 Surrounded by
104 Star witnesses?
105 "You gotta be kidding!"
106 Drop down?
107 Margery of rhyme
108 Acerb herb
110 The Jazz, for one
111 Spigot
112 John, in Scotland

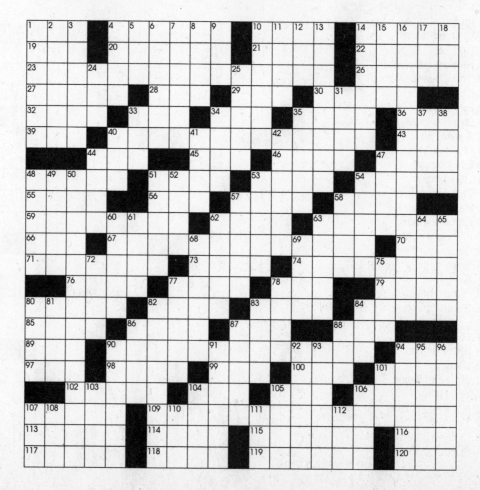

ACROSS

1 The thing here
5 First-anniversary gift
10 Took the hook
13 Monkees' "__ Believer"
16 Poultry perch
17 Uncle Tom's tormentor
18 "Self" starter
19 Hollywood's Heflin
20 Suggest
21 Possible urban myth?
24 __ carotene
25 Earn a citation?
26 Bit of marginalia
27 Deep blue dyestuff
28 Deadlock
30 Out of the way
32 Steakhouse option
33 Musketeers' oath word
35 Brown brew
36 __-ump (puh-lenty)
37 Crack the case
38 __ vous plaît
39 Excruciating accordion standard?
42 Wine label word
43 ATM essential
45 Gershwin's Concerto __
46 Richard the Anonymous
47 Caesar of the screen
51 Schnoz
52 Williams' streetcar
54 Halles or Miserables lead-in
55 Pastoral place
56 Avail yourself of
57 'enry 'iggins' pupil
58 Finish third
60 A long way off
61 1917 revolutionaries
63 Sleepy British conservative?
65 Kissing couple?
66 Section section
67 Basilica section
68 Von Richthofen's rank
69 Comic strip sound
70 Golf tutor
71 Clear tables
72 The Karate Kid 's Pat
73 More than adequate
76 Really excellent
78 John the Anonymous
80 TV monitor?
81 1965 Van Morrison spellout
82 __ Aviv
83 Tormented by pistachios?
86 Gives the go-ahead
87 Fireplace frame
89 Piano piece
90 Before Vadis or after status
91 Doc for ducks
92 Gave a hand
93 Euphoria
94 Butt head?

97 Beatles' "__ Love Her"
98 Where the boyz are
99 Juliet's betrothed
100 Latin lesson word
103 The need to discover, perhaps?
107 Search
108 Ballad ending
109 Ham's A
110 Grow a few feet?
111 Banks of Chicago
112 Agcy. discontinued in 1973
113 Car since 1989
114 Crow's nest?
115 Diskette contents

DOWN

1 Voluminous volume
2 Rabbit's life plan?
3 Riyadh religion
4 Uncouth coop
5 Reiser and Rose
6 Come to terms
7 Cow poke
8 Unfinny fish
9 Fam. reunion attender
10 Montana metropolis
11 Spillane's __ Jury
12 Nail site
13 Chekhov's first play

14 Semper fi guy
15 Place for a bracelet
16 Sticking spot?
17 Expired
18 Pain assuager
22 Ab __ (from the beginning)
23 Insipid prose
25 Caesar, for one
29 Sense of taste
30 Rock band blaster
31 It's in the trunk for a change
32 Chicano bulls?
33 Invites out
34 Legal claim
36 Florence palace
37 Nutso
40 Investor's concerns
41 Where blueprints become buildings
44 Oater chasers
48 Santa seminar subject?
49 Swing a scythe
50 Dinghy dippers
52 Abysses
53 Sly character?
54 Doone of literature
58 Hard and fast
59 Thatched hut
60 Avis alternative

61 Talks syncopatedly
62 Raw silk's color
63 Trinket
64 Criticism quantity
69 Election day list
71 Kansas City baseballer George
72 Honey beverages
74 Feel fondness for
75 Needle point?
77 And others
78 Former senior's certificate
79 Lake near Syracuse
81 Oversupplies
84 Sodium symbols
85 Zebra or donkey
87 Categories
88 Traffic trackers
92 Prom partners
93 Comic strip "Mister __"
94 Room in a maison
95 Hunger after
96 Palmer or Petrie
98 Place for an ace
99 Raindrop sound
101 Home to billions
102 Fr. religious figure
104 Place for a price
105 Obtain
106 Second Edenite
107 Where E is erat

ACROSS

1 Quick cash mach.
4 *Viet Rock* playwright Terry
9 Bailey's partner
15 Blow by Bowe
18 Queen's address
20 Cara or Castle
21 Speech-song composition
22 "May __ on?"
23 Nevada town
24 Elvis' sew-sew plaint?
26 Only U.S. voters till 1920
27 Vamoose
29 Enter
30 Like some chess moves
32 Bristly organs
33 Without
34 More adorable
35 Abbey Theater playwright
37 Before hand or eye
39 Bathsheba's boy
41 Sends e-mail
42 Self-important
43 European chain
45 Outspoken
47 Deuce beater
48 Mild, weatherwise
49 Civil wrong
50 Make haste
51 "__ man answers . . ."
52 Film classic on a sew-and-sew?
56 Stowe's little one
57 Like massy clouds
59 Lake Victoria's outlet
60 Overjoyed
62 Tiny parasite
63 Zestful
65 Place for a slicker
66 Howdy Doody, e.g.
69 Devonshire dweeb
70 Mustard and Potter
74 Satyajit Ray hero
75 Sew-sew Rat Pack movie?
79 Workout unit
80 Netanyahu's repub.
81 Folklore fiend
82 Was an omen
83 Los Angeles settler Pio
84 Southwest competitor
87 Gardener's bane
88 Went "ptui"
89 Chip for a dip
90 Weather report?
92 House of Lords member
93 Box Tops classic "The __"
94 Intro to math?
95 Downtown street
97 95 Across crosser
98 Landau or Luther
100 "Old story" adjective
101 Moseyed

105 Globe
106 Sewer's imprecation?
109 Have trust
110 Car named for Olds
111 Says
112 Please, in Potsdam
113 What you go by
114 Musician's asset
115 Eliot and Loch
116 Photographer Adams
117 PC system

DOWN

1 Iowa State site
2 Grilling order?
3 Is a public sew-and-sew?
4 Noon
5 Disintegrate
6 Col.'s superior
7 Pot grower?
8 It's S of S.D.
9 Actor Kevin
10 Gallico's *Mrs. __ Goes to Paris*
11 Nothing, to Nanette
12 This very second
13 Coming in handy
14 Fiery cocktail
15 Songwriter who had success sewn up?

16 1958 Pulitzer author
17 *Golden Eye* spy
19 "Aw, shucks" attitude
25 Wodehouse expletive
28 Old-time actor Roscoe
31 Riviera resort San __
33 Panasonic competitor
34 __ Brava
35 Some kind of nerve
36 Ionian isle
37 Big bashes
38 Life partner?
39 Binge
40 Too trusting
42 What it's worth
43 Overhead expanse?
44 Humble
46 X-ray vision blocker
48 Three sheets to the wind
52 Outlander
53 Hands and feet
54 Wearing the chador
55 John who sang of Daniel
58 There's one at home
61 Writer Rand
63 Talked a blue streak?
64 Felt nostalgic
65 Break a Commandment
66 Was profitable

67 Cause to capsize
68 Safe place for stitchery?
69 Bengal beast
70 Fragrant evergreen
71 Sew-sew explorer?
72 Milk, in Málaga
73 Animal track
76 Part of some PC's
77 He played Jed Clampett
78 Giraffe's gait
83 China design
85 Grass clump
86 Like Brady Bill supporters
89 Barber's call
91 Signify
92 Gangplank terminus
93 Architectural load bearer
95 *Tia*'s sis
96 Accumulate
97 Furniture set
98 Oliver Twist's request
99 Side squared, for a square
100 Some babies
101 Before deep or dive
102 Ubiquitous insects
103 Tickle Me doll
104 Indigo and henna
107 M and N, in D.C.
108 Jordan's organization

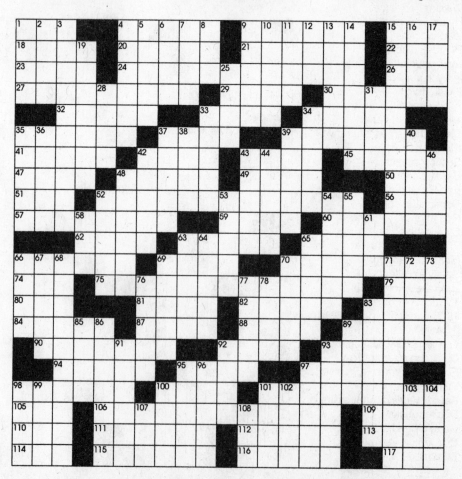

ACROSS

1 Prospect
6 South African archbishop
10 River to the Caspian
14 Shoemakers' holemakers
18 Detroit pros
19 Country on the Caspian
20 Italy's San __
21 Burmese's neighbor
22 With 75 Down, lovesick pizzamaker's song?
25 Singer k.d.
26 Composer Siegmeister
27 Start of a Cash title
28 Year in Antoninus' reign
29 Take off the hook, perhaps
31 Contracts
32 With 52 Across, voice of many toons
33 Cornhusker rival
35 Map in a map
36 Geneviève or Jeanne
37 Burt Reynolds film about pizza?
39 Like LAX or JFK
40 Doleful
41 Gull friend?
42 __ pooped to pop
44 Sets one's sights
47 Irritable
50 A Yemen capital
52 See 32 Across
54 "March Madness" org.
55 Draw closer
56 Law against crisp pizza?
59 Bit of work
60 Dyed-in-the-wool
62 Major suffix
63 Exhorts
65 "People" person
66 NAFTA and NATO
68 Kind of code or colony
70 O with a bar through it
72 Actress Ward
73 Procrastinating
76 Castling notation
77 Beatles' paean to pizza?
82 The Supremes, for one
83 Grass clump
85 Lies in wait
86 Be out of
87 Louisiana marsh
88 Art Deco designer
89 Kimono accessory
90 Geol. or anat.
91 Bit of wit
92 Tin lizzie
94 Crazy about pizza with everything?
99 See 113 Across
102 Minotaur's home
104 Twenty minutes of hockey
105 Mae West role
106 Compact combos
107 Party's main party
109 Come together
110 Where couch potatoes are planted
111 "__ a Spell on You"
112 "Where __ written that . . .?"
113 After 99 Across, what the man on the flying trapeze wants on his pizza?
117 Uris' __ 18
118 Strong-ox link
119 Cardinals or Orioles
120 "Hotel California" group
121 Open an orange
122 God, to Galba
123 Saturnalia
124 Lost a lap

DOWN

1 ROYGBIV's last
2 Set afire
3 Two-time U.S. Open champ
4 Subject to strain
5 Guilt-ridden
6 Copenhagen park
7 1934 chemistry Nobelist
8 Click up your heels?
9 Lion-tailed beast of myth
10 Like Mama, Papa and Baby?
11 Ump's cousin
12 Affaire du coeur
13 Desolate
14 Martin Luther King, Jr., for one
15 "That's some piece of pizza!"
16 Cavalry weapon
17 Tour highlight
18 Former cover girl Cheryl
23 The third man
24 Time Machine people
30 Vietnam Memorial designer Maya
33 Glacial ridge
34 What you will
37 Rotation duration
38 Beginning of Caesar's boast
39 "The Things We Do for Love" band
40 Way across town?
43 "Put __ Happy Face"
45 Former filly
46 Gives in to gravity
47 Bam-boom sticks?
48 For aye
49 African pizza's secret ingredient?
50 Cold-shoulder
51 Broke bread
52 Ram
53 D-day GI carriers
56 Pale potable
57 Sum up
58 Casserole standard
61 Lesage hero Gil __
64 Wickerwork palm
66 Sneak a look
67 Yodeler's range
68 Mighty like a rosé
69 Connecticut collegian
70 Be a caddy
71 Appointed time
72 7Up rival
73 Wyatt's OK Corral ally
74 1947 Road destination
75 See 22 Across
78 Squishy stuff
79 Three-man craft?
80 Spain's national hero
81 Prince's was purple
84 Abstaining from alcohol
87 Future flower
90 Arts festival site
91 Queens' quarters
93 Irish airline __ Lingus
95 Liver and lungs
96 Artist Mondrian
97 Melancholy
98 Tick off
99 Van Morrison's "__ Honey"
100 Provided shelter
101 Simon of the opera
102 Arboreal ape
103 Oprah colleague
104 As such
106 Muralist Rivera
108 Yikes!
110 Daddy deer
114 Evian water
115 Cont. story
116 Boater or sailor

ACROSS

1 As well
7 Emporium
11 Home for 91 Down
15 Top quality?
19 __ kind (nonpareil)
20 Mansard feature
21 Oscar-winning Patricia
22 Entreat
23 W.S. Gilbert play, sans souchong?
26 First-rate
27 TV Sales?
28 What slanderers sling
29 Wyatt of the West
30 Feline four
32 Town on the Colorado
33 *Fantasia* frame
34 Treaty partner
35 Peccadillo
38 Routine response?
40 Parthenon porch
41 Navelless man?
42 Chor or chlor ender
43 Yeltsin's yeas
46 Rending, lacking Lapsang?
49 Get the picture
50 Of races
52 *Outbreak*'s Romeo
53 Certain Prot.
54 Columbus' home
55 You can believe it
56 Monsieur Le Moko
57 Play horseshoes
58 Every 24 hours
59 Famed freebooter
60 It's right on the farm
61 Sylvester, to Tweety
62 Fishhook part
63 USAF arm
64 Town on the Hudson, saying "So long, oolong"?
69 Hard water?
72 Baba au __
74 __ Jima
75 "Caught you!"
76 A bit they can split
77 __-Hawley Tariff Act
79 Top with tar
81 Franklin's flyer
83 Bear out
84 Cantina snack
85 Nonchalance
86 Drink with sashimi
87 Safari servant
88 At the crest
89 Grabbing the spotlight, with gunpowder gone?
92 Ham sweet home?
93 Greenspan's grp.
94 In the Red?
95 Mate for Oop
96 Freeborn feline
98 Patted down
100 *Con mucho dinero*
101 Warm the bench
102 After 25 Down, exiled Asian leader
106 Rawboned
107 Sex Pistols' forte
108 It may be made in clubs
109 Submitted 1040's
110 Crowd, in Cologne?
112 Classroom credential, after Earl Gray goes?
116 Early TV quiz host Jack
117 The way Cain went
118 1950s film critic
119 Member of a very old kingdom
120 Choir recess
121 Gallows reprieve
122 Column crossers
123 Capable of being accomplished

DOWN

1 *Uncle Tom's Cabin* girl
2 "I've got my eye __!"
3 Indian VIP
4 Tuba tones
5 Obsolete epithet
6 *¿Qué __, amigo?*
7 Korean capital
8 It's out on a limb
9 Fertility clinic concerns
10 She waited for Odysseus
11 Hopping mad
12 Bound away
13 Calvin, to Hobbes
14 Careless
15 Rad comic character
16 Diet supplements, missing chamomile?
17 1981 Tony winner McKellen
18 TV science guy
24 "Know what __?"
25 See 102 Across
31 USN VIP
33 In the mode
34 Make amends
35 *Golden Boy* writer
36 Slowness symbol
37 Old Indian mercenary
39 Dry as dust
40 Dance unit
41 Leaders in suits
43 Places for 41 Down
44 Heart parts
45 Show false emotion, bereft of bohea?
47 Zorba or Zeno
48 Overact
49 Fly high
51 Old Nick
56 Chest muscle, for short
57 __ Mahal
58 Dennis, Doris or Morris
60 Ring thing
61 Sugar-lump option
62 Arthur who played Dorothy
64 Crackpot
65 He played Fogg
66 Ma that maas
67 Gives stars to
68 Ursula Andress role
70 Break a Commandment
71 Filer's aid
73 Croquet wicket
76 Constellation near Scorpio
77 Fill job openings
78 Etonian's mum
79 Went white
80 China setting?
81 Rivera's wife Frida
82 Household furnishings chain
83 Seats in St. Vibiana's
85 Hearts and souls
86 Racing Chevy
87 It may be from the blue
90 Auctioneer's word
91 Swiss miss
94 Alias
97 Silverstone of the silver screen
99 Confiscate
100 Puny
101 Locations
103 As gentle as __
104 Mercury, for one
105 *Fledermaus* maid
107 Tower town
108 Prepare tea
109 Dry Spanish sherry
110 Gene ID
111 Song from the hood
113 Bean covering?
114 Psyche section
115 Brief sensation

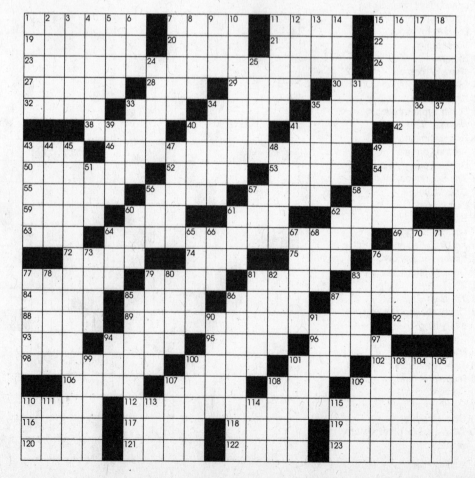

ACROSS

1 It may be underfoot or overhead
4 *Waiting for Lefty* writer
9 CD readers
15 Shortwave operator
18 Word of mouth?
20 __ Verdes Estates
21 A house may be in it
22 Judah's third king
23 Kind of culture?
24 1970 Lennon number
26 Weasel's prey
27 Osmosis sites
29 Pause filler
30 Throw a line?
32 Poet's inspiration
33 Vista
34 Largo or lento
35 House on the Hill
37 Sign on a staff
39 They're up to date
41 Background actor
42 Toot your own horn
43 Show muscle
45 Bombing on the boards
47 Like Dorothy's slippers
48 Good, in Guadalajara
49 Autobahn auto
50 Item for a rowlock
51 Ala. neighbor
52 Tutti-frutti entertainer
56 Altdorf's canton
57 Legendary dragon-slayer
59 Relative of etc.
60 Taped over
62 Eyes, to poets
63 Concisely cogent
65 B.C. currency
66 A star's lookalike
69 Turn off the sound
70 Melting pot, of a sort
74 Thor's stepson
75 1975 LaBelle toe-tapper
79 Holidayless mo.
80 You might get it for effort
81 Airline to Ben-Gurion
82 Place for a pimento
83 On or ola opener
84 Unmetric measures
87 Colleen
88 Hollywood crosser
89 Recapitulate
90 Do a slow burn
92 Horny bill
93 Court authority
94 Artist Oldenburg
95 Vocal nag
97 Impressionist Claude
98 Most repulsive
100 Music's Gang leader
101 Astronomer

105 Assent of a woman?
106 Like happy endings
109 XIX times III
110 Fudd, to Bugs
111 Resonated
112 Gymnast's prop
113 Cooking fat
114 Genre
115 Steadfastly
116 Double curves
117 Half a laugh?

DOWN

1 Ramble
2 Yen
3 Plane carry-on
4 Religion, to Marx
5 "Book 'em, __!": "Hawaii Five-O"
6 Other than this
7 Sandbox set
8 Retirement-check assn.
9 River of forgetfulness
10 Out of alignment
11 Con game
12 Act human
13 Gamboled
14 Flocked, like flies
15 Not at all discordant
16 Quickly, quickly
17 "Friend" LeBlanc
19 Book store?
25 Babe in the woods
28 Pro __ (proportionately)
31 Nashville attraction
33 Strict non-meateater
34 It can make you sick
35 Medieval menials
36 Shout "Yes!"
37 __ de cacao
38 Penny or Memory
39 Purple Heart, e.g.
40 Catch in a trap
42 One-horse towns
43 First of three virtues
44 Virginia's __ Caverns
46 Lock opener
48 Rosie's favorite celeb
52 Reef component
53 Olympic race unit
54 Bamboozle
55 In __ against time
58 Goddess of the dawn
61 Fragonard's friend
63 Mountain lions
64 Slanted ltrs.
65 Hunger for
66 Yacht's landing
67 Arm bones
68 Nightstand prop

69 Polyester film
70 Post-toast sound
71 Rite for a *mensch*
72 Pacific picnics
73 Alexandria's land
76 Drops a line?
77 Pulled up stakes
78 Saturn trailer?
83 Panacea
85 Onetime Kansas senator
86 Zorro's Z's
89 Done some doo-wop
91 Do Spade work?
92 Martin's *Ed Wood* role
93 Novelist Amado's namesakes
95 Roomy place?
96 Out of control
97 Parsonage
98 Word in great Caesar's boast
99 Role model
100 Mee __ (Thai menu item)
101 Urban haze
102 Run out of gas
103 De Valera's republic
104 Take mass transit
107 Sleuth's shout
108 P, to Plato

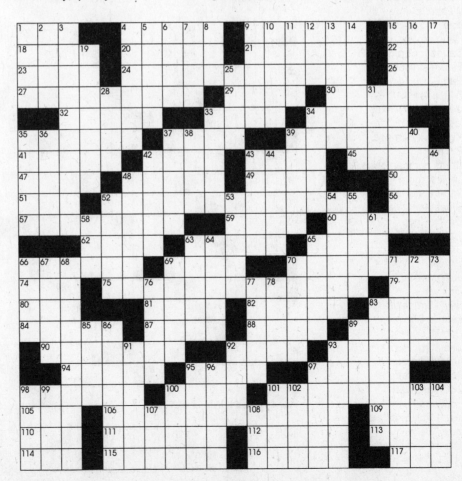

ACROSS

1 Mythical monster
5 Eight hundred preceder
8 Festal
12 It may come to shove
16 Treats meats
17 Inner ear?
18 Modern energy type
19 Video game plumber
20 ". . . and thereby hangs __"
21 Recontoured power base?
24 Gemini's mother
25 Zip or pop
26 Moccasin without a sole
27 One-time bridge
28 Dissipate
30 Ruin a shutout
31 Peanut butter option
35 Broadway luminary
36 Urban eyesore
37 Luke's sister
38 Tint
39 Joker
41 Remodeled mystery spot?
45 "__ Little Teapot"
46 Piano key material
48 Old World pref.
49 Degas contemporary
50 Box at the gym
51 Turner of film
52 Auction offers
53 Weasel's kin
54 Boo Boo or Bugs
55 Hang around
56 Cause for brooding?
57 Future stallion
58 Ego
59 With it, once
60 New type of Texas
   topography?
64 Not neut. or masc.
67 FYI part
69 Crafts companions
70 Ladies' room?
71 Sphere starter
72 Gloat
73 Tie the knot
75 Increase
76 Crack from the cold
77 Louver
78 Street on TV
79 Pink wine
80 New Hampshire town
81 Tennis' Shriver
82 Rebuilt London site?
85 Like some socks
86 Action-film gun
87 Barrett or Jaffe
88 SLC students
89 Royal, to Raúl
91 Giant California native
93 Jabs, often
95 The movies
98 The Eiger, e.g.

99 1940s wonder drug
100 Command to Fido
101 Actor Ray
102 Reformed relations?
107 Busybody
108 Wrong
109 Fletcher's creation
110 Life support?
111 Like a lot
112 Coming up
113 Twixt 12 and 20
114 Where swine dine
115 Lacunae

DOWN

1 Further away
2 Repatterned prof's
   practice?
3 Tie in
4 Malt or Chin ender
5 Transpire
6 Any thing
7 A drop in the ocean
8 Make much progress
9 Similar
10 Byway
11 Canine comment
12 Hymn of praise
13 Decorative vase
14 Often-bracketed word
15 Tiller's tool
16 Herd newcomer
18 Wine-growing county
19 Shared in common
22 Portuguese peso
23 Will Rogers prop
25 Tunney or Tierney
29 Shakespeare's Sir __
   Belch
30 Mumbles' kin
31 Rome's Demeter
32 Restructured offspring?
33 Kind of rights, relations
   or resources
34 Sophomore or senior
36 Blur an outline
37 Coupling
39 Like Dylan Thomas
40 Let up
42 Throne time
43 Puts on a happy face
44 Three-piece piece
47 Vote from a con
50 Helios, to Romans
52 "To __ not to . . ."
53 1997 Britpic *The Full* __
54 Summer shirt
57 OK, e.g.
58 Getz or Kenton
60 "Ya big __"
61 "Cheers" waitress
62 Says "Salud"

63 Fifi's farewell
65 "Read __ weep"
66 Motorized bike
68 Trough remnant
71 Zinger from Hingis
72 Trail marking
73 "__ Bobby McGee"
74 __ Romeo
75 Tipper and Al
77 Short branch track
78 Dejected
79 Switch material
80 Naval base?
82 Bridge beasties
83 Belly laugh
84 Bloke from Blighty
90 Actress Plummer
92 Spare tire site
93 It may be filthy
94 "Rocket Man" singer John
95 Full of flames
96 Olfactory stimuli
97 Be gloomy
99 Very dry
100 Cat's eye, at times
102 Air circulator
103 Soul, by the Seine
104 Baker's shortcut
105 Pack animal?
106 Krypton, e.g.
107 Slump

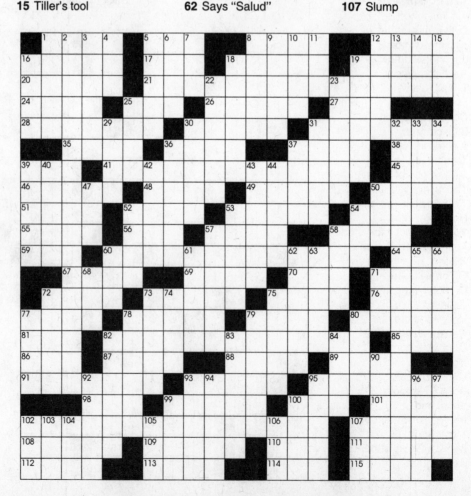

ACROSS

1 London derrière
4 Insignificant matter
10 Diminutive dog
13 New Mexico town
17 "A __ plan, a canal . . ."
18 Expired
19 Farm fixture
20 A Chekhov sister
21 Nuts and bolts
22 Risqué maritime musical?
24 Like a duck's back
25 Job-seeker's concern
27 Kiwi kin
28 Largest U.S. union
29 Montana city
31 Faith formula
32 Drs.' co-workers
33 Hockey's Mikita
34 Fire proof
35 Latin dances
37 Moreno Valley neighbor
39 Burns' sweet stream
43 In imitation of
45 Controversial fictional vessel?
47 Brontë's governess
48 Get into the game
50 Chair-man Charles
51 Adorn anew
54 Settles a loan
55 Half the time
56 Before group or freak
57 "__ only joking"
58 Begin fighting
60 Raintree, e.g.
61 House of Leo?
62 Blue plate vessel?
65 It runs in the spring
68 Speeders' nemeses
69 Waters down
70 "__ said was . . ."
71 1960s militant Carmichael
73 Manhattan transit till 1955
74 Sure thing
76 Kerflooey
77 Make coleslaw
80 Barn attic
81 "Three men in __"
82 Sailing wordplay?
85 Vine veggie
86 Cuban coins
88 Unfroze
89 Started the bidding
91 Fire follows it
93 Ospreys' kin
94 Au __
95 Minor no more
98 Extremist
100 Vintage vehicle
101 Beseech
102 I Kings prophet
103 Alliance

104 How to address a destroyer?
108 Move to yawns
109 Not fooled by
110 Short cuts
111 Job history
112 He wrote the Book
113 Vespiary denizen
114 Sister of Selene
115 Treeless tract
116 Hosp. areas

DOWN

1 Storybook elephant
2 Asia's seagoing symbol?
3 Dead Sea tourism must
4 Ilium, later
5 Encouraging word
6 Holy smoke?
7 Firefighters' options
8 Berg opera
9 And the list goes on
10 1998 box-office blast
11 Word toreadors adore
12 Nixon birthplace __ Linda
13 Vessel for commuting dentists?
14 Dismounted
15 Cast an amorous eye
16 For example
17 Like some Sp. nouns
19 T.S. Eliot's S
23 Not faithful
26 Hugh __ AKA Wavy Gravy
30 NAFTA initiator
32 Croupier's prop
33 Petticoat junction?
36 Cricket equipment
37 __ the gallery
38 Masks, as in mystery
40 Beginner
41 Face-to-face exam
42 Marshal at Waterloo
43 Unpleasantly pungent
44 Camelot co-writer
46 At __ door (in critical condition)
49 Ballet step
52 Central Sicilian city
53 D.A., e.g.
55 Disapprove of
56 Fargo writers
58 Superlatively unfresh
59 Less than e'er
60 Byron's __ Harold
62 Japanese persimmon
63 Times book critic Richard
64 Famous last words
65 Featured vessel?
66 "Get __!"

67 Columbus caravel
68 Lagoon lawman?
70 One way to the WWW
71 Overfill
72 1960 Olympian Wyomia
74 Enclosure with a ms.
75 Sunday songbook
76 WWII general Arnold
77 You may play with their toys
78 "__, brown cow!"
79 Unnamed litigants
80 Shorts supports
83 Little angels
84 Manhandle
87 Dubbed one
90 Fit to be tried
92 Weasel word
94 Rev. Jackson
96 Capers
97 Second person in the Bible?
98 Forearm feature
99 Things to draw
101 Mister Maverick
102 Olympic event since 1900
103 Acknowledge applause
105 Reset readout
106 __ gratia artis
107 Rascal

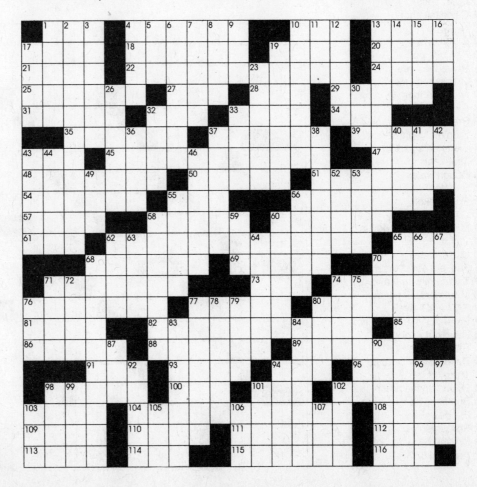

ACROSS

1 Papeete's place
7 Get out of shape
11 Duel prelude
15 Musical composition
19 Met set?
20 Solidifying agent
21 Bear with a hard bed
22 A son of Eve
23 KEEP away
26 1950s Pulitzer novelist
27 Sharon of "Cagney & Lacey"
28 Bacillus shape
29 Pub purchase
30 Polynesian image
32 On this spot
33 Bob and Carol or Ted and Alice
34 Sailor's port
35 CFO's concern
38 Make cotton candy
40 Categorize
41 Wind indicator
42 Throwing ability
43 Director Craven
46 SALT away
49 Field yield
50 Not virtual
52 "Your mileage may __"
53 "I've Gotta __"
54 Parasite's need
55 Loud
56 Miller option
57 City desk shout
58 No-good
59 Citron or salmon suffix
60 Part of a pod
61 Poseidon's realm
62 Crossword category
63 N.J. neighbor
64 RIGHT away
69 Pres. who started NASA
72 Stop making a scene?
74 Siegfried's partner
75 Timespan
76 Rough water
77 Sedate
79 Poker token
81 Gael's gal
83 Mario of New York
84 Vittles
85 Use the mall
86 Fed. act about insurance
87 Two-family house
88 Merriment
89 FAR AND away
92 Perennial starlet Williams
93 Hang out to dry
94 Bake in kilns
95 Descartes or Lacoste
96 Throw of the dice
98 Roped on the ranch
100 Bumbling beasts
101 Put down
102 Shy worshiper's place
106 Dratted
107 Arrive at LAX
108 Ham, to Noah
109 Rigg or Ross
110 It's out on a lime
112 THROW away
116 Alt.
117 1967 Montreal event
118 Stream or spring starter
119 Muse of astronomy
120 Meerschaum
121 Caught in the act
122 Agile
123 Hertz patron

DOWN

1 "Too bad!"
2 Singer Fiona
3 Lumberjack, often
4 Ornamental flowers
5 Edges doilies
6 O'clock or so
7 "Yippie!"
8 Like fine sherry
9 British rule in India
10 It can be hot or private
11 Paid out
12 Like omega
13 Large copier?
14 Potpourri
15 Honshu port
16 SQUARE away
17 Colorado Indian
18 Ayesha, to Haggard
24 Brits call it boot
25 "Keen!"
31 Press coverage
33 Push-button predecessor
34 French castle river
35 Like surf
36 Pen name
37 You can't run on it for long
39 The thing, to Hamlet
40 Vamoose
41 Assembly phase
43 Ebbed
44 School for Raoul
45 RUN away
47 Spa near Lake Geneva
48 Tin-can target
49 Grub
51 Beach Boys' "Surfin' __"
56 Maui memento
57 Mark that's an arc
58 Yule fuel
60 Weasel word?
61 Demure
62 Genetic initials
64 Ward, to Beaver
65 Complaint
66 Outperform
67 "Abraham looked up and there __ a ram. . ."
68 Apr. addressee
70 Like the Griffith Observatory
71 Adhesive ingredient
73 Bailiff's order
76 Tea service unit
77 George of "Just Shoot Me"
78 *Rocky*'s Shire
79 Set of keys?
80 Diamond pentagon
81 Detroit gridders
82 Ne plus ultra
83 Snooker sticks
85 Botany and biology
86 Roosevelt's numbered four
87 Normandy landing date
90 Soprano Mirella
91 "__ Stop Loving You"
94 Voting aye
97 Island China
99 Burn balm
100 Stick for Salonen
101 Daft
103 Dim
104 Hall of fame?
105 Leadfoot catcher
107 Early Hollywood's Velez
108 Move deeply
109 Marty Allen line "Hello __!"
110 Get-up-and-go
111 Bulldogs' backer
113 Firefighter's tool
114 Suede feature
115 Biblical epic *Ben-__*

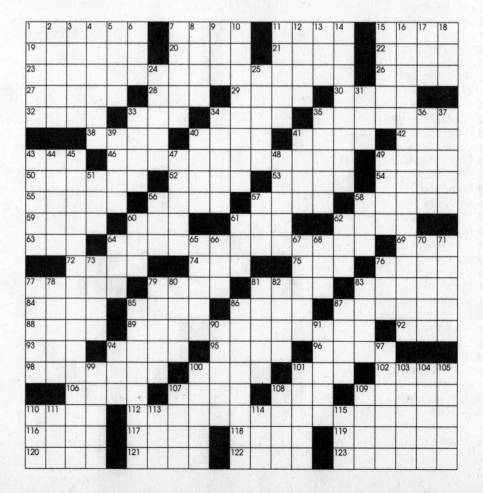

ACROSS

1 Place for a home game?
4 Debris asea
10 They go over your part
14 Town east of Perris
19 Commotion
20 It doubles in division
21 Out of control
22 Sheepish?
23 Be suspicious of guests?
26 Out of order
27 Character created by 48A's père
28 Call from the Andrea Doria
29 It may have 6 rms, riv vu
30 Stevedores' site
32 Active one
33 TD signaler
34 Late starter
35 Beer ad amphibian
36 It has a taxing job
39 Do a human thing
40 "Dang! The gun didn't work!"?
43 Boot tip
44 Shake a tail
45 Silver of the screen
46 Liturgy
47 "Spin City's" Michael __
48 Camille writer
51 Modern Milquetoast
53 Sonny Crockett's squad
54 Ditzy
55 Prowl car, to cops
56 __ moment's notice
57 Fine fiber
58 Marina mooring
59 On cloud nine
62 Pie-cooling place
63 Floaty
66 Monument for Mahal?
67 Fumble at Fort Knox?
70 Cassis-wine apéritif
71 Splendiferous
73 Hateful
74 Resembling Hyde or Griffith
76 Word above WALK
77 Precious stone
78 Adversary
79 Durante's "__ Dinka Doo"
80 Uncompromising
82 Cunning
83 Heading for the fifth set
84 On the up and up
85 Change for a fiver
86 Deep sleep
87 __ Nidre
88 Added fuel to
89 Croissant shape
90 Write M-E-I-D-A?
94 Kisser
97 Aachen article
98 Aesthetically pretentious
99 Abbr. by a phone no.
100 Nasser's org.
101 Tree trunk
102 Pear type

104 Canvas coat?
105 Give the gun
106 Courageous
107 Threepio's pal
109 Gets the Mirandas wrong?
113 "20/20" journalist Lynn
114 Perry's creator
115 "Pata Pata" singer Miriam
116 Ruff female
117 Kibbutznik's dances
118 Cars named for Olds
119 Big Red, once
120 Amtrak abbr.

DOWN

1 Injure
2 Manuscript mender
3 Deli diner
4 Preserve preservers
5 Kiwi kin
6 Has a restless night
7 Depart
8 First-grader's lesson
9 See 119A
10 Kind of stance?
11 She loves, to Livy
12 Cargo unit
13 Do airmail?
14 Tribute
15 Green or glade lead-in
16 The buzz about George III?

17 Lt.'s subordinate
18 Mystery writer Josephine
24 Hilltop
25 "Nash Bridges" co-star Cheech
31 Use a whetstone
33 Offshore structure
34 Stagehand's tote
35 Film, familiarly
37 Castle, to some
38 Like double-entendres
40 More, to Moreno
41 La Douce
42 Auto ornament
44 Volt-ampere product
47 Kangaroo kid
48 "__ circumstances beyond . . ."
49 Prepare to use Pepsodent or Pepsi
50 Underestimate an abyss?
51 Belt site
52 Hankering
53 Town, in Tours
54 "Keys made" structure
57 Move crabwise
58 Engine hum
60 Alter a bill
61 Paint-mixing option
62 Slyly insinuating
63 Spoke sheepishly
64 Sixx of Mötley Crüe

65 October handout
68 Deity's incarnation
69 Fraternal org.
72 Clark's colleague
75 Told tall tales
77 On edge
78 The reel stuff
80 Hope-Crosby title word
81 Legal memo phrase
82 Edith Head, e.g.
83 Trike riders
84 Meadowland
86 Erstwhile Strip club owner
87 Prepared to propose
88 Oregon state tree
90 The big leagues
91 Pupils' surroundings
92 N. California town
93 Young woman
94 Japanese movie monster
95 Long, loose overcoat
96 Spouting spring
101 Program problem
103 An Asta master
104 It's south of Lillehammer
105 Rat- __
106 Composer __ Carlo Menotti
107 Before tray or tree
108 P, to Pericles
110 Choler
111 Morning hrs.
112 Scorecard stat

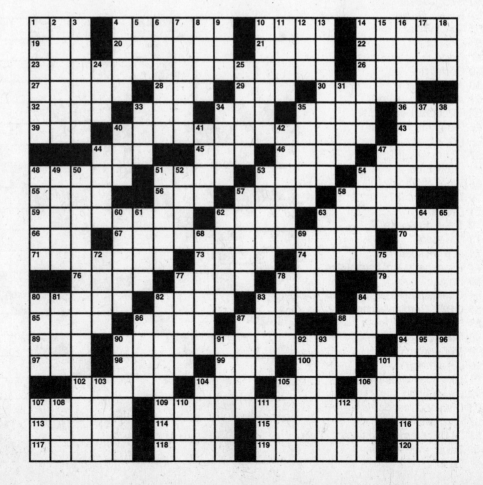

ACROSS

1 The reel thing
5 Diamond shape
9 Flower forerunners
13 Bub or cap lead-in
16 Cobb and Caesar
18 Disney pachyderm
19 Pre-med course
20 Pioneer performance artist
21 Not from here
22 Photog Diane or actor Alan
23 Abounding
24 The even prime
25 GREEN sailor's rest stop?
28 Is suffering from
29 Quiver
30 Field of work
31 Cutely saucy
32 Cleaning cloth
35 Howard or Drabowsky
36 Floppy disk contents
38 Moldy stuff?
39 PINK pachyderm's restraint?
44 Tennyson dramatic poem
45 Like *Reservoir Dogs*
46 Flooded
47 Airport surface
49 Have title to
50 Sect leader?
51 Misery cause
52 Trail the pack
54 Coddle
57 Rockers __ for Pyros
59 Socializes
60 Aussie avian
61 Adam's __ (water)
62 YELLOW pea coats?
65 Sleep stage meas.
66 River inlet
67 Gold standard
68 Lubricated
69 Word of whoa?
70 Do road work?
71 Chichi
72 To be, to Bonita
73 "So there!"
75 In a whisper
77 *Passage to India* character
80 Bruited about
84 Chemistry Nobelist Harold
85 GRAY Cardinal's concern?
87 Walk of Fame figure
88 Criticize slyly
89 Menu words
90 Jet setting?
91 Like bees or beavers
92 Jack Sprat's diet
93 Diamond rounds
97 Farm worker?
98 BLUE attorney's jotting?
104 Laker sportscaster Lantz
105 Paramecium shape
106 Yearn for
107 Rabid supporter
108 Small amount
109 Like some straits
110 *Tap*'s Gregory
111 Mystery
112 One, no matter which
113 Hodgepodge half
114 General under Dwight
115 Tabletop, perhaps

DOWN

1 Danza-DeVito sitcom
2 Sleep like __
3 Walkers' ways
4 Chanteuse Piaf
5 Compact container
6 Future ash
7 Meet end to end
8 Went towards the top
9 Obstacle
10 Local groups?
11 *English Patient*'s Willem
12 Pipe section
13 RED warning for the short-tempered?
14 Heedless
15 Prop up
16 *Poivre* partner
17 Rhenish Symphony composer
18 Novelist Alphonse
26 It means teeth
27 Abdul's Almighty
31 Choice assignment
32 Give it the gas
33 "Rumble in the Jungle" victor
34 Prizm producer
36 Where St. Pete is
37 Provence pronoun
38 Rub the right way?
40 Artful dodge
41 Cut down
42 A source?
43 Outstanding, as debt
44 Olympia painter
47 Strained
48 It's a relief
50 "Good Morning, America"'s competition
51 Harley rider
53 Big role for Hanks
54 S.F. subway
55 Billy the Kid, e.g.
56 Prove research, in BROWN?
57 Libertarian, e.g.
58 Iberian eye
59 "American Pie" man Don
62 Kwan or Kerrigan
63 Premature
64 Bridal path
69 Layup or jump
73 Soothe the savage breast?
74 Grp. with a caduceus
76 Rub away
77 Containing NH_2
78 Dance floor move
79 180° from WSW
80 Piece of the past
81 ACLU concerns
82 Shrieker's sound
83 Prohibition promoter
85 Makes possible
86 Where Césars are given
87 Basker's goal
88 Alaska was his "folly"
91 Enough, to Enzo
92 Linda of "Alice"
93 Early Pepsodent rival
94 Cry of defiance
95 Secluded valleys
96 Kind of mail
98 Band of gold, perhaps
99 *Siete y uno*
100 AmFAR's Dr. Mathilde
101 One of Chekhov's Three Sisters
102 Last place?
103 Guess at LAX

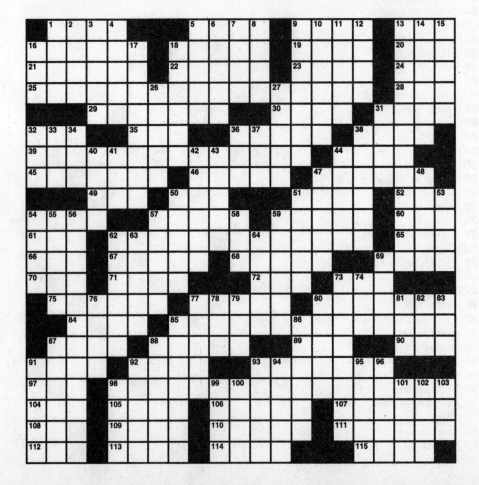

ACROSS

1 Slumgullion
5 P, R, D and N
10 Kind of fair
15 Turn left
18 Singer Amos
19 Cause trouble
20 Digital alternative
21 "You __ here"
22 Sigher's word
23 Sauntered
25 Thrice LXVII
26 Looked like
28 AIDS memorial project
29 Dagger-carrying sect members
31 Finery
32 Besmirch
33 Gives a ring
34 Multi-purp. truck
35 Vouchers
36 One who finds a loss a gain
37 Like doilies
40 *To Kill a Mockingbird* character
42 Expense
43 "Sort of" suffix
44 Rafter of note
48 Greek vowel
51 "'Tis __ to be jolly"
53 Like Seattle
54 Mild cheese
55 Like a psychedelic submarine
56 "Semper fi" guy
58 Key letter
59 Hotsy-totsy folk
61 The more it dries, the wetter it gets
62 Satellite receivers
63 Fives and tens
64 Expressed derision
66 Just a little more?
68 Coffee houses?
69 Humeri neighbors
70 Bubble up
73 15A opposite
74 Memorable danseur
77 Girl in an '05 song
78 Hotdog
80 "__ Mio"
81 *Poule* product
82 Rinse and wash
83 Was overfond
85 Battle stat
87 Investigations
88 Honeybunch
89 Be the life of the party
93 __ cum laude
94 Foot marker
95 Take the show on the road
97 "__ was going to St. Ives . . ."
98 Bond's golden girl
101 To laugh, in Toulouse
102 Chaney of old Hollywood
103 Philly footballers
104 Kind of drab
105 Youngest Greek god
106 PC capacity unit
107 Remains
108 Toledo title
109 Slim swimmers

DOWN

1 Cassiopeia component
2 Post-Oland Chan
3 Remove graffiti
4 Smart aleck
5 Procter's partner
6 Gastroenterologist's concern
7 Between ports
8 Wished one hadn't
9 Watch from hiding
10 Escargots
11 Keep a count
12 Quite a bit
13 It can be long or gross
14 Shade shade
15 The trite thing to say
16 Sagittarius, e.g.
17 *Marat/Sade* writer Peter
20 No longer a teen
24 Actors' group
27 Slam softener
30 Scintilla
32 Elisabeth of *Leaving Las Vegas*
33 To the point
35 Harry or Roy
36 "Rebel Rouser" rocker Eddy
37 English subj.
38 Butt end?
39 Laramie County seat
40 Not good, not bad
41 Caw caller
42 Frigga's mate
44 Where Brits can see the BBC
45 Laughing Cavalier painter Frans
46 Miscomputed
47 Fence at Santa Anita
49 Sprinter's goal
50 *Amo, __, amat*
52 Hingis rival
54 Display stand
56 Recurring theme
57 Leave open-mouthed
58 Noted ballet company
59 Self-satisfied
60 Sported
61 Slave away
62 "Galloping dominoes"
64 Pluto, to Plato
65 Nostril nudger
66 Use taction
67 Gross, of early "Ellen"
69 Dead letters?
70 Poke
71 Fraternity T
72 A little cobbler?
74 Liberates
75 Certificate certifier
76 Mouse manipulator
79 Nuclear delivery syst.
81 Acorn's origin – or destiny
82 His work was done by Friday
83 D.C. airport
84 Expressions for arches?
85 Way
86 Return receiver
87 The 23rd, for one
88 Churlish
89 Like Duke Ellington's doll
90 Utah university site
91 French river
92 Swashbuckler Flynn
94 Baryshnikov's birthplace
95 Bundle, as straw
96 Meal in a hall
99 Band or box lead-in
100 Aurora, to some

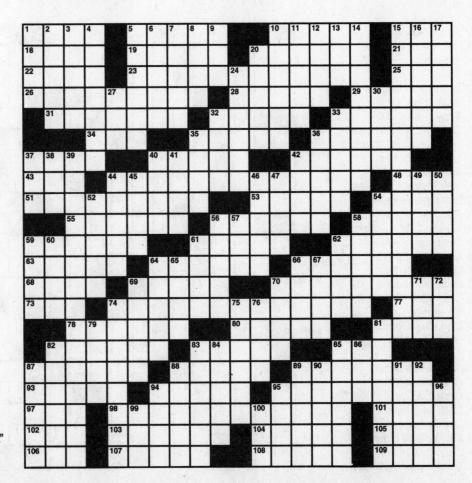

ACROSS

1 Cornrow alternative
5 __ up (neaten)
10 Miami's Marino
13 Rocker Scaggs
16 Ocarbon opener
17 Using words
18 Singer at Woodstock
19 What makes God good?
20 Nissan competitor
21 '76 Abba hit
24 8A or 12D, e.g.
25 Not at all rad, dude
26 Non-Arabic 1007
27 Part of Krupa's kit
28 Made long-distance calls?
30 Halfhearted
32 Coppers
33 EMT technique
35 "Open sesame" utterer
36 Pamplona pineapples
37 Particular
38 Wish otherwise
39 Kids' street game
42 Apr. collectors
43 Jughead's pal
45 Irish Coronation Stone
__ Fail
46 Hockey great Bobby
47 National or American
51 Village center
52 A land was named
for him
54 Pitch in
55 Script ending?
56 He'll make a hog of
himself
57 Ria
58 Incantation opener
60 Glum drop
61 They play at Shea
63 Get oneself to a nunnery
65 Sonja Henie's birthplace
66 Labyrinth goal
67 Word of woe
68 WWII bomber — Gay
69 Luncheon leaving
70 Address for an NCO
71 Greetings at meetings
72 Donnybrooks
73 Mayer or Madison
76 Situs for an itis
78 Haggard heroine
80 Skier Tommy
81 Bill and coo
82 Canada's Grand __
83 Bath necessity
86 Anti's answer
87 '94 Reeves hit
89 Studio sign
90 Carte preceder
91 HMO employees
92 Used an auger
93 Composers' closers
94 Grumpy Old Men star
97 Saga of generations
98 Simpsons creator
Groening
99 Chalet features
100 Picket-line pariah
103 Poe mansion
107 It always makes page 1
108 Las' followers
109 Launch sight
110 Sites for rites
111 Take as one's own
112 Quit fasting
113 Go for it
114 Marsh ducks
115 Forfeiter's score

DOWN

1 Jai __
2 TV watcher's woe
3 Calf-roping contest
4 ". . . __ mouse?"
5 Marsh plant
6 Using the bragging
rights
7 Egyptian sacred bird
8 The Macarena, e.g.
9 Mr. Ziegfeld
10 Artoo Detoo, e.g.
11 Et __ (and others)
12 Affirm silently
13 Scot's tots
14 Working
15 Barrels along
16 NPR radio bands
17 Concertmaster's
instrument
18 Counselor
22 Damage
23 Midland neighbor
25 Misrepresent
29 Having moxie
30 It hangs by the neck
31 Embassy employee
32 Better again
33 Steep rock
34 Sound of contentment
36 Trek stop?
37 Relating to offspring
40 A Life for the Tsar
composer
41 Supermarket sections
44 The Brink's job, e.g.
48 Rattle at the
Philharmonic, e.g.
49 Russian river
50 Eliel Saarinen's son
52 Old channel changers
53 Old-time knockout
54 La Scala solos
58 Take __ poverty
59 Ball stars
60 Human trunk
61 After dead or red
62 Montreal athlete
63 Followed furtively
64 Inflame with love
69 Tuba tones
71 Filled an opening
72 Lebanese valley
74 Rent- __
75 Wide Sargasso Sea
writer Jean
77 Oration
78 Phil Rizzuto's
nickname
79 Live from __ mouth
81 Sailors
84 Frozen wasser
85 Tom Mix flicks
87 La Loren
88 Father figure?
92 '81 hit "__ Davis Eyes"
93 Mudville's hope
94 Shah Jahan's wife,
Mumtaz __
95 Says for the record
96 Stage line
98 Sierra Club's
co-founder
99 ¿ Cómo __ ?
101 Friskies rival
102 Vegas venture
104 Choose
105 What most dieters
avoid
106 Glob or gran ender
107 Bugs' toon bane

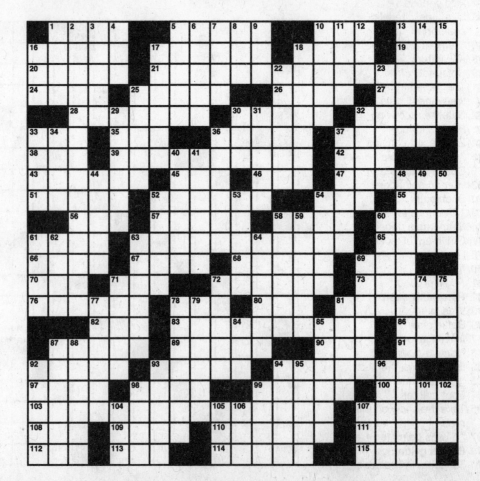

ACROSS

1 Yesterday's "is"
4 A sister of Erato
10 Toasting term
15 Colleague of Lassie
19 Animal shelter?
20 Sea of the Cyclades
21 Edo, today
22 Tiny bit
23 Early Olds
24 Appalachian range
26 Pool table material
27 Figure, in a way
29 Sunscreen ingredient
30 Safari steerer
31 "Why do __ my time . . .?"
32 "Uh . . . pardon me"
33 Engorged
35 "May I speak __?"
37 First English American settlement
39 Chambord's river
40 Memorable singer Bailey
42 mehitabel's friend
43 Start of a Shakespeare title
44 Superlatively bad
45 Roman ode writer
47 Shake it or break it
50 Toothpaste type
51 Site Matthew Perry visited
53 It often follows you
54 Hardens
56 "I'll make __ of that"
57 Mini-play
58 Snack on toast
60 Hoodwinks
62 Fare exchanges?
64 Sitting on
65 Afghan language
67 Atelier
69 Maui chow
70 Town a ways from Okmulgee and Muskogee
74 Malay isthmus
77 MGM has two
78 Speak ill of
79 '36 Olympics hero
80 Some are split
81 SST center
82 __ -four (common board)
83 They make a row in the field
84 Marshall Islands component
89 Big-billed bird
90 *Lakmé* composer Leo
91 KP, e.g.
92 Hindquarter
94 Half a Washington town?
95 Soccer's *Perla Negra*
96 Works the room at a banquet

99 Seed protector
100 Oregon inlet
103 Feathery scarf
104 Old learning method
105 Firefighter Red
106 Lorne or Mean Joe
107 Many millennia
108 Slave Scott
109 Born-again Frenchwoman?
110 Gave lip
111 Benevolent brother

DOWN

1 Microwave briefly
2 Amount of space
3 Chicago neighbor
4 Weekend yard event
5 Galileo's crime
6 Intermediary
7 Letter paper?
8 Med or dev closer
9 Prob. solver
10 Hot, in a way
11 Hoosier State city
12 Tom Joad, e.g.
13 Word said in passing?
14 Part of UCLA
15 Very much
16 Meredith MacRae's mother
17 Tennis' "Big Bill"
18 Be there
25 Taj __
28 Washstand items
30 "Land o' __!"
32 It comes from the heart
33 It's a wrap in Durango
34 Benevolent sorcery
35 Ross national product?
36 Jack, for DiCaprio
37 Prickly heat
38 Gold unit
40 __ fun at (mock)
41 Cupid's counterpart
44 Was garbed in
45 "King of the Hill's" Hill
46 Spanish eyes
47 Kissimmee River receiver
48 Poetic Ireland
49 *As Good As It* __
51 Gary Cooper assent
52 Art of *True Lies*
55 Tot's timeout
57 Cross-country runner
58 Horn, for one
59 Mighty mite
60 Toot your own horn
61 "When the big hand __ . . ."
62 Rolaids rival
63 Seraglio room

65 Big books
66 "I Get __ Out of You"
67 Wooley of "Purple People Eater" fame
68 Bennett or Dorsett
70 Protozoan
71 *Plume* owner
72 Humble
73 Away sans O.K.
75 __ avis
76 NAACP, e.g.
80 Shelter for a joey
81 Consumed like a hog?
82 Tribal emblem
83 Mellifluous, as tones
84 The Confessor King
85 "Whether __ far away"
86 Muscovite's crystal kin
87 Antarctic penguin
88 Visalia's county
89 Louisiana university
92 Cods' kin
93 Cluny clerics
95 Design
96 Pearl Harbor word
97 Fast Eddie Felson's game
98 Became submerged
100 Roofer's goo
101 Ox tail?
102 Certain hoods in the hood

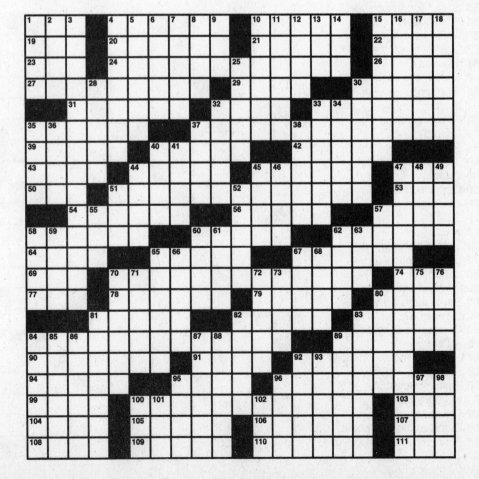

ACROSS

1 Observe Ramadan
5 __ and took notice
10 Adjective for Abner
13 AAA concern
16 "I __" ("beats me")
17 *Scarface* and *Serpico* star
18 Top-notch
19 Astral altar
20 Piece of Bacon
21 Age-determination spectacle?
24 It'll last for days
25 Does the Wright thing?
26 Whispers sweet nothings
27 Press secretary, for one
28 Foreign and American
30 Blackcap and bluebill kin
32 Dents slightly
33 Zeta-theta separator
35 Port near Stuttgart
36 Penurious
37 A piece of the pie
38 Jazz bassist Carter
39 Where Marlins and Mariners play?
42 House or wife lead-in
43 Not half bad
45 P-T bridge
46 U.K. legislators
47 Revolutionary evolutionist
51 It grows by degrees
52 Assumed appearances
54 Spanish chess piece
55 She's a deer
56 Accelerando's opp.
57 Most of "Deck the Halls"
58 "Your turn to talk"
60 Coolidge or Tushingham
61 "Diamonds and Rust" singer
63 Farmer's concern?
65 Coup d'__
66 *Baja* opposite
67 JFK's French cousin
68 *Diciembre* follower
69 Lanka lead-in
70 Application
71 Bulls do it
72 Natural, as hair
73 Talking heads group
76 Guyana gelt
78 TV football nt.
80 Want-ad abbr.
81 Put through the wringer
82 Piece of 8?
83 Correct the Dingbat?
86 A Clanton
87 Have a trying experience?
89 Stones' "__ Bleed"
90 Pasture parent
91 Neither's partner
92 Chummy
93 Stops on the way home?
94 Frequent soap plot device
97 *Et* __

98 Old Cadillac features
99 Coffeemaker's consideration
100 Lewd look
103 Unsuccessful carrier?
107 Bobbysoxer's spell
108 Chor or chlor ender
109 Win 4-3, e.g.
110 Equivocate
111 Monkey or pony
112 Ave. crossers
113 Half a gaffe
114 Less ordinary
115 County containing most of Death Valley

DOWN

1 Often-blown item
2 Fairy tale about photography?
3 Plumber's device
4 Poodle type
5 Lustrous fabric
6 Room to grow on
7 3-3 games, e.g.
8 A little French number
9 __ *favor*
10 Arches and alligators
11 Cousins of Ltds.
12 Hula hoop?
13 In the 10K
14 Walk ploddingly

15 De-stresses
16 Drops on the lawn
17 Pigeon, to Pedro
18 Noms de plume
22 Like wintry windows
23 Freebooter
25 Debone
29 Seam insert
30 Make marry
31 French cathedral city
32 Little dents
33 *Cope Book* aunt
34 Bugs or Mickey
36 Bahamian capital
37 Waterproof boots
40 Raise a ruckus, to some
41 Hat named after a novel
44 She could have danced all night
48 Author's angst?
49 Least bit
50 Not on ice
52 Magnificence
53 Big Bertha's birthplace
54 Fix the fairway
58 "...only hurt the __ love"
59 Entertainer Ben
60 Showed in syndication
61 Modem speed term

62 Too
63 Origin
64 Owing
69 Bowler's marks
71 Hollywood vet Billy
72 Marx's exhortation
74 Nevada city
75 To read, to toreadors
77 She saved Timmy
78 Gallimaufry
79 Black Sea port
81 Spoke Persian?
84 'Twas, now
85 Board-and-care for cairns
87 Casting director's concern
88 Arlo's early hangout
92 Louvre locale
93 Dog in a spell-out
94 Be mentioned
95 Coal porter
96 Hawkeye
98 Dog tag?
99 Elated
101 Plumb crazy
102 More E than N
104 She has a ball
105 __ Jima
106 Rover or River preceder
107 '80s Pentagon letters

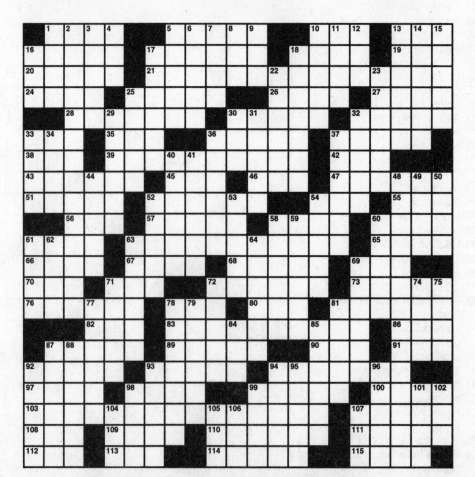

ACROSS

1 PC screen
4 Frozen dew
8 He scared Skywalker
13 Put a lid on
16 Beavis and Butt-head soundbite
17 After 94D, lone star?
18 John lost his head for her
19 Blue ox or pink pig
20 Stock or block ender
21 Take __
23 More than
24 Compassion
26 Sheeplike
27 Lubricated
29 Olivia's *GWTW* role
30 Brushed leather
31 Search
32 Prime the pot
33 Lisa of "Ellen"
34 As __ (in itself)
35 Add a soundtrack
38 Schlepp
39 Leave __
43 Ham on the hoof
44 Bonkers
46 Contra contraband
47 Kick off
48 Bat wood
49 Memorable sportscaster Caray
50 Verve, to Vittorio
51 Use the crosshairs
52 Spike heel's thinner kin
54 Joan of Art
55 Didn't depart
59 "... a __ 'clock scholar"
60 Take __
64 __ of the above
65 Luanda is its capital
67 Once it was enough
68 Give heart
70 Bed
71 Brown, in Brittany
72 Fred Allen's medium
73 Tear along
74 '60s supergroup
77 Col. Mustard's game
78 In a beelike manner?
79 Mike holders
80 Leave __
83 Metro maker
84 Frost bite
85 Character builder?
86 "Phooey!"
87 Webb of the NBA
89 Candace Gingrich's brother
90 What Friday wanted
92 Dew time
95 Timid
97 Chef's topper
98 It makes a Luger less loud

99 New Year's Day game
100 Take leave __
103 "__ had it!"
104 City south of Moscow
105 Tourist's car
106 Appears to be
107 Angler's gear
108 Trade rings
109 Where jeans may be worn
110 Gull friend?
111 B.C.E. ender

DOWN

1 Abyss
2 Go back to blonde
3 Leave __
4 McDaniel of *GWTW*
5 "The Lady __ Tiger?"
6 Start of a Cash title
7 Balderdash!
8 In force
9 Frock shape
10 Fuller figure?
11 British recording label
12 Fiddle with a photo
13 Spelunker's site
14 Tucked in for the night
15 MPH center
17 James Dean film

18 Arduous
19 Something from the blue
22 Every 60 minutes
25 Hunger reminder
28 Live in
30 Smacking of the sea
31 Embraces
33 Too much
34 Heavyweight wrestling
35 Collie or corgi
36 A quarter of quadri-
37 Writer-actor Affleck
38 Hark!
39 "The __ end all ..." (WWI)
40 Short of breadth?
41 Betelgeuse's constellation
42 French racecourse
43 Naples staple
44 Who blows thar?
45 Kitty's z's?
50 Plains Indian mainstay
51 Attack
53 Regard
54 Graceful old dance
56 Take __
57 Caruso or Fermi
58 The Mariana Trench, etc.
61 Play it again
62 Makes a clean slate

63 Overhauled
66 French porcelain center
69 Tofu base
71 Color, or off-color
72 Puny pups
74 News letters
75 *Duc*'s king
76 Second sight or sixth sense
77 "Red" coin
78 Yahoos
81 "Seinfeld" setting
82 Go back to straight hair
83 Moses of the movies
87 Like some oaths
88 Basketball defense
89 Not in force
90 Screenwriter Horton
91 Blue-green tints
92 Skinflint
93 Defier's cry
94 See 17A
95 Glutton's cry
96 Took credit
97 Newcastle's river
98 Snicker follower
99 Fiddle stick
101 Marshland
102 *Compas* point

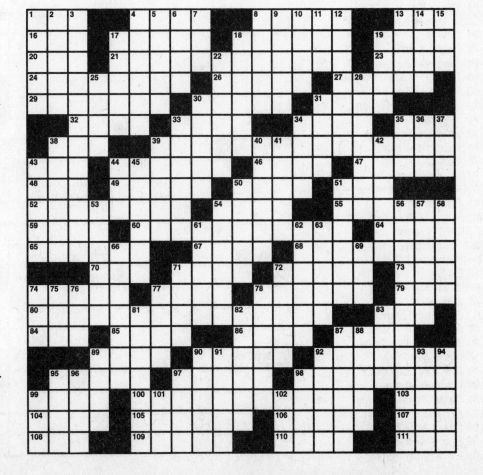

ACROSS

1 Sixes, to Sextus
4 He's hailed outside hotels
10 Check the water
13 Thumb nail?
17 Frigate feature
18 Plateau
19 Carson City neighbor
20 Jersey or Guernsey
21 In some other way
22 Dust jackets?
24 Comparison word
25 Squashes, e.g.
27 Allowing alcohol
28 Abbr. on a Fr. envelope
29 Star that came out in 1997
31 Combat zone
32 Hare hair
33 Ocelot feature
34 Get it
35 Harrison in '64, for one
37 Let off the hook
39 Like Martina Hingis
43 She adopted Soon-Yi
45 March of the manuscripts?
47 "Take __ from me"
48 Rorschach feature
50 Lets off steam
51 Wit's proverbial soul
54 Crossed swords
55 Emolument
56 Pulitzer poet Wallace
57 Ethereal
58 Therefore
60 Colossus' island
61 City rds.
62 Unghosted?
65 Tongues and tails do it
68 Coffeemaker's concerns
69 Acts as usher
70 Cheeseboard choice
71 Violin and viola
73 What CLU's sell
74 Runs the meeting
76 Gratified
77 "__ my big mouth!"
80 He 54A with Hamlet
81 Shofar, e.g.
82 "Sittin' by the Book of the Day" singer?
85 Equi's equal
86 Worshiped one
88 Displayed alarm
89 "Star Trek" rank
91 One of D.C.'s 100
93 Basketball and boxing orgs.
94 Rankle
95 Tom Brown's school
98 Ms. Midler
100 Brothers and others
101 Infamous Amin
102 Regis' former co-host __ Lee
103 *Camelot* actor Franco
104 Czech book?
108 She played Ginger
109 Element element
110 River to the Caspian
111 DNA expert's concern
112 McMuffins' stuffin'
113 Home, for one
114 Military address
115 Dog star
116 P, to Plato

DOWN

1 Decoration justification
2 Editors who cobble books together?
3 Canned heat brand
4 Ernie Banks' bunch
5 V-mail handler
6 Enlargements
7 Holmes' street
8 "Meet Me __ Louis"
9 Old English letter
10 What expletives may be
11 "What happened next?"
12 Baby in the bulrushes
13 Publisher's current lists?
14 Onetime UCLA tennis star
15 Rob Roy led one
16 He's a doll
17 MHz's M
19 Shark-suckers
23 Disclose
26 Mottle-marked mare
30 Article in *Paris Match*
32 Territory of most rulers
33 Extend across
36 Stepped on
37 Valedictory, e.g.
38 They owe
40 Get __ the neck
41 Tends toddlers
42 Hari or Harriet
43 Touchy fellow?
44 Where "kayak" came from
46 Some are blessed
49 Muckraker Nellie
52 Demond's '70s co-star
53 Holiday preludes
55 Interfamily fights
56 Slap and sling enders
58 Dejected
59 Greek dawn goddess
60 Kigali is its capital
62 Crocus kin
63 Half a golf course
64 Restrained
65 Creating pot boilers?
66 Buenos __
67 Plaster of Paris
68 Ulysses' epic?
70 Mixologist's milieu
71 Blackthorn fruit
72 *Tomorrow Never Dies*' Hatcher
74 Inspiration for Warhol
75 Mohammad's Mecca-Medina move
76 Third degree, often
77 Send the wrong invoice
78 Picasso's *país*
79 Greek Mars
80 One in a long line of sausages
83 Railroad oil carrier
84 Originates (from)
87 However
90 It runs along a lane
92 Birthmark
94 Baal, et al.
96 "You've got it!"
97 Pro votes
98 Constellation's second brightest
99 He goes for the heart
101 *To Live and Die* __
102 Bauhaus artist
103 Collar a con
105 Greek nickname
106 *The Saint*'s Kilmer
107 Biblical judge

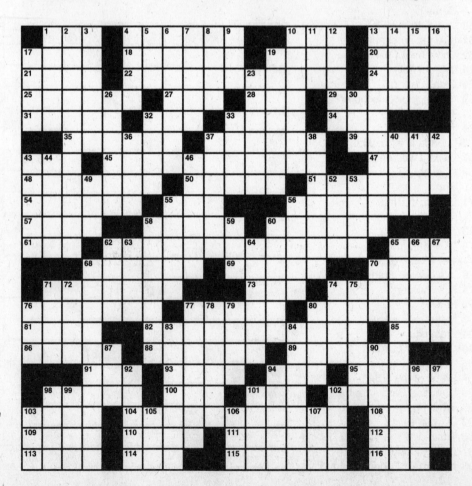

ACROSS

1 Moriarty's nemesis
7 Store
11 Chowder chunk
15 Future fuchsias
19 Regulars' orders
20 Engine hum
21 Rhea's anagrammatic daughter
22 At the crest of
23 Surrealist's battle scenes?
26 La __ Tar Pits
27 "__ Kick Out of You"
28 Pennant-waver's cry
29 Ligament injury
30 H.H. Munro
32 He played Ricky
33 Elbow-bending joint
34 Pants part
35 Opera's Renata
38 Present time
40 Some can't take it
41 Minimal money
42 *My Name Is Asher __*
43 Certain GI
46 Cubist's cat portrait?
49 TV eye or peacock
50 "Stop!"
52 Hankering
53 *Don Juan DeMarco*'s Dunaway
54 Bavarian river
55 Loosen a brogue
56 Name on a '97 comet
57 Point __ return
58 Cottontail's sibling
59 One mo' time
60 Diving bird
61 One of the girls
62 Singer Mitchell or James
63 Ewe said it
64 Abstract artist's seascapes?
69 Statute
72 Nil, to *el niño*
74 Sgt. Preston's horse
75 Jet- __ (padded mailer)
76 Painter Paul
77 Bob of *All That Jazz* fame
79 Tattle
81 Stocking stuffers
83 Norwegian inlet
84 Sugar unit
85 Algerian city
86 Bern's river
87 Name on Ringo's drum
88 "How sweet __!"
89 Flemish food still-lifes?
92 Keep company with
93 *Independence Day* invaders
94 Seeks answers
95 Rudiments
96 Screen detective Rawlins
98 Ornamental badge
100 Follow orders
101 Alfred E. Neuman's magazine
102 Promise to tell the truth
106 "Eureka!" evoker
107 Pipe joints

108 Former Mideast initials
109 A lot, in Veracruz
110 L.A. flaw
112 Impressionist's dance scenes?
116 Start of a Welk count
117 Margarita fruit
118 Was in the hole
119 "Boy, it's hot __!"
120 Terrarium growth
121 First place?
122 It may be baking
123 Deputized groups

DOWN

1 Like greenhouse air
2 Siouan language
3 Backslider's sleds?
4 Music's Freddy, Frank or Dean
5 Lamb by another name
6 TU-144, e.g.
7 Use a fork
8 Sudden silence
9 Former fort near Monterey
10 Make-believe
11 Copy cat
12 Jet-set jet
13 Life may imitate it
14 She kneads you
15 Coffeecake cousin
16 French boudoir works?
17 Bambi's mom, e.g.

18 Jacuzzi kin
24 Short refrain
25 Excellent exploits
31 Situps strengthen them
33 Sesame Street denizen
34 Blockade kin
35 Metropolis trashed by Godzilla
36 Impressionist Edgar
37 Camay competitor
39 Off-Broadway award
40 Throw
41 Go up and down the dial
43 Poultry dish
44 Din in India?
45 Venetian's Old California series?
47 Shake from shock
48 Negotiation starter
49 Britain's emblem
51 Solder or soldier material
56 Mauve, e.g.
57 Surprised expressions
58 Yr.'s dozen
60 Rap sheet abbr.
61 Reason for an R
62 NYC airport
64 "To Autumn," e.g.
65 French bread?
66 Cal. page
67 Blunted swords
68 Corrode

70 Cliff hanger
71 Pie slice
73 Small cobras
76 A little butter?
77 Speculative venture
78 __ lunch
79 Devoid of dinero
80 Dundee damsel
81 Take a shine to
82 Passion personified
83 Ado
85 Hindrance
86 EPA and OSHA concern
87 Juiciest part, usually
90 Se __ *español*
91 "I __ Symphony"
94 Put away groceries
97 Lads and 80D's
99 Noses out
100 *Hellzapoppin'* star
101 One of the Gabors
103 Sets of *scènes*
104 Limerick opener
105 Waters down
107 Salinger dedicatee
108 Pre-owned
109 One-track
110 Spade or Snead
111 Cattle call
113 Help out
114 Seesaw quorum
115 Limo rider, often

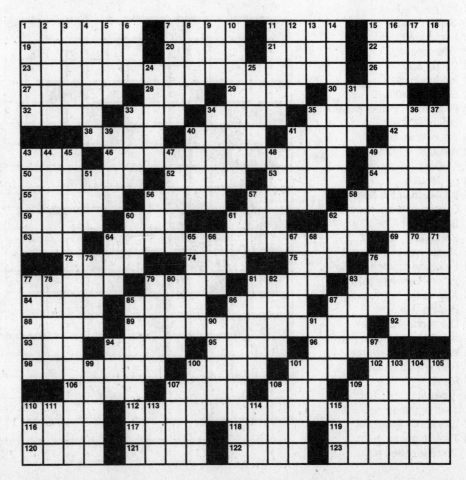

ACROSS

1 Sheriff's emblem
5 *The Bell Jar* writer
10 Swing the camera
13 Stock the arsenal
16 Marianne, Michael or Melba
17 Silverstone of the screen
18 Prince Charles' game
19 *Evita* character?
20 Ignore the script
21 Hatless Gable-Powell classic?
24 Miami-__ county
25 Acts grandmotherly
26 Eye of the wolf?
27 Dash
28 Out of focus
30 Gumbo veggies
32 Skyscraper unit
33 Buddy
35 4 o'clock service?
36 Convenes
37 Express gratitude
38 Boyle Hts. neighbor
39 Hats off to saying "Enough"?
42 Jackie's second
43 Artist M.C.
45 It seems like forever
46 Minnesota twins
47 John or Paul
51 Fireside aid
52 "It's __ Night for Singing"
54 Pat gently
55 *Señor*'s shout
56 Some are grand
57 '60s greeting
58 Venus' son
60 Mountain cat
61 Be a bellwether
63 Hats off to "Penny for your thoughts"?
65 Sauce thickener
66 Anxious
67 McCarthy's obsession
68 __ Janeiro
69 It's heard in the herd
70 Groove-billed cuckoo
71 Switch to low beams
72 Benny's "__ Bloom"
73 Mega- kin
76 Extortion or bootlegging
78 When France is bakin'
80 Atty. assn.
81 Braked a bit
82 Diamonds, to Legs
83 Bareheaded Indian hero?
86 Wash.-Mont. separator
87 Henry VIII's house
89 Priss
90 -y plural
91 Joad or Jones
92 Like some speakers
93 They're gonna get it
94 Texas leaguer, e.g.

97 Semicircular recess
98 Klingon on the *Enterprise*
99 Delight in
100 Evans or Carnegie
103 Hatless safety glass?
107 Rouse from sleep
108 Start of many odes
109 Stevedore's sight
110 Beginning
111 To come
112 Elver's elder
113 Porking lot?
114 Oasis' asset
115 Have a bagel

DOWN

1 RC or 7Up
2 Hatless Mercer-Arlen evergreen?
3 *The Tempest* sprite
4 CSA soldier
5 Cover with gold
6 Like notebook paper
7 Gospels follower
8 *Padre*'s sib
9 Solo in space?
10 Spin-doctor's concerns
11 Healing plant
12 Where Cain dwelt
13 Catalina community

14 Notice
15 Longtime labor leader
16 Magazine since '52
17 Without principle
18 High horse?
22 Storyville's Jelly Roll
23 Keep on the payroll
25 Gloomy
29 Speaks
30 Anthem contraction
31 In E or G, e.g.
32 Woody plant
33 Slightest sound
34 In addition
36 Where Grimaldis rule
37 *Canterbury Tales* inn
40 Sleepy Hollow had one
41 Raids
44 Exhilarating
48 Hatless Dave Clark Five fave?
49 Opera's Gluck
50 In the vicinity
52 ". . .__ lovely as a tree"
53 Pref. meaning nerve
54 *Indiscreet* director Stanley
58 It multiplies by dividing
59 Abraham's son
60 Francesca's *Inferno* fellow

61 Shakespearean king
62 Ferber or Millay
63 Glasgow or London
64 Normandy beach
69 Obstinate
71 Ersatz eider
72 Madagascar mammal
74 Take it from the top
75 Economist Smith
77 Reeves : Kent : : __ : Lane
78 Napoleon, e.g.
79 Import duty
81 See-through
84 Sponsors' spots
85 Let out the heir?
87 "__ Through the Tulips"
88 Open envelopes
92 Disposables
93 Bunkum
94 Friday's was 714
95 To have, in Le Havre
96 86A, spelled out
98 Mandamus or mittimus
99 Fit of anger
101 Mother of Judah
102 Denouement
104 Afterthought #2
105 Knock one's socks off
106 George's lyricist
107 Pallid

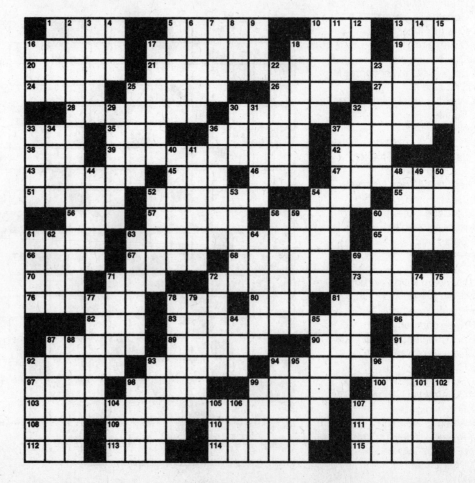

ACROSS

1 Be catty?
4 95D's former name
10 Most of a Cuba libre
14 Taj __
19 Feast-famine fIller
20 Indie filmmaker Roger
21 Trim snaps
22 Dateless
23 Comical *Copperfield* character?
26 Christine of "Chicago Hope"
27 Ride in orbit
28 Capp and Capone
29 "Diamond" dame
30 Disk jockey's medium
32 Wheelchair obstacle
33 Chi.-Miami heading
34 Show conclusion?
35 Slip a Mickey
36 The way
39 Knack for melody
40 Merry musical immortal?
43 *Metal precioso*
44 What the Getty's got
45 Down-under bird
46 The Jazz and Big Band, e.g.
47 Slash mark?
48 Seder staple
51 Fiddler on the reef
53 Give an F
54 "__ I lie to you?"
55 The bouncing bawl
56 Quarterback's bark
57 Auction actions
58 Carries the day
59 Promotes
62 Trait determiner
63 Cousteau's craft
66 Margarine container
67 Willis' killer comedy?
70 Regatta blade
71 More sordid
73 Scallopini meat
74 KO causer
76 Boyz' town?
77 'Bama's Bryant
78 MPG center
79 Cord or Ford
80 Truth twisters
82 Hair splitter?
83 Galileo's birthplace
84 "He is __"
85 N.Y.C. stadium name
86 Makes memos
87 X rating?
88 Poor Richard, really
89 Paesano's possessive
90 Cackling Carolinian?
94 "Neato!" updated
97 Hair color
98 __ out (withdraws)
99 Wintry chill
100 Give a leg up
101 Subcompact car
102 Tours ta-ta

104 Band booking
105 Item for the disposal
106 Buddy's erstwhile White House buddy
107 "Cosby kid" Malcolm-__ Warner
109 Mirthful Mongol?
113 Dumbfound
114 Leading man?
115 Monty Python's John
116 Before, before
117 Headquartered
118 "__ smile be . . ."
119 *Nostromo* novelist
120 Utter

DOWN

1 Eat it or wear it
2 Proof goofs
3 Bob Marley backup
4 Needing liniment
5 Yokohama drama
6 Musical about the '50s
7 Egg dish
8 Rallying cries
9 Purchase from Sajak
10 Wildly eccentric
11 Dodger Hershiser
12 Female rabbit
13 Go-ahead
14 *On the Waterfront*'s Karl
15 Jai __

16 Risible razzle-dazzle?
17 Social worker?
18 *Malihini*'s gift
24 Climber's challenge
25 A Job interviewer
31 Barbary beasts
33 Matched batch
34 Lay an egg
35 Rock's frequent co-star
37 Vaccine type
38 Tidings
40 Soul man?
41 Track trial
42 Type of tumble
44 Sea the Don flows into
47 Big name in Culver City
48 Comes upon
49 Without __ (in the dark)
50 Chortling Carib chain?
51 Greet the hero
52 "High priority!"
53 Crucial test
54 Oscar or Cornel
57 Joy of daytime's "The View"
58 Weft crosser
60 Toledo toodle-oo
61 At deuce
62 Like Gatsby or Gretzky
63 *Meet John Doe* director
64 Pan-fry
65 *Loot* playwright Joe

68 Disinclined
69 Shades
72 Oliver Twist's request
75 Drops from the sky
77 Saturday activities, in oaters
78 Fragrant tree
80 *Kundun* character
81 Egyptian goddess
82 Lusitania, today
83 Chick's chirp
84 Sib, e.g.
86 Practical joke
87 Choice at KFC
88 Before spring or spread
90 Worked hard
91 Puzzle
92 Listen respectfully
93 Indecisive choice
94 Wealth
95 Turkish capital
96 ABC's owner
101 Early bird
103 Stupefy
104 Blackfly
105 King Olaf's seat
106 After wood or water
107 Haymaker setup
108 GPs' gp.
110 Gelderland commune
111 Commerce regulating gp.
112 Simile center

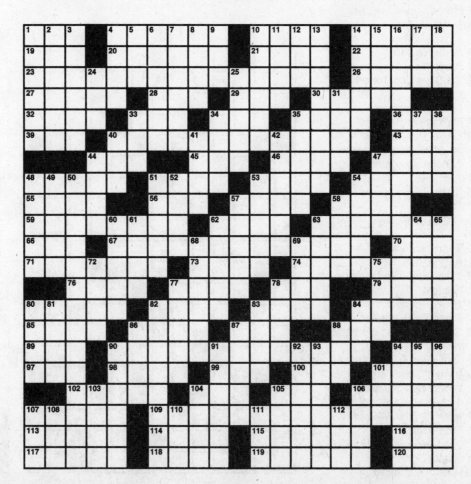

ACROSS

1 Excitement
6 Salary limit
9 Bus. degree
12 Fashion designer Arnold
18 Indian menu word
19 Piccadilly potable
20 CGS unit
21 Letterman list
22 Wynonna's sister
23 Elvis' dressy ditty?
26 Big Ben feature
27 Coiled hairdo
28 Actor Quinn
29 Baptism sites
30 Proverbial also-ran
31 Wordplayer's ploy
32 Function
33 Valhalla VIP
35 Fad mini-doll
37 ". . . __ man about a dog"
38 Jack-o'-lantern feature
39 NCO Pepper or Preston
42 Perfectly put
44 Ode to *Exorcist* accessories?
47 "Cosby Show" kid
48 Ripken broke his record
50 Sparks on the screen
51 DDE's WWII command
52 "Nuts!"
54 Vicinities
55 Go to the mat?
57 Constitution designers
58 N.Y.C. daily
59 "__ me timbers!"
60 Forest features
61 Anglo-Saxon letter
62 '64 Dixie Cups' chart topper?
65 Mr. Clampett
68 Delicate or decadent
70 *Ghost* star Patrick
71 Joust for giant Japanese
72 London emporium
74 Perfume
76 "Stayin' Alive" genre
77 Idle
78 One Wednesday
79 __ -Cone
80 Pearl harborer
81 Abundant
82 Hit buttoned up by the Eagles?
86 *Enero,* for one
87 Treas. Dept. bureau
88 San Francisco's memorable Harvey
89 Nov. electee
90 "I Am Woman" singer
92 Island east of Java
93 19th-century pseudonym
94 Blues Brother Aykroyd
95 From this date
98 John Jacob or Mary
101 Skater Sonja
103 Have the deed to
104 All together, at the Phil
105 Air Supply's wrap number?
108 A river runs through it
109 Put through a blender
110 Mt. measurement
111 Name tag?
112 '40s prime minister Clement
113 Caught in a trap
114 Tra trailers
115 Celestial sphere
116 Diamond corners

DOWN

1 Buckwheat porridge
2 Clapton's ode to haberdashers?
3 Less ruffled
4 Arp contemporary
5 Pronounce
6 Hot cuisine
7 Economist Greenspan
8 JFK Library architect
9 archy's chum
10 Nutrition writer Jane E.
11 Quito quaff
12 Jeanne d'Arc title
13 Dracula's day-bed
14 Blacksmith's garment
15 Like __ of bricks
16 Breakaway body
17 Renews stamp pads
18 Jet speed term
24 "Today" 's Matt
25 Sot's shot
27 Syringe section
31 Spark or fire follower
32 Scroll discovery site
34 Show it isn't so
36 Skinner of the stage
37 Place for an ace
38 Day- __ colors
39 Hit Gary Lewis wrote on his feet?
40 Will of "The Waltons"
41 Some are tops
42 Yawning
43 Reform Party biggie
45 Green
46 It's *chaud* time
47 Heavy reading
49 Squealer – or squeaker
53 One of the wealthy
55 Bugs' question opener
56 Tie up
57 Stopped dead
59 '89 Streep-Roseanne comedy
60 Antifreeze ingredient
62 Corp. money bosses
63 "Yes, I do think the world __ living"
64 Burney and Brice
66 Roast host
67 Step and stop lead-ins
69 Cleaving tool, to some
71 Nickname in the family
72 Sabra dance
73 Keep __ (persevere)
74 Ballpark fig.
75 Steals from stores
76 Used red #2 on
78 "Don't __"
80 Pizzeria part
83 Mr. Yale
84 Irish playwright Brian
85 N. African port
88 Oscar-winner Matlin
91 Dismays
92 Secluded arbor
93 Famous plane's first name
94 Simp
96 Native Oklahomans
97 Dandy companion
98 Pharaonic symbols
99 Steer clear of
100 Scarlett's spread
102 It may be last on the list
103 Finished
104 "See you, Reginald"
106 Unmatched
107 Lennon's widow
108 Metered rental

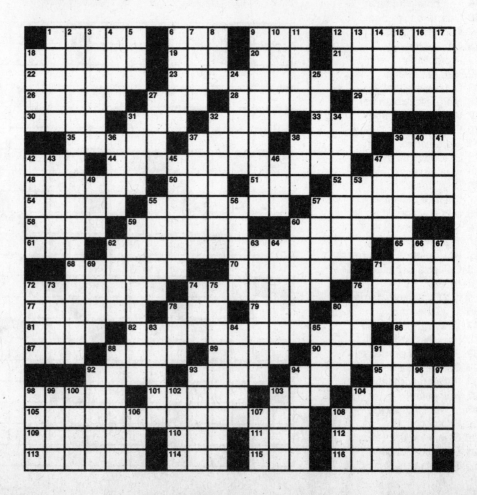

ACROSS

1 Peter, Paul and Mary, for short
4 Uses a finger bowl
10 Debilitate
13 Spellbound
17 Do smithy work
18 Wagnerian heroine
19 First river, alphabetically
20 Peter Fonda's Golden Globe role
21 Madison's home
22 Dessert specialty
24 Sans mixer
25 They may be liquid or frozen
27 B&O stop
28 Waste watchers
29 Yokum yokel
31 Pola's rival
32 Parisian season
33 Restrain
34 Minstrel's song
35 *Wag the Dog*'s Robert
37 Sentence shortener
39 Lake into the Zambezi
43 Dodgers' '60s nemesis?
45 Dolmas' wrappers
47 Movie whale
48 White wine
50 Beatrice's beloved
51 Rents from a renter
54 Heavenly headwear
55 Remaindered-book holder
56 Humbert Humbert's creator
57 Stole or shawl
58 Fabulous fellow
60 Mystery writer Dorothy
61 Subsidize
62 Bar basic
65 Slam dunk
68 Writer Rushdie
69 Fine fiddle
70 Cosmonaut Gagarin
71 Kirk or Kangaroo
73 Wyo. neighbor
74 Cities in Florida and Oklahoma
76 Lurch's line
77 Nubia, today
80 Highwayman
81 Pro's con
82 Rice-pork dish
85 Bar opener?
86 Double-flowered plant
88 Mosque feature
89 Navy officer
91 Thing on a ring
93 Stands on the course
94 Club on a diamond
95 Bowie's Stardust
98 Wasting no words
100 Club for driving
101 Mule of song
102 Belgrade is its capital
103 Late Congressman Sonny
104 Chinese dinner opener
108 Sugar substitute?
109 False god
110 Low digits
111 Read
112 Touch down
113 Be a kegler
114 Sea plea
115 Back-combed
116 Gateway abbr.

DOWN

1 __ -kebab
2 Green side dish
3 Leave the union
4 They may be short or spare
5 This __ test
6 Sans layover
7 Chalkboard
8 Fiction's Ferber
9 Sargasso or Galilee
10 Ready for the market
11 First name in '60s shipping
12 Potpourri part
13 Sunny-side up option
14 Out of the gale
15 Bosc or Anjou
16 Hanoi holiday
17 Try for a fly
19 Be in favor
23 Pointillist painter
26 Twisted mass
30 There's one on DDT
32 Time frames
33 Calvados capital
36 Rainbow
37 __ attack (strategy)
38 Made an attempt
40 Prefix meaning Mars
41 "Great White North" network
42 __ in apple
43 "Uh" sound indicator
44 Lewis or Belafonte
46 Stock ticker inventor
49 Charlie Parker's genre
52 Opposite of unter
53 Round Table knight
55 Irish playwright Brendan
56 Of birth
58 "__ be expected. . ."
59 "Sesame St." site
60 Powerful
62 Spreadsheet fodder
63 NASA's Shepard
64 Lewis' __ *Happen Here*
65 Certain Mexican seed
66 Handel bars?
67 Err
68 Chinese meal munchie
70 Sun __ -sen
71 Tepee shape
72 Opel or Citroën
74 Mineral hardness scale
75 Charge atoms
76 Snappish bark
77 Bed and breakfast items
78 Rise
79 Flops at the box office
80 Typesetter's concern
83 They'll turn off your lights
84 Green-eyed
87 Ado Annie's reply
90 Middle manager?
92 Has a rendezvous
94 Iraqi port
96 Filmed Ferber epic
97 Three rulers could make one
98 Kind of list
99 Once it was enough
101 Noted *Graf*
102 Burned up the road
103 Dribble guard
105 Oversentimentality
106 Make up your mind
107 Manipulate

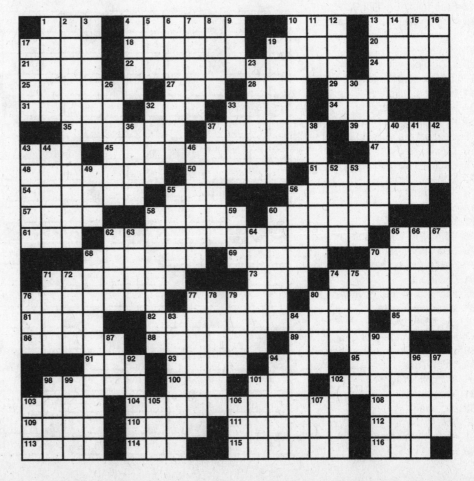

ACROSS

1 Guy's date
4 Corona rival __ Blanca
9 "Route 66" writer Bobby
14 Words for the pros?
18 Sacrifice fly result
19 Winner at Antietam
20 Stimulate
21 Sacred Hindu collection
22 Go back down
23 Balkan dwarf plant?
25 Former Uganda ruler
26 Land by bypaths
28 Reproach mildly
29 Chin chink
30 Transept projections
31 Tend the hearth
32 Delaware, at first
34 Old length measures
36 Petrarch's inspiration
37 Great shortage
38 Fashion's Hardy
39 Tropical tree
40 Skillful lawmaker
41 Couch quickie
44 100 dinars
45 Congo River watch style?
48 JFK info
49 Close friend
50 Kermit's color
51 Camel cousin
52 Bad atmosphere?
53 Free-falls from flights
55 Like some topaz or quartz
56 Correct on the keyboard
58 Heron's cousin
59 Ladd's classic Western
60 It goes across Hollywood
61 Highly motivated
64 Mme. de Poitiers
65 Famous far and wide
69 Beatles' meter maid
70 Ulee's Gold star
71 Bag and box lead-ins
72 Sooner than
73 __ standstill
74 Neat island?
77 Minor falling-out
78 With 79A, a mild soft cheese
79 See 78A
80 Iliad god who favored Troy
81 Cut it out
82 Mimieux of the movies
84 More agreeable
86 Old silver coins
87 Finishes in the money
88 Wag the Dog's Anne
89 Titleholder
90 Cockpit array
91 Namely
92 Big bag
95 Tel __
96 Jerusalem soap opera?
99 Paleo's opposite
100 Big bag
101 Far from cheerily
102 Medea's aunt
103 Señora Perón
104 Lully opera
105 Pungs and luges
106 Piccolos' kin
107 Trunk top

DOWN

1 Expanded
2 Popsters from Stockholm
3 North African roll?
4 Braque and Gris
5 Cell terminals
6 Stands up
7 Heavy weights
8 "Wheel of Fortune" buy
9 Three-person ruling body
10 "Chevaliers de la Table __"
11 Yorkshire river
12 Letters on stamps
13 Canadian prov.
14 Funicello's friend
15 Arab foe?
16 Uplift
17 Good Will Hunting director Gus Van __
20 Really hate
24 Not virtual
27 Sales talk
29 It may be static
31 Hair care lair
32 Lily variety
33 Novel set in Tahiti
34 Cavils
35 Inuit craft
36 Box seats
37 Big-headed?
39 They're bent in pliés
40 Weave in and out
42 Perched on
43 Volume unit?
45 Bakersfield neighbor
46 Poor Richard's book
47 Single-handedly
50 Scoff
52 Hearty dish
54 Met star
55 Not quite kosher
56 Orange coats
57 Seth's son
59 Subsequently
60 Tennis' Williams
61 Uninteresting
62 Baptism, e.g.
63 Romans, except for the Vatican?
64 Drown, in a way
65 More seldom seen
66 Himalayan discussion group?
67 Get the lead out?
68 Inhibit
70 Lute markings
71 Spendthrift's specialty
74 Info for builders
75 It is chopped liver
76 America's Cup entries
77 Unwholesome
81 Boston's river
83 Cardiologist's concerns
84 Staircase supports
85 In a frigid manner
86 North-of-the-Aegean region
87 Center's move
88 Store up supplies
89 African capital
90 Quantities of dope?
91 Unfeigned
92 Baby's bed
93 Jacob's son
94 Pack the Mack
96 Nametags, e.g.
97 Sonoran sun
98 Italian novelist

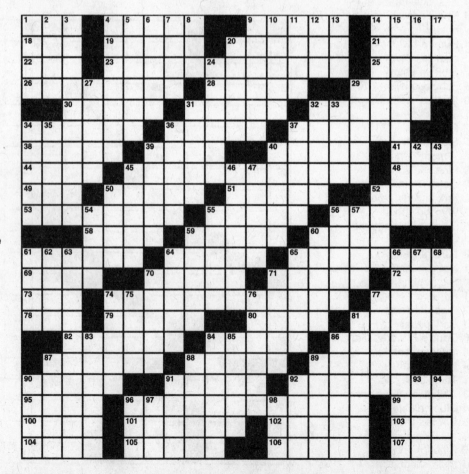

ACROSS

1 PST pt.
4 MRI exam
8 Raise, as anchors
13 Rambo rescuee
16 Toothpaste-approving gp.
17 Swiftly
18 "He that hath __ hear . . .": Matt. 11
19 WWII Japanese general
20 Cute cutup
21 Life with Billy+David?
23 Pizazz
24 Strong currents
26 "__ it" ("Happy Days" expression)
27 Light yellow-brown
29 Got going
30 Get into the computer
31 *Who's Who* entries
32 "__ I say more?"
33 Tin Man and Toto's creator
34 Tallow source
35 Mini-whopper
38 '60s activist org.
39 Desk set Sean+Rosa?
43 Scott Joplin opus
44 Said "cheese"
46 Not home
47 Entertainer Abdul
48 Where speedometer needles rest
49 Chinese weights
50 Clothier's diagonal
51 South, south of the border
52 Gershwin's __ in F
54 Sound from Simba
55 Like Dickens' Dodger
59 Cubic Rubik
60 Round trip with J.S.+Harrison?
64 *The Mission* author Hans
65 Engine type
67 Responsibility
68 Wagnerian *Ring* role
70 It's west of G.B.
71 Fudd's frustrater
72 Peggy Lee classic
73 Bloodshot
74 Beach near San Luis Obispo
77 Loblolly, e.g.
78 Cable senders
79 Some former IBM PC's
80 Explosive Marge+Maximilian?
83 Even one
84 Curling surface
85 Van Gogh painting part
86 Not at all stuffy
87 Bungee, e.g.
89 Rain pollutant
90 French actress Ardant
92 Entrance or exit
95 Earthling
97 The life, in Lille

98 Turnovers, to Turgenev
99 Thigh-high skirt
100 Top 40's Ray+Esther?
103 Get one's goat
104 Like the Negev
105 Oregon college town
106 Saab rivals
107 Nail site
108 Thus far
109 Midnight meeting
110 Humorist Lebowitz
111 No one has two

DOWN

1 Makes the twain?
2 Word on a ticket
3 Graduates Al+Maud?
4 Dug up the dirt?
5 Was empathetic
6 They'll make a play for you
7 Napoleon's marshal
8 "It __ Be You"
9 Bean of "Dr. Quinn . . ."
10 "When the Frost __ the Punkin"
11 Alphabetical nickname
12 He wrote of Frodo
13 President during the Mexican War
14 Ventura Co. musicfest site
15 Copped the cup
17 "Take __ out of crime"
18 Puzzler
19 Gunpowder, etc.
22 "Shh, don't make __!"
25 Very, to Verlaine
28 Henry Percy, in *Henry IV*
30 Nathan and Memory
31 Harbor marker
33 Writer Hilaire
34 Steamy spots
35 Winter woe
36 Kind of wind or wlll
37 She played Maude
38 Zen enlightenment
39 Michelangelo masterwork
40 River nymphs
41 Minute man?
42 Crude
43 Drove at Indy
44 Start of many Quebec place names
45 Elgin collection item
50 Gravy bread?
51 Barry who sang of Green Berets
53 Medicis' "the Elder"
54 They're cooking with gas
56 Extensive Jamie+Betty?

57 State of being in place
58 It's on the Aire
61 Huckleberry, e.g.
62 To excess
63 "Boléro" writer
66 Ovid's *Art of Love,* etc.
69 Krypton symbols
71 Bargain holders
72 Like really hot chili
74 Trident-shaped letter
75 Bus. regulating org.
76 Yonder lass
77 Stamp word
78 Said "Are we *there* yet?"
81 Gewgaw
82 Premolar neighbor
83 Olympian aggressor
87 Satirist George
88 Early Oklahomans
89 Encompassed by
90 Clock fronts
91 __ -garde
92 Comic Radner
93 Tire town
94 "Omigosh!"
95 Give employment to
96 Sergeant's command
97 It means study
98 Rain in buckets
99 Merry month
101 Classic Čapek play
102 Brits' air arm

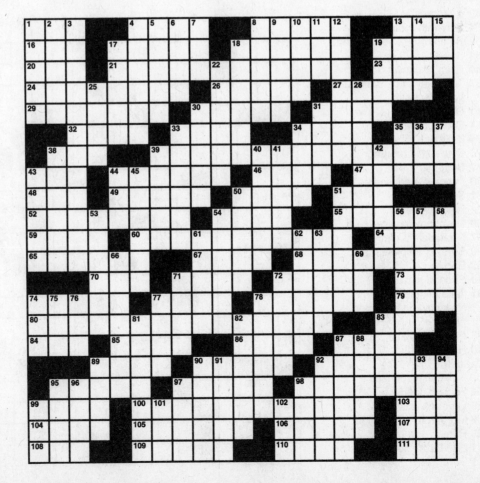

ACROSS

1 Butt
4 Eulogize
10 "How can __?"
15 Didn't discard
19 Shin or pay ender
20 He pays for stays
21 Ship of fuels?
22 Fencing category
23 It's inspired
24 Pip of a novel?
26 Antibes neighbor
27 Utmosts
29 Harass
30 Buddy's buddy
31 Like Paul Pry
32 Olds' oldies
34 What hands wear on their legs
36 Moonlight, e.g.
39 They're Super in Seattle
41 Passes
45 Led Zep's ode to gambling?
48 See 23A
49 James or Jimmy's middle name
50 Tu and tu together
51 Anka tune "__ Beso"
53 Filling of some knishes
54 Phonograph part
55 QE2 milieu
57 Small change
59 Yards of yarn
60 TVA cousin
61 Play with robots
62 Before meat, heat or beat
64 Secret WWII gp.
66 Evan or conval closer
67 Tune played before a full house?
71 Salami salon
74 Conan Doyle title
75 Kelly or Krupa
76 Byte's little brother
77 Beat-nik?
80 Improve manuscripts
82 Series sample
84 Perspicacious
86 Royal possessive
87 Guadalajara girlfriend
88 Brian of ambient music
89 Bric-a- __
90 Second glove
91 Take minutes
93 New spin on a guiding principle?
98 Piled pancakes
100 Removed rind
101 Idea
102 Roll-call responses
104 Feeling good
105 Lift or off lead-in
106 More than sometimes
109 Rate
111 Like Lahr's lion
115 Berth place
116 Bankable composer?
119 Shad delicacy
120 Open some
121 Historian Durant
122 Drawing power
123 It's put before the carte
124 Plant with pads
125 Thickly packed
126 Lowered the lights
127 Mindless card game

DOWN

1 Wander
2 Inter or et follower
3 Manifesto maker
4 Raise in rank
5 Act of denying
6 "Me __ big mouth!"
7 Like __ (candidly)
8 Short time?
9 Cockney present
10 Bald Soprano playwright
11 Eye shades
12 Ancient Mexican
13 Be 25D
14 Atlantic bird
15 Chancy convention orator?
16 It's a long story
17 Bushel quarter
18 Pegs with concave tops
25 Like water at 212°
28 "__ my days, I never . . ."
30 Telegrapher's nickname
32 Getty Center feature
33 Hazzard County lawman
35 It's worn under a chasuble
36 Say "#@!*"
37 Chicago stopover
38 Marilyn, at first
39 Porch for Pericles
40 Cinematographer Nykvist
42 Freelancers' encls.
43 Professional standard
44 Classic cowboy film
46 Like brown bananas
47 Bar legally
52 Braised veal dish
55 Nickel in a pocket?
56 Lead-ins
57 Sign of omission
58 Innocent state
63 Start of a conclusion
65 "SNL" staple
67 Chancy bit of produce?
68 BYOB opener
69 Erudite
70 When the French fry?
71 Darlings
72 Ant, to some
73 German camera brand
77 Coon's kin
78 Lunch preceders?
79 Pose proudly
81 Lower the lights
83 Insiders are in it
85 Jokester
89 Boris and Lon's colleague
90 Taxi ticker
92 Alemannic article
94 Easy to read
95 Mekong, e.g.
96 Not cognizant
97 Found
99 Coy
103 Canary kin
105 Kings play here
106 Milky-white stone
107 Suva is its capital
108 Color close to aqua
110 AAA offerings
111 Unruffled
112 Gunslinger's dare
113 Dancer Montez
114 Subscription term
116 Good, in street talk
117 He's no gentleman
118 MDX ÷ X

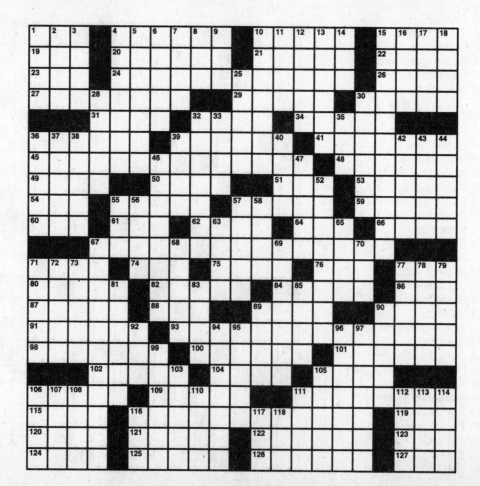

ACROSS

1 Get the 7-10 split
6 Rearwards, on boats
9 Eliza D.'s creator
12 "Altogether ooky" family
18 Grievous
19 More than a cold
20 Stephen of *The Crying Game*
21 Ga-ga go-with
22 Northern Ireland district
23 Family cult classic?
26 Tacitus' tongue
27 Make martinis
28 __ meal out (dines in a diner)
29 Ravens' havens
30 Roving redhead
31 T. follower
32 They reduce a mtge.
33 Spreads the frosting
35 Log lodge
37 Newborn's head covering
38 Have a falling out?
39 Is past?
42 *Nixon in China* role
44 Procession of sex appeal series?
47 Fronded plant
48 Rolls with the punches
50 Pref. meaning outside
51 Young Billy, or young billy
52 Aviator Earhart
54 Great Dame?
55 Curled the lip
57 Patella
58 T on a test
59 Curie or Cardin
60 "You don't know what that __ me!"
61 Abby's twin
62 Sitcom starring Dumbo?
65 "Spy Vs. Spy" magazine
68 Sings lullabies
70 Archie Bell's backup group
71 FYI circulator
72 City east of Pittsburgh
74 Oakland's environs
76 Pencil-chewing, for one
77 Pencil-chewing, for one
78 Son of a Bush
79 Andorra neighbor __ de Urgel
80 Take it all back
81 Lotion ingredient
82 Western series that was all the rage?
86 Coquettish
87 Sought office
88 Donnybrook
89 Fiefdom owner
90 It goes with alas
92 Power-line pipe
93 Deadly septet
94 Tongue-in-cheek
95 Werewolf's wail
98 "There's __ line between ..."
101 Ludwig wrote *für* her
103 Unassertive
104 Soak in the tub
105 Series about a swing-shift worker?
108 Uri, e.g.
109 Clan's plaid
110 Bovary or Butterfly
111 Break ground
112 Reach, in a way
113 Seco or Grande
114 Cat's flat
115 Sagacity symbol
116 Off that way

DOWN

1 Echolocation device
2 Sitcom with the rite stuff?
3 Chad's home
4 Athens attraction
5 Shade tree
6 -ed, e.g.
7 Linseed source
8 Famous Memphis king
9 Erie, e.g.
10 Lahr and Convy
11 Fifth Avenue landmark
12 Before this time
13 Swallowed
14 Medication measures
15 Ever so long
16 Between half and all
17 AA candidates
18 Ridge
24 Take skirts to new lengths
25 Natatory nymph
27 Snack preview?
31 Branco and Bravo
32 Couturier's cutout
34 Where those who are taken get taken?
36 Mac morsel
37 Rome's greatest orator
38 Misbehaving
39 Conservationist's favorite sitcom?
40 Diva's ditty
41 Halve a pretzel
42 Devilfish
43 Bedeck
45 Asks for more *Time*?
46 Disencumber
47 Podiatrist's concern
49 Post opp.
53 Military meal
55 Chianti region
56 "I Am Woman" warbler
57 Qantas mascot
59 By the sound of it?
60 Ponce __
62 Awl or maul
63 Delete-key punchers
64 Perused anew
66 Of certain acids
67 Daft
69 Choir attire
71 Big Apple – or burger
72 Not nearly near
73 Kinks classic
74 Canto intro
75 Stamped out
76 Zeus' consort
78 Deep black
80 Be dependent
83 Suite spot
84 Work for nine
85 Far Side's Larson
88 Airstrip – or stripper's strip
91 Tinker to Evers to __
92 "Me, too"
93 Letter from Greece
94 Unicycle, mostly
96 "__ woods these are ..."
97 One of your contacts
98 Start for girl or boy
99 Whar she blows?
100 Man of the *Haus*
102 Walk like Frasier's dad
103 Kind of man or job
104 Cantata composer
106 Cadmus' daughter
107 "Well, well, *well*"
108 Ailurophobe's bane

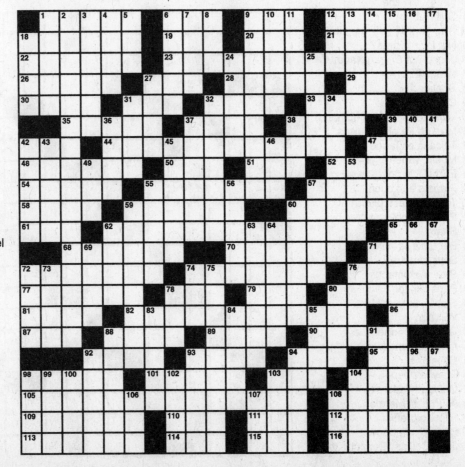

ACROSS

1 Now, later
5 It'll hold water
10 Dandelion, for one
14 Asgard god
18 Out of wind?
19 Bunk
20 Bloomers with hips
22 Rioja or rouge
23 __ up (be mum)
24 "The day the music died" hit
26 Quipu maker
27 Block of stamps
29 Dinful?
30 Sheen
32 Toy for a tot
35 Kilt feature
37 Irritant
38 "Stop __ shoot!"
39 Exhausted from talking
43 Hyannis' cape
46 Plays the knight?
48 Khayyám creations
49 Pinta poles
50 Beatle spouse
51 Where the Storting meets
52 Back up on disk
53 Courteous bloke
54 One-pot meal
55 A score of quires
56 Animal Alice encountered
60 Lay __ the line
61 Shirt fabric
63 New York's __ Fisher Hall
64 Not in __ words
66 Joseph of *Citizen Kane*
67 Wings it?
68 Shelter
69 Opt for
70 World Series maximum
71 Ma and Pa of '50s films
72 Titicaca or Tahoe
73 Muslin variety
76 Early Dr. J do
79 Planets and such
80 Toastmaster's place
81 Put on edge?
82 Snare
83 Begum's spouse
84 Says seriously
86 Steers' stomachs
88 Paris divider
89 F or G, but not H
90 Win big
93 Dusk, to Donne
94 It may be critical
95 Echelons
96 They're deep
98 Old Getty address
101 Journalist Mannes
103 Piloting prefix
104 Cameo component
105 Joan Collins' "Dynasty" role
109 Shirk work
113 *Mère*'s mate
114 Detroit dud
115 Sarge's superior
116 Disgusting
117 It'll hold water
118 Percussion instrument
119 Enclose closely
120 Verve

DOWN

1 Campaign contribution gp.
2 100%
3 Place for swells
4 Be seductive
5 No. 5's maker
6 Vatican surroundings
7 Hula accompaniment
8 Bottom of the *mapa*
9 Famous
10 Gossamer ghost
11 Almost forever
12 TV sports award
13 Agnus or Mater follower
14 Dickens' Oliver
15 Tip-off
16 Not quite never
17 Kind of guard or end
21 See 69A
25 Lacquer layers
28 Vestry vestments
31 Puts to work
32 Power mower part
33 Come to pass
34 Historic Oregon site
35 Annoyances
36 Actor's dialog
37 Fusilli or fettucine
40 Area code 801 resident
41 Bahrain bigwigs
42 Imagine
43 Hash browns alternative
44 Low draw score
45 Soft and fluffy
47 Beefsteak and cherry
52 Lengthy discourse
53 Environmentalists
54 Fake or feign
57 The Super Bowl has two
58 Like some halls or walls
59 Fly in the tropics
62 *Lost Weekend* syndrome
65 Much more than ne'er
66 Put on plastic
67 Obsession
68 Take another shot
69 Spy's cover?
70 Kick off
71 Some newsstands
74 *Golden Boy* writer
75 Show clout?
77 Indian VIP
78 Bids a club
84 Great white hunter?
85 A-V's V
86 "Love Train" soul singers
87 *Cool Hand Luke* prop
88 Red giant or white dwarf
91 Going amiss
92 Was a good boy
94 Get-acquainted dance
97 Get x
98 Be in the mood to brood
99 From scratch
100 Instrument for Erato
101 "From the desk of" note
102 Nerve-cell process
103 Hero of a '22 play
106 Chicken choice
107 Transvaal leader __ Paul Kruger
108 Heart throb
110 Castor or canola
111 Near Miss.?
112 Bog

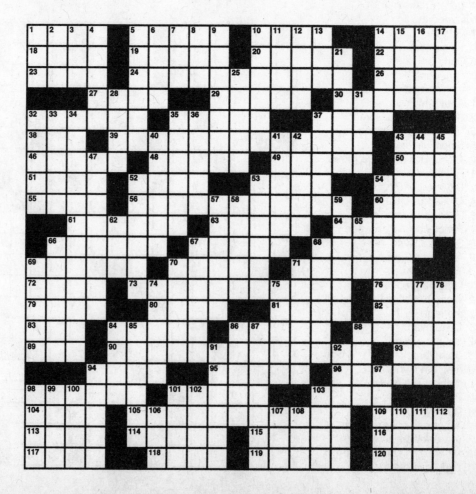

ACROSS

1 "__ next?"
5 Union Jack, for one
9 Psyche's opposite
13 Drag the bottom
18 Throw a bash
19 Come apart
21 Cheese that's made backward?
22 Longtime entertainer Blake
23 Temporary vessel?
26 "__ to bed"
27 Getting warmer
28 Like Lewis' professor
29 Creeks
30 In the old days
31 Opera boxes
32 Fleshy herb
33 Clumsy
36 Low point on the Titanic
37 Touching off
40 Trudge
41 TV's Jeannie, e.g.
42 Defunct treaty org.
43 Long of *Soul Food*
44 Try-square shape
45 Sinew-ous Sinatra film?
48 "Just __ suspected!"
49 Cambodia's Lon
50 Spouts off
51 Decant the Darjeeling
52 Narrow valley
53 Mob member
55 Aviary sound
57 Pro or dia ender
59 Santa follower
60 Monastery monody
61 Jumbo shrimp
62 Well-mannered
64 River of Cologne
65 River of Limerick
67 Foster a felon
68 Connery or O'Casey
69 "Let's flip __"
70 Verb of the past?
72 Tremayne or Crane
73 Connective tissue policy?
77 Unaccounted-for GI
78 Fairy queen
79 Infamy
80 Quite enough
81 He was in *Misery*
82 Summer coolers
84 Take it past the limit
85 What trespassers are out of
87 They can brake a bronc
88 Clipped, as sheep
89 Postprandial potable
90 Sculptor and actor George
92 Prentiss or Poundstone
93 It's a drag

97 Cheri of "SNL"
98 Gristly exams?
101 *Pollo* partner
102 Burundi native
103 Ursa Major neighbor
104 Spill the beans
105 Brasselle of '60s TV
106 Sit suddenly
107 Countenance
108 Seeing things

DOWN

1 How soon
2 Second of three virtues
3 Workplace safety org.
4 Athlete's temptation
5 Camus wrote in it
6 Spacious
7 Palindromic name
8 It could make your hair stand on end
9 Loveseat
10 Playwright Clifford
11 Queen of Long Beach
12 Writer Lowell or Tan
13 Diamond shape
14 Elapse
15 Gutsy yeti?
16 Tide rival
17 Most August birthday boys
20 Wool grease
24 They have lots of secs.
25 Robust
29 " . . . __ path to your door"
31 Notebook paper feature
32 Brenda, Belle or Bart
33 Unwrap
34 Stand for
35 Hairy burlesque?
36 Rubble or Grable
37 Entrap
38 Some second-generation Americans
39 Makes progress
41 Class, or kind
42 Stable sound
45 Foot the bill
46 Holland's The __
47 Voice a view
52 Commencement rental
54 Use a letter opener
55 Hutch contents
56 Star Wars' Solo
57 Galahad's quest
58 Drescher persona
60 Bracelet bangle

61 Car option
62 Where dates are made
63 Witchcraft branch
64 Picture puzzle
65 Tongue-lash
66 Natatory nymph
68 Jimmy of "NYPD Blue"
69 Quaker in the grove?
71 __ *souci* (carefree)
73 Prepare for war
74 Paradise paradigms
75 Campania's province
76 Oz's __ City
81 Bargain
83 "Please step to the __ the bus"
84 "Oh hush!"
85 Fondant candy
86 Hydrox rival
88 Painter Andrea del __
89 Bishop or knight
90 Lie in the tub
91 French I infinitive
92 Rhymin' Simon
94 Carhop's burden
95 Unengaged
96 Invites
98 I-5 patrollers
99 Sling contents
100 Moo goo __ pan

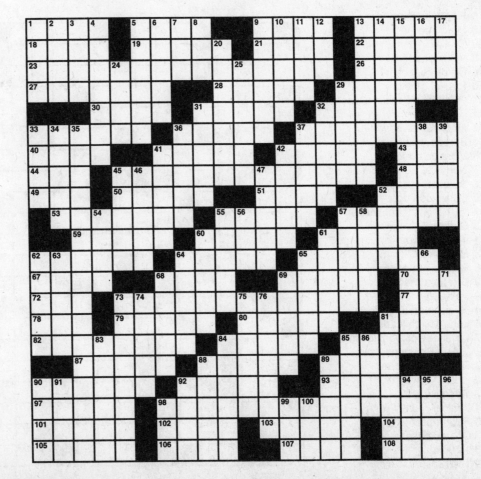

ACROSS
1 Drops at daybreak
4 Roadside assist
7 Thumb nail?
11 Water lily
16 It's long in fashion
17 Strasbourg street
18 Pythias' pal
19 Niles Crane's flame
20 Venomous provocateurs?
23 Throws out
24 In good spirits
25 Performance record
26 Unimprovable
28 New Zealand parrot
29 Flit fetcher of old ads
30 You get it with your order
31 Some babies
32 Chum
34 Farm butter
35 Anomalous
36 Kyoto cash
37 Stylishness
38 Reuben bread
39 Is more than one?
40 Singularly slithery era?
45 Trigger puller?
47 Knights' counterparts
49 John, to Jock
50 Skew
52 Material for Strauss
53 Dandy
55 *El* pluralized
56 Fixed, as elections
59 Make merry
60 On fire
63 VW preceders
65 On one's rocker?
66 Path of a pass
67 Poisonous Puritan preacher?
71 La-la leader
72 *Madre's hermanos*
74 Barbecue leftover
75 More on edge
76 Nancy of *Sunset Boulevard*
78 "I swear!"
80 Düsseldorf dessert
82 "Simpsons" shopkeeper
83 Gideons' giveaway
84 It has drawers for drawers
86 Babe in a '98 film
88 Record material
89 Box for a cracker?
90 Polite viper?
94 Noah's porky son?
95 Long March leader
97 Levensen or Donaldson
98 __ -en-Provence
99 Royal flush starter
102 Letter "Y" wearer
103 Tentative taste
104 Ironically funny
105 Pewter part
106 Coated cheese
108 1,200 mos.
109 The press, TV, etc.

111 Sweetie
112 Chessplayer's ploy
113 Three-bagger
116 Biting biopic?
119 Hardened
120 Kick back
121 It lacks refinement
122 It gets decked in December
123 Hale-Bopp, e.g.
124 Serve *Time*
125 Method
126 Meth or eth ending

DOWN
1 Ran the 100-meter
2 Put out
3 More Solomonic
4 City on the Hudson
5 Sharer's pronoun
6 Ecologist's concern
7 Cross-shaped letter
8 Present all around
9 Incurable diseases
10 Dummy's seat
11 Far from stringent
12 Antonym syn.
13 Reptilian Redford role?
14 Forget about it?
15 Tahini ingredient
16 More than just masculine
18 Borzoi or basenji

19 Gridlock result
21 Playwright Christopher
22 Theater ticket datum
27 "__ moi, le déluge"
30 Grassy mead
31 Cornucopia
33 Louis Quatorze, till 1715
36 Aye, ashore
37 World's most popular drink
40 Include's antonym
41 Corin of "Parker Lewis Can't Lose"
42 It means double
43 Altar answer
44 Bad move
46 Dyne-centimeters
47 Dolores of *Cheyenne Autumn*
48 Constrictive herpetological home?
51 Faithful, or factual
52 Controversial sentence
53 Antoine Domino or Thomas Waller
54 Gershwins' "__ Sing"
55 Ponce's birthplace
57 Matriculate
58 Ben Franklin cohort Silas
61 Myrmecologist's topic
62 Monsieur's Mrs.
64 "No __ traffic"
68 Silver filling?

69 Lexicographer's concern
70 Hood who did good
73 Doer of the lord's work?
77 It's trapped in the dryer
79 Strikes one as
81 Sportscaster Cross
85 Sub's viewer
86 Bill or boy lead-in
87 Suffix in poli sci
88 Raise dander
89 Sept. '43 landing site
91 Sabra, e.g.
92 Water colors?
93 Neatness standard
94 Busy as a beehive
96 Sought targets
99 Underground Railroad leader
100 Fit for the feast
101 Durban's province
104 Overcaffeinated
105 Mix of old films
106 Looker's leg
107 D-day beach
110 Calamitous
111 Put the whammy on
112 Zanesville's Zane
114 Sent or vent lead-in
115 Not the best service
117 It welcomes you at the door
118 Roaring Twenties, e.g.

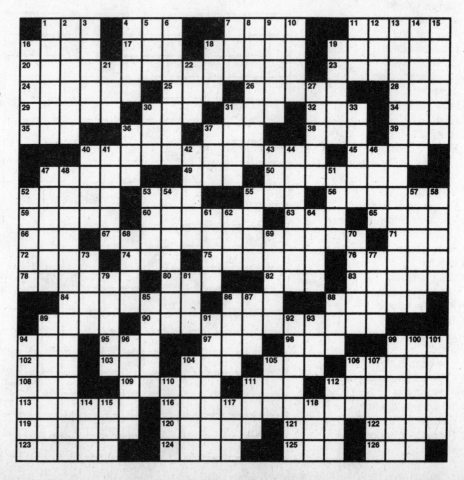

ACROSS

1 Spill the beans
5 Christmas in Calais
9 Baby's bed
13 Motown creation
16 Combined
18 All-time bestseller
19 Betting setting
20 Notre Dame name
21 '97 action flick
22 *Elève*'s milieu
23 Makes choices
24 Michael, to Kirk
25 Mention overdue debts?
28 Cling to
29 Puts under
30 Where most people live
31 Give the slip to
32 Pop favorite?
35 Dozen doz.
36 Be cyclical
38 Joe from France?
39 Comments of interest?
44 Coagulate
45 Beluga and sevruga
46 Huey and Howie
47 Like some talk shows
49 Fresh fish?
50 Was winning
51 Shades
52 Time beyond measure
54 Be borne on a breeze
57 Window parts
59 Toyland denizens
60 Twosome
61 Getty adviser Huxtable
62 Debt counselor's service?
65 The Eiger, e.g.
66 Take this and you'll be sick
67 He was Smart
68 Pound sounds
69 Noah of "ER"
70 Christmas contraction
71 Composer Bartók
72 Liverpool lav
73 Pizarro's gold
75 Din
77 It's a natural
80 Redolent
84 Kind of rind
85 Immature account?
87 Mr. Rogers
88 Piece of the pie
89 Bit in a horse's mouth
90 He had a salty wife
91 Far from loaded
92 Stylish, in teenspeak
93 "Red __ is she": "Ancient Mariner"
97 He wears very little clothing
98 Austen's banking book?
104 "__ was saying . . ."
105 Like old lettuce

106 Gives berth?
107 Where to find Eugene
108 Army bed
109 Biathlon supply
110 Come to terms
111 Arabian Peninsula countries, once
112 Letters from Mom?
113 Cellist Ma
114 Add shading
115 Give a G, e.g.

DOWN

1 Churlish chap
2 Jennifer of WKRP
3 Hales, Jr. and Sr.
4 Restful color
5 Specialized market
6 English horns' kin
7 Queen of scat
8 Satyric glance
9 Richness criterion
10 Fix
11 Mural or venous opener
12 Head honcho
13 Per diem?
14 Excite
15 Where the buffalo roam
16 An OSHA concern
17 Scut work
18 Tout's target
26 Saddle pals
27 Pinions' partners
31 Ho Chi Minh Trail locale
32 PC alternative
33 Edible tuber
34 Non-Arabic 1105
36 Campaigned
37 Joule ten-millionth
38 Elegant
40 Schism
41 Egypt and Syria, briefly
42 Italian queen's namesakes
43 Fashion figure
44 Inch along
47 Brass band biggies
48 "__ never regret this"
50 MOMA's West Coast kin
51 Movie mime
53 Not yep
54 Tend tables
55 Improvise
56 Paper gains?
57 David's creation
58 Swine suite
59 Fit in
62 Legendary

63 Optimal
64 She went to Paris
69 Function
73 Choral Symphony part
74 Charles Dutton sitcom
76 Forest fauna
77 Torrent
78 Cross i's?
79 Join the competition
80 Alternative to Midway
81 Dressing ingredient
82 *Cero* follower
83 NCO Club patron
85 Salon service
86 Unrefined
87 Cash sang its blues
88 Front-wheel wobble
91 Dove's goal
92 Excellent, dude
93 Decorate
94 Spendthrift's outing
95 Less iffy
96 Plant swelling
98 Portray
99 Latin I verb
100 Not A-OK
101 Beach Boys' "__ Around"
102 Road-hazard marker
103 Nus to you

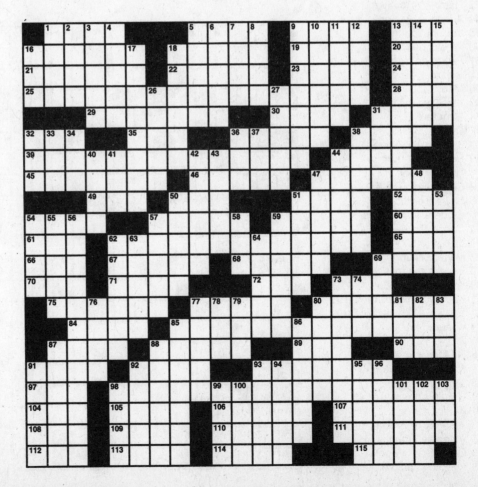

ACROSS

1 Be a poor loser
5 Answer to the Sphinx's riddle
8 Young yippers
12 Hoodwink
16 Former enemy capital
17 A number's homophone
18 Bridal path
19 Soup sound
20 Lander at 50A
21 Certain household help
24 Locationally challenged, perhaps
25 Swissair competitor
26 Siouan language
27 Breadth of fresh hair?
28 "Hart to Hart" pooch
30 Assumed appearance
31 WWII cartoon GI
35 Shot through the chest?
36 Gets all choked up
37 Dance partner
38 Tchrs.' union
39 Sarcastic "I knew *that*"
41 Be treated justly
45 Elev.
46 Strike dumb
48 Warp crosser
49 Atlanta university
50 De Gaulle alternative
51 Sacred bird in old Egypt
52 Cotton cube
53 Ramp alternative
54 A long way to go?
55 Vaccination fluids
56 Weeks per *annum*
57 Fee to be free
58 Soft rock
59 Many mos.
60 *Arrowsmith* author
64 Gym ball
67 Take a tumble
69 It vies with *Vogue*
70 Beaver's oeuvre
71 Horn or Fear
72 Cannon of *Bob & Carol* . . .
73 Mops the orlop
75 Cinderella's helpers
76 Comic Rudner
77 Like Toledo?
78 Military uniform material
79 Laze in the rays
80 Ira Gershwin opus
81 Kobe cummerbund
82 Erstwhile "Masterpiece Theatre" host
85 Zinger from Hingis
86 Hit the jackpot
87 Iron coating, often
88 Sign gas
89 Cardinal's residence
91 Femur, for one
93 Anthony or Anton
95 Acted as arsonist
98 Onassis, to People
99 "Olympia" painter
100 Put two on the nose
101 Treaty partner
102 Canadian novelist
107 King Minos' domain
108 Pandora's escapees
109 Gold mold
110 Low-tech propeller
111 Walken or Danson
112 Rather ripe
113 Bank's claim
114 Sit in judgment
115 Doogie Howser was one

DOWN

1 Enjoy
2 Sign in some salons
3 Pillager
4 Family reunion attendees
5 In furious fashion
6 Molecule mite
7 Just in or out
8 Hummus holders
9 Customary practice
10 Bend, at the barre
11 To-be-cont. story
12 Old Glory, etc.
13 Ypres yes
14 Municipal req.
15 CD ancestors
16 Five to ten, e.g.
18 St. Francis' town
19 Dab
22 Milky Way center
23 Posh
25 Movie Mitty
29 Carry on
30 Social blunder
31 Skyrockets
32 One indoor sports spectator
33 Ma plays it
34 *High Noon*'s Jurado
36 Of Scots Highlanders
37 Emporium
39 Dagwood's dog
40 "Burnt" color
42 Country singer Shania
43 Call it a career
44 Nasal appraisal
47 Half sister of Eva Gabor?
50 Tin Woodsman's need
52 It's seen on a screen
53 Leaves port
54 Most of "Deck the Halls"
57 San Diego park
58 Frequent flyer?
60 Moral misdeed
61 Tilted, in Tottenham
62 Prolific inventor
63 Wild and crazy
65 Of eyes
66 Tolstoy topic
68 Focus group member?
71 Have a bawl
72 "Drift Away" singer Gray
73 Give a gloss
74 The Badger St.
75 Dry red or white wine
77 Ginsberg's magnum opus
78 Mayo spread?
79 Something to catch or save
80 To read, to Reynaldo
82 Islands off Portugal
83 Six-footer?
84 Nautical mile
90 Hard to come by
92 Not at all well
93 What Bilko answered to
94 Coalition
95 Bathrobe fabric
96 "Crocodile Rock"-er John
97 Textile worker
99 Skimpy skirt
100 Carry, on safari
102 Columnist Greenfield
103 *In vitro* items
104 Periphery
105 Be below snuff?
106 Sodom fleer
107 Hipster

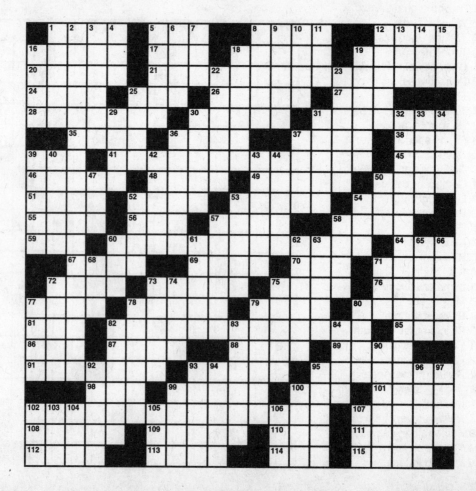

ACROSS

1 Cold mold
6 Win going away
10 Use a button
14 Workplace-inspecting org.
18 Corroborate
19 Cult figure
20 Dueling piece
21 Grande and Bravo
22 More baroque banker?
25 Serengeti sights
26 Right wing workplace?
27 Auditioner's goal
28 Portable bed
29 Uneasy feeling
31 José's hurrays
32 UK award
33 Dry, dry again
35 Commencement
36 One of the jet set
37 Steals blue eggs?
39 Door to daylight
40 Coll. entrance exam
41 Frequent "further" follower
42 Sound of distress
44 Abysmal test score
47 Indian chief
50 Pretense
52 With 118A, a French oath
54 Name for a colleen
55 France's Côte d'__
56 Two-bit sticker?
59 Terra's star
60 Opening in the Titanic
62 Candlestick base?
63 Friendship
65 Vernon's dance partner
66 Investigation
68 Mountain lions
70 Say "Yay!"
72 Super dry
73 Newspapers
76 Isn't out of
77 Italian fawns?
82 Lop the crop
83 Bit of eye makeup?
85 Contract parts
86 "__ that a shame?"
87 Contaminated
88 Five, to a Fauve
89 __ shoestring
90 Dribble guard
91 Questionnaire datum
92 Evita's husband
94 Moment of silence?
99 Bellhop's burden
102 Same old thing
104 Actor Ed's kin
105 Period of note
106 Took a trip?
107 Big name in dictionaries
109 School org.
110 Quatrain schedule?
111 Katmandu's continent
112 Cheese from France
113 Gunfire alerts?

117 Robert Knievel, to most
118 See 52A
119 Catchall abbr.
120 Sidesteps
121 Optimistic
122 Safecracker
123 Facts and figures
124 Mall events

DOWN

1 Helps
2 "Ozymandias," e.g.
3 They get slapped around
4 Paris, in Paris
5 Square-cut cigar
6 Long arms?
7 Garfield's foil
8 Sun. follower
9 Powerless pill
10 Fruit jelly base
11 News letters
12 Half a Tommy tune title
13 Zeus' wife
14 Place in order
15 Evil twin, perhaps?
16 Monopoly buy
17 It's on the plus side
18 Hair dos
23 LBJ son-in-law
24 "__ lay me down . . ."

30 Fish near a knish
33 Event producing big bucks?
34 Cupid's love
37 The old college cry?
38 Devil-may-care
39 Water vessel
40 De Beauvoir's beau
43 Guadalajara gold
45 Run amok
46 Unique
47 Criminal charge
48 Of a carbon-nitrogen group
49 Results of disorder in the courts?
50 Carpet quality
51 Letterless phone button
52 Snooty sort
53 "Don't look __ that way!"
56 Bon follower
57 Valerie Harper series
58 Roster entry
61 Rosemary, for one
64 Rectangular array
66 Stiff-necked
67 Barbecue specialty
68 Huff and puff
69 Mideast weapon

70 Fashionable
71 Mata __
72 Army's Creighton
73 Totter sauce?
74 Have the fare
75 KGB or CIA operative
78 "This must weigh __"
79 Singers Boyz II __
80 Disfigures
81 Actress Osterwald
84 On the button
87 Balmoral river
90 Scolded
91 Mares' nests?
93 Baba or Pasha
95 Go acoustic
96 French bean?
97 Spiral or Horsehead
98 Russian river
99 In addition to
100 Some frocks' shapes
101 Kundun composer Philip
102 Brown earth tone
103 Mechanism lead-in
104 Stubborn as __
106 Deadly
108 "Dear" lady
110 Like __ out of hell
114 Charley horse site
115 WKRP or KPFK
116 Stowe's little one

ACROSS

1 Orange tuber
4 '97 Val Kilmer role
9 Talk over again
15 Fielders' flings
19 In the past
20 *Zoo Story* writer
21 Actor Estevez
22 The greatest place on earth?
23 Tie the knot
24 Gable-Shearer interface?
26 TV tapers
27 Heckled
29 Publisher Nast
30 Cries like calves
31 It's shot in hearts
32 Starr of the comics
34 Wither away
36 Work a wedding
38 Hunter's hideaway
39 Judicial writ
40 Bush and Clinton, e.g.
41 Poe peripheral?
45 Current craze
48 Headlight setting
49 Dull finishes
50 Clapton's "__ the Sheriff"
51 Big Mack
52 Homer Simpson's dad
53 Preminger and Klemperer
54 Sadat of Egypt
55 Letter or mail preceder
56 Seasoned rice dish
58 To the side of a ship
59 "My kingdom for __"
60 Iconic Chaney film?
64 E or G, e.g.
67 Aviary
68 EDT opener
72 Not listed above
73 Stravinsky and Sikorsky
74 Socko synonym
76 School lobby
77 Nonpareil
78 Prefix meaning solid
79 Cookwear coating
80 Pro __ (for now)
81 Hippie's home
82 Film about Rommel's hard drive?
84 Golfer Ballesteros
85 Troy, to some
87 Label anew
88 Tear to bits
89 Declares
91 See the world
93 Orioles or Eagles
94 "Bell Song" opera
95 Final authority
96 Tell practiced it
99 Likewise
100 A la a graphic screen writer?
104 San Diego attraction
105 Cinematographer Nykvist
106 Maine metropolis
107 Three minutes in the ring
108 Half a turn
109 Prepares the table
110 They can create a stir
111 Leave Nod?
112 *Cat __ Hot Tin Roof*

DOWN

1 Show sleepiness
2 '58 Pulitzer author
3 Chaplin's baudy opus?
4 Barnacle Bill, e.g.
5 Standish's stand-in
6 See above
7 Avant-gardist
8 Asian occasion
9 King Harbor's beach
10 Improve
11 Imagist poet Doolittle
12 Sheltered, at sea
13 Tend tots
14 Weeder's tool
15 He got dogs into condition
16 De Niro's power surge?
17 Saddle strap
18 Impudent
25 Happening places
28 Bunnies' moms
30 Relative of Remus?
32 "Popeye" villain
33 Leaves the couch
34 Loathe
35 Allowance for waste
36 Closet-lining wood
37 "I was home alone," e.g.
38 Nadir
41 Be significant
42 Most excellent
43 Onetime Army org.
44 Sea World star
46 *Lucky Jim* writer
47 Sup in style
49 Whistler subject
51 Vertically challenged?
54 Bottomless pit
55 Korea, to Koreans
57 Water-loving weasel
58 Florentine affairs
59 Smart __
61 Pressed for
62 Dinty or Dudley
63 Single out for attention again
64 Dub onto a soundtrack
65 Europe's highest volcano
66 Hepburn-Tracy personas displayed onscreen?
69 Film in which Bergman and Howard merge?
70 Cinema Superman
71 Not anonymous
73 List bits
74 A screen Davis
75 Rubbish
78 Close
79 *Key Largo*'s Claire
82 Retread or radial
83 Errata removers
84 He ran Iran
86 Clinkers
88 Leave the federation
89 "Amo, amas, I love __"
90 Burn balm
91 "Jealousy," e.g.
92 Newcastle neighbor
93 Tree stem
95 __ -Japanese War
96 Kind of marine
97 Horse hue
98 Meditation method
100 Big Bird's network
101 Some MTV music
102 The Renaissance, e.g.
103 Porker parent

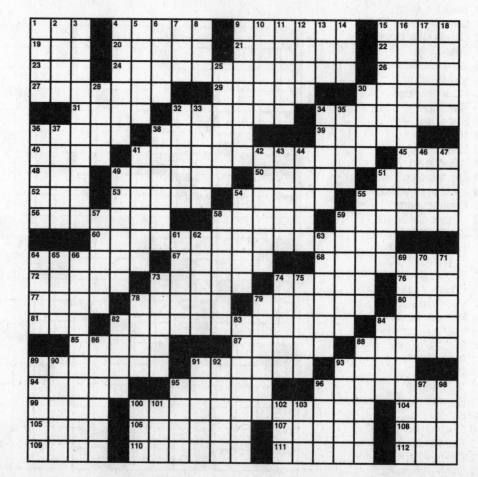

ACROSS

1 Guest greeter
5 Study hard
9 Disgorge a video
14 Forgo food
18 Unoriginal reply?
19 Cantina menu item
20 Language of the Eddas
21 Certain sax
22 From SIDE to SIDE
26 Practice surgery
27 Lane, in Lorraine
28 Rulers' lengths
29 Competes at Henley
30 Mystery writer's prize
31 Cap complement
32 In force
35 Acknowledges
36 Bunch of flowers
39 Uganda's Idi
40 From SIDE to SIDE
43 Beethoven preceder
45 Did a ditty
46 "That's one small step for __"
47 Ober and opus lead-ins
48 Sacrum or scapula
49 Bastille Day season
50 Where the toys are
51 Cans or sacks
53 Common Sense author
54 Culiacán is its capital
56 Of a certain cereal grass
57 Unposed photo
58 From SIDE to SIDE
62 Golfer's position
65 Matriculate
66 Emulate Hollywood Hulk Hogan
70 R.U.R. writer
71 Praise
72 Unexciting
74 Eyeglass frame
75 General Bradley
76 Four Tops' Stubbs
77 Lawrence Welk intro intro
78 Aerie utterance
79 Gumshoe
80 From SIDE to SIDE
84 La Bohème, updated
85 Relaxing of tension
87 Nanette's notions
88 In shambles
89 Father of Harmonia
90 Take home after deductions
91 Ukrainian capital
93 Hurling, curling and birling
96 Cobbled, in a way
97 Conestoga passenger
100 From SIDE to SIDE
104 The African Queen screenwriter
105 Mickey or Mighty
106 Daytime TV host
107 Mah-jongg piece
108 Larboard
109 Adds a fringe
110 Directors' domains
111 Charon's river

DOWN

1 Chiffons' "__ So Fine"
2 Twice cuatro
3 Boutique
4 Overwhelming
5 Schmoozes
6 Paella base
7 Falstaff's quaff
8 Japanese emperors
9 Embrace
10 The wild one
11 Nova Scotian language
12 Zone of Ark.
13 Fragrant bush flowers
14 Losing strength
15 ". . . as falling off __"
16 Flabbergast
17 Small fry
19 Pincer
23 Nudge
24 David Dubinsky's union
25 More recent
30 Program part
31 Ruling bodies, for short
32 Hydrangea holders
33 Cremona craftsman
34 Napery
35 Tabletalk collections
36 The __ Creed
37 Steer clear of
38 Tesh contemporary
40 Pakistani city
41 "See what __?"
42 "Air Music" composer
44 Hunger for
48 Hall of Famer Ernie
50 Henhouse sound
51 Confronts
52 Believe __ not
53 Walked nervously
55 Daisy Mae's man
56 Palindromic emperor
57 Gleason's TV sidekick
59 Lifework
60 Nullified
61 Safari supervisor
62 Free start?
63 Domesticated
64 At a good clip
67 Tamarind and tamarisk
68 Legal attachments
69 Let it all out
71 Urn odist
72 Holmes' street
73 Troughs in graphs
76 Like McMurtry's dove
78 Forestalls
80 Bed on board
81 Creeps
82 Take __ breath
83 Conductors
86 Clay pigeon, e.g.
88 Meal-order catalog
90 Thicket
91 New Zealanders
92 Actress Skye
93 Shot or stick starter
94 Porkypine's pal
95 Humdinger
96 Cozy
97 VFW branch
98 Change a Life sentence?
99 Depend
101 Gat
102 Deer girl
103 Nurse June's hubby

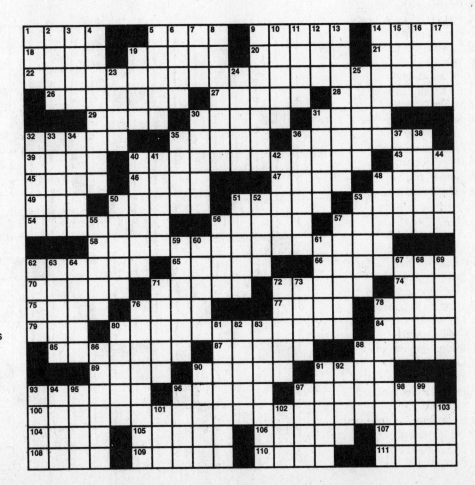

ACROSS

1 Spacecraft compartment
4 '94 trade treaty
9 They're quickly spread
15 Not up yet
19 A piece of Freud's mind?
20 Time for a shower?
21 Actress Plummer or Blake
22 Be *really* impatient
23 Weapon
24 Era predating shell money?
26 "__ homo"
27 Small spore
29 Sub
30 Prepared pizza
31 Passing remarks?
32 Unimposing
34 Toast containers
36 Eateries
38 Mario Puzo subject
39 Bee and Em
40 Atacama adjective
41 Fork over a small fee?
45 Take tiffin
48 M.L.K.'s title
49 Says it's not so
50 Before hop or hog
51 Baylor University site
52 Half and half
53 Singer Bonnie or John
54 Conductor Koussevitzky
55 French underground?
56 Hanna's partner
58 __ meal out (dines in a diner)
59 Venom
60 Frugal mogul?
64 It's a funny business
67 Writer Godden
68 American marsupial
72 Says it's so
73 Goes up against
74 Place of berth?
76 Nurses' org.
77 Landlocked land
78 Small, to Simone
79 Boring tools
80 It may be flipped
81 Under the weather
82 Money of many notes?
84 Drain problem
85 Indoor patios
87 Calls on the beeper
88 Mansfield or Meadows
89 Devil, to some
91 Bouquet throwers
93 One-horse town
94 Tournament type
95 Immoderate imbiber
96 Hissy fit
99 It can take a shuttle
100 Green team's coach?
104 The second Mrs. Sinatra
105 Seagirt spot

106 Diverted
107 Chihuahua chum
108 Bottom-line figure
109 Pouring parties
110 Lower in quality
111 Come to the point?
112 __, to Morse

DOWN

1 Shooter ammo
2 Grimm villain
3 Request to a small-time counterfeiter?
4 City near Vesuvius
5 __ -ski
6 Guitar bar
7 Two before toe
8 Half and half
9 Marjorie of old Hollywood
10 Ear membrane parts
11 Corday's victim
12 "I'll get right __"
13 Initials on Centrum
14 Saint, in Salamanca
15 "Enough is as good as __"
16 Costly tickets?
17 Intro giver
18 Monopoly cards
25 TV sound systems

28 Went blonde
30 Nemesis
32 "__ please the court . . ."
33 As __ (so far)
34 It may go from E to F
35 Big *Time* operator
36 Locust bean
37 Where the action is
38 Lunatic
41 Like heavenly gates
42 Eloquent speaker
43 '75 Kurosawa film __ *Uzala*
44 Impressionist Degas
46 It means height
47 Yosemite Sam, e.g.
49 Feels fear
51 "The Pretender" 's Michael T.
54 Receipts receptacles
55 GM division
57 Defense system acronym
58 Legendary clown Kelly
59 Scots musicians
61 Speak formally
62 Desi Jr.'s sis
63 Arbors
64 Colombia city
65 Like Bush's office

66 Business school song?
69 Big-money dancer?
70 AFT or AFL
71 Palmolive-plugging manicurist
73 Wild
74 Make a stab at?
75 Arch types
78 Silvers or Spitalny
79 Garland, once
82 Tonsorial touch-up
83 Seinfeld's last was in May 1998
84 Tea wagon
86 London Bridge crossed it
88 Eleventh-grader
89 Small wine bottle
90 Came up
91 __ nova
92 Is in charge
93 Copper's "tin"
95 High-hat
96 Voyage
97 Bit of eye makeup?
98 SAT section
100 Pet rocks or pogs
101 George Harrison's "__ Mine"
102 Diamond club
103 Healers' group

ACROSS

1 Ripoff
5 *The Doctor* director Haines
10 Key personnel
15 Act as "it"
19 Goya's duchess
20 Elvis' "__ Your Love Tonight"
21 Bay window
22 Out of work
23 TIGER
27 "Yo!"
28 Sir or tender ender
29 Festivals
30 Potential lox
31 Teen trauma
32 The end
33 Intents
34 Least exciting
37 Number of *mousquetaires*
38 Kind of soda or sandwich
39 __ Na Na
42 TIGER
46 __ sci
47 Mary Todd's mate
48 Nanty __, Pa.
49 Garbo role
50 TIGER
58 Q.b.'s gain or loss
59 Charlie Brown expletive
60 Heckler, often
61 Little Lulu, e.g.
62 *Palais* dwellers
63 Artist Jasper
64 All men except Adam
65 They're for suckers
68 Jacques Tati's character
69 *Leaving Las Vegas* star
70 Ankh letter
73 TIGER
77 British princess
78 Jazz great Tatum
79 It's slippery when wet
80 Queen City team
81 TIGER
89 Mag wheels?
90 Functions
91 Bridge beastie
92 Fast breakers
93 Head the bill
94 Greene of the screen
95 Salinger title ending
96 Shoeless
99 Spook of the devil?
100 AKA opener
102 Unc's bro
105 TIGER
109 Deadlocked
110 Vatican treasure
111 "England's Rose" singer John
112 '04 Nobelist Pavlov
113 Corrida cries
114 Plain people
115 Leather colors
116 Nonchalance

DOWN

1 Obi, e.g.
2 Give a lead
3 Pauline Esther Friedman
4 Lt. col.'s subordinate
5 Cannelloni component
6 Not pro
7 Garish light
8 3 on the dial
9 Slow movements
10 Rather indifferent
11 They may be coded
12 Lowers the beams
13 One of Lee's men
14 Paradise
15 Soprano Beverly
16 Wax-coated cheese
17 Nevada town
18 Mourn aloud
24 Beethoven wrote for her
25 Lose it
26 Ritchie Valens' "La __"
31 '83 Woody Allen film
32 Released
33 Metal mix
34 Not quite high
35 Give a wide berth to
36 Standish, to some
37 Diodes and triodes
38 Blush or flush
39 Rascal
40 Goddesses of the seasons
41 Not quite upright
43 Trot and pace
44 Grendel's ilk
45 Sends off
51 Make head lines
52 Former Soviet first lady
53 __ from the blue
54 Not at all
55 "__ know it!"
56 Love by the Loire
57 "Read my lips: __ taxes!"
62 Nearer extinction
63 Coup group
64 Mobil rival
65 Opera's Frederica Von __
66 Firmed the muscles
67 Undersized ones
68 Henbane and horehound
69 '60s Olympic runner Peter
70 See eye __ (agree)
71 Venomous viper
72 Of Brezhnev's bailiwick
74 Mom, to Maugham
75 Writer Zora __ Hurston
76 Take the stump
82 Lacking
83 Dancer Duncan
84 Tolerate
85 Fielding flub
86 More fair, in Ayr
87 Men, women and children
88 The __ the land
93 Discards
94 Mr. Strauss' trousers
96 "__ us a child is born"
97 Polish target
98 *Peter Pan* pirate
99 Surreal Salvador
100 "__ boy!"
101 Where the Rhone meets the Saône
102 Met luminary
103 Sad to say
104 Force unit
106 Type of sleep
107 "Xanadu" singers
108 Polygraph detection

ACROSS

1 Parboils
7 *Catulli Carmina* composer
11 "Take __ from the pros"
15 SEATO or SALT
19 Poor excuse for an excuse
20 Preside at tea
21 Dover domestic
22 Shy worshiper's place
23 Shaffer's contrived-ending play?
26 *The __ Reader* (eclectic magazine)
27 Frigid floaters
28 Have a go at
29 Isolated valley
30 Having an off day?
32 Stuff to the gills
33 Kind of bee, cow or horse
34 JFK and RFK, e.g.
35 Large sheepdogs
38 Loafer or sneaker
40 Cat hair
41 Crack wise
42 Words before T
43 Shea man
46 Wilder's urban drama?
49 Like this
50 *1984* author
52 Part of a set
53 Taradiddles
54 Fly catchers
55 Finest part
56 "So what __ is new?"
57 Indolent
58 Neat!
59 Gothic novelist Victoria
60 *Treasure Island* auth.
61 Its tip may be felt
62 Bank deposits?
63 Kennel cry
64 Creepy Lerner-Loewe musical?
69 Hundredweight pts.
72 Dogwood or redwood
74 Marshal at Waterloo
75 "Isn't that beautiful?"
76 Envelope closer
77 Playwright Fugard
79 Cat-o'-no-tails?
81 Pop art?
83 Dudley or Demi
84 Howard and Brown
85 Lily of Utah
86 Handle adversity
87 Reddish brown
88 Center of a rotation
89 Aristophanes' appetizing comedy?
92 Poet Hughes
93 Oversized
94 Domino that's round
95 Wile E. Coyote's supplier
96 Boat's landing place
98 Astronaut Wally
100 *The Egyptian* author Waltari
101 Estelle and Betty's co-star
102 Had a rivalry
106 What that isn't
107 Model's assumption
108 By way of
109 Party line?
110 Caesar's cohort
112 Chase's intoxicating comedy?
116 He succeeded Haakon
117 Nanette's notion
118 Facilitate
119 Mariel's grandfather
120 Use a camcorder
121 Uncorking sounds
122 Changed clothes?
123 Warns

DOWN

1 They'll cross the line
2 __ cropper (fail big)
3 Here and there?
4 Gives quarters to
5 Membership fees
6 Erwin of '50s TV
7 Gluck work
8 Famed NYC moviehouse
9 Fee fie fo follower
10 Sweet-smelling
11 Post-workout woes
12 Add turpentine
13 With 39D, *Alien* android actor
14 Mega-meadows
15 Comic Poundstone
16 Miller's apocalyptic drama?
17 Film container
18 *Uno, due, __*
24 Head for the ranch?
25 Loin cover
31 Short swim
33 James Brown's realm
34 "Rebel Rebel" rocker
35 *Under Siege*'s Gary
36 Emulate Thomas
37 Cheeky
39 See 13D
40 Pen pals?
41 Interrogate
43 Joe from Arabia
44 Diamond flaw
45 Shakespeare's comedy subtitled *What You Swill*?
47 Oklahoma city
48 Pre-Toler Chan
49 Nincompoop
51 Have a hero
56 Pointy shoe wearer
57 Low land?
58 Emulate Xanthippe
60 Potent potable
61 Wood thickness
62 Simpleton's syllable
64 Pam Tillis' pa
65 *The __ the Sixth Happiness*
66 "The Wonder Horse"
67 Off-peak call?
68 Herpetological hugger
70 Ballet studio prop
71 Pay out
73 Bill and Bob's opponent
76 Shipping abbr.
77 Faisal and Farouk
78 Kind of a waste?
79 Bombay-born conductor
80 Grows up
81 Inflexible teaching
82 Part of Notre Dame
83 Werfel's *The Forty Days of __ Dagh*
85 Jefferson Airplane, later
86 Topsy-turvy
87 Malarial woe
90 Reach on the radio
91 Sweet'n Low rival
94 TGIF pt.
97 The Munsters' De Carlo
99 "__ a dream . . ."
100 Formally proposes
101 Irritated
103 Stevens of '60s TV
104 Perspire, e.g.
105 Saloon harpoons
107 Attend Andover
108 Ming thing
109 Astronomer Sagan
110 Barracks sack
111 Intensive suffix
113 Foofaraw
114 System
115 Estelle and Betty's co-star

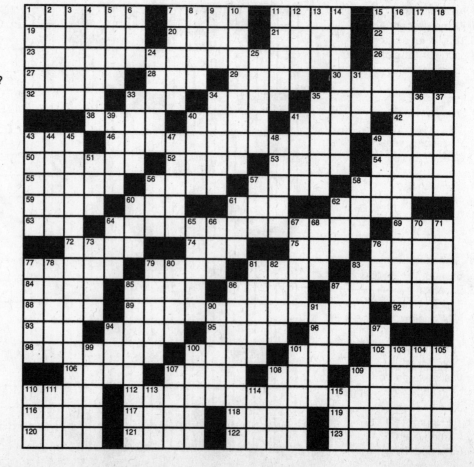

ACROSS

1 Autumn pear
5 Demonstrate derision
10 Pry
15 Illegal block
19 "... beauty is __ forever"
20 Discussion group
21 Momma's man
22 Western U.S. dance
23 "... should I have __ still and been quiet . . .": Job 3:13
24 Ryan or Cara
25 Sheik's peer?
26 Confederate
27 Dustin Hoffman's college student role?
31 Eclipse sight
32 Sectarians' suffixes
33 Spanish assents
34 Stir on the water?
36 Hops heater
38 Spaciousness
40 In the doldrums
43 Alarming dinner entrée?
49 Act like a sap?
50 Danny Kaye's __ Arms
51 Reacts to yeast
52 Jekyll on a bad night
53 Writer Beattie
54 Give X's and R's
55 More like a bug's ear?
56 "All My Exes Live in __"
57 More hanky-intensive
60 Allayed
61 Provence pronoun
62 Chaplin's marching song?
69 Big thing in London?
70 Prior location?
71 More irritated
72 Rehab requisite
75 Dough for pasta?
76 Delhi dress
78 Essay
79 Sung soliloquy
80 Depth-defying device
81 Netman Nastase
82 Del __ Fashion Center
83 Solid South city?
89 Equi- equivalent
90 Two fives for __
91 Forearm feature
92 Demeanor
93 Lab order?
94 It has an edible shell
96 Half a toast?
98 Composer of "The Lady Is a Tutti-Frutti"?
107 Pop star?
108 Schedule section
109 Rubber rollers
110 Midterm, e.g.
111 Takes one's time?
112 Dogie's domain
113 Shake a tail?

114 Houston campus
115 A Spice Girl
116 Did a farrier's job
117 They're fit to be tried
118 Mulligan, e.g.

DOWN

1 Round dance?
2 SoCal festival site
3 "__ would seem"
4 Novelist Ozick
5 Barker's babble
6 Runner's "load"
7 "Dedicated to the __ Love"
8 __ shui (art of placement)
9 Many Belgians
10 Exhausted
11 Hurler Hideo's kin
12 Debut
13 The UAE belongs to it
14 Sunshades
15 Wrangler's wear
16 Old comics' Little __
17 Woes
18 Be worth the effort
28 Falls back
29 Spot of wine?
30 Puccini heroine
34 Sultanate in Borneo

35 Cheesemaker's preparation
36 "The thing __ is . . ."
37 Unpopular spots?
38 Northridge neighbor
39 'Rithmetic, perhaps
40 Underground river
41 He was Hawkeye
42 Grades in the 60's
43 Free-for-all
44 Big bowl for soup
45 Some MoMA works
46 Like most pizza
47 Bad-check passer
48 His and hers
55 Spits in the ocean?
56 Canine from Kansas
58 JFK's was 109
59 Holly
60 Set off
61 More agile
63 "Don't __ My Parade"
64 Bric- __
65 Big Mac kin
66 "Peace is . . . __ of mind": Spinoza
67 Memorable Broadway belter
68 Comic Richard
72 "Persistence of Memory" painter

73 Discordia's Greek counterpart
74 Emperor in a Mozart opera
75 Traditional tales
76 Write on the dotted line
77 Inter __
80 Shane good guys
84 Brest milk
85 "That smarts!"
86 Was borne by water
87 In the thick of
88 Doesn't dissipate
93 Secret store
94 Color nuance
95 Wasn't passive
96 Words to live by
97 Waters, as lawns
98 Corporate symbol
99 Balladeer Burl
100 High Society's "Well, Did You __"
101 Truckee stop?
102 Rub the wrong way
103 Roll or stick lead-in
104 Turnoff
105 After foot or arms
106 Diving duck
107 The rest of the afternoon?

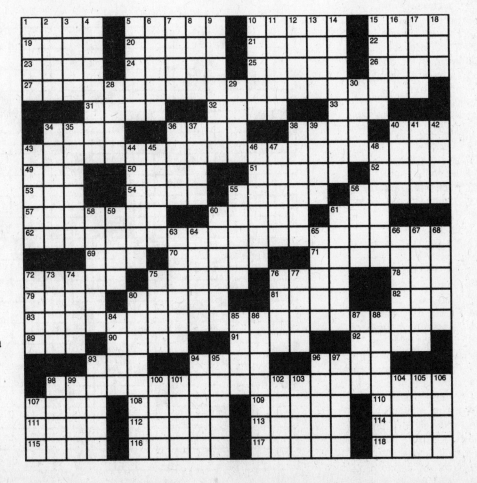

ACROSS

1 Fine, per hip-hoppers
4 Rhea, on "Cheers"
9 Certain Cubans
15 It retains water
18 Start of a Shakespeare title
20 Be of use
21 Spongy fungi stuff
22 "__ lazy river . . ."
23 Boor
24 Explosive retaliation?
26 Old boys?
27 Worse than puerile
29 Understudy's study
30 L.A. soccer team
32 He gave us the slip
33 Bay Area's __ City
34 Mystical markings
35 *Lone Star* director John
37 Cervine creatures
39 Short snoozes
41 The color of honey
42 Fireplace fuel
43 Crosspatch
45 Fencing rapiers
47 Melee
48 Actress San Giacomo
49 Souvlaki ingredient
50 Root word?
51 Muslim title
52 Dog that takes a turn at the cookout?
56 Touchdown time
57 Filbert
59 Hamelin vermin
60 Saul Bellow title
62 Work on the docks
63 Lions and tigers and bears, e.g.
65 Verve
66 Flower in a Ladd-Lake flick
69 NFL pro
70 Mentors' followers
74 Guidonian note
75 Rock ode to Egypt?
79 Capitol Records label
80 Have it bad
81 Take __ the limit
82 "Sailing to Byzantium" poet
83 Hidden hindrance
84 Floats downriver
87 Toque wearer
88 Nathan of "Encore! Encore!"
89 Jammed with the band
90 Like mud or mush
92 Auctioneer's last word
93 *Planet of the Apes* novelist
94 They parallel radii
95 "__ there, done that"
97 Well-quaffed one
98 Arboreal marsupials
100 Hildegarde's "Darling, Je Vous __ Beaucoup"
101 Antony's word for Brutus

105 Underestimate, e.g.
106 Erotic version of Dorothy's saga?
109 Grandpa Walton portrayer
110 Grouper grabber
111 Least processed
112 Accustom
113 Chisholm Trail town
114 From A __
115 *Sí sí*, at sea
116 Irritating ones
117 Eva Gabor's half sister?

DOWN

1 Limp watchman?
2 North Carolina college
3 Lightweight man who hung on Ruth's neck?
4 Sonora flora
5 Sidestep
6 Memorable actor Julia
7 Pickup shtick
8 After 9D, Cindy Crawford colleague
9 See 8D
10 Suggest
11 Beaufort scale "8"
12 Fuss and feathers
13 Hooch
14 Vega or Pleshette

15 *Three Musketeers Can't Jump* writer?
16 Peak point
17 Lots
19 Yet unknown actress
25 Significant times
28 Not e'er
31 Do a jeté
33 Cul- __ (dead end)
34 Mishnah authority
35 Singer Vaughan
36 Early computer
37 Have reservations
38 Beanstalk baddie
39 Tenting grounds
40 Alliance ended in '77
42 Lash the movie cowboy
43 Fair, as fights
44 Dreadlocks wearer
46 Layered hairstyle
48 Oscar winner Martin
52 Non-Tory Tony
53 Pit viper
54 Pangs
55 Leipzig neighbor
58 Old Nick's 'eadquarters
61 School starters
63 Special talent
64 Detached
65 Savage

66 Cherished one
67 You can go by it
68 Pints of crystal?
69 Guisewite – or her heroine
70 Mind your __ Q's
71 Motorized TV bear?
72 Send with a click
73 Actress Hasso
76 Special spot
77 Stocking stuff
78 Fair or square follower
83 It's the wurst
85 Seed-planting drill inventor Jethro
86 "Old Blue Eyes"
89 Like Aesop's grapes
91 Square-dance move
92 Prescient person
93 Hits the sauce
95 Teeny
96 Rage onstage
97 Short shot
98 *Daily Planet* reporter
99 Snack since '12
100 Using clippers?
101 Fine-tune
102 "Just the Two __"
103 Hula Bowl items
104 Teutonic earth goddess
107 Dolly the clone
108 Sound from the pound

CONTAINING CONTAINERS 181

ACROSS

1 Like Jean-Luc Picard
5 Salesperson's incentive
10 Couples clubs?
15 First name in country
19 Colleague of Hap and Ike
20 Asian mountain range
21 Fable feature
22 12/24 and 12/31
23 Italian dessert
25 19th-c. political behavior
27 Mileage measurer
28 Slip cover?
30 England's last king
31 Waxes Bryanesque
32 Be coquettish
33 Substance from seaweed
34 Sun shade
35 Give the benediction
36 CIA head
40 Unspoken
43 Danish philosopher
46 Boar's Head order
47 They often clash
48 Tosspots
49 Cutlass maker
50 U.S. theater org.
51 Shutout spoiler
52 Druggist
56 Arizona flattops
57 Resembling nets
59 Oxford tie
60 Queeg portrayer
61 Key material
62 Televised
63 Photo finish?
64 Comeback performance?
66 Thunder god
67 Bota material
70 Certain averages
71 Obstinately
73 Choler
74 Certain Semite
75 En route to Catalina
77 Intuit
78 Eat corn on the cob
79 Russian Blue or Havana Brown
80 Reporter, often
84 Mezzanine sections
85 "Hath not the potter power over __?": Rom. 9
87 "__ His Kiss"
88 Pavarotti possessive
89 Everybody, in Baden-Baden
90 Pamphlet
91 Grapevine product
94 Elapse
97 __ Vista
98 Hot pie shop
100 Herman's Herds, e.g.

102 Freebooters
104 *Time Machine* people
105 Livid
106 What -vore means
107 Small fly
108 Revelers paint it red
109 Generational novels
110 He was in CONTROL
111 *Hope Floats* actress Rowlands

DOWN

1 Dumb guy
2 Novelist Jorge
3 Garage charge
4 __ personae (cast list)
5 Bambi's creator
6 Bolshoi bends
7 "Believe __ Not"
8 Circulation increaser
9 Pops' Arthur
10 Dip
11 Get out of bed
12 ILO and OAS
13 "I'm agin' it"
14 Heavy hitters
15 Student's grade card
16 At any time
17 Arctic Ocean sighting

18 "__ sow, so shall . . ."
24 Suggest
26 "__ my big mouth!"
29 Put on the line
32 ". . . but the __ is weak"
33 USNA pt.
35 Please, in Potsdam
37 Plundering
38 Sacrifice site
39 Most unlike most
40 Four years at 1600
41 Fever symptom
42 Make holy
43 Like the Addamses
44 Torn by a horn
45 One of Rita's exes
48 Backbone
50 Sponsorship
52 *Zut __!*
53 Peace Nobelist Root
54 Locust bean
55 Biting
56 Python of satire
58 Nuclear threat
60 __ ears (listen attentively)
62 Perfume from petals
63 He's history
64 Make into law
65 Lofts the novelist

67 Inexperienced
68 Of wrath, in a hymn
69 Brokaw's broadcast
71 Get the picture
72 "A pun is the lowest form __"
75 Freud's specialty
76 Eye sore
78 Bump on the noggin
80 "Well __ darned!"
81 Computer bugaboos
82 *Like this, for short*
83 Getaways
84 *Les Préludes* composer
86 Redeem chips
88 *Amadeus* subject
90 "Ain't __ Shame"
91 Donor
92 Actress Dunne
93 Slovenian seaport
94 Coffeehouse performer
95 Woody's heir
96 Clumsy craft
97 Rocky outcrop
98 Pocket bread
99 Tinseltown terrier
101 Musical syllable
103 Aries symbol

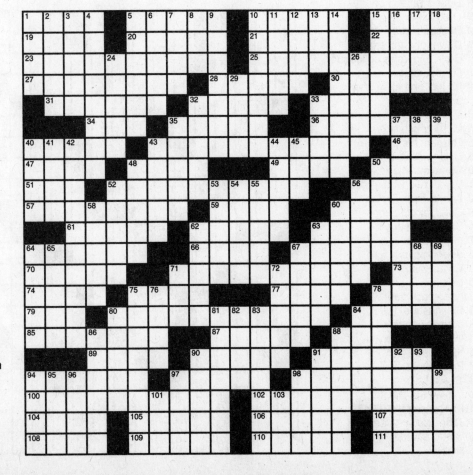

ACROSS

1 LAPD alert
4 Director Kurosawa
9 Hands on hips
15 Like Peck's boy
18 Pager noise
20 Nubia, now
21 Musician's echo effect
22 Southern st.
23 Aptly-named spa
24 Forgo excuses?
26 It's no bull
27 Spacecraft steerer
29 Abbr. on an env.
30 Lose power
32 Isle SW of Majorca
33 He and she
34 Quotable catcher
35 Of borzois and basenjis
37 Where Mets meet
39 Butler's business
41 Pond plants
42 B, as in backup?
43 "Git!"
45 Hines and Holliman
47 Guys in sties
48 Fad
49 It could be living
50 Away, in a way
51 Old French coin
52 Sacrifice business?
56 Sultana's chamber
57 Indexer's concerns
59 Does a takeoff on
60 Gofer
62 Despair's opposite
63 Downright unpleasant
65 Boris and Lon's colleague
66 Dakota dialect
69 It's just one thing after
another
70 Made over
74 Man-mouse link
75 Torment the sunburnt?
79 Use one's scull
80 Chest muscle
81 Perspiration passageway
82 Acrylic fiber
83 Color, or off-color
84 Drinks with sushi
87 In due time
88 Sticking place
89 Enhances
90 Lids
92 Keep occupied
93 Stalinesque
housecleanings
94 Walk destination
95 "How sad!"
97 Pinch or lift
98 '60s TV toon
100 Played the plaintiff
101 Princess of the '60s?
105 John Jr.'s stepdad
106 Tantalus' order to
Niobe?

109 Biblical twin
110 *He Got Game*
director
111 Sci-fi writer Ursula
112 Etonian's dad
113 Swizzle
114 Aragon article
115 Campfire sweet
treats
116 Union unit
117 One mo?

DOWN

1 Israel's Eban
2 __ de soie
3 Gambler?
4 Judicial inquest
5 Friend of Fran
6 Syncrasy starter
7 Absorbed
8 Formicary resident
9 Sharp crest
10 "Love Letters" singer
Lester
11 Lendl of tennis
12 Danny's "lethal"
co-star
13 Stout fellow?
14 Watch carefully
15 Be an abettor?
16 Sunscreen ingredient
17 Time for a duel

19 Irrational fears
25 It's a laugh
28 Needle holder
31 Musical soliloquy
33 Basic part
34 Pepper plant, or
palm
35 *R.U.R.* writer
36 Tennis great Marble
37 Serbs and Moravians
38 Persecute a pledge
39 "Star Trek," etc.
40 Trick tailers
42 First deadly sin
43 Won gold, silver and
bronze
44 Mudville slugger
46 Hang on
48 __ tunnel syndrome
52 She wrote *To the
Lighthouse*
53 Speeders make it
54 Prime time's end
55 Leaves for lunch
58 "Huh?"
61 Machine disk
63 Dynamite stuff
64 Beyond the pale?
65 Topside's opposite
66 Klutz's cry
67 Like Alexander and
Peter

68 Dessert deficiency?
69 Lugdunum, today
70 Pass on
71 Survey specters?
72 __ *vie* (brandy)
73 Mother Hubbard,
for one
76 Disconnected
77 Cadabra counterpart
78 Misjudges
83 Robert Frost poem
85 Heroic saga
86 Lies all over the place
89 Big swig
91 Value
92 Grammy winner
Erykah
93 Midwest capital
95 WWII hero Murphy
96 Puts at an angle
97 Armada
98 Like most NBA
players
99 Sandwich cookie
100 Texas basketballer
101 "Been there, done __"
102 Sundance Kid's girl
103 It's at your fingertip
104 EU money
107 Freudian factor
108 Many AMA
members

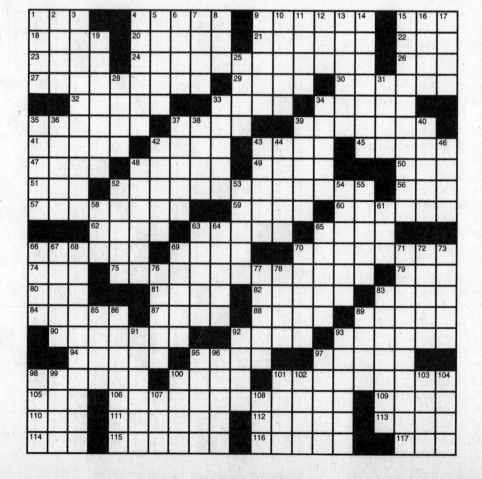

ACROSS

1 Tore up the road
5 Japanese WWII leader
9 Jeb of Florida
13 Naval initials
16 Make airtight
18 Toast toppings
19 Golden Rule word
20 Slave leader Turner
21 Of the sea
22 Harpo Productions head
23 Eastern Nigerians
24 Poetic pugilist
25 Along with 13D, our subject's "final word in reality"
28 Wood of the Stones
29 Arduous laborers
30 Do nothing
31 Photochemical haze
32 Car sticker stat
35 Jailbird
36 A to Z
38 Demeanor
39 Where he said "I've been to"
44 Sidekick
45 Indonesian Island
46 They take a beating
47 Unprecedented events
49 Holy Fr. woman
50 Jersey girl?
51 Singer Mitchell
52 Big to-do
54 New Testament book
57 Hyperactive
59 Busy artery
60 Sky light?
61 Greek P
62 What he was not, on 4/3/68
65 Pewter component
66 Space station in '98 news
67 Journalist Molly
68 Job particulars
69 Tête-à-tête
70 Still and all
71 It's inherited
72 Phon or morph ending
73 Roast pig side dish
75 It's coming
77 Moses' mount
80 Ozzie's wife
84 Crew team
85 " . . . but by the content of __": his 8/28/63 speech
87 She's an inspiration
88 Dimmesdale's daughter
89 I-strain?
90 Many jigsaw pieces
91 Halloween purchase
92 Hoot
93 Takes it easy
97 Call a spade a club
98 What he said "injustice anywhere" threatens
104 Sir Elton's john
105 Old man, in Oldenburg
106 Refuge
107 Former Met pitcher Tom
108 Tight wrapper?
109 It may have a big head
110 Rehab candidates
111 Our subject, sans "Dr." and "Jr."
112 Moreover
113 Quick-moving
114 Turn to slush
115 Singer-actor Lovett

DOWN

1 Penn name
2 Paris green
3 George, née Mary Ann
4 "I __" ("Beats me")
5 Piglike animal
6 Other ones, to Juan
7 Simmons or Seberg
8 Workplace inspection org.
9 Hype's purpose
10 Lift the latch
11 Franklin invented one
12 Haberdashery section
13 See 25A
14 Alco-hall?
15 Gordon Sumner, to most
16 The Mustangs, for short
17 Work on your feet?
18 Powerful
26 Massey of the screen
27 Capacious cars
31 Round Table titles
32 Washington and McKinley, for short
33 Dien Bien __
34 Topaz or turquoise
36 Endangered antelope
37 Where to use a PIN
38 Robin Hood's "maid"
40 Matter for Einstein
41 Cooperstown's Mel
42 Gorgeous guy
43 Novelist Shaw
44 15th-century caravel
47 1040 and W-2
48 East European capital
50 "Laugh-In"'s Judy
51 *Finnegans Wake* writer
53 Custom
54 General assembly?
55 CEO opener
56 What led him from Alabama to a Nobel Prize
57 Penobscot's state
58 Metric abbrs.
59 Insipid
62 Calculate
63 Myrlie or Medgar
64 " . . . partridge in __ tree"
69 Newspaper stat
73 Convulsion
74 60 *minuti*
76 To-do item
77 Lamb Chop's memorable Lewis
78 Comparative suffix
79 This amounts to nothing
80 Comics' __ the Horrible
81 "__ never too late"
82 Comic-book scream
83 Have a go at
85 Unstable
86 Washington's Mount St. __
87 Strand
88 Annoy
91 Moore of Broadway's *Purlie*
92 Dixie drink
93 Have a ball
94 Turn inside out
95 Tom of *The Seven Year Itch*
96 See 85D
98 Bowe blows
99 Fish bait bit
100 Deftness
101 Like Lex Luthor
102 Painter Magritte
103 Unit in a joule

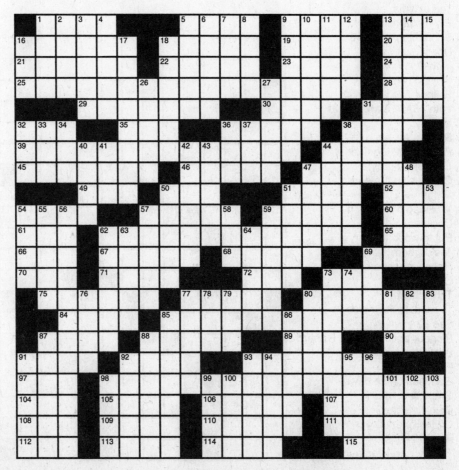

ACROSS

1 Nile reptiles
5 Bargain holders
9 Okra bits
13 "Peel __ grape"
16 Tips off
18 __ four (small iced cake)
19 Freeway ramp sign
20 Hankering
21 Meryl of *One True Thing*
22 Set things right
23 St. Petersburg's river
24 Buddy, in brief
25 '67 Dionne Warwick winner
28 Trunk top
29 Stung
30 Drinks after darts
31 I before E, e.g.
32 Red-lobster center
35 Base of computer operations
36 The right stuff?
38 Long of Louisiana
39 '70 Norman Greenbaum evergreen
44 This, *and* that
45 Headlight lamp type
46 Arranges in lines
47 "Pop!" goer
49 High hill crest
50 Rock and Roll Hall of Fame architect
51 Teri of films
52 Pie-mode middle
54 Something to heave
57 Does impressions?
59 Malt-drying kilns
60 Moving vehicle
61 Palindromic singer
62 With 85A, '78 Meat Loaf melody
65 Six-foot Aussie runner
66 Put 2 and 2 together
67 *Our Town* heroine
68 Oedipus, in the end
69 Midge
70 '47 Road destination
71 Declines
72 Put to work
73 Joey's mom
75 Fishes, or schemes
77 On the ball
80 Tchotchkes
84 To read, to Reynaldo
85 See 62A
87 Pioneer polar explorer Richard
88 Epsilon preceder
89 Round starter
90 Goddess of the dawn
91 One-liner
92 Coin collector?
93 Cratchit's employer
97 Raggedy miss
98 '81 Juice Newton number

104 Troops' troupers
105 Craziness criterion
106 City of Lights
107 Superfluous
108 'Course not
109 Aphrodite's son
110 Go off
111 Incredible bargains
112 Christmas contraction
113 Relinquish
114 Has, after expenses
115 It flows through Florence

DOWN

1 Mt. statistics
2 Antitoxins
3 Victimizes
4 Watt's power
5 Davis or Midler
6 "__ you so!"
7 729's cube root
8 Part of a flight
9 Kind of hockey box
10 Certain daisies
11 Honky-tonks
12 Antares, e.g.
13 '56 Fats Domino ditty
14 A la King?
15 Battery terminal
16 "__ live and breathe!"
17 Paint like Pollock
18 "Old Blood and Guts"
26 Hale the golfer
27 Ribs servings
31 Truck tracks
32 Good firewood?
33 Masseuse's work site
34 Be bedridden
36 Marshland
37 Pop the question
38 Raspy-voiced
40 Portnoy's creator
41 "May __ on?"
42 In, for now
43 Western Hispaniola
44 Built-in bunk
47 Fritter away
48 Alpaca kin
50 Rings out
51 Loretta Lynn's singing sister
53 "Sometimes you feel like __ . . ."
54 Go up and up
55 Home to 1 in 6 people
56 '66 Beach Boys biggie
57 Small amounts
58 Fresno-L.A. dir.
59 Bishop, in Baja
62 Removed the rind

63 Color between red and green
64 Commuter's community
69 "The Wayward Wind" singer Grant
73 Tall timber
74 Nocturnal predator
76 *Red Corner* actor
77 Coastal shrub
78 President from Mo.
79 Cry of triumph
80 Former fiancé
81 Mellow the madeira
82 Sci-fi doctor
83 42nd, etc.
85 It's 50% of sport
86 Cop's collar
87 Japanese art
88 Drive your karma up?
91 Pleasure trip
92 Sound asleep?
93 Cakewalk kin
94 Fergie's fries
95 Garbo
96 Key in type
98 Billy Baldwin's brother
99 Admitting customers
100 Paying passenger
101 Former shahdom
102 __ contendere
103 Family MD's

ACROSS

1 Beetle juice?
4 Sword handles
9 Gave a makeover
14 So bad it's good
18 Greenlander's knife
19 Chopin's Impromptu No. 29 in __ Major
20 Utah's erstwhile country
21 Squished circle
22 Wild bunch
23 Mirren's detective series
25 Horne of music
26 Some cyclists
28 King of wartime Troy
29 Shroud city
30 "__ my case"
31 Puffery part
32 Landing surface
34 Very generous
36 Service error
37 Tanksgiving?
38 Not right
39 Understands
40 Hypnotist's order
41 Colorful amphibian
44 Portend
45 According to the rules
48 __ alai
49 Get a lode of this
50 Dimwits
51 Iroquois' enemies
52 James Brown's sound
53 Jean Henri Dunant founded it
55 Quarter back?
56 Get your bearings
58 Not at all clear
59 Berlin is on it
60 Item in an *iglesia*
61 M.A.S.H. procedure
64 Risk tickets
65 Standards
69 It's out on a lime
70 Looks through keyholes
71 Chases away
72 Eye, poetically
73 Not on duty
74 Kind of juice plant?
77 He picked pairs
78 "__ dern tootin'"
79 Cat- __ -tails
80 Chicken bite
81 Numbers-matching game
82 Bear witness
84 Printer's proof
86 Twister or stomper
87 Clue category
88 Safe place
89 Bible prophet
90 Textile-dyeing method
91 It's a natural in Vegas
92 Make alcohol undrinkable
95 Actor Bogosian or Stoltz
96 Worst-seller's fate

99 On the down side
100 Removed from the board
101 Automotive about-faces
102 Bedding
103 It runs when broken
104 Dancers Miller and Reinking
105 Film FX shot
106 Battle field?
107 Call, in poker

DOWN

1 Big role for Hanks
2 Tonic-yielding plant
3 Prepared to build on lots
4 Unlucky
5 All over
6 Coquette
7 Caledonian caps
8 Hagiographer's abbr.
9 Put up a fight
10 Gertrude Stein, for one, for short
11 Per __ (daily payment)
12 Trade-regulating org.
13 Part of an E-mail address
14 Art Buchwald specialty
15 Mr. Typical
16 Wired, in a way
17 Blueprint
20 Wall art
24 Husband or wife
27 Leave the couch
29 Vacation options
31 Old Saturday night activities
32 Balsa and balsam
33 U.S. citizen
34 Repair bill item
35 Love, Italian style
36 Celebrates
37 *Tiny Alice* playwright
39 Musical featuring Mama Rose
40 Face lift?
42 Horned deity
43 Knight fight
45 The hard stuff
46 Dearest companion
47 Exhorted
50 Camp clothes?
52 Tag datum
54 Jeremy's singing partner
55 Swashbucklers' weapons
56 Pursuer of the Pleiades
57 Driving hazards
59 Steeple

60 Hook alternative
61 City of Paris
62 More than abundant
63 Violation
64 Used up
65 Young *hombre*
66 Origins
67 Hopping mad
68 Be revulsed by
70 Guard or chard preceder
71 Back of the bark
74 *The Chosen* writer
75 Eleven ingredients?
76 Tack on
77 Octet with a guest
81 Potluck staple
83 Bridge hand parts
84 Small narrow valley
85 Equalizes
86 Pass or party of lore
87 Moses' brother
88 Artichoke center
89 Writer Helnrich
90 Outmoded VCR
91 V-chips block it
92 Sink sound
93 Fury, or fad
94 Move by inches
96 Daiquiri liquor
97 OINSHRDLU opener
98 "I'm Alive" musicians

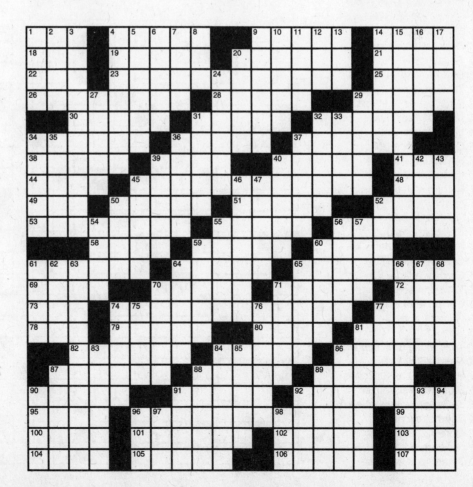

ACROSS

1 Rose family fruit
5 "Let It Be" or "Let It Bleed"
10 Joltless joe
15 Just one of those things?
19 Former Minnesota governor Carlson
20 Longtime labor leader
21 Melodramatize
22 Take back to the drawing board
23 Irritating actor?
25 Organic comedian?
27 Let go
28 Gauzy linen
30 Trial separation?
31 More nimble
32 Comeback
33 Singer Lovett
34 -y plural
35 City SW of Cleveland
36 "Ventura Highway" singers
40 Maps out
43 Ribald folk-rocker?
46 Pro __
47 Funny lady Martha
48 Plumb crazy
49 *The Godfather*'s son's portrayer
50 850 *anni* ago
51 It lacks refinement
52 Boyish action hero?
56 "__ Coy Mistress"
57 Deadbolts' shelfmates
59 Be short of
60 Shearer and Talmadge
61 '97 Fonda film __ *Gold*
62 What you take at spas
63 Mideast peninsula
64 Lords' lodgings
66 Coin no longer minted
67 Sir Ian the actor
70 "Love Train" rockers
71 Extreme "Deep Space Nine" star?
73 Reed or Rawls
74 Red-light or blue
75 Runner Sebastian's kin
77 Chancellor Von Bismarck
78 Give for a time
79 Time-line section
80 Gallant lead singer?
84 Chapter and __
85 Up
87 They make up a score
88 New Jersey fort
89 Rarae __ (unusual ones)
90 Stopwatch squeezer
91 SoCal canyon or colony
94 Butt-head's pal
97 More like Solomon
98 No-work work
100 Texas A&M actress?
102 Gung-ho rock star?
104 Story made of whole cloth?
105 $10 coin
106 Faint color
107 In the vicinity
108 Smelting refuse
109 Ampule amounts
110 Rarin' to go
111 Last of a 1/1 lyric

DOWN

1 Make matches
2 Made faux pas
3 Spats spot
4 Find new meaning
5 Entertains
6 Cubist Fernand
7 Have a falling out?
8 One for *los libros*
9 Diana Riggs' gig
10 Samson's downfall
11 Etiquette arbiter Post
12 Sheltered nook
13 Had a bite
14 Charon, e.g.
15 Bright bullet
16 Epitaph opener
17 Pens a P.S.
18 *Small Soldiers* characters
24 Popish Plot figure
26 British actress Mirren
29 Crude gp.?
32 Mil. survey
33 The priest, not the beast
35 Non-linesmen
37 Restless bandleader?
38 *As You Like It* lass
39 Out of whack
40 Play thing
41 Her theme was a hit
42 Agreeable actress?
43 Jewelry, slangily
44 Litmus reddeners
45 Jed Clampett and John Walton
48 *Fortune* founder's family
50 Fable follow-up
52 Nursery workers, at times
53 Broadcast sign
54 Evaluate anew
55 Post-op period
56 Phone drones
58 Early comic star Harold
60 Honshu shrine site
62 Hallow
63 George C. or Martha
64 KGB and CIA concerns
65 "What __!" ("Turkey!")
67 Nocturnal wool gatherers
68 A long, long time
69 Clothing-optional option
71 "Oy __!"
72 Mudd or Moore
75 Touched tenderly
76 Santa Anita stat
78 Dictionaries
80 "__ en Rose"
81 Fairfax noshes
82 Alaskan port
83 Repeat
84 More disgusting
86 Giving the Hi sign
88 Hoofer
90 Championship
91 Tiny fly
92 Actor Gary or Jake
93 Of cities
94 Shrimping areas
95 On a par, in Paris
96 Pearl Mosque site
97 Foreign strands?
98 Cop to the cops
99 Brontë's governess
101 Chinese chairman
103 Routing preposition

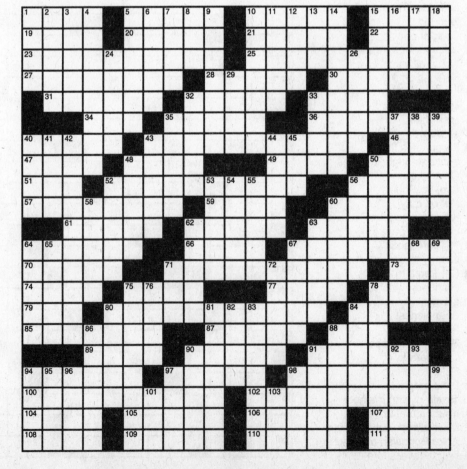

ACROSS

1 Remote forerunner
5 Bar mitzvah dance
9 Composer Khachaturian
13 It's often glossed over
16 Low-slung hound
18 Accomplish completely
19 Megaphone shape
20 Cat __ Hot Tin Roof
21 '87 Beatty-Hoffman epic
22 Paris' __ la Cité
23 Square on campus
24 Hitchcock film, for short
25 Ignoring Valentine's Day?
28 Ruckus
29 Says "OK"
30 Commits perjury
31 Family men?
32 Quick to learn
35 Ballerina's strong point
36 British quarters
38 Called up
39 Cupid's arsenal?
44 Tennyson poem
45 Petite pianos
46 Kunta Kinte's saga
47 It tolls by the Thames
49 Together with 50A, polar feature
50 See 49A
51 Isle east of Java
52 It's 21% oxygen
54 Faked a handoff
57 Shows to the world
59 Anthony or Anton
60 Dauphin's dad
61 Each, in tennis
62 Bette Davis' romantic movie cry?
65 Arab name part
66 Actress LeGallienne
67 It's nothing, to some
68 Three squares?
69 Look for
70 Designer Claiborne
71 Revelers' romp
72 Give it a shot
73 Unduly
75 Rationality
77 Mubarak's predecessor
80 Light particles
84 Lacking
85 The Scourge of God, to his darling?
87 Baby branch
88 Made well
89 Show-ticket datum
90 Possess
91 Sense
92 Moreover
93 Aspect of every element
97 Low note?
98 Porgy's paean to Bess?
104 Cause for a Band-Aid
105 Donated
106 Banks of baseball

107 Correction section
108 That Geller feller
109 In charge of
110 Sunday rejoinders
111 The girls from uncle?
112 Call, in cards
113 Lévesque or Lacoste
114 Lyricist Lorenz
115 Titles on Fr. envelopes

DOWN

1 Morse morsel
2 "The Last of His Tribe"
3 Latin stars
4 CIA concerns
5 Spartan slave
6 Buck of country music
7 Uncivil
8 Tarzan's friends
9 Lets the accused off
10 Postal beats
11 Delta of Venus author Nin
12 Ancient Asian
13 U.K. darling?
14 Diamond round
15 Kasparov sacrifices
16 Again, in music
17 East Coast weathercaster's adjective
18 Not anonymous

26 Broadway lights
27 Harpy's weapons
31 Paint poorly
32 What situps strengthen
33 Oomph
34 __ chi ch'uan
36 To's correlative
37 Building site
38 Fulminating
40 Course division
41 NYSE watchdog
42 Biblical landfall
43 Lassoed
44 Home of La Scala
47 Foundation
48 Fabulous weeper
50 Frazzled comic character
51 Schoolyard menace
53 Right wing workplace?
54 Film critic Pauline
55 Lisa Marie's father
56 Darling Neil Simon comedy?
57 Like trendy teens' trousers
58 Cogito, ergo __
59 Peloponnesian War winner
62 Pressing a suit?
63 Screen's John, William and Mary Beth

64 Tin or zinc
69 Explorer Hernando de __
73 '39 Crawford-Shearer comedy
74 Fireworks watcher's cry
76 It gets hit on the head
77 Barbershop prop
78 Had elevenses
79 Served the purpose
80 Start for finish?
81 Double Fantasy star
82 Avant-garde
83 Thesaurus wd.
85 Not nearly ornate
86 Old Champagne capital
87 Prof's prize
88 Like some hooves
91 Cry to the projectionist
92 Cadmus' daughter
93 Before tube or circle
94 Be frugal
95 Feast of Lots
96 Stephanie Zimbalist's dad
98 Borodin's prince
99 Mother of Judah
100 La Bombeck
101 Confront
102 Suffixes in rock groups?
103 Sodium symbols

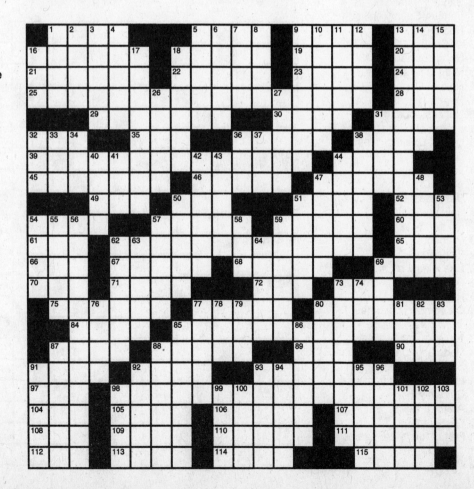

ACROSS

1 He's no gentleman
4 Casino job
10 "Oh, fudge!"
14 Have an inkling
19 Cry partner
20 Shoe part
21 Per person
22 Cutthroat, for one
23 Gridder who plays with food?
26 Sly character?
27 Look and look and look
28 Mad. or Lex.
29 Kabuki kin
30 "Don't Cry for Me . . ." musical
32 Surrender stipulation
33 Lode stone
34 Tiny tunneler
35 Dis-tress sound?
36 Blight
39 Tolkien's Treebeard
40 Crazy country veggies?
43 It climbs the wall
44 Catch on
45 Raise dander
46 Discombobulate
47 Get the news
48 "The Great George M"
51 Scrambled, as type
53 Don't go
54 Pickup line?
55 Kazakhstan river
56 Santa __ winds
57 Ventura County valley
58 Had on
59 Of Brother Cadfael's life
62 Helm position
63 Fight loser's demand
66 Neither Dem. nor Rep.
67 Deadly dressing?
70 Duffer's doodad
71 Beans, or beans' alternative
73 One of Chekhov's three sisters
74 Lens opening
76 *Battle Cry* author
77 Bee Gees, e.g.
78 Pair of 501's?
79 On the rocks
80 Malodorous
82 Flopperoo
83 Like jokers, often
84 Sanctify
85 Heavy file
86 Camembert casemate
87 Transgress
88 Tun of a kind
89 Rodman's *Bad __ Wanna Be*
90 Salad daze?
94 Lobster eater's neckwear
97 Certainly
98 Aretha's realm
99 Wish undone
100 Part of four state names
101 ¿__ está?
102 Made long swinging strides

104 Defeat at bridge
105 Battle stat
106 Plucked instruments
107 Jonah's three-day prison
109 Herb categories?
113 Corinthian cousin
114 X-ray vision blocker
115 Like the Rose Parade
116 Keats feat
117 Beckett's no-show
118 Lay eyes on
119 Orchid organ
120 Make one

DOWN

1 Celibate
2 *Emma* author
3 Go
4 Ominous
5 Spain's last queen
6 Norse gods' home
7 Slat
8 If not
9 One of 435 in Cong.
10 Old Chrysler line
11 Allergic reaction
12 Score 100 on
13 Lamenter's song
14 Screws up a screw
15 Q.E.D. center
16 Veggie for Donny only?
17 Teacher du jour

18 WWII area
24 Escort's offering
25 Supplementary structure
31 Chianti, in the Monti Chianti
33 Stable particle
34 Tucked in for the night
35 Moses' mount
37 Track shape
38 Mentor's charge
40 Only U.S. voters till '20
41 Eye area
42 Pumpkin pie spice
44 Benefit, often
47 Juno's counterpart
48 Rosemary rackmate
49 Maine college town
50 Circular dressing?
51 Buckets
52 Andean Indian
53 Chianti region
54 Simpson patriarch
57 Connacht county
58 "__ Got Tonight"
60 One-colored
61 Bow and bolo
62 Wing it
63 BART part
64 Rome's Demeter
65 Listens to
68 Everyday

69 Train track
72 Plumbing problem
75 Compete at Camelot
77 All-out
78 Make money
80 Start to unravel
81 Naturalness
82 Confuse
83 Like the Magi
84 Pole-vault prop
86 Frigid floater
87 Cook mushrooms, perhaps
88 I do, e.g.
90 Appearance
91 Elm St.'s "nightmare"
92 Local groups?
93 Goober
94 Take awhile
95 Hamper
96 Gave the orders
101 Bud holder?
103 Miscellaneous mix
104 Pass the breaking point
105 Bigger than micro-
106 War, to Sherman
107 Locks you can pick
108 After yoo-
110 Loser to DDE
111 Overtake on the track
112 Glad, to Gauls

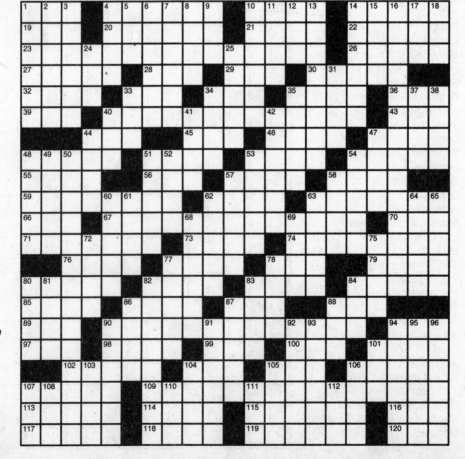

ACROSS

1 Face with hands
5 Gets top billing
10 "Ka-pow!"
14 Karate move
18 Twice halved
19 The Bible, before Joshua
20 Paella part
21 Asian capital
22 Mercer-Arlen detective ditty?
25 Warm, in a way
26 Curry or Rice
27 Eris' brother
28 Spillane's __ Jury
29 Took steps
30 Countdown penultimate
31 Capote, familiarly
32 The Nazarene author
34 Hide or hair lead-in
35 Ransom's Russo
37 The Drifters' D.A. ditty?
41 Sr., to Jr.
44 Get up and it's gone
46 Accomplishment
47 Play area
48 Word on a February card
49 Glitch result
52 Babies in blue
53 Swines' confines
54 A second time
55 City Hall habitué
56 Beach Boys' hymn to a hawkshaw?
59 Part with
60 Its point is to make holes
61 Arena level
62 Altar answers
63 Evasive
64 Muff or fluff
66 U.N. leader Kofi __
68 Use a fire extinguisher
69 Fantasy writer Ursula
71 Custard dessert
72 Poulet product
73 Nonprofessional
76 City south of Gainesville
77 Irving Berlin's excuse for a song?
80 IOU part
81 Be weak-minded
82 Rugged rocks
83 It lasts for months
84 Country roads
86 "Whiffenpoof" singers
87 Prop for Harpo
88 Old Glory, for one
89 R&R pt.
90 Paleo's opp.
91 Doris Day's mystery melody?
94 The cart before the ores
98 End of the line, for some
100 Caddie alternative
101 Tokyo, once
103 Carte start
104 Taste
106 Dreamscape artist

108 Elated
109 It may be made in clubs
110 WWII ocean menace
111 The Fantasticks' judgmental song?
115 Car co-ops
116 Autobahn auto
117 In solitary
118 Wrist-to-elbow bone
119 Phoenix netters
120 He wanted a loaf and a jug
121 Small salamanders
122 Chow palace

DOWN

1 After play or spin
2 Like some skates
3 Shrewdness
4 Wilderness Campaign leader
5 You really put your foot in it
6 Firm the muscles
7 BA part
8 The old college cry
9 It might end with a bang
10 Twist in agony
11 Weathercast word
12 Head or heart attachment
13 Where Cav and Pag are played
14 Honeycomb components
15 B.J. Thomas' paean to perps?
16 Yorkshire river
17 Pressed a suit?
21 Neck protector
23 Sank into the sofa
24 Nuremberg negative
29 Tiger on the grass
32 In regard to
33 Stoner's supply
34 Mountain in Ex. 3:1
36 A little cobbler?
38 "Days __ Lives"
39 Herpetological crusher
40 Casablanca's Claude
42 Turn away
43 He lost to Truman
45 Linz's land
48 __ lazuli
49 Where fat cats get thin
50 This very second
51 Patti Page's accusatory song?
52 Cassandra, e.g.
53 Splash with Scotch
57 Silverdome pro
58 Muslim folklore character
59 Clear the deck?
63 Sam & Dave's sound
65 Robert wrote them

66 Corrects the wheels
67 Hooks crooks
68 A lot of bucks?
69 Dark green cloth
70 Maître's milieu
71 Bell-bottom bottom
72 River to the Missouri
74 Strike dumb
75 No alternative
77 "__ by any other name . . ."
78 Balloon material
79 Matzo's lack
82 A funny Chevy
85 Be in a cast
88 Delicate
89 107D's lover
91 Certain .45s
92 Napoleon kin
93 Give some slack
95 Commoners, to snobs
96 Klingons and Vulcans
97 Coromandel Coast port
99 Australian exports
102 Poetic paean
104 Dines at eight
105 "__ Ben Adhem"
106 Roll or stick lead-in
107 Verdi princess
108 Increase
111 Lao-tse's way
112 Soak up rays
113 Flamenco shout
114 Tight-lipped

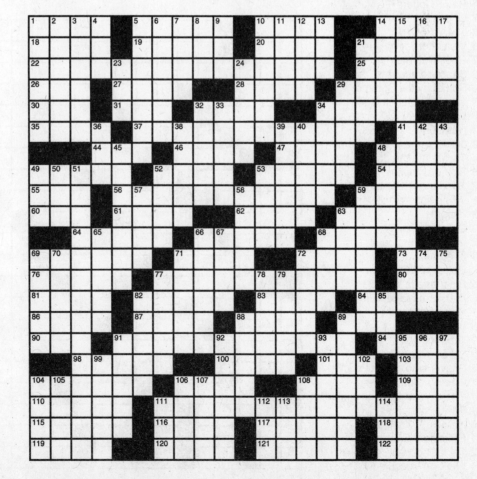

ACROSS

1 Be in summer stock
4 "Taxi" troubadour Harry
10 Goblet part
14 Physique
19 Auto-front protector
20 Ease up
21 She was Lois to Dean's Clark
22 Irk
23 '77 Waylon Jennings song
26 Tennis great Don
27 Crooked
28 __ heartbeat (immediately)
29 Turn state's evidence
30 Model Campbell
32 Dreyfus defender
33 That fella Pinella
34 Poitier, to pals, perhaps
35 Martial arts studio
36 Welsh rabbit ingredient
39 Sign of bigfoot?
40 '67 Neil Diamond ditty
43 Improved's frequent partner
44 "Just add water" product
45 Mystery writer Grafton
46 Tip top
47 Barry or Brubeck
48 Esther's enemy
51 Pesky plant
53 Remus' Rabbit or Fox
54 Jerry or Jerry Lee
55 Goddess of discord
56 Return letters?
57 One in the L column
58 114A's __ 18
59 Visa alternative
62 Roosevelt matriarch
63 Sausage shapers
66 Some, by the Somme
67 Truman's favorite song
70 La-la lead-in
71 Nutrition
73 John Diamond's nickname
74 Throw into the drink
76 Compos mentis
77 Saddle or step start
78 When spr. starts
79 Except
80 Cornerstone
82 Important PC command
83 Exec's extra
84 Good, in Guadalupe
85 Big name in Valhalla
86 Dietrich's Marlene
87 Plea at sea
88 Barbell abbr.
89 Tube top
90 '69 Bee Gees hit
94 Shaver who doesn't shave
97 Gear for Pearl Jam
98 One-named folk-pop singer
99 Bowler or boater
100 Israel's __ Vashem
101 Folksinger Seeger
102 "__ for Adonais": Shelley
104 Work on the quilt

105 Dr. Ruth's forte
106 Huffs and puffs
107 Pass word
109 '77 Eagles classic
113 Get extra wear from
114 Exodus author
115 Off the subject
116 City reg.
117 Mormon VIP
118 Like some losers
119 Roosevelt and
    Pendergrass
120 Originally known as

DOWN

1 In flames
2 He worked Friday
3 Sack, e.g.
4 Shell occupants
5 Egg manufacturer
6 England's old name
7 __ gallery (cheap seats)
8 Peruvian person
9 Highest degree
10 Regular date
11 It's in the book
12 Timeline segment
13 Ted, for Todd, e.g.
14 Fierce African monkey
15 Latin quarter word?
16 '70 R. Dean Taylor tune
17 Flight record
18 Anil or woad
24 New Zealand parrot
25 Three-wheeler
31 Comet competitor
33 Tarzan Barker
34 Gulf War missile
35 Nitwits
37 Matchmaker Dolly
38 Some bighorns
40 Relations
41 Takes habitually
42 Polish pact city
44 Not neut. or fem.
47 Pastrami purveyor
48 Hopper of old Hollywood
49 Historian Durant
50 '27 Paul Whiteman
   number
51 Horse Whisperer's
   Dianne
52 Reckons wrongly
53 Yeltsin
54 Hungarian rhapsodist
57 T-shirt size
58 Mr. Dillon
60 Foretokens
61 It crosses Hollywood
62 Like Elvis' song shoes
63 Sales staffer
64 Vault line
65 Holy hombre
68 Ma Walton

69 Open a crack
72 Anytown USA st.
75 Letters of debit?
77 Zippy dip
78 Sup with soldiers
80 __ Raton, Fla.
81 Gen. 2:7 subject
82 He had a rock to roll
83 Make moues
84 Air gun ammo
86 Freeway division
87 Shoulder warmer
88 Inc. cousin
90 Greeter go-with
91 Packer fan's headgear
92 Liner location
93 Headed for the
   runway
94 "Imagine" imaginer
95 Garb
96 Malefic marquis
101 Between birdie and
    bogey
103 Solomonic
104 Flurry of activity
105 In under the tag
106 Pea jackets?
107 Modern art?
108 The Diamond St.
110 Conquistador's quest
111 Jiver
112 Wing it?

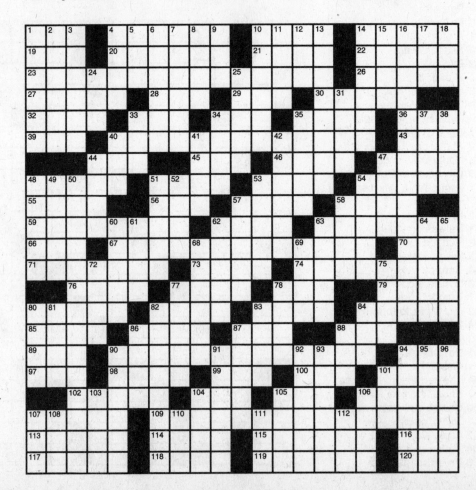

ACROSS

1 Clown for the camera
4 Bettor's method
10 Guinness from London
14 Staff breaks?
19 Book before Jer.
20 Unrefined
21 *Corrida* combatant
22 Swallow the story
23 Wig-flipping composer?
26 Old pal
27 Secret vocabulary
28 Connections
29 Cockney's cottage
30 Cannes coin
32 Artist Alice
33 In this env.
34 A quarter of quadri-
35 Adjective for 2000
36 CIA counterpart
39 Luncheon leaving
40 Unmaned animal-help group?
43 Y-chromosomed
44 Spanish pair
45 Not agin'
46 Uses a shuttle
47 Two make 2
48 Denounce
51 Spur on
53 Certain bond, for short
54 Birthday suit modelers
55 Marie Wilson radio-TV role
56 "A certain *je ne __ quoi*"
57 Maidenhair or asparagus
58 Dweller by the Morava
59 Vivid
61 Ahab, in Ray Stevens' song
62 '50s Italian star Anna
65 Stop start?
66 Dis-tressed Superman citadel?
69 *Wind in the Willows* animal
70 Capricorn and Cancer
72 Dear me!
73 Cosmos
75 Asparagus spearer
76 Oft-patched pants part
77 Farm fraction
78 Countersink
79 Pugilist's quest
81 Faulty firecrackers
82 NE Nevada county
83 Mini-mountains
84 Ken of "Wiseguy"
85 Anti-DUI school gp.
86 Parisian prom
87 Northern seabird
88 Goes from green to ripe
89 Hank leaves expression of gratitude?
93 *Casablanca* pianist
96 Cry convulsively
97 Second-stringers
98 Some tag players
99 SUV
100 This is one
101 Better – or best
103 Mach 1 exceder
104 Enthusiast
105 Pours down
106 In the know
108 In agreement, without a wave?
112 Brink
113 Historic actor Edmund
114 Hardened
115 Run along
116 Did simple math
117 '40s film star from India
118 Engenders
119 Koppel or Kennedy

DOWN

1 City in northern Italia
2 High-interest lender
3 Gizmo
4 Ella's specialty
5 Hither and __
6 Old Italic language
7 Doughboy's defense
8 Linguists' suffixes
9 Convened
10 AEC's A
11 Part of a marriage vow
12 Before, of yore
13 Celebrant's sprinkle
14 It's on the road again
15 Work for
16 The whole thing, unlocked?
17 Capacious cask
18 Secret agent
24 One in an encycl. series
25 See 11D
31 X and gamma
33 Requests to come again?
34 Pre-owned
35 Singer Rimes
37 Jubilation
38 Catfish Row woman
40 *Small Soldiers* character
41 Fleet from far away?
42 Memorable pianist José
43 Grieve
44 Wee drop
48 Ink Spots' "If I __ Care"
49 Fielding flub
50 Hairless Sinatra?
51 Puts together
52 With *mucho dinero*
53 Like old apples
54 Most of Israel
56 Broth base
57 Ethan of literature
58 Beatles' "Sexy __"
60 Blazing
61 Arson aftermath
62 Saki's real name
63 Twangy-sounding
64 Inventory lines
67 __ Lac, Wis.
68 Take care of loose ends
71 Opinion samplers
74 Composer Satie
76 Praise
77 Join forces
79 "__ ever thus"
80 Shakespeare villain
81 Diaries
82 What otoscopes examine
83 "Say what?"
85 Stable mate
86 Midler of *The Rose*
87 Flexible blackjack card
90 Hindu preserver
91 Caftan kin
92 Says
93 Lacking substance
94 Mame, relatively speaking
95 Dovetailed
97 Peel's "Avengers" partner
100 Give the sack
102 Argue for
103 Wild guess
104 Grandma, affectionately
105 Beatty biggie
106 Actress Gardner
107 Tie the knot
109 PBS benefactor
110 Attack command
111 Peggy or Pinky

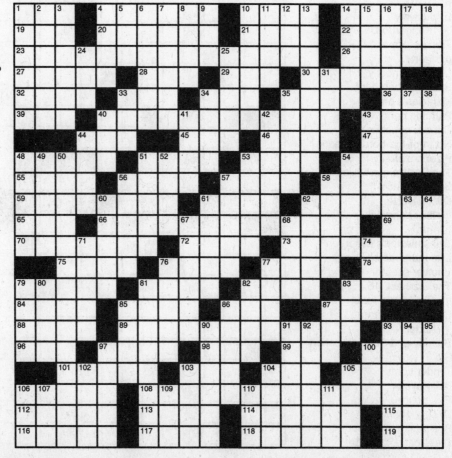

ACROSS

1 Wingding
5 TV plug
10 Whack or wagon opener
15 Like some Cheddar
19 This, *señorita*
20 __ Olay
21 ". . . __ horse to water . . ."
22 Showroom model
23 Jed Clampett's Beverly Hills mansion?
26 Treater's phrase
27 Stand for Woods
28 Nos. in a travel guide
29 Tickle Me dolls
30 Mason's material
32 Fills with fury
34 __ one's style (inhibit)
35 Less genteel
36 Shropshire chap
37 Cease-fire
38 Like a berserker
41 Leprechaunlike
44 Blindman's buff moves?
46 Cambodian's neighbor
47 Hard to come by
48 Barrymore of *Ever After*
49 Sultry Sommer
50 Be facetious
51 New homonym
52 Friendly farm animals?
56 Down-filled comforter
57 Winter Olympics sites
59 FYI part
60 Exclusively
61 "__ Kangaroo Down, Sport"
62 Franz's former "NYPD Blue" partner
63 Unicycle, mostly
64 Brit's bumbershoot
66 Magician's prop
67 Piercing pang
70 Certain punches
71 North-of-the-border Beatle?
74 Pizarro's plunder
75 The Earth's quadrillion
76 Betting bunch
77 Dust particle
78 Letter openers
79 "Uh-uh"
80 Transmission's assertion?
84 Like tearjerkers
85 Shower scourer
87 The 6:22 at 6:15
88 It's Big up the coast
89 Caricaturist George
90 __ Abdel Nasser
91 Spanky and Stymie's cohort
95 Big Sky capital
97 Tender spots
98 Baby oyster
99 Pub potion
100 Like __ of bricks
101 Bus pass?
105 Classical colonnade
106 Words before vie or cologne
107 Cry of defeat
108 Congregation's comeback
109 They may be let down
110 Valuable violin
111 Kyoto quaffs
112 Old video format

DOWN

1 '98 film *Cousin* __
2 Not at all ruddy
3 Take the helm
4 "And pigs fly!"
5 Looked sullen
6 Does standup?
7 José's hurrays
8 Barn bellow
9 Present, as evidence
10 Drop sharply
11 Man of morals?
12 Morse T's
13 RMN was his VP
14 Skullcap or shul cap
15 Actress Renée
16 Posh positions?
17 Oscar winner Thompson
18 Wrong end?
24 It's played at Dodger Stadium
25 Iced, as fruit
31 Tote board info
33 "It's a Sin to Tell __"
34 Director Cameron
35 Haystacks
37 Tough trips
38 Great Laker Chamberlain
39 It may stand at a meeting
40 A bit barmy
41 10,000,000 make a joule
42 Limp, as locks
43 Dreary output?
44 Raisin, once
45 Raises
48 Crash-test casualty
50 Dixie drink
52 French adjective
53 Erstwhile Opry auditorium
54 Auctioneer's warning
55 Perform better than
56 Boston baseballer Bobby
58 Disengages?
60 Portion
62 Slop
63 "__ up, Doc?"
64 *Vin* option
65 Of the kidneys
67 Tale
68 St. Louis landmark
69 Wine or hair quality
71 Morticia's man
72 Din from a den
73 Baby size
76 Northwest and Middle
78 Certain air
80 Conspiring
81 Got wind of
82 Played at Vegas
83 16th-century Swiss theologian
84 Civilian clothes
86 Bullrings, e.g.
88 Puts on the schedule
90 Coated cheese
91 Orange mismatch
92 "Bell Song" opera
93 Fast on the feet
94 Farmers competitor
95 Yesterday's roast, today
96 -ess kin
97 Go bad
98 Feeling poorly
102 Before or after pack
103 Cytoplasm stuff
104 Semi front

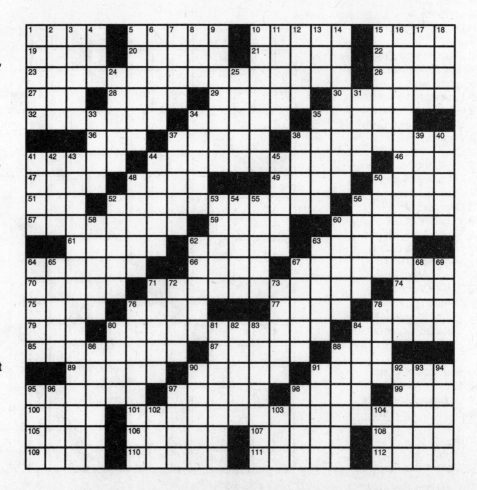

ACROSS

1 __ de combat
5 Sewing or cooking term
10 *Red River* co-star
15 Your, among Friends
18 Considerably
19 AMPAS award
20 Twain of song
21 Weal's opposite
22 After 40A, *Kundun* subject
23 A la *Buddenbrooks*?
25 Out __ limb
26 Classic WWI tune
28 Sherman and Pershing
29 Midwest hoopster
31 Ann of Malsie movies
32 *Pride and Prejudice* suitor
33 Personal pat
34 Racket or rocket ender
35 Big name above Brentwood
36 Don sackcloth
37 '97 Jim Carrey persona
40 See 22A
42 Most minimal
43 TV "Batman" sound
44 Bookstore stocking *The Deer Park*?
48 Stirrup site
51 Green dip
53 Lies in loops
54 Early Bond foe
55 Defy Bligh
56 IV league?
58 Personal records
59 Made the twain meet
61 Stacks
62 Flutist James
63 Governs
64 Joanie, in Doonesbury
66 Way past tipsy
68 Saharan
69 Ballet studio prop
70 Rash
73 Ewe said it
74 Irving Stone's shining opus?
77 Likewise
78 Oxford benefactor
80 The tipping type, for short
81 "Glad *that's* over!"
82 Cognac not from Cognac
83 Bowler's bad break
85 __ polloi
87 Form-fitting
88 Directs square dances
89 Ate like a king
93 Hits the horn
94 "__ Want to Be a Rock & Roll Star"
95 Riverside County saline spot
97 *The Ice Storm* director Lee
98 Gretzky's kiss?
101 Catchall abbr.
102 Verse on a vase
103 Atheist Madalyn's family

104 *Common Sense* writer
105 Individuality
106 Spanish I verb
107 Voluminous volumes
108 Virtuoso's violin
109 __ precedent

DOWN

1 Light headwear?
2 Some Norwegian kings
3 After 96D, Italian speedster
4 First-team member
5 Take the trouble
6 Tribe in Joshua 19
7 Reject with contempt
8 Bring to heel
9 Time piece
10 Not at all a sure thing
11 Rawboned
12 Wayhouses
13 "Bah!"
14 Roofing material
15 The value of a couple of cagers?
16 No fooling!
17 '00 and MM
20 Chic
24 Radio "noise"

27 Word indexers ignore
30 God who favored the Trojans
32 Letter opener
33 Agriculture goddess
35 Gaiety
36 They're bound by ties
37 Yule fuel
38 Gambler's chit
39 Well-known impostor?
40 The Belmonts backed him
41 Unite
42 Yuppie nosh
44 Chichester chums
45 Surrounded by
46 Growing room
47 Colonial flagmaker
49 Theater org.
50 Promising
52 Well again
54 TWA rival
56 More genteel
57 Director Grosbard
58 Wash all over
59 Hyde Park stroller
60 New Age emanation
61 Unadulterated
62 "A good walk spoiled"
64 DJ Kasem
65 Some are fine

66 Weevil's target
67 Lane of Metropolis
69 Partner
70 Greek-letter org.
71 Buck's mate
72 "Ouch!"
74 Dark horse
75 Give it the gas
76 Cole Porter miss
79 Williams senior or junior
81 '85 Harrison Ford flick
82 Fair of hair
83 Mystery writer Dorothy
84 Clever tactics
85 Detestation
86 Barcelona bear
87 Pre-Creation state
88 News commentator Roberts
89 Muslim ascetic
90 Italian saint
91 Lauder lady
92 Passed out?
94 Run a game on
95 Go shoo-be-doo – or just shoo
96 See 3D
99 Taunting cry
100 P.O. alternative

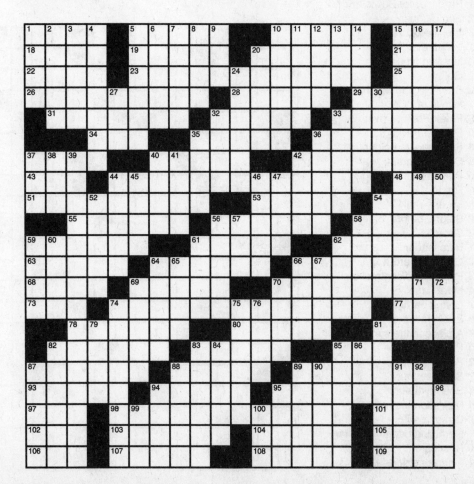

ACROSS

1 Woofer or tweeter
4 Boutonniere spot
9 Ballroom dance
15 Come to the plate
18 Arab sultanate
20 Show a good time
21 *My Sister* __
22 Kind of trip taken by one person
23 Doonesbury
24 Steinbeck opus
26 Sammy Sosa, e.g.
27 Jumping the gun
29 Elbow-wrist connection
30 Anthropologist Louis
32 When pigs fly
33 Walked on
34 A pretty piece of change?
35 Less fettered
37 "Yippee!"
39 Parsley, often
41 Eye-related
42 It means anger
43 Bovine bunch
45 Longtime bestseller *Angela's* __
47 Slapstick missiles
48 Troy, to Romans
49 Isaac's elder son
50 Astral altar
51 Producer for Bowie and U2
52 Sumptuously
56 Whistle blower
57 Lets the air out
59 Molding type
60 Go by
62 Brooklyn and Manhattan followers
63 Patek Philippe rival
65 Follow furtively
66 Philadelphia neighbor
69 Cousin's mom
70 Pulsed with pain
74 Regret
75 Military rank
79 Before, before "before"
80 Seraglio
81 Blue leader
82 Gets the hard way
83 Pessimistic contraction
84 More sagelike
87 Give a party
88 Put in jeopardy
89 A place in the sun
90 Prom rentals
92 Perkily pretty
93 Square corner
94 Speedy trials?
95 Meir's foreign minister
97 Genesis wife
98 Gambling game __ de fer
100 Resting on
101 Itinerary entries
105 Santa syllables
106 Court
109 Seed enclosure
110 Bird on an Aussie coin
111 Creating concupiscence
112 Noticeably less friendly
113 Valley for vintners
114 Bench press iteration
115 Blazers' rivals
116 Common pizzeria name
117 Sunday seat

DOWN

1 Ostentation
2 Dune biggie
3 Observe
4 Second of two
5 Love, by the Louvre
6 Well-tuned engine's sound
7 Where *el sol* rises
8 Haole's wear
9 Yo-Yo's plaything?
10 Comics' __ Lois
11 __ -Romeo
12 *Lion King* frame
13 One who makes good by making well
14 Rabbit ears, e.g.
15 *Vanity Fair* female
16 Chills and fever
17 Collectible jug
19 Vengeance goddess
25 It's at the end of the line
28 Not *sans*
31 Cuckoo birds
33 Hopkins of "Family Matters"
34 *Kiss Me, Kate* setting
35 Took easy strides
36 State one's view
37 Tyler and Taylor
38 Noon or midnight
39 Prayer ere fare
40 Roll-call replies
42 Sculptor Oldenburg
43 Thicket fence
44 Raleigh's rival
46 Hole in the wall?
48 Purpose
52 Writer Joyce Carol __
53 Nick of flicks
54 Gets wind of
55 Girl George?
58 Pot top
61 Cleric's vestment
63 Name meaning red-haired
64 Commencement
65 Express gratitude to
66 Food for the humble
67 Book review?
68 Makes the grade
69 Jackson Five features
70 Laconic
71 Get off scot-free
72 "Sesame Street" regular
73 Rehab result
76 One of a Dumas trio
77 TV encore
78 Way of walking
83 Pack of camels
85 It's held for questioning
86 *Joy of Cooking* contents
89 But, to Bernardo
91 Travis Bickle portrayer
92 Guitarist's gizmo
93 Fog, mist and steam
95 Value system
96 Certain pears
97 Hog-caller's holler
98 Chastity's mom
99 Run or spun lead-in
100 Broadway opening?
101 Arroyo __
102 Doublemint ad feature
103 Pluckable
104 Chopped cabbage
107 Stylishness
108 Caltech counterpart

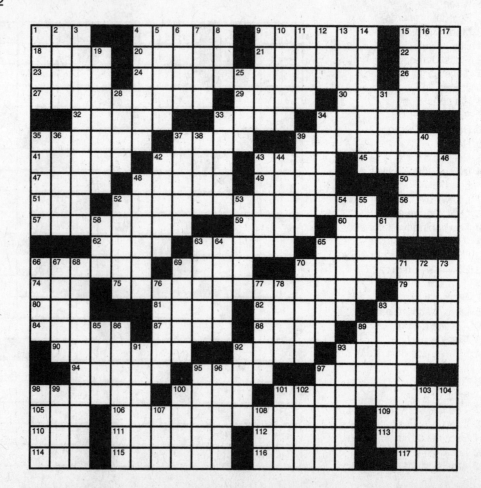

ACROSS

1 They'll make your day
6 Stagehand
10 Hit with lightning
13 Say it is so
17 Palmer, to his army
18 Hunt illegally
19 Finish line
20 Dino's tail?
21 Union organizer's autobiography?
23 Machu Picchu dweller
24 Actress Swenson
25 Like hot property
26 French or Italian alternative
28 Marina moorer
29 Like loads
32 *Delta of Venus* writer
33 Mudder's fodder
34 Whom Uncle Sam wanted
36 Anglo-Saxon letter
37 *Sí*, to Simone
38 Country club employee
39 "There's __ gold at the end of the rainbow"
41 Spot on a screen
43 Wise men's speech?
47 Runs up the phone bill
50 What I may mean
51 Native of Liberia
52 "99 Luftballons" singer
53 "... Raymond" co-star Peter
54 Urban pall
56 Characterized
58 Raged
60 Ivory shelfmate
61 Of Paxos' neighbor
62 Where 'dos are done
64 One with a sheepish look?
65 Cash dispenser
66 Spooky beaver clan?
68 ... fish __ fowl
69 Expected
70 Secondary study
71 "I hate to __ run"
72 Cals. counterparts
73 Dolce's designing partner
75 Cruising cyberspace
76 Early Beatle Pete
77 About-face
78 Not __ many words
81 Chip circuit abbr.
82 What Tell took
83 "Simple Simon __ pieman"
84 Boring Midwest landscape?
90 Inexperienced one
92 Defame
93 "Acid"
94 Cob's mate
95 Get no return?
97 Tot's timeout
99 Riches
100 For shame!
101 UHF or VHF
102 Escapades
104 Backslide
106 Shape for a pool
108 Breathing spell?
109 Make jerky
110 Outdoor number?
115 Airport near Paris
116 Include's opposite
117 PC symbols
118 Author Lofts
119 Little dogs
120 __ Xing
121 Starting four
122 Emulate Izaak Walton

DOWN

1 Bacon kin
2 Heavy metal rock?
3 Form or corn lead-in
4 Shampoo sequel
5 County capital
6 Big name in bridge
7 Seattle forecast
8 Trade-regulating org.
9 Tut, e.g.
10 Electrode element
11 Literary cockroach
12 Shell game prop
13 Kublai Khan's domain
14 Some "I Love Lucy" checks?
15 The figure zero
16 Ire
18 Mt. Ossa neighbor
19 Charming
22 Bandleader Vaughn
27 Be there
28 Bald Brynner
29 Parliament head?
30 Pair's pronoun
31 Rome's Appia or Veneto
33 Ideal
35 *Shogun* apparel
38 Unsound engine's sound
39 "It is __ better thing ..."
40 Bleachers bellower
42 Frankenstein aide
44 "Home Improvement" prop
45 Go to extremes
46 Fuel conduit
48 Trounced
49 Ceremonial dinners
53 Unfilleted
54 Put in place
55 Roz Russell's opera role?
56 Polish target, for some
57 To munch, in München
59 Broke a military rule
60 Consarn kin
61 Pull yourself up to the bar?
62 Make content
63 "He's __ a million"
66 U.S. sleuth
67 Diminish
72 Altar space
74 Jenny's cry
75 Scads
76 Grouse or snipe
79 Pt. of USNA
80 Small scrap
82 AWOL opener
84 Feathered stole
85 Region on the Oder
86 Omits vowels
87 Spring for drinks?
88 Mattel male
89 *King-I* connector
91 IV attachers
95 Mete out
96 Capital near Alexandria
98 Fluffy feather
100 Addict
101 *Don Juan* author
103 Custodian's collection
105 Like Mongolia
106 Longtime McDonald's CEO
107 Actress __ May Oliver
109 Beat pounder
111 "Respect" letters
112 Bit of work
113 "My gal" of song
114 Pronoun for a ship

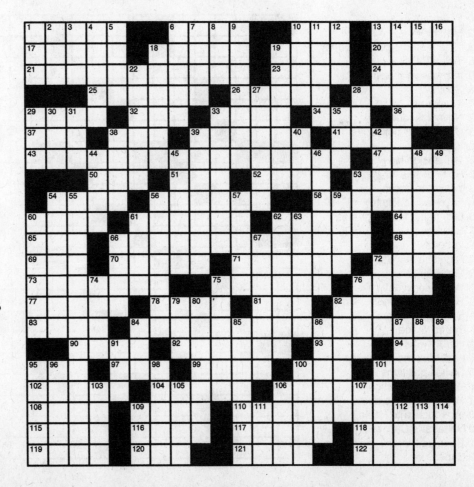

ACROSS

1 Phil Jackson, to the Lakers
6 Arthur Marx's instrument
10 Proper partner
14 Go no further
18 Cloaklike rainwear
19 Sometime still-life subject
20 Punjab princess
21 Seven presidents' birthplace
22 Context
25 One from Wales
26 Opera-house box
27 Sneaker brand
28 Toonsmith's product
29 Riviera resort
31 Articles in Le Monde
32 Multipurp. truck
33 Ancient Aegean
35 Role for Clint
36 Long-nosed fish
37 Houseguests' quarters
39 Country bumpkin
40 Hirschfeld and Hirt
41 Tibetan ox
42 Lump option
44 __ Land (L.A., to some)
47 Irritable
50 Rapierlike
52 Unpleasingly pungent
54 __ out (barely makes)
55 Steam engine pioneer
56 They're left on the road
59 Granola bit
60 Water
62 Mouthy?
63 "The Metamorphosis" writer
65 Ticked off
66 Impressive assembly
68 Spooky
70 Keepsake
72 Noisy takedown
73 Colleagues' colloquy
76 Is for two?
77 Dickensian kids
82 Roll-call misser
83 Wield the baton
85 Feydeau specialty
86 Like half a team's games
87 Searches
88 Lung division
89 A geisha ties one on
90 Gotcha!
91 Woodstock feature
92 Breaks a rule in the Army
94 Sewing kit staple
99 Young Yorkie
102 Hardly windy
104 New York Indian people
105 Switch positions
106 Break in the action
107 Young actress's role
109 Introduction to Paulo
110 Baseball's Canseco
111 Bear, up there
112 Expensive

113 Shares evenly
117 Give vent to
118 Place for banquet
    biggies
119 Frequent flier?
120 Philly fliers?
121 Ant. antonyms
122 Dismounted
123 The pokey
124 Laundromat machine

DOWN

1 Blunt-ended cigar
2 Medieval catapult
3 Zeniths
4 Guerilla Guevara
5 RV needs
6 Cattle caller
7 Astounds
8 Field marshal?
9 Get ready to eat later
10 Ring opener
11 Operated
12 From early Peru
13 Appearance
14 Gregarious
15 Early light
16 He was at home in the
   Astrodome
17 Sidewalk game
18 Jo Ann of *M*A*S*H*

23 Greek cheese
24 Blackjack burg
30 Fri. preceder
33 Afghan's neighbor
34 Of the stars
37 Showing shrewdness
38 Peers at
39 Took the trolley
40 Finery
43 Get the gold
45 Plumbing problem
46 Famed film dog
47 Pref. with light or night
48 Sonic receptor
49 Agree on a deal
50 Moss on the runway
51 Chin attachment?
52 Taj town
53 Moldy material?
56 Soft touch
57 Averages
58 Pass up
61 The Daltons, e.g.
64 "Total theater's" Antonin
66 Waugh or Wilder
67 Less than medium
68 Muffet diet part
69 Dawn deity
70 Like the Sears Tower
71 It may get a good
   licking

72 Part of Old Glory
73 Place for hydrotherapy
74 Studio area
75 Kiloliters, for short
78 Aerial enigmas
79 Pickup in a bar?
80 Aztec, e.g.
81 "__ only joking"
84 Trifles with tarts?
87 Attila follower
90 Approaches
91 Walked in a Western
93 Nonliving doll
95 Refuse to relent
96 Well-groomed
97 Vaudeville dancer
98 *Meet Me __ Louis*
99 Ornamental border
100 Heavy overcoat
101 Portrays
102 Ocean's motions
103 Other side
104 Calyx leaf
106 Boccherini or
    Cherubini
108 Beef-rating gp.
110 Hendrix at
    Woodstock
114 Card count, to Cato
115 Be appropriate
116 A long way

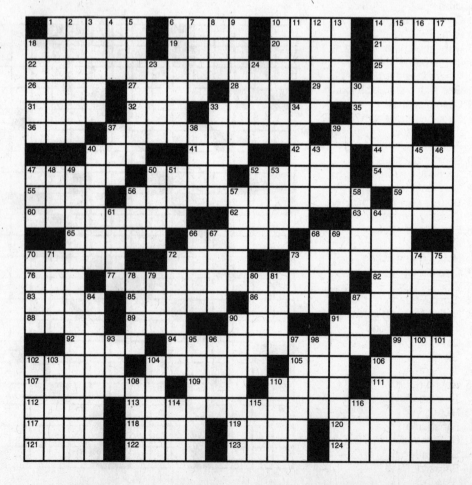

ACROSS

1 Mustard family member
5 Accra is its capital
10 Got or hot ender
13 Unimportant matter
19 "__ to differ"
20 Coty and Clair
21 Dr Dre's specialty
22 *Grand Illusion* director Jean
23 Strategies for the future
26 Reversals in Rollses
27 Twaddle
28 Lip
29 *Little Women* matriarch
30 Lark or light lead-in
31 Big Red, once
32 1 to 10, e.g.
34 Porcupine quill
35 Big sensation
37 Grown-up pullet
38 Plato's P
41 Prey
44 Tailless simians
45 Timber trees
46 Gift-tag word
47 Inuit's canoe
48 Footfall
49 HST's first
51 Walk wearily
52 Make bread?
53 Ex-GI-to-be
55 Take the shuttle?
56 Not quite yet
57 Gung-ho
58 Less flabby
59 Graceful antelope
63 Managed
65 Hesitates
66 Carved canyons
67 Bust a bronco
68 Like the Negev
69 Flubbed one
70 "Designing Women" surname
73 Fad that went-went?
77 Utah national park
78 Enrage
79 To laugh, to Lafayette
80 REM opener
81 H.B. Stowe's little one
82 Table-talk collections
83 *Quo Vadis?* emperor
84 Mother's whistler
85 In medias __
86 Brew milieu
87 A painting's papers
90 Vibrato
92 Is footloose
93 Thai tongue
94 East is right here
97 Only just
99 Director Vittorio De __
100 Cortes' co-conquistador
102 Casts out
103 Hitting on all cylinders
106 Julia's "Seinfeld" role
107 Roman candle's path
108 They can bog you down
109 Condo, e.g.
110 Crosses foils
111 Pref. meaning muscle
112 Poet Sylvia
113 Scratches the surface

DOWN

1 Potters' bakers
2 "I could write __!"
3 Squiggy's pal
4 Ova here?
5 Where the Plains' grain stays, mainly
6 Pioneer Muppeteer
7 Cherbourg cherub
8 Born, in Bordeaux
9 Cleopatra's feller?
10 Rock gently
11 Cleaner's freebie
12 Basilica section
13 Twaddle
14 Doesn't give up
15 Store ashes
16 Past paramour
17 Queue
18 Language that gave us "whiskey"
24 Casual comment
25 Emulates Pisa's landmark
32 He may live in Apt. 1A
33 Moved stealthily
34 Bake eggs
35 High-fiber food
36 Relay stick
39 First Quaker president
40 Franciscans and Jesuits
41 French-speaking prov.
42 Thurman of *The Avengers*
43 Hang on the clothesline
45 Mr. Mertz
48 Tootsy wrapper?
49 Bee flats
50 In the thick of
51 Saucy
53 Auctioneer's "amen"
54 Flare's opposite
55 Feral
56 Tireless vehicle
58 Diamond decision
59 Eccentric oldster
60 Get there
61 Mazdaism adherent
62 Churchill successor
63 Hamster's home
64 General under Dwight
65 Bingo card's center word
67 Big jerks
68 Rubber hub
70 Hair or traffic problem
71 Short-vowel mark
72 Buenos __
73 Ticket take
74 End the indecision
75 Evans of jazz
76 Praiseful poem
78 Freudian's fortes
80 Paint again
82 Texas town
83 Kim of *Vertigo*
84 Rascally
87 Abbey branch
88 Like Chippendale furniture
89 Completely wrong
91 Venerated object
94 __ cum laude
95 Firefighter Red
96 Fence supports
97 Rhubarb source?
98 Chassis component
99 Job for the bunco squad
100 Uttar Pradesh tourist spot
101 Baba au __
104 Little dickens
105 Nada

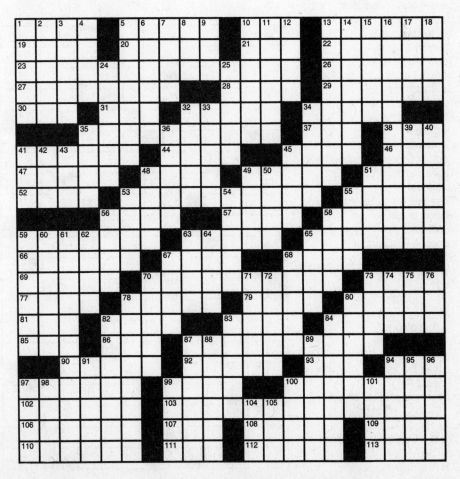

ACROSS

1 Dance like the monkey
5 Bill Nye's subj. on TV
8 Hammett hound
12 Borscht or bisque
16 Scandinavian hotspot
17 Mine, in Milano
18 Poe preceder
19 Neigh sayer
20 Bloomer from a bulb
21 Round at the bar?
24 Articles written by Proust
25 Put to the test
26 Wetlands bird
27 Three-time ring king
28 Double on the diamond, e.g.
30 Kilmer poem
31 They were into heavy metal
35 Plow pullers
36 Embodiment
37 Mediocre
38 Stupefaction
39 Start of many California place names
41 Gardening comic strip?
45 Compete
46 Total, in a way
48 Yard-long fish
49 "__ get a kick out of this"
50 Select
51 "__ it would seem"
52 Make goo-goo eyes
53 Cereal grass diseases
54 Batman creator Bob
55 Whitewater craft
56 Trilby or tricorne
57 Tests the water?
58 Chicken chomper's choice
59 Storm center
60 Trip segment?
64 Max. opposite
67 Dog breed Lhasa __
69 Unnamed litigants
70 Book between Chron. and Neh.
71 Typesetter's unit
72 Dateless
73 They may be stripped
75 Mouse target
76 WWII alliance
77 London nightlife area
78 Strauss specialty
79 He was terrible
80 Swift
81 S.F.-Tahoe dir.
82 John Gay's ursine opus?
85 Barring alcohol
86 Basketball center
87 Incense
88 Leaves the straight and narrow
89 Mideast A
91 Army mule and UCLA bruin
93 "...and __ all of us"
95 Like Hester's letter
98 What a Cockneyed optimist 'as?
99 J.R. Ewing's mom
100 Seashell seller
101 Veni, __, vici
102 With 110A, slogan of Grafton's soap?
107 It lets things swing
108 Son of Abraham
109 Corday's victim
110 See 102A
111 Bring to a boil
112 Née
113 Has an evening meal
114 Chance
115 Clutter

DOWN

1 The animal kingdom
2 Controls the means of flight?
3 For him or her
4 Lacuna
5 Fashionable
6 Newport or Salem
7 Letters of credit?
8 Actress Woodard
9 Plums' kin
10 Pucker-provoking
11 Picnic pest
12 Edna Ferber novel
13 Groundbreaking discovery?
14 Manipulate
15 Pricing word
16 Ticket part
18 Jessica's longtime portrayer
19 Greek sun god
22 Déjà vu causes?
23 Fairy-tale house-eater
25 She didn't like Ike
29 It's not as bad as hell
30 Linen fabric
31 Newport and Salem rivals
32 Whooping it up with everyone?
33 Now and again?
34 Act as It
36 Gracefully slender
37 Up front?
39 Cussed
40 Dress up
42 Copier setting
43 Satyrs' consorts
44 Put out the fire
47 WAC's sack
50 Shepherd's deity
52 Louisville's river
53 Venues
54 "Here's looking at you, __"
57 Da Vinci's employer
58 Offer a caveat
60 N.Y.C. sports arena
61 Speechify
62 Brief summaries
63 Earth protector
65 More glacial
66 '86 Janet Jackson hit
68 Kung __ chicken
71 Good buddy
72 Screen's Braga
73 Men of Man
74 River to the North Sea
75 Key material
77 Jeans joint
78 Blanch
79 The '48 state
80 FDR's Scottie
82 Capricorn or Cancer
83 Turn from temptation
84 Tour de France, e.g.
90 Home of the Anteaters
92 That "Yankee Doodle" boy
93 Soup sound
94 __ the hills
95 Dolly the clone, e.g.
96 Moves hesitantly
97 Ticket datum
99 Son of 108A
100 Large shorebird
102 Pen part
103 Bear in a bosque
104 Pitch source
105 Baseball VIP's
106 O'clock or so
107 Son of Noah

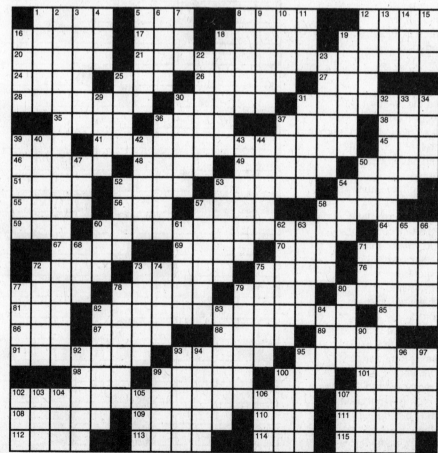

ACROSS

1 They need work
5 Magazine digest *The __ Reader*
9 Old Hollywood's Novello
13 The one yonder
17 City SSE of New Delhi
18 Can't do without
19 Foch of films
20 Queen Latifah's colleague
22 Supportive liqueur?
25 José's hurrah
26 Plop kin
27 Screwball or slider
28 Taking more time
29 Valley girl?
30 Snail's snack
31 Marx Brothers foil Margaret
32 Equivalence
35 Detroit gridders
36 Japanese noodles
37 Cat- __ -tails
38 Candy bear type
39 To be in Berlin
40 Uncommon bills
44 Unexpected impediment
45 Dessert starter?
47 Despise
48 Put in rollers
49 Well-known
50 Risqué
51 "__ people . . ."
52 Probes
54 Bedevil
56 Compass direction
57 Roadside rests
58 Baking quantity
59 Clinton Cabinet's Janet
60 Actress Elizabeth
63 It may be passing
64 What big leaguers play
68 Eye catchers?
69 "Your mileage may __"
70 Lifting device
71 '88 Dennis Quaid film
72 Nervous
73 Cushiony loaf?
76 Squinter's eye
77 It may be critical
78 Wharton degrees
79 Recess in the shore
80 Ream twentieth
81 Used a squeegee
83 Urge forward
84 Before check or chicken
85 Henley Regatta site
87 Jordan's capital
88 Female kudus
89 Missal item
90 Mold on the buffet table?
91 Caroline and John, Jr.
95 Golf course __ Beach
96 Spring dish?
98 Caesar and Cobb
99 Fringe benefit
100 Feller with Teller
101 Poi, essentially
102 Skater Lipinski
103 They'll get you there PDQ
104 Bowls over
105 No longer ajar

DOWN

1 Dieter Sprat
2 Grimm character
3 Relative of Remus?
4 Hip-hop DJ's technique
5 Excessively
6 Weeny head?
7 Buss in the car?
8 Old English letter
9 Chevrons or bars
10 Prospects
11 In reserve
12 Sign of sensitivity
13 "All roads lead __"
14 Food for a sweet toot?
15 Get it straight?
16 Everest locale
20 Defamation
21 Dinghy thingie
23 Best of a group
24 Poise
30 Set one's sights
31 Milk-producing plant
32 Group of Westerns
33 Architectural afterthought
34 Vaquero's rope
35 Skywalker namesakes
36 Volleyball champ Gabrielle
38 Go and Go Fish
39 Secret deposit
41 Engine inventor James
42 Emperor after Galba
43 Oracle
45 Shrewd
46 Singer Chapman
49 Ticket prices?
51 George who played Norm
53 Snack that reduces your roll?
54 Country singer Tucker
55 And so on
56 Poetry
58 Fishhooks' features
59 Singer Bonnie
60 Throat-clearing sound
61 Bubbly beverage
62 Refuses to share
63 Capacitance unit
64 Radisson or Ramada
65 Stray from the script
66 French châteaux region
67 Not yet
69 Hamp's instrument
70 Love of Paris
73 They may be shocking
74 Advertisers' angles
75 Take out the garb?
76 Nourishes oneself
80 Pacify
82 She of many shoes
83 Bring into the U.S.
84 Williams and Hood
85 Give medical attention
86 "*Aquí se __ español*"
87 Phoenix source
88 Woody's Annie
89 Additional addendum
90 Small cobras
91 Ragout or burgoo
92 Ark-itect
93 Spiritual adviser
94 Dick's dog
97 Mineral spring

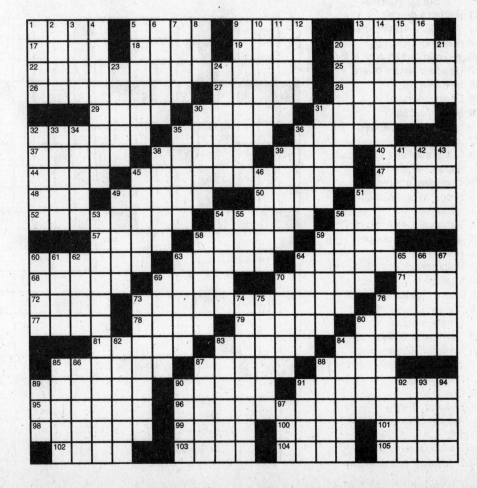

ACROSS

1 Schmooze
5 Moving man?
10 Native of old Peru
14 Half Miss Muffet's meal
18 "That smarts!"
19 Pit viper
20 Army discharge?
22 Lie low
23 Elk's ilk
24 Call out for produce?
26 Swenson of "Benson"
27 Sooner St.
29 Chair arm protector
30 Make a difference
32 Hack
35 '41 hit "Maria __"
37 Be gloomy
38 Singer DiFranco
39 Winery wiseacres?
43 Reporter's query
46 Bombay neighbor
48 *Beloved* star
49 Tough outer layers
50 Warm welcome
51 Venetian resort
52 Peau de __
53 Highland hillside
54 Pepper grinder
55 *Mi casa __ casa*
56 On-line countries?
60 Spot in the ocean
61 The Era __ Feeling
63 Pitcher's perch
64 With 68A, *The Homecoming* playwright
66 You can get an A or E for it
67 Used an emery board
68 See 64A
69 Curvy course
70 Medicine balls?
71 Software bootlegger
72 Jackie, to Jack
73 "All in the Family" actress shows her stuff?
76 Olympian aggressor
79 Brooklyn and Manhattan followers
80 Baseball's Aparicio or Tiant
81 "Don't throw bouquets __"
82 Prime raters?
83 Potpie morsel
84 Leaf part
86 Kafka character Gregor
88 "Deep Space Nine" 's Shimerman
89 Cornerstone abbr.
90 Garb for '60s activists?
93 When the mouse ran down
94 Hera's husband
95 Damp
96 Hoffman-Beatty mega-nonhit
98 Tell
101 Undamaged
103 Biblical preposition
104 Within arm's reach
105 Drunken racketeers?
109 __ carotene
113 Baby's bed
114 Emporium
115 Steve's singing wife
116 Sweat site
117 "Hava Nagila" dance
118 Go after flies – or hit them
119 Breathers
120 Ketch kin

DOWN

1 Ppd.'s opposite
2 Tint
3 Shoot one
4 Beat strongly
5 Centerpieces?
6 Scottish miscellany (ROAR anagram)
7 Very, in Veracruz
8 ABA member
9 Intestine sections
10 Song of Solomon follower
11 Of the U.S. or U.K.
12 Fill to excess
13 Hail, to Caesar
14 Chess opener
15 Word to the wise
16 Periphery
17 A dozen 25D's
21 Donny or Marie
25 It'll last for weeks
28 Fruit from Down Under
31 Boulle's *Planet* occupants
32 CNN opener
33 Diarist Nin
34 Accomplished avians?
35 Caught sight of
36 Sophia of *El Cid*
37 Got the lead out
40 __ to handle
41 Gofer's task
42 Choice dish
43 Painter's pithy remark?
44 Removed pea pods
45 Girl watcher
47 Collapsible dishes
52 Rants and raves
53 Most melancholy
54 Mythical maze monster
57 Dickinson and Post
58 Marks the hour
59 Thinly scattered
62 Gunk
65 CPA's suggestion
66 Haute monde members
67 Due from a daughter
68 *Prizzi's Honor* role
69 Put a credit card through
70 Put in the pipes
71 __ ease (relaxes)
74 Medicinal plants
75 Cloverleaf parts
77 Minneapolis suburb
78 Less loco
84 Hip or tip ender
85 Tests melons
86 Teatime treat
87 "Don't kid __"
88 Off. aide
91 Talisman
92 Color nuances
94 Kazantzakis' Greek
97 Philately, for some
98 What " may mean
99 Claudius' successor
100 Inside the foul line
101 Refuse transport
102 Creole veggie
103 One of a kind
106 Word often mispunctuated
107 Grain in a Salinger title
108 They show your age
110 Proposed 27th Amendment
111 Auto club service
112 You might find it boring

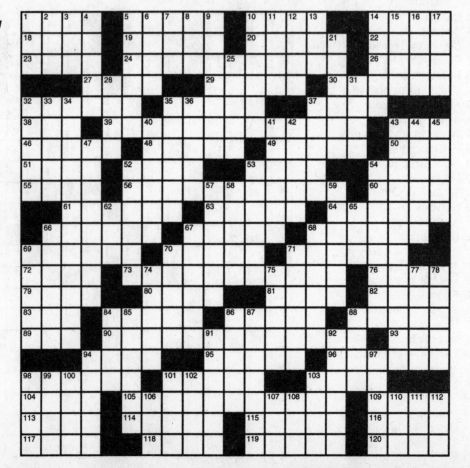

ANSWERS

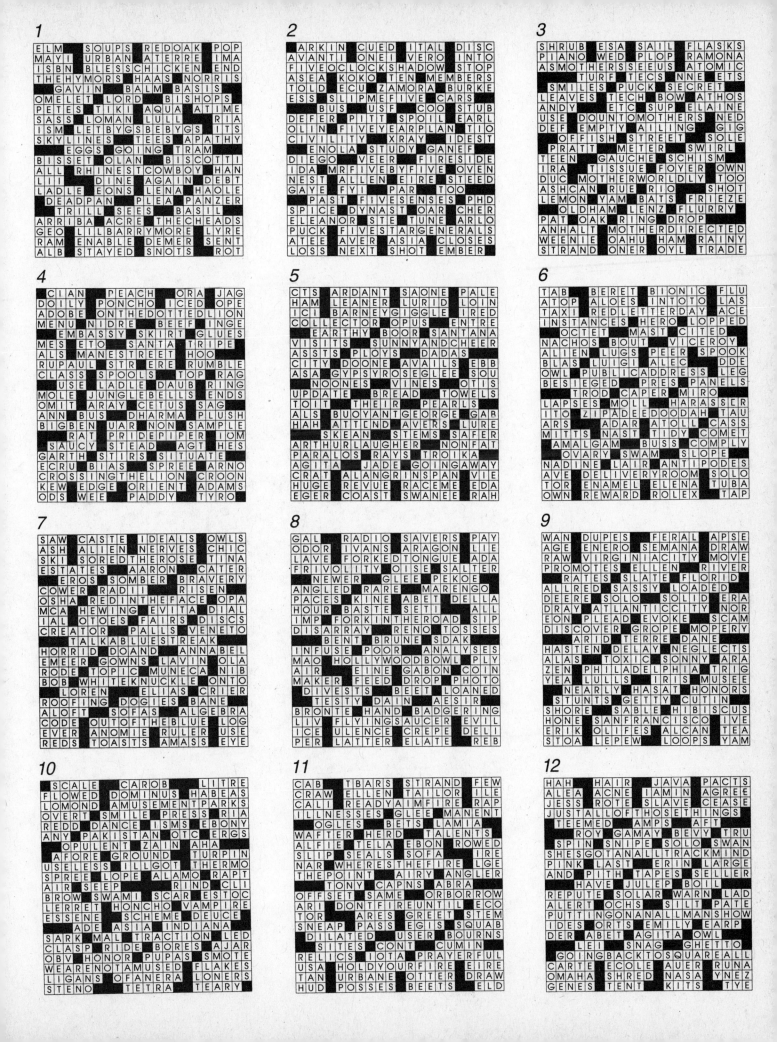

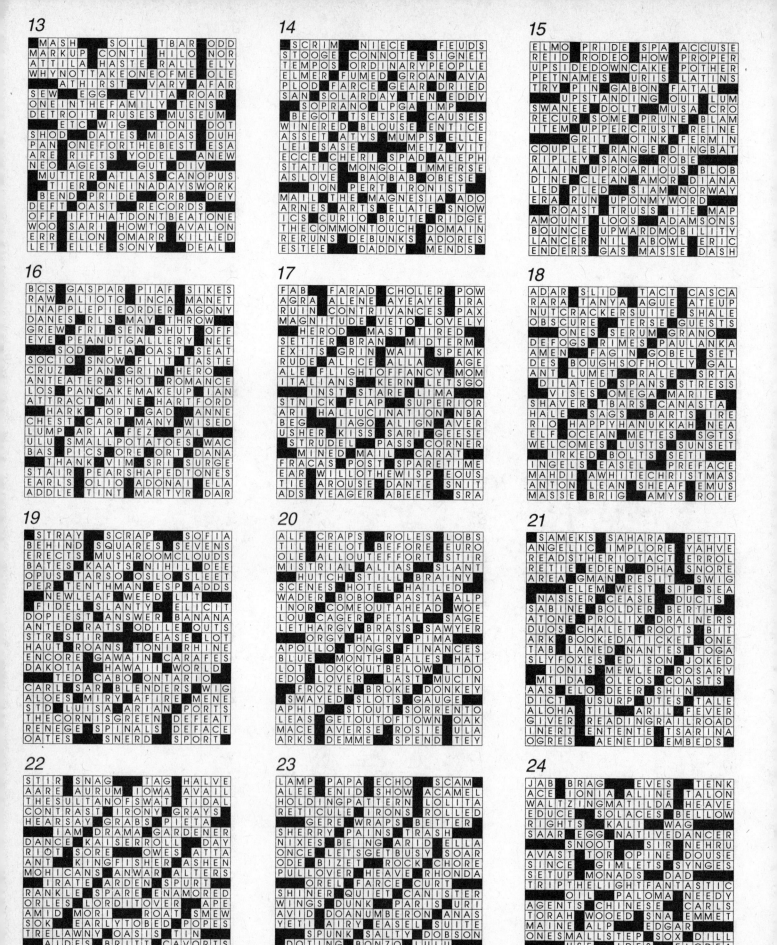

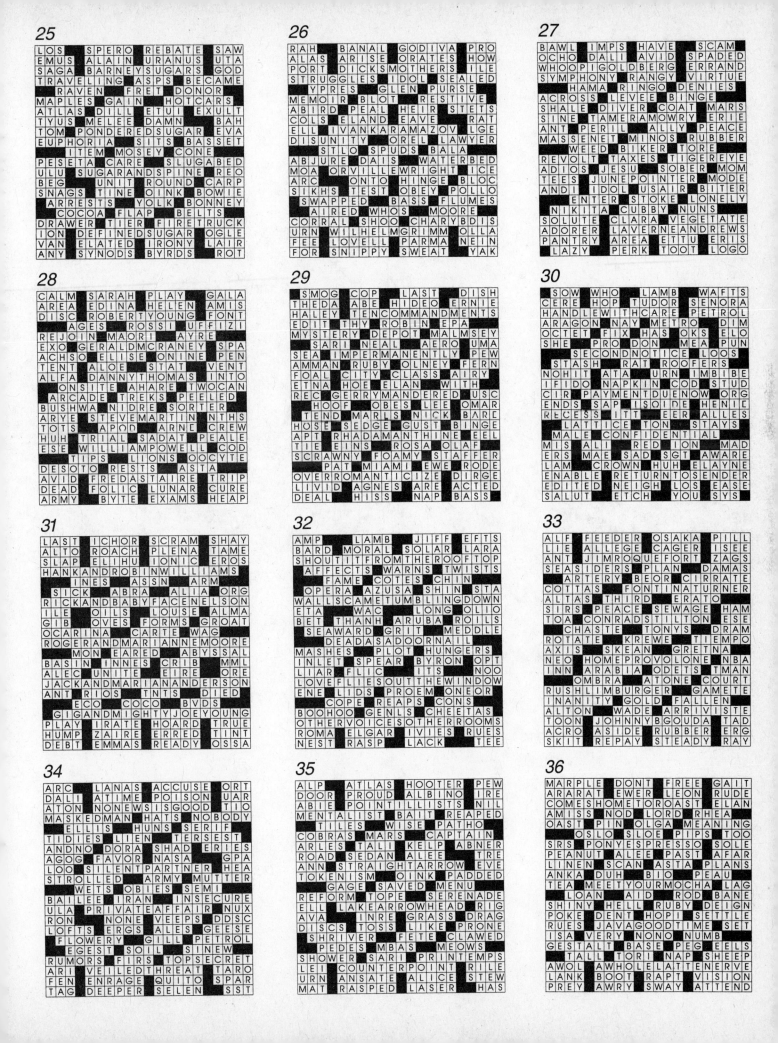

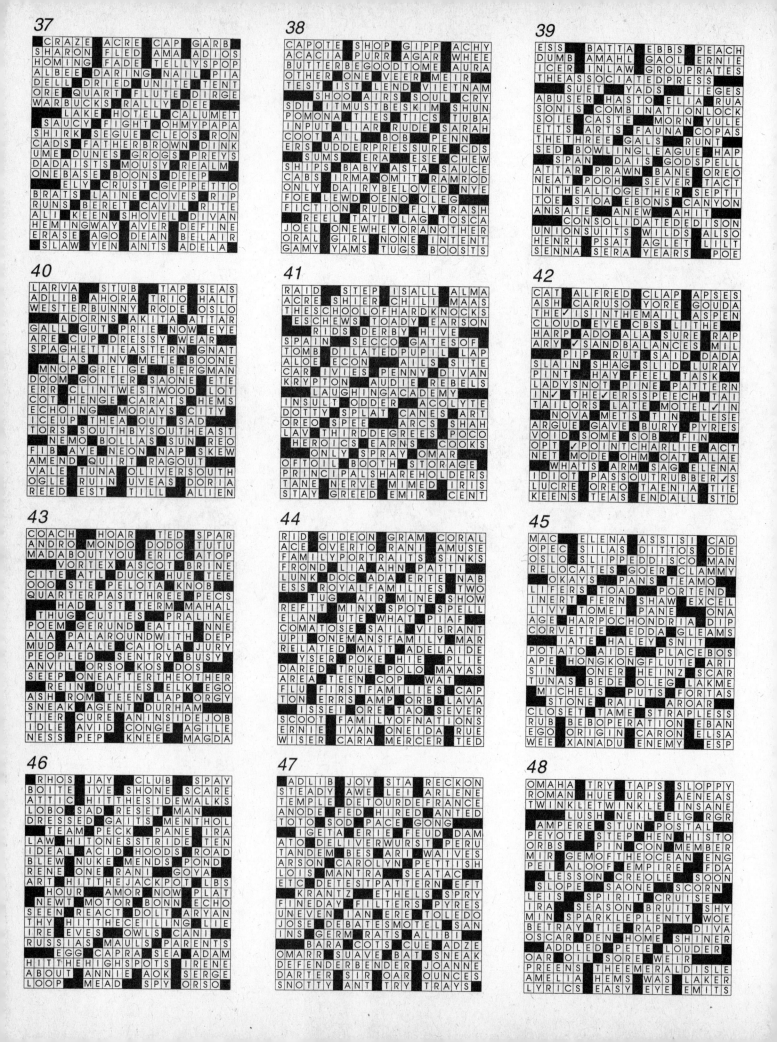

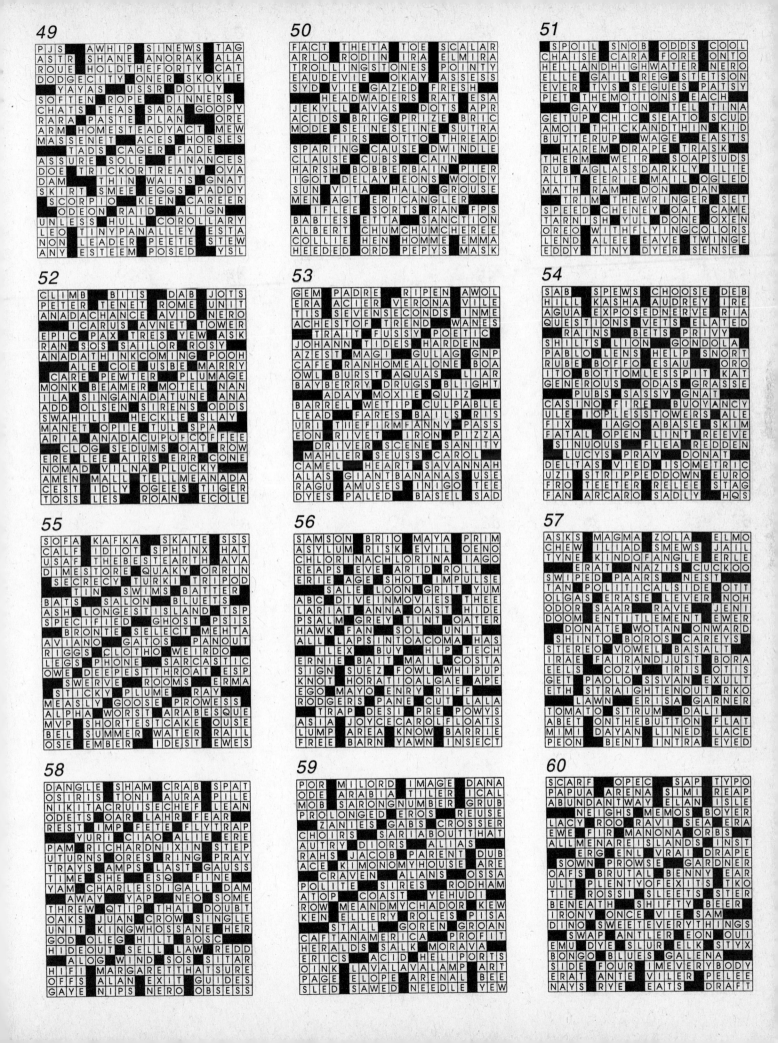

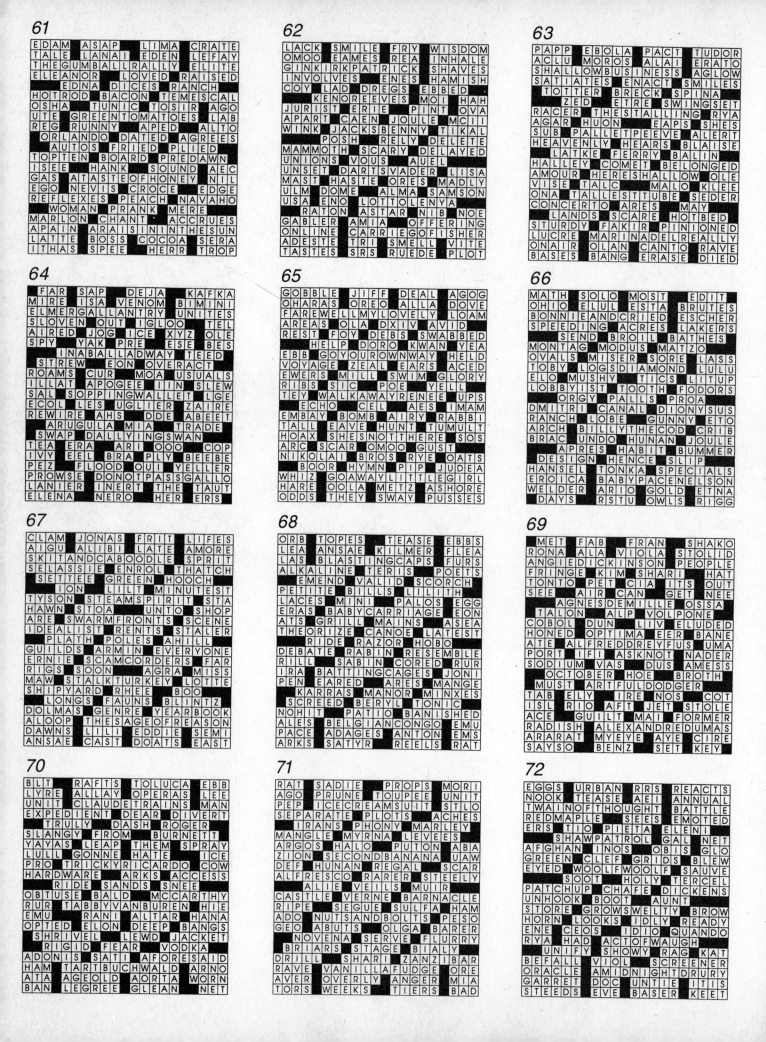

73

```
BRAC BEBOP  FETED  RST
REDO ALIKE  AERATE EVE
OLEA REBATESMOTEL  BEN
WILLINGLY  STUDS  ITOLD
CATSEYE SCORE  SCOUTS
    AMY  GEARS  JOANNE
PURR  SHARP  VOICED
ARE  REMEMBERSONLY  FRO
DICHOTOMY  ATLAS  LOAD
UBANGI CADETS  CARGO
CORONA MILAN  RANGER
HARMS  RAIDER SPIRAL
OREB  MILNE  ELECTIONS
USN  REPAIROFSOCKS  REO
TEASES  ROSES  DYED
MEDIAN LADLE  DEE
HAVENS TIRED  SLEEPIN
UPEND  SAVOR  THINKOVER
NON  REPRESSAGENT  SAVE
TUT ORIOLE GILDA  INES
STS PATTY  OFFAL  TART
```

74

```
WISPS DIP SASE  SARONG
ADIEU USE TIPS  ELINOR
GETALLTANKEDUP  TUPELO
   TOCK  EWER  MOM  SAW
SPLASH  MRED  SONICS
EQUINE BIND PHI  NUTTY
LUMP  ODE CIA  CURARE
MAP ANNUALPREMIUM  TIM
OBI POETS RACIAL  IVE
NOISES  GOVERN  COEN
AGONY  VIBES  STUNT
BUFF  LEONID  WAPITI
LSU MALIGN COLIN  NON
ATL LUBECKGERMANY  LAY
RELIED CEO JOE  RISE
ENOLA LTD PEON  PROFIT
FORGES  SACK  FLUTES
SAL NET CURT  GRUB
CREDIT  PRESSUREGROUPS
ALAINS REDO RIA  INSET
BODEGA OWEN INK  CASTS
```

75

```
ARCH SIDLE EDAM  STATE
MIRO CREEP RARE  ARBOR
INAMORALDILEMMA RESOD
ESTIVATE  TOWNS PAMELA
ESCAPE  BATHS  BACON
IRE  UPTO  PAPERCUT
CANDY AFGHANISTAN  ETA
ALOE ELAL GATS  MOIS
AIR UNIVERSALLY RIFLE
NAMESAKE EPSOM MUMMER
ACUTE  SPANO  MANIA
GALORE SORTA  PERICLES
AMPLY ATMOSPHERIC ILA
TIRE CLAM ERGO  SCAN
ENE ROLLERSKATE SAENS
DOGGEREL EWER  STU
NINNY  SPENT  TEASES
SHAFTS HELEN  SATIATES
TANTE BUDAPESTHUNGARY
ULCER ALAN DROOP EGIS
BOYDS RANT YIPES SENT
```

76

```
CAFTAN EPIC ALEC  AVON
HORACE RENO SILO  LIFE
ERICHVONSTROHEIM OCTO
STATE KIT NNES  MOOT
SARI RAE WITS  BONFIRE
COOP EACH DUNE  MOD
END CLIMBTHEWALL SLUG
QUICHE ERTE ORGY PETE
URGES TAOS FREE MOSES
AMEN HIS PAL  EATS
LIS NICKELANDDIME CAP
TROT POW RVS  ARIA
AMIES BEST SWEE PAILS
NAVE SUMO HAHA FLAMES
TREK PRIMEEXAMPLE EYE
ICE BENT FROM  READ
CONDUCT ERIN FAX AJAR
ZEST ABET BOW  SPARE
RAYE ROSEMARYANDTHYME
HEMP USER GERM DONNED
ORES MEAT EDDY TWEEDS
```

77

```
DREW SKIMP CRIES ASTA
RENE INNER HAMMY VTOL
AFTERNOONOFAFAUN EARL
MEE ANTS BATTY CANNES
ARRIVES PACES  ALOUD
KER MALTA  EMINENCE
FANON NOCLOUDNINE OHM
IRON FIFE ENTE  SCAM
BIT HALFMONOBAY CLETE
SAOPAULO VIDA THIRST
PARRY SAVER  CHINE
BRONTE TRET  YOUNGMAN
LOFTS PLAYNOWORDS ONO
ATTY IRAN RYES  GNAT
NOH KNOCKONWOOD BLYTH
CREVASSE ODETS  COO
WITTY  SMOTE  DRYWALL
SCOTTI SWIRL AUEL DIA
AURA NOPINSANDNEEDLES
NELL CHAFE NAACP IATE
ODDS TORTE DYNES DIOR
```

78

```
HEMS BONE SHAG  SCOT
ERIK ELIE OAHU  CLOVER
SIREONMCKELLEN HAMITE
SNOWSHOE DIVAN EVENED
ECUS CITED  BRIDES
FARRAR LOTUS  PRICY
OTHER BORED THUS OLDS
GEED DECADETOOTH FOOT
UNI SEGAL IONE  CEASE
PONYTAIL BETTY CURFEW
EARN PAPAS  BARA
LOGANS DAYAN  ARTISTRY
AWARD JUNO IDAHO HEE
RELY CENTURYDUTY HILL
KNEE OWES HULLS VIGIL
ACHES COMET  NIGHTS
WARHOL LADYS  RICH
MAGYAR SOYOU ROMANCED
ARREST HOURMISSBROOKS
STEAMS INGA EVIL OLEO
SERS PSAS SPEE  NESS
```

79

```
LIFTS REF REAP SCAMPS
INERT EGO AIRS ORDURE
ENDURINGENIGMA NESSIE
ICES ASHY DIA  IMP
SHADOW SPIT  ARCTIC
STEVEN JOAN EMS IRATE
LOWE ALL SAO  FOALED
ALA SITCOMVETERAN WAG
YES NOOKS ICEBOX USA
GIANTS DVORAK  ONER
PERPS BEANY  HANDS
LAOS HERALD  MOUSSE
APR DUNORD HALLS RHO
BAG VERSATILEJEAN KID
EYELET ICH ONO  MIND
LABOR UGH PURR SWINGS
AUTUMN TINY  PARADE
SDI IMA SONG  LOLA
TOLUCA SCREENANTIHERO
ARENAS ROSA BIZ TUTOR
ROYALS AWOL ARI HEADY
```

80

```
NARC DEARS BUTCH CAP
USER AEGIS MANRAY AMI
MALO BRENTWOTWOOD NUN
BLACKBIRD HOMEY RAISE
EXHALES SALAD CONNED
EYE MILAN  SIGNED
DEFT SEINE  SPLEEN
OAR TENTENDERLOIN IDS
CREDITORS RIATA SNAP
IODATE SWINGS LEEZA
MIGUEL SHOCK  TINTED
ITHAS HELENA  TACTOE
CITY MORAL  BOTHERERS
ASE PETITFOURFOUR TOP
ICICLE PNEUM  WHEY
AGENCY SEPIA  BEE
ATHENA GODOT  CHAGALL
LOTSA SELES SHANGRILA
INE CONEONESTOGA OVAL
VCR LOUSES RERAN FEMA
EES EMBED OPERA FRAN
```

81

```
STUBS ASH FAR  OBERON
GNARLY DOE ATO ALLURE
RIGGED DOMINOSDRIVERS
APTED TUT RAMAR MIDST
BEEN GAP EATS  IMPS
ATOLL ANTI DEUS WAY
LAM FACTCHECKERS VALE
EDWARD ITA AHA KIERON
FORMA BRINDLE NOTICES
TREY PRANCE  GIGOLO
YES BRIDGEBUILDER RTE
TALESE INSURE  BRAN
POLLOCK HOTDATE GUEST
YVETTE BAR RIE GEYSER
RARA POOLCLEANERS PRY
ELS ETNA HUSH  DITTO
BAST GEMS WET  ONCE
AMOUR ANOSE TON MIDAS
SEVENUPBOTTLER TALENT
HAINES CUR EAR AGENDA
ENDORA STA TRY DIRTY
```

82

```
SAC SPRAY  SCREW STAB
ETH PROBE  SCHEME PARE
AMI HABEASCORPUS ABIE
MONKEYED MARIO DRESS
AIRED HORNS  MAITRE
FABLED POKES  OILCAN
REELS WAVE BUGLE ASH
IRRS SABERTOOTHED COO
SIR SCULL EGRET CLUB
KEYLARGO ALDER BOLERO
UTAH MULES  MACE
SHALOM RADON DOGHOUSE
HALL SERIF NUDES NIN
ASP TOWEROFBABEL DIME
HHH EDIFY ANAS BROOM
ARNESS MERCI  GRANNY
ABHORS HOBBY  CRAWL
SHEER BATOR  GLOSSARY
TITI DAYTONABEACH BOO
AKIM ARTERY ARIEL ELK
RECS WEEDS GERRY LEE
```

83

```
JOB SOCIAL STEM TASTE
ALI ORACLE CORE WIPER
BELITTLEBIGHORN EDUCE
BALOO ACS AOK  SPEAR
ERIN MIA ITO SWAT NET
DYE DESPISELIKEUS BRO
BAG HID NEAL  TAIL
MODEM AMOS FAIR MABEL
OMIT ZIP TURN  SEXY
WASHOUTS REDO VENISON
ERD SNEERINGWHEEL PRE
DRASTIC ALEE EXPOSURE
INIT GILT ORE  ARID
MANIA FUSS QUAD BUNNY
ABET ALAI GUS  AUK
MUD SCORNFRITTERS PAC
EGG THUD LIP ASK MILA
LOREN GUN ANT BEGUN
STAGE DERIDINGACADEMY
AISLE EGAD DELTAS ONO
ONSET ROBS SWEETS NAN
```

84

```
CABBY TOT CDS  DOODAH
FIGURE UAW LAP EUNICE
INURES THISALEOFTEARS
ADEPT LOU TRACK FILES
TYPE AIR TIKI  APOS
REACT SALK APEX TDS
PRE LIEANDLETLIE SHAH
LIMPID LIP NIP RACEME
AGORA RETORTS GALAHAD
TONY CIRCLE  FIGARO
TRI LADTHEIMPALER MAC
THAMES GOURDS  MEMO
OPIATES CENTERS HOOFS
LIONEL BUM INA CONFAB
LEND LEERBROTHERS TRY
ADS FIXE AONE  DUTCH
FEAT PROS MIX  HEFT
ERROL REARS HOT DEBRA
THEOLGABOATMEN BARREL
TESTER ALS ARE ISRAEL
EATERS NOS PAY SHYER
```

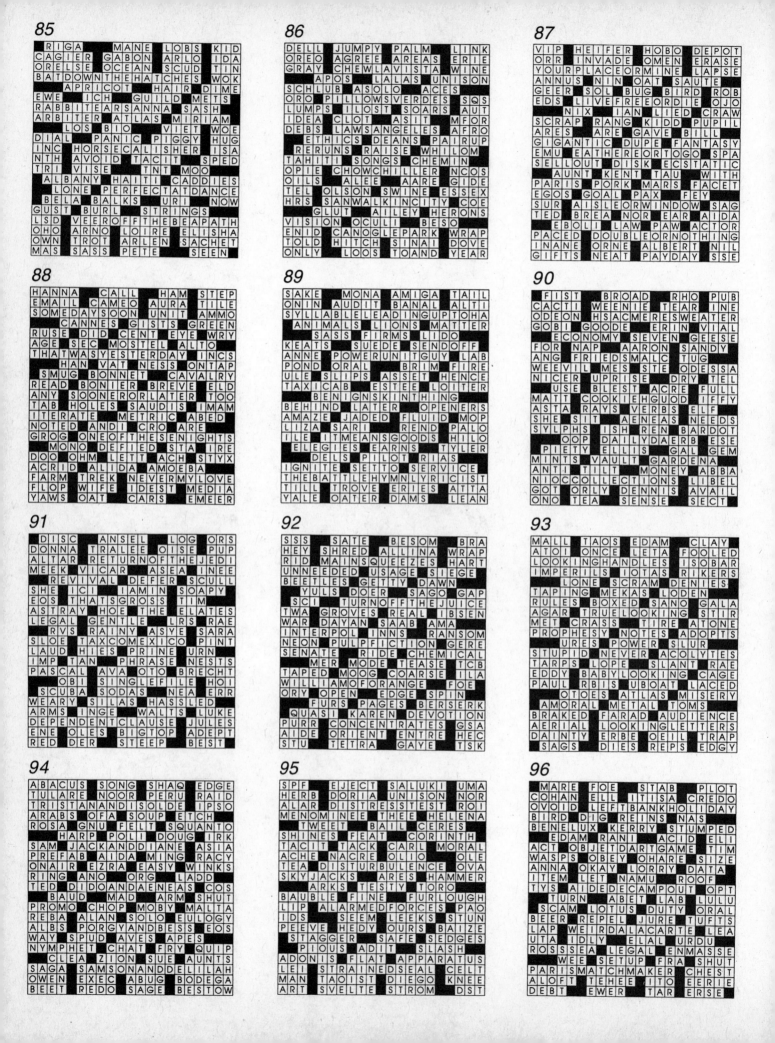

97

```
TRES  CANWE   BOARD    WON
HURT  OVOID   SUNDAY   EPA
OMAR  WEBFOOTSTATE     BET
ROSEMARIE  URBAN   MOUNT
RETORTS   STOOP   FAMILY
COD    FILMY    LIKELY
BACH   UVULA    TALENT
IRA   DANIELWEBSTER    TAD
ZINFANDEL  DOATS   CHOU
TRICOT   FEWARE   CAINE
BEWARE   MERIT   SUBSET
ENEMY   BREMEN   BALTIC
TOBE   GLOOM    ORDAINING
AWE   WHATWEBELIEVE   TIE
FRIEZE   ANGEL    DYNE
PRYNNE   GOLDA    ROI
PLIANT   MEZZO   CLAUSES
HYENA   GINZA   SHAMROCKS
IIN   BEATRICEWEBB    BOUT
AND   LEGREE   NAVEL   ELLE
LGS   ELSES   STYLE    YELP
```

98

```
PHI  SHOPPE   DITCH    JAWS
RON  HARLAN   AMOUR    OREE
OOF  INFANCYPANTS     BRAC
STRINGENT   OPRY     CLOSE
INDIOS    RULE    ONEEYED
DANCIN   FILETOFINSOLE
UNGAG    WEALL    PLOTS
AYES  NOTRE   STROBE    IDS
LAG  INWARDCLEAVER     NIA
RECESS   LATHE    AFEW
STONES   FLUTE   FAMOUS
LOUD    SWOON    OCULAR
ARP  TRIALBYINJURY    MOW
YES  ROTHKO   DOORS    LEVI
LACTO    FIRST    DIRER
INVOICEOFDOOM    BELFRY
REALTOR   LOOM    ARENAL
ORRIS   GEOL   AMERICANA
NUIT  DARTHINVADER    MAW
IDEA  ABACA   EASYTO    ERA
CASS  BRUHN   ASSESS    SKY
```

99

```
PROOF  OGLE   SINK     ATEN
SAHARA  ROIL  AREA     CHAO
PRESENTSASUMMARY     HERD
ELSE  TOIL  SAP    VEHICLE
NOUS  AWN  MILLAY    ALLES
DRS   MINIMOVIES     LILI
SAL    INE    YEA    ENDS
BOGUS  TELE  SOLON    STOP
OLAN  TREATSWOUNDS    OVA
PASSBOOK   PALM    INNER
PERRY   PLAYA    KUDOS
HASTA   ALIT   SILENCED
ARF  GARDENSTAPLE    FAVA
SNOW  MARAT  ELAN    FATED
HORA   AMI    BEE    SIT
BTUS   ALBUMCOVER    AMP
MARES  KNEADS  RED    ISAR
EMERSON  MID  DATA    FINO
DIAL  VOCALIZETOTHEMAX
INTO  ALAN  NOME    EULOGY
COHO  LLDS  GOOD    DELVE
```

100

```
MASS  SHELF   LOFT     GRAM
AREA  EASEL   AURAS    RUSE
REEL  STAGYOUREIT      ANEW
AVAS   BURST    APPEAL
WISDOM   AMATI    UTAH
ENO  CERVINECAMPUS    FAT
EDUCE  EELER  TATES    ASE
MIRO  ACNE   STLO     SWIM
SADR  FOUROFAHIND     ANAP
ONLINE   DENIS   ASLANT
DEBITS   POTTS   CUBANS
SABADO   DANCE   CUNARD
CURL  FROMTHEHART     IGOT
ABEL  OREO   OSIS     EAVE
LEA  CECIL   SANTA    ADMIT
ADD  ELKCAMINOREAL    ENE
MOBY   INTRO    ROUSES
CARUSO   ALTAI    ICES
ATOM  WAPITIQBACH     HAIR
ROAM  SLIME   URIEL    ECRU
SPRY  ANON   EARLY    REAM
```

101

```
DEEP  RIDE   CAPS    METRO
OLLA  EMOTE  OILY    ATHOL
DEBTOFASALESMAN     THEME
OVERBIG   EVIAN    STILES
IONE    SCENT    MERCI
NICOLE  TITLE   TAPESTRY
ERAT  SORRY   ARIAS    TEE
RID  GUISEANDDOLLS    LEA
ONO  OLGAS   ILLS     PEST
ANARCHY   PANEL   SLOPES
ACMES   SABER    SKOSH
MAHLER   GLUED   SHUTTLE
ABOU  LOIS  SHALT    OLA
CAT  THEAWEDCOUPLE    XED
EFT  OOHLA  ORATE    VENA
STIMULUS   GRIPE   CAESAR
NORMA   PIETY    HASH
SARDIS   NAOMI   ARTICLE
OTOES  HAITICHRONICLES
BOOST  ISNT  SMILE    LOOT
SIFTS  PASO  OBEY    EDNA
```

102

```
ACTS  CLODS   CIA      PAP
SPARE  DRAGEE  OUST    AGO
ASPIC  YOURFIRSTLETTER
MEIN  SNORE  OPIE    AINT
TIJUANA   ANDRE    PLODS
BAA  ARM   BLAME    BALSA
ALL   CLOSEOFDAY     EGO
SPOOKY  TNT  INS   LAWYER
HOFFA  BURANA  HON    ORO
YUL  OMANI   EDEN     JUNO
PIES  HAPPYENDING    ATOM
ROME   ASST   CIGAR    PCH
EWE  PIT   REMEDY    LOFTS
SANGER  BMI  ROE    KABUKI
RED  LASTOFMANY      LOT
BRAVO   OREAD    TIE    LSU
LEAVE   AWING    SETFREE
ANTE  AGUA   DIXIE    LAMB
PHILOSOPHYFINAL    RODEO
SUN  WENS  ALPACA    OPERA
ERG  LAY   POSIT    WERE
```

103

```
PESOS  DASH   KURT     SMOG
SHRINK  ANTIE  ELIE    PEGO
COFFEEANDUGHNUTS     OSHA
ABUT  PRAY  HUN    ETHICAL
DIRS  TIN  THREES    SLAMS
SAT   NIAGARALLS     STAT
DEC    HIT    PET    GERE
TEVYE  REAP  SWIPE    EDIT
ARAB  MEMBERTHEAMO    ANN
SANBRUNO   HEED    PANDA
GUIDE   ELOPE    HOURI
SICKO   OVID   BALSAMIC
IDA  THEMEMACHINE    MAMA
KELP  ADORE  LANG    PILAR
HAIR   TOR    SOL    IRS
FUME   PYSTYFORME     SEE
SCORE  CHEERS  NIP    DING
MARINER  AMI  URAL    IGGY
ACNE  MEANINGFULONSHIP
SHIN  MALE  GOOS    DOCENT
HEAT  AMID  SASH    ERODE
```

104

```
SAME  HASTA   FAR    STATES
CLIP  ICHOR  LEO    ARCHIE
ALLIGATORPEARS     RECENT
LANCELOT   LUIS    PARSES
DYE  OER  TWINE    RETAN
GRASSROOTS   EDE     APA
SLEIGH  TART  PLOD    KIN
EAGLE  WEPT  TRAIN    BERG
AWOL  MARSHAHUNT     PAPAL
PORN   BUDS    FINITE
CABOOSE  DANDY   TIPSTER
AVOCET   TELE    VINE
NIGHT  ROBERTREED     PEAL
DADS  FORTE  OOLA    DUNCE
ITA  FAWN  INGE    FORGET
DEN  IMA   GASGUZZLER
ONEON  ERASE  EOS     STU
HAVASU   SADA   PAWNSHOP
OLIVOS  CROCODILETEARS
RECALL  OUR  HONOR    ERSE
ASHLEY  TPS  MEETS    RIOT
```

105

```
DOWN  SPACE   MESA     BLEW
ODIE  ILIUM  ALEPH    LECH
GANG  MURRAYDECAY     ONCE
EMPS   NUEVO    PHOOEY
MARVEL   SHAKO    SHAM
ULU  DECEITOFPOWER    SCH
NONCE  ARLEN  USAND    IRA
DOOR  ARIL  CRAT    STUD
INFO  SEESDELIGHT     LOSE
DULLES   REESE   RHINOS
METIER   SALEM   COUPDE
REMOTE   SAGES   BOUNCE
ODIN  PUTTODETEST     AFAR
PALS  SPIN  RAMS    SERA
ELL  CLEAR  SWAMI    GENET
SSE  ROTTENTODECOR    SNO
CABO   EARED    KOREAN
APLOMB   SHANK    MAGI
WAIL  ENTERDEFRAY     GRAY
ALSO  DRILL  ROUTE    HIRE
YEAR  ARMY  SPEED    TOES
```

106

```
BLED  TEETH   NACHO    FRAS
YOLO  ALCOA  OILOF    EAST
GREATBARRIERREEF     MICA
UNG  HUTU  TIMES    SMUSHY
MAYPOLE   CIGAR    OHARE
ERA   SHAHN   CLOISTER
TITAN  GIANTSLALOM     HAE
EGOS  SIGN   OMIT     LESE
SOW  MIGHTYMOUSE      SATES
TREMOLOS   OATS    SIMILE
REPOT   CURRY    BLEAT
ABIDES   OLIO   FRAGRANT
LINED  ENDLESSLOVE     NOR
ALGA  PRIE   TOWS     RISE
RBI  GRANDCANYON     CACHE
MONGOOSE   EMEND    CON
FORTE   SLATE   ROUGHLY
BYEBYE   GLESS   RING   EEE
EARL  COLOSSUSOFRHODES
ARNE  TWEET  KOALA    OGRE
KNOT  SENSE  ENDED    HESS
```

107

```
FLING  OLAF   SUFI     ACRE
SOIREE  FARO  PLAN    SHAM
MIMEANOLDCOWHAND     TARP
OLIN  ERIE  TOE    CORONET
TETE  REF  SPORTY    ANGRY
EDS   MIMEREADER     OPIE
SIC    ELD    ODD    SYNE
ROMEO  MANE  FRODO    HOOD
ERIS  MIMESWEEPERS    UMA
COMANECI   RAGS    HAREM
EMOTE   CLOTS    CHASM
SHEER   RUIN   LAUGHING
LIV  MIMEBOGGLING    OMOO
ARES  SAGAN  RAZE    TREND
BERT   ARG    SAT    ARE
YEAR   AUNTIEMIME     MAD
PAWNS  BESEEN  COM    DICE
ROOMIER  USA  ALTO    INON
ERMA  YOURSMIMEANDOURS
STAR  ROSE  ELIA    IODINE
SANK  EDER  DERN    ABETS
```

108

```
LEAF  LEASH   COMIC    TSAR
ACRE  OLLIE  LAURA    AQUI
SLEETDEPRIVATION     RUED
TAN  EGGS  FEVER    TAMALE
STANLEY   HELEN    GAMAL
ALS   BETEL   ARTICLES
BATTY  DRIZZLYBEAR     ORO
OCHO  SUIS   ALES     AFAR
SHE  OWENTWISTER      SKATE
SYBARITE   ATIE    POISON
LIAMS   BRADS    BANTU
GRILLS   EINE   GUNGADIN
OOZES  HUMIDBEINGS     DRY
OZZY  POLA   LLDS     BEAN
CSA  CLOUDYDOODY     NANNY
HARDHATS   IONIA    EAR
DEANS   DEBTS   CLOBBER
GROSSE  JULIA  BEAM    EMU
RAFT  THUNDERSUSPICION
ODOR  OUNCE  IOTAS    OGRE
HAZY  FREED  OUTRE    BEYS
```

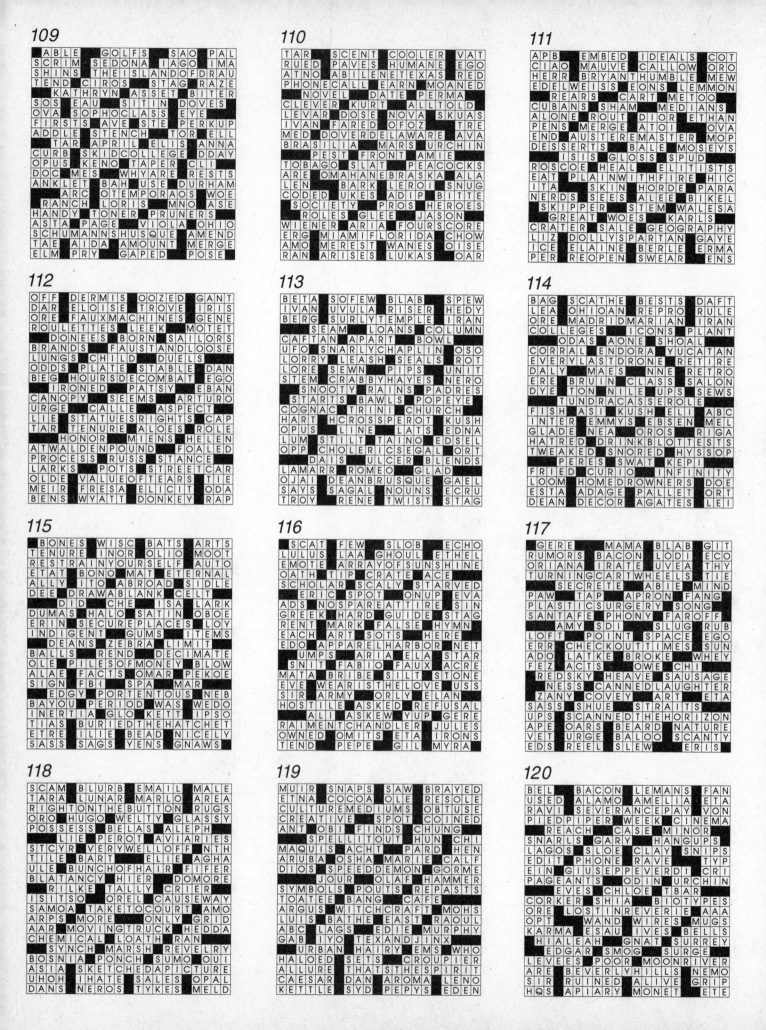

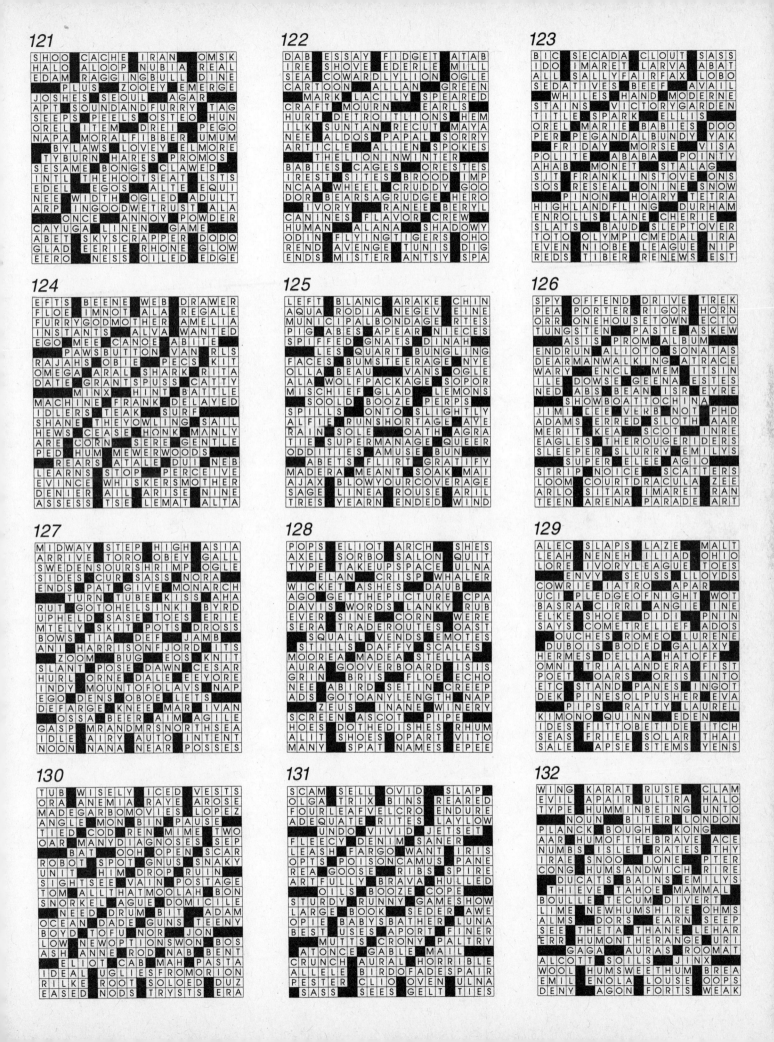

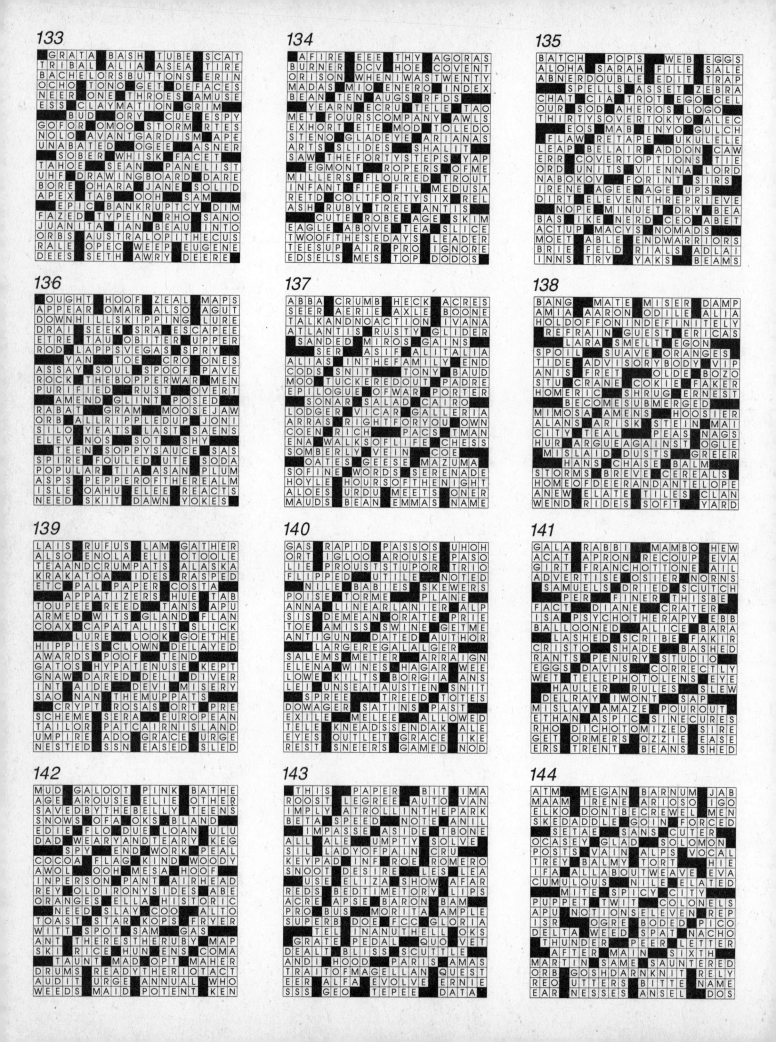

145

```
VISTA TUTU URAL AWLS
TIGERS IRAN REMO THAI
IONLYHAVEPIESFOR LANG
ELIE ABOY CLI UNLATCH
GETS MEL SOONER INSET
STE DELIVERIES INTL
SAD ERN TOO AIMS
TESTY SANA BLANC NCAA
NEAR ANTICRUSTACT ERG
TRUEBLUE ETTE URGES
CELEB PACTS PENAL
THETA SELA DILATORY
OOO SGTPEPPERONI TRIO
TUFT LURKS LACK BAYOU
ERTE OBI SCI PUN
HEAP TOPPINGMAD THE
CRETE PERIOD LIL DUOS
HONOREE GEL SOFA IPUT
ISIT GREATESTOFCHEESE
MILA ASAN TEAM EAGLES
PEEL DEUS ORGY STOOD
```

146

```
TOBOOT SHOP ALPS SPIN
ONEOFA EAVE NEAL PRAY
PYGMALIONANDGALA AONE
SOUPY MUD EARP PAWS
YUMA CEL ALLY ODDNESS
HAHA STOA ADAM INE
DAS RINGTOPIECES SNAP
ETHNIC RENE METH OHIO
CREED PEPE TOSS DAILY
KIDD GEE TAT BARB
SAC NECKNEWJERSEY ICE
RHUM IWO AHA ATOM
SMOOT PAVE KITE PROVE
TACO EASE SAKE BEARER
ATOP SLINGTHESHOW STY
FED ASEA OOLA ELSA
FRISKED RICO SIT LAMA
LEAN PUNK BID FILED
DREI CHINGCERTIFICATE
NARZ EAST AGEE ANIMAL
APSE STAY ROWS DOABLE
```

147

```
RUG ODETS LASERS HAM
ORAL PALOS ESCROW ASA
AGRI INSTANTKARMA RAT
MEMBRANES AHEM PROMPT
ERATO VIEW TEMPO
SENATE CLEF MODERNS
EXTRA BRAG FLEX DYING
RUBY BUENA AUDI OAR
FLA CARMENMIRANDA URI
STGEORGE ETAL ERASED
ORBS PITHY CLAM
QUASAR MUTE CRUCIBLE
ULL LADYMARMALADE AUG
ANA ELAL OLIVE CRAY
YARDS LASS VINE SUMUP
SMOLDER BEAK JURIST
CLAES MRED MONET
VILEST KOOL STARGAZER
IDO HEARTWARMING LVIII
DOC ECHOED HORSE LARD
ILK STABLY OGEES HEE
```

148

```
OGRE ONE GALA PUSH
CURES COB SOLAR MARIO
ATALE GUN SNAKE ATA
LEDA CUBEOFINFLUENCE
FRITTER SCORE CRUNCHY
NEON SLUM LEIA HUE
WAG BERMUDASPIRAL IMA
EBONY EURO MANET SPAR
LANA BIDS MINKS TOON
STAY EGG COLT SELF
HEP LONECONESTATE FEM
YOUR ARTS ODA ATMO
BRAG MARRY GAIN CHAP
SLAT DELLA ROSE KEENE
PAM TRAFALGARTUBE ODD
UZI RUNA UTES REAL
REDWOOD LEFTS FILMDOM
ALP SULFA SIT ALDO
FAMILYRECTANGLE SNOOP
AMISS ARROW AIR ADORE
NEXT TEEN STY GAPS
```

149

```
BUM TRIFLE TOY TAOS
MANA RANOUT SILO OLGA
ABCS OHCALCUTTER OILY
SALARY EMU NEA BUTTE
CREDO RNS STAN ASH
SAMBAS PERRIS AFTON
ALA NAKEDLAUNCH EYRE
COMPETE EAMES REARRAY
REPAYS DAY CONTROL
IWAS SETTO COUNTY
DEN KETCHOFTHEDAY SAP
RADARS THINS ALLI
STOKELY ELS SHOOIN
HAYWIRF SHRED HAYLOFT
ATUB SCHOONERISM PEA
PESOS THAWED OPENED
AIM ERNS JUS ADULT
ULTRA REO BEG ELIJAH
BLOC YOURWARSHIP BORE
ONTO BOBS RESUME LUKE
WASP EOS STEPPE ERS
```

150

```
TAHITI WARP SLAP OPUS
OPERAS AGAR PAPA SETH
UPWITHTHEJONESES AGEE
GLESS ROD PINT TIKI
HERE DUO LEFT FINANCE
SPIN SORT SOCK ARM
WES LAKECITYUTAH CROP
ACTUAL VARY BEME HOST
NOISY LITE COPY LOUSY
ELLA PEA SEA DOWN
DEL DOINGTHETHING DDE
WRAP ROY ERA CHOP
STAID CHIP LASS CUOMO
EATS SHOP FICA DUPLEX
GLEE COMEFROMWIDE EDY
AIR FIRE RENE CAST
LASSOED BEES LAY AFAR
DARN LAND SON DIANA
PEEL CAUTIONTOTHEWIND
ELEV EXPO MAIN URANIA
PIPE SEEN SPRY RENTER
```

151

```
DEN JETSAM HATS HEMET
ADO AMOEBA AMOK OVINE
MISTRUSTCOMPANY MESSY
ATHOS SOS APT WHARF
GOER REF PRE FROG IRS
ERR MISFIRINGLINE TOE
WAG RON RITE JFOX
DUMAS WIMP VICE KOOKY
UNIT ATA SILK PIER
ECSTATIC SILL BUOYANT
TAJ MISHANDLEBARS KIR
OPULENT VILE PARKLIKE
DONT JADE FOE INKA
RIGID CUTE TIED LEGIT
ONES COMA KOL FED
ARC MISPRINTMEDIA MUG
DER ARTY RES UAR BOLE
ANJOU OIL ARM GUTSY
ARTOO MISSTATESRIGHTS
SHERR ERLE MAKEBA REE
HORAS REOS STALIN ARR
```

152

```
TAPE PEAR BUDS HUB
SALADS DUMBO ANAT ONO
EXOTIC ARBUS RIFE TWO
LIGHTHOUSETEAROOM HAS
SHUDDER LINE PERT
RAG MOE FILES CLAY
ELEPHANTCOLLAR MAUD
VIOLENT AWASH TARMAC
OWN TRI BANE LAG
BABY PORNO MIXES EMU
ALE SEADOGJACKETS REM
RIA KARAT OILED STOP
TAR ARTY SER MAH
SOFTLY ADELA RUMORED
UREY EMINENCEMATTER
STAR SNIPE ALA SKY
BUSY LEAN INNINGS
ANT LAWBOOKPENCILNOTE
STU OVAL CRAVE ZEALOT
TAD DIRE HINES ENIGMA
ANY ENDS OMAR SLAB
```

153

```
STEW GEARS STATE HAW
TORI ACTUP ANALOG ARE
ALAS MOSEYEDALONG CCI
RESEMBLED QUILT SIKHS
REGALIA SULLY PHONES
UTE CHITS DIETER
LACY SCOUT OUTLAY
ISH THORHEYERDAHL ETA
THESEASON RAINY EDAM
YELLOW MARINE KAPPA
SWELLS TOWEL DISHES
MONEY HOOTED FAIRER
URNS RADII PERCOLATE
GEE RUDOLFNUREYEV SAL
WIENER OSOLE OEUF
CYCLES DOTED MIA
PROBES SUGAR SPARKLE
SUMMA RULER BARNSTORM
ASI SHIRLEYEATON RIRE
LON EAGLES OLIVE EROS
MEG STAYS SENOR EELS
```

154

```
AFRO SPIFF DAN BOZ
FLUOR VERBAL ARLO ANO
MAZDA IDOIDOIDOIDOIDO
SIZE BOGUS MVII DRUM
YODELED TEPID CENTS
CPR ALI PINAS FUSSY
RUE RINGALEVIO IRS
ARCHIE LIA ORR LEAGUE
GREEN DISNEY AID URE
PIG INLET ABRA TEAR
METS TAKETHEVEIL OSLO
EXIT ALAS ENOLA ORT
APO HIS BRAWLS OSCAR
TONSIL SHE MOE SMOOCH
PRE CAKEOFSOAP NAY
SPEED ONAIR ALA DRS
BORED CODAS MATTHAU
EPIC MATT EAVES SCAB
THEHOUSEOFUSHER TITLE
TIS PIER ALTARS ADOPT
EAT TRY TEALS ZERO
```

155

```
WAS THALIA SKOAL ASTA
ARK AEGEAN TOKYO WHIT
REO GREATSMOKIES FELT
MAKESENSE ALOE GUIDE
IWASTE AHEM SWOLLEN
FREELY ROANOKEISLAND
LOIRE PEARL ARCHY
ALLS WORST HORACE LEG
GEL YOKOHAMAJAPAN ARE
INURES ANOTE SKIT
CANAPE BILKS TOKENS
ATOP FARSI STUDIO
POI ATOKAOKLAHOMA KRA
EMS MALIGN OWENS PEAS
SONIC TWOBY HOERS
ENIWETOKATOLL TOUCAN
DELIBES DUTY HAUNCH
WALLA PELE TABLEHOPS
ARIL TILLAMOOKBAY BOA
ROTE ADAIR GREENE EON
DRED RENEE SASSED ELK
```

156

```
FAST SATUP LIL RTE
DUNNO PACINO AONE ARA
ESSAY ATREERINGCIRCUS
WEEK FLIES COOS AIDE
LEGIONS WRENS DINGS
ETA ULM NEEDY WEDGE
RON SEASTADIUM ALE
MODEST QRS MPS DARWIN
ANGLE GUISES REY ROE
RIT LALAS OVER RITA
BAEZ SOWBUSINESS ETAT
ALTA ORLY ENERO SRI
USE BUY UNDYED PANEL
DOLLAR MON EOE MANGLE
ARC EDITBUNKER IKE
TASTE LETIT EWE NOR
PALSY BASES AMNESIA
ALII FINS GRIND OGLE
RECEDINGAIRLINE SWOON
INE EDGE WEASEL DANCE
STS BOO ODDER INYO
```

157

```
CRT  HOAR  VADER  CAP
HEH  GARBO  SALOME  BABE
ADE  ITTOTHELIMIT  OVER
SYMPATHY  OVINE  OILED
MELANIE  SUEDE  HUNT
ANTE  DARR  SUCH  DUB
LUG  WELLENOUGHALONE
PIG  SCATTY  ARMS  BEGIN
ASH  HARRY  BRIO  AIM
STILETTO  MIRO  STAYED
TENO  NOPRISONERS  NONE
ANGOLA  ENOW  REASSURE
KIP  BRUN  RADIO  RIP
CREAM  CLUE  BUSILY  MGS
NOSTONEUNTURNED  GEO
NIP  GENE  NUTS  SPUD
NEWT  FACTS  MORNING
MOUSY  TOQUE  SILENCER
BOWL  OFYOURSENSES  IVE
OREL  RENTAL  SEEMS  NET
WED  KNEES  TERN  ERA
```

158

```
VIS  CABBIE  DAM  TACK
MAST  UPLAND  RENO  ISLE
ELSE  BOOKSHIELDS  THAN
GOURDS  WET  MME  ELLEN
ARENA  FUR  SPOT  SEE
MOPTOP  SPARED  SWISS
MIA  PROSEPARADE  ATIP
INKBLOT  VENTS  BREVITY
DUELED  FEE  STEVENS
AIRY  HENCE  RHODES
STS  INAUTHORWORDS  WAG
GRINDS  SEATS  BRIE
STRINGS  INS  CHAIRS
PLEASED  MEAND  LAERTES
HORN  OTISREADING  ISO
DEITY  GASPED  ENSIGN
SEN  NBAS  IRK  RUGBY
BETTE  KIN  IDI  KATHIE
NERO  VACLAVNOVEL  TINA
ATOM  URAL  ALLELE  EGGS
BASE  SIR  LASSIE  RHO
```

159

```
HOLMES  SHOP  CLAM  BUDS
USUALS  PURR  HERA  ATOP
MAGRITTESDEFEATS  BREA
IGETA  RAH  TEAR  SAKI
DESI  BAR  SEAT  TEBALDI
NOEL  HINT  SOUS  LEY
SGT  BRAQUESSOCKS  LOGO
QUITIT  URGE  FAYE  ISAR
UNTIE  HALE  OFNO  MOPSY
AGIN  AUK  SHE  JONI
BAA  OKEEFFESREEFS  LAW
NADA  REX  PAK  KLEE
FOSSE  BLAB  FEET  FIORD
LUMP  ORAN  AARE  LUDWIG
ITIS  BOSCHSNOSHES  SEE
ETS  ASKS  ABCS  EASY
ROSETTE  OBEY  MAD  OATH
IDEA  ELLS  UAR  MUCHO
SMOG  CASSATTSGAVOTTES
AONE  LIME  OWED  INHERE
MOSS  EDEN  SODA  POSSES
```

160

```
STAR  PLATH  PAN  ARM
MOORE  ALICIA  POLO  VEE
ADLIB  MANTANMELODRAMA
DADE  DOTES  OGLE  ELAN
BLURRED  OKRAS  STORY
PAL  TEA  MEETS  THANK
ELA  TALLFORYOU  ARI
ESCHER  EON  ENS  BUNYAN
POKER  AGRAND  DAB  OLE
MAS  PEACE  AMOR  PUMA
LEAD  WONYOURMIND  AGAR
EDGY  REDS  RIODE  MOO
ANI  DIM  LOVEIN  ULTRA
RACKET  ETE  ABA  SLOWED
ICE  MAMAGANDHI  IDA
TUDOR  PRUDE  IES  TOM
WINDY  HEIRS  BASEHIT
APSE  WORF  SAVOR  DALE
STERPROOFWINDOW  WAKEN
TOA  PIER  ORIGIN  AHEAD
EEL  STY  WATER  NOSH
```

161

```
MEW  ANGORA  SODA  MAHAL
ORA  CORMAN  CROP  ALONE
URIAHHEEHEEHEEP  LAHTI
SALLY  ALS  LIL  RADIO
STEP  SSE  BIZ  DOPE  HOW
EAR  BEETHOHOHOVEN  ORO
ART  EMU  ERAS  SCAR
MATZO  CRAB  FAIL  WOULD
ECHO  HUT  BIDS  WINS
ELEVATES  GENE  CALYPSO
TUB  DIEHARHARHARD  OAR
SEAMIER  VEAL  UPPERCUT
HOOD  BEAR  PER  AUTO
LIARS  PART  PISA  RISEN
ASHE  JOTS  TEN  BEN
MIA  TARHEEHEEHEEL  RAD
ASH  OPTS  NIP  AID  MINI
ADIEU  GIG  ORT  SOCKS
JAMAL  GENGHISKHAHAHAN
AMAZE  ADAM  CLEESE  ERE
BASED  LETA  CONRAD  SAY
```

162

```
KICKS  CAP  MBA  SCAASI
MASALA  ALE  ERG  TOPTEN
ASHLEY  JAILHOUSEFROCK
CHIME  BUN  AIDAN  FONTS
HARE  PUN  DUTY  ODIN
TROLL  SEEA  GRIN  SGT
APT  TUBULARBELTS  THEO
GEHRIG  NED  ETO  PHOOEY
AREAS  WRESTLE  FRAMERS
POST  SHIVER  GROVES
ETH  CHAPEAUOFLOVE  JED
EFFETE  SWAYZE  SUMO
HARRODS  ESSENCE  DISCO
OTIOSE  ASH  SNO  OYSTER
RIFE  VESTOFMYLOVE  MES
ATF  MILK  PRES  REDDY
BALI  ELIA  DAN  ASOF
ASTOR  HENIE  OWN  TUTTI
SHAWLOUTOFLOVE  CANYON
PUREED  ALT  NEE  ATTLEE
SNARED  LAS  ORB  BASES
```

163

```
STS  RINSES  SAP  RAPT
SHOE  ISOLDE  AARE  ULEE
WISC  BANANASPLIT  NEAT
ASSETS  STA  EPA  ABNER
THEDA  ETE  CURB  LAY
DENIRO  PAROLE  NYASA
SSS  GRAPELEAVES  ORCA
CHABLIS  DANTE  SUBLETS
HALOES  BIN  NABOKOV
WRAP  AESOP  SAYERS
AID  DASHOFBITTERS  JAM
SALMAN  STRAD  YURI
CAPTAIN  COL  MIAMIS
YOURANG  SUDAN  FOOTPAD
ANTI  HOPPINGJOHN  ISO
PEONY  TURRET  ENSIGN
GEM  TEES  BAT  ZIGGY
TERSE  AAA  SAL  SERBIA
BONO  EGGDROPSOUP  DEAR
IDOL  TOES  PERUSE  LAND
BOWL  SOS  TEASED  ENT
```

164

```
GAL  CARTA  TROUP  AYES
RBI  UNION  AROUSE  VEDA
EBB  BOSNIABONSAI  AMIN
WAYSIDES  CHIDE  CLEFT
APSES  STOKE  COLONY
CUBITS  LAURA  FAMINE
AMIES  KOLA  SOLON  NAP
RIAL  ANGOLAANALOG  ETA
PAL  GREEN  LLAMA  SMOG
SKYDIVES  SMOKY  RETYPE
IBIS  SHANE  VINE
DRIVEN  DIANE  RENOWNED
RITA  FONDA  SANDS  ERE
ATA  SPRUCYCYPRUS  SPAT
BEL  PAESE  ARES  CEASE
YVETTE  NICER  THALER
PLACES  HECHE  CHAMP
DIALS  TOWIT  CARRYALL
AVIV  ISRAELSERIAL  NEO
TOTE  DOURLY  CIRCE  EVA
ATYS  SLEDS  OBOES  LID
```

165

```
PAC  SCAN  HOIST  POW
ADA  APACE  EARSTO  TOJO
IMP  BARTYANDSOUL  ELAN
RIPTIDES  SITON  KHAKI
STARTED  LOGON  BIOS
NEED  BAUM  SUET  FIB
SDS  PENNANDPONSELLE
RAG  SMILED  AWAY  PAULA
ATO  TAELS  BIAS  SUR
CONCERTO  ROAR  ARTFUL
ERNO  BACHANDFORD  HABE
DIESEL  ONUS  VALKYRIE
IRE  BUGS  FEVER  RED
PISMO  PINE  WIRERS  ATS
SCHOTTANDSCHELL  ANY
ICE  IRIS  AIRY  CORD
ACID  FANNY  GATEWAY
HUMAN  LAVIE  PIROSHKI
MINI  KROCANDROLLE  IRK
ARID  EUGENE  AUDIS  TOE
YET  TRYST  FRAN  ENS
```

166

```
RAM  PRAISE  ILOSE  KEPT
OLA  RENTER  OILER  EPEE
AIR  OFDICEANDMEN  NICE
MAXIMUMS  BESET  SOCKS
NOSY  REOS  CHAPS
SONATA  SONICS  ELAPSES
WHOLELOTTOLOVE  BREATH
EARL  VOUS  ESO  KASHA
ARM  OCEAN  CENTS  SKEIN
REA  RUR  DEAD  OSS  ESCE
BEERBARRELPOKER
DELI  SIR  GENE  BIT  COP
EMEND  PILOT  ACUTE  OUR
AMIGA  ENO  BRAC  MATE
RECORD  GOLDENROULETTE
STACKED  PEELED  NOTION
HERES  GLAD  FACE
OFTEN  MERIT  COWARDLY
PIER  BURTBACCARAT  ROE
AJAR  ARIEL  ALLURE  ALA
LILY  DENSE  DIMMED  WAR
```

167

```
SPARE  AFT  GBS  ADDAMS
WOEFUL  FLU  REA  GOOGOO
ANTRIM  FATHERKNOWSEST
LATIN  MIX  EATSA  NESTS
ERIC  REX  PMTS  ICES
CABIN  CAUL  BALD  WAS
MAO  YOURITPARADE  FERN
ADAPTS  ECT  KID  AMELIA
NOTRE  SNEERED  KNEECAP
TRUE  PIERRE  DOESTO
ANN  THEWONDEREARS  MAD
CROONS  DRELLS  MEMO
ALTOONA  BAYAREA  HABIT
FOIBLE  JEB  SEO  RECANT
ALOE  THELONEANGER  COY
RAN  RIOT  LORD  ALACK
DUCT  SINS  WRY  HOWL
ATHIN  ELISE  SHY  BATHE
THETWILIGHTONE  CANTON
TARTAN  MME  HOE  ACCESS
ARROYO  PAD  OWL  THERE
```

168

```
PAST  CRUSE  WEED  THOR
ALEE  HOKUM  ROSES  WINE
CLAM  AMERICANPIE  INCA
PANE  NOISY  LUSTER
RATTLE  PLEAT  PEST
ORI  BLUEINTHEFACE  COD
TILTS  TENTS  MASTS  ONO
OSLO  SAVE  GENT  STEW
REAM  CHESHIRECAT  ITON
MADRAS  AVERY  SOMANY
COTTEN  FLIES  REFUGE
CHOOSE  SEVEN  KETTLE
LAKE  DOTTEDSWISS  AFRO
ORBS  DAIS  HONE  TRAP
AGA  AVERS  OMASA  SEINE
KEY  HITTHEJACKPOT  EEN
MASS  RANKS  BASSES
MALIBU  MARYA  AERO
ONYX  ALEXISCOLBY  LOAF
PERE  LEMON  LOUIE  VILE
EWER  GONG  EMBED  ELAN
```

169

```
WHOS  FLAG   SOMA   TRAWL
HOST  RAVEL  EDAM   EUBIE
EPHEMERALARTERY    ANDSO
NEARING  NUTTY   BROOKS
     ONCE  LOGES  SEDUM
OAFISH  BILGE  STARTING
PLOD  GENIE  SEATO   NIA
ELL  THETENDONTRAP   ASI
NOL  RANTS   POUR   GLEN
WISEGUY  CHIRP  GNOSIS
  CLAUS   CHANT   PRAWN
POLITE  RHINE  SHANNON
ABET  SEAN   ACOIN   WAS
LES  MEMBRANESONLY   MIA
MAB  ODIUM  AMPLE   CAAN
SHERBETS  SPEED  BOUNDS
   REINS  SHORT   PORT
SEGALS  PAULA  INERTIA
OTERI  CARTILAGEBOARDS
ARROZ  HUTU  DRACO   TALK
KEEFE  PLOP   MIEN   EYES
```

170

```
DEW   TOW   TACK   LOTUS
MAXI  RUE   DAMON  DAPHNE
ASPSFORTROUBLE    EXPELS
CHEERY  LOG  IDEAL    KEA
HENRY  LAW  HES  PAL  RAM
ODD   YEN   TON   RYE  ARE
   ONEADDERTIME    REIN
   DAMES   IAN   DISTORT
DENIM  FOP   LOS   RIGGED
ELATE  AFLAME  STU   SANE
ARC  COTTONMOUTHER   TRA
TIOS  ASH  TENSER  OLSON
HONEST  EIS   APU   BIBLE
   DRESSER  PIG   VINYL
   SAFE  CIVILSERPENT
HAM  MAO  SAM  AIX   TEN
ELI  SIP  WRY  TIN  GOUDA
CEN   MEDIA  HES  GAMBIT
TRIPLE  IREMEMBERMAMBA
INURED  RELAX  ORE  HALL
COMET   EDIT   WAY   ANE
```

171

```
BLAB   NOEL   CRIB    CAR
POOLED  BIBLE  RENO   ARA
CONAIR  ECOLE  OPTS   SON
BRINGUPTHEARREARS    HUG
   SEDATES   ASIA   LOSE
MOM  GRO  RECUR    CAFE
ACCRUEDREMARKS     CLOT
CAVIARS  LONGS  TRASHY
   FRY  LED  HUES   EON
WAFT  PANES  BABES   DUO
ADA  FISCALTHERAPY   ALP
ILL  ADAMS  YELPS   WYLE
TIS   BELA   LOO    ORO
BEDLAM  SEVEN  ODOROUS
PEEL  SPRINGCHECKING
FRED  SHARE   OAT    LOT
POOR  PHAT    ASAROSE
ELF  PRIMEANDPREJUDICE
ASI  LIMP  MOORS  OREGON
COT  AMMO  AGREE  YEMENS
EMS  YOYO   TONE   RATE
```

172

```
SULK   MAN   PUPS    FOOL
HANOI  ATE  AISLE   SLURP
AVION  DOWNSTAIRSMAIDS
LOST  KLM  OSAGE    WIG
FREEWAY  GUISE  SADSACK
XRAY  GAGS   SONG    NEA
DUH  GETAFAIRSHAKE   ALT
AMAZE  WEFT  EMORY  ORLY
IBIS  BALE  STEPS   LIMO
SERA  LII  BAIL    TALC
YRS  SINCLAIRLEWIS   HOP
TRIP   ELLE  DAM   CAPE
DYAN  SWABS  MICE   RITA
HOLY  CHINO  BASK  LYRIC
OBI  ALISTAIRCOOKE   ACE
WIN  ZINC   NEON   NEST
LEGBONE  SUSAN  TORCHED
ARI  MANET   BET   ALLY
MORDECAIRICHLER  CRETE
EVILS  INGOT  OAR  ACTOR
GAMY   LIEN   TRY   TEEN
```

173

```
ASPIC  ROMP   PUSH   OSHA
AVOUCH  IDOL  EPEE   RIOS
FANCIERFINANCIER   GNUS
RINK  ROLE  COT  MALAISE
OLES  OBE  REWIPE  ONSET
SST  ROBSROBINS   EXIT
   SAT  ADO  YOW   ZERO
RAJAH  POSE  SACRE  ERIN
AZUR  TINHORNTHORN   SOL
PORTHOLE  HOME   AMITY
   IRENE  PROBE  PUMAS
CHEER   ARID   GAZETTES
HAS  BAMBIBAMBINI   REAP
IRIS  TERMS  AINT  DIRTY
CINQ   ONA   BIB    SEX
   JUAN  MUTEMINUTE  BAG
USUAL  ASNERS  ERA  FELL
MERRIAM  PTA  ABAB  ASIA
BRIE  BULLETSBULLETINS
EVEL  BLEU  ETAL  EVADES
ROSY  YEGG  DATA  SALES
```

174

```
YAM   SAINT  REHASH   PEGS
AGO   ALBEE  EMILIO   ASIA
WED  IDIOTSDELETE   VCRS
NEEDLED  CONDE    BLATS
   MOON  BRENDA  ATROPHY
CATER  BLIND     BREVE
ELIS  MOUSEOFUSHER   FAD
DIM  MATTES  ISHOT   SEMI
ABE  OTTOS  ANWAR  CHAIN
RISOTTO  ABEAM  AHORSE
   THEMUMMYSCURSOR
LETTER  ROOST   EASTERN
OTHER  IGORS  BOFFO   NEA
ONER  STERE  TEFLON   TEM
PAD  THEDESERTFAX   SEVE
   ILIUM  RETAG   SHRED
ASSERTS  TRAVEL   TEAM
LAKME  SAYSO   ARCHERY
ALSO  PRINTERESQUE   ZOO
SVEN  BANGOR  ROUND   ZAG
SETS  SPOONS  AWAKE   ONA
```

175

```
HOST   CRAM  EJECT   FAST
ECHO  CHILI  NORSE   ALTO
SHOWPLACEKICKSTANDOUT
OPERATE  ALLEE  REIGNS
   ROWS  EDGAR   GOWN
VALID  AVOWS  NOSEGAY
AMIN  LINESUPRIVER   VAN
SANG  AMAN  OCTS   BONE
ETE  CHEST  FIRES  PAINE
SINALOA  OATEN  CANDID
   BURNOUTCOMEBACK
STANCE  ENTER  WRESTLE
CAPEK  KUDOS  BLAND   RIM
OMAR  LEVI  AONE   PEEP
TEC  BOARDWALKWAY   RENT
DETENTE  IDEES   MESSY
   ARES  CLEAR   KIEV
SPORTS  SOLED  PIONEER
LONGHORNPIPEDOWNUNDER
AGEE  MOUSE  ROSIE   TILE
PORT  EDGES  SETS   STYX
```

176

```
POD  NAFTA  RUMORS   ABED
EGO  APRIL  AMANDA   FUME
ARM  PRECLAMBRIAN   ECCE
SEEDLET  UBOAT    BAKED
   AYES  MODEST  GLASSES
CAFES  MAFIA    AUNTS
ARID  PAYYOURDEUCE   EAT
REV  DENIES  HEDGE   WACO
ONE  RAITT  SERGE  METRO
BARBERA  EATSA  POISON
   MALCOLMFOURBITS
COMEDY  RUMER  OPOSSUM
AVOWS  FACES  LOWER   ANA
LAOS  PETIT  AUGERS   LID
ILL  THREETENNERS   CLOG
   ATRIA  PAGES  JAYNE
SAMHILL  BRIDES   BURG
PROAM  SOUSE   TANTRUM
LOOM  FINSLOMBARDI   AVA
ISLE  AMUSED  AMIGO   NET
TEAS  DEBASE  TAPER   DAH
```

177

```
SCAM  RANDA  CADRE   SEEK
ALBA  INEED  ORIEL   IDLE
SUBJECTOFAPOEMBYBLAKE
HEY  LOIN  GALAS  SALMON
   ZIT  FINIS   AIMS
TAMEST  TROIS  CLUB   SHA
IVYLEAGUESCHOOLMASCOT
POLI  ABE   GLO    HARI
SIEGFRIEDANDROYANIMAL
YDS  RATS  BOOER  MOPPET
   ROIS  JOHNS   SONS
STRAWS  HULOT  SHUE   TAU
TOURNAMENTWINNERWOODS
ANNE   ART   EEL    REDS
DETROITBASEBALLPLAYER
EDS  USES  TROLL  EATERS
   STAR  LORNE   RYE
UNSHOD  DEMON  ALSO   DAD
NAMEFORAVARIETYOFLILY
TIED  RELIC  ELTON   IVAN
OLES  AMISH  ROANS   EASE
```

178

```
SCALDS  ORFF  ATIP   PACT
COPOUT  POUR  CHAR   AFAR
AMADEUSEXMACHINA   UTNE
BERGS  TRY   GLEN   IDLE
SATE  SEA  BROS  BRIARDS
SHOE  COAT  QUIP    TOA
MET  OURTOWNHOUSE   THUS
ORWELL  UNIT  LIES   WEBS
CREAM  ELSE  LAZY  NIFTY
HOLT  RLS   PEN    DATA
ARF  MYFAIRLADYBUG   LBS
TREE   NEY   OOH   FLAP
ATHOL  MANX  DADA  MOORE
RONS  SEGO  COPE  AUBURN
AXIS  THEFROGSLEGS   TED
BIG  FATS  ACME   QUAY
SCHIRRA  MIKA  RUE  VIED
THIS   POSE   VIA  CONGA
COCA  HARVEYWALLBANGER
OLAV  IDEE  EASE  ERNEST
TAPE  POPS  DYED  ALERTS
```

179

```
BOSC  SCOFF  SNOOP   CLIP
AJOY  PANEL  POPPA   HULA
LAIN  IRENE  EMEER   ALLY
LITTLEBIGMANONCAMPUS
   HALO  ISTS   SIS
BRIG  OAST  ROOM    SAD
BREASTOFCHICKENLITTLE
RUN  UPIN  RISES   HYDE
ANN  RATE  CUTER  TEXAS
WEEPIER  EASED   SOI
LITTLETRAMPTRAMPTRAMP
   BEN  ABBEY  CROSSER
DETOX  LIRAS  SARI   TRY
ARIA  SONAR  ILIE   AMO
LITTLEROCKOFGIBRALTAR
ISO  ATEN  ULNA   MIEN
   SIT  TACO   CHIN
LITTLERICHARDRODGERS
NOVA  EVENT  TIRES   EXAM
AGES  RANGE  ELUDE   RICE
POSH  SHOED  DEMOS   STEW
```

180

```
DEF   CARLA  CIGARS   DAM
ALLS  AVAIL  AMADOU   UPA
LOUT  COUNTERPLOTZ   MEN
INFANTILE  ROLE  GALAXY
   FREUD  DALY   RUNES
SAYLES  DOES  CATNAPS
AMBER  LOGS  CRAB  EPEES
RIOT  LAURA  LAMB    RAH
AGA  BARBECUESPITZ   ETA
HAZELNUT  RATS  HERZOG
   LADE  FAUNA   BRIO
DAHLIA  COLT  PROTEGES
ELA  RUNAROUNDSUEZ   EMI
AIL  ITTO  YEATS   SNAG
RAFTS  CHEF  LANE  SATIN
SQUISHY  SOLD   BOULLE
   ULNAE  BEEN   SOUSE
KOALAS  AIME  HONORABLE
ERR  THESTORYOFOZ   GEER
NET  RAWEST  INURE   ENID
TOZ  AYEAYE  PESTS   ZSA
```

181

```
BALD  SPIFF  IRONS  REBA
OMAR  ALTAI  MORAL  EVES
ZABAGLIONE  MUGWUMPERY
ODOMETER  DRESS  GEORGE
ORATES  FLIRT  AGAR
TAN  BLESS  CENTRAL
TACIT  KIERKEGAARD  ALE
EGOS  SOTS  OLDS  ANTA
RUN  APOTHECARY  MESAS
MESHLIKE  LACE  BOGART
EBONY  AIRED  GENIC
ENCORE  THOR  GOATSKIN
NORMS  STUBBORNLY  IRE
ARAB  ASEA  FEEL  GNAW
CAT  INTERVIEWER  LOGES
THECLAY  ITSIN  MIO
ALLE  TRACT  GOSSIP
PASSBY  CHULA  PIZZERIA
ORCHESTRAS  PRIVATEERS
ELOI  IRATE  EATER  GNAT
TOWN  SAGAS  SMART  GENA
```

182

```
APB  AKIRA  AKIMBO  BAD
BEEP  SUDAN  REVERB  ALA
BATH  SKIPTHETALES  COW
AUTOPILOT  ATTN  WEAKEN
IBIZA  THEY  BERRA
CANINE  SHEA  SERVICE
ALGAE  PLAN  SCAT  EARLS
PIGS  CRAZE  WAGE  OUT
ECU  WAIVETHESALES  ODA
KEYWORDS  APES  LACKEY
HOPE  NASTY  BELA
OGLALA  LIST  REVAMPED
ORA  FLAYTHEPEELED  OAR
PEC  PORE  ORLON  BLUE
SAKES  ANON  CRAW  GILDS
TOPPERS  BUSY  PURGES
FIRST  ALAS  FILCH
TOPCAT  SUED  TELEPHONE
ARI  WEEPDAUGHTER  ESAU
LEE  LEGUIN  PATER  STIR
LOS  SMORES  STATE  SLO
```

183

```
SPED  TOJO  BUSH  USS
SEALUP  PATES  UNTO  NAT
MARINE  OPRAH  IBOS  ALI
UNCONDITIONALLOVE  RON
TOILERS  IDLE  SMOG
MPG  CON  GAMUT  MIEN
THEMOUNTAINTOP  PARD
SUMATRA  DRUMS  FIRSTS
STE  COW  JONI  ROW
ACTS  MANIC  AORTA  UFO
RHO  FEARINGANYMAN  TIN
MIR  IVINS  SPECS  CHAT
YET  GENE  EME  POI
FUTURE  SINAI  HARRIET
OARS  THEIRCHARACTER
MUSE  PEARL  EGO  SKY
MASK  JEER  RELAXES
ERR  JUSTICEEVERYWHERE
LOO  ALTE  HAVEN  SEAVER
BOA  BEER  USERS  MLKING
AND  SPRY  MELT  LYLE
```

184

```
ASPS  BINS  PODS  MEA
ALERTS  PETIT  EXIT  YEN
STREEP  ATONE  NEVA  BRO
ISAYALITTLEPRAYER  LID
SMARTED  ALES  RULE
ASA  TWO  FACTS  HUEY
SPIRITINTHESKY  BOTH
HALOGEN  RANKS  WEASEL
TOR  PEI  GARR  ALA
SIGH  DENTS  OASTS  VAN
ONO  PARADISEBYTHE  EMU
ADD  EMILY  EXILE  GNAT
RIO  EBBS  USE  ROO
ANGLES  SHARP  GEWGAWS
LEER  DASHBOARDLIGHT
BYRD  DELTA  ROW  EOS
JOKE  SOFA  SCROOGE
ANN  ANGELOFTHEMORNING
USO  LOON  PARIS  DETROP
NAW  EROS  ERUPT  STEALS
TIS  CEDE  NETS  ARNO
```

185

```
GAS  HAFTS  REDID  CAMP
ULU  AFLAT  MEXICO  OVAL
MOB  PRIMESUSPECT  LENA
PEDALERS  PRIAM  TURIN
IREST  BOAST  TARMAC
LAVISH  FAULT  ARMING
AMISS  GETS  SLEEP  EFT
BODE  BYTHENUMBERS  JAI
ORE  DOPES  ERIES  SOUL
REDCROSS  EAGLE  ORIENT
HAZY  SPREE  CRUZ
TRIAGE  SPEED  CRITERIA
RIND  SPIES  SHOOS  ORB
OFF  POWERSTATION  NOAH
YER  ONINE  PECK  LOTTO
ATTEST  REPRO  DANCER
ACROSS  HAVEN  HOSEA
BATIK  SEVEN  DENATURE
ERIC  REMAINDERING  SAD
TOOK  UTURNS  LINEN  EGG
ANNS  MATTE  OPERA  SEE
```

186

```
PEAR  ALBUM  DECAF  THAT
ARNE  MEANY  EMOTE  REDO
IRKDOUGLAS  LIVERHARDY
RELEASED  TOILE  RECESS
DEFTER  REPLY  LYLE
IES  BEREA  AMERICA
PLANS  RACYCHAPMAN  TEM
RAYE  LOCO  CAAN  MCLI
ORE  HUCKNORRIS  TOHIS
PADLOCKS  NEED  NORMAS
ULEES  BATHS  SINAI
MANORS  LIRA  MCKELLEN
OJAYS  VERYBROOKS  LOU
LEWD  COES  OTTO  LEND
ERA  LADYSKNIGHT  VERSE
SKYWARD  NOTES  DIX
AVES  TIMER  MALIBU
BEAVIS  WISER  SINECURE
AGGIESMITH  AVIDCROSBY
YARN  EAGLE  TINGE  NEAR
SLAG  DOSES  EAGER  SYNE
```

187

```
DIAL  HORA  ARAM  LIP
BASSET  SEWUP  CONE  ONA
ISHTAR  ILEDE  QUAD  NNW
SHIRKINGONESCUTIE  DIN
ASSENTS  LIES  DONS
APT  TOE  FLATS  RANG
BEAUSANDARROWS  MAUD
SPINETS  ROOTS  BIGBEN
ICE  CAP  BALI  AIR
KEPT  BARES  SUSAN  ROI
ALL  WHATADUMPLING  IBN
EVA  OUGHT  MEALS  SEEK
LIZ  ORGY  TRY  TOO
SANITY  SADAT  PHOTONS
SANS  ATTILATHEHONEY
TWIG  CURED  ROW  OWN
FEEL  ALSO  ISOTOPE
ONE  IGOTPLENTYOMUFFIN
CUT  GAVE  ERNIE  ERRATA
URI  OVER  AMENS  NIECES
SEE  RENE  HART  MMES
```

188

```
CAD  DEALER  DRAT  SENSE
HUE  INSOLE  EACH  TROUT
ASPARAGUSPASSER  RAMBO
STARE  AVE  NOH  EVITA
TERM  ORE  ANT  SNIP  ROT
ENT  MADRUBEONIONS  IVY
GET  VEX  UNDO  HEAR
COHAN  PIED  STAY  HELLO
URAL  ANA  SIMI  WORE
MONASTIC  ALEE  REMATCH
IND  OILANDINGRAVE  TEE
NOODLES  OLGA  APERTURE
URIS  TRIO  MII  ICED
FETID  BOMB  WILD  BLESS
RASP  FETA  SIN  VAT
ASI  ALFALFASTUPOR  BIB
YES  SOUL  RUE  NEW  COMO
LOPED  SET  MIA  HARPS
WHALE  DANDELIONGENRES
IONIC  LEAD  ANNUAL  ODE
GODOT  ESPY  PISTIL  WED
```

189

```
DIAL  STARS  WHAM  CHOP
ONCE  TORAH  RICE  SEOUL
CLUESINTHENIGHT  CLOSE
TIM  ARES  ITHE  WALKED
ONE  TRU  ASCH  HORSE
RENE  UPONTHEPROOF  DAD
LAP  FEAT  YARD  LOVE
SNAFU  SONS  STIES  ANEW
POL  SLEUTHJOHNB  SPARE
AWL  TIER  IDOS  SHIFTY
ERROR  ANNAN  DOUSE
LEGUIN  FLAN  OEUF  LAY
OCALA  ALIBIMYSELF  OWE
DOTE  CRAGS  YEAR  LANES
ELIS  HORN  FLAG  REC
NEO  CASESERASERA  TRAM
NOOSE  CART  EDO  ALA
SAMPLE  DALI  GLAD  BID
UBOAT  TRIALTOREMEMBER
POOLS  AUDI  ALONE  ULNA
SUNS  OMAR  NEWTS  MESS
```

190

```
ACT  CHAPIN  STEM  BUILD
BRA  RELENT  TERI  ANNOY
LUCKENBACHTEXAS  BUDGE
ASKEW  INA  RAT  NAOMI
ZOLA  LOU  SID  DOJO  ALE
EEE  KENTUCKYWOMAN  NEW
MIX  SUE  APEX  DAVE
HAMAN  WEED  BRER  LEWIS
ERIS  IRS  LOSS  MILA
DISCOVER  SARA  CASINGS
DES  MISSOURIWALTZ  TRA
ALIMENT  LEGS  JETTISON
SANE  SIDE  MAR  OMIT
BASIS  SAVE  PERK  BUENO
ODIN  LILI  SOS  LBS
CAP  MASSACHUSETTS  LAD
AMP  ENYA  HAT  YAD  PETE
IWEEP  SEW  SEX  PANTS
ADMIT  HOTELCALIFORNIA
REUSE  URIS  AFIELD  ORD
ELDER  SORE  TEDDYS  NEE
```

191

```
MUG  SYSTEM  ALEC  RESTS
ISA  COARSE  TORO  EATUP
LUDVANBEETHOVEN  CRONY
ARGOT  INS  OME  FRANC
NEEL  ENC  UNI  LEAP  KGB
ORT  THEHUSOCIETY  MALE
DOS  FER  TATS  ONES
DECRY  PROD  MUNI  NUDES
IRMA  SAIS  FERN  SERB
DRAMATIC  ARAB  MAGNANI
NON  FOROFSOLITUDE  RAT
TROPICS  OHMY  UNIVERSE
FORK  KNEE  ACRE  REAM
TITLE  DUDS  ELKO  HILLS
WAHL  SADD  BAL  AUK
AGES  TYOUVERYMUCH  SAM
SOB  SUBS  ITS  UTE  CLUE
OUTDO  SST  NUT  RAINS
AWARE  ONTHESAMELENGTH
VERGE  KEAN  INURED  HIE
ADDED  SABU  CAUSES  TED
```

192

```
BASH  PROMO  PADDY  AGED
ESTA  OILOF  LEADA  DEMO
THEHOUSEOFGUSHER  ONME
TEE  RTES  ELMOS  MORTAR
ENRAGES  CRAMP  RUDER
LAD  TRUCE  WILDEYED
ELFIN  GROPETRICKS  LAO
RARE  DREW  ELKE  JEST
GNU  QUAKERGOATS  DUVET
SKIJUMPS  YOUR  SOLELY
TIEME  SMITS  WHEEL
BROLLY  WAND  SHARPJAB
LEFTS  GRINGOSTARR  ORO
ANTS  POOL  MOTE  ABCD
NAH  IAMALLGEARS  MUSHY
CLEANSER  EARLY  SUR
GROSZ  GAMAL  ALFALFA
HELENA  SORES  SPAT  ALE
ATON  GROUNDTRIPTICKET
STOA  EAUDE  UNCLE  AMEN
HEMS  STRAD  SAKES  BETA
```

193

```
HORS  BASTE  CLIFT  THY
ALOT  OSCAR  SHANIA  WOE
LAMA  THOMASMANNER  ONA
OVERTHERE  TANKS  PACER
SOTHERN  DARCY  CARESS
EER  GETTY  REPENT
LIAR  DALAI  BAREST
OOF  MAILERCARRIER  EAR
GUACAMOLE  COILS  DRNO
MUTINY  NURSES  BESTS
PAIRED  PILES  GALWAY
RULES  CAUCUS  BLOTTO
ARID  BARRE  FOOLHARDY
MAA  LUSTERFORLIFE  TOO
RHODES  ITALS  WHEW
BRANDY  SPLIT  HOI
CLINGY  CALLS  FEASTED
HONKS  SOYOU  SALTONSEA
ANG  HOCKEYPUCKER  ETAL
ODE  OHAIRS  PAINE  SELF
SER  TOMES  STRAD  SETA
```

194

```
PET  LAPEL  CHACHA  BAT
OMAN  AMUSE  EILEEN  EGO
MIKE  TORTILLAFLAT  CUB
PREMATURE  ULNA  LEAKEY
NEVER  TROD  PENNY
LOOSER  WHEE  GARNISH
OPTIC  CHOL  HERD  ASHES
PIES  ILIUM  ESAU  ARA
ENO  ONAGRANDSCALE  REF
DEFLATES  OGEE  ELAPSE
ITES  ROLEX  TAIL
CAMDEN  AUNT  THROBBED
RUE  STAFFSERGEANT  ERE
ODA  TRUE  EARNS  CANT
WISER  HOST  RISK  PATIO
TUXEDOS  CUTE  VERTEX
RACES  EBAN  SARAH
CHEMIN  ATOP  STOPOVERS
HOS  PITCHSOMEWOO  ARIL
EMU  EROTIC  ICIER  NAPA
REP  SONICS  TONYS  PEW
```

195

```
HOURS  GRIP  ZAP  AVOW
ARNIE  POACH  WIRE  SAUR
MEINAMERICA  INCA  INGA
STOLEN  RANCH  YACHT
LOVE  NIN  OATS  YOU  ETH
OUI  PRO  APOTOF  BLIP
ORATIONOFTHEMAGI  GABS
ONE  VAI  NENA  BOYLE
SMOG  TERMED  STORMED
DIAL  CORFUS  SALON  EWE
ATM  THEDAMSFAMILY  NOR
DUE  MINOR  EATAND  BTUS
GABBANA  ONLINE  BEST
UTURN  INSO  LSI  AIM
META  BLANDSOFNEBRASKA
TYRO  VILIFY  LSD  PEN
ACE  NAP  PELF  FIE  BAND
LARKS  LAPSE  KIDNEY
LIFE  CURE  STREETDRESS
ORLY  OMIT  ICONS  NORAH
TOYS  PED  ABCD  ANGLE
```

196

```
COACH  HARP  PRIM  GTOP
PONCHO  EWER  RANI  OHIO
FRAMEOFREFERENCE  CELT
LOGE  KEDS  CEL  ANTIBES
UNES  UTE  IONIAN  HARRY
GAR  SPAREROOMS  RUBE
ALS  YAK  TWO  LALA
TESTY  KEEN  ACRID  EKES
WATT  PASSINGLANES  OAT
IRRIGATE  ORAL  KAFKA
IRATE  ARRAY  WEIRD
TOKEN  SLAM  SHOPTALK
ARE  GUTTERSNIPES  AWOL
LEAD  FARCE  AWAY  HUNTS
LOBE  OBI  AHA  MUD
ASKS  PINCUSHION  PUP
TERSE  SENECA  ONS  LULL
INGENUE  SAO  JOSE  URSA
DEAR  SPLITSFIFTYFIFTY
EMIT  DAIS  TIME  EAGLES
SYNS  ALIT  STIR  DRIER
```

197

```
KALE  GHANA  CHA  TRIFLE
IBEG  RENES  RAP  RENOIR
LONGRANGEPLANS  UTURNS
NONSENSE  EDGE  MARMEE
SKY  MAO  SCALE  SPINE
BARNBURNER  HEN  RHO
QUARRY  APES  FIRS  FOR
UMIAK  STEP  HARRY  PLOD
EARN  SHORTTIMER  WEAVE
SOON  AVID  FIRMER
GAZELLE  COPED  FALTERS
ERODED  TAME  ARID
ERRED  SUGARBAKER  GOGO
ZION  ANGER  RIRC  RAPID
EVA  ANAS  NERO  KETTLE
RES  BAR  PROVENANCE
TRILL  ROVES  LAO  MAP
BARELY  SICA  ALVARADO
EXILES  COOKINGWITHGAS
ELAINE  ARC  MIRES  UNIT
FENCES  MYO  PLATH  MARS
```

198

```
FRUG  SCI  ASTA  SOUP
SAUNA  MIO  ALLAN  HORSE
TULIP  ATURNFORTHEBEER
UNES  TRY  EGRET  ALI
BASEHIT  TREES  KNIGHTS
OXEN  SOUL  SOSO  AWE
SAN  CALVINANDHOES  VIE
WRECK  EELS  YOULL  PICK
ORSO  OGLE  SMUTS  KANE
RAFT  HAT  SIPS  WING
EYE  MILEOFTHEROAD  MIN
APSO  ROES  EZR  PICA
STAG  GEARS  ICON  AXIS
SOHO  WALTZ  IVAN  FLEET
ENE  THEBEARSOPERA  DRY
AIR  RILE  ERRS  ALIF
MASCOTS  SOSAY  SCARLET
OPE  ELLIE  SHE  VIDI
NOTHINGSUDSLIKE  HINGE
ISAAC  MARAT  SUE  ANGER
BORN  SUPS  HAP  MESS
```

199

```
JOBS  UTNE  IVOR  THAT
AGRA  NEED  NINA  COOLIO
CREMEDECHASSIS  ARRIBA
KERPLUNK  PITCH  LONGER
LILY  ALGAE  DUMONT
PARITY  LIONS  RAMEN
ONINE  GUMMI  SEIN  TWOS
SNAG  CAKEBATTERY  HATE
SET  FAMED  RACY  WETHE
EXAMINES  TEASE  VECTOR
INNS  BATCH  RENO
ASHLEY  FANCY  HARDBALL
HOOKS  VARY  HOIST  DOA
EDGY  AIRBAGUETTE  SLIT
MASS  MBAS  INLET  QUIRE
WIPED  IMPEL  RUBBER
THAMES  AMMAN  DOES
PRAYER  ASPIC  SIBLINGS
PEBBLE  SHOCKSTAILSOUP
SALADS  PERK  PENN  TARO
TARA  SSTS  AWES  SHUT
```

200

```
CHAT  NOMAD  INCA  WHEY
OUCH  URUTU  SALVO  HIDE
DEER  CRYTOMATOES  INGA
OKLA  DOILY  MATTER
CABBIE  ELENA  MOPE
ANI  WITSONTHEVINE  WHO
BARSI  OPRAH  RINDS  HUG
LIDO  SOIE  BRAE  MILL
ESSU  THENETLANDS  ISLE
OFGOOD  MOUND  PINTER
EFFORT  FILED  HAROLD
SLALOM  PILLS  PIRATE
WIFE  SALLYSTRUTS  ARES
ITES  LUIS  ATME  USDA
PEA  STOMA  SAMSA  ARMIN
EST  THEBLACKPANTS  ONE
ZEUS  MOIST  ISHTAR
INFORM  SOUND  UNTO
NEAR  PICKLEDRING  BETA
CRIB  STORE  EYDIE  BROW
HORA  SWAT  RESTS  YAWL
```

RANDOM HOUSE CROSSWORD ORDER FORM

VOL.	ISBN	QUANT.	PRICE	TOTAL

New York Times Sunday Crosswords

New York Times Sunday Crossword Puzzles
Volume 24 • 978-0-8129-3647-6 ___ $8.95 ___

New York Times Sunday Crossword Puzzles
Volume 25 • 978-0-8129-3648-3 ___ $8.95 ___

New York Times Sunday Crossword Puzzles
Volume 26 • 978-0-8129-3649-0 ___ $8.95 ___

New York Times Toughest Crossword Puzzles
Volume 7 • 978-0-8129-3650-6 ___ $8.95 ___

New York Times Crossword Tribute to Eugene T.
Maleska • 978-0-8129-3384-0 ___ $13.99 ___

Los Angeles Times Sunday Crosswords

Los Angeles Times Sunday Crossword Omnibus
Volume 5 • 978-0-8129-3683-4 ___ $12.95 ___

Los Angeles Times Sunday Crossword Omnibus
Volume 6 • 978-0-375-72248-6 ___ $12.95 ___

Los Angeles Times Sunday Crossword Puzzles
Volume 25 • 978-0-375-72156-4 ___ $9.95 ___

Los Angeles Times Sunday Crossword Puzzles
Volume 26 • 978-0-375-72174-8 ___ $9.95 ___

Los Angeles Times Sunday Crossword Puzzles
Volume 27 • 978-0-375-72175-5 ___ $9.95 ___

Los Angeles Times Sunday Crossword Puzzles
Volume 28 • 978-0-375-72176-2 ___ $9.99 ___

Los Angeles Times Sunday Crossword Puzzles
Volume 29 • 978-0-375-72177-9 ___ $9.99 ___

Washington Post Sunday Crosswords

Washington Post Sunday Crossword Omnibus
Volume 3 • 978-0-375-72187-8 ___ $12.95 ___

Washington Post Sunday Crossword Puzzles
Volume 15 • 978-0-8129-3492-2 ___ $9.95 ___

Boston Globe Sunday Crosswords

Boston Globe Sunday Crossword Omnibus
Volume 3 • 978-0-375-72186-1 ___ $12.95 ___

Boston Globe Sunday Crossword Puzzles
Volume 14 • 978-0-8129-3487-8 ___ $9.95 ___

Boston Globe Sunday Crossword Puzzles
Volume 15 • 978-0-8129-3488-5 ___ $9.95 ___

New York Magazine Crosswords

New York Magazine Crossword Puzzles
Volume 6 • 978-0-8129-3526-4 ___ $9.95 ___

New York Magazine Crossword Puzzles
Volume 7 • 978-0-8129-3684-1 ___ $9.95 ___

New York Magazine Crossword Omnibus
Volume 1 • 978-0-375-72153-3 ___ $12.99 ___

Chicago Tribune Crosswords

Chicago Tribune Daily Crossword Omnibus
978-0-375-72219-6 ___ $12.95 ___

Chicago Tribune Daily Crossword Puzzles
Volume 5 • 978-0-8129-3560-8 ___ $9.95 ___

Chicago Tribune Daily Crossword Puzzles
Volume 6 • 978-0-8129-3561-5 ___ $9.95 ___

Chicago Tribune Sunday Crossword Omnibus
978-0-375-72209-7 ___ $12.99 ___

Chicago Tribune Sunday Crossword Puzzles
Volume 5 • 978-0-8129-3563-9 ___ $9.95 ___

Random House Vacation Crosswords

Random House All Weather Crossword Omnibus
978-0-375-72200-4 ___ $12.95 ___

Random House Harvest Moon Crosswords
978-0-8129-3628-5 ___ $6.95 ___

Random House Springtime Crosswords
978-0-8129-3626-1 ___ $6.95 ___

Random House Summer Nights Crosswords
978-0-8129-3627-8 ___ $6.95 ___

Random House Winter Treat Crosswords
978-0-8129-3623-0 ___ $6.95 ___

Random House Year Round Crossword Omnibus
978-0-375-72201-1 ___ $12.95 ___

Random House Crosswords

Random House Casual Crossword Omnibus
978-0-375-72244-8 ___ $12.95 ___

Random House Casual Crosswords
Volume 3 • 978-0-8129-3666-7 ___ $9.95 ___

Random House Casual Crosswords
Volume 4 • 978-0-8129-3673-5 ___ $9.95 ___

Random House Casual Crosswords

Random House Casual Crosswords
Volume 5 • 978-0-8129-3674-2 ___ $9.95 ___

Random House Crosswords
Volume 5 • 978-0-8129-3501-1 ___ $9.95 ___

Random House Casual Crosswords
Volume 6 • 978-0-8129-3675-9 ___ $9.95 ___

Random House Casual Crosswords
Volume 7 • 978-0-375-72331-5 ___ $9.99 ___

Random House Casual Crosswords
Volume 8 • 978-0-375-72332-2 ___ $9.99 ___

Wall Street Journal Crosswords

Wall Street Journal Crossword Puzzle Omnibus
978-0-375-72210-3 ___ $12.95 ___

Wall Street Journal Crossword Puzzles
Volume 4 • 978-0-8129-3640-7 ___ $9.95 ___

Wall Street Journal Crossword Puzzles
Volume 5 • 978-0-375-72154-0 ___ $9.95 ___

Specialty Crosswords and Puzzle Reference

Mel's Weekend Crosswords
Volume 1 • 978-0-8129-3502-8 ___ $9.95 ___

Mel's Weekend Crosswords
Volume 2 • 978-0-8129-3503-5 ___ $9.95 ___

Random House Webster's Crossword Puzzle Dictionary
4th Edition • 978-0-375-72131-1 ___ $19.99 ___

Random House Webster's Large Print
Crossword Puzzle Dictionary
978-0-375-72220-2 ___ $24.95 ___

Stanley Newman's Crosswords Shortcuts
978-0-375-72306-3 ___ $12.95 ___

Stanley Newman's Movie Mania Crosswords
978-0-8129-3468-7 ___ $7.95 ___

The Puzzlemaster Presents: Will Shortz's Best
Puzzles from NPR
978-0-8129-3515-8 ___ $13.95 ___

15,003 Answers: The Ultimate Trivia Encyclopedia
2nd Edition • 978-0-375-72237-0 ___ $24.95 ___

To place your order, fill out this coupon and return to:
RANDOM HOUSE, INC., 400 HAHN ROAD, WESTMINSTER, MD 21157
ATTENTION: ORDER PROCESSING

☐ Enclosed is my check or money order payable to Random House
☐ Charge my credit card (circle type): AMEX Visa Mastercard

[ ][ ][ ][ ][ ][ ][ ][ ][ ][ ][ ][ ][ ][ ][ ][ ]

Credit Card Number

NAME _____ SIGNATURE _____

ADDRESS _____ CITY _____ STATE _____ ZIP _____

To order, call toll-free 1-800-733-3000

Handling	
CARRIER	ADD
USPS	$5.50
UPS	$7.50

Total Books ___

Total Dollars $ ___

Sales Tax * $ ___

Postage
& Handling $ ___

Total Enclosed $ ___

* Please calculate according to your state sales tax rate